Commercial Application Development Using

ORACLE

DEVELOPER 2000

IVAN BAYROSS

B-14, CONNAUGHT PLACE, NEW DELHI-110001

FIRST EDITION 1997
Distributors:

MICRO BOOK CENTRE
2, City Centre, CG Road,
Ahmedabad-380009 Phone: 6421611

COMPUTER BOOK CENTRE
12, Shrungar Complex, M. G. Road,
Bangalore-560001 Phone: 5587923, 5584641

MICRO BOOKS
Shanti Niketan Building, 8, Camac Street,
Calcutta-700017 Phone: 2426518, 2426519

BUSINESS PROMOTION BUREAU
8/1, Ritchie Street, Mount Road,
Chennai-600002 Phone: 834796, 8550491

BPB BOOK CENTRE
376, Old Lajpat Rai Market,
Delhi-110006 Phone: 2961747

DECCAN AGENCIES
4-3-329, Bank Street,
Hyderabad-500195 Phone: 512280, 593826

MICRO MEDIA
Shop No. 5, Mahendra Chambers, 150 D.N. Road, FORT,
Mumbai-400001 Phone: 2078296, 2078297, 2002732

INFO TECH
G-2, Sidhartha Building, 96 Nehru Place,
New Delhi-110019 Phone: 643825, 6415092, 6234208

INFO TECH
B-11, Vardhman Plaza, Sector-16, Electronics Nagar,
Noida-201301 Phone: 8531346

COMPUTER BOOK CENTRE
SCF No.-65, Sector-6,
Panchkula-134109, Chandigarh Phone: 561613, 567538

© BPB Publications

No part of this publication can be stored in any retrieval system or reproduced in any form or by any means without the prior written permission of the publishers.

Limits of Liability and Disclaimer of Warranty
The Author and Publishers of this book have tried their best to ensure that the programmes, procedures and functions contained in the book are correct. However, the author and the publishers make no warranty of any kind, expressed or implied, with regard to these programmes or the documentation contained in the book. The author and publishers shall not be liable in any event for any damages, incidental or consequential, in connection with, or arising out of the furnishing, performance or use of these programmes, procedures and functions. Product name mentioned are use for identifications purposes only and may be trademarks of their respective companies.

All trademarks referred to in the book are acknowledged as properties of their respective owners.

ISBN 81-7029-899-7

Published by Manish Jain for BPB Publications, B-14, Connaught Place,
New Delhi-110001 and Printed by him at Pressworks, Delhi.

FOREWORD

The need of today's software development is competence in a G.U.I. based front-end tool, which can connect to Relational Database engines. This gives the programmer the opportunity to develop client server based commercial applications.

These applications give users the power and ease of use of a G.U.I. with the multi user capabilities of Novell or Unix based RDBMS engines such as Oracle.

From the array of G.U.I based front-end tools Oracle Developer 2000 stands out. Many clients are looking for people with Oracle Developer coding capabilities today. Oracle Developer 2000 offers a host of technical advantages over Oracle Forms 3.0, which was an excellent tool in itself. This book focuses on the new features available in Oracle Developer 2000 and has many applications that explain the commercial application development techniques used with Oracle Developer 2000.

All the important coding techniques used by programmers, in OOPS based coding is brought out in full and in great detail. This is coupled with material on how to use the various tool sub sets available in Oracle Developer 2000. The examples given in this book also focus on standards that have to be maintained in a software project and how a programmer can maintain these standards whilst coding in Oracle Developer 2000.

The book pre - supposes that the person reading it has a DBMS background and that the basic concepts of DBMS commercial application development are already in place. The combination of a sharp drop in hardware prices and quantum jump upward in software technology makes working in Client/Server very much within the financial budgets of most organizations. This release's to users, the power of working with a G.U.I. based front end to manipulate data in any RDBMS back end. Programmers capable of writing fine tuned code are really invaluable today.

I have found DBMS/RDBMS to be the most exciting environments to work with. With the availability of powerful, easy to use G.U.I based, Client/Server tools; commercial applications have really taken a quantum jump forward in 'ease of use'.

This foreword would not be complete without my thanking the many people who encouraged me and put up with my many revisions and updations of the material with patience.

My Sincere thanks goes to:

1) My Publisher Mr. Manish Jain. Manish who has criticized me and made me redo my work sometimes; but each time I really have improved. Thanks Manish I'm getting better each day thanks to you.

2) Mita Engineer who really sweated to complete this book from the time it was conceived.

3) The many graduate engineers who studied Oracle Developer 2000 at SCT. Each time you found a mistake and suggested a correction, you helped me towards perfection. A very big thank-you.

4) The many programmers who read this book. I would welcome your brickbats or bouquets. Without you I would not be an author. You can contact me via Mr. Manish Jain at BpB New Delhi.

IVAN N. BAYROSS

TABLE OF CONTENTS

1. INTRODUCTION TO MANAGING DATA 1

BASIC DATABASE CONCEPTS 4
What is a database ? 4
Characteristics of a Database Management System 4

HOW THE CONCEPT OF RDBMS CAME ABOUT 4

CHARACTERISTICS OF A RELATIONAL DBMS MODEL 5

E.F. TED CODD'S LAWS FOR A FULLY FUNCTIONAL RELATIONAL DATABASE MANAGEMENT SYSTEM 8

ORACLE 7 .... THE PRODUCT PHILOSOPHY 10
Introduction to Oracle Tools 10
Oracle DBA 11
*SQL*Plus* 11
Oracle Forms 11
Report Writer 11
Oracle Graphics 12

2. INTERACTIVE SQL 13

INVOKING SQL*PLUS 13

DATA MANIPULATION IN DATA BASE MANAGEMENT SYSTEMS 16

THE ORACLE DATATYPES 17

TWO DIMENSION MATRIX CREATION 17
Creating a table 18
Creating a table from a table 19

INSERTION OF DATA INTO TABLES 19
Inserting a single row of data into a table 19
Inserting data into a table from another table 20
Insertion of selected data into a table from another table 20

UPDATING THE CONTENTS OF A TABLE 20

DELETION OPERATIONS 21
Deletion of all rows 21
Deletion of a specified number of rows 21

THE MANY FACES OF THE *SELECT* COMMAND 22
Global data extract 22
The retrieval of specific columns from a table 22
Elimination of duplicates from the Select statement 22
Sorting of data in a table 22

Selecting a data set from table data..*23*

MODIFYING THE STRUCTURE OF TABLES 24
Adding new columns..*24*
Modifying existing columns...*24*
Restrictions on the Alter table...*24*

REMOVING / DELETING / DROPPING TABLES 24

DATA CONSTRAINTS 25
Column Level and Table Level Constraints...*25*
NULL value concepts..*25*
Primary Key concepts..*26*
Unique Key concepts..*27*
Default value concepts...*27*
The Foreign Key/References constraint...*28*
CHECK Integrity constraints...*29*
Defining different constraints on the table..*31*
Defining Integrity constraints in the ALTER TABLE command................*32*
Dropping Integrity constraints in the ALTER TABLE command..............*32*

COMPUTATIONS IN EXPRESSION LISTS USED TO SELECT DATA 33
Arithmetic operators..*33*
Renaming Columns Used With Expression Lists......................................*34*

LOGICAL OPERATORS 34

RANGE SEARCHING 35

PATTERN MATCHING 35
The use of the like predicate..*35*
The in and not in predicates..*36*

ORACLE FUNCTIONS 37

GROUPING DATA FROM TABLES IN SQL 42
The concept of grouping..*42*

MANIPULATING DATES IN SQL 43

JOINS 43
Joining Multiple Tables (Equi Joins)..*43*
Joining A Table to Itself (Self Joins)...*46*

CONSTRUCTING AN ENGLISH SENTENCE WITH DATA FROM TABLE COLUMNS ...48

SUBQUERIES 49

USING THE UNION, INTERSECT AND MINUS CLAUSE ....
Union Clause..*50*
Intersect Clause..*51*
Minus Clause..*56*

INDEXES 57
Creating an Index for a table 57
Dropping Indexes 57

VIEWS 58
Creation of views 58
Renaming the columns of a view 58
Using Views (visual concept) 59
Selecting a data set from a view 59
Updateable Views 59
Destroying a view 59

SEQUENCES 60
Creating Sequences 60
Referencing a Sequence 61
Altering A Sequence 62
Dropping A Sequence 62

GRANTING PERMISSIONS 63
Permission on the objects created by the user 63
Granting permissions using GRANT statement 63
Object Privileges 63
With Grant Option 64
Referencing a table belonging to another user 64
Granting permissions to users when the grantor has been given GRANT permission 64

REVOKING THE PERMISSIONS GIVEN 64
Revoking permissions using the REVOKE statement 65

CREATION OF REPORTS IN SQL*PLUS 66
*Formatting commands used in SQL*Plus* 66

SELF REVIEW EXERCISES IN SQL 68
Tables For Exercises 69
Sixty Self Review SQL Sentence Constructs For Practice 70
Single Table Retrieval 74

3. PL/SQL 77

INTRODUCTION 77
Performance 77
Performance Improvement 77
Portability 74
PL/SQL datatypes 78
What PL/SQL can do for programmers 78

THE PL/SQL EXECUTION ENVIRONMENT 79
PL/SQL in the Oracle RDBMS 79

- Using PL/SQL Blocks in the SQL*PLUS Environment 80
- Running a PL/SQL block written via any editor 80

THE PL/SQL SYNTAX 80
- The character set 80
- Literals 81
- Comments 81
- Data Types 81
- Variables 82
- Assigning Values to Variables 82
- Picking up a Variable's Parameters from a table cell 83
- Declaring a constant 83
- Using logical comparisons in PL/SQL 83

UNDERSTANDING THE PL/SQL BLOCK STRUCTURE 84
- An identifier in the PL/SQL block 85
- Displaying user Messages on the Screen 86
- Conditional control in PL/SQL 86
- Iterative Control 86

ORACLE TRANSACTIONS 89
- Using commit 89
- Using rollback 89
- Using Savepoint 90

CONCURRENCY CONTROL IN ORACLE 92

LOCKS 92
- Types of locks 92
- Implicit locking 92
- Explicit locking 93
- Who can explicitly lock ? 93
- Using the select...for update statement 93
- Using lock table statement 94
- When locks are released 95

CURSORS 96
- How are SQL statements processed by Oracle ? 96
- What is a cursor ? 96
- Use of cursors in PL/SQL 97
- Explicit Cursor 97
- Why use an Explicit Cursor ? 97
- Explicit Cursor Management 98
- Declaring a Cursor 99
- Opening a Cursor 99
- Fetching a record from the Cursor 100
- Closing a Cursor 101
- Explicit Cursor Attributes 101
- Cursor for loops 104

- Implicit Cursor 107
- Implicit Cursor Attributes 107

  Parameterized Cursor *109*

ERROR HANDLING IN PL/SQL 114
 Declaring Exceptions (i.e. user-defined error conditions) *114*
 Pre-determined internal PL/SQL exceptions *115*

4. STORED PROCEDURES 119

WHAT ARE PROCEDURES ? 119
 Declarative part *119*
 Executable part *119*
 Exception Handling part *119*

WHERE DO PROCEDURES RESIDE ? 119

HOW ORACLE CREATE A PROCEDURE ? 119

HOW ORACLE EXECUTES PROCEDURES ? 120

ADVANTAGES OF PROCEDURES 120

SYNTAX FOR CREATING STORED PROCEDURE 121
 Keywords and Parameters *121*

AN APPLICATION USING A PROCEDURE 122

DELETING A STORED PROCEDURE 125

5. STORED FUNCTIONS 126

WHAT ARE FUNCTIONS ? 126
 Declarative part *126*
 Executable part *126*
 Exception Handling part *126*

WHERE DO FUNCTIONS RESIDE ? 126

HOW ORACLE CREATES A FUNCTION ? 126

HOW ORACLE EXECUTES A FUNCTIONS ? 127

ADVANTAGES OF FUNCTIONS 127

SYNTAX FOR CREATING A STORED FUNCTION 128
 Keywords and Parameters *128*

AN APPLICATION USING A FUNCTION 129

DELETING A STORED FUNCTION 132

6. DATABASE TRIGGERS 133

INTRODUCTION 133
USE OF DATABASE TRIGGERS 133
Database Triggers vs. Procedures *133*
*Database Triggers vs. SQL*Forms* *133*
Database Triggers vs. Declarative integrity constraints *134*

HOW TO APPLY DATABASE TRIGGERS 134

TYPES OF TRIGGERS 135
Row Triggers *135*
Statement Triggers *135*
Before VS. After Triggers *135*
Before Triggers *135*
After Triggers *136*
Combinations *136*

SYNTAX FOR CREATING TRIGGER 137
Keywords and Parameters *137*

DELETING A TRIGGER 138

AN APPLICATION USING DATABASE TRIGGERS 139

RAISE_APPLICATION_ERROR PROCEDURE 143

7. WORKING WITH FORMS 145

BASIC CONCEPTS 145

APPLICATION DEVELOPMENT IN FORMS 145
Forms *146*
Menu *146*
Library *146*

FORM MODULE 146
Blocks *146*
Items *147*
Canvas-view *149*
Windows *149*

USING THE FORMS DESIGNER 151
Parts of Forms Designer Window *151*
Tools Available with the Forms Designer *152*

CREATING A FORM 153

GENERATING AND RUNNING A FORM 158
Data Retrieval and Manipulation Operations *159*

(x)

USING THE LAYOUT EDITOR 160
   Positioning and Sizing an Item 160
   Setting the Properties of the Items 161
   Placing Push buttons on the Form 161

CONSTRAINTS DEFINED AT THE TIME OF CREATION OF A BLOCK 163

8. MASTER FORM 164

PRODUCT MASTER DATA ENTRY SCREEN 164

TRIGGERS 165
   Interface Events 166
   Internal Processing Events 166
   The sequence of trigger execution 166
   Writing Triggers 166

THE BEHAVIOR OF AN ORACLE FORM IN A COMMERCIAL APPLICATION 168
   Form Behavior While Viewing Data 169
   Form Behavior While Updating Data [Primary Key problems] 169
   Form Behavior While Deleting Data 169
   Form Behavior While Inserting Data 169
   The Forms Mode Of Operation 169

DATA NAVIGATION VIA AN ORACLE FORM 169
   Multiple Rows Being Retrieved From The Table 169
   A Single Row Being Retrieved From The Table 170

PROCEDURES 174
   Writing Procedures 174

VALIDATIONS 178
   Table Data Input / Output Validations 178

INCLUDING SEARCH FUNCTION IN THE MASTER FORM 184

9. PROPERTY CLASS AND VISUAL ATTRIBUTES 185

MAINTAINING STANDARDS IN FORMS 185
   Standards In A Commercial Application 185
   Setting Standards in Oracle Forms 185

PROPERTY CLASS 186
   Creating Property Class object 187

VISUAL ATTRIBUTES 193
   Setting the visual attributes of an object 193
   Creating Named Visual Attributes and applying the same on the objects 194

10. LIBRARIES AND ALERTS 198

LIBRARY FILE FORMATS 198
.PLL *198*
.PLX *198*
.PLD *198*

CREATING AND ATTACHING A LIBRARY TO A MODULE 199
Creating a Library *199*
Attaching a Library to Another Module *199*

HANDS ON 202

ALERTS 205
Creating an Alert *205*
Displaying an Alert *207*

DISPLAYING CONTEXT SENSITIVE HELP 223
Display Context Sensitive Help on the message line at runtime *223*
Displaying balloon Help *223*

11. MASTER DETAIL FORM 225

CREATING A MASTER-DETAIL FORM 226
The Relation Object *228*

RUNNING A MASTER DETAIL FORM 230
Data Retrieval and Manipulation Operations *230*

MASTER DETAIL DATA ENTRY SCREEN 242
Relation Object and its Properties *242*
Master Deletes Property *242*
Setting the properties of the relation object *242*
Creating a Display Item *248*

WORKING WITH LOV OBJECTS 249
Creating A List of Values *250*

USING A RADIO BUTTON GROUP 253

CREATING AND USING A LIST ITEM 262
Poplist *262*
Text List *262*
Combo List *262*
Creating A List Item *263*

INCLUDING SEARCH FUNCTION IN THE MASTER DETAIL FORM 266

CROSS TABLE UPDATIONS 303
Cross table updation in Insert Mode *303*
Cross table updation in Modify Mode *303*
Cross table updation in Delete Mode *303*

12. PARAMETER PASSING IN FORMS 309

SPECIFYING THE PARAMETER LIST IN THE CALLING FORM 309
Creating a Parameter List 309
Adding Parameter to the Parameter List 310
Types of Parameters 310
TEXT_PARAMETER 310
DATA_PARAMETER 310
Specifying the parameters in the called form 311
Using the parameters in the called form 312

DIFFERENCES BETWEEN GLOBAL VARIABLES / PARAMETER VARIABLES ... 313

13. USING MULTIPLE CANVASES ON A FORM 321

WORKING WITH CANVAS VIEWS 321
Types of Canvas Views 321
Creating a Stacked Canvas 323
Displaying a Stacked Canvas 324

14. WORKING WITH MENUS 328

USING THE DEFAULT MENU 328

USING THE CUSTOM MENU 329
Creating A Menu Module 330
To Assign a Command to a Menu Item 333

ATTACHING A MENU MODULE TO A FORM 337

OPENING A FORM THROUGH THE MENU 338
Invoking Other Products From Oracle Forms Or Menus 338

CHECKED, ENABLED AND DISPLAYED PROPERTY OF MENU ITEMS 347
Checked Property 347
Enabled Property 347
Displayed Property 347
Getting the Value of the Menu Property 347
Setting the Properties of the menu item 348

15. TOOLBARS 351

BASIC CONCEPTS 351

CREATING A TOOLBAR 351

16. WORKING WITH REPORTS 361

FEATURES 361
- Basic Concepts 362

DEFINING A DATA MODEL FOR A REPORT 363
- Queries 363
- Groups 363
- Columns 363
- Parameters 364
- Data Links 364

SPECIFY THE LAYOUT FOR A REPORT 364
- Repeating Frames 365
- Frames 365
- Fields 365
- Boilerplate 365
- Anchors 365

SPECIFY A RUNTIME PARAMETER FORM FOR A REPORT ... 366
- Fields 366
- Boilerplate 366

USE THE ORACLE REPORTS INTERFACE 367
- Property Sheets 367
- Object Navigator 367
- Editors 368
- Palettes and Toolbars 368

CREATING A DEFAULT TABULAR REPORT 369
- Creating a new Report Definition 371
- Connecting to the Database 371
- Specifying the Data for the Report 372
- Specify a Default Layout for the Report 377
- Save and run the Report 378

CREATING COMPUTED COLUMNS 380
- Summaries columns 380
- Formula columns 380
- Create a Formula using the Formula Column Tool 381
- Create serial nos. field using Summary Column Tool 383
- Create a Report Summary using Summary Column Tool 385

CREATING USER PARAMETERS 388

ARRANGING THE LAYOUT 394
- Change Layout Settings 394
- Fill Color Tool 394
- Line Color Tool 394
- Text Color Tool 395

17. CREATING A BREAK REPORT 403
Creating a new Report Definition 405
Creating a Break Group 406
Creating summary column 409
Specifying default layout 410
About Repeating Frames 412
Arranging The Layout 413

18. MASTER/DETAIL REPORT 417
CONCEPTS 417
Data Link Object 417
Data Relationships 418
Layout 418

CREATING A MASTER/DETAIL REPORT 418
Creating the report definition 420
Queries Object 421
Data Link Object 422
Creating Formula And Summary Columns 424
Formula Column 424
Default Layout 425
Arranging the Layout 427
Accepting Parameter Values 431

19. CREATING A MATRIX REPORT 436
MATRIX DATA MODEL 437
Number Of Queries 437
Group Structure 437
Summaries and Product Order 438
Matrix Layout 439
Matrix / Cross Product Object 439
Creating Query 442
Creating groups 443
Creating Default Layout 444
Creating Summary columns 446
Adding Zeroes in place of non-existent values 448
Adding a Grid 451
Creating User Parameters 452

20. WORKING WITH GRAPHS 454
INTRODUCTION 454
Functionality of Oracle Graphics 454
Working with Charts 455
DISPLAY 455
LAYOUT 455
QUERIES 455
Chart Properties 456
Chart Types 456
Chart Templates 457

USING THE GRAPHICS DESIGNER 458
Tools Available with the Graphics Designer 458

CREATING A GRAPH 459

PASSING PARAMETERS IN ORACLE GRAPHICS 468

21. DRILL DOWN CHARTS 473

1. INTRODUCTION TO MANAGING DATA

Since you are reading this material I'm sure that you are already a programmer or have decided to be a programmer. Hence, you will earn your living by managing other people's data for them. To achieve this you have made a clear decision to use a computer and a programming environment to manage human data.

Let's take a very brief look at human data. Our purpose in doing so is to try and understand whether human data is very complex, if this is so, then by default any system designed to manage this data would in turn be very complex. On the other hand if the data we wish to manage is not complex at all then any system designed to manage it need not be complex at all.

If we look hard enough, we should begin to understand that any kind of human data we would wish to manage can be expressed either in *Characters* or *Numbers*. Only *Numbers* may be of two distinct types either *Whole Numbers* or *Floats*, (i.e. Numbers with decimal points). Hence, basically all human data that we will ever manage can be grouped under two distinct types. This is simple enough, projecting from this, any system used to manage human data cannot be extremely complex.

However, we really face a major problem when we attempt to manage human data using a computer. Human data is traditionally *Free Form*.

Lets take a very simple example of someone's name. A name can be as small as, let's four to six characters, e.g. Jane, Jude, Jyoti or as long as you want it to be e.g. Venkateshwarlu Velamakanni a very common Telegu name from Andhra Pradesh. The human mind can immediately perceive all these characters as *'Names'* the computer cannot.

Hence, we have to be able to somehow get *'Free Form'* human data to appear *'Rigid'* to a computer, so that the data can be managed by the computer. To achieve this we need to understand the methods we use to manage other *'Free Form'* human materials in day to day life. Then find out if an *'Equivalent Method'* exists using a computer and a *'Programming Environment'*. If such a method does exist, then it should be relatively simple to manage free form human data using a computer.

A simple example of *'Free From'* human material is water i.e. a *liquid*. To manage liquids, human beings place liquids in a container, such as a glass, if you want a drink of water. Then they manage the glass, which in turn allows the *'Free Form'* material to be managed. Using this as a base, lets see if we can do the same thing or something similar with computers and *'Free Form'* human data.

The idea being to place *'Free Form'* human data into a container of some kind and then get the computer to manage the container. The container being created, maintained and managed via the programming environment we have chosen to work with.

Any programming environment used to create containers, to manage human data, can be conceptualized as a Data Management System. Traditionally, the block of human data being managed is called a Database. Hence, in very simple terms these programming environments can be conceptualized as DataBase Management Systems, in short **DBMSystems.**

All Database Management Systems (**i.e. Oracle** is a DBMS) allow users to create containers for data storage and management. These containers are called '*Cells*' The minimum information that has to be given to Oracle for a suitable container to be constructed which can hold free form human data is

- The Cell Name
- The Cell Length
- The type of Data that can be placed in to the Cell

Cell Name
When we wish to view the contents of a cell later all we need to do is tell the programming environment the cell name. The programming environment is intelligent enough to fetch for us *contents of the cell* rather than the cell itself.

Cell Length
This is the manner we '*Rigidize*' free form human data. We create a container of a pre-determined length into which we will store '*Free Form*' human data for management. If we map this, to the example on names we were looking at earlier, this automatically puts a limit on the length of a person's '*Name*' that we can hold in the container. We will have to try our best and decide on the longest name we wish to manage and decide on the container length accordingly.

Cell Data Type
As we had a look earlier, human data is mainly of two types, Character or Numbers, if Numbers then we can have Whole numbers or Floats. We would then have to inform the programming environment, which is creating the cell for us, what kind of data we will store in the cell when it is being used. The simplest reason being that we would have to separate Character and Number data types.

Another name that programming environments use for a '*Cell*' is '*Field*' these names can be used interchangeably and generally mean the same thing. This can be conceptualized as follows :

INTRODUCTION TO MANAGING DATA 3

Lets use Oracle to create several '*Fields*' (or '*Cells*') in the same horizontal plane. This will look like :

Name	Age	TelephoneNo
20 Characters	2 N	8 Numbers

This really means that we have asked Oracle to create three '*Fields*' for us. The name of the first field is '*Name*', the name of the second field is '*Age*' and the name of the last field is '*Telephoneno*'. The first field can take a maximum of **20** characters, the second field can take a maximum of **2** numbers, the third field can take a maximum of **8** numbers.

After we have filled data in the set of three fields and we have more data to manage, Oracle will oblige us by giving us another set of three fields to fill up. These three fields will be stored exactly below the other set of three fields. This will look like the diagram 1.1 below.

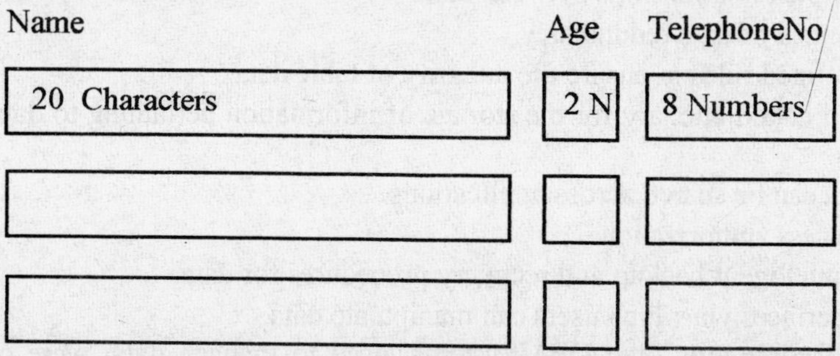

Name	Age	TelephoneNo
20 Characters	2 N	8 Numbers

Diagram 1.1 : Multiple sets of fields placed one below the other

We could imagine that each field was an *object* created for us by Oracle. Then the three fields created for us in the same horizontal plane would be another distinct object created for us by Oracle. Multiple fields placed in the same horizontal plane is an object called a '*Record*' by Oracle. Several '*Records*', of equal length, placed one below the other to enable users to continue to store data is called a '*Table*'.

Hence a '*Table*' can be visualized as a two dimensional matrix, consisting of '*Rows and Columns*' used for storing data. The '*Table*' therefore becomes the third object after '*Field*' and '*Row*' that Oracle will create for users to help us manage human data.

A **group** of '*Tables*' with '*Related*' data in them is called a '*Database*'

BASIC DATABASE CONCEPTS
What is a database ?
It is a coherent collection of data with some inherent meaning, designed, built and populated with data for a specific purpose. A database stores data that is useful to us. This data is only a part of the entire data available in the world around us.

To be able to successfully design and maintain databases we have to do the following :
1) Identify which part of the world's data is of interest to us.
2) Identify what specific objects in that part of the world's data are of interest to us.
3) Identify a relationship between the objects.

Hence, the objects, their attributes and the relationship between them that are of interest to us are stored in the database that is designed, built and populated with data for a specific purpose.

Characteristics of a Database Management System :
- It represents complex relationships between data.
- Keeps a tight control of data redundancy.
- Enforces user-defined rules to ensure the integrity of table data.
- Has a centralized data dictionary for the storage of information pertaining to data and its manipulation.
- Ensures that data can be shared across applications.
- Enforces data access authorization.
- Has automatic, intelligent backup and recovery procedures for data.
- Has different interfaces via which users can manipulate data.

In the early days of computing the DBMSystems, used to manage data, were of the Hierarchic or Network model. When these were placed onto network operating systems and multiple users began to access table data concurrently the DBMSystem responded to these user requests very sluggishly and was not totally stable when the number of users exceeded four or five.

This caused commercial application developers to abandon the use of DBMSystems to manage data and switch over to other programming environments, such as Cobol, or 'C' to develop software that had to be used by multiple users concurrently.

About the time while all this was happening, (a very disappointing time for DBMS programmers) the was a mathematician called E.F.T. Codd who was working with IBM doing research in statistics.

HOW THE CONCEPT OF RDBMS CAME ABOUT :
He applied the principles of relationships in statistics to data management and came up with twelve laws. Using mathematics, he proved that if all these 12 laws were incorporated into database core technology, there would be a revolution in the speed of any DBMSystems while managing data, even when used on network operating systems. All of a sudden new life was injected into software houses who had devoted large sums of money in developing DBMSystems that programmers could use to manage data.

These software houses took up the challenge and many products came into existence which propounded that they followed Codd's laws; products like Oracle, Ingres, Sybase, Unify, Informix and so on.

However, none of these products have been successful implementing all of Codds 12 laws into their DBMS core technology. The lesser the number of Codd's laws implemented in a product's core technology, greater are the overheads the product will place on the hardware used for running it.

Oracle 6.0 implements around *seven* of Codd's laws, Ingres *nine*, Sybase *ten and a half*. However, research and development is constantly going on at all these vendor sites. Each vendor is striving to implement all of Codd's laws in their products. This constantly leads to product upgrades being brought out by the product vendors. This is really good news for programmers. Currently Oracle 7.1 implements all rules fully or partially. The programming world is constantly getting easier and easier.

The cost per transaction (i.e. unit of work done by the DBMSystem) is always getting less and less. When this is viewed in the light of the advances made in hardware, programmers are really getting more and more powerful hardware platforms to work with on which faster and more flexible DBMSystems are being developed and implemented.

Since E.F.T. Codd was a statistician and in statistics relationships play a key role the newer products that came into existence in which several of Codd's laws were used were called Relational DataBase Management Systems, RDBMS for short.

CHARACTERISTICS OF A RELATIONAL DBMS MODEL

- The relational data management model eliminated all parent-child relationships and instead represented all data in the database as simple row/column tables of data values.
- A relation is similar to a table with rows/columns of data values. The rows of a table are referred to as Tuples and the columns are referred to as Attributes. Several tuples of equal length placed one below the other create a table.
- Each table is an independent entity and there is no physical relationship between tables.
- Most data management systems based on the relational model have a built-in support for query languages like ANSI SQL or QBE (Query By Example). These queries are simple English constructs that allow adhoc data manipulation from a table.
- Relational model of data management is based on set theory. Built-in query language is designed in the RDBMS, so that it can manipulate sets of data (one or more tuples).
- The user interface used with relational models is non-procedural because only what needs to be done is specified and not how it has to be done. Using any of the other methods, you have not only to specify what needs to be done but how it has to be done as well.

Data as well as Data Security come under the central control of the RDBMSystem. A very great deal of these requirements are built directly into the RDBMS environment itself. Gradually 4thGeneration RDBMSystems came into sharp focus. These systems are in great demand today. Programmers who can write in 4thGeneration Language's, that work with RDBMS are in equally great demand.

In a RDBMS, all user requests to Insert data in a table or to Update, Delete or View data in a table must be routed through the RDBMS engine only. Direct calls for data, cannot be made to the tables themselves. Hence there is a single point of control when it comes to data manipulation, this gives rise to excellent data security.

This means that unless the RDBMS engine is loaded and running in a computers memory user requests for table data are simply not entertained.

In a single user environment only one user can manipulate data in a table through the Oracle DBA. No other user can share the data in the table being used for manipulating data. This is quite wasteful from the point of view of data. There will have to be multiple tables all carrying the *very same data* on different computers. This redundant data being held on different computers is eliminated or very sharply reduced by shifting to computers and operating systems capable of working with multiple users concurrently.

In a multi user environment, an RDBMS engine capable of functioning on a multi user operating system is used. Now, multiple user's requests for table data will be responded to by the RDBMS engine. In this scenario, the computer on which the RDBMS engine is loaded and run, which responds to multiple user requests for table data concurrently, is called the RDBMS Server. If Oracle is the RDBMS engine being used then this is called the **Oracle Server**.

Since this book is about Oracle, we are going to focus only on the Oracle engine. This engine will be loaded on a multi user operating system mounted on a computer that can take the multi user operating system. Hence, we are going to focus on an Oracle Server.

Diagram 1.2 illustrates the interaction between a multi-user operating system and the hard disk of the computer. The DBA system is a block of code loaded from the hard disk drive by the person who organizes all information that sits on the hard disk. By default this person becomes the Oracle **DataBase Administrator**. This person is responsible for administrating all of Oracle's resources on the hard disk drive and allowing user access to these resources.

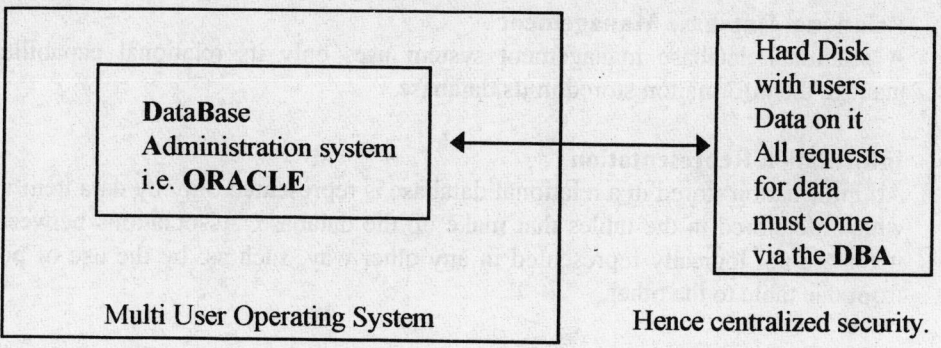

Diagram 1.2 : Interaction between Oracle, a multi-user O/S and the hard disk drive with data on it.

The DBA takes care of the following:
- Updating the database.
- Retrieving information from the database.
- Accepting query language statements.
- Enforcing security specifications.
- Enforcing data integrity specifications.
- Enforcing transaction consistency.
- Managing data sharing.
- Optimizing queries.
- Managing system catalogs.

E.F. TED CODD'S LAWS FOR A FULLY FUNCTIONAL RELATIONAL DATABASE MANAGEMENT SYSTEM

> These set of rules are given here more for knowledge purposes that for any other reason. They are not in any way directly applicable to the actual study of commercial application development using Oracle as the programming environment.

- **Relational Database Management**
  A relational database management system uses only its relational capabilities to manage the information stored in its database.

- **Information Representation**
  All information stored in a relational database is represented only by data item values, which are stored in the tables that make up the database. Associations between data items are not logically represented in any other way, such as, by the use of pointers from one table to the other.

- **Logical Accessibility**
  Every data item value stored in a relational database is accessible by stating the name of the table it is stored in, the name of the column under which it is stored and the value of the primary key that defines the row in which it is stored.

- **Representation of null values**
  The database management system has a consistent method for representing null values. For example, null values for numeric data must be distinct from zero or any other numeric value and for character data it must be different from a string of blanks or any other character value.

- **Catalog facilities**
  The logical description of a relational database is represented in the same manner as ordinary data. This is done so that the facilities of the relational database management system itself can be used to maintain database description.

- **Data Language**
  A relational database management system may support many types of languages for describing data and accessing the database. However, there must be at least one language that uses ordinary character strings to support the definition of data, the definition of views, the manipulation of data, constraints on data integrity, information concerning authorization and the boundaries for recovery of units.

- **View Updatability**
  Any view that can be defined using combinations of base tables, that are theoretically updatable, is capable of being updated by the relational database management system.

- **Insert, Update and Delete**
  Any operand that describes the results of a single retrieval operation is capable of being applied to an insert, update or delete operation as well.

- **Physical data independence**
  Changes made to physical storage representations or access methods do not require changes to be made to application programs.

- **Logical data independence**
  Changes made to tables, that do not modify any data stored in that table, do not require changes to be made to application programs.

- **Integrity Constraints**
  Constraints that apply to entity integrity and referential integrity are specifiable by the data language implemented by the database management system and not by the statements coded into the applications program

- **Database Distribution**
  The data language implemented by the relational database management system supports the ability to distribute the database without requiring changes to be made to application programs. This facility must be provided in the data language, whether or not the database management system itself supports distributed databases.

- **Non Subversion**
  If the relational database management system supports facilities that allow application programs to operate on the tables a row at a time, an application program using this type of database access is prevented from bypassing entity integrity or referential integrity constraints that are defined for the database.

ORACLE 7....... THE PRODUCT PHILOSOPHY
Introduction to Oracle Tools :

Conceptually, Oracle is a kernel package that has a number of tools that can be purchased separately and integrated with the kernel as *'Addons'*. These tools allow the user to create database objects, forms, reports, graphs etc. Some of the tools of Oracle are *SQL*Plus, Oracle Forms, Oracle Report Writer, Oracle Graphics, SQL Precompilers for C and Cobol*

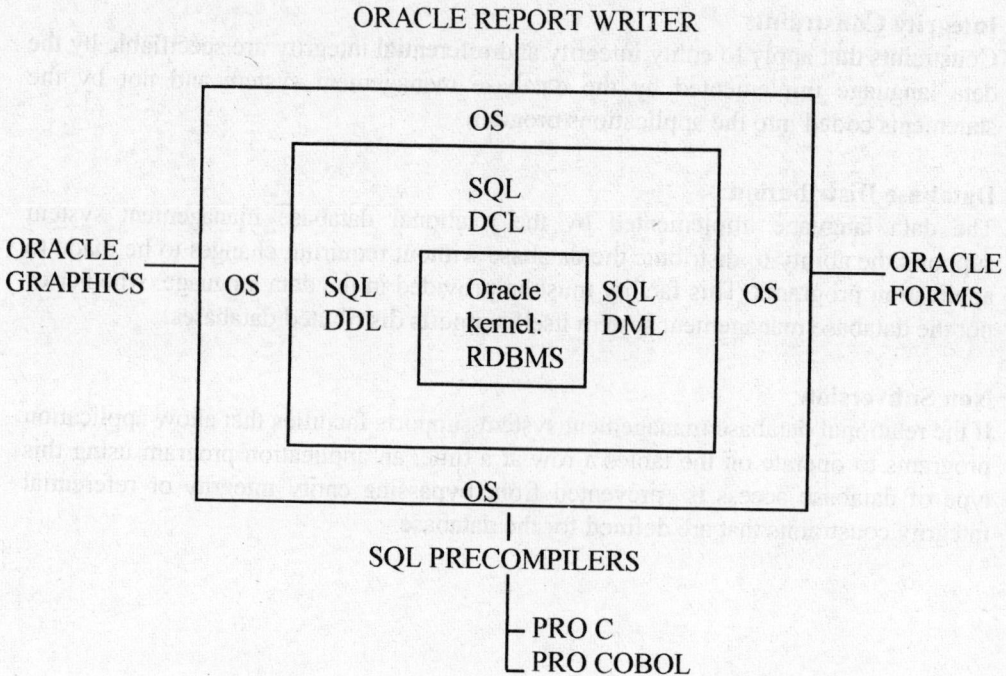

Diagram 1.3 : Various tools connected to the Oracle kernel.

Oracle DBA:

The Oracle DBA can compile and execute SQL sentences issued by a user. If the SQL sentence is unsuccessful, the Oracle DBA returns an appropriate error message to the user.

Very briefly this is shown in diagram 1.4

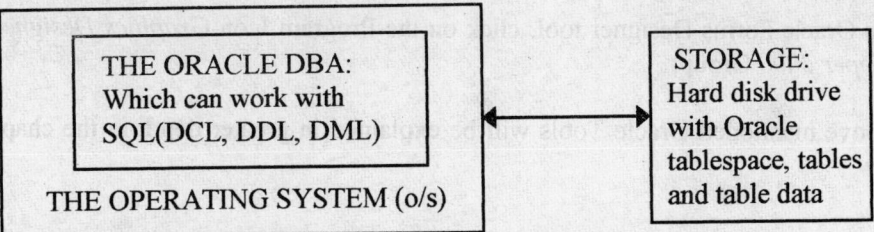

Diagram 1.4 : Working with the Oracle DBA.

Once the Oracle DBA is loaded in memory, users of the network can connect to the DBA and get work done.

SQL*Plus :

SQL*Plus is made up of two distinct parts. These are
- Interactive SQL
- PL/SQL

Interactive SQL is designed to create, access and maintain all data structures like tables, indexes etc. It can also be used for interactive, data manipulation.

Programmers can use PL/SQL to create programs for validation and manipulation of table data. PL/SQL adds to the power of interactive SQL and provides the user with all the facilities of a standard, modern day (4GL) programming environment.

To invoke SQL*Plus, click on the Program Icon *SQL*Plus 3.1* in the *Oracle* Group.

Oracle Forms :

This Tool allows you to create a data entry screen along with suitable menu objects. Thus it is the Oracle Forms Tool, that handles data gathering and data validationin a commercial application.

To invoke the Oracle Forms designer tool, click on the Program Icon *Forms Designer* in the *Developer 2000* Group.

Report Writer :

Report Writer allows programmers to prepare innovative reports using data from the Oracle Structures like tables, views etc. Thus it is the Report Writer Tool that handles the reporting section of a commercial application.

To invoke the Oracle Report Designer tool, click on the Program Icon *Reports Designer* in the *Developer 2000* Group.

Oracle Graphics :
Some of the data can be better represented in the form of graphs. The Oracle Graphics Tool allows programmers to prepare graphs using data from Oracle Structures like tables, views etc. Oracle Graphics can also be considered as a part of the reporting section of a commercial application.

To invoke Oracle Forms Designer tool, click on the Program Icon *Graphics Designer* in the *Developer 2000* Group.

All the above mentioned Oracle Tools will be explained in greater depth in the chapters that follow.

2. INTERACTIVE SQL

INVOKING SQL*PLUS

To work in Oracle, the user should be able to effectively communicate with the Oracle DBA. The user can communicate with the Oracle DBA by using ANSI SQL, the natural language of DBA.

Oracle provides an Interactive SQL tool i.e. SQL*Plus, which allows users to enter the ANSI SQL sentences and pass them to the DBA for execution. These sentences allow the user to create, access and maintain data structures like tables, indexes etc.

This is the first tool to be used by most programmers when they begin their study in Oracle.

The steps in invoking SQL*Plus are as follows :

1. Start Windows in the normal way.

2. Click on the **Start** button as shown in diagram 2.1 and click on **Programs**. It displays a list of programs. Click on **Oracle** and then select **SQL*Plus 3.1**.

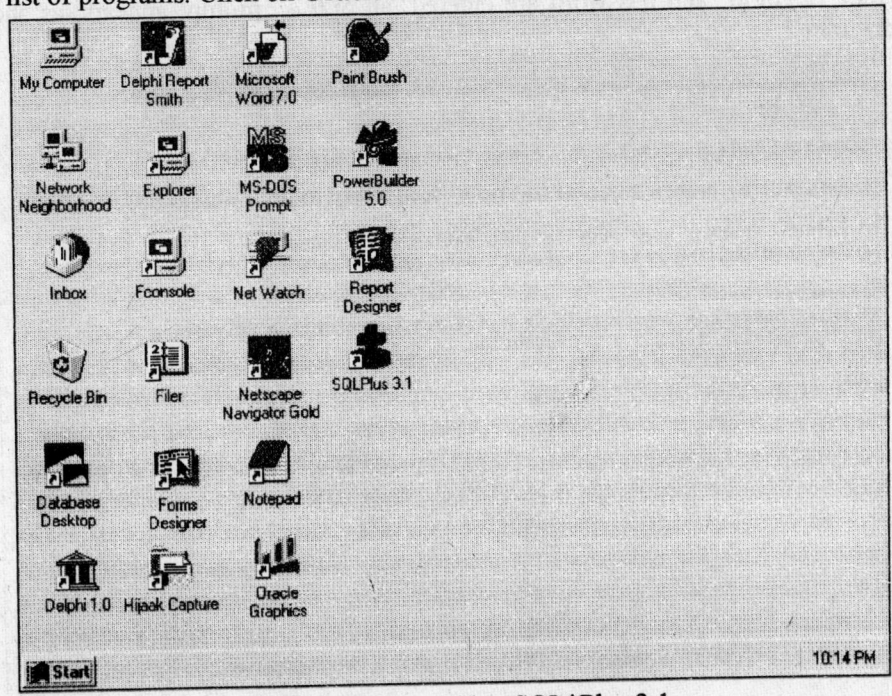

Diagram 2.1 : Invoking SQL*Plus 3.1

3. You are prompted for your Login-id and password (Oracle) as shown in diagram 2.2.

14 COMMERCIAL APPLICATION DEVELOPMENT USING ORACLE 7, DEVELOPER 2000

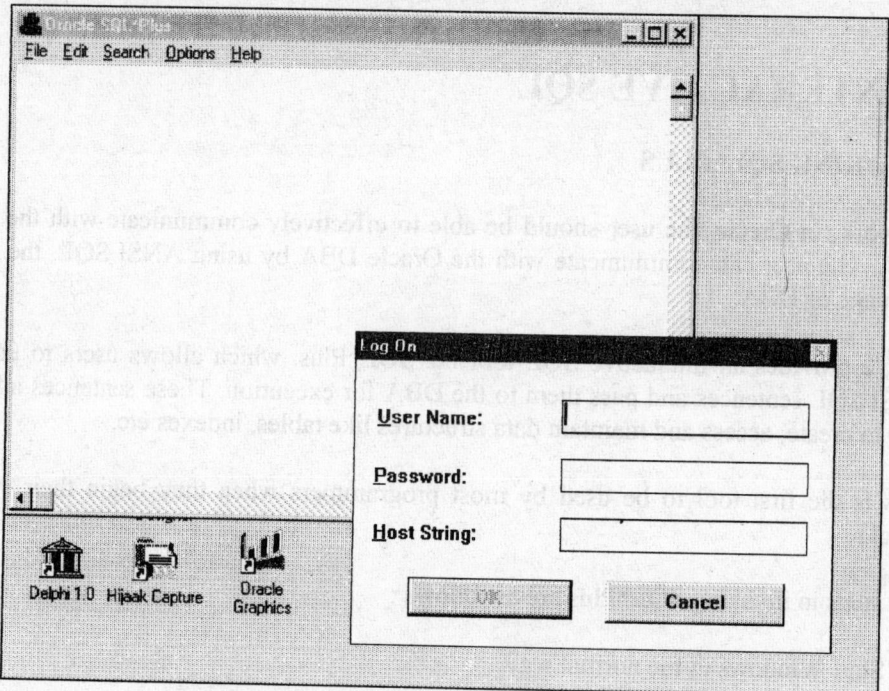

Diagram 2.2 : Entering user id and password

4. Once Login-id and password are entered, an *SQL>* prompt appears, as shown in diagram 2.3.

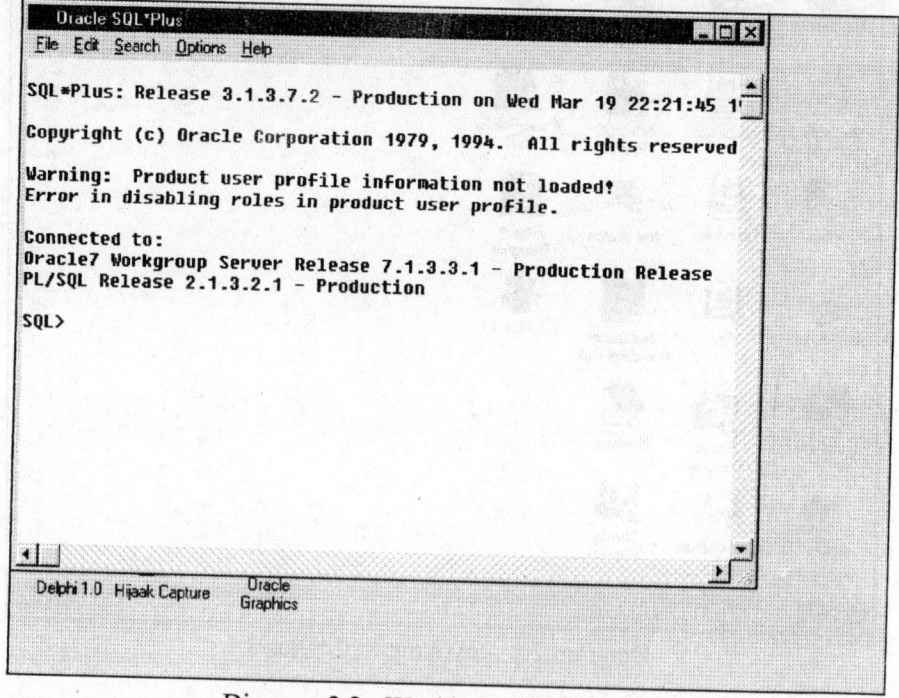

Diagram 2.3 : Working with SQL*Plus

INTERACTIVE SQL 15

At this point in time, you are connected to the Oracle DBA. Oracle's SQL*Plus tool allows you to pass SQL statements to the DBA. It also allows you access to *PL/SQL* i.e. the *Procedural Language* of Oracle which we shall learn in later chapters.

The methods via which you can construct SQL sentences and pass them to the DBA are.
- Use the SQL editor, which is automatically invoked and running while the SQL prompt is on the screen. This editor is similar to the DOS edlin editor and the commands are nearly identical.
- Invoke Windows's full page Notepad editor and create a command file containing the SQL sentences that you send to the DBA using suitable ISQL commands.

An example of both methods is described below :
FIRST METHOD: (Using the SQL editor)
- At the SQL> prompt, you can execute any valid SQL statement. e.g. : *select * from client_master;*
- If you want to save the SQL statement in a file, type in : *save f1* where f1 is the filename. This command creates a file by the name of *f1.sql* in the current directory.
- At any later point of time, if you want to execute the same sql statement, give the command : *get f1* which gets the file in the buffer and returns back to the SQL> prompt.
- Then at the SQL> prompt type, / using SQL's editor
- This executes the SQL statement which is stored in the buffer.
- You can also edit the file *f1.sql* using the standard line editor commands.

SECOND METHOD: (Using Windows Notepad editor)
- Invoke Notepad from the Accessories group icon in program manager. This opens a new file in Notepad.
- Write your SQL sentence into the file. For e.g. *select * from client_master*
- Terminate the SQL statement with a / (backslash) **in the first column of the next line**.
- To run this file, after saving it in notepad as *f1.sql*, at the SQL> prompt
  - type the command *get f1*
    or
  - Click on **Open** from the **File** menu item. It displays the *File Open* dialog box. Select the name of the file and click on OK.
- To execute the file *f.sql* at the SQL> prompt type,
  -
    or
  - Click on **Run** from the **File** menu item.
- Everytime you make changes to the *.sql* file, you have to open the file and run the file
- The *.sql* file can be compiled and executed using *start <filename>* at the SQL > prompt.

Via SQL you can create and maintain data manipulation objects such as tables, views, joins etc. These data manipulation objects will be created and stored in a tablespace to which you have been assigned by the Oracle DBA.

DATA MANIPULATION IN DATA BASE MANAGEMENT SYSTEMS
The CPU of a computing system requires that user data be held in a very rigid format for high speed data manipulation.

All DBMSystems store user data in what is called a *table*. A *table* is really a two dimensional matrix that consists of rows and columns. Each column consists of a cell which is created by the **DataBase Administrator**.

A cell is also called a field. A number of such fields placed in the horizontal plane is called a record or row. A number of rows, of equal length placed one below the other is called a table.

To create a cell in which a user can store and maintain data, the DBA requires a minimum of three parameters to be passed by the user. These parameters are *cell name*, *cell length* and *cell data type*.

These parameters are passed to the DBA via its natural language, SQL. There are other parameters that the user can pass to the DBA at cell creation time. These parameters place various constraints on the kind of data that the user can load the cell with.

THE COMPONENT PARTS OF A TWO DIMENSIONAL MATRIX

```
Tablename : candidates

Name          Age          Telno

Sunita        12           6124371
Mita          20           3452670
Carol         21           4456132
```

Diagram 2.4 : The components of a two dimensional matrix.

The field *Name* is of type char (character) with length 20, the field *Age* is of type number with length 2 and the field *Telno* is of type number with length 8.

The two dimensional matrix will have a unique name, (in diagram 2.4, the name is *candidates*) when we create it via which it can be referred to, after its creation. The rigidity of data stored in such a format is sufficient for the CPU to enable very high speed data manipulation.

THE DATATYPES THAT A CELL CAN HOLD
- CHAR

Values of this datatype are fixed length character strings of maximum length 255 characters. ORACLE7 compares CHAR values using blank-padded comparison semantics.

- VARCHAR / VARCHAR2

Values of this datatype are variable length character strings of maximum length 2000. ORACLE7 compares VARCHAR values using non-padded comparison semantics.

- NUMBER

The NUMBER datatype is used to store numbers (fixed or floating point). Numbers of virtually any magnitude maybe stored up to 38 digits of precision. Numbers as large as 9.99 * 10 to the power of 124, i.e. 1 followed by 125 zeros can be stored.

- DATE

The standard format is DD-Mon-YY as in 13-NOV-88. To enter dates other than the standard format, use the appropriate functions. DateTime stores date in the 24-hour format. By default, the time in a date field is 12:00:00 am, if no time portion is specified. The default date for a date field is the first day of the current month.

- LONG

Cells defined as LONG can store variable length character strings containing upto 65,535 characters. Long data can be used to store arrays of binary data in ASCII format.

TWO DIMENSION MATRIX CREATION

This can be done by communicating with the DBA using the natural language of the DBA, namely ISQL. Hence, by using an ISQL sentence we can command the DBA to create a matrix with cell parameters of our choice.

Here, it is necessary to understand how to construct sentences via which you can communicate with the DBA. We must take a look at a generic SQL sentence to understand the SQL syntax.

The Generic SQL Sentence Construct :
        VERB [parameter 1], [parameter 2], ... [parameter n];
Note : A comma delimits one parameter from another.
        A semi colon indicates the end of an sql sentence.

The Create Table Command

Creating a table :
<u>Syntax</u> :   CREATE TABLE tablename
                (columnname datatype(size), columnname datatype(size));

<u>Examples</u> :
1. Create client_master table where :

Column Name	Data Type	Size
client_no	varchar2	6
name	varchar2	20
address1	varchar2	30
address2	varchar2	30
city	varchar2	15
state	varchar2	15
pincode	number	6
remarks	varchar2	60
bal_due	number	10,2

CREATE TABLE client_master
  (client_no varchar2(6), name varchar2(20), address1 varchar2(30),
    address2 varchar2(30), city varchar2(15), state varchar2(15),
    pincode number(6), remarks varchar2(60), bal_due number(10,2));

2. Create product_master table where

Column Name	Data Type	Size
product_no	varchar2	6
description	varchar2	25
profit_percent	number	2,2
unit_measure	varchar2	10
qty_on_hand	number	8
reorder_lvl	number	8
sell_price	number	8,2
cost_price	number	8,2

CREATE TABLE product_master
(product_no varchar2(6), description varchar2(25),
profit_percent number(2,2), unit_measure varchar2(10), qty_on_hand number(8),
reorder_lvl number(8), sell_price number (8,2), cost_price number (8,2));

Creating a table from a table :
Syntax :   CREATE TABLE tablename
                [(columnname, columnname)]
                    AS SELECT columnname, columnname FROM tablename;

Note : If the Source table from which the Target table is being created, has records in it then the target table is populated with these records as well.

Example :
1. Create table supplier_master from client_master. select all fields and rename client_no with supplier_no and name with supplier_name.

        CREATE TABLE supplier_master
                (supplier_no, supplier_name, address1,
                    address2, city, state, pincode, remarks)
                AS SELECT client_no, name, address1, address2,
                    city, state, pincode, remarks
                FROM client_master;

INSERTION OF DATA INTO TABLES
Inserting a single row of data into a table :
Syntax :   INSERT INTO tablename
                    [(columnname, columnname)]
                    VALUES (expression, expression);

Example :
1. Insert a record in the client_master table as *client_no* = C02000, *name* = Prabhakar Rane, *address1* = A-5, Jay Apartments, *address2* = Service Road, Vile Parle, *city* = Bombay, *state* = Maharashtra, *pincode* = 400057;

        INSERT INTO client_master
                (client_no, name, address1, address2, city, state, pincode)
                VALUES ('C02000', 'Prabhakar Rane', 'A-5, Jay Apartments',
                    'Service Road, Vile Parle', 'Bombay', ' Maharashtra', 400057);

Note : The character expressions must be in single quotes.

Inserting data into a table from another table :
Syntax :   INSERT INTO tablename
              SELECT columnname, columnname,
              FROM tablename ;

Example :
1. Insert records in table supplier_master from table client_master;

   INSERT INTO supplier_master
         SELECT client_no, name, address1, address2,
                 city, state, pincode, remarks
         FROM client_master;

Insertion of selected data into a table from another table:
Syntax :   INSERT INTO tablename
              SELECT columnname, columnname
              FROM tablename
              WHERE column = expression;

Example :
1. Insert records into supplier_master from table client_master where client_no = 'C01001';

   INSERT INTO supplier_master
         SELECT client_no, name, address1, address2,
                 city, pincode, state, remarks
         FROM client_master
         WHERE client_no = 'C01001' ;

UPDATING THE CONTENTS OF A TABLE
Syntax :   UPDATE tablename
              SET columnname = expression, columnname = expression...
              WHERE columnname = expression;

Example :
1. Update table client_master set name = 'Vijay Kadam' and address = 'SCT Jay Apartments' where client_no = 'C02000';

   UPDATE client_master
         SET name = 'Vijay Kadam' , address1 = 'SCT Jay Apartments'
         WHERE client_no = 'C02000' ;

DELETION OPERATIONS
Deletion of all rows :
Syntax :   DELETE FROM tablename;

Example :
1. Delete all records from table client_master;

   DELETE FROM client_master ;

Deletion of a specified number of rows :
Syntax :   DELETE FROM tablename WHERE search condition;

Example :
1. Delete from table client_master where client_no = 'C02000';

   DELETE FROM client_master WHERE client_no = 'C02000' ;

THE MANY FACES OF THE *SELECT* COMMAND

Global data extract :

<u>Syntax</u> :   SELECT * FROM tablename;

Example :
1. Select all records from table client_master;

   SELECT * FROM client_master;

The retrieval of specific columns from a table :

<u>Syntax</u> :   SELECT columnname, columnname
            FROM tablename;

Examples :
1. Select client_no and name from client_master

   SELECT client_no, name
        FROM client_master ;

Elimination of duplicates from the Select statement :

<u>Syntax</u> :   SELECT DISTINCT columnname, columnname
            FROM tablename;

Example :
1. Select unique rows from client_master;

   SELECT DISTINCT client_no, name
        FROM client_master;

Sorting of data in a table :

<u>Syntax</u> :   SELECT columnname, columnname
            FROM tablename
            ORDER BY columnname, columnname;

Example :
1. Select client_no, name, address1, address2, city, pincode from client_master sort in the ascending order of client_no;

   SELECT client_no, name, address1, address2, city, pincode
        FROM client_master
        ORDER BY client_no;

Selecting a data set from table data :

Syntax :   SELECT columnname, columnname
                    FROM tablename
                    WHERE search condition;

Example :
1. Select client_no, name from client_master where client_no is equal to 'C01234';

         SELECT client_no, name
                    FROM client_master
                    WHERE client_no = 'C01234';

Note : In the *search condition* all standard operators such as logic, arithmetic, predicates etc. can be used. We shall see their usage in SQL sentences used in later chapters.

MODIFYING THE STRUCTURE OF TABLES
Adding new columns :
Syntax :   ALTER TABLE tablename
            ADD (newcolumnname datatype(size), newcolumnname datatype(size)...);

Example :
1. Add fields client_tel number(8), client_fax number(15) to table client_master;

    ALTER TABLE client_master
        ADD (client_tel number(8), client_fax number(15));

Modifying existing columns :
Syntax :   ALTER TABLE tablename
            MODIFY (columnname newdatatype(size));

Example :
1. Modify field client_fax as client_fax varchar2(25);

    ALTER TABLE client_master
        MODIFY (client_fax varchar2(25));

Restrictions on the Alter table :
Using the alter table clause you cannot perform the following tasks :
- Change the name of the table.
- Change the name of the column.
- Drop a column.
- Decrease the size of a column if table data exists.

Note :
Oracle will not allow constraints defined using the alter table, if the data in the table, violates such constraints.

Example : The Primary key constraint on the column that has duplicate values will not be allowed.

REMOVING / DELETING / DROPPING TABLES :
Syntax :   DROP TABLE tablename;

Example :
1. Delete table client_master;

    DROP TABLE client_master;

DATA CONSTRAINTS

Besides the cell name, cell length and cell data type, there are other parameters i.e. other data constraints, that can be passed to the DBA at cell creation time.

These data constraints will be connected to a cell by the DBA as flags. Whenever a user attempts to load a cell with data, the DBA will check the data being loaded into the cell against the data constraints defined at the time the cell was created. If the data being loaded fails any of the data constraint checks fired by the DBA, the DBA will not load the data into the cell, reject the entered record, and will flash an error message to the user.

These constraints are given a constraint name and the DBA stores the constraints with it's name and instructions internally along with the cell itself.

The constraints can either be placed at the column level or at the table level.

Column Level Constraints :
If the constraints are defined along with the column definition, it is called as a column level constraint. Column level constraint can be applied to any one column at a time i.e. they are local to a specific column. If the constraint spans across multiple columns, the user will have to use table level constraints.

Table Level Constraints :
If the data constraint attached to a specific cell in a table references the contents of another cell in the table then the user will have to use table level constraints. Table level constraints are stored as a part of the global table definition.

Examples of different constraints that can be applied on the table are as follows :

NULL value concepts :
While creating tables, if a row lacks a data value for a particular column, that value is said to be null. Columns of any data types may contain null values unless the column was defined as *not null* when the table was created.

Principles of NULL values :
- Setting a null value is appropriate when the actual value is unknown, or when a value would not be meaningful.
- A null value is not equivalent to a value of zero.
- A null value will evaluate to null in any expression. e.g. null multiplied by 10 is null.
- When a column name is defined as *not null*, then that column becomes a *mandatory* column. It implies that the user is forced to enter data into that column.

Example : Create table client_master with a not null constraint on columns *client_no*, *name, address1, address2*.
NOT NULL as a column constraint :
    CREATE TABLE client_master
    (client_no varchar2(6) NOT NULL,
    name varchar2(20) NOT NULL,
    address1 varchar2(30) NOT NULL,
    address2 varchar2(30) NOT NULL,
    city varchar2(15), state varchar2(15), pincode number(6),
    remarks varchar2(60), bal_due number (10,2));

Primary Key concepts :
A primary key is one or more columns in a table used to uniquely identify each row in the table. Primary key values must not be null and must be unique across the column.

A multicolumn primary key is called a *composite* primary key. The only function that a primary key performs is to uniquely identify a row and thus if one column is used it is just as good as if multiple columns are used. Multiple columns i.e. (composite keys)are used only when the system designed requires a primary key that cannot be contained in a single column.

Examples :
PRIMARY KEY as a column constraint :
Create client_master where client_no is the primary key.

    CREATE TABLE client_master
    (client_no varchar2(6) PRIMARY KEY,
    name varchar2(20), address1 varchar2(30), address2 varchar2(30),
    city varchar2(15), state varchar2(15), pincode number(6),
    remarks varchar2(60), bal_due number (10,2));

PRIMARY KEY as a table constraint :
Create a sales_order_details table where

Column Name	Data Type	Size	Attributes
s_order_no	varchar2	6	Primary Key
product_no	varchar2	6	Primary Key
qty_ordered	number	8	
qty_disp	number	8	
product_rate	number	8,2	

    CREATE TABLE sales_order_details
    (s_order_no varchar2(6), product_no varchar2(6),
    qty_ordered number(8), qty_disp number(8),
    product_rate number(8,2),
    PRIMARY KEY (s_order_no, product_no));

Unique Key concepts :

A unique key is similar to a primary key, except that the purpose of a unique key is to ensure that information in the column for each record is unique, as with telephone or driver's license numbers. A table may have many unique keys.

Example : Create Table client_master with unique constraint on column client_no

UNIQUE as a column constraint :

    CREATE TABLE client_master
       (client_no varchar2(6) CONSTRAINT cnum_ukey UNIQUE,
      name varchar2(20), address1 varchar2(30), address2 varchar2(30),
      city varchar2(15), state varchar2(15), pincode number(6),
      remarks varchar2(60), bal_due number(10,2), partpay_yn char(1));

UNIQUE as a table constraint :

    CREATE TABLE client_master
      (client_no varchar2(6), name varchar2(20),
      address1 varchar2(30), address2 varchar2(30),
      city varchar2(15), state varchar2(15), pincode number(6),
      remarks varchar2(60), bal_due number(10,2),
      CONSTRAINT cnum_ukey UNIQUE(client_no));

Default value concepts :

At the time of cell creation a 'default value' can be assigned to it. When the user is loading a 'record' with values and leaves this cell empty, the DBA will automatically load this cell with the default value specified. The data type of the default value should match the data type of the column. You can use the default clause to specify any default value you want.

Create sales_order table where :

Column Name	Data Type	Size	Attributes
s_order_no	varchar2	6	Primary Key
s_order_date	date		
client_no	varchar2	6	
dely_Addr	varchar2	25	
salesman_no	varchar2	6	
dely_type	char	1	delivery : part(P) / full (F) Default 'F'
billed_yn	char	1	
dely_date	date		
order_status	varchar2	10	

```
CREATE TABLE sales_order
    (s_order_no  varchar2(6) PRIMARY KEY,
     s_order_date date, client_no varchar2(6),
     dely_Addr varchar2(25), salesman_no varchar2(6),
     dely_type char(1) DEFAULT 'F',
     billed_yn char(1), dely_date date,
     order_status varchar2(10)) ;
```

Foreign Key concepts :
Foreign keys represent relationships between tables. A foreign key is a column (or a group of columns) whose values are derived from the primary key of the same or some other table.

The existence of a foreign key implies that the table with the foreign key is related to the primary key table from which the foreign key is derived. A foreign key must have a corresponding primary key value in the primary key table to have a meaning.

For example, the *s_order_no* column is the primary key of table *sales_order*. In table *sales_order_details*, *s_order_no* is a foreign key that references the *s_order_no* values in table *sales_order*.

The Foreign Key/References constraint :
- rejects an INSERT or UPDATE of a value, if a corresponding value does not currently exist in the primary key table;
- rejects a DELETE, if it would invalidate a REFERENCES constraint;
- must reference a PRIMARY KEY or UNIQUE column(s) in primary key table;
- will reference the PRIMARY KEY of the primary key table if no column or group of columns is specified in the constraint;

- must reference a table, not a view or cluster;
- requires that you own the primary key table, have REFERENCE privilege on it, or have column-level REFERENCE privilege on the referenced columns in the primary key table;
- doesn't restrict how other constraints may reference the same tables;
- requires that the FOREIGN KEY column(s) and the CONSTRAINT column(s) have matching datatypes;
- may reference the same table named in the CREATE TABLE statement;
- must not reference the same column more than once (in a single constraint).

Example : Create table sales_order_details with primary key as s_order_no and product_no and foreign key as s_order_no referencing column s_order_no in the sales_order table.

FOREIGN KEY as a column constraint :
    CREATE TABLE sales_order_details
    (s_order_no varchar2(6) REFERENCES sales_order,
    product_no varchar2(6),
    qty_ordered number(8), qty_disp number(8),
    product_rate number(8,2),
    PRIMARY KEY (s_order_no, product_no));

FOREIGN KEY as a table constraint :
    CREATE TABLE sales_order_details
    (s_order_no varchar2(6),
    product_no varchar2(6),
    qty_ordered number(8), qty_disp number(8),
    product_rate number(8,2),
    PRIMARY KEY (s_order_no, product_no),
    FOREIGN KEY (s_order_no) REFERENCES sales_order);

CHECK Integrity constraints :
Use the CHECK constraint when you need to enforce integrity rules that can be evaluated based on a logical expression. Never use CHECK constraints if the constraint can be defined using the not null, primary key or foreign key constraint.

Following are a few examples of appropriate CHECK constraints :
- a CHECK constraint on the client_no column of the client_master so that no client_no value *starts with 'C'*.
- a CHECK constant on name column of the client_master so that the name is entered in *upper case*.
- a CHECK constraint on the city column of the client_master so that only the cities *"BOMBAY", "NEWDELHI", "MADRAS" and "CALCUTTA"* are allowed.

```
CREATE TABLE client_master
  ( client_no varchar2(6) CONSTRAINT ck_clientno
   CHECK (client_no like 'C%'),
    name varchar2(20) CONSTRAINT ck_cname
    CHECK (name = upper(name)),
    address1 varchar2(30), address2 varchar2(30),
    city varchar2(15) CONSTRAINT ck_city
    CHECK (city IN ('NEWDELHI', 'BOMBAY', 'CALCUTTA', 'MADRAS')),
    state varchar2(15), pincode number(6),
    remarks varchar2(60), bal_due number(10,2));
```

When using CHECK constraints, consider the ANSI / ISO standard which states that a CHECK constraint is violated only if the condition evaluates to *False, True and unknown values do not violate a check condition.* Therefore, make sure that a CHECK constraint that you define actually enforces the rule you need to enforce.

For example, consider the following CHECK constraint for *emp* table :
   CHECK (sal > 0 or comm >= 0)

At first glance, this rule may be interpreted as "do not allow a row in *emp* table unless the employee's salary is greater than 0 or the employee's commission is greater than or equal to "0". However, note that if a row is inserted with a null salary and a negative commission, the row does not violate the CHECK constraint because the entire check condition is evaluated as unknown. In this particular case, you can account for such violations by placing *not null* integrity constraint on both the *sal* and *comm* columns.

<u>CHECK with *not null* integrity constraints</u> :
According to the ANSI / ISO standard, a *not null* integrity constraint is an example of a CHECK integrity constraint, where the condition is, CHECK (column_name IS NOT NULL). Therefore, the *not null* integrity constraint for a single column can, in practice be written in two forms, by using the *not null* constraint or by using a CHECK constraint. For ease of use, you should always choose to define the *not null* integrity constraint instead of a CHECK constraint with the *is not null* condition.

Here we shall look at the method via which data constraints can be attached to the cell so that data validation can be done at table level itself using the power of the DBA.

A constraint clause restricts the range of valid values for one column (a column constraint) or for a group of columns (a table constraint). Any INSERT, UPDATE or DELETE statement evaluates a relevant constraint; the constraint must be satisfied for the statement to succeed.

Constraints can be connected to a table by CREATE TABLE or ALTER TABLE command. Use ALTER TABLE to add or drop the constraint from a table. Constraints are recorded in the data dictionary. If you don't name a constraint, it is assigned the name SYS_C*n*, where *n* is an integer that makes the name unique in the database.

Restrictions on *CHECK* Constraints :
A CHECK integrity constraint requires that a condition be true or unknown for every row of the table. If a statement causes the condition to evaluate to false; the statement is rolled back. The condition of a CHECK constraint has the following limitations:
- The condition must be a Boolean expression that can be evaluated using the values in the row being inserted or updated.
- The condition cannot contain subqueries or sequences.
- The condition cannot include the SYSDATE, UID, USER or USERENV SQL functions.

Defining different constraints on the table :
Create a sales_order_details table where

Column Name	Data Type	Size	Attributes
s_order_no	varchar2	6	Primary Key, Foreign Key references s_order_no of sales_order table.
product_no	varchar2	6	Primary Key, Foreign Key references product_no of product_master table.
qty_ordered	number	8	not null
qty_disp	number	8	
product_rate	number	8,2	not null

```
CREATE TABLE sales_order_details
( s_order_no varchar2(6) CONSTRAINT order_fkey
         REFERENCES sales_order,
  product_no varchar2(6) CONSTRAINT product_fkey
         REFERENCES product_master,
  qty_ordered number(8) NOT NULL,
  qty_disp number(8),
  product_rate number(8,2) NOT NULL,
  PRIMARY KEY (s_order_no, product_no));
```

Defining Integrity constraints in the ALTER TABLE command :
You can also define integrity constraints using the constraint clause in the ALTER TABLE command. The following examples show the definitions of several integrity constraints :

1. Add PRIMARY KEY constant on column supplier_no in table supplier_master;

    ALTER TABLE supplier_master
        ADD PRIMARY KEY (suppplier_no);

2. Add FOREIGN KEY constraint on column s_order_no in table sales_order_details referencing table sales_order, modify column qty_ordered to include NOT NULL constant;

    ALTER TABLE sales_order_details
        ADD CONSTRAINT order_fkey
            FOREIGN KEY (s_order_no) REFERENCES sales_order
    MODIFY (qty_ordered number(8) NOT NULL);

Dropping Integrity constraints in the ALTER TABLE command :
You can drop an integrity constraint if the rule that it enforces is no longer true or if the constraint is no longer needed. Drop the constraint using the ALTER TABLE command with the DROP clause. The following examples illustrate the dropping of integrity constraints:

1. Drop the PRIMARY KEY constraint from supplier_master;

    ALTER TABLE supplier_master
        DROP PRIMARY KEY;

2. Drop FOREIGN KEY constraint on column product_no in table sales_order_details;

    ALTER TABLE sales_order_details
        DROP CONSTRAINT product_fkey;

Note : Dropping UNIQUE and PRIMARY KEY constraints drops the associated indexes.

COMPUTATIONS IN EXPRESSION LISTS USED TO SELECT DATA
Arithmetic operators :

+	Addition	*	Multiplication
-	Subtraction	**	Exponentiation
/	Division	( )	Enclosed operation

Example :
1. Select product_no, description and compute sell_price * 0.05 and sell_price * 1.05 for each row retrieved;

    SELECT product_no, description, sell_price * 0.05, sell_price * 1.05
        FROM product_master;

Here, *sell_price * 0.05* and *sell_price * 1.05* are not columns in the table *product_master*, but are calculations done on the contents of the column *sell_price* of the table *product_master*.

By default, the DBA will use the column names of the table *product_master* to display output to the user on screen.

Since there are no columns with names as *sell_price * 0.05* and *sell_price * 1.05* in the table *product_master*, the DBA will perform the required operations and use these names as the default column names when displaying the output as shown below :

Product No	Description	Sell Price * 0.05	Sell Price * 1.05
P00001	1.44 Floppies	25	525
P03453	Monitors	600	12600
P06734	Mouse	50	1050
P07865	1.22 Floppies	25	525
P07868	Keyboards	150	3150
P07885	CD Drive	250	5250
P07965	HDD	400	8400
P07975	1.44 Drive	50	1050
P08865	1.22 Drive	50	1050

Renaming Columns Used With Expression Lists :

The default output column names can be renamed by the user if required.

<u>Syntax</u> : SELECT columnname result_columnname, columnname result_columnname
FROM tablename ;

<u>Example</u> :
1. Select product_no, description and compute sell_price * 0.05 and sell_price * 1.05 for each row retrieved. Rename sell_price * 0.05 as Increase and salary * 1.05 as New_Price;

SELECT product_no, description,
sell_price * 0.05 Increase, sell_price * 1.05 New_Price
FROM product_master;

Product No	Description	Increase	New Price
P00001	1.44 Floppies	25	525
P03453	Monitors	600	12600
P06734	Mouse	50	1050
P07865	1.22 Floppies	25	525
P07868	Keyboards	150	3150
P07885	CD Drive	250	5250
P07965	HDD	400	8400
P07975	1.44 Drive	50	1050
P08865	1.22 Drive	50	1050

LOGICAL OPERATORS

The logical operators that can be used in SQL sentences are :

    and   *all of* must be included
    or   *any of* may be included
    not   *none of* would be included

<u>Examples</u> :
1. Select client information like client_no, name, address1, address2, city and pincode for all the clients in 'BOMBAY' or 'DELHI';

SELECT client_no, name, address1, address2, city, pincode
FROM client_master WHERE city = 'BOMBAY' OR city = 'DELHI';

2. Select client information like client_no, name, address1, address2, city and pincode for all the clients in Santacruz(w) or Vile Parle (E) ;

   SELECT client_no, name, address1, address2, city, pincode
   FROM client_master WHERE city = 'BOMBAY' AND
   (pincode = 400054 OR pincode = 400057) ;

3. Select product_no, description, profit_percent, sell_price where profit_percent is between 10 and 20 both inclusive;

   SELECT product_no, description, profit_percent, sell_price
   FROM product_master
   WHERE profit_percent >= 10 AND profit_percent <= 20;

RANGE SEARCHING
Examples :
1. Select product_no, description, profit_percent, sell_price where profit_percent is between 10 and 20 both inclusive;
   SELECT product_no, description, profit_percent, sell_price
   FROM product_master
   WHERE profit_percent BETWEEN 10 AND 20;

2. Select product_no, description, profit_percent, sell_price where profit_percent is not between 10 and 20 ;

   SELECT product_no, description, profit_percent, sell_price
   FROM product_master
   WHERE profit_percent NOT BETWEEN 10 AND 15;

PATTERN MATCHING
The use of the *like* predicate :
For character data types : % matches any string
   _ (underscore) matches any single character

Examples :
1. Select supplier_name from supplier_master where the first two characters of name are 'ja';

   SELECT supplier_name FROM supplier_master
   WHERE supplier_name LIKE 'ja%';

2. Select supplier_name from supplier_master where the second character of name is 'r' or 'h';

   SELECT supplier_name
       FROM supplier_master
       WHERE supplier_name LIKE '_r%' OR supplier_name LIKE '_h%';

3. Select supplier_name, address1, address2, city and pincode from supplier_master where name is 3 characters long and the first two characters are 'ja';

   SELECT supplier_name, address1, address2, city, pincode
       FROM supplier_master WHERE supplier_name like 'ja_';

The *in* and *not in* predicates :
Example :
1. Select supplier_name, address1, address2, city and pincode from supplier_master where name is 'ramos', 'clark', 'pramada' or 'aruna' ;

        SELECT supplier_name, address1, address2, city, pincode
            FROM supplier_master
            WHERE supplier_name IN ('Ramos', 'Clark', 'Pramada', 'Aruna');

ORACLE FUNCTIONS

Functions are used to manipulate data items and return a result. Functions follow the format of : function_name(argument1,argument2,..). An argument is a user-supplied variable or constant. The structure of functions is such that it accepts zero or more arguments.

Examples :

AVG	Syntax	AVG([DISTINCT|ALL] n)
	Purpose	Returns average value of n, ignoring null values.
	Example	SELECT AVG(sell_price) "Average" FROM product_master,
	Output	Average

		2012.3654

Note : In the above SELECT statement, AVG function is used to calculate the average selling price of all products. The selected column is renamed as 'Average' in the output.

MIN	Syntax	MIN([DISTINCT|ALL] expr)
	Purpose	Returns minimum value of expr.
	Example	SELECT MIN(s_order_date) "Minimum Date" FROM sales_order ;
	Output	Minimum Date

		26-Jan-93

COUNT(expr)	Syntax	COUNT([DISTINCT|ALL] expr)
	Purpose	Returns the number of rows where expr is not null.
	Example	SELECT COUNT(order_no) "No of Orders" FROM sales_order;
	Output	No of Orders

		5

COUNT(*)	Syntax	COUNT(*)
	Purpose	Returns the number of rows in the table, including duplicates and those with nulls.
	Example	SELECT COUNT(*) "Total" FROM client_master;
	Output	Total

		15

MAX	Syntax	MAX([DISTINCT|ALL] expr)
	Purpose	Returns maximum value of expr.
	Example	SELECT MAX(qty_ordered) "Maximum" FROM sales_order_details ;
	Output	Maximum

		5000.00

SUM	Syntax	SUM([DISTINCT|ALL] n)
	Purpose	Returns sum of values of n.

	Example	SELECT SUM(qty_ordered) "Total Qty"
		     FROM sales_order_details
		     WHERE product_no = 'P00001';

	Output	Total Qty ------------- 29025.00
ABS	Syntax	ABS(n)
	Purpose	Returns the absolute value of n.
	Example	SELECT ABS(-15) "Absolute" FROM dual;
	Output	Absolute ------------ 15
POWER	Syntax	POWER(m,n)
	Purpose	Returns m raised to nth power. n must be an integer; else an error is returned.
	Example	SELECT POWER(3,2) "Raised" FROM dual;
	Output	Raised --------- 9
ROUND	Syntax	ROUND(n[,m])
	Purpose	Returns n rounded to m places right of the decimal point: if m is omitted, to 0 places. m can be negative to round off digits left of the decimal point. m must be an integer.
	Example	SELECT ROUND(15.19,1) "Round" FROM dual;
	Output	Round --------- 15.2
SQRT	Syntax	SQRT(n)
	Purpose	Returns square root of n; if n<0 , NULL. SQRT returns a *real* result.
	Example	SELECT SQRT(25) "Square Root" FROM dual;
	Output	Square Root -------------- 5
LOWER	Syntax	LOWER(char)
	Purpose	Returns char, with all letters in lowercase
	Example	SELECT LOWER('IVAN BAYROSS') "Lower" FROM dual;
	Output	Lower ---------------- ivan bayross

INITCAP	Syntax	INITCAP(char)	
	Purpose	Returns string with the first letter in upper case.	
	Example	SELECT INITCAP('IVAN BAYROSS') "Title Case" FROM dual;	
	Output	Title Case	

		Ivan Bayross	
UPPER	Syntax	UPPER(char)	
	Purpose	Returns char, with all letters forced to uppercase.	
	Example	SELECT UPPER('Ms. Carol') FROM dual;	
	Output	UPPER('Ms. Carol')	

		MS. CAROL	
SUBSTR	Syntax	SUBSTR(char,m[,n])	
	Purpose	Returns a portion of char, beginning at character m, n characters long (if n is omitted, to the end char). The first position of char is 1.	
	Example	SELECT SUBSTR('ABCDEFG',2,3) "Substring" FROM dual;	
	Output	Substring	

		BCD	
LENGTH	Syntax	LENGTH(char)	
	Purpose	Returns the length of char.	
	Example	SELECT LENGTH('ELEPHANT') "Length" FROM dual;	
	Output	Length	

		8	
LTRIM	Syntax	LTRIM(char[,set])	
	Purpose	Removes characters from the left of char with initial characters removed upto the first character not in set.	
	Example	SELECT LTRIM('xxxXxxLAST WORD','x') "Left trim example" FROM dual;	
	Output	Left trim example	

		XxxLAST WORD	
RTRIM	Syntax	RTRIM(char,[set])	
	Purpose	Returns char, with final characters removed after the last character not in the set. set is optional it defaults to ''.	
	Example	SELECT RTRIM('TURNERxxXxx','x') "RTRIM Example" FROM dual;	
	Output	RTRIM Example	

		TURNERxxX	

LPAD	Syntax	LPAD(char1,n [,char2])
	Purpose	Returns char1, left padded to length n with the sequence of characters in char2; char2 defaults to blanks.
	Example	SELECT LPAD('Page 1',14,'*') "Lpad" FROM dual;
	Output	Lpad

```
----------------------
********Page 1
```

RPAD	Syntax	RPAD(char1,n[,char2])
	Purpose	Returns char1, right-padded to length n with the characters in char2, replicated as many times as necessary; if char2 is omitted, right-pad with blanks.

	Example	SELECT RPAD(name,10,'x') "RPAD Example"
		  FROM client_master
		    WHERE name = 'TURNER';

	Output	RPAD Example

```
----------------------
TURNERxxxx
```

TO_NUMBER	Syntax	TO_NUMBER(char)
	Purpose	Converts char, a character value containing a number, to a value of NUMBER datatype.
	Example	UPDATE product_master SET sell_price = sell_price + TO_NUMBER(SUBSTR('$100',2,3));

TO_DATE	Syntax	TO_DATE(char [, fmt])
	Purpose	Converts a character field to a date field.
	Example	INSERT INTO sales_order (s_order_no, s_order_date) VALUES ('O87650', TO_DATE('30-SEP-85 10:55 A.M.', 'DD-MON-YY HH:MI A.M.'));

If the date has to be entered in any other format other than 'DD-MON-YY' then we need to use the TO_DATE function. To enter the time portion of a date, the TO_DATE function must be used with a format mask indicating the time portion.

TO_CHAR (number conversion)	Syntax	TO_CHAR(n[,fmt])
	Purpose	Converts a value of NUMBER datatype to a value of CHAR datatype, using the optional format string. fmt must be a number format. If fmt is omitted, n is the converted to a char value exactly long enough to hold significant digits.
	Example	SELECT TO_CHAR(17145,'$099,999') "Char" FROM dual;
	Output	Char

```
-------------
$017,145
```

TO_CHAR	Syntax	TO_CHAR(d[,fmt])
(date conversion)	Purpose	Converts a value of DATE datatype to CHAR value in the format specified by the char value fmt. fmt must be a date format. If fmt is omitted, d is converted to a character value in the default date format, i.e. "DD-MON-YY".
	Example	SELECT TO_CHAR(s_order_date,'Month DD, YYYY') "New Date Format" FROM sales_order WHERE s_order_no = 'O42453';
	Output	New Date Format --------------------- January 26, 1996

The above Oracle functions are just a few selected from the many functions that are in built into Oracle. These are the Oracle functions that are most commonly used in commercial application development. They will serve to indicate how Oracle functions are used. Before you develop your own functions using SQL or PL/SQL refer to the Oracle manuals and check to see if an in built Oracle function already exists that would allow you to process your data as required.

GROUPING DATA FROM TABLES IN SQL

The concept of grouping :

From sales_order_details table, we will create a set containing several sets of rows grouped together based on a condition.

Table name : **sales_order_details**

S Order No	Product No	Qty Ordered	Qty Disp
O19001	P00001	10	10
O19001	P03453	3	3
O19001	P06734	3	3
O46865	P06734	4	4
O46865	P03453	10	10
O46865	P00001	2	2
O73965	P03453	2	2
O73965	P00001	1	1
O73965	P06734	1	1

Example :
1. Select product_no, total qty_ordered for each product;

    SELECT product_no, sum(qty_ordered) "Total Qty Ordered"
    FROM sales_order_details
    GROUP BY product_no;

The following is the output displayed :

Product No	Total Qty Ordered
P00001	13
P03453	15
P06734	8

A condition can be imposed on the *group by* clause, using the *having* clause as done in the following example :

1. Select product_no, total qty_ordered for products 'P00001', 'P03453';

    SELECT product_no, sum(qty_ordered) "Total Qty Ordered"
    FROM sales_order_details
    GROUP BY product_no
    HAVING product_no = 'P00001' OR 'P03453';

The following output displayed :

Product No	Total Qty Ordered
P00001	13
P03453	15

MANIPULATING DATES IN SQL

1. Display order information like s_order_no, client_no, s_order_date for all the orders placed by the client in the ascending order of date. The S_order_date should be displayed in 'DD/MM/YY' format'.

Table name : **sales_order**

S Order No	Client No	S Order Date
O19001	C00001	12-oct-95
O19002	C00341	25-nov-95
O19003	C23001	03-jul-96
O46865	C00001	18-feb-96
O46866	C00871	20-mar-96
O46867	C00001	12-jan-95

Note : *sysdate* represents the system date or today's date.

Example : SELECT s_order_no, client_no , to_char(s_order_date,'DD/MM/YY')
FROM sales_order
ORDER BY to_char(s_order_date, 'DD/MM/YY');

The output will be as displayed below :

```
S Order No      Client No       S Order Date
-----------     -----------     ------------
O46867          C00001          12/01/95
O19001          C00001          12/10/95
O19002          C00341          25/11/95
O46865          C00001          18/02/96
O46866          C00871          20/03/96
O19003          C23001          03/07/96
```

JOINS
Joining Multiple Tables (Equi Joins) :
Sometimes we require to treat more than one table as though it were a single entity. Then a single SQL sentence can manipulate data from all the tables as though the tables were not separate objects, but one single entity.

To achieve this, we have to join tables. Tables are joined on columns that have the same data type and data width in the tables.

Example 1 : Display order information like s_order_no, client name, s_order_date for all the orders placed by the client in the ascending order of date. The s_order_date should be displayed in 'DD/MM/YY' format'

Here the data required is in two tables *sales_order* and *client_master*. These tables have to be accessed as though they were one entity.

Table name : **sales_order**

S_Order_No	Client_No	S_Order_Date
O19001	C00001	12-oct-95
O19002	C00341	25-nov-95
O19003	C23001	03-jul-96
O46865	C00002	18-feb-96
O46866	C00871	20-mar-96
O46867	C00003	12-jan-95

Table name : **client_master**

Client_No	Name
C00001	Ivan Bayross
C00341	Pradeep Mathew
C23001	Mili Parikh
C00002	Norma Fernandes
C00871	Rahul Desai
C00003	Arjun Shetty

Note : Data from relevant fields are displayed in the above tables.

Example :   SELECT s_order_no, name , to_char(s_order_date,'DD/MM/YY')
FROM sales_order , client_master
WHERE client_master.client_no = sales_order.client_no
ORDER BY to_char(s_order_date, 'DD/MM/YY');

Note : Here we use the technique of specifying the tablename prior the columnname, separated by a period in the WHERE condition because the columnname in both tables are identical.

The output will be as displayed below :

S Order No	Name	S Order Date
O46867	Arjun Shetty	12/01/95
O19001	Ivan Bayross	12/10/95
O19002	Pradeep Mathew	25/11/95
O46865	Norma Fernandes	18/02/96
O46866	Rahul Desai	20/03/96
O19003	Mili Parikh	03/07/96

Example 2 : Select product_no, product_description and total qty_ordered for each product;

Table name : **sales_order_details**

S_Order No	Product_No	Qty_Ordered	Qty_Disp
O19001	P00001	10	10
O19001	P03453	3	3
O19001	P06734	3	3
O46865	P06734	4	4
O46865	P03453	10	10
O46865	P00001	2	2
O73965	P03453	2	2
O73965	P00001	1	1
O73965	P06734	1	1

Table name : **product_master**

Product No	Description
P00001	1.44 Floppies
P03453	Monitors
P06734	Mouse
P07865	1.22 Floppies
P07868	Keyboards
P07885	CD Drive
P07965	HDD
P07975	1.44 Drive
P08865	1.22 Drive

```
SELECT sales_order_details.product_no, description,
       sum(qty_ordered) "Total Qty Ordered"
FROM sales_order_details , product_master
WHERE product_master.product_no = sales_order_details.product_no
GROUP BY sales_order_details.product_no, description ;
```

The output will be as displayed below :

Product No	Description	Total Qty Ordered
P00001	1.44 Floppies	13
P03453	Monitors	15
P06734	Mouse	8

Joining A Table to Itself (Self Joins):

In some situations, you may find it necessary to join a table to itself, as though you were joining two separate tables. This is referred to as a self-join. In the self-join, the combined results consists of two rows from the same table.

To join the table to itself, the table name appears twice in the FROM clause. To distinguish between the appearance of the same tablename, a temporary name, called an alias or a correlation, is assigned to each mention of the tablename in the FROM clause. The form of the FROM clause with an alias is :   FROM tablename [alias1], tablename [alias2] ....

Example 1 :
Our task here is to extract the names of the employees along with their managers from the *employee* table.

Table name : **employee**

Employee_No	Name	Manager_No
E00001	Basu Navindgi	E00002
E00002	Rukmini	E00005
E00003	Carol D'Souza	E00004
E00004	Cynthia Bayross	-
E00005	Ivan Bayross	-

The Query :   SELECT emp.name, mngr.name manager
                            FROM employee emp, employee mngr
                            WHERE emp.manager_no = mngr.employee_no;

results in :   Name   Manager
                          ----------   ----------
                          Basu Navindgi   Rukmini
                          Rukmini   Ivan Bayross
                          Carol D'Souza   Cynthia Bayross

In this query, the employee table, using the alias feature of SQL, is treated as two separate tables named emp and mngr, as shown here:

Table name : **emp**

Employee No	Name	Manager No
E00001	Basu Navindgi	E00002
E00002	Rukmini	E00005
E00003	Carol D'Souza	E00004
E00004	Cynthia Bayross	-
E00005	Ivan Bayross	-

Table name : **mngr**

Employee No	Name	Manager No
E00001	Basu Navindgi	E00002
E00002	Rukmini	E00005
E00003	Carol D'Souza	E00004
E00004	Cynthia Bayross	-
E00005	Ivan Bayross	-

The join operation is evaluated as follows :

1. Using the compound condition : emp.manager_no = mngr.employee_no

where, each manager_no record (E00002, E00005, E00004) from the *emp* table is joined with the employee_no record (E00001, E00002, E00003, E00004, E00005) from the *mngr* table to form the following intermediate result :

Table name : **emp**

Employee No	Name	Manager No
E00001	Basu Navindgi	E00002
E00002	Rukmini	E00005
E00003	Carol D'Souza	E00004

Table name : **mngr**

Employee No	Name	Manager No
E00001	Rukmini	E00002
E00002	Ivan Bayross	E00005
E00003	Cynthia Bayross	E00004

<u>Example 2</u> :   Find the Order No, Client No and Salesman No where a client has been serviced by more than one salesman.

Our task here is to extract the Order No, Client No and Salesman No from the *Sales_order* table.

Table name : **sales_order**

S_Order_No	Client_No	Salesman_No
O19001	C00001	S00002
O46865	C00001	S00001
O73965	C00003	S00004
O46865	C00002	S00003
O57575	C00001	S00003
O46462	C00001	S00002
O86723	C00002	S00003

The Query :   SELECT DISTINCT c_order.order_no, c_order.client_no,
                              c_order.salesman_no
                    FROM sales_order c_order, sales_order s_order
                    WHERE c_order.client_no = s_order.client_no AND
                          c_order.salesman_no <> s_order.salesman_no

Results In :

Order No	Client No	Salesman No
O46865	C00001	S00001
O19001	C00001	S00002
O46462	C00001	S00002
O57575	C00001	S00003

CONSTRUCTING AN ENGLISH SENTENCE WITH DATA FROM TABLE COLUMNS

Example : SELECT INITCAP(name) || ' has placed orders worth Rs. ' ||
     sum(qty_ordered * sell_price)
    FROM sales_order_details , product_master, client_master, sales_order
    WHERE product_master.product_no = sales_order_details .product_no
     and client_master.client_no = sales_order .client_no
     and sales_order_details .s_order_no = sales_order .order_no
    GROUP BY name;

Since the above SELECT column is taken as a single string, the column title of the above result will appear as follows :

INITCAP(NAME)||'HASPLACEDORDERSWORTHRS.'||SUM(QTY_ORDERED*SELL_PRICE)

Mili Parikh has placed orders worth Rs. 1600
Pradeep Mathew has placed orders worth Rs. 1600
Rahul Desai has placed orders worth Rs. 400

Whereas, if you can rename the whole string as, something like say, :

    SELECT INITCAP(name) || ' has placed orders worth Rs. ' ||
     sum(qty_ordered * sell_price) "Orders Placed"
    FROM sales_order_details , product_master, client_master, sales_order
    WHERE product_master.product_no = sales_order_details .product_no
     and client_master.client_no = sales_order .client_no and
     sales_order_details .s_order_no = sales_order .order_no
    GROUP BY name;

The output will appear as follows :

Orders Placed

Mili Parikh has placed orders worth Rs. 1600
Pradeep Mathew has placed orders worth Rs. 1600
Rahul Desai has placed orders worth Rs. 400

SUBQUERIES

A subquery is a form of an SQL statement that appears inside another SQL statement. It is also termed as *nested query*. The statement containing a subquery is called a *parent* statement. The rows returned by the subquery are used by the *parent* statement.

It can be used by the following commands :
- To insert records in the target table.
- To create tables and insert records in this table.
- To update records in the target table.
- To create views.
- To provide values for the conditions in the WHERE, HAVING IN, SELECT, UPDATE and DELETE statements.

Examples :
1. Creating *client_master* table from the *oldclient_master* table :

>   CREATE TABLE client_master
>   AS SELECT * FROM oldclientmaster;

2. select orders placed by 'Rahul Desai'.

>   SELECT * from sales_order
>   where client_no =
>   (SELECT client_no FROM client_master
>   WHERE name = 'Rahul Desai')

3. To determine the non moving products in the product_master table :

>   SELECT product_no, description
>   FROM product_master
>   WHERE product_no NOT IN
>   (SELECT product_no FROM sales_order_details);

The above examples show two levels of nesting. If the user wants the information from a table depending upon the information from another table, which in turn is also dependent, then the user will have to go in for the next level of query.

Example : To select the names of persons who are in Mr. Pradeep's department and who have also worked on an inventory control system.

>   SELECT ename, deptno
>   FROM emp
>   WHERE deptno IN (SELECT deptno FROM emp
>   WHERE ename = 'Pradeep')
>   AND ename IN (SELECT ename
>   FROM inv_sys);

USING THE UNION, INTERSECT AND MINUS CLAUSE
Union Clause :
The user can put together multiple queries and combine their output using the union clause. The Union clause merges the output of two or more queries into a single set of rows and columns.

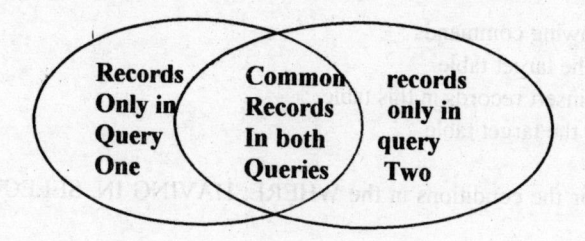

Diagram 2.5 : Output of the Union Clause

The output of both the queries will be as displayed above. The final output of the union clause will be:

Output = Records only in query one + records only in query one +
A single set of records which is common in both queries.

Example : select all the clients and the salesman in the city of 'Bombay';

        SELECT salesman_no "ID", name
        FROM salesman_master
        WHERE city = 'Bombay'
UNION
        SELECT client_no "ID", name
        FROM client_master
        WHERE city = 'Bombay' ;

The output of the query will be as follows :

ID	Name
S00001	Arjun Shetty
S00002	Rahul Desai
S00003	Rahul Rao
C00001	Ivan Bayross
C00002	Pradeep Mathew

The Restrictions on using a union are as follows :
- No. of columns in all the queries should be the same.
- The datatype of the columns in each query must be same.
- Unions cannot be used in subqueries.
- You cannot use aggregate functions in a union.

INTERACTIVE SQL 51

Intersect Clause :
The user can put together multiple queries and combine their output using the intersect clause. The *Intersect* clause outputs only rows produced by both the queries intersected i.e. the output in an Intersect clause will include only those rows that are retrieved by both the queries.

Common Records In both Queries

Diagram 2.6 : Output of the Intersect Clause

The output of both the queries will be as displayed above. The final output of the Intersect clause will be:

Output = A single set of records which are common in both queries.

Example : select salesman name in 'Bombay' who has atleast one client located at 'Bombay'.

```
SELECT name FROM salesman_master
    WHERE city = 'Bombay'
INTERSECT
SELECT name FROM salesman_master
    WHERE 'Bombay' IN
    (SELECT city FROM client_master
        WHERE client_master.client_no IN
        (SELECT client_no FROM sales_order
        WHERE salesman_no = salesman_master.salesman_no)) ;
```

The diagram shown below shows the columns from different tables required in the intersect example. It shows all the tables and the relation between each of these tables.

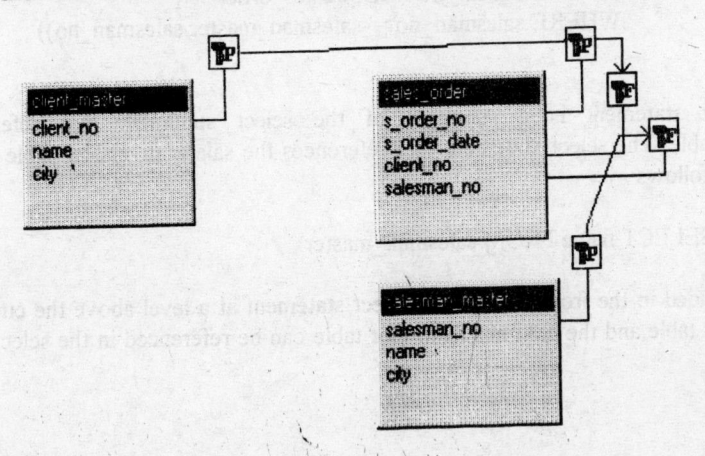

client_master
- client_no
- name
- city

sales_order
- s_order_no
- s_order_date
- client_no
- salesman_no

salesman_master
- salesman_no
- name
- city

The Data in each of these tables is as follows:

Table Name: Client_Master

Client No	Name	City
C00001	Ivan Bayross	Bombay
C00002	Vandana Saitwal	Madras
C00003	Pramada Jaguste	Bombay
C00004	Basu Navindgi	Bombay
C00005	Ravi Sreedharan	Delhi
C00006	Rukmini	Bombay

Table Name: Salesman_Master

Salesman No	Name	City
S00001	Kiran	Bombay
S00002	Manish	Bombay
S00003	Ravi	Delhi
S00004	Ashish	Madras

Table Name: Sales_order

S Order No	S Order Date	Client No	Salesman No
O19001	12-jan-96	C00001	S00001
O19002	25-jan-96	C00002	S00003
O46865	18-feb-96	C00003	S00003
O19003	03-apr-96	C00001	S00001
O46866	20-may-96	C00004	S00003
O10008	24-may-96	C00005	S00004

The select statement is:

```
SELECT name FROM salesman_master
    WHERE 'Bombay' IN
    (SELECT city FROM client_master
        WHERE client_master.client_no IN
        (SELECT client_no FROM sales_order
        WHERE salesman_no = salesman_master.salesman_no)) ;
```

Note:
The above select statement is a subquery of the select statement that references the salesman_master table. The select statement that references the salesman_master table without its where clause is as follows:

SELECT name FROM salesman_master

If any table is included in the from clause of a select statement at a level above the current select statement then that table and the columns from that table can be referenced in the select statement at lower levels.

> Thus **we do not need to include the salesman_master table** in the **From** clause of the **subquery** even if the columns is referenced in the where clause as shown in the query below.
>
> SELECT client_no FROM sales_order
>   WHERE salesman_no = salesman_master.salesman_no

How does a subquery work?
The top-level select statement retrieves Names from the salesman_master table as seen in part of the select statement i.e. **SELECT name FROM salesman_master**.

The salesman_no from the salesman_master table is used in the where clause for the lowest level of subquery i.e. **WHERE salesman_no = salesman_master.salesman_no**.

Oracle required two fields i.e. *Salesman_No* and *Name* from the salesman_master table. This target table will be as follows:

Salesman No	Name
S00001	Kiran
S00002	Manish
S00003	Ravi
S00004	Ashish

The second level query retrieves city from the client_master table as seen in part of the select statement i.e. **SELECT city FROM client_master**.

The client_no from the client_master table is used in the where clause for the same query i.e. **WHERE client_master.client_no in**.

Thus Oracle requires two fields i.e. *client_No* and *City* from the Client_Master table. This target table will be as follows:

Client No	City
C00001	Bombay
C00002	Madras
C00003	Bombay
C00004	Bombay
C00005	Delhi
C00006	Bombay

The lowest level subquery retrieves client_no from the sales_order table as seen in part of the select statement i.e. **SELECT client_no FROM sales_order**.

The salesman_no from the Sales_Order table is used in the where clause for the same query i.e. the salesman_no is compared with the salesman_no in the Salesman_Master table as in **WHERE salesman_no = salesman_master.salesman_no**.

Thus Oracle requires two fields i.e. *client_No* and *salesman_no* from the Sales_Order table. Note that both these fields form a part of the where clause for the higher level queries. These values will only be used to supply values for the WHERE clause. This target table will be as follows:

Client No	Salesman No
C00001	S00001
C00002	S00003
C00003	S00003
C00001	S00001
C00004	S00003
C00005	S00004

Once the tables and the required columns form the target table, Oracle eliminates records, not required after the application of the where clause.

Oracle applies the where clause in reverse order i.e. **WHERE salesman_no = salesman_master.salesman_no** will be first applied to the data set to eliminate records. As per this clause, Since all the salesman_no are present in the salesman_master table the target sales_order table remains the same when the where clause is applied to the last subquery segment i.e.

      SELECT client_no FROM sales_order
             WHERE salesman_no = salesman_master.salesman_no

The query must pick up client's from the client_master who have placed an order. The client_no for each client who has placed an order is recorded in the sales_order table. Thus the client_no must be present in both the client_master and the sales_order tables.

Record with client_no 'C00006' will be eliminated from the target table of client_master because client 'C00006' has not placed any orders.

Thus the result will be:

Client No	City
C00001	Bombay
C00002	Madras
C00003	Bombay
C00004	Bombay
C00005	Delhi

The client numbers from the resulting data set will be applied to the client_master table to pickup only those records where city = 'Bombay'.

Thus the target client_master table will be

Client No	City
C00001	Bombay
C00003	Bombay
C00004	Bombay

Finally we need the names of salesman who have serviced clients in Bombay i.e. 'C00001', 'C00003', 'C00004'. Salesman_No 'S00001' and 'S00004' have serviced these clients. Thus the final output for the salesman_master table will be

Salesman No	Name
S00001	Kiran
S00003	Ravi

The first query in the intersect example is as follows:
    SELECT name FROM salesman_master
        WHERE city = 'Bombay'

The Target Table will be as follows:

Salesman No	Name	City
S00001	Kiran	Bombay
S00002	Manish	Bombay

We need all the salesman who are in 'Bombay' i.e. the target table of the first query and the serviced client's must be in 'Bombay' i.e. the output of the second query.

Intersect clause picks up records that are common in both the queries. Thus the output after applying the intersect clause will be

Salesman No	Name	City
S00001	Kiran	Bombay

Salesman_no and city were used in the where clause for comparison with data from the client_master and the sales_order table. Thus the final output will be

Name

Kiran

Minus Clause :

The user can put together multiple queries and combine their output using the minus clause. The *Intersect* clause outputs only rows produced by both the queries intersected i.e. the output in an intersect clause will include only those rows that are retrieved by both the queries.

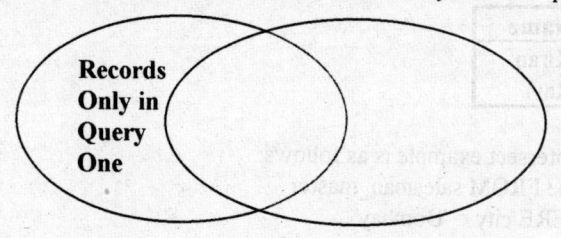

Diagram 2.7 : Output of the Minus Clause

The output of both the queries will be as displayed above. The final output of the minus clause will be:

Output = Records only in query one

Example 1 : select all the product_no of non-moving items in the product_master table.

        SELECT product_no FROM product_master
        MINUS
        SELECT product_no FROM order_details;

Example 2 : select the product_no, description, qty_on_hand, cost_price of non-moving items in the product_master table.

        SELECT product_no, description FROM product_master
        MINUS
        SELECT order_details.product_no, description
            FROM order_details, product_master
            WHERE product_master.product_no = order_details.product_no;

INDEXES

An *Index* is an ordered list of contents of a column or group of columns in a table. An index created on the single column of the table is called *Simple Index*. When multiple table columns are included in the index it is called *composite Index*.

Creating an Index for a table:

Simple Index :   CREATE INDEX indexfilename
                   ON tablename (columnname);

Example : Create an index on the table client_master, field client_no.

        CREATE INDEX client_ndx
            ON client_master(client_no);

Composite Index :   CREATE INDEX indexfilename
                      ON tablename (columnname, columnname);

Example : Create a composite index on the sales_order_details table for the columns s_order_no and product_no.

        CREATE INDEX sales_order_details _ntx
            ON sales_order_details (s_order_no, product_no);

The indexes in the above examples do not enforce uniqueness i.e. the column included in the index can have duplicate values. To create a unique index, the keyword UNIQUE should be included in the *Create Index* command.

Syntax : CREATE UNIQUE INDEX indexfilename
            ON tablename(columnname);

Example : Create a unique index on the table client_master, field client_no.

        CREATE UNIQUE INDEX client_ndx
            ON client_master(client_no);

When the user defines a primary key or a unique key contraint, Oracle automatically creates unique indexes on the primary key column or unique key.

Dropping Indexes :

An index can be dropped by using the DROP INDEX command.

Syntax : DROP INDEX indexfilename ;

Example : Drop index client_ndx on table client_master;

        DROP INDEX client_ndx ;

When the user drops the primary key, unique key constraint or the table, Oracle automatically drops the indexes on the primary key column, unique key or the table itself.

VIEWS

Logical data is how we want to see the current data in our database. Physical data is how this data is actually placed in our database.

Views are masks placed upon tables. This allows the programmer to develop a method via which we can display predetermined data to users according to our desire.

In a concurrent environment, where several people are querying a database different people will want to look at data differently, i.e. each group of people will want to see different fields of the same table.

To make the querying of the table easier, Oracle provides for the generation of views. A view is created unique, according to the needs of each user, where the user can then, only access those fields of the database allowed by the view. This goes a long way in providing security for data within a table.

The DBA treats a view just as it would treat a base table. Hence you can query a view exactly as though it were a base table. The query fired on a view would naturally run faster than if it were fired on the base table, as the view will be a subset of the total number of columns in the table.

It is a programming convention that a view name begins with *vw_* to allow one to distinguish a view from a table when the name is used in the FROM clause of the SQL sentence.

Views may be created for the following reasons:
- The DBA stores the view as a definition only. Hence, there is no duplication of data.
- Simplifies queries.
- Can be queried as a base table itself.
- Provides data security.
- Avoids data redundancy.

Creation of views :

<u>Syntax</u>: CREATE VIEW viewname AS
            SELECT columnname, columnname
            FROM tablename
            WHERE columnname = expression list ;

<u>Example</u> : Create view on client_master for the admin department.

    CREATE VIEW vw_clientadmin AS
        SELECT name, address1, address2, city, pincode, state
        FROM client_master ;

This creates a view by the name of *vw_clientadmin* based on the table *client_master*.

Renaming the columns of a view :
<u>Example</u> : CREATE VIEW vw_clientadmin AS
            SELECT name, addr1, addr2, city, pincode, state
            FROM client_master ;

Here the columns of the table are related to the view on a one-to-one relationship. The columns of the view can take on different names from the table columns, if required.

Using Views: (visual concept)
Table name : **Client_Master**(This is the base table from which the view is created)

client_no	name	address1	address2	city	pincode	state

Example :   CREATE VIEW vw_clientadmin AS
                    SELECT name, address1, address2, city, pincode, state
                    FROM client_master ;

vw_clientadmin, the view created from *client_master* will look as follows :

name	address1	address2	city	pincode	state

Selecting a data set from a view :
Example :   SELECT name, address1, address2, city, pincode, state
                    FROM vw_clientadmin
                    WHERE city IN ('BOMBAY', 'DELHI');

Updateable Views :
Views can also be used for data manipulation i.e. the user can perform the Insert, Update and the Delete operations on the view. The views on which data manipualtion can be done are called *Updateable Views*. Views that donot allow data manipuation are called *Reasonly* views. When you give a view name in the Update, Insert or Delete statement, the modifications to the data will be passed to the underlying table.

For the view to be updateable, it should meet the following criteria :
- The view must be created on a single table.
- The Primary key column of the table should be included in the view.
- Aggregate functions cannot be used in the select statement.
- The select statement used for creating a View should not include DISTINCT, GROUP BY or HAVING clause.
- The select statement used for creating a View should not include use subqueries for the creation of views.
- if a view is defined from another view, the second view should be updateable.
- It must not use constants, strings or value expressions like sell_price * 1.05.
- For insert, it should include all the NOT NULL fields.

Destroying a view :
A view can be dropped by using the DROP VIEW command.

Syntax : DROP VIEW viewname;

Example :   DROP VIEW vw_clientadmin;

SEQUENCES

Most applications require the automatic generation of a numeric value. The technique used by some developers is to create table with two columns. One column would contain the table name and the other column would contain the maximum value stored. The table's max. Value could be updated whenever the next highest value is requested. This technique would increase disk I/O.

ORACLE provides an automatic sequence generator of numeric values, which can have a maximum value of upto 38 digits. A sequence can be defined to

- generate numbers in ascending or descending,
- provide intervals between numbers,
- caching of sequence numbers in memory etc.

Sequence numbers are used by SQL statements that reference the sequence. Sequences are created independent of the tables that it may be used.

Creating Sequences :

A sequence can be created by issuing the following statement in an interactive SQL environment like SQL*Plus.

<u>Syntax</u> : CREATE SEQUENCE *sequence_name*
          [INCREMENT BY *integervalue*
          START WITH *integervalue*
          MAXVALUE *integervalue* / NOMAXVALUE
          MINVALUE *integervalue* / NOMINVALUE
          CYCLE / NOCYCLE
          CACHE *integervalue* / NOCACHE
          ORDER / NOORDER]

KEYWORDS AND PARAMETERS

sequence_name
Sequence is the name given to the sequence so that it can be referenced later.

INCREMENT BY
Increment By specifies the interval between sequence numbers. It can be any positive or negative value but not zero. If this clause is omitted, the default value is 1.

MINVALUE
Specifies the sequences minimum value.

NOMINVALUE
NOMINVALUE specifies a minimum value of 1 for an ascending sequence and $-(10)^{26}$ for a descending sequence.

MAXVALUE
Maxvalue specifies the maximum value that a sequence can generate.

NOMAXVALUE
NOMAXVALUE specifies a maximum of 10^{27} for an ascending sequence or -1 for a descending sequence. This is the default clause.

START WITH
Specifies the first sequence number to be generated. The default for an ascending sequence is the sequences minimum value and for descending it is the maximum value.

CYCLE
Cycle specifies that the sequence continues to generate values after reaching either its maximum or minimum value.

NOCYCLE
Nocycle specifies that a sequence cannot generate more values after reaching the maximum or minimum value.

CACHE
Cache specifies how many values of the sequence ORACLE preallocates and keeps in memory for faster access. The minimum value for this parameter is two.

NOCACHE
Nocache specifies that the values of the sequence are not preallocated. If the CACHE / NOCACHE clause is omitted ORACLE caches 20 sequence numbers by default.

ORDER
Order guarantees that sequence numbers are generated in order of request. This is only necessary if you are using exclusive mode option as it will always be in order.

NOORDER
Noorder does not guarantee sequence numbers are generated I order of request. If the ORDER / NOORDER clause is omitted it takes the NOORDER clause by default.

Example :
To create a sequence order_seq which will start generating numbers from 1 to 9999 in ascending order with an interval of 1.

```
CREATE SEQUENCE order_seq
    INCREMENT BY 1
    START WITH 1
    MAXVALUE 9999
    CYCLE ;
```

Referencing a Sequence :
Once defined, the user must be able to access a unique sequence number. This can be done by using SELECT statement.

Refer to the next value : SELECT *sequence_name*.NEXTVAL FROM dual ;

Refer to the current value : SELECT *sequence_name*.CURRVAL FROM dual ;

Every time NEXTVAL is referenced the sequence is automatically incremented from the old value to the new value and gives you the new value. The next new value is generated only if NEXTVAL is used again.

Example : Insert values in the sales_order table. The s_order_no must be generated by using the order_seq sequence.

```
INSERT INTO sales_order
        (s_order_no, s_order_date, client_no )
        VALUES (order_seq.nextval, sysdate, 'C00001');
```

NEXT_VALUE is used in the SQL statement to get the next sequence number. Every time NEXTVAL is referenced the sequence is automatically incremented from the old value to the new value and gives you the new value. The next new value is generated only if NEXTVAL is used again.

To get the current sequence number the user must use CURRVAL as shown below :

```
SELECT sequence_name.CURRVAL FROM dual ;
```

Altering A Sequence :

Sequence can be altered by using the ALTER SEQUENCE statement. This way, any of the parameters are already defined at creation of the sequence.

Syntax : ALTER SEQUENCE *sequence_name*
      [INCREMENT BY *integervalue*
      MAXVALUE *integervalue* / NOMAXVALUE
      MINVALUE *integervalue* / NOMINVALUE
      CYCLE / NOCYCLE
      CACHE *integervalue* / NOCACHE
      ORDER / NOORDER   ]

Note : The starting value of the sequence cannot be altered.

Example :
Change the caching of the sequence *order_seq* to 30 and interval between two numbers as 2.

```
ALTER SEQUENCE order_seq
       INCREMENT BY 2
       CACHE 30 ;
```

Dropping A Sequence :

A sequence can be dropped by using the statement DROP SEQUENCE.

Syntax : DROP SEQUENCE sequence_name ;

Example : Drop the sequence *order_seq*.

```
DROP SEQUENCE order_seq ;
```

GRANTING AND REVOKING PERMISSIONS

Permission on the objects created by the user :
The Objects created by one user are not accessible by another user unless the owner of those objects gives such permission to other users. These permissions can be given by using the **Grant** statement. One user can grant permission to another user if he is the owner of the object or has the permission to grant access to other users.

Granting permissions using GRANT statement :
The Grant statement provides various types of access to database objects such as tables, views and sequences.

Syntax : GRANT {object privileges}
ON objectname
TO username
[WITH GRANT OPTION];

Object Privileges :
Each object privilege that is granted authorizes the grantee to perform some operation on the object. The user can grant all the privileges or grant only specific object privileges.

The list of object privileges is as follows :

- ALTER   : allows the grantee to change the table definition with the ALTER TABLE command.

- DELETE   : allows the grantee to remove the records from the table with the DELETE command

- INDEX   : allows the grantee to create an index on the table with the CREATE INDEX command.

- INSERT   : allows the grantee to add records to the table with the INSERT command.

- SELECT   : allows the grantee to query the table with the SELECT command.

- UPDATE   : allows the grantee to modify the records in the tables with the UPDATE command.

With Grant Option :
The WITH GRANT OPTION allows the grantee to grant object privileges to other users.

Example 1 : Grant all privileges on the table product_master to the user Pradeep.

        GRANT ALL
            ON product_master
            TO pradeep ;

Example 2 : Grant *Select* and *Update* privileges on table client_master to Mita.

        GRANT SELECT, UPDATE
            ON client_master
            TO mita ;

Example 3 : Grant all privileges on the table client_master to the user Ivan with the grant option.

        GRANT ALL
            ON client_master
            TO ivan
            WITH GRANT OPTION ;

Referencing a table belonging to another user :
The Objects created by one user cannot be used by another user unless the owner of those objects gives object privileges to other users. Once the permission is given by the owner, the user can access the table by prefixing the table with the name of the owner.

Example : Select all records from *product_master* table belonging to *Sunita*.

        SELECT * from
            sunita.product_master ;

Granting permissions to users when the grantor has been given GRANT permission :
If the users wants to grant permission to other users, he must be the owner of the object or must be given the GRANT option by the owner of the object. If the user is not the owner of the object, the user can access the object by prefixing the table with the name of the owner.

Example : Carol has GRANT OPTION on table product_master that belongs to Sunita. Grant *SELECT* privilege on product_master to Mili.

        GRANT SELECT
            ON sunita.product_master
            TO mili ;

REVOKING THE PERMISSIONS GIVEN
Permissions once given can be denied to the user using the REVOKE command. One user can revoke the permission granted to another user, if he is the owner of the object or the user had granted the permission to another user.

Revoking permissions using the REVOKE statement :

The REVOKE statement is used to deny the grant given on an object.

<u>Syntax</u> : REVOKE { object privileges }
                ON objectname
                FROM username ;

The list of object privileges is as follows :

- ALTER   : allows the grantee to change the table definition with the ALTER TABLE command.

- DELETE   : allows the grantee to remove the records from the table with the DELETE command

- INDEX   : allows the grantee to create an index on the table with the CREATE INDEX command.

- INSERT   : allows the grantee to add records to the table with the INSERT command.

- SELECT   : allows the grantee to query the table with the SELECT command.

- UPDATE : allows the grantee to modify the records in the tables with the UPDATE command.

Note :

You can use the revoke command to revoke object privileges that you previously granted directly to the Revokee.

You cannot use the REVOKE command to perform the following operations :
- revoke the object privileges that you didn't grant to the revokee.
- revoke the object privileges granted through the operating system.

<u>Example 1</u> : Revoke *Delete* privilege on supplier_master from Florian.

        REVOKE DELETE ON supplier_master
        FROM florian ;

<u>Example 2</u> : Revoke the remaining privileges on supplier_master that were granted to Florian.

        REVOKE ALL ON bonus
        FROM florian ;

<u>Example 3</u> : Revoke *SELECT* privilege on product_master from Norma. Sunita is the owner of product_master.

        REVOKE SELECT ON sunita.product_master
        FROM norma ;

CREATION OF REPORTS IN SQL*PLUS

SQL*Plus is usually thought of as a kind of interactive report writer. It uses SQL to get information from the ORACLE database, and lets you create polished well-formatted reports by giving you easy control over titles, column headings, subtotals and totals, reformatting of numbers and text, and much more.

SQL*Plus is most commonly used for simple queries and printed reports. Getting SQL*Plus to format information in reports according to your taste and requires using only a handful of commands, or key words that instruct SQL*Plus about how to behave. They are listed below:

Formatting commands used in SQL*Plus :

1. **Ttitle** — Sets the top **title** for each page of a report.

   Syntax — ttitle [left] {text} [right] {text} [centre] {text}

2. **Btitle** — Sets the bottom **title** for each page of a report.

   Syntax — btitle [left] {text} [right] {text} [centre] {text}

3. **Skip** — Skips as many blank lines.

   Syntax — skip {number}{page}

4. **Set Pause** — Makes screen display stop in between pages of display.

   Syntax — set pause on

5. **Column** — Gives SQL*Plus a variety of instructions on the heading, format and treatment of the column.

   Syntax — column {col. name} [format] {format instruction} [justify] {justification} [heading] {text}

6. **SQL.pno** — Displays the page number.

   Syntax — sql.pno

7. **Break On** — Tells SQL*Plus where to put spaces between sections of a report, or where to break for subtotals and totals.

   Syntax — break on {column}

8. **Compute Sum** — Makes SQL*Plus calculate subtotals.

   Syntax — compute sum of {column} on {column}

Example : Create a productwise sales report that displays product no, description, unit of measure, quantity, rate and total value. The report should display the page no in the report header.

The output is as shown in diagram 2.8:

```
Page No:  1              PRODUCTWISE SALES

Product No      Description        UOM      Quantity      Rate       Total
-----------     --------------     -----    ---------    --------   --------
P00001          1.44 FLOPPIES      Piece       22          500       11000
P03453          1.22 FLOPPIES      Piece        6          500        3000
P06734          HDD                Piece        8         8000       64000
```

Diagram 2.8 : Productwise Sales Report

The steps in creating a report are :

1. Open the notepad editor and key in the following code :

```
ttitle left 'Page No: ' format 99 sql.pno center 'PRODUCTWISE SALES' skip 4
set pause 'More....'
set pause on
column product_no format a15 justify center
column product_no heading 'Product No.'
column description heading 'Description'
column description format a25 justify center
column unit_measure heading 'UOM'
column qty_ordered justify right
column sell_price justify right
column sell_price heading 'Rate'
SELECT product_master.product_no, description, unit_measure,
     sum(qty_ordered) "Quantity", sell_price, sum(qty_ordered) * sell_price "Total"
     FROM sales_order_details , product_master
     WHERE product_master.product_no = sales_order_details.product_no
     GROUP BY product_master.product_no, description, unit_measure, sell_price ;
```

2. Save the file. Run the file using the start command. It will display the output as shown in diagram 2.8.

SELF REVIEW EXERCISES IN SQL

Tables For Exercises
1. Create the following tables:
1) Create the following tables using the SQL create statement

Table Name : Client_master
Description : Use to store information about clients.

Column Name	Data Type	Size	Attributes
client_no	varchar2	6	Primary Key / first letter must start with 'C'.
name	varchar2	20	Not Null
address1	varchar2	30	
address2	varchar2	30	
city	varchar2	15	
state	varchar2	15	
pincode	number	6	
bal_due	number	10,2	

Table Name : product_master
Description : Use to store information about products.

Column Name	Data Type	Size	Attributes
product_no	varchar2	6	Primary Key / first letter must start with 'P'.
description	varchar2	5	Not Null
profit_percent	number	2,2	Not Null
unit_measure	varchar2	10	Not Null
qty_on_hand	number	8	Not Null
reorder_lvl	number	8	Not Null
sell_price	number	8,2	Not Null, cannot be 0.
cost_price	number	8,2	Not Null, cannot be 0.

Table Name : salesman_master
Description : Use to store information about salesmen working in the company.

Column Name	Data Type	Size	Attributes
salesman_no	varchar2	6	Primary Key / first letter must start with 'S'.
salesman_name	varchar2	20	Not Null
Address1	varchar2	30	Not Null
Address2	varchar2	30	
city	varchar2	20	
pincode	varchar2	6	
State	varchar2	20	
sal_amt	number	8,2	Not Null, cannot be 0
tgt_to_get	number	6,2	Not Null, cannot be 0
ytd_sales	number	6,2	Not Null
Remarks	varchar2	60	

Table Name : sales_order
Description : Use to store information about order

Column Name	Data Type	Size	Attributes
s_order_no	varchar2	6	Primary Key / first letter must start with 'O'.
s_order_date	date		
client_no	varchar2	6	Foreign Key references client_no of client_master table.
dely_Addr	varchar2	25	
salesman_no	varchar2	6	Foreign Key references salesman_no of salesman_master table
dely_type	char	1	delivery : part(P) / full (F), Default 'F'
billed_yn	char	1	
dely_date	date		cannot be less than s_order_date
order_status	varchar2	10	values ('In Process', 'Fulfilled', 'BackOrder', 'Canceled')

Table Name : sales_order_details
Description : Use to store information about products ordered.

Column Name	Data Type	Size	Attributes
s_order_no	varchar2	6	Primary Key / Foreign Key references s_order_no of sales_order table.
product_no	varchar2	6	Primary Key / Foreign Key references product_no of product_master table.
qty_ordered	number	8	
qty_disp	number	8	
product_rate	number	10,2	

Table Name : Challan_Header
Description : Use to store information about challans made for the orders.

Column Name	Data Type	Size	Attributes
challan_no	varchar2	6	Primary Key / first two letters must start with 'CH'.
s_order_no	varchar2	6	Foreign Key references s_order_no of sales_order table
challan_date	date		Not Null
billed_yn	char	1	values('Y', 'N'). Default 'N'.

Table Name : Challan_Details
Description : Use to store information about challan details.

Column Name	Data Type	Size	Attributes
challan_no	varchar2	6	Primary Key / Foreign Key references challan_no of challan_header table.
product_no	varchar2	6	Primary Key / Foreign Key references product_no of product_master table
qty_disp	number	4,2	Not Null

2 Insert the following data into their respective tables using the SQL insert statement :

1 Data for **client_master** table :

Client No	Name	City	Pin code	State	Bal. Due
C00001	Ivan Bayross	Bombay	400054	Maharashtra	15000
C00002	Vandana Saitwal	Madras	780001	Tamil Nadu	0
C00003	Pramada Jaguste	Bombay	400057	Maharashtra	5000
C00004	Basu Navindgi	Bombay	400056	Maharashtra	0
C00005	Ravi Sreedharan	Delhi	100001		2000
C00006	Rukmini	Bombay	400050	Maharashtra	0

2 Data for **product_master** table:

Product No	Description	Profit Percent	UOM	Qty on hand	Reorder Level	Sell Price	Cost Price
P00001	1.44 Floppies	5	Piece	100	20	525	500
P03453	Monitors	6	Piece	10	3	12000	11280
P06734	Mouse	5	Piece	20	5	1050	1000
P07865	1.22 Floppies	5	Piece	100	20	525	500
P07868	Keyboards	2	Piece	10	3	3150	3050
P07885	CD Drive	2.5	Piece	10	3	5250	5100
P07965	540 HDD	4	Piece	10	3	8400	8000
P07975	1.44 Drive	5	Piece	10	3	1050	1000
P08865	1.22 Drive	5	Piece	2	3	1050	1000

3. Data for salesman_master table :

Salesman No	Salesman Name	Address 1	Address 2	City	Pincode	State	Salamt	Tgt_To Get	Ytd sales	Remarks
S00001	Kiran	A/14	Worli	Bombay	400002	MAH	3000	100	50	Good
S00002	Manish	65	Nariman	Bombay	400001	MAH	3000	200	100	Good
S00003	Ravi	P-7	Bandra	Bombay	400032	MAH	3000	200	100	Good
S00004	Ashish	A/5	Juhu	Bombay	400044	MAH	3500	200	150	Good

4. Data for **sales_order** table :

S Order No	S Order Date	Client No	Dely Type	Bill Yn	Salesman No	Dely Date	Order Status
O19001	12-jan-96	C00001	F	N	S00001	20-jan-96	IP
O19002	25-jan-96	C00002	P	N	S00002	27-jan-96	C
O46865	18-feb-96	C00003	F	Y	S00003	20-feb-96	F
O19003	03-apr-96	C00001	F	Y	S00001	07-apr-96	F
O46866	20-may-96	C00004	P	N	S00002	22-may-96	C
O10008	24-may-96	C00005	F	N	S00004	26-may-96	I P

5. Data for **sales_order_details** table :

S Order No	Product No	Qty Ordered	Qty Disp	Product Rate
O19001	P00001	4	4	525
O19001	P07965	2	1	8400
O19001	P07885	2	1	5250
O19002	P00001	10	0	525
O46865	P07868	3	3	3150
O46865	P07885	3	1	5250
O46865	P00001	10	10	525
O46865	P03453	4	4	1050
O19003	P03453	2	2	1050
O19003	P06734	1	1	12000
O46866	P07965	1	0	8400
O46866	P07975	1	0	1050
O10008	P00001	10	5	525
O10008	P07975	5	3	1050

6. Data for **challan_header** table:

Challan No	S Order No	Challan Date	Billed
CH9001	O19001	12-dec-95	Y
CH6865	O46865	12-nov-95	Y
CH3965	O10008	12-oct-95	Y

7. Data for **challan_details** table:

Challan No	Product No	Qty Disp
CH9001	P00001	4
CH9001	P07965	1
CH9001	P07885	1
CH6865	P07868	3
CH6865	P03453	4
CH6865	P00001	10
CH3965	P00001	5
CH3965	P07975	2

Hands-On Exercise

a. Add the following record into the challan_details table and check if the record gets added or not. Note the observation for each of them

    CH9001   P00001   5
    P785341   P06734   9
    P00001   CH9001   1

b. Drop the table product_master. Can the product_master be dropped. If not, note the error message.

c. Drop the table challan_details, challan_header and product_master in the specified sequence.

What conclusions can you draw, performing the above tasks?

SIXTY SELF REVIEW SQL SENTENCE CONSTRUCTS FOR PRACTICE

Single Table Retrieval :
1. Find out the names of all the clients.
2. Print the entire client_master table.
3. Retrieve the list of names and the cities of all the clients.
4. List the various products available from the product_master table.
5. Find the names of all clients having 'a' as the second letter in their names.
6. Find out the clients who stay in a city whose second letter is 'a'.
7. Find the list of all clients who stay in city 'Bombay' or city 'Delhi' or city 'Madras'.
8. List all the clients who are located in Bombay.
9. Print the list of clients whose bal_due are greater than value 10000.
10. Print the information from sales_order table of orders placed in the month of January.
11. Display the order information for client_no 'C00001' and 'C00002'.
12. Find the products with description as '1.44 Drive' and '1.22 Drive'.

13. Find the products whose selling price is greater than 2000 and less than or equal to 5000.
14. Find the products whose selling price is more than 1500 and also find the new selling price as original selling price * 15.
15. Rename the new column in the above query as new_price.
16. Find the products whose cost price is less than 1500.
17. List the products in sorted order of their description.
18. Calculate the square root of the price of each product.
19. Divide the cost of product '540 HDD' by difference between its price and 100.
20. List the names, city and state of clients not in the state of 'Maharashtra'.
21. List the product_no, description, sell_price of products whose description begin with letter 'M'.
22. List all the orders that were canceled in the month of March.

Set Functions and Concatenation :
23. Count the total number of orders.
24. Calculate the average price of all the products.
25. Calculate the minimum price of products.
26. Determine the maximum and minimum product prices. Rename the title as max_price and min_price respectively.
27. Count the number of products having price greater than or equal to 1500.
28. Find all the products whose qty_on_hand is less than reorder level.
29. Print the information of client_master, product_master, sales_order table in the following format for all the records :-
{cust_name} has placed order {order_no} on {s_order_date}.

Having and Group By :
30. Print the description and total qty sold for each product.
31. Find the value of each product sold.
32. Calculate the average qty sold for each client that has a maximum order value of 15000.00.
33. Find out the total sales amount receivable for the month of jan. It will be the sum total of all the billed orders for the month.
34. Print the information of product_master, order_detail table in the following format for all the records :- {description} worth Rs. {total sales for the product} was sold.
35. Print the information of product_master, order_detail table in the following format for all the records :-
{description} worth Rs. {total sales for the product} was ordered in the month of {s_order_date in month format}.

Joins and Correlations :
36. Find out the products which has been sold to 'Ivan Bayross'.
37. Find out the products and their quantities that will have to delivered in the current month.
38. Find the product_no and description of moving products.
39. Find the names of clients who have purchased 'CD Drive'.

40. List the product_no and s_order_no of customers having qty_ordered less than 5 from the order details Table for the product '1.44 Floppies'.
41. Find the products and their quantities for the orders placed by 'Vandana Saitwal' and 'Ivan Bayross'.
42. Find the products and their quantities for the orders placed by client_no 'C00001' and 'C00002'.

Nested Queries :
43. Find the product_no and description of non-moving products.
44. Find the customer name, address1, address2, city and pincode for the client who has placed order no "O19001".
45. Find the client names who have placed orders before the month of May, 96.
46. Find out if product '1.44 Drive' is ordered by any client and print the client_no, name to whom it is was sold.
47. Find the names of clients who have placed orders worth Rs. 10000 or more.

Queries using Date :
48. Display the order number and day on which clients placed their order.
49. Display the month (in alphabets) and date when the order must be delivered.
50. Display the s_order_date in the format 'dd-month-yy'. e.g. 12-February-96.
51. Find the date, 15 days after today's date.
52. Find the number of days elapsed between today's date and the delivery date of the orders placed by the clients.

Table Updations :
53. Change the s_order_date of client_no 'C00001' to 24/07/96.
54. Change the selling price of '1.44 Floppy Drive' to Rs. 1150.00.
55. Delete the record with order number 'O19001' from the order table.
56. Delete all the records having delivery date before 10th July '96
57. Change the city of client_no 'C00005' to 'Bombay'.
58. Change the delivery date of order number 'O10008' to 16-08-96.
59. Change the bal_due of client_no 'C00001' to 1000.
60. Change the cost price of '1.22 Floppy Drive' to Rs. 950.00.

3. PL/SQL

While SQL is the natural language of the DBA, it does not have any procedural capabilities such as looping and branching nor does it have any conditional checking capabilities vital for data testing before storage. For all this, Oracle provides PL/SQL. Programmers can use it to create programs for validation and manipulation of table data. PL/SQL adds to the power of SQL and provides the user with all the facilities of a programming environment.

INTRODUCTION

PL/SQL bridges the gap between database technology and procedural programming languages. It can be thought of as a development tool that extends the facilities of Oracle's SQL database language. Via PL/SQL you can insert, delete, update and retrieve table data as well as use procedural techniques such as writing loops or branching to another block of code.

PL/SQL is really an extension of SQL. It allows you to use all the SQL data manipulation statements as well as the cursor control operations and transaction processing. PL/SQL blocks can contain any number of SQL statements. It allows you to logically group a number of SQL sentences and pass them to the DBA as a single block.

Performance :
Without PL/SQL, DBA has to process SQL statements one at a time. This results in calls being made to the DBA each time an SQL statement is executed. It slows down table data processing considerably, especially when several users are firing SQL statements at the same time, as done in a multi-user environment. Each time an SQL statement is fired, it causes traffic to originate on the network and places quite a bit of overhead on the hardware.

With PL/SQL, an entire block of statements can be sent to the RDBMS engine at any one time. This dramatically reduces the communication between the developed software and the DBA (i.e. it reduces the traffic on the network).

Performance Improvement :

```
                   Block
                   PL/SQL begin
 ┌───────────┐     SQL statement     ┌───────────┐
 │APPLICATION│ ──► SQL statement ──► │ORACLE DBA │
 └───────────┘     PL/SQL end        └───────────┘


 ┌───────────┐     SQL sentence ───► ┌───────────┐
 │APPLICATION│ ──► SQL sentence ───► │DBA OF ANY │
 └───────────┘     SQL sentence ───► │OTHER RDBMS│
                                     └───────────┘
```

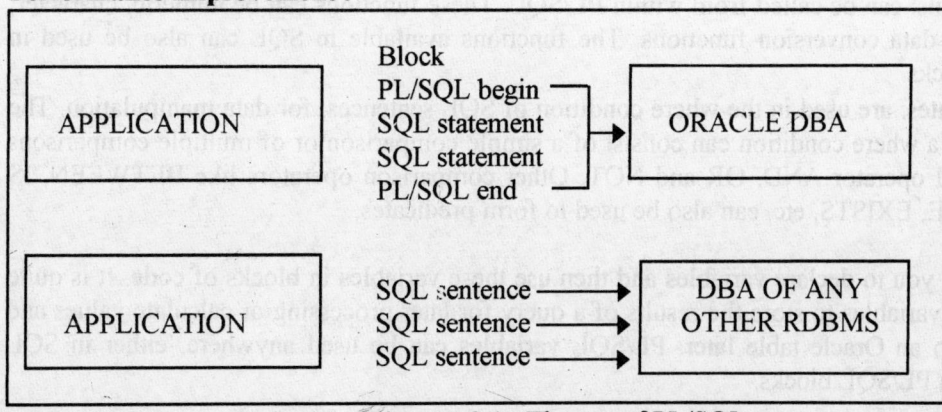

Diagram 3.1 : The use of PL/SQL.

Via diagram 3.1, it is obvious that when the DBA gets SQL code as a single block, it exercises this code much faster than if it got the code one sentence at a time. Hence, there is a definite improvement in the performance time of the DBA.

PL/SQL can also be used in SQL*FORMS. Its procedural capabilities can be used for writing complex triggers that will validate data before it is placed in the table. Here, the trigger code will be treated by the DBA as a block and processed in the same manner. Via PL/SQL you can do all sorts of calculations, quickly and efficiently without the use of the DBA. This considerably improves transaction performance.

Portability :
Applications written in PL/SQL are portable to any computer hardware and operating system, where Oracle is operational. Hence, PL/SQL code blocks written for a DOS version of Oracle will run on it's UNIX version, without any modifications made to it.

PL/SQL datatypes :
Both PL/SQL and Oracle have their foundations in SQL. Most PL/SQL datatypes are native to Oracle's data dictionary. Hence, there is a very easy integration of PL/SQL code with the Oracle RDBMS.

The %TYPE attribute provides for further integration. PL/SQL can use the %TYPE attribute to declare variables based on definitions of columns in a table. Hence, if a column's attributes change, the variable's attributes will change as well. This provides for data independence, reduces maintenance costs and allows programs to adapt to changes made to the table.

What PL/SQL can do for programmers
PL/SQL offers procedural methods of code writing for accessing the database and manipulating data in its table with flexibility and ease. This is because PL/SQL supports the following :
- SQL data manipulation statements: are those statements via which table data can be manipulated.
- SQL transaction processing statements: are a set of SQL statements that are treated as a single block by the DBA, so that all changes made to the data in the table are done or undone all at once.
- SQL functions: can be called from within PL/SQL. These functions can be numeric, character, and date or data conversion functions. The functions available in SQL can also be used in PL/SQL blocks.
- SQL predicates: are used in the where condition of SQL sentences, for data manipulation. The predicate to a where condition can consist of a simple comparison or of multiple comparisons using logical operator AND, OR and NOT. Other comparison operators like BETWEEN, IS NULL, LIKE, EXISTS, etc. can also be used to form predicates.

PL/SQL allows you to declare variables and then use these variables in blocks of code. It is quite possible to use variables to store the results of a query for later processing or calculate values and insert them into an Oracle table later. PL/SQL variables can be used anywhere, either in SQL statements or in PL/SQL blocks.

THE PL/SQL EXECUTION ENVIRONMENT

Wherever the PL/SQL technology is required i.e. in the RDBMS core or in its tools, the PL/SQL engine accepts any valid PL/SQL block as input. The PL/SQL engine executes procedural statements in the block and SQL statements are sent to the SQL statement executor in the Oracle RDBMS.

PL/SQL in the Oracle RDBMS :

When the PL/SQL engine resides in the Oracle RDBMS, the RDBMS can process not only single SQL statements but entire PL/SQL blocks.

These blocks are sent to the PL/SQL engine, where procedural statements are executed; and SQL statements are sent to the SQL executor in the RDBMS. Since the PL/SQL engine resides in the RDBMS, this is an efficient and swift operation.

You need to call the RDBMS only once to execute any number of SQL statements, if you bundle them inside a PL/SQL block.

Diagram 3.2 will give you an idea of how these statements are executed and how convenient it is to bundle SQL code within a PL/SQL block. Since the RDBMS is called only once for each block, the speed of SQL statement execution is vastly enhanced, when compared to the RDBMS being called for each SQL sentence.

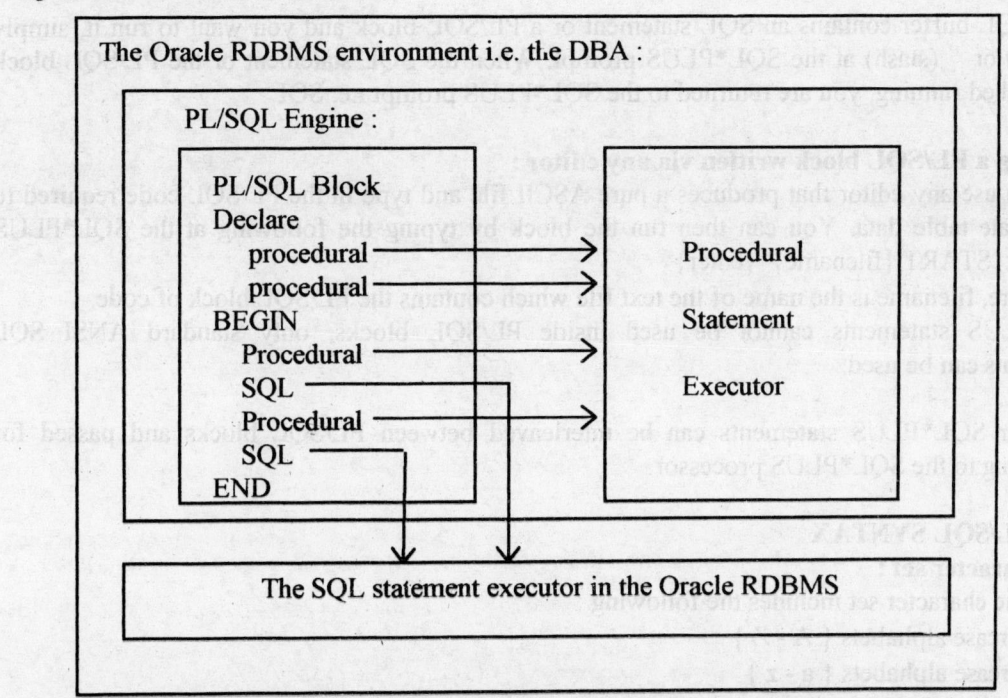

Diagram 3.2 : The PL/SQL execution environment.

USING PL/SQL Blocks in the SQL*PLUS ENVIRONMENT

PL/SQL can also be run from within the SQL*Plus environment. After invoking SQL*Plus, you can run a PL/SQL block in any one of the following ways :
- key it in directly using the SQL*PLUS editor, then run it.
- load it from a previously created ASCII file.

Either of the two methods require you to be within the SQL*PLUS environment first. All PL/SQL blocks start with the reserved word DECLARE or if the block has no declaration part, it will start with the reserved word BEGIN.

Typing either of these words at the SQL*PLUS prompt (SQL>) informs the SQL*PLUS code (held in ram) to do the following:
- Clear the SQL buffer,
- Enter into INPUT mode,
- Ignore semicolons, i.e. the SQL statement terminator.

You can then key in your entire PL/SQL block and use the normal SQL*PLUS editing features to edit the block. Terminating your PL/SQL block with a period (.) stores the block in the SQL buffer. If you terminate the PL/SQL block with a slash (/), it causes the PL/SQL block to be stored in the SQL buffer and then be executed.

If the SQL buffer contains an SQL statement or a PL/SQL block and you want to run it, simply type *run* or / (slash) at the SQL*PLUS prompt. When the SQL statement or the PL/SQL block has finished running, you are returned to the SQL*PLUS prompt i.e. SQL>

Running a PL/SQL block written via any editor :
You can use any editor that produces a pure ASCII file and type in the PL/SQL code required to manipulate table data. You can then run the block by typing the following at the SQL*PLUS prompt : START {filename} {enter}
- where, filename is the name of the text file which contains the PL/SQL block of code.

SQL*PLUS statements cannot be used inside PL/SQL blocks, only standard ANSI SQL statements can be used.

However SQL*PLUS statements can be interleaved between PL/SQL blocks and passed for processing to the SQL*PLUS processor.

THE PL/SQL SYNTAX
The character set :
The basic character set includes the following :
- uppercase alphabets { A - Z }
- lowercase alphabets { a - z }
- numerals { 0 - 9 }
- symbols : ( ) + - * / < > = ! ; : . ' @ % , " # $ ^ & _ \ { } ? [ ]

Words used in a PL/SQL block are called lexical units. You can freely insert blank spaces between lexical units in a PL/SQL block. The spaces have no effect on the PL/SQL block.

The ordinary symbols used in PL/SQL blocks are: ( ) + - * / < > = ; % ' " [ ] :

Compound symbols used in PL/SQL blocks are: < > != ~= ^= <= >= := ** .. || << >>

Literals :
A literal is a numeric value or a character string used to represent itself.

NUMERIC LITERAL
These can be either integers or floats. If a float is being represented, then the integer part must be separated from the float part by a period.
Example : 25, 6.34, 7g2, 25e-03, .1, 1., 1.e4, +17, -5

STRING LITERAL
These are represented by one or more legal characters and must be enclosed within single quotes. You can represent the single quote character itself, in a string literal by writing it twice. This will not be the same as a double quote.
Example : 'Hello World', 'Don''t go without saving your work'

CHARACTER LITERAL
These are string literals consisting of single characters.
Example : '*', 'A', 'Y'

LOGICAL (BOOLEAN) LITERAL
These are predetermined constants. The values it can take are: TRUE, FALSE, NULL

Comments :
A comment can have two forms:
- The comment line begins with a double hyphen (--). The entire line will be treated as a comment.
- The comment line begins with a slash followed by an asterisk (/*) till the occurrence of an asterisk followed by a slash (*/). All lines within, are treated as comments. This form of specifying comments can be used to span across multiple lines, which means that you can use this to surround a section of a PL/SQL block that you temporarily do not want to execute.
  Note : Comments cannot be nested.

Data Types :
The default data types that can be declared in PL/SQL are *number* (for storing numeric data), *char* (for storing character data), *date* (for storing date and time data), *boolean* (for storing TRUE, FALSE or NULL). *number*, *char* and *date* data types can have NULL values.

%TYPE declares a variable or constant to have the same datatype as that of a previously defined variable or of a column in a table or in a view. When referencing a table, you may name the table and column, or the owner of the table and column.

NOT NULL causes creation of a variable or a constant that cannot have a null value. If you attempt to assign the value NULL to a variable or a constant that has been assigned a NOT NULL constraint, it is an exception that Oracle senses automatically and an internal error condition is returned.

Note : As soon as a variable or constant has been declared as NOT NULL, it must be assigned a value. Hence every NOT NULL declaration of a variable or constant needs to be followed by a PL/SQL expression that loads a value into the variable or constant declared.

Variables :
Variables in PL/SQL blocks are *named* variables. A variable name must begin with a character and can be followed by a maximum of 29 other characters.

Reserved words cannot be used as variable names unless enclosed within double quotes. Variables must be separated from each other by at least one space or by a punctuation mark.

The case is insignificant when declaring variable names. A space cannot be used in variable name.

You can declare a variable of any data type either native to the Oracle DBA such as number, char, date, etc. or native to PL/SQL such as boolean (i.e. logical variable content).

Example :
* Declare a numeric variable that can hold 11 digits, two of which is to the right of the decimal point: *bonus number(11,2)*;
* Declare a variable that can hold boolean values true or false: *in_stock boolean*;

Assigning Values to Variables :
The assigning of a value to a variable can be done in two ways :
- Using the assignment operator ':=' (i.e. a colon followed by an equal to sign).

Example :   tax := price * tax_rate;
                  bonus := current_salary * 0.10;

- Selecting or fetching table data values into variables.

Example :   SELECT sal INTO current_salary
                  FROM emp
                  WHERE ename = 'SMITH';

you can calculate a 10% bonus for SMITH as follows :

                  bonus := current_salary * 0.10;

It is also possible to use the power of the DBA to perform calculations for you and then load a variable with a value.

>   Example : SELECT sal * 0.10 INTO bonus
>   FROM emp
>   WHERE ename = 'SMITH';

At this point you could use the variable bonus in another calculation, if required.

An interesting point to note here is that if you use PL/SQL code blocks for loading and calculating variables, the power of the DBA is not used. This frees up the DBA for other work and considerably improves response time.

Picking up a Variable's Parameters from a table cell :
The basic building block of a table is a cell that can be used to create records. When cells are being created by the Oracle DBA, under the instructions of the user, certain cell attributes are passed by the user and attached to the cell.

These attributes can be passed onto the variables being created in PL/SQL. This simplifies the declaration of variables and constants.

The *%type* attribute is used in the declaration of a variable when the variable's attributes must be picked up from a table column (i.e. a cell).

Example :   title   book_info.book_title%type;

Declaring a variable with the *%type* attribute has two advantages :
- You do not need to know the data type of the table column.
- If you change the parameters of the table column, the variable's parameters will change as well.

Declaring a constant :
Declaring a constant is similar to declaring a variable except that you have to add the keyword 'constant' and immediately assign a value to it. Thereafter, no further assignments to the constant are possible.
Example: bonus_multiplier constant number(3,2) := 0.10;

This constant can be used anywhere in the code.
Example: bonus := current_salary * bonus_multiplier;

Using logical comparisons in PL/SQL :
PL/SQL supports the comparison between variables and constants in SQL and PL/SQL statements. These comparisons, often called boolean expressions, generally consist of simple expressions separated by relational operators (<, >, =, < >, >=, <= that can be connected by logical operators (AND, OR, NOT). A boolean expression will always evaluate to TRUE, FALSE or NULL.

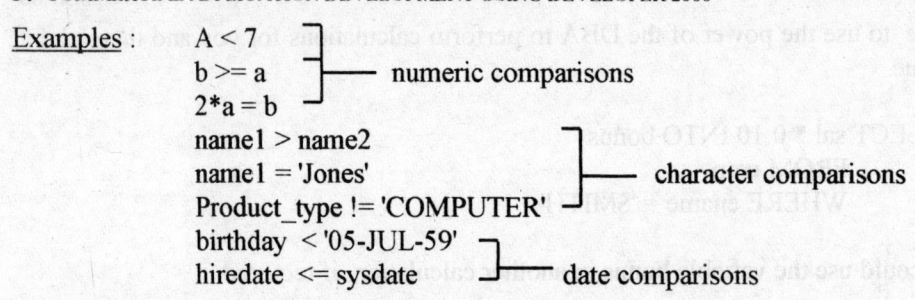

Examples :   A < 7 ⎤
              b >= a ⎬— numeric comparisons
              2*a = b ⎦
              name1 > name2   ⎤
              name1 = 'Jones'   ⎬— character comparisons
              Product_type != 'COMPUTER' ⎦
              birthday < '05-JUL-59' ⎤
              hiredate <= sysdate   ⎦— date comparisons

UNDERSTANDING THE PL/SQL BLOCK STRUCTURE

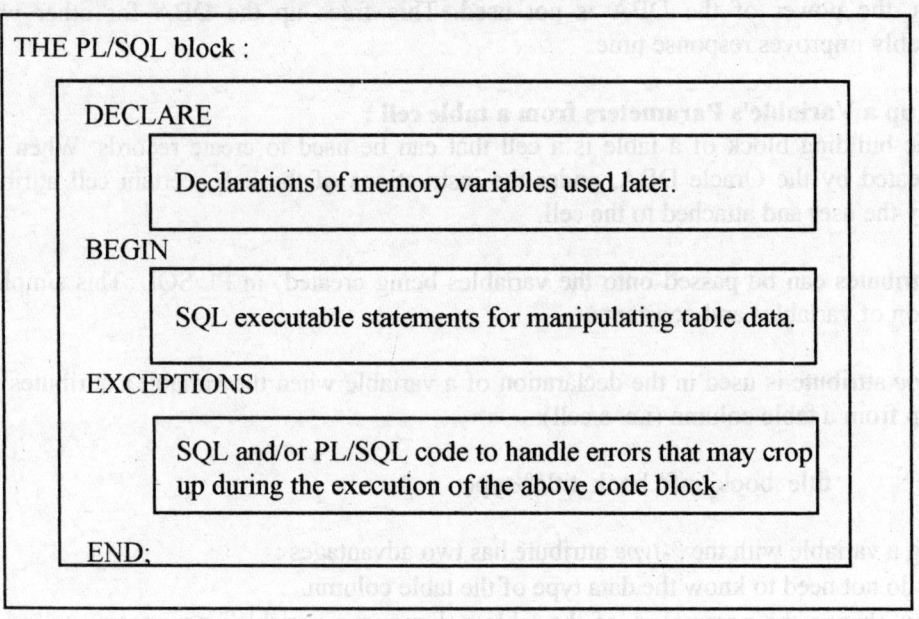

```
THE PL/SQL block :

  DECLARE
    ┌─────────────────────────────────────────────────┐
    │ Declarations of memory variables used later.    │
    └─────────────────────────────────────────────────┘
  BEGIN
    ┌─────────────────────────────────────────────────┐
    │ SQL executable statements for manipulating table data. │
    └─────────────────────────────────────────────────┘
  EXCEPTIONS
    ┌─────────────────────────────────────────────────┐
    │ SQL and/or PL/SQL code to handle errors that may crop │
    │ up during the execution of the above code block │
    └─────────────────────────────────────────────────┘
  END;
```

Diagram 3.3 : The PL/SQL block structure.

To begin to use PL/SQL code skillfully, you have to understand how to write its blocks and know the scope of what PL/SQL blocks can do.

In diagram 3.3, the PL/SQL block parts are logical. Blocks start with a declaration section in which memory variables and other Oracle objects can be declared. Once declared they can be manipulated in the SQL statements that are used for data manipulation.

If data validation is required or if internal or user-defined errors are encountered, the code written in the EXCEPTION section takes care of it.

Each block can contain other blocks, i.e. blocks can be nested. A nested block is a sub-block and is within an enclosing block. Blocks of code cannot be nested in the declaration section.

An identifier in the PL/SQL block :
The name of any Oracle object (variable, constant, record, cursor etc.) is known as an identifier. The following laws have to be followed while working with identifiers :
- An identifier cannot be declared twice in the same block.
- The same identifier can be declared in two different blocks.

If you follow the second law, the two identifiers are unique and any change in one does not affect the other. An identifier can be declared in a sub-block of another sub-block in which case it is local to that sub-block alone.

Example :
```
          DECLARE
                  account number(5);
                  credit_limit number(9,2);
          BEGIN
                  DECLARE
                          account char(20);
                          new_balance number(9,2);
                  BEGIN
                          The identifiers available to this block are
                          account char(20), credit_limit, new_balance
                  END;
                  DECLARE
                          old_balance number(9,2);
                  BEGIN
                          /* The identifiers available to this block are
                          account number(5), credit_limit, old_balance */
                  END;
                  /* The identifiers available here are
                  account number(5), credit_limit */
          END;
```

Displaying user Messages on the Screen :
Any programming tool requires a method through which messages can be displayed to the user.

dbms_output is a package that includes a number of procedure and functions that accumulate information in a buffer so that it can be retrieved later. These functions can also be used to display messages to the user.

Put_line: Put a piece of information in the buffer followed by an end-of-line marker. It can also be used to display message to the user.

put_line expects only one parameter of character datatype. If used to display message, it will be the message string.

To display messages to the user the SERVEROUTPUT should be set to ON. SERVEROUTPUT is a SQL*PLUS environment parameter that displays the information passed as a parameter to the put_line function.

Example : Setting the server output on :

SET SERVEROUTPUT ON

Example : Write the following code in the PL/SQL block to display message to the user.

DBMS_OUTPUT.PUT_LINE (' Displaying User Message ') ;

Conditional control in PL/SQL :
In PL/SQL, the *if* statement allows you to control the execution of a block of code. In PL/SQL you can use the IF - THEN - ELSIF - ELSE - END IF statements in code blocks that will allow you to write specific conditions under which a specific block of code will be executed.

Syntax :
```
IF < Condition > THEN
        < Action >
ELSIF < Condition >
        < Action >
ELSE
        < Action >
END IF;
```

Example :
```
DECLARE
        acct_balance number(11,2)
        acct constant number(2) := 3;
        debit_amt number(5) := 2000;
        min_bal constant number(5,2) := 500.00;
BEGIN
        select bal into acct_balance from accounts
                where account_id = acct;
        acct_balance := acct_balance - debit_amt;
        if acct_balance >= MIN_BAL then
                update accounts set bal = bal - debit_amt
                        where account_id = acct;
        end if;
END;
```

Iterative Control :
This is the ability to repeat or skip sections of a code block.

A loop repeats a sequence of statements. You have to place the keyword *loop* before the first statement in the sequence of statements that you want repeated and the keywords *end loop* immediately after the last statement in the sequence. Once a loop begins to run, it will go on forever. Hence loops are always accompanied by a conditional statement that keeps control on the number of times the loop is executed.

You can build user defined exits from a loop, where required.

THE *WHILE LOOP* :

Syntax :   WHILE < Condition >
           LOOP
                < Action >
           END LOOP;

Example : Inversing a given number e.g. number 5639 when inverted must display output as 9365.

```
DECLARE
    given_number varchar(5) := '5639';
    cntr number(2);
    inverted_number varchar(5);
BEGIN
    cntr := length(given_number);
    while cntr > 0
    loop
        inverted_number := inverted_number ||
                    substr(given_number, cntr, 1);
        cntr := cntr - 1;
    end loop;
    dbms_output.put_line ('The Given number is ' ||
                    given_number );
    dbms_output.put_line ('The Inverted number is ' ||
                    inverted_number );
END;
```

THE *FOR LOOP* STATEMENT

Syntax :   FOR variable IN [REVERSE] start..end
           LOOP
                < Action >
           END LOOP;

Example : Inversing a given number e.g. number 5639 when inverted must display output as 9365.

```
DECLARE
    given_number varchar(5) := '5639';
    str_length number(2);
    inverted_number varchar(5);
BEGIN
    str_length := length(given_number);
```

```
                for cntr in reverse 1..str_length  /* variables used as counter in for
                loop need not be declared i.e. cntr declaration is not required*/
                loop
                        inverted_number := inverted_number ||
                                       substr(given_number, cntr, 1);
                end loop;
                        dbms_output.put_line ('The Given number is ' ||
                                       given_number );
                        dbms_output.put_line ('The Inverted number is ' ||
                                       inverted_number );
        END;
```

THE *GOTO* STATEMENT

The *goto* statement allows you to change the flow of control within a PL/SQL block.

Example : If the prices of product 'P00001' is < 4000 then change the price to 4000. The price change is recorded in the old_price_table along with product_no and the date on which the price was changed last.

```
                DECLARE
                        Sell_price number(10,2) ;
                BEGIN
                        select sell_price into sell_price from product_master
                                where product_no = 'P00001';
                        if sell_price < 4000 then
                                goto add_old_price;
                        else
                                goto same_price;
                        end if;

                << add_old_price >>
                        update product_master
                                set sell_price = 4000
                                where product_no = 'P00001';
                        insert into old_price_table
                                (product_no, change_date, raise ) values
                                ( 'P00001', sysdate, 4000) ;
                        dbms_output.put_line('The new Price of P00001 is 4000' );
                << same_price>>
                        dbms_output.put_line('Current Price of P00001 is ' || sell_price);
                END ;
```

The entry point of the block is defined within << >> as shown in the above example.

ORACLE TRANSACTIONS

A transaction is a user-defined series of one or more logically related statements or operations to be performed on the Oracle table data. This is also termed as a logical unit of work. It is a sequence of SQL statements that Oracle treats as a single entity. A transaction begins with the first executable SQL statement after a *commit*, *rollback* or *connection* made to the database. All changes made to an Oracle table data via this unit of work (i.e. a transaction) are made or undone at any time.

Specifically, a transaction is a group of events that occurs between any of the following events:
- Connecting to Oracle.
- Disconnecting from Oracle.
- Committing changes to the database.
- Rollback.

Closing Transactions :
You close a transaction by using either a *commit* or a *rollback* statement. By using these statements you can ensure that all or none of the changes are made to the data in the Oracle table.

Example : Transferring money from one bank account to another. The logical units of work are :
Debit account 'A'; Credit account 'B' .

This typically requires two SQL updates. However the entire block is viewed as a single transaction.

Using *commit* :
A *commit* ends the current transaction and makes permanent any changes made during that transaction. While a transaction is in progress no other user can see the data being processed.

Syntax : COMMIT;

Using *rollback* :
The *rollback* statement does the exact opposite of the *commit* statement. It ends the transaction but undoes any changes made during the transaction. *Rollback* is useful for two reasons :

1. If you have made a mistake, such as deleting the wrong row for a table, you can use *rollback* to restore the original data. *Rollback* will take you back to an intermediate statement in the current transaction, which means that you do not have to erase the entire transaction.

2. *Rollback* is useful if you have started a transaction that you cannot complete. This might occur if you have a logical problem or if there is an SQL statement that does not execute successfully. In such cases, *rollback* allows you to return to the starting point to allow you to take corrective action and perhaps try again.

Syntax :   ROLLBACK [WORK] [TO [SAVEPOINT] savepoint]

where,

WORK	: is optional and is provided for ANSI compatibility.
SAVEPOINT	: is optional and is used to rollback a partial transaction, as far as the specified savepoint.
savepoint	: is a savepoint created during the current transaction.

Using rollback without *savepoint* clause:
- Ends the transaction.
- Undoes all the changes in the current transaction.
- Erases all savepoints in that transaction.
- Releases the transaction locks.

Using rollback with the *to savepoint* clause :
- Rolls back just a portion of the transaction.
- Retains the save point rolled back to, but loses those created after the named savepoint.
- Releases all table and row locks that were acquired since the savepoint was taken.

For example :

1. To rollback entire transaction: ROLLBACK;
2. To rollback to savepoint *sp5* :   ROLLBACK TO SAVEPOINT sp5;

Using Savepoint :
Savepoint marks and saves the current point in the processing of a transaction. Used with the *rollback* statement, savepoints can undo parts of a transaction. By default the maximum no of savepoints per transaction is 5. An active savepoint is the one that is specified since the last commit or rollback.

Syntax :   SAVEPOINT savepoint;

After a savepoint is created, you can either continue processing, commit your work, rollback the entire transaction, or rollback to the savepoint.

Example :
Update Blake's and Clarks's salary, check that the total company salary does not exceed 20000. If total salary > 20000 then rollback.

```
DECLARE
        total_sal number(9);
BEGIN
        update emp
            set  sal = 2000
            where ename = 'Blake';
```

```
            savepoint Blake_sal;
            update emp
                    set sal = 1500
                    where ename = 'Clark';

            savepoint Clark_sal;
            select sum(sal) into total_sal from emp;
            if :total_sal > 20000 then
                    rollback to savepoint Blake_sal;
            end if;
            commit;
    END;
```

Example : The following PL/SQL code block processes an order for 540 HDD :

```
DECLARE
        num_in_stock number(5);
BEGIN
        select quantity into num_in_stock from product_master
                where product = '540 HDD';
        If num_in_stock > 0 then
                update product_master set quantity = quantity - 1
                        where product = '540 HDD';
                insert into purchase_record
                        values ('ONE 540 HDD PURCHASED', sysdate);
        else
                insert into purchase_record
                        values ('NO 540 HDD AVAILABLE', sysdate);
        end if;
        commit;
END;
```

The above block of PL/SQL code does the following:
- It determines how many 540 HDD are left in stock.
- If the number left in stock is greater than zero, it updates the inventory to reflect the sale of the product.
- It stores the fact that a 540 HDD was purchased on a certain date.
- If the stock available is zero, it stores the fact that there are no more 540 HDD for sale and the date on which such a situation occurred.

In this sample block, there is a clear illustration of conditional control, one of the basic features of a procedural language. The declaration of variables, their data types etc. are also visible.

CONCURRENCY CONTROL IN ORACLE

Users manipulate Oracle table data via SQL or PL/SQL sentences. Hence, these sentences cause the DBA/CPU combination to perform a unit of work. This unit of work is called a transaction.

It is possible to have a unit of work done via a single SQL sentence or it maybe necessary to have several SQL sentences to get the unit of work done. This gives rise to Single Query Transactions and Multiple Query Transactions. i.e. SQT and MQT (DML's).

These transactions (whether SQT or MQT) all access an Oracle table or tables. Since we are working with Oracle on a multi-user platform like Unix, it is more than likely that several people will be firing DML's at the same time.

The DBA would have to allow multiple people to access data from the Oracle table at the same time. The Oracle table is therefore a global resource.

When several people are accessing a global resource a technique called concurrency control has to be employed by any RDBMS to prevent damage to the global resource or to its contents.

Several methods have been tried and tested for concurrency control. A method called **Locking** has been accepted and is universally used. Hence Oracle uses automatic locking for concurrency control.

LOCKS

Locks are mechanisms intended to prevent destructive interaction between users accessing the same resource, i.e. interaction which leads to incorrect data or incorrect alteration to a datastructure. The resource could be a table or a row in the table. Thus, locks are used to ensure data integrity while allowing maximum concurrent access to the data by unlimited users.

Oracle's locking is fully automatic and requires no user action. DBA locks the Oracle data while executing SQL statements. This type of locking is called *implicit* locking. When a lock is put by user it is called *explicit* locking.

Types of locks :
There are two levels of locks that a DBA can be applied. They are :
- Shared   : Multiple users can hold various share locks on a single resource.
- Exclusive   : It prohibits all sharing of resources (table or row), i.e. only the first user has the sole ability to alter the resource until the locks are released.

Implicit locking
Oracle applies different locks automatically based on the DDL or DML processed. This results in a high degree of data concurrency. Readers of data do not wait for writers. Writers of data do not wait for readers. Writers only wait for other writers, if they attempt to update the same rows at the same time.

A table can be decomposed into rows which can be further decomposed into items. Hence, if an automatic locking system is designed so as to be able to lock the items of a record, it will be the most flexible locking system available.

It would mean that more than one user can be working on a single record in a table i.e. each on a different item of the same record in the same table.

Oracle provides two levels of automatic locking, table level and row level. The DBA decides on what level to use by the presence or absence of a *where* condition in the SQL sentence as explained below :

Following are the locking characteristics for *update*, *delete* and the *insert* SQL statements:
- It acquires exclusive locks on the rows to be modified and row exclusive lock on the table containing those rows.
- Other users can query the rows to be modified but cannot alter until the locks are released. They can work on other rows.
- Locks on Rows and tables are released on commit.
- A rollback to savepoint, releases all locks acquired, upto the named savepoint, are released.

When a *select* statement is fired without using the *for update* clause, no locks are put. Hence it is from the SQL sentence itself that the DBA recognizes the exact type and level of lock to fire upon a global resource such as an Oracle table.

Explicit locking
When a lock is put by an operator or trigger it is called explicit locking.

Who can explicitly lock ?
- The DBA can lock any table.
- Other users can lock tables they own or any tables on which they have been granted table privileged (such as *select*, *insert*, *update*, *delete*).

Users can explicitly lock either table(s) or row(s) using the *select...for update* statement or *lock table* statement.

You can start a *read only* transaction by the *set transaction read only* statement and override the default locking.

Using the *select...for update* statement :
The *select...for update* can also be used to override locks. It is used in anticipation of performing updates and acquiring exclusive row locks.

Example :   SELECT * FROM emp WHERE emp_no < 'E00001' FOR UPDATE;

The *select... for update* cannot be used with the *distinct* and the *group by* clause. It cannot be used with set operators and group functions. This clause signals that you intend to update data but do not require that the update operation be performed. It is often followed by one or more *update* statements with the *where* clause.

Note:
1. The columns specified in the *select* statement signify only the rows to be locked, the specific columns are not significant. The tables locked must be located on the same database.
2. If the rows are already locked by another user, then Oracle will wait for the lock to be released by a commit or rollback statement. However you can use the NOWAIT option to cause Oracle to terminate the statement.
3. It terminates at the *commit* or *rollback* statement. It is better to use it for a few rows than for many.

Using *lock table* statement :
It manually overrides the default locking by creating a data lock in the mode specified.

Syntax :   LOCK TABLE table [,table]...
            IN {ROW SHARE|ROW EXCLUSIVE|SHARE UPDATE|
                SHARE|SHARE ROW EXCLUSIVE|EXCLUSIVE }
            MODE [NOWAIT]

where,

- **table** : indicates the name of table(s), view(s) to be locked. In case of views, the lock is placed on underlying tables;
- **MODE** : decides what other locks on the same resource can exist simultaneously. For example, if there is exclusive lock on the table no user can update rows in the table. Data locks can be obtained in one of the two ways :

  - **EXCLUSIVE** : They allow query on the locked resource but prohibit any other activity;
  - **SHARE** : It allows queries but prohibits updates to a table;
  - **ROW SHARE SHARE UPDATE** : Row share locks allow concurrent access to a table. They prohibit other users to lock entire table exclusively;
  - **ROW EXCLUSIVE** : Row exclusive locks are the same as row share locks, but also prohibit locking in shared mode. These locks are acquired when updating, inserting or deleting.
  - **SHARE ROW EXCLUSIVE** : They are used to look at a whole table, to selective updates and to allow other users to look at rows in the table but not lock the table in share mode or to update rows.
  - **NOWAIT** : indicates that you do not wish to wait, if resources are unavailable. If omitted, the DBA will wait till resources are available.

Example   : Lock emp table in exclusive mode

```
LOCK TABLE emp
IN EXCLUSIVE MODE
NOWAIT;
```

When locks are released :
All locks are released under the following circumstances:
- The transaction is committed successfully.
- A *rollback* is performed.
- A *rollback to a savepoint* will release locks set after the specified *savepoint*.

Note :
- All the data is released on *commit* or *unqualified Rollback*.
- Table locks are released by rolling back to a savepoint.
- Row-level locks are not released by rolling back to a savepoint.

CURSORS
How are SQL statements processed by Oracle ?
Whenever an SQL statement is executed, Oracle DBA performs the following tasks :

- Reserves an area in memory called private SQL area
- Populates this area with the appropriate data.
- Processes the data in the memory area.
- Frees the memory area when the execution is complete.

Let us assume that the user executes an SQL statement that selects *employee code, employee name, job* and *salary* from table *employee* and displays the same in the ascending order of employee name.

The SQL select statement will be as follows :

    Select emp_code, emp_name, job, salary
        from employee
        order by emp_name ;

To execute the above statement, Oracle will reserve an area in memory and populate it with the records from employee table. These records are then sorted in the ascending order of employee name and displayed to the user. When all the records from the employee table are displayed, Oracle will free the memory area used for retrieving and sorting the data.

What is a cursor ?
We have seen how Oracle executes an SQL statement. Oracle DBA uses a work area for its internal processing. This work area is private to SQL's operations and is called a **Cursor**.

The data that is stored in the cursor is called the **Active Data Set**. The size of the cursor in memory is the size required to hold the number of rows in the Active Data Set. However this is further subject to the control that the Oracle DBA exercises over the main memory of the computer.

Oracle has a pre-defined area in main memory set aside, within which it opens cursors. Hence the cursor's size will be limited by this pre-defined area. Should the SQL statement return more rows than can be held in the cursor, cursor data and the retrieved data is swapped under the control of the DBA according to user requests. i.e. the request to view more data or EXIT.

Example :
When a user fires a select statement as,

    select empno, ename, job, salary from employee where deptno = 20;

the resultant data set will be as displayed in diagram 4.

Active Data Set	3456	IVAN	MANAGER	10000
	3459	PRADEEP	ANALYST	7000
	3446	MITA	PROGRMR	4000
	3463	VIJAY	CLERK	2000
	3450	ALDRIN	ACCTANT	3000

Diagram 3.4 : Contents of a cursor.

When a query returns multiple rows, in addition to the data held in the cursor, Oracle will also open and maintain a row pointer. Depending on user requests to view data the row pointer will be relocated within the cursor's Active Data Set. Additionally Oracle also maintains cursor variables loaded with the value of the total no. of rows fetched from the active data set.

Use of cursors in PL/SQL :
While SQL is the natural language of the DBA, it does not have any procedural capabilities such as condition checking, looping and branching. For this, Oracle provides the PL/SQL. Programmers can use it to create programs for validation and manipulation of table data. PL/SQL adds to the power of SQL and provides the user with all the functionality of a programming environment.

A PL/SQL block of code includes the Procedural code for looping and branching along with the SQL statement. If records from a record set created using a select statement are to be evaluated & processed one at a time, then the only method available is by using Explicit Cursors.

Also cursors can be used to evaluate the success of updates and deletes and the number of this affected (Implicit).

Explicit Cursor :
You can explicitly declare a cursor to process the rows individually. A cursor declared by the user is called **Explicit Cursor**. For queries that return more than one row, you must declare a cursor explicitly.

Why use an Explicit Cursor ?
Cursors can be used when the users wants to process data one row at a time.

Example :
Update an Acctmast table and set a value in its *Balance amount* column depending upon whether the account has an amount debited or credited in the *Accttran* table. The records from the Accttran table will be fetched one at a time and updated in the Acctmast table depending upon whether the account is debited or credited.

PL/SQL raises an error if an embedded select statement retrieves more than one row. Such an error forces an abnormal termination of the PL/SQL block. Such an error can be eliminated by using a cursor.

Explicit Cursor Management :

The steps involved in declaring a cursor and manipulating data in the active set are :
- Declare a cursor that specifies the SQL select statement that you want to process
- Open a cursor.
- Fetch data from the cursor one row at a time.
- Close the cursor.

A cursor is defined in the declarative part of a PL/SQL block by naming it and specifying a query. Then, three commands are used to control the cursor : *open, fetch* and *close*.

First, initialize the cursor with the *open* statement, this ;
> defines a private SQL area
> executes a query associated with the cursor
> populates the **Active Data Set**.
> Sets the **Active Data Set's** row pointer to the first record.

The *fetch* statement retrieves the current row and advances the cursor to the next row. You can execute *fetch* repeatedly until all rows have been retrieved.

When the last row has been processed, close the cursor with the *close* statement. This will release the memory occupied by the cursor and its Data Set.

Focus : The HRD manager has decided to raise the salary for all the employees in department No. 20 by 0.05. Whenever any such raise is given to the employees, a record for the same is maintained in the emp_raise table. It includes the employee number, the date when the raise was given and the actual raise. Write a PL/SQL block to update the salary of each employee and insert a record in the emp_raise table.

The table definition is as follows :
Table name : **employee**

Column name	Data Type	Size	Attributes
emp_code	varchar	10	Primary Key, via which we shall seek data in the table.
ename	varchar	20	The first name of the candidate.
deptno	number	5	The department number.
Job	varchar	20	Employee job details.
salary	number	8,2	The current salary of the employee.

Table name : **emp_raise**

Column name	Data Type	Size	Attributes
emp_code	varchar	10	is the part of a composite key via which we shall seek data in the table.
raise_date	date		The date on which the raise was given
raise_amt	number	8,2	The raise given to the employee.

Emp_code and raise_date together form a composite primary key.

Declaring a Cursor :
To do the above via a PL/SQL block it is necessary to declare a cursor and associate it with a query before referencing it in any statement within the PL/SQL block. This is because forward references to object are not allowed in PL/SQL.

Syntax :   CURSOR cursorname **IS**
                    SQL statement ;

Example :   DECLARE
                    /* Declaration of the cursor named c_emp
                    The active data set will include the names, department numbers
                    and salaries of all the employees belonging to department 20 */
                    **cursor c_emp is
                        select emp_code, salary from employee
                        where deptno = 20;**

The cursor name is not a PL/SQL variable; it is used only to reference the query. It cannot be assigned any values or be used in an expression.

Opening a Cursor :
*Open*ing the cursor executes the query and identifies the active set, that contains all the rows which meet the query search criteria.

Syntax :   OPEN cursorname ;

Example :   DECLARE
                    cursor c_emp is select emp_code, salary from employee
                        where deptno = 20;
                BEGIN
                    /* Opening cursor c_emp */
                    open c_emp;
                END;

Open statements retrieves the records from the database and places it in the cursor (private SQL area).

Fetching a record from the Cursor :

The *fetch* statement retrieves the rows from the active set to the variables one at a time. Each time a *fetch* is executed, The focus of the DBA cursor advances to the next row in the Active Set.

One can make use of any loop structure (Loop-End Loop along with While, For, IF-End If) to fetch the records from the cursor into variables one row at a time.

Syntax :   FETCH cursorname INTO variable1, variable2, ... ,

For each column value returned by the query associated cursor, there must be a corresponding variable in the *into* list. And, their datatypes must match. These variables will be declared in the DECLARE section of the PL/SQL block.

Example :   DECLARE
                    cursor c_emp is select emp_code, salary from employee
                        where deptno = 20;

```
            /* Declaration of memory variable that holds data fetched from
                the cursor */
            str_emp_code            employee.emp_code%type;
            num_salary              employee.salary%type;
        BEGIN
            open c_emp;

            /* infinite loop to fetch data from cursor c_emp one row
                at a time */
            loop
                fetch c_emp into str_emp_code, num_salary;

                /* Updating the salary in the employee table as
                    current salary + raise */
                update employee set salary = num_salary + (num_salary * .05)
                    where emp_code = str_emp_code ;

                /* Insert a record in the emp_raise table */
                insert into emp_raise values
                    (str_emp_code, sysdate, num_salary * 0.05)
            end loop;
            commit ;
        END ;
```

Note that the current program will result into an *indefinite loop* as there is no exit provided from the loop. The Exit from the loop can be provided using cursor variables as explained on page 101 section <u>*Explicit Cursor Variables*</u>. Also note if you execute a *fetch* and there are no more rows left in the *active data set*, the values of the Explicit cursor variables are indeterminate.

Closing a Cursor :

The *close* statement disables the cursor and the active set becomes undefined. This will release the memory occupied by the cursor and its Data Set. Once a cursor is *close*d, the user can re*open* the cursor using the open statement.

Syntax :   CLOSE cursorname ;

Example :   DECLARE
                   cursor c_emp is select emp_code, salary from employee
                       where deptno = 20;
                   str_emp_code employee.emp_code%type;
                   num_salary employee.salary%type;
               BEGIN
                   open c_emp;
                   loop
                       fetch c_emp into str_emp_code, num_salary;
                       update employee set salary = num_salary + (num_salary * .05)
                           where emp_code = str_emp_code ;
                       insert into emp_raise values
                           (str_emp_code, sysdate, num_salary * 0.05)
                   end loop;
                   commit ;
                   /* Close cursor c_emp */
                   close c_emp ;
               END ;

Explicit Cursor Attributes :

Oracle provides certain attributes / cursor variables to control the execution of the cursor. Whenever any cursor (explicit or implicit) is opened and used Oracle creates a set of four system variables via which Oracle keeps track of the 'Current' status of the cursor. You can access these cursor variables. They are described below.

- **%NOTFOUND** : evaluates to *true*, if the last *fetch* has failed because no more rows were available; or to *false*, if the last *fetch* returned a row.

Syntax : cursorname%NOTFOUND

Example :
```
DECLARE
        cursor c_emp is select emp_code, salary from employee
                where deptno = 20;
        str_emp_code employee.emp_code%type;
        num_salary employee.salary%type;
BEGIN
        open c_emp;
        loop
                fetch c_emp into str_emp_code, num_salary;

                /* If no. of records retrieved is 0 or if all the records are
                   fetched then exit the loop. */
                exit when c_emp%notfound ;
                update employee set salary = num_salary + (num_salary * .05)
                        where emp_code = str_emp_code ;
                insert into emp_raise values
                        (str_emp_code, sysdate, num_salary * 0.05)
        end loop;
        commit ;
        close c_emp ;
END;
```

- **%FOUND** : is the logical opposite of *%notfound*. It evaluates to *true*, if the last fetch succeeded because a row was available; or to *false*, if the last fetch failed because no more rows were available.

Syntax : cursorname%FOUND

Example : The PL/SQL block will be as follows :

```
DECLARE
        cursor c_emp is select emp_code, salary from employee
                where deptno = 20;
        str_emp_code employee.emp_code%type;
        num_salary employee.salary%type;
BEGIN
        open c_emp;
        loop
                fetch c_emp into str_emp_code, num_salary;
```

```
                    /* If no. of records retrieved > 0 then
                            process the data
                       else exit the loop. */
                    if c_emp%found then
                        update employee set salary = num_salary + (num_salary * .05)
                            where emp_code = str_emp_code ;
                        insert into emp_raise values
                            (str_emp_code, sysdate, num_salary * 0.05)
                    else
                        exit;
                    end if;
                end loop;
                commit ;
                close c_emp ;
        END;
```

- **%ISOPEN** : evaluates to *true*, if an explicit cursor is *open;* or to *false*, if it is *close*d.

    Syntax :   cursorname%ISOPEN

    Example :   DECLARE
```
                    cursor c_emp is select emp_code, salary from employee
                        where deptno = 20;
                    str_emp_code employee.emp_code%type;
                    num_salary employee.salary%type;
                BEGIN
                    open c_emp;

                    /* If the cursor is open
                            continue with the data processing
                       else
                            display an appropriate error message */
                    if c_emp%isopen then
                        loop
                            fetch c_emp into str_emp_code, num_salary;
                            exit when c_emp%notfound ;
                            update employee set salary = num_salary + (num_salary * .05)
                                where emp_code = str_emp_code ;
                            insert into emp_raise values
                                (str_emp_code, sysdate, num_salary * 0.05)
                        end loop;
                        commit ;
                        close c_emp ;
                    else
                        dbms_output.put_line ('Unable to open Cursor ');
                    end if ;
                END;
```

%ROWCOUNT : returns the number of rows *fetch*ed from the active set. It is set to zero when the cursor is *open*ed.

Syntax :   cursorname%ROWCOUNT

Example :   Display the names, department name and salary of the first 10 employees getting the highest salary.

```
DECLARE
    cursor c_emp is
            select ename, deptno, salary from employee, deptmaster
            where deptmaster.deptno = employee.deptno
            order by salary desc ;
    str_ename employee.ename%type ;
    num_deptno employee.deptno%type ;
    num_salary employee.salary%type ;
BEGIN
    open c_emp ;
    dbms_output.Put_line ('Name          Department        Salary');
    dbms_output.Put_line ('--------      ---------------   ---------');
    loop
            fetch c_emp into str_ename, num_deptno, num_salary;
            dbms_output.Put_line (str_ename || '    ' ||
                                  num_deptno || '    ' || num_salary);
            exit when c_emp%rowcount = 10 ;
    end loop;
END ;
```

Cursor *for* loops :
In most situations that require an explicit cursor, you can simplify coding by using a cursor *for* loop instead of the *open, fetch* and *close* statements.

A cursor *for* loop implicitly declares its loop index as a *%rowtype* record, opens a cursor, repeatedly fetches rows of values from the active set into items in the record, and closes the cursor when all rows have been processed.

Example : The PL/SQL block will be rewritten as follows :

```
DECLARE
    cursor c_emp is select emp_code, salary from employee
            where deptno = 20;
```

```
BEGIN
    for emp_rec in c_emp
    loop
        update employee
            set salary = emp_rec.salary + (emp_rec.salary * .05)
            where emp_code = emp_rec.emp_code;
        insert into emp_raise values
            (emp_rec.emp_code, sysdate, emp_rec.salary *.05)
    end loop;
    commit ;
END;
```

When you use a cursor for loop, the cursor *for* loop
- implicitly declares *emp_rec* as belonging to type *c_emp%rowtype* and retrieves the records as declared in the cursor *c_emp*.
- The sequence of statements inside the loop is executed once for every row that satisfies the query associated with the cursor. with each iteration, a record will be fetched from *c_emp* into *emp_rec*. Dot notation should be used to make a reference to individual items.
  Example : emp_rec.emp_code
  where emp_rec is a row type variable and emp_code is the name of the field.
- When you leave the loop, the cursor is closed automatically. This is true even if you use an *exit* or *goto* statement to leave the loop prematurely, or if an *exception* is raised inside the loop. Thus, When you exit the loop it closes the cursor *c_emp*.

Note :
The record is defined only inside the loop. You cannot refer to it's item outside the loop. The reference in the following example is illegal:

```
BEGIN
    for c1rec in c1 loop
    ....
    end loop;
    result := c1rec.n2 + 3; /* referencing c1rec outside for loop is illegal */
END;
```

Focus : A bank has an 'ACCTMAST' table where it holds the current status of a client's bank account (i.e. currently what the client has in the savings bank account.)

Another table called the ACCTTRAN table holds each transaction as it occurs at the back. i.e. Deposits / Withdrawals of clients. A client can deposit money which must be then 'ADDED' to the amount held against that specific clients name in the ACCTMAST table. This is referred to as a 'CREDIT' type transaction.

A client may withdraw money from his account. This must be 'SUBTRACTED' from the amount held against that specific client's name in the ACCTMAST table. This is referred to as a 'DEBIT' type transaction.

The ACCTTRAN table must therefore hold a 'flag' that indicates whether the transaction type was 'CREDIT' or 'DEBIT'.

Based on this flag define a cursor which will update the ACCTMAST 'Balance' field contents.

Write a PL/SQL block that updates the acctmast table and sets the balance depending upon whether the account is debited or credited. The updation should be done only for those records that are not processed i.e. the processed flag is 'N' in the accttran table.

1. Create the following tables

Table name : acctmast

Column name	Data Type	Size	Attributes
Acctno	varchar2	4	Primary Key
Name	varchar2	20	Account Name
Balance	Number	8	The balance in the account.

Table name : Accttran

Column name	Data Type	Size	Attributes
Acctno	varchar2	4	is the foreign key field which references table **acctmast**.
TrnDate	date		The Transaction Date.
deb_crd	char	1	The Dr / Cr Flag.
Amount	number	7,2	
Processed	char	1	A flag indicating whether the record is processed or not

The following PL/SQL code updates the acctmast table depending upon the daily transactions entered in the accttran table.

```
DECLARE
        cursor acc_updt is
                select acctno, deb_crd, amount from accttran
                where processed = 'N';
                acctnum char(4);
                db_cd char(1);
                amt number(7,2);
BEGIN
        open acc_updt ;

        /* perform the updation for all the records retrieved by the cursor */
        loop
                fetch acc_updt into acctnum, db_cd, amt;
                /* if the account is debited then update the
                   acctmast table as balance = balance - amt */
                if db_cd = 'd' then
                        update acctmast
                        set balance = (balance - amt)
                        where acctno = acctnum;
                else
                        /* if the account is credited then update the
                           acctmast table as balance = balance + amt */
                        update acctmast
                        set balance = (balance + amt)
                        where acctno = acctnum ;
                end if;
                update accttran set processed = 'Y'
                        where acctno = acctnum;
                exit when acc_updt%notfound ;
        end loop;
        close acc_updt;
        commit ;
END;
```

Implicit Cursor :
Oracle implicitly opens a cursor to process each SQL statement not associated with an explicitly declared cursor. PL/SQL lets you refer to the most recent implicit cursor as the SQL cursor. So, although you cannot use the *open, fetch,* and *close* statements to control an implicit cursor, you can still use cursor attributes to access information about the most recently executed SQL statement.

Implicit Cursor Attributes :
The SQL cursor has four attributes as described below. When appended to the cursor name (i.e. SQL), these attributes let you access information about the execution of *insert, update, delete* and single-row *select* statements. Implicit cursor attributes return the boolean *null* value, until they are set by a cursor operation.

The values of the cursor attributes always refer to the most recently executed SQL statement, wherever the statement appears. It might be in a different scope (in a sub-block). So, if you want to save an attribute value for later use, assign it a *boolean* variable immediately.

- **%NOTFOUND** : evaluates to *true*, if an *insert*, *update* or *delete* affected no rows, or a single-row *select* returns no rows. Otherwise, it evaluates to *false*.

Syntax : SQL%NOTFOUND

Example : The HRD manager has decided to raise the salary of employees by 0.15. Write a PL/SQL block to accept the employee number and update the salary of that employee. Display appropriate message based on the existence of the record in the employee table.

```
BEGIN
    update employee set salary = salary * 0.15
        where emp_code = &emp_code;
    if sql%notfound then
        dbms_output.put_line('Employee No. Does not Exist');
    else
        dbms_output.put_line('Employee Record
                Modified Successfully ');
    end if;
END;
```

- **%FOUND** : is the logical opposite of *%notfound*. Note, however that both attributes evaluate to *null* until they are set by an implicit or explicit cursor operation. *%found* evaluates to *true*, if an *insert*, *update* or *delete* affected one or more rows, or a single-row *select* returned one or more rows. Otherwise, it evaluates to *false*.

Syntax : SQL%NOTFOUND

Example : The example in sql%notfound will be written as follows :

```
BEGIN
    update employee set salary = salary * 0.15
        where emp_code = &emp_code;
    if sql%found then
        dbms_output.put_line('Employee Record
                Modified Successfully ');
    else
        dbms_output.put_line('Employee No. Does not Exist');
    end if;
END;
```

- **%ROWCOUNT** : returns the number of rows affected by an *insert*, *update* or *delete*, or select into statement.

    Example : The HRD manager has decided to raise the salary of employees working as 'Programmers' by 0.15. Write a PL/SQL block to accept the employee number and update the salary of that employee. Display appropriate message based on the existence of the record in the employee table.

    ```
    DECLARE
        rows_affected char(4) ;
    BEGIN
        update employee set salary = salary * 0.15
            where job = 'Programmers' ;
        rows_affected := to_char(sql%rowcount)
        if sql%rowcount > 0 then
            dbms_output.put_line(rows_affected || 'Employee Records
                    Modified Successfully ') ;
        else
            dbms_output.put_line('There are no Employees
                    working as Programmers');
        end if;
    END;
    ```

- **%ISOPEN** : Oracle automatically closes the SQL cursor after executing its associated SQL statement. As a result, *sql%isopen* always evaluates to *false*.

Parameterized Cursors :

So far we have used cursors querying all the records from a table. Sometimes records are brought in memory selectively. While declaring a cursor, the select statement must include a where clause to retrieve data conditionally.

We should be able to pass a value to cursor only when it is being opened. For that the cursor must be declared in such a way that it recognizes that it will receive the requested value(s) at the time of opening the cursor. Such a cursor is known as **Parameterized Cursor**.

Syntax : CURSOR cursor_name (variable_name datatype) is
            select statement...

The scope of cursor parameters are local to that cursor, which means that they can be referenced only within the query declared in the cursor declaration. The values of cursor parameters are used by the associated query when the cursor is *open*ed.

For example,

>   cursor c_emp (num_deptno number) is
>   select job, ename from emp where deptno > num_deptno;

The parameters to a cursor can be passed in the open statement. They can either be constant values or the contents of a memory variable.

For example,

>   OPEN c_emp (30)
>   OPEN c_emp (num_deptno)

Note : The memory variable should be declared in the DECLARE section and the value should be assigned to that memory variable.

Each parameter in the declaration must have a corresponding value in the *open* statement. Remember that the parameters of a cursor cannot return values.

Example :

Allow insert, update and delete for the table **itemmast** on the bases of the table **itemtran** table.

1. Create the following tables

Table name : itemmast

Column name	Data Type	Size	Attributes
itemid	number	4	Primary Key
description	varchar	20	The item description
Bal_stock	number	3	The balance stock for an item

Table name : **ItemTran**

Column name	Data Type	Size	Attributes
Itemid	number	4	Foreign key via which we shall seek data in the table.
Description	varchar	30	item description
Operation	char	1	The kind of operation on ItemMast table i.e. Insert, Update, Delete(I, U, D)
Qty	number	3	The Qty sold
Status	varchar	30	The status of the Operation.

Based on the value in the **operation** column of table **itemtran** the records for table **itemmast** is either inserted, updated or deleted. On the basis of success/failure of insert, update and delete operation the status column in the table **itemtran** is updated with appropriate text indicating success or reason for failure. Following are the 3 cases which are to be taken care of.

1) If Operation = ' I ' then the **itemid** against along with **description** and **qty** is inserted into the required columns of the table **itemmast**. If insert is successful then the status field of **itemtran** table is updated to ' SUCCESSFUL ' else it is updated as 'ITEM ALREADY EXIST'.

2) If Operation = ' U ' then the **qty** against this operation column is added to **bal_stock** column of the table **itemmast** where itemid of table **itemmast** is same as that of **itemtran**. If update is successful then the **status** column of **itemtran** table is updated to ' SUCCESSFUL ' else it is updated as ' ITEM DOES NOT EXIST '.

3) If Operation = ' D ', then a row from **itemmast** is deleted whose **itemid** is equal to the **itemid** in the table **itemtran** with the **operation** column having the value ' D '. If delete is successful then the **status** column of **itemtran** table is updated to 'SUCCESSFUL ' else it is updated as 'ITEM DOES NOT EXIST'.

The following PL/SQL code takes care of the above three cases.

```
DECLARE
        /* Cursor scantable retrieves all the records of table itemtran */
        cursor scantable is
                select itemid, operation, qty, description from itemtran;

        /* Cursor Itemchk accepts the value of item id from the current row of cursor
           scantable */
        cursor itemchk(mastitemid number) is
                select itemid from item_mast
                where itemid = mastitemid;

        /* variables that hold data from the cursor scantable */
        itemidno number(4);
        descrip varchar2(30);
        oper char(1);
        quantity number(3);

        /* variable that hold data from the cursor itemchk */
        dummyitem number(4);
BEGIN
        /* open the scantable cursor */
        open scantable;
        loop
                /* Fetch the records from the scantable cursor */
                fetch scantable into itemidno, oper, quantity, descrip;
```

/* Open the itemchk cursor
   Note that the value of variable passed to the itemchk cursor
   is set to the value of item id in the current row of cursor scantable */
open itemchk(itemidno);
fetch itemchk into dummyitem;

/* if the record is not found and the operation is insert then
   insert the new record and set the status to 'Successful' */
if itemchk%notfound then
    if oper = 'I' then
        insert into item_mast(itemid, bal_stock, description)
           values(itemidno, quantity, descrip);
        update itemtran
           set itemtran.status = 'SUCCESSFUL'
           where itemid = itemidno;
    /* if the record is not found and the operation is update/delete then
       set the status to 'Item Not Present' */
    elsif oper = 'U' or oper = 'D' then
        update itemtran
           set itemtran.status = 'ITEM NOT PRESENT'
           where itemid = itemidno;
    end if;
else
    /* if the record is found and the operation is insert then
       set the status to 'Item Already Exists' */
    if oper = 'I' then
        update itemtran
           set itemtran.status = 'ITEM ALREADY EXISTS'
           where itemid = itemidno;

    /* if the record is found and the operation is update/delete then
       perform the update or delete operation
       set the status to 'Successful' */
    elsif oper = 'D' then
        delete from item_mast where item_mast.itemid = itemidno;
        update itemtran
           set itemtran.status = 'SUCCESSFUL'
           where itemid = itemidno;
    elsif oper = 'U' then
        update item_mast
           set item_mast.bal_stock = quantity
           where itemid = itemidno;
        update itemtran
           set itemtran.status = 'SUCCESSFUL'
           where itemid = itemidno;
    end if;

```
            end if;
        close itemchk;
        exit when scantable%notfound;
    end loop;
    close scantable;
    commit ;
END;
```

ERROR HANDLING IN PL/SQL

Whenever a SQL*Plus statement is executed, if it results into an error condition, Oracle returns an error number and an error message stating the Oracle error. These Oracle errors and messages are included in the *Oracle 7 Messages and Codes Manual*.

PL/SQL has the capabilities of dealing with Oracle errors. It has a number of conditions that are pre-programmed into it that are recognized as error conditions. These are called internally-defined exceptions. You can also program PL/SQL to recognize user-defined exceptions.

The method used to recognize user-defined exceptions is as follows:
- Declare a user-defined exception in the declaration section of the PL/SQL block.
- In your main program block, for the condition that needs special attention, execute a *raise* statement.
- Define a user exception that will be invoked automatically when a specified condition occurs. In such a case the exception name and the event have to be defined.

This stops the normal processing of the PL/SQL block of code and control passes to an error handler block of code at the end of the PL/SQL program block.

Declaring Exceptions : (i.e. user-defined error conditions)

An exception declaration declares a name for a user-defined error condition that the PL/SQL code block recognizes. It can only appear in the DECLARE block of the PL/SQL code which precedes the keyword BEGIN.

A user-defined exception name is the lead up to a block of PL/SQL code that will process the exception condition. This code specifies what action has to be taken when the named exception condition occurs.

The action that has to be taken has to be raised by the user. When this occurs, PL/SQL stops normal execution of the block of code and passes control to an appropriate exception handler. The exception handling part of a PL/SQL code block is optional. It is ended with the same END statement that ends the executable part.

Example : The salesman_master table records the salesman_no, name, commission along with the minimum sales for which the commission is given. If the sales made is greater than the target he is to commission. The commission amount along with the salesman_no is recorded in commissison_payable table.

```
DECLARE
    less_than_target exception;
    salesman_no salesman_master.salesman_no%type ;
    target salesman_master.target_sales%type;
    actual_sales salesman_master.actual_sales%type;
    commission salesman_master.comm%type;
```

```
            BEGIN
                    select salesman_no, comm, target_sales, actual_sales
                            into salesman_no, commission, target, actual_sales
                            from salesman_master
                            where salesman_no = & salesman_no;
                    If actual_sales < target_sales then
                            raise less_than_target;
                    else
                            insert into commisison_payable
                                    values (salesman_no,
                                    actual_sales * commission / 100);
                    end if ;
            EXCEPTION
                    when less_than_target then
                            dbms_output.put_line('Salesman No' || salesman_no ||
                                    'is not entitled to get commission');
            END;
```

Some exceptions (i.e. internal error conditions) are pre-defined and need not be declared. The naming convention for exception names are exactly the same as those for variables or constants. All the rules of accessing an exception from PL/SQL blocks are the same as those for variables and constants.

However, it should be noted that exceptions cannot be passed as arguments to functions or procedures like variables or constants.

Pre-determined internal PL/SQL exceptions :
- DUP_VAL_ON_INDEX : Raised when an *insert* or *update* attempts to create two rows with duplicate values in column/s constrained by a *unique* index.
- LOGIN_DENIED: Raised when an invalid username/password was used to log onto Oracle.
- NO_DATA_FOUND: Raised when a *select* statement returns zero rows.
- NOT_LOGGED_ON: Raised when PL/SQL issues an Oracle call without being logged onto Oracle.
- PROGRAM_ERROR: Raised when PL/SQL has an internal problem.
- TIMEOUT_ON_RESOURCE: Raised when Oracle has been waiting to access a resource beyond the user-defined timeout limit.
- TOO_MANY_ROWS: Raised when a *select* statement returns more than one row.
- VALUE_ERROR: Raised when the data type or data size is invalid.
- OTHERS: stands for all the other exceptions not explicitly named in the exception handler.

Example : The salesman_master table records the salesman_no, name, commission along with the minimum sales for which the commission is given. If the sales made is greater than the target he is to commission. The commission amount along with the salesman_no is recorded in commisison_payable table.

If the user enters a salesman no. that is not in the salesman_master table, It must display appropriate error messages.

```
DECLARE
    less_than_target exception;
    salesman_no salesman_master.salesman_no%type ;
    target salesman_master.target_sales%type;
    actual_sales salesman_master.actual_sales%type;
    commission salesman_master.comm%type;
BEGIN
    select  salesman_no, comm, target_sales, actual_sales
            into salesman_no, commission, target, actual_sales
            from salesman_master
            where salesman_no  = & salesman_no;
    If actual_sales < target_sales then
            raise less_than_target;
    else
            Insert into commissison_payable
                    values (salesman_no,
                        actual_sales * commission / 100);
    end if ;
EXCEPTION
    when less_than_target then
            dbms_output.put_line('Salesman No' || salesman_no ||
                        'is not entitled to get commission');
    when no_data_found then
            dbms_output.put_line('Salesman No' || salesman_no ||
                        'is not present in the salesman_master
                        table');
END;
```

The internal exceptions like NO_DATA_FOUND, TOO_MANY_ROWS etc. are associated with the internal Oracle error and are referenced by the name given to them.

For Example : The exception NO_DATA_FOUND is associated with Oracle's internal error number ORA-01403.

All Oracle errors are not associated with an exception name. When such error conditions occur, Oracle looks for exception named OTHERS. As seen earlier, exception OTHERS take care of all exceptions that are not defined in the exception block.

Example :	BEGIN
		insert into client_master (client_no, name, bal_due)
			values (&client_no, &name, &bal_due);
	EXCEPTION
		when others then
			dbms_output.put_line('Invalid datatype...
				No records inserted');
	END;

In the above example, Oracle will display 'Invalid datatype... No records inserted' and the PL/SQL block will be terminated.

Using exception OTHERS is justified if the action to be taken is general. This method will fail if the user wants to trap a specific error for which no exception name is defined. In the example given above, it will display the same message even if the insert has failed due to some other error.

To eliminate this problem, the user can define an exception for the error number and use the exception like any other user defined exception.

The steps in declaring an exception to trap errors are as follows :

1. In the DECLARE section of the PL/SQL block declare a new exception as follows :

    DECLARE
        err_invalid exception ;

2. This exception has now to be associated with the Oracle integer_error number. For this we make use of EXCEPTION_INIT in the DECLARE section. This command takes two parameters; first the exception name just declared, and the integer_error number. The integer_error number should be negative if the error code is negative (true for fatal errors).

    Note that the format of this command requires the word PRAGMA before EXCEPTION_INIT. A pragma is an instruction to the PL/SQL compiler, rather than executable code. The pragma must be in the DECLARE section of a PL/SQL block, and must be preceded by an exception declaration.

    DECLARE
        invalid_datatype exception ;
        pragma exception_init (invalid_data, -4646)

    Example : The following code traps the error message that appears when a value of invalid data type is inserted into a column. If an error occurs then an error message is displayed to the users.

```
DECLARE
        invalid_datatype Exception;
        pragma exception_init(invalid_datatype, -1722);
BEGIN
        Insert into client_master (client_no, name, bal_due )
                values (&client_no, &name, &bal_due);
        Commit;
EXCEPTION
        when invalid_datatype then
                dbms_output.put_line(' Invalid datatype... Record not inserted ' );
END;
```

Note : Whenever a user enters a value which does not match the datatype of the column, it returns error number -1722.

4. STORED PROCEDURES

WHAT ARE PROCEDURES ?
Procedures are named PL/SQL blocks that can take parameters, perform an action and can be invoked. A procedure is generally used to perform an action and to pass values.

Procedures are made up of :
1. A declarative part,
2. An executable part, and
3. An optional exception-handling part.

Declarative part :
The declarative part may contain declarations of cursors, constants, variables, exceptions and subprograms. These objects are local to the procedure. The objects become invalid once you exit from it.

Executable part :
The executable part contains a PL/SQL block consisting of statements that assign values, control execution and manipulate ORACLE data. The action to be performed is coded here and data that is to be returned back to the calling environment is also returned from here. Variables declared are put to use in this block.

Exception Handling part :
This part contains code that performs an action to deal with exceptions raised during the execution of the Executable part. This block can be used to handle Oracle's own exceptions or the exceptions that are declared in the Declarative part. One cannot transfer the flow of execution from the Exception Handling part to the Executable part or vice versa.

WHERE DO PROCEDURES RESIDE ?
Procedures in ORACLE are called stored procedures. Procedures are stored in the database and are invoked or called by any anonymous block (the PL/SQL block that appears within an application). Before the procedure is created, ORACLE parses the procedure. Then this parsed procedure is stored in the database.

HOW ORACLE CREATE A PROCEDURE ?
When a procedure is created, ORACLE automatically performs the following steps :

1. Compiles the procedure.
2. Stores the compiled code.
3. Stores the procedure in the database.

The PL/SQL compiler compiles the code. If an error occurs, then the procedure is created but it is an invalid procedure. ORACLE displays a message during the time of creation that the procedure was created with compilation errors.

It does not display the errors. These errors can be viewed using the *select* statement :

SELECT * FROM *user_errors*;

ORACLE loads the compiled procedure in the memory area called the System Global Area (SGA). This allows the code to be executed quickly. The same procedure residing in the SGA is executed by the other users also.

HOW ORACLE EXECUTES PROCEDURES ?
ORACLE performs the following steps to execute a procedure :

1. Verifies user access.
2. Verifies procedure validity.
3. Executes the procedure.

ORACLE checks if the user who called the procedure has the *execute* privilege for the procedure. If the user is invalid, then access is denied otherwise Oracle proceeds to check whether the called procedure is valid or not. The user can view the validity of the procedure by using the *select* statement as :

SELECT *object_name, object_type, status*
FROM *user_objects*;
WHERE *object_type* = 'PROCEDURE';

Only if the status is *valid*, then the procedure can be executed. Once the procedure is found valid, ORACLE then loads the procedure into memory (i.e. if it is not currently present in memory) and executes the PL/SQL code.

ADVANTAGES OF PROCEDURES
1. **Security** : Stored procedures can help enforce data security. For e.g. you can grant users access to a procedure that can query a table, but not grant them access to the table itself.

2. **Performance** : It improves database performance in the following ways :
   - Amount of information sent over a network is less.
   - No compilation step is required to execute the code.
   - As procedure is present in the shared pool of SGA retrieval from disk is not required.

3. **Memory Allocation** : Reduction in memory as stored procedures have shared memory capabilities so only one copy of procedure needs to be loaded for execution by multiple users.

4. **Productivity** : Increased development productivity, by writing a single procedure we can avoid redundant coding and increase productivity.

5. **Integrity** : Improves integrity, a procedure needs to be tested only once to guarantee that it returns an accurate result. Hence coding errors can be reduced.

SYNTAX FOR CREATING STORED PROCEDURE

Syntax :   CREATE OR REPLACE
　　　　　PROCEDURE [schema.] procedurename
　　　　　　　(argument { IN, OUT, IN OUT} datatype, ...) {IS, AS}
　　　　　　　variable declarations ;
　　　　　　　constant declarations ;
　　　　　BEGIN
　　　　　　　PL/SQL subprogram body ;
　　　　　EXCEPTION
　　　　　　　exception PL/SQL block ;
　　　　　END;

Keywords and Parameters:
The keywords and the parameters used for creating database procedures are explained below :

REPLACE	recreates the procedure if it already exists. You can use this option to change the definition of an existing procedure without dropping, recreating and regranting object privileges previously granted on it. If you redefine a procedure ORACLE recompiles it.
schema	is the schema to contain the procedure. ORACLE takes the default schema to be the current schema, if it is omitted.
procedure	is the name of the procedure to be created.
argument	is the name of an argument to the procedure. Parentheses can be omitted if no arguments are present.
IN	specifies that you must specify a value for the argument when calling the procedure.
OUT	specifies that the procedure passes a value for this argument back to its calling environment after execution.
IN OUT	specifies that you must specify a value for the argument when calling the procedure and that the procedure passes a value for this argument back to its calling environment after execution. By default it takes IN.
datatype	is the datatype of an argument. It supports any datatype supported by PL/SQL.

PL/SQL subprogrambody is the definition of procedure consisting of PL/SQL statements.

AN APPLICATION USING A PROCEDURE

Focus :
Perform insert, update and delete for the table **itemmast** on the basis of the table **itemtran** table.

1. Create the following tables

    Table name : itemmast

Column Name	Data Type	Size	Column Description
itemid	number	4	Primary Key via which we shall seek data in the table
description	varchar	20	The item description
Bal_stock	number	3	The balance stock for an item.

    Table Name : ItemTran

Column Name	Data Type	Size	Column Description
Itemid	number	4	which we shall seek data in the table.
Description	varchar	30	item description
Operation	char	1	kind of operation on the ItemMast table i.e. Insert, Update, Delete(I, U, D)
Qty	number	3	The Qty sold
Status	varchar	30	The status of the Operation

Based on the value in the **operation** column of table **itemtran** the records for table **itemmast** is either inserted, updated or deleted. On the basis of success/failure of insert, update and delete operation the status column in the table **itemtran** is updated with appropriate text indicating successes or reason for failure.

1) If Operation = ' I ' then the **itemid** along with **description** and **qty** is inserted into the required columns of the table **itemmast**. If insert is successful then the status field of **itemtran** table is updated to ' SUCCESSFUL ' else it is updated as 'ITEM ALREADY EXISTS'.

2) If Operation = ' U ' then the **qty** is added to **bal_stock** column of the table **itemmast** where itemid of table **itemmast** is same as that of **itemtran**. If update is successful then the **status** column of **itemtran** table is updated to ' SUCCESSFUL ' else it is updated as ' ITEM NOT PRESENT '.

3) If Operation = ' D ', then a row from **itemmast** is deleted whose **itemid** is the same as the **itemid** in the table **itemtran** with the **operation** column having the value ' D '. If delete is successful then the **status** column of **itemtran** table is updated to 'SUCCESSFUL ' else it is updated as ' ITEM NOT PRESENT '.

Write a database procedure which will check for the existence of *item_id* in the table *itemmast*. The procedure must have one argument which receives a value for which a matching pattern for *item_id* in the table *itemmast* and another which will return value indicating whether a match has been found or not. This value returned by the procedure can be used to make a decision to perform further processing or not.

Creating A Procedure for use:

To create a procedure to perform an item id check operation. *p_itemidchk* is the name of the procedure which accepts a variable *itemid* and returns a variable *valexists* to the host environment. The value of *valexists* changes from *0* (itemid does not exist) to *1* (itemid exists) depending on the records retrieved.

```
CREATE or replace PROCEDURE p_itemidchk(vitemidno IN number,
                     valexists OUT NUMBER) AS

        /* variable that hold data from the itemmast table */
        dummyitem number(4);
BEGIN
        select itemid into dummyitem
            from itemmast where itemid = vitemidno ;

        /* if the select statement retrieves data, valexists is set to 1 */
        valexists := 1;
EXCEPTION
        /* if the select statement does not retrieve data, valexists is set to 0 */
        when no_data_found then
            valexists := 0;
END;
```

Any PL/SQL block can be used to call this procedure to perform the check. To do this the contents of the variable *vitemidno* is passed on as an argument to the procedure *p_itemidchk*. The return value is then checked and appropriate action is taken.

The following PL/SQL code takes care of what needs to be done as expressed on pages 119-120.

```
DECLARE
        /* Cursor scantable retrieves all the records of table itemtran */
        cursor scantable is
                select itemid, operation, qty, description from itemtran;

        /* variables that hold data from the cursor scantable */
        vitemidno number(4);
        descrip varchar2(30);
        oper char(1);
        quantity number(3);

        /* variable that stores 1 or 0. It is set in the procedure p_itemidchk */
        valexists number(1);

BEGIN
        open scantable;
        loop
                fetch scantable into vitemidno, oper, quantity, descrip;

                /* Call procedure p_itemidchk to check if item_id is present in
                 itemmast table */
                p_itemidchk(vitemidno, valexists);

                /* if itemid does not exists */
                if valexists = 0 then
                        /* if mode is insert then
                           insert a record in itemmast table and set the status in the
                           itemtran table to 'SUCCESSFUL' */
                        if oper = 'I' then
                                insert into itemmast(itemid, bal_stock, description)
                                        values(vitemidno, quantity, descrip);
                                update itemtran
                                        set itemtran.status = 'SUCCESSFUL'
                                        where itemid = vitemidno;
                        /* if the record is not found and the operation is update/delete then
                           set the status to 'Item Not Present' */
                        elsif oper = 'U' or oper = 'D' then
                                update itemtran
                                        set itemtran.status = 'ITEM NOT PRESENT'
                                        where itemid = vitemidno;
                        end if;
```

```
            else
                    /* if the record is found and the operation is insert then
                            set the status to 'Item Already Exists' */
                    if oper = 'I' then
                            update itemtran
                                    set itemtran.status = 'ITEM ALREADY EXISTS'
                                    where itemid = vitemidno;

                    /* if the record is found and the operation is update/delete then
                            perform the update or delete operation
                            set the status to 'Successful' */
                    elsif oper = 'D' then
                            delete from itemmast where itemmast.itemid = vitemidno;
                            update itemtran
                                    set itemtran.status = 'SUCCESSFUL'
                                    where itemid = vitemidno;
                    elsif oper = 'U' then
                            update itemmast
                                    set itemmast.bal_stock = quantity
                                    where itemid = vitemidno;
                            update itemtran
                                    set itemtran.status = 'SUCCESSFUL'
                                    where itemid = vitemidno;
                    end if;
            end if;
            exit when scantable%notfound;
    end loop;
    close scantable;
    commit ;
END;
```

The advantage of using the above procedure is that the procedure can even check for the same product in some other application, provided the user has the privilege. There is also a saving of memory area as no matter how many users are using this procedure, there is only one copy of the procedure is being executed by the system in memory.

DELETING A STORED PROCEDURE

A procedure can be deleted from the database by using the following command :

        DROP PROCEDURE p_itemidchk;

5. STORED FUNCTIONS

WHAT ARE FUNCTIONS ?
Functions are named PL/SQL blocks that can take parameters, perform an action and returns a value to the host environment. A function can only return one value.

Functions are made up of :
1. A declarative part,
2. An executable part,
3. And an optional exception-handling part.

Declarative part :
The declarative part may contain declarations of type, cursors, constant, variables, exceptions, and subprograms. These objects are local to the function. The objects become invalid once you exit from the function. Here the datatype of the return value is also declared.

Executable part :
The executable part contains a PL/SQL block consisting of statements that assign values, control execution, and manipulate Oracle data. The action to be performed is coded here and data that is to be returned back to the calling environment is also returned from here. Variable declared are put to use in this block. The return value is also passed back in this part.

Exception Handling part :
This part contains code that performs an action to deal with exceptions raised during execution of the Executable Part. This block can be used to handle Oracle's own exceptions or the exceptions that are declared in the Declarative Part. One cannot transfer the flow of execution from the Exception Handling Part to the Executable Part and vice versa. The return value can also be passed back in this part.

WHERE DO FUNCTIONS RESIDE ?
Functions in Oracle are called stored functions. Functions are stored in the database and are invoked or called by any anonymous block (a PL/SQL block that appears within an application) Before the function is created, Oracle parses the function. Then this parsed function is stored in the database.

HOW ORACLE CREATES A FUNCTION ?
When a function is created, Oracle automatically performs the following steps :

1. Compiles the function.
2. Stores the compiled code.
3. Stores the function in the database.

The PL/SQL compiler compiles the code. If an error occurs then the function is created but its an invalid function. Oracle displays a message during the time of creation that the function was created with compilation errors. It does not display the errors. These errors can be viewed by using the *select* statement :

SELECT * FROM *user_errors*;

Oracle loads the compiled function in the memory area called the System Global Area (SGA). This allows the code to be executed quickly. The same function residing in the SGA is executed by the other users also.

HOW ORACLE EXECUTES A FUNCTIONS ?
Oracle performs the following steps to execute an function

1. Verifies user access.
2. Verifies function validity.
3. Executes the function.

Oracle checks if the user who called the function has the *execute* privilege for the function. If the user is invalid, then access is denied else if the user is valid, then it proceeds to check whether the called function is valid or not. The user can view the validity of the function by using the *select* statement as :

SELECT *object_name, object_type, status*
FROM *user_objects*;
WHERE *object_type* = 'FUNCTION';

Only if the status is *valid*, the function can be executed. Once the function is found valid, Oracle loads the function into memory (i.e. if it is not currently present in memory) and executes the PL/SQL code.

ADVANTAGES OF FUNCTIONS
1. **Security** : Stored functions can help enforce data security. For e.g. you can grant users access to function that can query a table, but not grant them access to the table itself.

2. **Performance** : It improves database performance in the following ways :
   - Amount of information sent over a network is less.
   - No compilation step is required to execute the code.
   - As function is present in the shared pool of SGA, retrieval from disk is not required.

3. **Memory Allocation** : Reduction in memory as stored functions have shared memory capabilities so only one copy of function needs to be loaded for execution by multiple users.

4. **Productivity** : Increased development productivity, by writing a single function we can avoid redundant coding and increase productivity.

5. **Integrity** : Improves integrity, a function needs to be tested only once to guarantee that it returns an accurate result. So committing coding errors can be reduced.

SYNTAX FOR CREATING A STORED FUNCTION

<u>Syntax</u> :   CREATE OR REPLACE
          FUNCTION [schema.] functionname (argument IN datatype, ...)
          RETURN datatype {IS, AS}
              variable declarations ;
              constant declarations ;
          BEGIN
              PL/SQL subprogram body ;
          EXCEPTION
              exception PL/SQL block ;
          END;

Keywords and Parameters :
The keywords and the parameters used for creating database functions are explained below :

REPLACE   recreates the function if it already exists. You can use this option to change the definition of an existing function without dropping, recreating and regranting object privileges previously granted on it. If you redefine a function, Oracle recompiles it.

Schema   is the schema to contain the function. Oracle takes the default schema to be the current schema, if it is omitted.

function   is the name of the function to be created.

argument   is the name of an argument to the function. Parentheses can be omitted if no arguments are present.

IN   specifies that you must specify a value for the argument when calling the function.

RETURN *datatype*   is the datatype of the function's return value. Because every function must return a value, this clause is required. It supports any datatype supported by PL/SQL.

PL/SQL subprogram_body is the definition of function consisting of PL/SQL statements.

AN APPLICATION USING A FUNCTION

Focus :
Check for the duplicate itemid for the table **itemmast.**

1. Create the following tables

    Table name : itemmast

Column Name	Data Type	Size	Column Description
itemid	number	4	Primary Key via which we shall seek data in the table
description	varchar	20	The item description
Bal_stock	number	3	The balance stock for an item.

    Table Name : ItemTran

Column Name	Data Type	Size	Column Description
Itemid	number	4	which we shall seek data in the table.
Description	varchar	30	item description
Operation	char	1	kind of operation on the ItemMast table i.e. Insert, Update, Delete(I, U, D)
Qty	number	3	The Qty sold
Status	varchar	30	The status of the Operation

Based on the value in the **operation** column of table **itemtran** the records for table **itemmast** is either inserted, updated or deleted. On the basis of success/failure of insert, update and delete operation the status column in the table **itemtran** is updated with appropriate text indicating successes or reason for failure. Following are the 3 cases which are to be taken care of.

1) If Operation = ' I ' then the **itemid** along with **description** and **qty** is inserted into the required columns of the table **itemmast**. If insert is successful then the status field of **itemtran** table is updated to ' SUCCESSFUL ' else it is updated as 'ITEM ALREADY EXISTS'.

2) If Operation = ' U ' then the **qty** is added to **bal_stock** column of the table **itemmast** where itemid of table **itemmast** is same as that of **itemtran**. If update is successful then the **status** column of **itemtran** table is updated to ' SUCCESSFUL ' else it is updated as ' ITEM NOT PRESENT '.

3) If Operation = ' D ' , then a row from **itemmast** is deleted whose **itemid** is the same as the **itemid** in the table **itemtran** with the **operation** column having the value ' D '. If delete is successful then the **status** column of **itemtran** table is updated to 'SUCCESSFUL ' else it is updated as ' ITEM NOT PRESENT '.

Write a database function which will check for the existence of *item_id* in the table *itemmast*. The function must have one argument which receives a value for which a matching pattern for *item_id* in the table *itemmast*. The function will return value '1' indicating that a match is found and a value '0' indicating that no match is found. This value returned by the function can be used to perform the necessary operation.

Creating Function for use :
A stored procedure is now created to perform the item id check operation. *f_itemidchk* is the name of the function which accepts a variable *itemid* and returns a variable *valexists* to the host environment. The value of *valexists* changes from *0* (itemid does not exist) to *1* (itemid exists) depending on the records retrieved.

```
CREATE FUNCTION f_itemidchk(vitemidno IN number) RETURN number IS
    /* variable that hold data from the itemmast table */
    dummyitem number(4);
BEGIN
    select itemid into dummyitem
        from itemmast where itemid = vitemidno ;

    /* if the select statement retrieves data, valexists is set to 1 */
    return 1;
EXCEPTION

    /* if the select statement does not retrieve data, valexists is set to 0 */
    when no_data_found then
        return 0;
END;
```

The PL/SQL block is now modified to call a function to perform the check. To do this the contents of the variable *vitemidno* is passed on as an argument to the function *f_itemidchk*.

The return value is then checked and appropriate action is taken.

```
DECLARE
    /* Cursor scantable retrieves all the records of table itemtran */
    cursor scantable is
        select itemid, operation, qty, description from itemtran;

    /* variables that hold data from the cursor scantable */
    vitemidno number(4);
    descrip varchar2(30);
    oper char(1);
    quantity number(3);

    /* variable that stores the value returned by the f_itemidchk function i.e. 1 or 0 */
    valexists number(1);

BEGIN
    open scantable;
    loop
        fetch scantable into vitemidno, oper, quantity, descrip;

        /* Call function f_itemidchk to check if itemid is present in
           itemmast table */
        valexists := f_itemidchk(vitemidno);

        /* if itemid does not exists */
        if valexists = 0 then
            /* if mode is insert then
               insert a record in itemmast table and set the status in the
               itemtran table to 'SUCCESSFUL' */
            if oper = 'I' then
                insert into itemmast(itemid, bal_stock, description)
                    values(vitemidno, quantity, descrip);
                update itemtran
                    set itemtran.status = 'SUCCESSFUL'
                    where itemid = vitemidno;
            /* if the record is not found and the operation is update/delete then
               set the status to 'Item Not Present' */
            elsif oper = 'U' or oper = 'D' then
                update itemtran
                    set itemtran.status = 'ITEM NOT PRESENT'
                    where itemid = vitemidno;
            end if;
```

```
            else
                /* if the record is found and the operation is insert then
                    set the status to 'Item Already Exists' */
                if oper = 'I' then
                    update itemtran
                        set itemtran.status = 'ITEM ALREADY EXISTS'
                        where itemid = vitemidno;

                /* if the record is found and the operation is update/delete then
                    perform the update or delete operation
                    set the status to 'Successful' */
                elsif oper = 'D' then
                    delete from itemmast where itemmast.itemid = vitemidno;
                    update itemtran
                        set itemtran.status = 'SUCCESSFUL'
                        where itemid = vitemidno;
                elsif oper = 'U' then
                    update itemmast
                        set itemmast.bal_stock = quantity
                        where itemid = vitemidno;
                    update itemtran
                        set itemtran.status = 'SUCCESSFUL'
                        where itemid = vitemidno;
                end if;
            end if;
            exit when scantable%notfound;
        end loop;
        close scantable;
        commit ;
END;
```

The advantage of using the above function is that the function can even check for the same product in some other application, provided the user has the privilege. There is also a saving of memory area as no matter how many users are using this function, there is only one copy of the function that is being executed by the system in the SGA.

DELETING A STORED FUNCTION

A function can be deleted from the database by using the following command :

```
DROP FUNCTION f_itemidchk ;
```

6. DATABASE TRIGGERS

Database triggers are procedures that are stored in the database and are implicitly executed (fired) when the contents of a table are changed.

INTRODUCTION
Oracle allows the user to define procedures that are implicitly executed (i.e. executed by Oracle itself), when an insert, update or delete is issued against a table from SQL*Plus or through an application. These procedures are called database triggers. The major point that make these triggers stand alone is that they are fired implicitly (i.e. internally) by Oracle itself and not explicitly called by the user, as done in normal procedures.

USE OF DATABASE TRIGGERS
Database triggers support Oracle to provide a highly customized database management system. Some of the uses to which the database triggers can be put to customize management information in Oracle are as follows :
* A trigger can permit DML statements against a table only if they are issued, during regular business hours or on predetermined weekdays.
* A trigger can also be used to keep an audit trail of a table (i.e. to store the modified and deleted records of the table) along with the operation performed and the time on which the operation was performed.
* It can be used to prevent invalid transactions.
* Enforce complex security authorizations.

Note :
* When a trigger is fired, a SQL statement inside the trigger can also fire the same or some other trigger (if exists), called as cascading, which must be considered.
* Excessive use of triggers for customizing the database can result in complex interdependencies between the triggers, which may be difficult to maintain in a large application.

DATABASE TRIGGERS VS. PROCEDURES
There are very few differences between these two. In procedures its possible to pass parameters which is not the case with triggers. A trigger is executed implicitly by the Oracle itself upon modification of an associated table whereas to execute a procedure, it has to be explicitly called by the user.

DATABASE TRIGGERS VS. SQL*FORMS
The Oracle tool SQL*Forms can also define, store and execute triggers as part of an application developed using the tool. However they differ from the database triggers as described below :

* Database triggers are defined on a table, stored in the associated database and executed as a result of an insert, update or a delete statement being issued against a table, no matter which user, tool or application issues the statement.

* SQL*Forms triggers are part of SQL*Forms application and are fired only when a specific trigger point is executed within a specific application. If the transaction in the table is performed through some other tool like SQL*Plus, this triggers do not apply there.

SQL statements within an SQL*Forms application can implicitly cause any associated database trigger to be fired.

DATABASE TRIGGERS VS. DECLARATIVE INTEGRITY CONSTRAINTS

Triggers as well as declarative integrity constraints can be used to constraint data input. However both have significant differences as mentioned below :

* A declarative integrity constraint is a statement about a database that is always true. A constraint applies to existing data in the table and any statement that manipulates the table. Triggers constrain what transaction can do. A trigger does not apply to data loaded before the trigger was created, so it does not guarantee all data in table conforms to the rules established by an associated trigger.
* Also a trigger enforces transitional constraint which can not be enforced by a declarative integrity constraint.

e.g. Constraint such as " current level (i.e. quantity) of a product can not be less than reorder level" in stock maintenance can not be enforced by a declarative integrity constraints.

HOW TO APPLY DATABASE TRIGGERS

A trigger has three basic parts :

1. A triggering event or statement
2. A trigger restriction
3. A trigger action

Each part of the trigger is explained after the syntax.

1. **Triggering Event or Statement :**
   It is a SQL statement that causes a trigger to be fired. It can be INSERT, UPDATE or DELETE statement for a specific table. A triggering statement can also specify multiple DML statements.

2. **Trigger Restriction**
   A trigger restriction specifies a Boolean (logical) expression that must be TRUE for the trigger to fire. It is an option available for triggers that are fired for each row. Its function is to conditionally control the execution of a trigger. A trigger restriction is specified using a WHEN clause.

DATABASE TRIGGERS 135

3. **Trigger Action :**
A trigger action is the procedure (PL/SQL block) that contains the SQL statements and PL/SQL code to be executed when a triggering statement is issued and the trigger restriction evaluates to TRUE. It can contain SQL and PL/SQL statements; can define PL/SQL language constructs and can call stored procedures. Additionally, for row triggers, the statements in a trigger action have access to column values (new and old) of the current row being processed.

TYPES OF TRIGGERS
When you define a trigger, you can specify the number of times the trigger action is to be executed; once for every row affected by the triggering statement (such as might be fired by an UPDATE statement that updates many rows), or once for the triggering statement, no matter how many rows it affects. The types of triggers are as explained below.

Row Triggers :
A row trigger is fired each time the table is affected by the triggering statement. For example, if an UPDATE statement updates multiple rows of a table, a row trigger is fired once for each row affected by the UPDATE statement. If the triggering statement affects no rows, the trigger is not executed at all. Row trigger should be used when the trigger action code depends on the data provided by the triggering statement or rows that are affected.

e.g. if the trigger is keeping the track of all the affected records.

Statement Triggers :
A row trigger is fired once on behalf of the triggering statement, independent of the number of rows the triggering statement affects (even if no rows are affected). Statement triggers are useful if the code in the trigger action does not depend on the data provided by the triggering statement or the rows affected.

e.g. if the trigger makes the security check on the time or the user.

Before VS. After Triggers :
When defining a trigger you can specify the trigger timing, i.e. you can specify when the triggering action is to be executed in relation to the triggering statement. BEFORE and AFTER apply to both row and the statement triggers.

Before Triggers :
BEFORE triggers execute the trigger action before the triggering statement. These types of triggers are commonly used in the following situation :

* BEFORE triggers are used when the trigger action should determine whether or not the triggering statement should be allowed to complete. By using a BEFORE trigger, you can eliminate unnecessary processing of the triggering statement.

* BEFORE triggers are used to derive specific column values before completing a triggering INSERT or UPDATE statement.

After Triggers :

AFTER trigger execute the trigger action after the triggering statement is executed. These types of triggers are commonly used in the following situation :

* AFTER triggers are used when you want the triggering statement to complete before executing the trigger action.
* If a BEFORE trigger is already present, an AFTER trigger can perform different actions on the same triggering statement.

Combinations :

Using the options explained above, four types of triggers can be created :

1. **BEFORE statement trigger :**
   Before executing the triggering statement, the trigger action is executed.

2. **BEFORE row trigger :**
   Before modifying each row affected by the triggering statement and before appropriate integrity constraints, the trigger is executed if the trigger restriction either evaluated to TRUE or was not included.

3. **AFTER statement trigger :**
   After executing the triggering statement and applying any deferred integrity constraints, the trigger action is executed.

4. **AFTER row trigger :**
   After modifying each row affected by the triggering statement and possibly applying appropriate integrity constraints, the trigger action is executed for the current row if the trigger restriction either evaluates to TRUE or was not included. Unlike BEFORE row triggers, AFTER row triggers have rows locked.

SYNTAX FOR CREATING TRIGGER

Syntax :   CREATE OR REPLACE TRIGGER [schema.] triggername
            {BEFORE , AFTER}
            {DELETE, INSERT, UPDATE [OF column, ...]}
            ON [schema.] tablename
            [REFERENCING { OLD AS old, NEW AS new }]
            [FOR EACH ROW [WHEN condition]]
            DECLARE
                variable declarations ;
                constant declarations ;
            BEGIN
                PL/SQL subprogram body ;
            EXCEPTION
                exception PL/SQL block ;
            END;

Keywords and Parameters

The keywords and the parameters used for creating database triggers are explained below:

OR REPLACE   : recreates the trigger if it already exists. You can use this option to change the definition of an existing trigger without first dropping it.

schema   : is the schema to contain the trigger. If you omit the schema, Oracle creates the trigger in your own schema.

triggername   : is the name of the trigger to be created.

BEFORE   : indicates that Oracle fires the trigger before executing the triggering statement.

AFTER   : indicates that Oracle fires the trigger after executing the triggering statement.

DELETE   : indicates that Oracle fires the trigger whenever a DELETE statement removes a row from the table.

INSERT   : indicates that Oracle fires the trigger whenever an INSERT statement adds a row to table.

UPDATE   : indicates that Oracle fires the trigger whenever an UPDATE statement changes a value in one of the columns specified in the OF clause. If you omit the OF clause, Oracle fires the trigger whenever an UPDATE statement changes a value in any column of the table.

ON : Specifies the schema and name of the table on which the trigger is to be created. If you omit schema, Oracle assumes the table is in your own schema. You cannot create a trigger on a table in the schema SYS.

REFERENCING : specifies correlation names. You can use correlation names in the PL/SQL block and WHEN clause of a row trigger to refer specifically to old and new values of the current row. The default correlation names are OLD and NEW. If your row trigger is associated with a table named OLD or NEW, you can use this clause to specify different correlation names to avoid confusion between table name and the correlation name.

FOR EACH ROW : designates the trigger to be a row trigger. Oracle fires a row trigger once for each row that is affected by the triggering statement and meets the optional trigger constraint defined in the when clause. If you omit this clause, the trigger is a statement trigger.

WHEN : specifies the trigger restriction. The trigger restriction contains a SQL condition that must be satisfied for Oracle to fire the trigger. This condition must contain correlation names and cannot contain a query. You can specify trigger restriction only for the row triggers. Oracle evaluates this condition for each row affected by the triggering statement.

PL/SQL_block : is the PL/SQL block that Oracle executes to fire the trigger.

Note :
The PL/SQL block cannot contain transaction control SQL statements (COMMIT, ROLLBACK, and SAVEPOINT)

DELETING A TRIGGER

DROP TRIGGER triggername ;

Where triggername is the name of the trigger to be dropped.

An Application Using Database Triggers :

Focus :
Create a transparent audit system for a table *Client_master*. The system must keep track of the records that are being deleted or modified and when they have been deleted or modified.

The table definition is given below :

Table Name : Client_master
Description : Use to store information about clients. This is the table for which the auditing must be performed.

Column name	Data Type	Size	Attributes
client_no	varchar2	6	Primary Key / first letter must start with 'C'.
name	varchar2	20	Not Null
address1	varchar2	30	
address2	varchar2	30	
city	varchar2	15	
state	varchar2	15	
pincode	number	6	
bal_due	number	10,2	

Table name : auditclient
Description : This is the table in which keeps track of the records deleted or modified and when such an operation was carried out. Records in this table will be inserted when the database trigger fires due to an update or delete statement fired on the table *client_master*.

Column name	Data Type	Size	Attributes
client_no	varchar	6	Primary Key
name	varchar2	20	
bal_due	number	10,2	
operation	varchar2	8	
odate	date		

Valid **column contents** are explained as follows :
- Operation : The operation performed on the employee table.
- Odate : The date when the operation was performed.

Solution :

DATABASE TRIGGER *AUDIT_TRAIL*

This trigger is fired when an update or delete is fired on the table employee. It first checks for the operation being performed on the table. Then depending on the operation being performed, a variable is assigned the value 'update' or 'delete'. The previous values of the modified record of the table client_master are stored into variables. The contents of these variables are then inserted into the audit table *auditclient*.

```
CREATE TRIGGER  audit_trail
    AFTER UPDATE OR DELETE ON  client_master
    FOR EACH ROW
DECLARE
    /* The value in the oper variable will be used to insert a value for the
       operation field in the auditemployee table */
    oper   varchar2(8);

    /* These variables hold the previous value of client_no, name
       and bal_due */
    client_no number(4);
    name varchar2(20);
    bal_due number(2);
BEGIN
    /* if the records are updated in client_master table then oper is set to
       'update'. */
    if updating then
            oper := 'update';
    end if;

    /* if the records are deleted in client_master table then oper is set to
       'delete' */
    if deleting then
            oper := 'delete';
    end if;

    /* Store the previous values of client_no, name and bal_due in the
       variables. These variables can be used to insert data in
       auditclient table */
    client_no := :old.client_no ;
    name := :old.name ;
    bal_due := :old.bal_due ;
    insert into auditclient
            values(client_no, name, bal_due, oper, sysdate);
END;
```

The creation of the database trigger *audit_trail* results in the auditing system for the table *client_master*. The owner of the table can keep track of time of modification or deletion of a record that was modified or deleted in *client_master* by querying the table *auditclient*.

OBSERVATIONS
The actual working of the auditing system can be confirmed from the SQL sentences that have been issued.

This is the data in the table *client_master* before the Database Trigger had been fired.

```
SQL>   SELECT  client_no, name, bal_due
         FROM    client_master;
```

CLIENT_NO	NAME	BAL_DUE
C00001	Rahul	2100
C00003	Joyce	2000
C00004	Varsha	2300
C00005	Donald	2300
C00006	Jayesh	2400
C00007	Anoop	2300
C00008	Sunita	8000
C00009	Arjun	2200

This is the data in the table *auditclient* before the Database Trigger has been fired.

```
SQL>   SELECT  client_no, name, bal_due, operation, odate
         FROM    auditclient;
```

No Rows Selected

Case 1 :
When an update statement modifies a record in the table *client_master*.

The following update statement modifies the client_master Arjun's bal_due from 2200 to 2000.

```
UPDATE  client_master
   SET  bal_due = 2000
   WHERE  name = 'Arjun';
```

Once the update is complete the contents of the table *client_master* are modified as shown below. The contents of the column *bal_due* in the table *client_master* where the value was 2200 is updated to 2000.

```
SQL>   SELECT  client_no, name, bal_due
            FROM  client_master;
```

Client No	Name	Bal Due
C00001	Rahul	2100
C00003	Joyce	2000
C00004	Varsha	2300
C00005	Donald	2300
C00006	Jayesh	2400
C00007	Anoop	2300
C00008	Sunita	8000
C00009	Arjun	2000

The changes made to the table *client_master* must be reflected in the table *auditclient*. Records are inserted into this table when an update or delete operation is performed on the table. The table keeps track of the previous contents of the table client_master whose records were modified as well as the operation and the date when the operation was performed. This can be observed by the update operation performed on the client_master whose *name* is 'arjun'.

```
SQL>   SELECT  client_no, name, bal_due, operation, odate
            FROM  auditclient;
```

Client No	Name	Bal_Due	Operation	Odate
C00009	Arjun	2200	update	05-JUN-95

Case 2 :
When a record is deleted from the table *Client_master*.

The following delete statement deletes the records of all client_masters whose names start with 'j' from the table *Client_master*.

```
SQL>   DELETE FROM client_master
              WHERE name like 'J%' ;
```

The following select statement confirms that two records have been deleted, that of 'Jayesh' and 'Joyce'.

```
SQL>   SELECT  client_no, name, bal_due
            FROM  client_master;
```

Client No	Name	Bal Due
C00001	Rahul	2100
C00004	Varsha	2300
C00005	Donald	2300

C00007	Anoop	2300
C00008	Sunita	8000
C00009	Arjun	2000

The records deleted from the table *client_master* must be reflected in the table *auditclient*. Records are inserted into this table when an update or delete operation is performed on the table. It can be observed that two more records have been inserted into the table *auditclient*.

```
SQL> SELECT client_no, name, bal_due, operation, odate
        FROM auditclient_master;
```

Client No	Name	Bal_Due	Operation	Odate
C00009	Arjun	2200	update	05-JUN-95
C00003	Joyce	2000	delete	05-JUN-95
C00006	Jayesh	2400	delete	05-JUN-95

Note :
If the user performs a ROLLBACK after this, then the records which were modified and deleted from the table *Client_master* are restored to the original status. The table *auditclient* will not then contain the information of records for which an attempt was made to modify and/or delete.

RAISE_APPLICATION_ERROR PROCEDURE

In the previous chapters, we have seen how Oracle errors can be trapped by using pre-defined exceptions or define the exception by associating the oracle error number with an exception name.

Oracle provides a procedure named *raise_application_error*, that allows programmers to issue user-defined error messages.

<u>Syntax</u> :   raise_application_error(error_number, message) ;

where

ERROR_NUMBER   :   is a negative integer in the range -20000 .. -20999

MESSAGE   :   is a character string up to 2048 bytes in length.

An application can call "raise_application_error" only from an executing stored subprogram like stored procedures and functions, database triggers. Typically, "raise_application_error" is used in database triggers.

raise_application_error ends the subprogram, rolls back any database changes it made, and returns a user-defined error number and message to the application.

Example : write database triggers that checks that the qty_on_hand does not become negative.

Table Name : product_master
Description : Use to store information about products.

Column Name	Data Type	Size	Column Description
product_no	varchar2	6	Primary key via which we shall seek data in the table.
description	varchar2	25	product description
profit_percent	number	2,2	The profit percentage for the product
unit_measure	varchar2	10	Unit od measure of the product
qty_on_hand	number	8	quantity on hand.
reorder_lvl	number	8	re-order level.
sell_price	number	8,2	selling price of the product.
cost_price	number	8,2	cost price of the product.

```
/* For every row updated we need to check that qty_on_hand must not be less
   than 0. Thus we need to write a database trigger before an update is fired on
   qty_on_hand */
CREATE TRIGGER check_qty_on_hand
     BEFORE UPDATE OF qty_on_hand
     ON product_master
     FOR EACH ROW
DECLARE

     /* A variable that hold the new value of qty_on_hand */
     new_qty  number(8);
BEGIN

     /* Assigning the new qty_on_hand to a variable */
     new_qty := :new.qty_on_hand;

     /* If new qty_on_hand is less than 0 then it should abort the operation
        and display an error message */
     IF new_qty < 0 THEN
          raise_application_error(-20001, 'Quantity on Hand cannot
               be less than 0');
     END IF;
END ;
```

7. WORKING WITH FORMS

BASIC CONCEPTS
As commercial application developers our primary task is to design data-entry forms that look as close to the printed sheets of paper that the data entry operators use in the current manual system of data collection.

Hence when the data entry operators switch from paper / pen to keyboard / VDU what they see on the VDU will be familiar to them.

Oracle Forms Designer gives you a powerful graphical user interface to design such forms. All objects, properties, triggers can be selected by simply clicking on an appropriate icon. Oracle Forms Designer, a graphical tool lets you quickly create forms. This tool allows commercial application developers to design forms that will capture, validate and store data keyed in by the data entry operators with the very minimum of code.

Forms Designer, Oracle's GUI based forms creation tool comprises of the following components :
- Forms Designer
- Forms Generator
- Runform

Forms Designer is what the programmer needs to create a form. It allows the user use pre-created objects, design the layout of data entry screens and write code blocks that may be required for data manipulation and validation.

Forms Generator is required to compile the file created in Forms Designer and create a binary file which can be executed by the *Runform*.

Runform is used to run compiled code created by Forms Generator. To run an Oracle form that has passed quality control test and is fully functional only the runform module is required. Hence at the time of software deployment only the runform module needs to be installed on the machines used by the data entry operators.

To program and test / debug an Oracle form, a complete installation of Forms tool is required.

APPLICATION DEVELOPMENT IN FORMS 4.5
Applications built using Forms 4.5 will contain the following components
1. Form module
2. Menus
3. Libraries

Forms :

The primary object of *Form Designer* is the form. The Form module is nothing but a collection of objects such as windows, blocks, canvas, items and event based PL/SQL code blocks called triggers.

Menu :

The menu module is a collection of objects such as menu items, sub menus, sub menu items and PL/SQL code blocks.

Library :

The library module is a collection of PL/SQL functions and procedures stored in a single library file. This library file is then attached to a form / menu module. Hence all other objects on the form or in the menu can now access and share the collection of PL/SQL functions and procedures.

FORM MODULE

The form module consists of the following components
- Window
- Canvas View
- Block
- Item
- PL/SQL Code blocks

The components of an Oracle form module :

Blocks :

A form contains one or more blocks. Blocks are logical containers that have no physical representation--only the items contained in a block are visible in the form interface.

The block can be conceptualized as a container object that holds a related group of objects such as text items, lists, and push buttons for storing, displaying, and manipulating records. Just as tables in the database consist of related columns and rows, blocks contain related items that display data records. Each block has its own set of properties.

A block is logical grouping only; the items in a block can be placed on different canvas-views and can be displayed in different windows.

A block may or may not be connected to the table. A block that is not connected to the table is called **Control Block**.

Each block can be directly related to a *single database table*. This table is known as the **Base Table**. Hence each column of the base table will have an associated item bound to it. The association or binding of the items with the table columns is done via a block. This direct relationship allows the user to query, update, insert and delete data in the base table via the form.

Blocks have several characteristics that can be defined. Some of these are the attributes determine how to order the information that is retrieved into the block from the base table, the number of records that can be displayed in the block, etc.

Blocks can be related to each other by specifying a master-detail relationship. A master-detail relationship corresponds to a primary-foreign key relationship between the base tables of the two blocks. Whenever a row is retrieved in the master block from the master table, the master detail relationship automatically displays the corresponding set of rows from the detail table in the detail block, without adding any special processing command.

Items :
Items are objects contained in blocks. At the most basic level, items serve as containers for data within the form. The values in an item can be manipulated by the user. Item values can also be manipulated by a procedure or a trigger. An item is always associated with the block. Each block normally has one or more items.

The items in a block usually corresponds to the columns of in the base table. Entering data into such items will determine the values entered in the base table. Alternatively, items can be filled with data from the base table by performing an SQL query on the base table.

Items do not always correspond to the columns of a base table. Entering data into such items will determine the values entered in the base table. Alternatively, items can be filled with data from the base table by performing an SQL query on the base table.

Items can also hold calculated values, display related information from other tables or accept operator input for processing later. Items not connected to a base table are called **control items**

Items have attributes that can be user-defined via the items property sheet. These attributes may be set dynamically at runtime via code or statically via the programmer typing in a value into an item's property sheet at design time.

Oracle Forms supports nine types of interface items that you can use to build your forms interface. Each item is displayed below.

Text Item

A text item displays string values, and can be edited.

Display Item

The display item shows information that must be fetched or assigned programatically. These items are not navigable and cannot be edited.

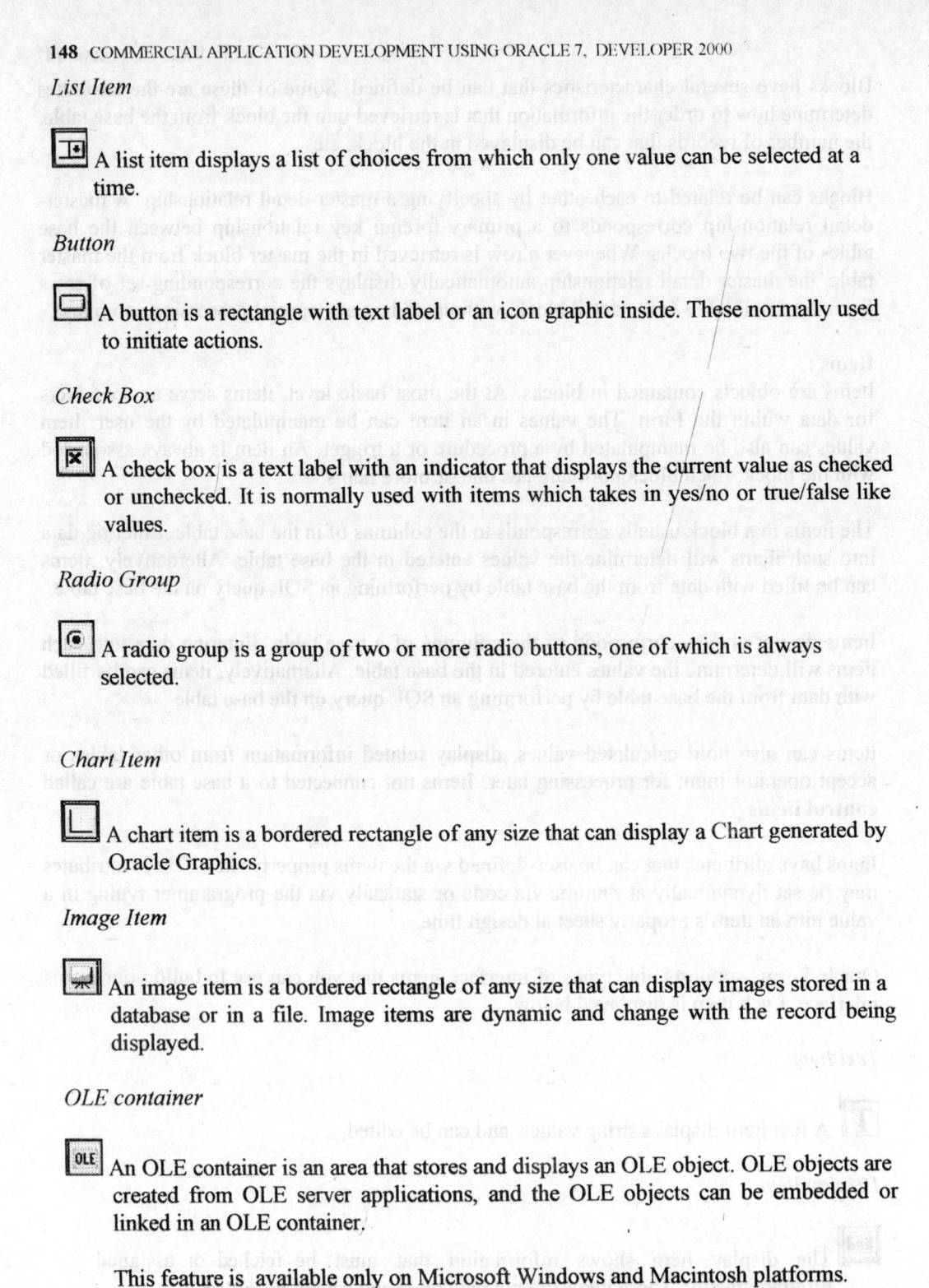

List Item

A list item displays a list of choices from which only one value can be selected at a time.

Button

A button is a rectangle with text label or an icon graphic inside. These normally used to initiate actions.

Check Box

A check box is a text label with an indicator that displays the current value as checked or unchecked. It is normally used with items which takes in yes/no or true/false like values.

Radio Group

A radio group is a group of two or more radio buttons, one of which is always selected.

Chart Item

A chart item is a bordered rectangle of any size that can display a Chart generated by Oracle Graphics.

Image Item

An image item is a bordered rectangle of any size that can display images stored in a database or in a file. Image items are dynamic and change with the record being displayed.

OLE container

An OLE container is an area that stores and displays an OLE object. OLE objects are created from OLE server applications, and the OLE objects can be embedded or linked in an OLE container.

This feature is available only on Microsoft Windows and Macintosh platforms.

VBX control

A VBX control is a custom control that simplifies the building and enhancing of user interfaces. This is available only in Microsoft Windows.

Canvas-view :

The canvas-view is the background on which you place interface items, text and graphics. The items in a block can be placed on different canvas-views and can be displayed in different windows.

Windows :

A form can include any number of windows. Every new form automatically includes a default window named WINDOW0. You can create additional windows as needed by inserting them in the Object Navigator under the Windows node.

For each window you create, you must also create at least one canvas-view. The canvas-view is the background on which you place items and labels. The canvas-view is linked to the window by setting the **Window** canvas-view property appropriately.

You can set properties to define the appearance and functionality of the windows you create, including their size, display position and title.

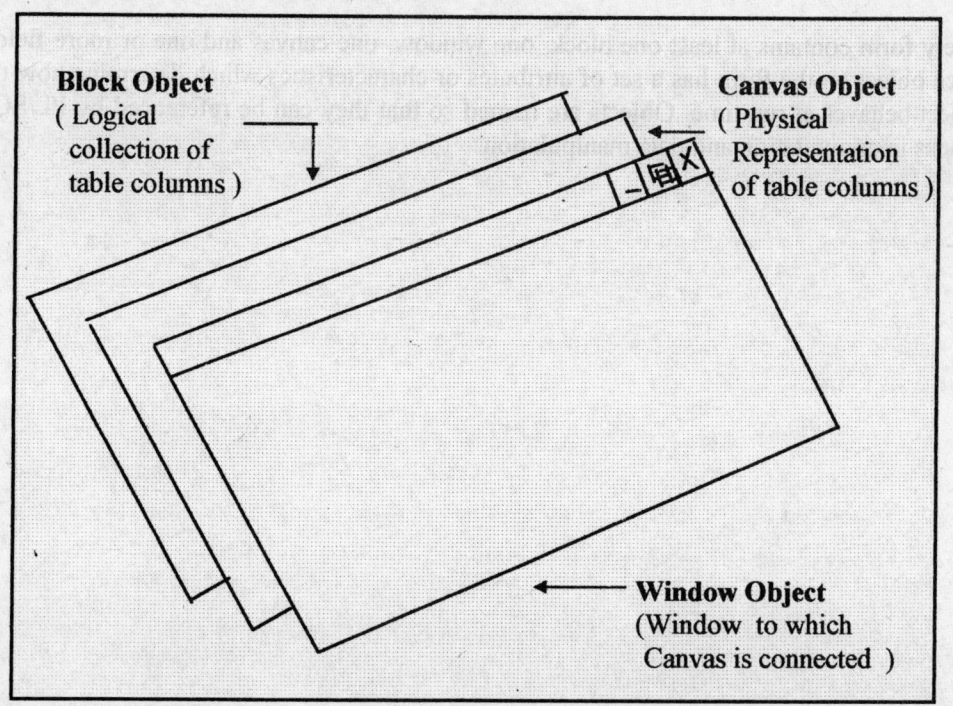

Diagram 7.1 : The Sectional View of the objects on the Form

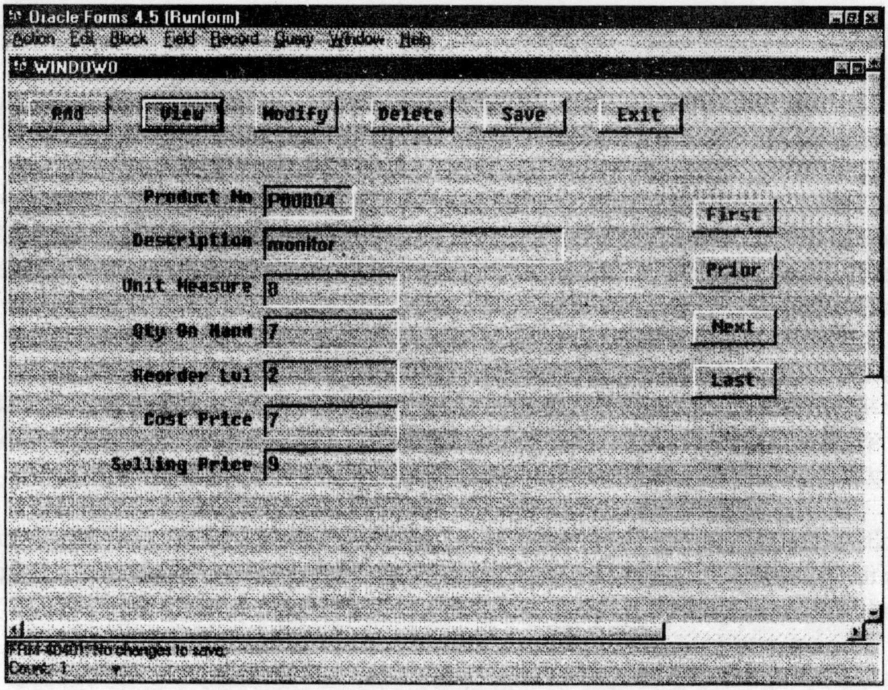

Diagram 7.2 : Data-entry form in Forms Tool

Every form contains at least one block, one window, one canvas and one or more fields. Each object on the form has a set of attributes or characteristics which determine how the object behaves at run time. Objects are named so that they can be referenced by PL/SQL blocks in computation and data manipulation.

USING THE FORMS DESIGNER
Parts of Forms Designer Window :
Before attempting to create a form, let us look at what is visible as part of a Forms Designer window.

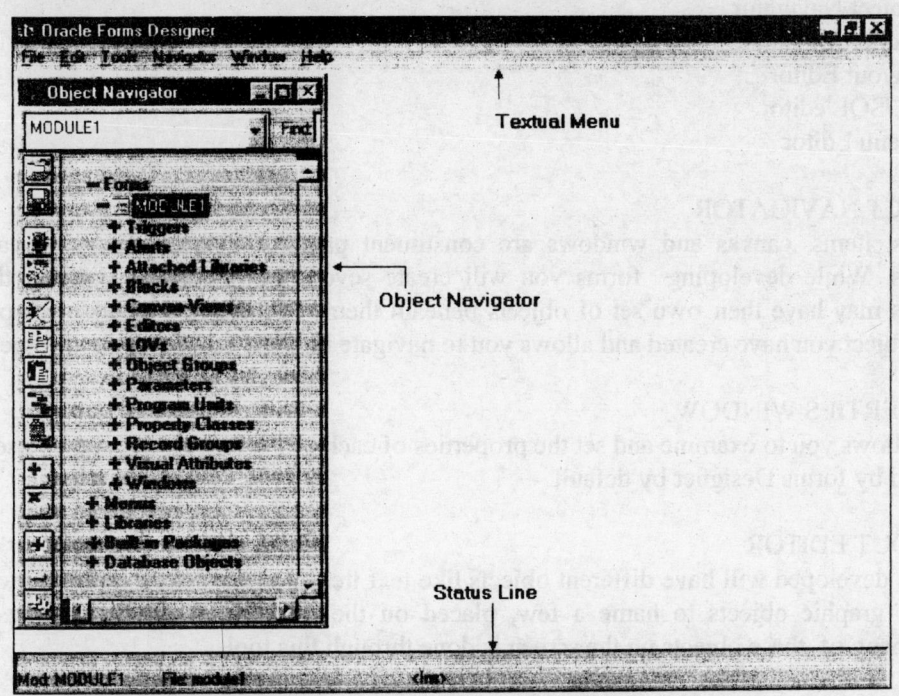

Diagram 7.3 : Layout of Forms Designer window

TEXTUAL MENU
The Forms Designer comes with a built-in menu which allows the user to access the different tools of the Form Designer.

OBJECT NAVIGATOR
Blocks, items, canvas and windows are the constituent parts of a form. They are called objects. While developing forms you may be creating several objects and each of these having their own set of objects beneath them. The Object Navigator allows you to navigate through this hierarchy of objects.

TOOLBOX
The Forms Designer comes with a built-in iconized menu which allows the user to access different tools of the Form Designer.

STATUS LINE
The status line at the bottom of the screen is the area which displays Oracle messages to the programmer / user. It also displays information about the selected object.

e.g.
if a form module is selected it displays the form name and the name of the file in which it is stored.

Tools Available with the Forms Designer :

Before attempting to create a form, let us look at what are the tools available with the Forms Designer so that life is made a little simpler for the developer. These are

1. Object Navigator
2. Properties Window
3. Layout Editor
4. PL/SQL editor
5. Menu Editor

OBJECT NAVIGATOR

Blocks, items, canvas and windows are constituent parts of a form. They are called objects. While developing forms you will create several such objects. Each of these objects may have their own set of objects beneath them. The Object Navigator displays each object you have created and allows you to navigate through this hierarchy of objects.

PROPERTIES WINDOW

This allows you to examine and set the properties of each of the objects defined by user or created by forms Designer by default.

LAYOUT EDITOR

Forms developed will have different objects like text items, check boxes, radio buttons, labels, graphic objects to name a few, placed on the screen. Sizing, positioning and alignment of these objects on the screen is done through this tool.

PL/SQL EDITOR

More often than not, tasks which are specific to an application must be performed. To achieve this appropriate PL/SQL code must be written. The PL/SQL Editor provides the interface in which PL/SQL code can be written and attached to an appropriate event.

MENU EDITOR

This tool is used to create user-defined menus. Oracle Forms automatically provides a default menu with default functionality like querying, inserting deleting records and navigating through different records. However for system specific functionality a user defined menu which overrides the default Oracle menu will be necessary.

WORKING WITH FORMS **153**

CREATING A FORM

1. Invoke *Forms Designer* by double clicking on the Forms Designer icon as displayed in diagram 7.4.

Diagram 7.4 : Invoking Forms 4.5

2. The opening screen is shown in diagram 7.5.

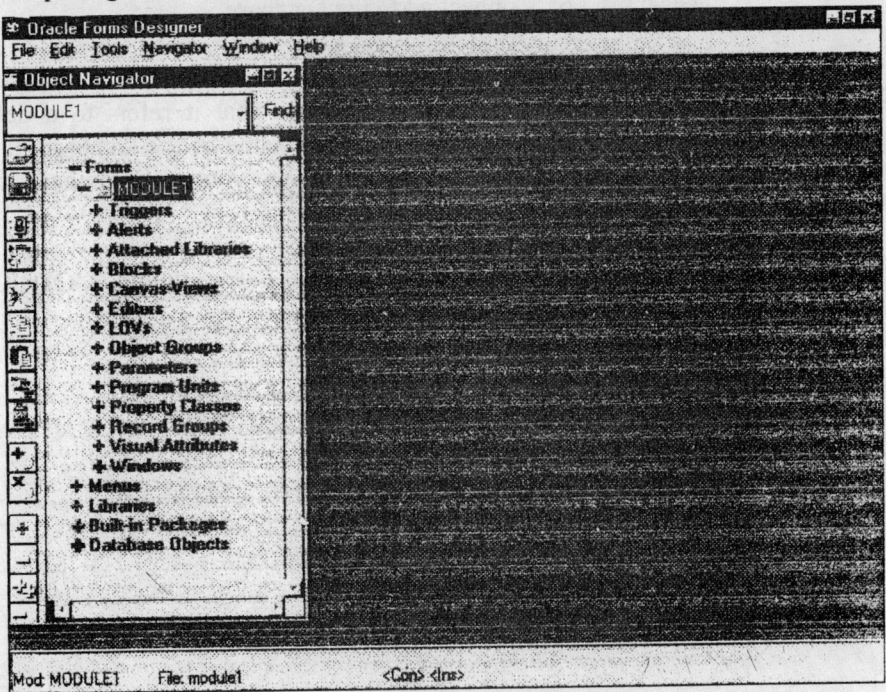

Diagram 7.5 : Forms Opening Screen

3. You must now connect to the Oracle Database. Click on **File** and select menu item **Conn_e_ct**.

4. Specify Login, Password and the name of Database. Click on the '**Connect**' PushButton. The completed connect information is displayed in diagram 7.6.

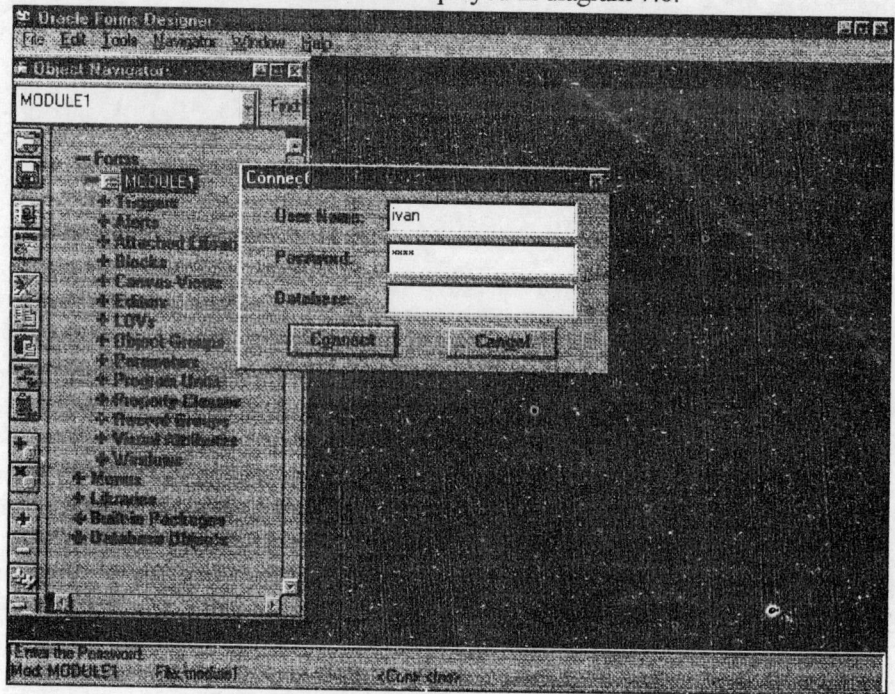

Diagram 7.6 : Connecting to the Database

Note :
The DBA may have configured the Client machine so that it refers to a default database. In that case you may not have to specify the name of the database. It will automatically connect to the default database allowing you to commence form building.

5. A new form is created by default. It displays the default Form module 'MODULE1' in the Object Navigator as shown in diagram 7.7.

WORKING WITH FORMS **155**

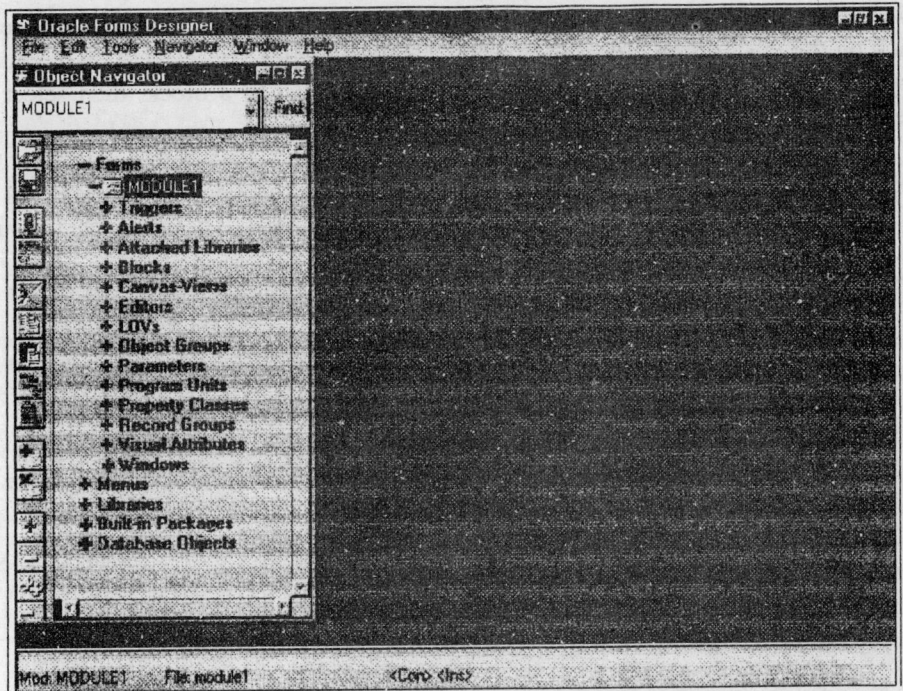

Diagram 7.7 : Default Form module 'MODULE1'

6. The next step would be to create a new block. Click on **Tools** and select **New Block...**. Specify the name of Base Table, the name of the block and the name of the canvas on which items of the blocks must be placed. The completed screen is displayed in diagram 7.8.

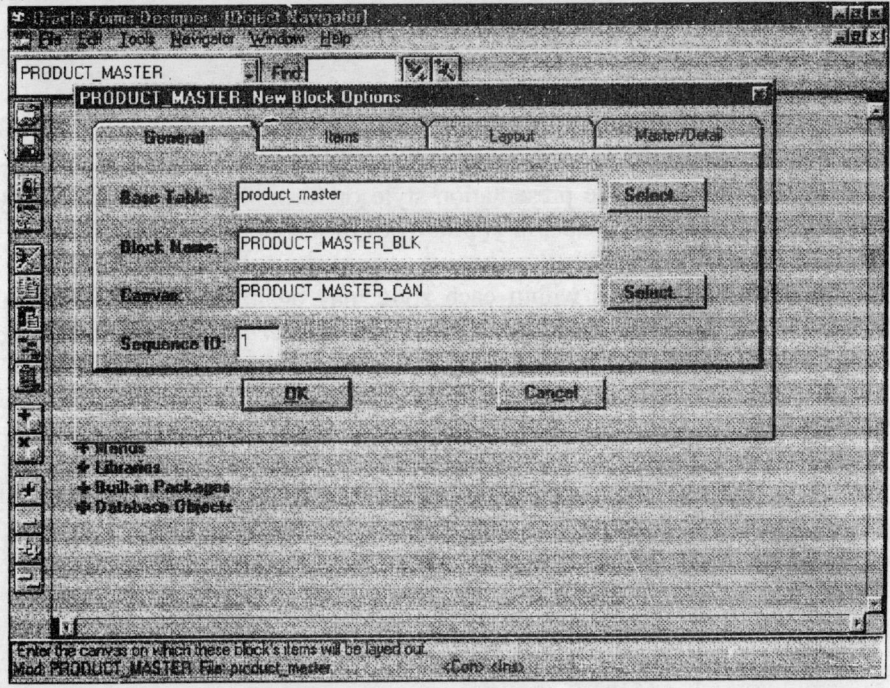

Diagram 7.8 : Creating a new block

7. Select the tab folder marked *Items*. The columns of the base table must be selected. Click on the PushButton **Select Colum**n**s**. All the columns are selected by default. If a specific table column is not to be logically connected to a block, then select the specific column and set the *include checkbox* off.

   The *label* for each column selected can be defined. The display type of the items can be specified by selecting from the dropdown list provided. The completed column selection screen is displayed in diagram 7.9.

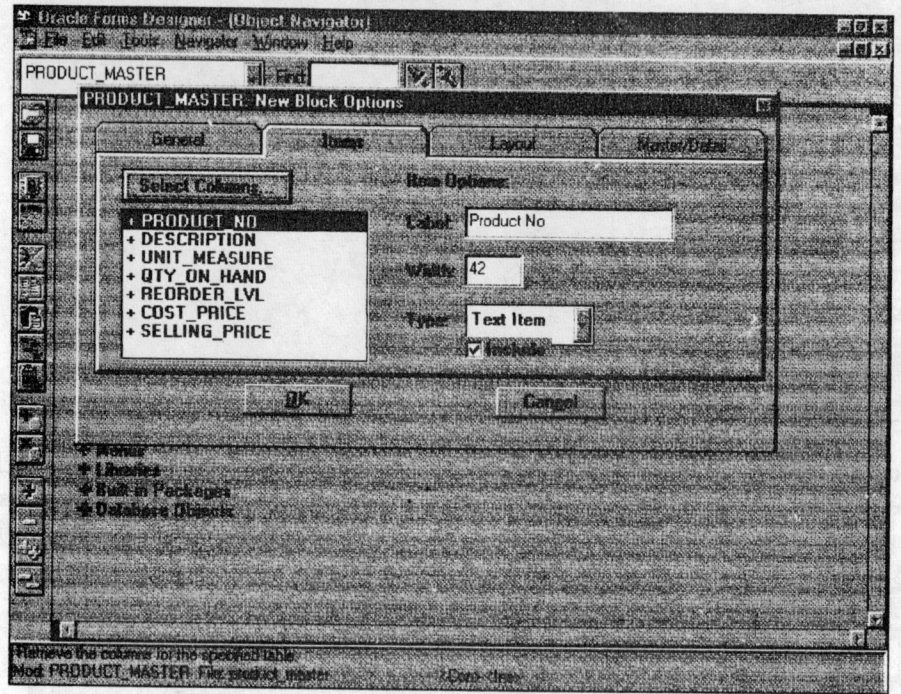

Diagram 7.9 : Column Selection

8. The last step is to specify the presentation style or form. The default form may be created with the Items and its label in *Tabular* or *Form* style.

   The Orientation of the Items within each style may again be either Horizontal or Vertical. Most of the time we will use *Form* style and *Vertical* Orientation as shown in diagram 7.10.

9. Click on OK.

WORKING WITH FORMS **157**

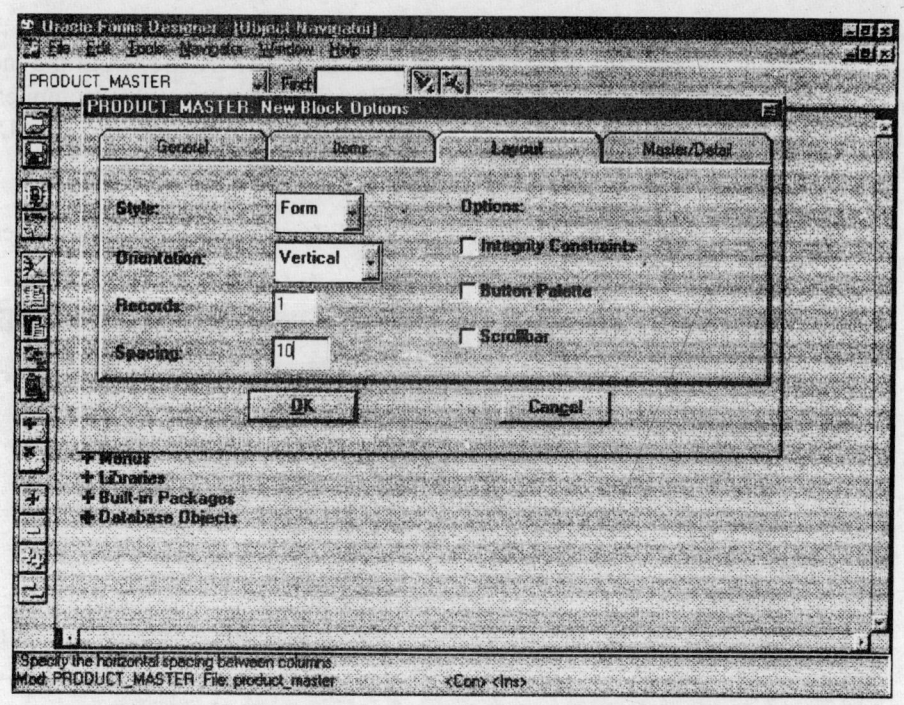

Diagram 7.10 : Form Presentation Style and Column Orientation

10. The master form is ready. Save the form module by Clicking on **File** and selecting **Save** menu item. Name the form and specify the directory where you want the file saved.

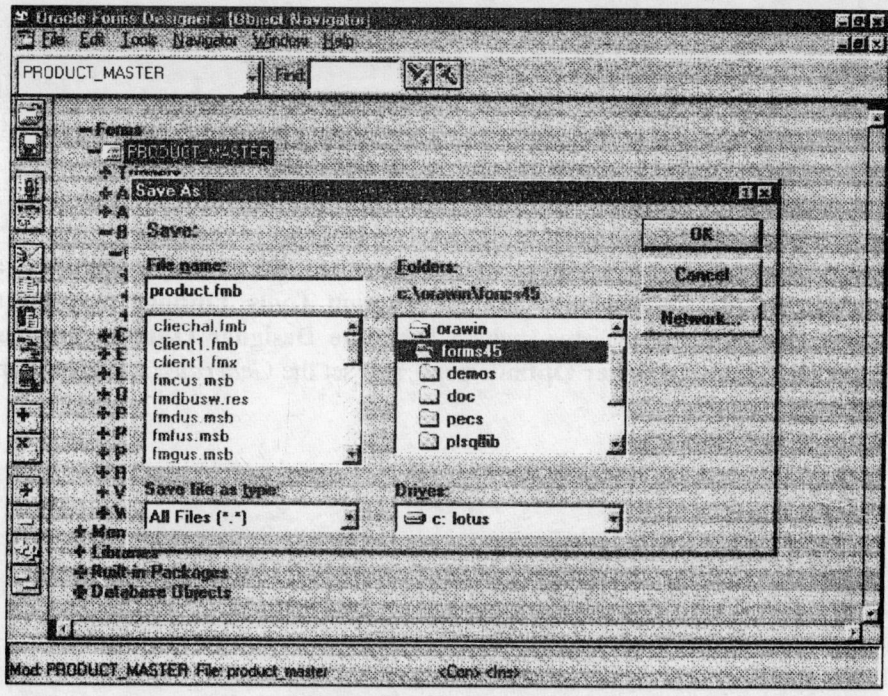

Diagram 7.11 : Save Form

GENERATING AND RUNNING A FORM

Before you can run a form, you must create an executable (.FMX file) from the module form created in the *Forms Designer* (.FMB file). Generating a form compiles any uncompiled program units and creates an executable runfile. To Generate a .FMX file from a .FMB file click on **File**, **Administration** and **Generate** menu option.

Run the Form by selecting the **Run** option under the **File** option. The default master data entry screen is displayed as shown in diagram 7.12.

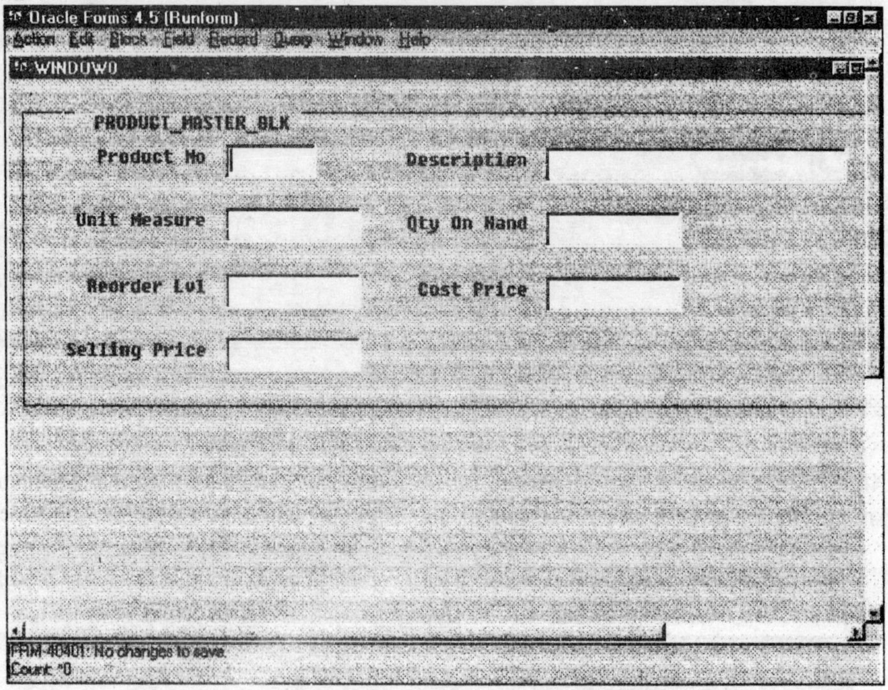

Diagram 7.12 : Default Master Data Entry Form

Setting the Default Environment :

The default environment setting can be set to ensure that Forms Designer generates a form before executing it. This can be done, by selecting **Tools**, **Options** from the textual menu. The options screen has two pages. These are **Designer Options** and **Runtime Options**. Click on the **Designer Options** page and set the *Generate Before Run* option ti true as shown in diagram 7.13.

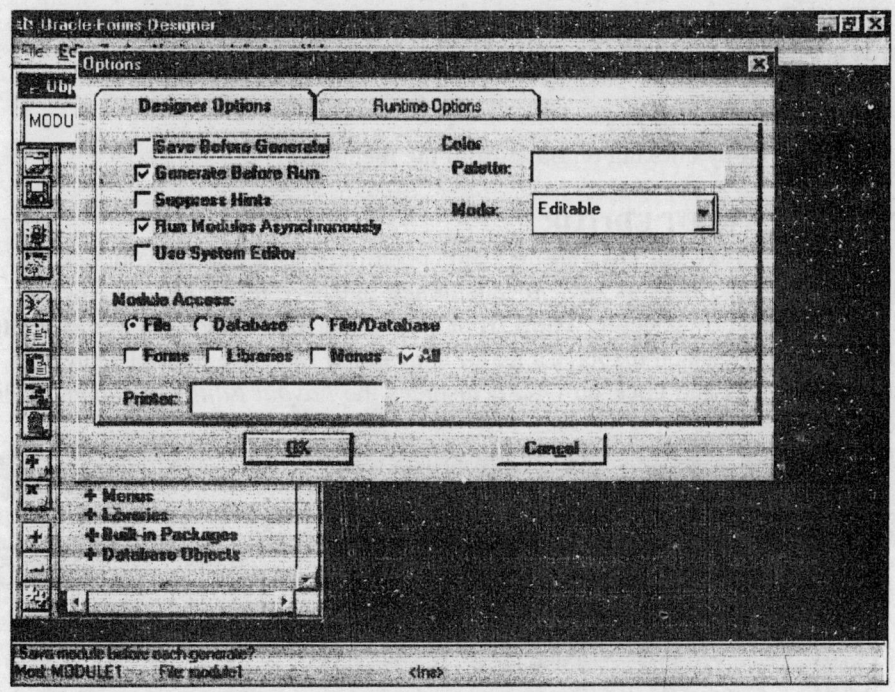

Diagram 7.13 : Setting the Designer Options

Data Retrieval and Manipulation Operations :
The runtime of the form comes with a default Menu system. The default menu system provides all the options for Navigating within the form and performing Data Manipulation.

DATA RETRIEVAL
Data can be retrieved by selecting the menu item **Query** and clicking on **Execute**. This would retrieve all the records from the table.

If a conditional query must be performed then select **Query** and click on **Enter**. It clears the block and allows the user to enter an Item Value. Type in the Item value in the appropriate item. By doing so, a condition is automatically defined at the block level. Execute the query by Clicking on **Execute** from **Query** Menu item.

The status line at the bottom of the screen will indicate the number of records retrieved.

NAVIGATION
If several records are queried, Click on **Records** and select **Previous** or **Next** to move to the previous or the next record.

INSERTING DATA
A record are inserted by first inserting a blank row. This is done by clicking on **Insert** from the menu item **Records**. Enter the values in the different items required. In this manner several records can be inserted.

DELETING DATA
Records are deleted by clicking on **Delete** from the **Record** menu item.

SAVING DATA
Records are saved by clicking on **Save** from the menu line.

USING THE LAYOUT EDITOR
The form created may not have all the items positioned and sized to your specific design needs. The Layout Editor is used to positioned and size items to your specific design needs. It is invoked by selecting **Tools** from the menu and clicking on **Layout Editor...** A dialog box appears which displays a list of canvases if there are multiple canvases. Select the required canvas and click on OK. It displays the *Layout Editor* as shown in diagram 7.14.

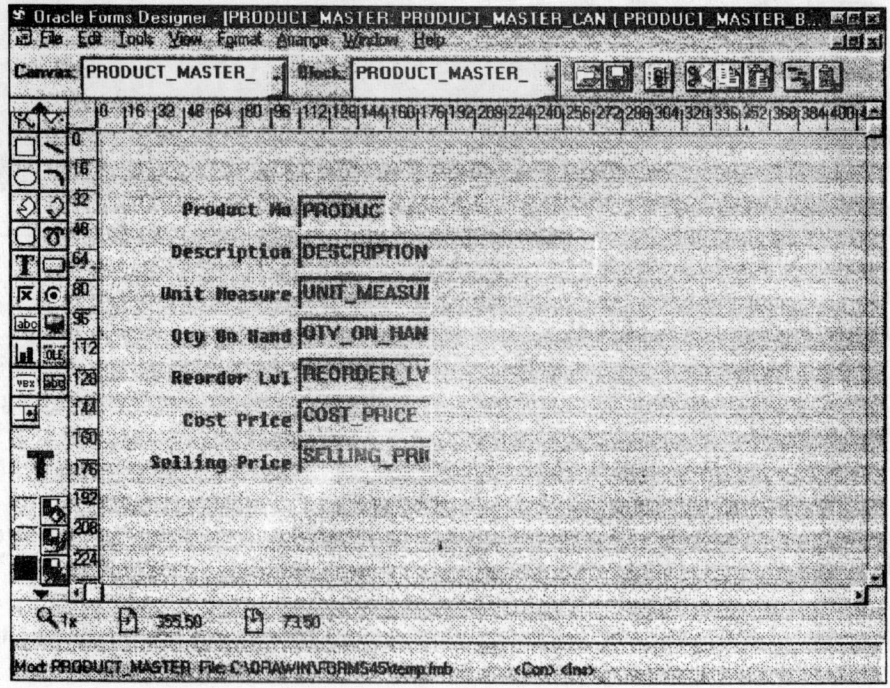

Diagram 7.14 : Layout Editor

Positioning and Sizing an Item :
The Layout editor opens up the canvas selected. Items can be positioned by selecting and dragging.

To size the items, select the item by clicking on it. Move the mouse cursor to the edge of the item and pull to required size.

The Layout Editor has a toolbox on the left side. Objects from the toolbox can be selected and pasted on to the canvas. Plain text can be pasted on to the canvas. The only way a plain text can be edited is by clicking on the text object from the toolbar and dropping it on the canvas. This provides a plain text area that can be edited.

Setting the Properties of the Items :
Double clicking on an item opens up the **Properties** window. Through this, the item's properties can be altered. The *Properties* dialog box is displayed in diagram 7.15.

To change the property select the property which is to be altered. Depending on the type of property a text box or a dropdown list box is available at top of all the properties. Type in or select the property value as the case might be.

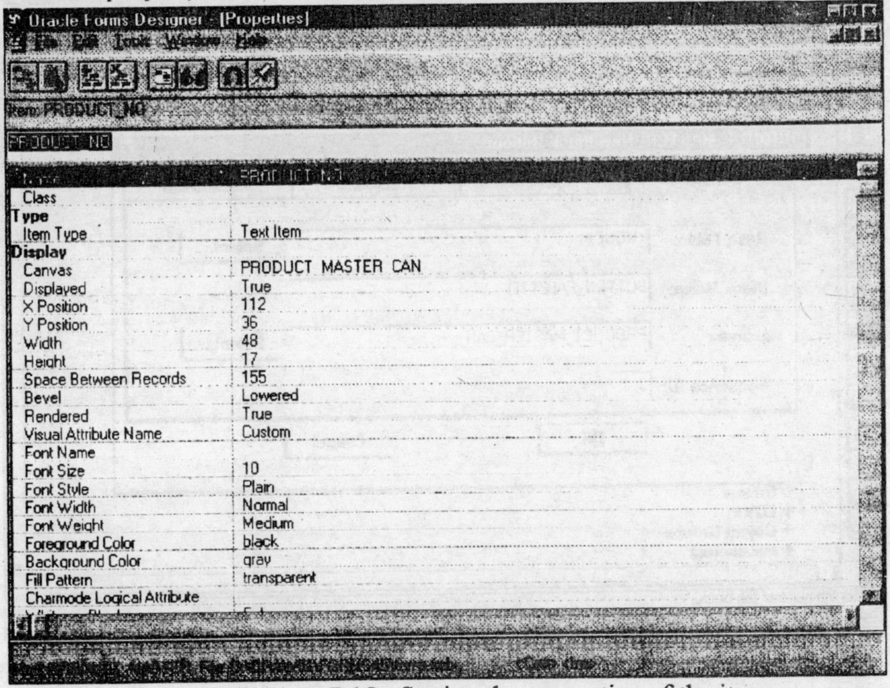

Diagram 7.15 : Setting the properties of the item

Placing Push buttons on the Form :
Screens developed are usually built based on a pre-determined GUI design. These designs very often include pushbuttons and items of different styles. If the design so demands, pushbuttons can be incorporated by selecting the *Button* icon from the toolbox of the layout editor and then pasting it.

A pushbutton is an item. The item must belong to some block. Thus any pushbutton pasted on the layout editor must belong to some block. The button when pasted on the layout editor will belong to the current block. The current block can be determined by the window title of the layout editor. It appears in parenthesis.

Note :
When the block connected to a table has the '*number of records displayed*' property set to multiple records, it will display a set of pushbuttons for each record displayed.

To avoid this create a new block by clicking on **New Block** from the **Tools** menu item. Specify the name of the block as Button_Palette. Leave the base table blank and name the block. The complete block information is displayed in diagram 7.16.

Open the Layout Editor and set the current block to Button_Palette.

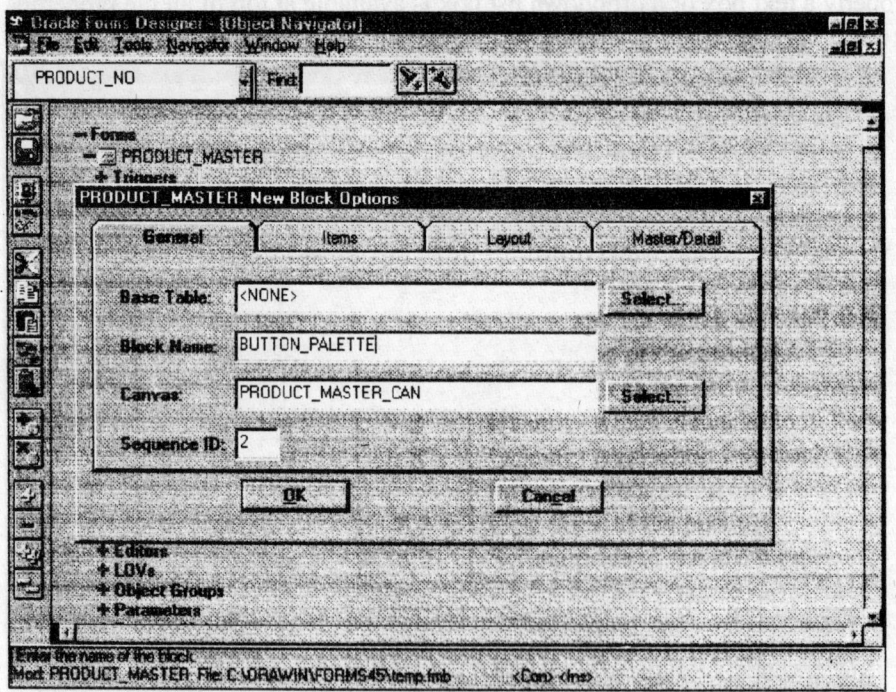

Diagram 7.16 : Creating a New Block for the Pushbuttons

Any button pasted on the form will belong to Button_Palette block since it is the current block. Set size and position of the buttons.

The text that must be displayed on the pushbutton can be set activating the **properties** window, locating the **label** property and filling in an appropriate value.

e.g. To set the label of push_button_add, open the property sheet of push_button_add and set the *Label* property to *Add*.

CONSTRAINTS DEFINED AT THE TIME OF CREATION OF A BLOCK

The *Integrity Constraints* option in the *Layout* tab page of *New Block* creation tool determines whether *Oracle Forms* should create a block that enforces the table and column constraints defined in the data dictionary for the block's base table. This option is valid only for base table blocks, not for control blocks. The integrity constraints option screen is shown in diagram 7.17.

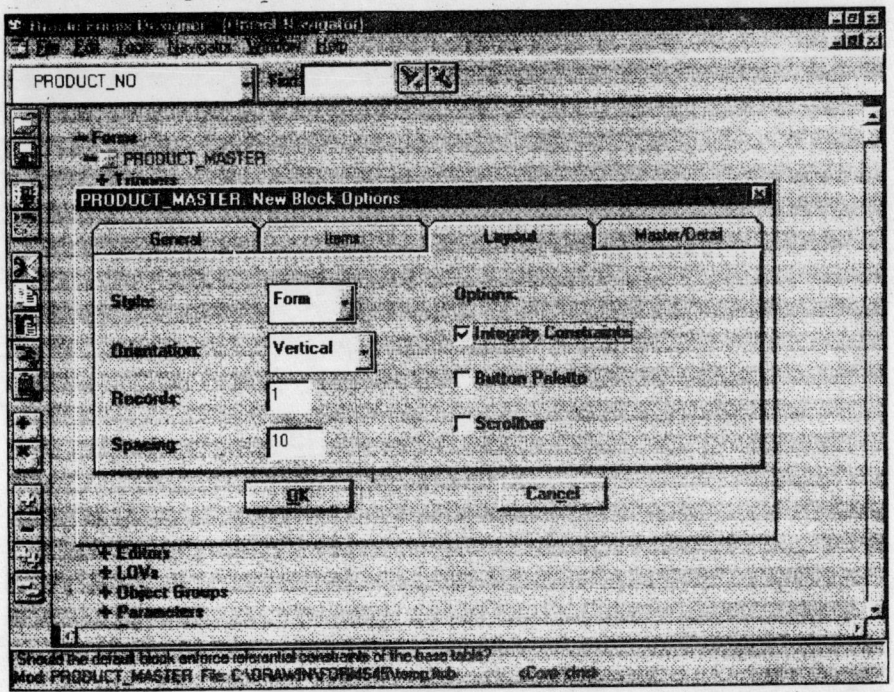

Diagram 7.17 : New block window with layout option

If you select the Integrity Constraints option when you create a base table block, Oracle Forms does the following:

1. Sets the *Primary Key* property to *True* and the *Update Allowed* property to *False* for items that correspond to primary key columns, and sets the Primary Key property equal to *True* for the block.

2. Creates a *When-Validate-Item* trigger to enforce NOT NULL constraints in items which corresponds to columns that have NOT NULL defined on the table. Similarly if CHECK constraints are defined at the table level then Oracle forms will create appropriate *When-Validate-Item* triggers for each of the CHECK constraints defined.

3. Creates a *Key-Delrec* trigger for the block if its base table is defined in the database as having a foreign key relationship with another table. The trigger prevents the deletion of a record when there are corresponding detail records in the foreign key table.

4. Sets the *Default* property for items that correspond to columns having default value constraints.

8. MASTER FORM

PRODUCT MASTER DATA ENTRY SCREEN
Create Product Master Form via which the user can manipulate the data being loaded into the table **product_master**. This is a single table taken from a Sales Order System.

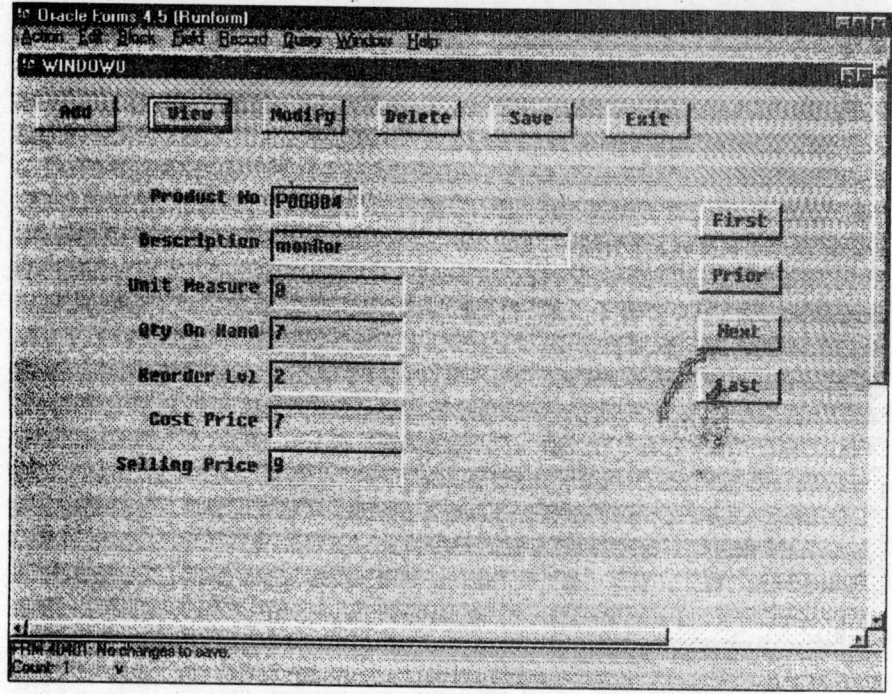

Diagram 8.1 : Product Master Data Entry Screen

Provide the user with complete data manipulation operations (Add, View, Modify, Delete). In the view mode, allow the user to browse through the data table, one record at a time i.e. First, Last, Previous, Next operations have to be provided for. Include search function that searches a record to match a product_no entered by the user.

Table Name : product_master
Description : Used to store information about products supplied by the company

Column Name	Data Type	Size	Column Description
product_no	varchar2	6	Access key via which we shall seek data.
description	varchar2	25	Description of the product.
unit_measure	varchar2	10	Unit by which the product is measured.
qty_on_hand	number	8	Quantity which is available in the stock.
reorder_lvl	number	8	Quantity level when the stock should be re-ordered.
cost_price	number	8,2	Cost price of the product.
selling_price	number	8,2	Selling price of the product.

Integrity Constraints :
- PK_Product_no Primary Key on product_no.

Validations in the product master data entry screen are as follows :
- product_no is a Primary Key i.e. duplicate values are not allowed in product_no. It cannot be left blank.
- first letter of product_no must start with 'P'.
- product description, unit_measure, selling_price and cost_price cannot be left blank
- qty_on_hand should have a default value of 0. Field qty_on_hand is not enterable.
- selling_price cannot be 0.
- cost_price cannot be 0
- selling_price cannot be less than cost_price.

SOLUTION
1. Create the default form as specified in CREATING A FORM.

2. Position and Size the items as shown in diagram 8.1.

3. Create a new control block to include the pushbuttons.

4. Place the pushbuttons on the canvas as shown in diagram 8.1 and set the *Name* and the *label* property of each pushbutton.

Push Button Name	Label	Push Button Name	Label
push_button_add	Add	push_button_exit	Exit
push_button_view	View	push_button_first	First
push_button_modify	Modify	push_button_prior	Prior
push_button_delete	Delete	push_button_next	Next
push_button_save	Save	push_button_last	Last

TRIGGERS
Code has to be written to add functionality to the default form. The code written is executed based on some event occurring in the application.

The code is written in PL/SQL blocks and is called a *Trigger*. A Trigger is executed when an event occurs. A trigger is written for an object. The object may be Form, Block or an Item.

Triggers are connected to Events i.e. when a block of code is executed. Thus while writing Triggers you must identify when you want the block of code to fire. Select the name of the Trigger from the list available. Oracle Associates the name of the trigger with the Event.

e.g.
When the cursor navigates from one field to the other Oracle fires a trigger named *Post-Text-Item*.

Several trigger names are available. To understand which trigger name to select, the events that occur may be classified as :

1. Interface Events
2. Internal Processing Events

Interface Events :
These events occur at the interface or the screen level. These usually occur when the operator has clicked on a button (*When-Button-Pressed*), Pressed a key sequence to **move the cursor** from one field to the other (*Key-Next-Item*).

Internal Processing Events:
These are fired as a result of runtime form processing. For example when **the cursor navigates** out of an item to another item *Post-Text-Item* for the current item and *Pre-Text-Item* for the item it moves into will fire.

The sequence of trigger execution :
When the user presses the tab or the enter key to navigate from one text item to another, the *Key-Next-Item* event fires. If the user has written any code in the *Key-Next-Item* trigger, Oracle executes the code specified by the user. If the *Key-Next-Item* trigger is not written, Oracle moves the cursor from the current item to the next navigation item.

Since the cursor actually navigates from the current item and enters the next item, it will fire the *Post-Text-Item* trigger for the item from which the cursor has moved out and the *Pre-Text-Item* trigger for the item in which the cursor has moved.

Thus the trigger hierarchy is as follows :

Key-Next-Item trigger of the current item
↓
Post-Text-Item trigger of the current item
↓
Pre-Text-Item trigger of the next item

Writing Triggers :
1. Select the object for which trigger code is to be written in the Object Navigator and click with the right mouse button. It displays a popup menu.

2. Click on *PL/SQL Editor* in the popup menu. It displays the *PL/SQL Editor* as shown in diagram 8.2.

MASTER FORM **167**

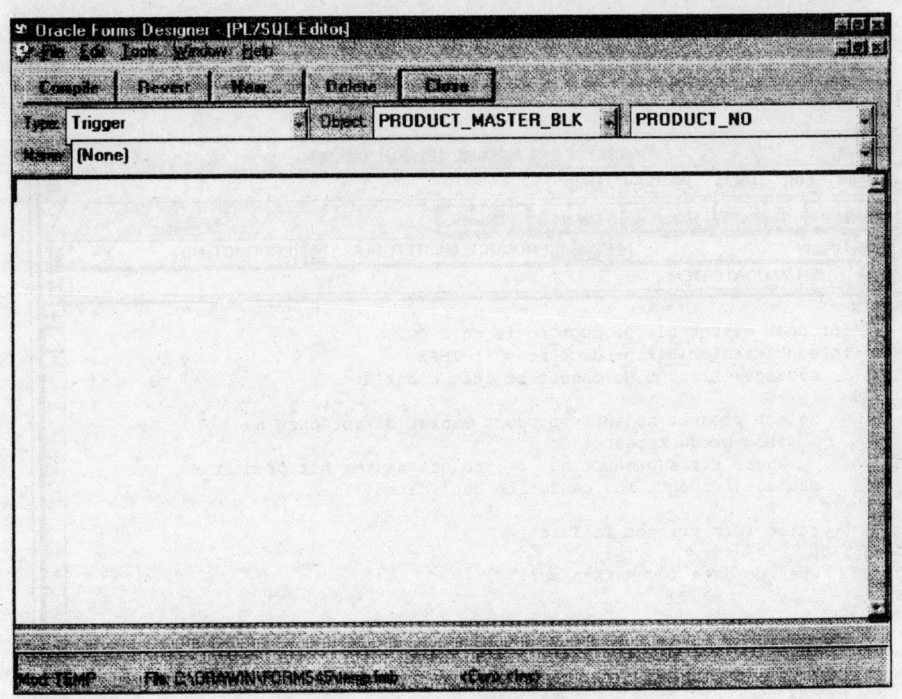

Diagram 8.2 : PL/SQL Editor

3. Select *Type* as *Trigger* and click on **New**. It displays a list of triggers as displayed in diagram 8.3. Specify the name of the trigger and click on OK.

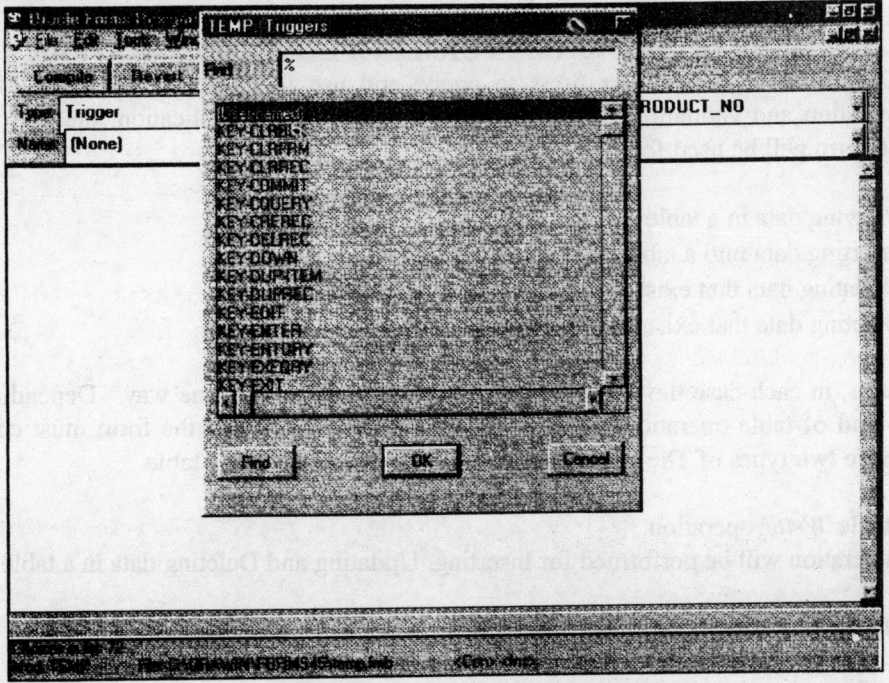

Diagram 8.3 : List of Trigger Names

4. Type in appropriate PL/SQL code in the text area of the PL/SQL Editor tool. The Completed *When-Button-Pressed* trigger on block button_palette and item push_button_first is displayed in diagram 8.4.

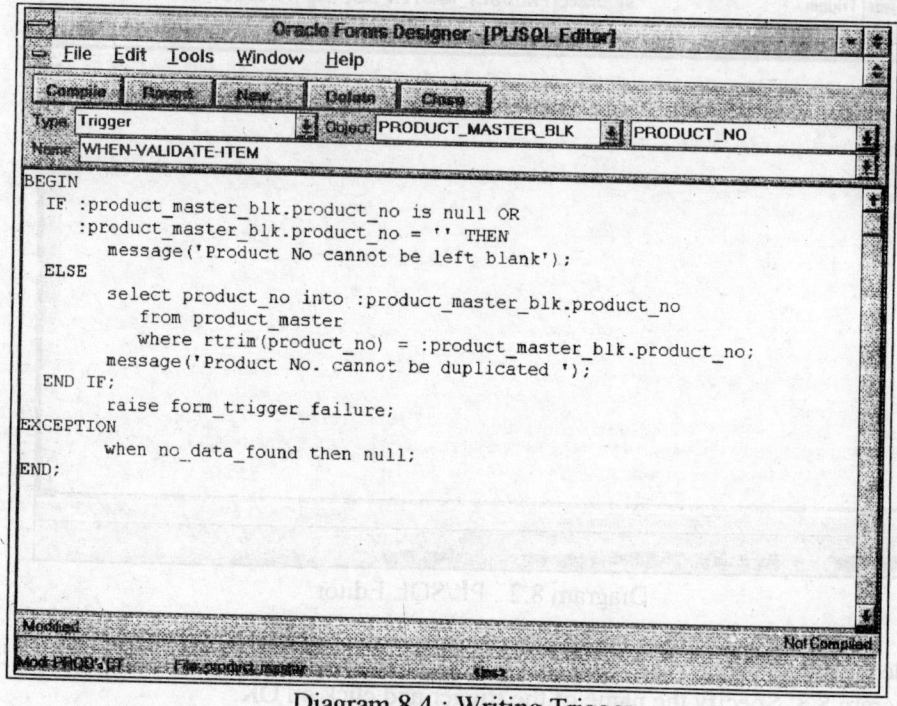

```
BEGIN
    IF :product_master_blk.product_no is null OR
       :product_master_blk.product_no = '' THEN
           message('Product No cannot be left blank');
    ELSE
           select product_no into :product_master_blk.product_no
              from product_master
              where rtrim(product_no) = :product_master_blk.product_no;
           message('Product No. cannot be duplicated ');
    END IF;
           raise form_trigger_failure;
EXCEPTION
           when no_data_found then null;
END;
```

Diagram 8.4 : Writing Trigger

THE BEHAVIOR OF AN ORACLE FORM IN A COMMERCIAL APPLICATION :

The Oracle forms tool allows users to create and use forms for the purpose of data manipulation and validation. Conceptually in a commercial application, the very same Oracle form will be used for

- Viewing data in a table
- Inserting data into a table
- Updating data that exists in a table
- Deleting data that exists in a table.

However, in each case the form cannot behave in exactly the same way. Depending on what kind of table operation is being performed the behavior of the form must change. There are **two** types of The operations that can be performed on a table.

1) A table *'Write'* operation.
This operation will be performed for Inserting, Updating and Deleting data in a table.

2) A table *'Read'* operation

This operation will be performed while Viewing data in a table. However, this operation must precede the Delete and Update operations. This is because unless you can see the data in the form you cannot really Delete or Update it.

Form Behavior While Viewing Data :
While Viewing data from a table the user of the form must not be allowed to make any changes to the data (*i.e. Data Updation*) and save these changes back into the table.

To update a record, the user must specifically make a request to the form to change the current mode of operation, from *View*, to *Update*.

Form Behavior While Updating Data : [*Primary Key problems*]
While Updating the contents of a form, the user should not be allowed to change the contents of the *Primary Key field*. In DBMSystems this is not allowed. If this is allowed by the system being created, then the DBA will not be able to maintain *Referential Integrity* of data between tables. A *mandatory change* in a Primary Key value generally always a *Delete* and an *Insert*.

Form Behavior While Deleting Data :
Deletion of data must be allowed at any instant in time.

Form Behavior While Inserting Data :
Insertion of data must be allowed at whenever required.

The Forms Mode Of Operation :
Changing between Viewing, Updating Deleting and Inserting data dynamically, is quite possible. The necessary control buttons exist on the form itself. Programmers have to take care to freeze the behavior of the form depending upon the user request received at the very first instance, through writing suitable code. Each form used in the commercial application will have the very same mode of behavior while manipulating and / or validating data. Hence instead of repeating the program code required to ensure behavior modes it is best to write a procedure that can be called by the programmer whenever required to ensure appropriate form behavior.

DATA NAVIGATION VIA AN ORACLE FORM
Multiple Rows Being Retrieved From The Table :
To navigate through several records via an Oracle form we use Push Buttons on the form appropriately labeled as *First, Next, Prior, Last*. Clicking on the push button will cause the *When-Button-Pressed* event to fire. Any code attached to this event will in turn execute. Hence, by clicking on the appropriate push button we can navigate through all the records we want to.

In Windows based applications navigational push buttons as mentioned are very commonly used. This gives rise to the need to super control the push buttons themselves. When the forms tool is focused on the *first* record the *Prior* and *First* push buttons should be disabled. When the forms tool is focused on the *Last* record the *Next* and *Last* push buttons should be disabled.

Having these push buttons enabled when the forms tool focus is on the *First* or *Last* record will achieve nothing if the user clicks on them. The movement is completely illogical.

Similarly, when the focus of the Forms tool is on any record *other than first* or *Last* it is necessary to have all the push buttons enabled. Having them disabled would now be considered completely illogical.

Every form will behave the same when it comes to navigating through several records. Hence writing a simple procedure that will scan the record buffer in memory and depending upon which record the focus of the forms tool is focused on, enable or disable navigational control push buttons would work very effectively.

A Single Row Being Retrieved From The Table :
The enabling or disabling of the scroll control buttons on the data entry form will be dependent on the number of data rows retrieved from the server.

If the SQL Select sentence retrieved only one row from the table, then the *First*, *Next*, *Prior*, *Last* scroll control buttons must be disabled. This is because there is really only one row in the data buffer.
Let us see how to write the triggers and procedures for data manipulation.

The Triggers are defined below :

Trigger Name : **WHEN-BUTTON-PRESSED** Form : product_master
Block   : button_palette   Item : push_button_view
Trigger Level : Field Level
Function   : Retrieve all the records and go to the first record in the product_master table.
Text   : BEGIN
                /* when we click on the push button view ,our focus is now on the button palette block hence we have to explicitly move the focus to the next block i.e. product_master_blk */
                next_block;

                /* execute query retrieves records for the current block. */
                execute_query ;
                item_enable_disable(property_off);
                END ;

MASTER FORM

Trigger Name	: **WHEN-BUTTON-PRESSED**	Form	: product_master
Block	: button_palette	Item	: push_button_first
Trigger Level	: Field Level		
Function	: Go to the first record in the product_master table.		
Text	: BEGIN		

```
        next_block ;

        /* position the cursor on the first record of the current block */
        first_record ;
   END ;
```

Trigger Name	: **WHEN-BUTTON-PRESSED**	Form	: product_master
Block	: button_palette	Item	: push_button_prior
Trigger Level	: Field Level		
Function	: Go to the previous record in the product_master table.		
Text	: BEGIN		

```
        next_block;

        /* position the cursor on the prior record of the current block */
        previous_record ;
   END ;
```

Trigger Name	: **WHEN-BUTTON-PRESSED**	Form	: product_master
Block	: button_palette	Item	: push_button_next
Trigger Level	: Field Level		
Function	: Go to the next record in the product_master table.		
Text	: BEGIN		

```
        next_block;

        /* position the cursor on the next record of the current block */
        next_record ;
   END ;
```

Trigger Name	: **WHEN-BUTTON-PRESSED**	Form	: product_master
Block	: button_palette	Item	: push_button_last
Trigger Level	: Field Level		
Function	: Go to the last record in the product_master table.		
Text	: BEGIN		

```
        next_block ;

        /* position the cursor on the last record of the current block */
        last_record ;
   END ;
```

Trigger Name	: **WHEN-BUTTON-PRESSED**	Form	: product_master
Block	: button_palette	Item	: push_button_add
Trigger Level	: Field Level		
Function	: Insert a record in the product_master table.		
Text	: BEGIN		

       next_block;

       /* *Insert a new record in the current block and position the cursor on that record* */
       create_record ;

       /* *Item_enable_disable is a user-defined procedure that enables the fields so that the contents of the field can be modified or new values can be entered in the add or modify mode and disable fields so that the contents of the field cannot be modified in view mode. This procedure is explained in the section PROCEDURE.* */
       item_enable_disable(property_on);

END ;

Trigger Name	: **WHEN-BUTTON-PRESSED**	Form	: product_master
Block	: button_palette	Item	: push_button_modify
Trigger Level	: Field Level		
Function	: Set the primary key i.e. product_no not updateable and set all other fields updateable so that the record in the product_master table can be modified.		
Text	: BEGIN		

       next_block;
       item_enable_disable(property_on);

       /* *In order to dynamically (at runtime) set the updateable property of product_no to false, we make use of a built-in subprogram i.e. set_item_property to set the value of specified property. It takes in three parameters. The parameters are :*
          Item Name optionally prefixed by block name
          Property Name
          Property Value

       If a property takes a Boolean value, the user can pass property_on i.e. True or property_off i.e. False */
       set_item_property('product_master_blk.product_no', updateable,
          property_off)

END ;

Trigger Name	: **WHEN-BUTTON-PRESSED**	Form	: product_master
Block	: button_palette	Item	: push_button_delete
Trigger Level	: Field Level		
Function	: Delete the current record in the product_master table.		
Text	: BEGIN		

```
        next_block;

        /* delete the current record in the block */
        delete_record ;

    END ;
```

Trigger Name	: **WHEN-BUTTON-PRESSED**	Form	: product_master
Block	: button_palette	Item	: push_button_save
Trigger Level	: Field Level		
Function	: Save the changes to product_master table.		
Text	: BEGIN		

```
        /* form status, a system variable holds the status of the form. It
           can take three values.
         These are :
         CHANGED (at least one record has changed in the form.
                  changes may be in the form of insert, update or
                  delete)
         NEW  (contains only blank records i.e. the user has insert new
                  rows but not values entered for the fields. Oracle
                  doesn't post blank records into the database
         QUERY ( contains records that have been queried but no
                 changes have been made. If the user changes the
                 value in any field, status changes to CHANGED. If
                 the commit is successful, status changes to QUERY */

         IF :system.form_status = 'CHANGED' THEN
         /* If the form status is changed then commit changes */
               commit_form ;
               IF :system.form_status = 'QUERY' THEN
                       item_enable_disable(property_off);
               END IF ;
         END IF;
    END ;
```

Note : Trigger *When-Button-Pressed* on field push_button_modify, push_button_delete, push_button_save calls a procedure named *item_enable_disable*. This procedure is explained in the section PROCEDURE.

174 COMMERCIAL APPLICATION DEVELOPMENT USING ORACLE 7, DEVELOPER 2000

Trigger Name : **WHEN-BUTTON-PRESSED**   Form : product_master
Block : button_palette   Item : push_button_exit
Trigger Level : Field Level
Function : Quit the product_master form.
Text : BEGIN
/* Close the form. If there are any changes in the form the system asks for confirmation to save changes */
exit_form ;
END ;

Set the next *navigational item property* of the last text item i.e. *selling price* to the name of the first text item i.e. *product no* .

PROCEDURES
Writing Procedures :
1. Click on **Tools**, **PL/SQL Editor** to invoke the PL/SQL Editor as shown in diagram 8.5.

2. Select *Type* as *Program Unit* and click on **New**. It displays *New Program Unit* dialog box as displayed in diagram 8.6. Select procedure and specify the name of the procedure and click on OK.

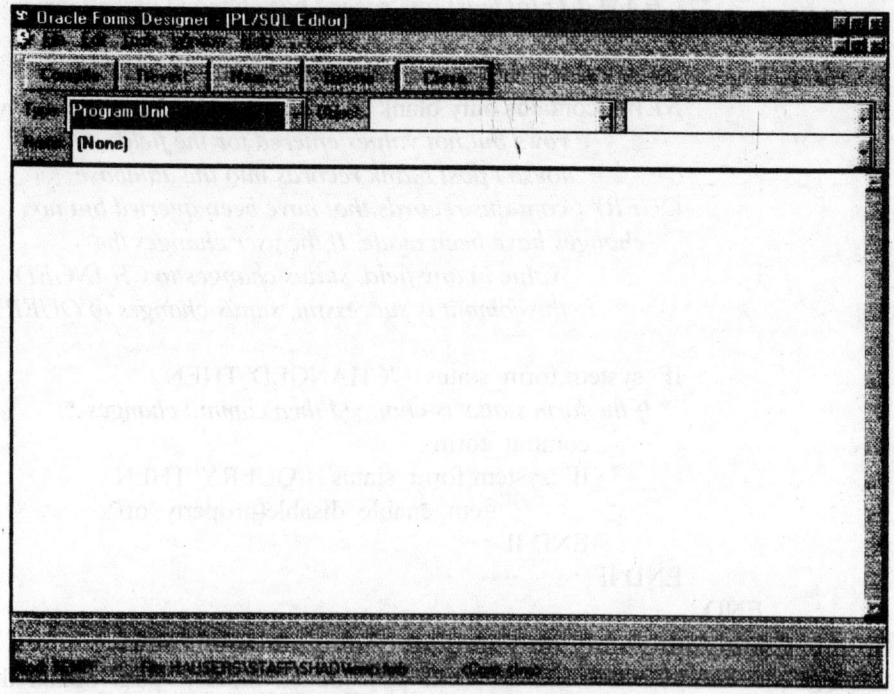

Diagram 8.5 : PL/SQL Editor

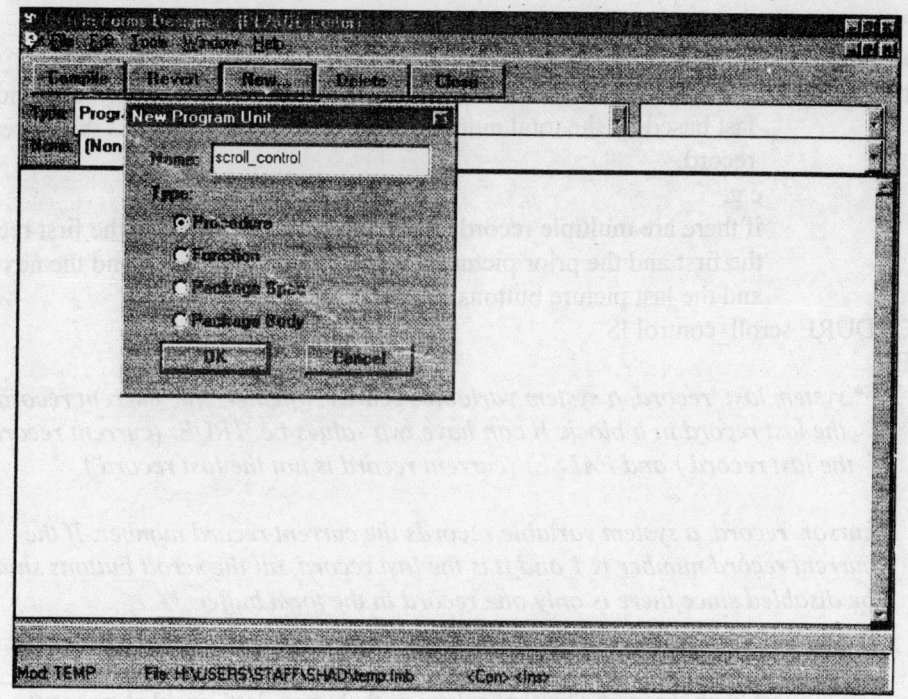

Diagram 8.6 : New Program Unit

3. Specify the procedure text. The *scroll_control* procedure is displayed in diagram 8.7.

```
PROCEDURE scroll_control IS
BEGIN
   PROCEDURE scroll_control IS
BEGIN
      IF :SYSTEM.LAST_RECORD='TRUE' AND :SYSTEM.CURSOR_RECORD='1' THEN
         SET_ITEM_PROPERTY('BUTTON_PALETTE.PB_FIRST',ENABLED,PROPERTY_OFF);
         SET_ITEM_PROPERTY('BUTTON_PALETTE.PB_NEXT',ENABLED,PROPERTY_OFF);
         SET_ITEM_PROPERTY('BUTTON_PALETTE.PB_LAST',ENABLED,PROPERTY_OFF);
         SET_ITEM_PROPERTY('BUTTON_PALETTE.PB_PRIOR',ENABLED,PROPERTY_OFF);
      ELSIF :SYSTEM.LAST_RECORD='TRUE' THEN
         SET_ITEM_PROPERTY('BUTTON_PALETTE.PB_FIRST',ENABLED,PROPERTY_ON);
         SET_ITEM_PROPERTY('BUTTON_PALETTE.PB_NEXT',ENABLED,PROPERTY_OFF);
         SET_ITEM_PROPERTY('BUTTON_PALETTE.PB_LAST',ENABLED,PROPERTY_OFF);
         SET_ITEM_PROPERTY('BUTTON_PALETTE.PB_PRIOR',ENABLED,PROPERTY_ON);
      ELSIF :SYSTEM.CURSOR_RECORD='1' THEN
         SET_ITEM_PROPERTY('BUTTON_PALETTE.PB_FIRST',ENABLED,PROPERTY_OFF);
         SET_ITEM_PROPERTY('BUTTON_PALETTE.PB_NEXT',ENABLED,PROPERTY_ON);
         SET_ITEM_PROPERTY('BUTTON_PALETTE.PB_LAST',ENABLED,PROPERTY_ON);
         SET_ITEM_PROPERTY('BUTTON_PALETTE.PB_PRIOR',ENABLED,PROPERTY_OFF);
```

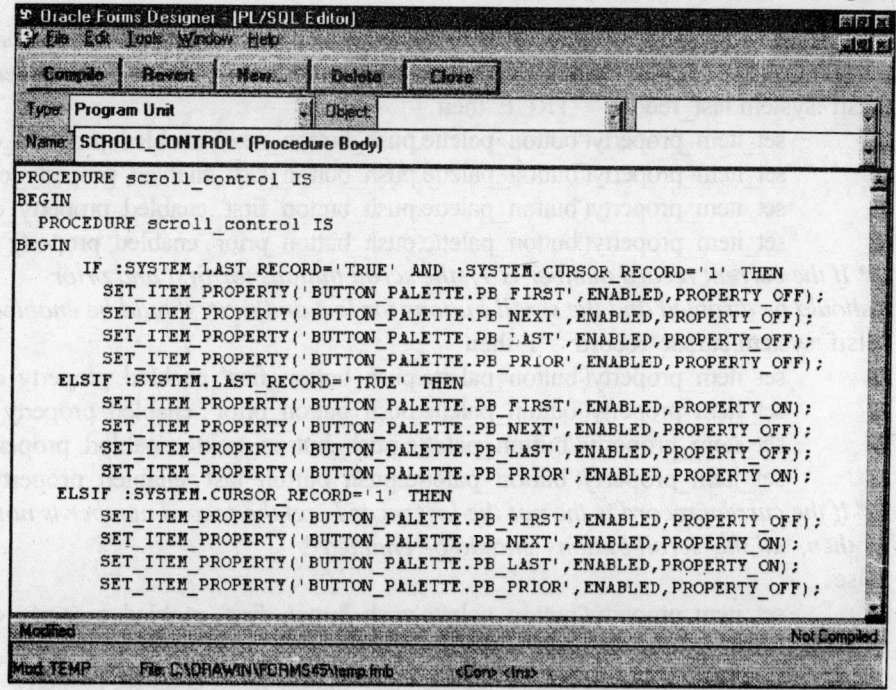

Diagram 8.7 : Writing Procedures

The Procedures are defined below :
Procedure Name : **SCROLL_CONTROL**
Function   : To enable or disable the scroll pushbuttons i.e. first, prior, next and last based on the total number of records on the form and the current record.

e.g.

if there are multiple records and the record pointer is on the first record the first and the prior picture button should be *disabled* and the next and the last picture buttons should be *enabled*.

```
PROCEDURE scroll_control IS
BEGIN
    /* system.last_record, a system variable records whether the current record is
       the last record in a block. It can have two values i.e. TRUE: (current record is
       the last record ) and FALSE: (current record is not the last record )

       cursor_record, a system variable records the current record number. If the
       current record number is 1 and it is the last record, all the scroll buttons should
       be disabled since there is only one record in the form buffer  */
    if :system.last_record = 'TRUE' and   :system.cursor_record = '1' then
        set_item_property('button_palette.push_button_next', enabled, property_off);
        set_item_property('button_palette.push_button_last', enabled, property_off);
        set_item_property('button_palette.push_button_first', enabled, property_off);
        set_item_property('button_palette.push_button_prior', enabled, property_off);

    /* If the current record is the last record,  the scroll buttons for first and prior
     should be enabled and the scroll buttons for last and next  should be disabled */
    elsif :system.last_record = 'TRUE' then
        set_item_property('button_palette.push_button_next', enabled, property_off);
        set_item_property('button_palette.push_button_last', enabled, property_off);
        set_item_property('button_palette.push_button_first', enabled, property_on);
        set_item_property('button_palette.push_button_prior', enabled, property_on);
    /* If the current record number is 1,  the scroll buttons for first and prior
     should be disabled and the scroll buttons for last and next  should be enabled */
    elsif :system.cursor_record = '1' then
        set_item_property('button_palette.push_button_first', enabled, property_off);
        set_item_property('button_palette.push_button_prior', enabled, property_off);
        set_item_property('button_palette.push_button_next', enabled, property_on);
        set_item_property('button_palette.push_button_last', enabled, property_on);
    /* If the current record is the not the last record and the record number is not 1
     then,  all the  scroll buttons  should be enabled */
    else
        set_item_property('button_palette.push_button_first', enabled, property_on);
        set_item_property('button_palette.push_button_prior', enabled, property_on);
        set_item_property('button_palette.push_button_next', enabled, property_on);
        set_item_property('button_palette.push_button_last', enabled, property_on);
    end if ;
END;
```

MASTER FORM   177

Note : The scroll control procedure must fire when the user moves from one record to the other. The change in the record position may be due to insert, retrieve, delete or scrolling. Trigger *When-New-Record-Instance* fires when the system performs insert retrieve, delete or scrolling operations.

Trigger Name	: **WHEN-NEW-RECORD-INSTANCE**	Form	: product_master
Block	: product_master_blk	Item	:
Trigger Level	: Block Level		

Function   : calls procedure scroll_control that enables or disables the scroll
                 pushbuttons i.e. first, prior, next and last based on the total number of
                 records on the form and the current record.
Text   : BEGIN
                    scroll_control ;
                 END ;

Procedure Name : **ITEM_ENABLE_DISABLE**
Function   : To enable the fields so that the contents of the field can be
                  modified or new values can be entered in the add or modify mode. To
                  disable fields so that the contents of the field cannot be modified in
                  view mode.

e.g. programming convention requires :
The primary key field product_no should be *updateable* in data insert mode and *non updateable* in the data modify mode.

```
PROCEDURE item_enable_disable (item_on_off  IN NUMBER) IS
BEGIN
        set_item_property('product_master_blk.product_no', updateable, item_on_off) ;
        set_item_property('product_master_blk.description ', updateable, item_on_off) ;
        set_item_property('product_master_blk.unit_measure', updateable, item_on_off);
        set_item_property('product_master_blk.qty_on_hand', updateable, item_on_off);
        set_item_property('product_master_blk.reorder_lvl', updateable, item_on_off);
        set_item_property('product_master_blk.cost_price ', updateable, item_on_off) ;
        set_item_property('product_master_blk.selling_price', updateable, item_on_off) ;
END;
```

VALIDATIONS

As programmers it is our responsibility to ensure table data integrity. Business decisions are made by managers based on the table data. If the table data is not valid then the business decision being made is going to be erroneous which is likely to cause the company to lose money.

To ensure table data integrity, it is necessary to validate data prior to it being stored in the table. What this really means is via our programming skills we ensure that the data conforms to a set of pre-defined rules before we store the data in a table cell.

These are really business rules and differ from business system to business system.

Not only must data be validated according to business rules but data also needs to be validated according to database input / output rules as well. This is because as programmers we are responsible both for table data integrity and the speed of table data extraction, this is where the input / output part comes in.

Table Data Input / Output Validations :

Rule 1 : One or more than one column of the table is set aside to uniquely identify a record in the table. This column /s must hold data that is *unique* and no cell in that column/s can be left blank. Such a column/s is referred to as primary key column.

In the product_master table, product_no is a primary key. Thus we need to write *When-Validate-Item* Trigger that will display an appropriate error if the product_no is left blank or it is duplicated. This trigger will fire when we navigate from the current item.

Whenever we look at validating the primary key field for unique values, there are two checks to be done . One is to check if the value entered is already present in the table and the other is to check if value entered is already present in the form buffer. The present code explained below ensures that the value entered is not present in the product master table. However the code to check the value in the form buffer is explained using a function in the next hands on.

Trigger Name	: **WHEN-VALIDATE-ITEM**	Form	: product_master
Block	: product_master_blk	Item	: product_no
Trigger Level	: Field Level		
Function	: Check for primary key i.e. product_no should not be left blank nor should it be duplicated.		
Text	: BEGIN		

        if :product_master_blk.product_no is null or
        :product_master_blk.product_no = '' then

        * message is a packaged procedure to display a message */
        message('Product No cannot be left blank');

```
        else
            select product_no into :product_master_blk.product_no
              from product_master
              where product_no = :product_master_blk.product_no;
            message('Product No. cannot be duplicated ');
        end if;

        /* raise form_trigger_failure aborts the trigger and positions the
           cursor on the same field */
        raise form_trigger_failure;
EXCEPTION
        /* when a select statement returns no records it fires an
           exception named no_data_found. In this validation, if the
           select statement retrieves no records, the value entered by the
           user is unique and thus no action has to be taken. */
        when no_data_found then null;
END;
```

Note :
If the column is defined as a primary key at the table level, Oracle Forms 4.5 sets the *Required* attribute to *True*. If the *Required* attribute is set to *True*, Oracle will display an error message if the user tries to leave the field blank. The *When-Validate-Item* will not be fired.

We have incorporated the not null check in the trigger and so we need to set the *Required* attribute to *False*. Select item product_no in the Object Navigator and click on **Tools**, **Properties**. It will display all the properties of product_no. Set the *Required* attribute to *False* as shown in diagram 8.8.

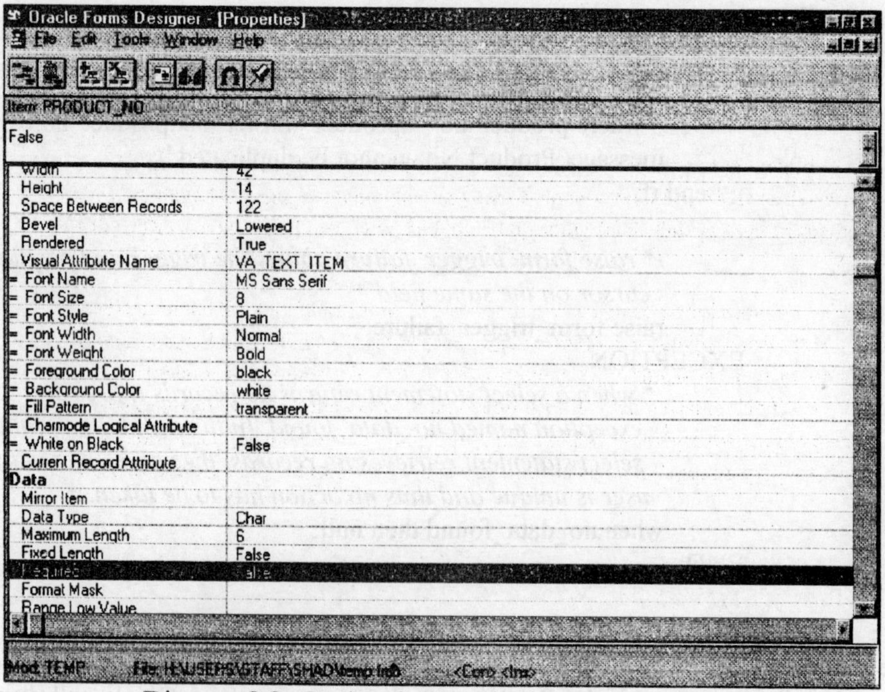

180 COMMERCIAL APPLICATION DEVELOPMENT USING ORACLE 7, DEVELOPER 2000

Diagram 8.8 : Setting the Required property to False.

Rule 2 : The first letter of product_no entered by the user must be 'P'.

The validation to check that the first letter of product_no is 'P', will be performed with the primary key validation. Thus we need to add PL/SQL code in the *When-Validate-Item* trigger :

Trigger Name : **WHEN-VALIDATE-ITEM**   Form : product_master
Block   : product_master_blk   Item   : product_no
Trigger Level : Field Level
Function   : Check for primary key i.e. product_no should not be left blank nor should it be duplicated. The first letter of product_no should be 'P'.
Text   : BEGIN

```
    if :product_master_blk.product_no is null or
       :product_master_blk.product_no = '' then
       message('Product No cannot be left blank');
    else
       if :product_master_blk.product_no not like 'P%'  then
          message('The first letter of Product No must be P.');
       else
         select product_no into :product_master_blk.product_no
            from product_master
            where product_no = :product_master_blk.product_no;
         message('Product No. cannot be duplicated ');
       end if;
    end if;
```

```
                    raise form_trigger_failure;
                EXCEPTION
                    when no_data_found then null;
                END;
```

Rule 3 : Product description and unit_measure should not be left blank.

```
Trigger Name   : WHEN-VALIDATE-ITEM          Form   : product_master
Block          : product_master_blk          Item   : description
Trigger Level  : Field Level
Function       : Check to see that Product description is not left blank.
Text           : BEGIN
                    if :product_master_blk.description is null or
                       :product_master_blk.description = '' then
                        message('Product Description cannot be left blank');
                        raise form_trigger_failure;
                    end if;
                END;
```

```
Trigger Name   : WHEN-VALIDATE-ITEM          Form   : product_master
Block          : product_master_blk          Item   : unit_measure
Trigger Level  : Field Level
Function       : Check to see that unit_measure is not left blank.
Text           : BEGIN
                    if :product_master_blk.unit_measure is null or
                       :product_master_blk.unit_measure = '' then
                        message('Unit of Measure cannot be left blank');
                        raise form_trigger_failure;
                    end if;
                END;
```

Rule 4 : Selling_price and cost_price cannot be 0 and the selling_price should be greater than cost_price.

```
Trigger Name   : WHEN-VALIDATE-ITEM          Form   : product_master
Block          : product_master_blk          Item   : cost_price
Trigger Level  : Field Level
Function       : Check to see that cost_price is not left blank. The value should not be 0
                 and it should be less than the selling price.
Text           : BEGIN
                    if :product_master_blk.cost_price is null then
                        message('cost price cannot be left blank');
                        raise form_trigger_failure;
                    elsif :product_master_blk.cost_price = 0 then
                        message('Cost Price cannot be 0');
                        raise form_trigger_failure;
```

/* Any comparison with a null value always evaluates to False. Thus if the selling price is null the comparison of selling price and cost price will evaluate to false and it will pass the validation test */
           elsif :product_master_blk.cost_price >
                    :product_master_blk.selling_price then
               message(' Cost Price cannot be greater than Selling Price');
               raise form_trigger_failure;
           end if;
        END;

Trigger Name	: **WHEN-VALIDATE-ITEM**	Form	: product_master
Block	: product_master_blk	Item	: selling_price
Trigger Level	: Field Level		
Function	: Check to see that selling_price is not left blank. The value should not be 0 and it should be greater than the cost price		
Text	: BEGIN		

        BEGIN
           if :product_master_blk.selling_price is null then
               message('Selling Price cannot be left blank');
               raise form_trigger_failure;
           elsif :product_master_blk.selling_price = 0 then
               message('Selling Price cannot be 0');
               raise form_trigger_failure;
           /* Any comparison with a null value always evaluates to False. Thus if the cost price is null the comparison of selling price and cost price will evaluate to false and it will pass the validation test */
           elsif :product_master_blk.cost_price >
                    :product_master_blk.selling_price then
               message(' Selling Price cannot be less than Cost Price');
               raise form_trigger_failure;
           end if;
        END;

Setting the default value to 0 :

qty_on_hand column in the product_master table, shows the balance quantity in the stock. The default value of qty_on_hand must be 0.

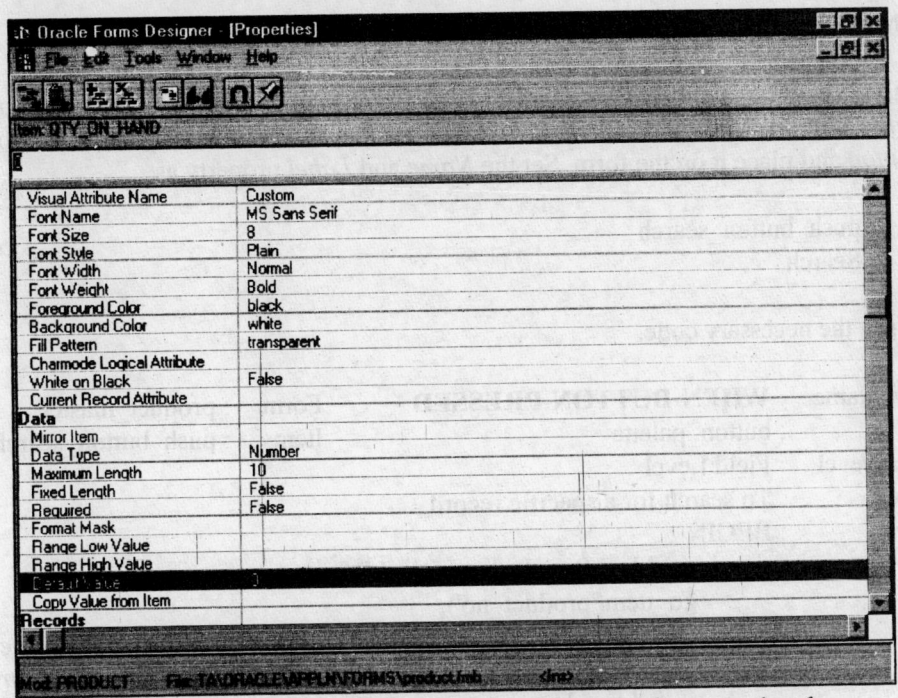

Diagram 8.9 : Changing the item type property of qyt_on_hand

Open the property sheet of qty_on_hand field and set the *default value* property to *0* as shown in diagram 8.9. Similarly, set the default value of Reorder_lvl to 0.

INCLUDING SEARCH FUNCTION IN THE MASTER FORM

To modify the form to include search function that searches a record to match the product_no entered by the user.

1. Check to see that the *Query Allowed* property for the field product_no is *True*.

2. Right click on button_palette block. It displays a popup menu. Click on *Layout Editor*. It displays the form layout. Click on the toolbox and select icon labeled *button* and place it on the form. Set the *Name* and *Label* property as

   Name : push_button_search
   Label : Search

3. Write the necessary code.

   Trigger Name : **WHEN-BUTTON-PRESSED**   Form : product_master
   Block   : button_palette   Item : push_button_search
   Trigger Level : Field Level
   Function   : To search for a specific record.
   Text   : BEGIN
           go_block('product_master_blk');
           go_item('product_no');
           /* enter query function flushes the current block and puts the form in the query mode. The user can enter the value in any field and execute a query. The query will use the values entered by the user in the where clause */
           enter_query;
       END;

9. PROPERTY CLASS AND VISUAL ATTRIBUTES

MAINTAINING STANDARDS IN FORMS
Now that we have created a Master form (i.e. one form attached to a single table) let us have a look at the facilities that Oracle Forms Tool offers us to help maintain standards across all our commercial applications.

Each form in our commercial application should look and behave alike irrespective of what data is being manipulated. This approach will help users of the commercial application to get quickly accustomed to how the forms work.

Standards are easy to apply across a commercial application because Oracle Forms Tool offers us an Object Oriented Programming System. Using any OOPS based system the facilities offered to maintain standards across entire commercial applications are simplified to a very large extent.

Standards In A Commercial Application :
To standardize all the objects on data entry forms would generally require the programmer to ensure that all the Aesthetic (Visual) and Data Control properties of each object on each data entry form are loaded with the same values.

A very simple example, would be that all the *data entry fields*, on the form must have the very same font type, font size, font weight assigned to them in addition to an appropriate background and foreground color.

This sort of standard is normally done by the forms create tool itself. There is a standard default *font type, font size and font weight* along with a default *foreground* and *background* color set by the forms create tool.

Should for any reason this require to be changed then the programmer must ensure that all the data entry fields on each and every form are changed as well. This maintains standards across the commercial application. This will be an incredibly tedious job generally leading to a drop in standards.

To help largely overcome this situation, Oracle Forms Tool offers us several simple but exceedingly effective methods. The correct use of these methods help programmers maintain standards right across the commercial application being developed.

Setting Standards in Oracle Forms :
Each data aware or data control object used in the forms, has an associated property sheet. This property sheet has a list of properties which either hold default values or NULL values.

Loading an appropriate value into a specific property on the object's property sheet, will cause the object to visually look different or change the way the object behaves when it handles data.

The simplest approach to apply standards across a commercial application, would be to create a User Defined property sheet and attach it to objects where required. The object would then take its visual and data handling properties from the user defined property sheet. This feature of Oracle is called *Property class inheritance*.

If the user defined property sheet, lists properties less than the default properties of the object, then for all the properties not listed in the user defined property sheet the object would be set to their default value obtained from the default property class.

PROPERTY CLASS

Property class inheritance is a powerful feature that allows you to quickly define objects that confirm to your own interface and functionality standards.

A *Property Class* is a named object that contains a list of properties and their settings.

Property classes allows you to make global changes to applications quickly. By simply changing the definition of a property class, you can change the definition of all objects that inherit properties from that class.

Once you create a property class you can base other objects on it. An object based on a property class can inherit the setting of any property in the class that makes sense for that object.

There can be any number of properties in a property class, and the properties in a class can apply to different types of objects.

Example :
You might define separate property classes for enterable items, required Items, and read-only items. When you want to change the appearance and functionality of all such items in an application, you need only update the properties in the appropriate class.

A property class might contain some properties that are common to all types of items, some that apply only to text items, and some that apply only to check boxes.

When you base an object on a property class, you have complete control over which properties the object should inherit from the class, and which should be overridden locally.

A property class can itself be based on a property class, to provide multiple levels of property inheritance.

Example :
You might create a BASE_FIELD class that contains standard property settings for all text items in your application, such as Font Name, Font Size, Height, etc., and a DATE_FIELD class for text items that display date values.

The DATE_FIELD class could inherit the properties defined for all items in the BASE_FIELD class, plus properties specific to date fields, such as Data Type and Format Mask.

Property classes are separate objects, and, as such, can be copied between modules as needed. Perhaps more importantly, property classes can be referenced in any number of modules.(refer to REFERENCING OBJECTS IN OTHER MODULES)

Creating Property Class object:
To create a user defined property sheet we have to first create a user defined *Property Class* object which will belong either to a form or a menu module. In the Object Navigator, property classes appear under the Property Classes node in the appropriate module.

There are two ways to create a property class.
- Create a new property class in the Object Navigator and then add properties to it
- Create a property class from an existing object's properties.

a) CREATING A PROPERTY CLASS IN THE OBJECT NAVIGATOR:
   1. In the Object Navigator, position the cursor on the Property Classes node and choose **Navigator, Create**. A property class object with a default name is inserted under the node.

   2. The new property class does not yet contain any properties. This object will have a property sheet having only two properties by default.
      - The Property *Name*
      - The Property *Class*.

   In the Properties window, add properties to the class as desired.

b) CREATING A PROPERTY CLASS IN THE PROPERTIES WINDOW:
   1. In the Object Navigator or layout editor, select one or more objects so that the Properties window displays the properties (and settings) that you want to be in the property class.

   2. In the Properties window, click the Property Class button on the toolbar. A messagebox is displayed to confirm the name of the class being created.

   3. The new property class includes all of the properties of the selected object. If certain properties of the selected object are not required in the Property Class, they can be deleted from the Property Class.

Example :
You might create a property class from the definition of an existing text item so you could apply the same font and height characteristics to other text items. However, the new property class would also contain the X Position and Y Position properties. Since these properties define display coordinates that would almost always need to be overridden for

each text item you base on the class, you might want to remove them from the class definition.

To view the definition of a property class i.e., the properties it contains, select the property class in the Object Navigator and see its properties displayed in the Properties palette. (If necessary, expand the Property Classes node by clicking the +.)

To this property sheet we can assign specific properties and assign values for those properties.

1. All that has to be done now is to assign this property class to an object on a data entry form. This will determine how the object will look visually and / or how it will handle data, if data aware. Simply by assigning the user defined property class to required objects on all data entry forms, standards will be applied across the commercial application. Should the standards ever require tweaking, making the change in the user defined property class will cause the new standard to be applied across the entire commercial application.

Oracle Forms Tool allows visual attributes of data aware objects to be set independent of the data handling attributes. This goes a long way in making it easy for the programmer to set standards in aesthetics on the data entry form which really are independent of the setting of data aware attributes.

An exercise that helps us deal with both the above i.e. the setting of aesthetics via the setting of visual attributes and the setting of data handling via assigning a user defined property class to the object of our choice will strongly reinforce our concept of the property class object and its associated property sheet.

PROPERTY CLASS AND VISUAL ATTRIBUTES **189**

Focus :

Create a property class object, with properties mentioned below and attach it to all the push buttons in the *product_master* form.

Name	: PClass_Button
Class	:
Item Type	: Button
Canvas	: Product_Master_Can
Displayed	: True
Width	: 23
Height	: 23
Enabled	: True
Navigable	: True
Mouse Navigate	: True
Iconic	: True

Solution :

1. Open the *product_master* form, if it is not open and connect to the database.

2. In the Object Navigator, position the cursor on the *Property Classes* node and choose **Navigator, Create**. A property class object with a default name is inserted under the node.

3. Open the property sheet of the newly created Property Class object and a property sheet as shown in the diagram 9.1 will open up. Change the name of the object to *PClass_Button*.

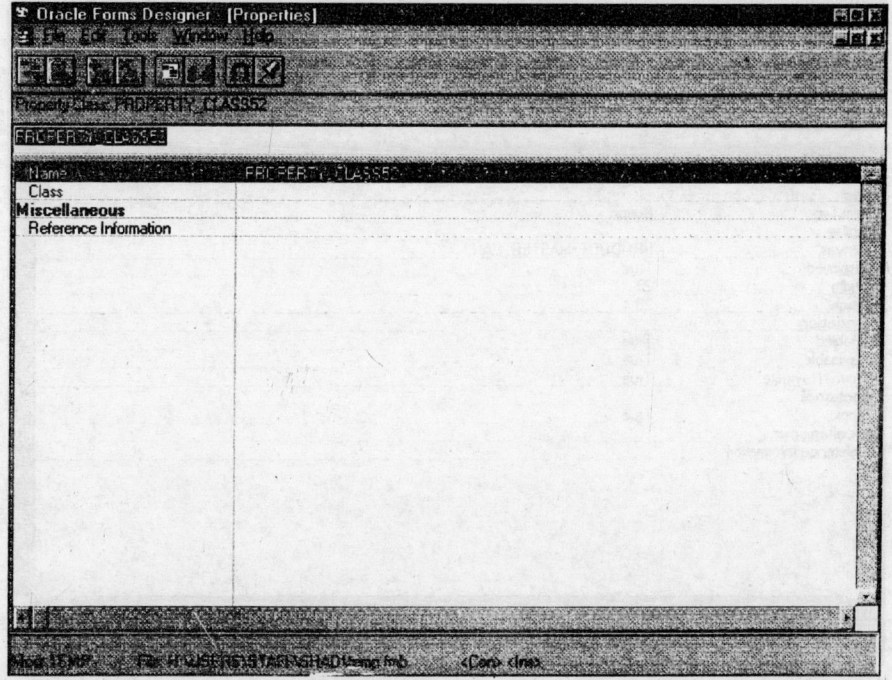

Diagram 9.1 : Property Sheet of newly created Property Class object

4. To add properties to the property class object, click on the **Add Property** button on the toolbar. A list of properties will pop up as shown in the diagram 9.2.

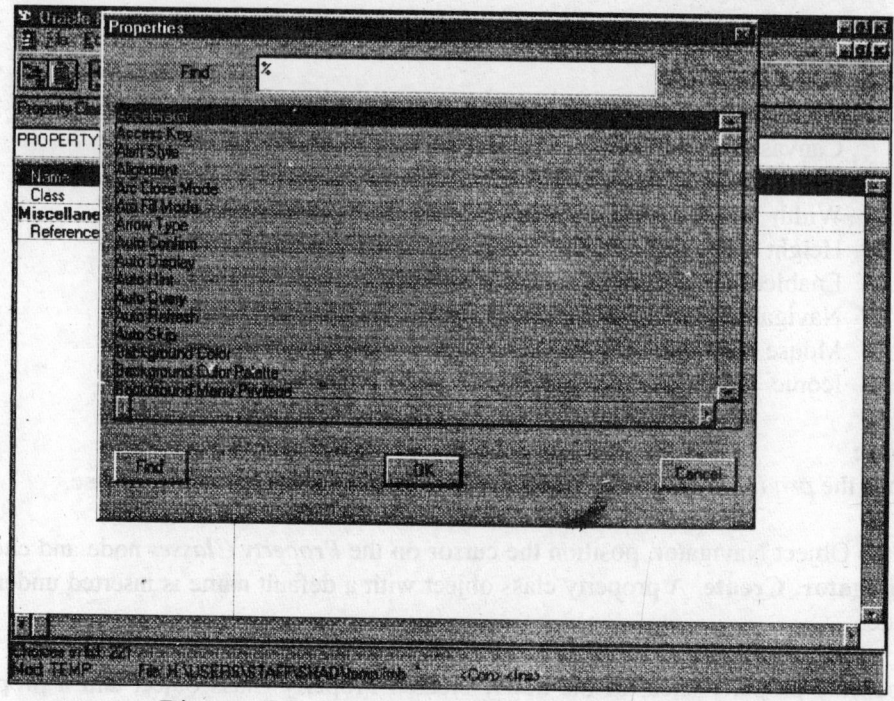

Diagram 9.2 : Adding properties in the property class

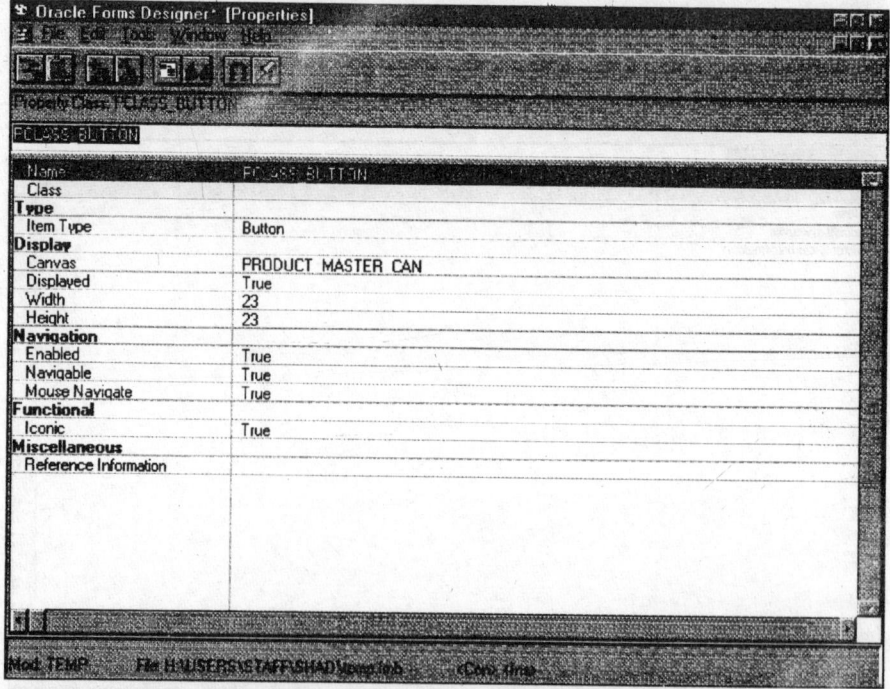

Diagram 9.3 : Property sheet after, adding required properties

PROPERTY CLASS AND VISUAL ATTRIBUTES 191

5. Select *Canvas* property from the list and click on the OK button. The Canvas property will be added to the properties of the property class object. Change the Canvas property value to *product_master_can* as given in the problem statement.

6. Similarly go on adding other properties and change each of their values as listed above. The final screen will be displayed as shown in the diagram 9.3.

7. To attach *PClass_Button* object to the buttons, select push_button_search button and open its property sheet.

8. Select and change the *Class* property of the button to *PClass_Button* using the list available. Change the *Icon Name* property to *view*.

9. Similarly change the *Class* property for the buttons listed below to *PClass_Button* and *Icon Name* property to as listed below :

Button Name	Icon Name
push_button_last	last
push_button_next	next
push_button_prior	prior
push_button_first	first
push_button_save	save
push_button_exit	close
push_button_delete	trash
push_button_modify	modify
push_button_view	retrieve
push_button_add	add
puss_button_search	search

Note :
  The icon files as specified in the *Icon Name* property must exist in the sub-directory specified in TK21_ICON.(refer to Changing the push buttons to iconic buttons)

10. Open the Layout Editor and you will find the push buttons changed to the picture buttons. Add labels to identify each of the buttons and align them as shown in the diagram 9.4.

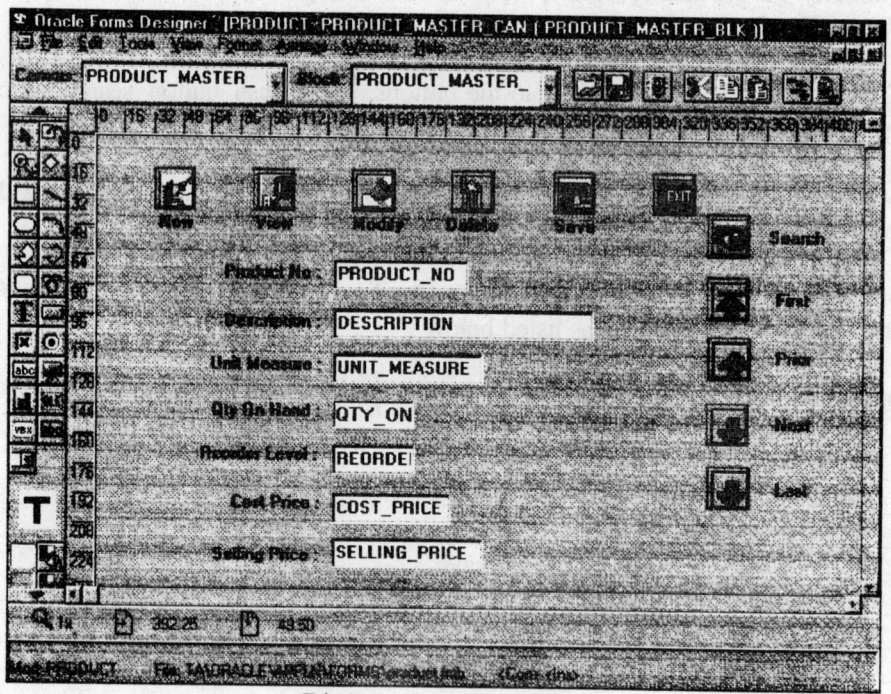

192 COMMERCIAL APPLICATION DEVELOPMENT USING ORACLE 7, DEVELOPER 2000

Diagram 9.4 : Final Layout

VISUAL ATTRIBUTES

Visual Attributes are the font, color and pattern properties that you set for form and menu objects that appear in your application's interface. Visual attributes include the following properties :

Color and pattern properties   : Foreground Color, Background Color, Fill Pattern, White on Black

Font properties   : Font Name, Font Size, Font Style, Font Width, Font Weight

Named Visual Attributes are similar to Property classes, the differences are :
1. Named Visual Attributes define only font, color and pattern attributes whereas property classes can contain these and any other properties.

2. You can change the appearance of objects at runtime by changing the named visual attribute programmatically whereas property class assignment cannot be changed programmatically.

3. When an object is inherited from both a property class and a named visual attribute, the named visual attribute settings take precedence, and any visual attribute properties in the property class are ignored.

Setting the visual attributes of an object :
There are several ways to set the visual attributes of objects in Oracle Forms Designer :
1. In the Properties window, set the Visual Attribute Name property as desired, then set the individual attributes (Font Name, Foreground Color, etc.) to the desired settings.

2. In the Layout Editor, select an item or a canvas and then choose the desired font, color, and pattern attributes from the Font dialog and Fill Color and Text Color palettes.

3. Define a named visual attribute object with the appropriate font, color, and pattern settings and then apply it to one or more objects in the same module. You can programmatically change an object's named visual attribute setting to change the font, color, and pattern of the object at runtime.

4. Create a property class that includes visual attribute properties and then base objects on it that inherit those properties.

Every interface object has a Visual Attribute Name property that determines how the object's individual visual attribute settings (Font Size, Foreground Color, etc.) are derived. The Visual Attribute Name property can be set to Default, Custom, or the name of a named visual attribute defined in the same module.

DEFAULT VISUAL ATTRIBUTES :

Setting the *Visual Attribute Name* property to *Default* specifies that that the object should be displayed with default color, pattern, and font settings. When Visual Attribute Name is set to Default, the individual attribute settings reflect the current system defaults. The actual settings are determined by a combination of factors, including the type of object, the resource file in use, and the window manager.

CUSTOM VISUAL ATTRIBUTES :

Setting the *Visual Attribute Name* property to *Custom* specifies that the object should be displayed with the attribute settings that you specify for the object explicitly at design time, either in the Properties window (by setting specific visual attribute properties) or in the Layout Editor (by selecting fonts, colors and patterns from menus and palettes).

NAMED VISUAL ATTRIBUTES :

Setting the *Visual Attribute Name* property to a named visual attribute defined in the same module specifies that the object should use the attribute settings defined in a *Named Visual Attribute*.

A *Named Visual Attribute* is a separate object in a form or menu module that defines a collection of visual attribute properties. Once you create a named visual attribute, you can apply it to any object in the same module. This way you can standardize the way all objects look in the application. To change any visual property, you only need to make a change only to the visual attribute object for the change to reflect it throughout the application.

Creating Named Visual Attributes and applying the same on the objects :

A named visual attribute is a separate object that defines a set of visual attribute settings. You can create named visual attributes in form and menu modules, and then apply them to objects in modules as desired.

When you apply a named visual attribute to an object, only those attributes that make sense for that object take effect.

CREATING A NAMED VISUAL ATTRIBUTE:

1. In the Object Navigator, position the cursor on the *Visual Attributes* node and choose **N**avigator, C**r**eate. Oracle Forms inserts a new named visual attribute.

2. In the Properties window, set the font, color, and pattern attributes of the named visual attribute as desired.

APPLYING A NAMED VISUAL ATTRIBUTE TO AN OBJECT :

1. In the Object Navigator or the Layout editor, select the desired object.

2. In the Properties window, set the *Visual Attribute Name* property to the name of the desired visual attribute object.

PROPERTY CLASS AND VISUAL ATTRIBUTES **195**

Note : When you explicitly set the visual attributes of an object in the Layout Editor or the Properties window, Oracle Forms converts the object's Visual Attribute Name setting to *Custom*, and the association with the named visual attribute is lost.

Focus :
Create a visual attribute, with properties mentioned below and attach it to the *product_no* text object, in the *product_master_blk* block, in the *product_master* form to make the primary key field look different than the other fields.

Name	: VA_TEXT_ITEM
Class	:
Font Name	: MS Sans Serif
Font Size	: 8
Font Style	: Plain
Font Width	: Normal
Font Weight	: Bold
Foreground Color	: black
Background Color	: white
Fill Pattern	: transparent
Charmode Logical Attribute	:
White On Black	: False
Reference Information	:

Solution :
1. Open the *product_master* form, if it is not open and connect to the database.

2. In the Object Navigator, position the cursor on the *Visual Attributes* node and choose **N**avigator, C**r**eate. Oracle Forms inserts a new named visual attribute.

3. In the properties window of the visual attribute object, set the font, color, and pattern attributes as listed above. The final screen will be as shown in the diagram 9.5.

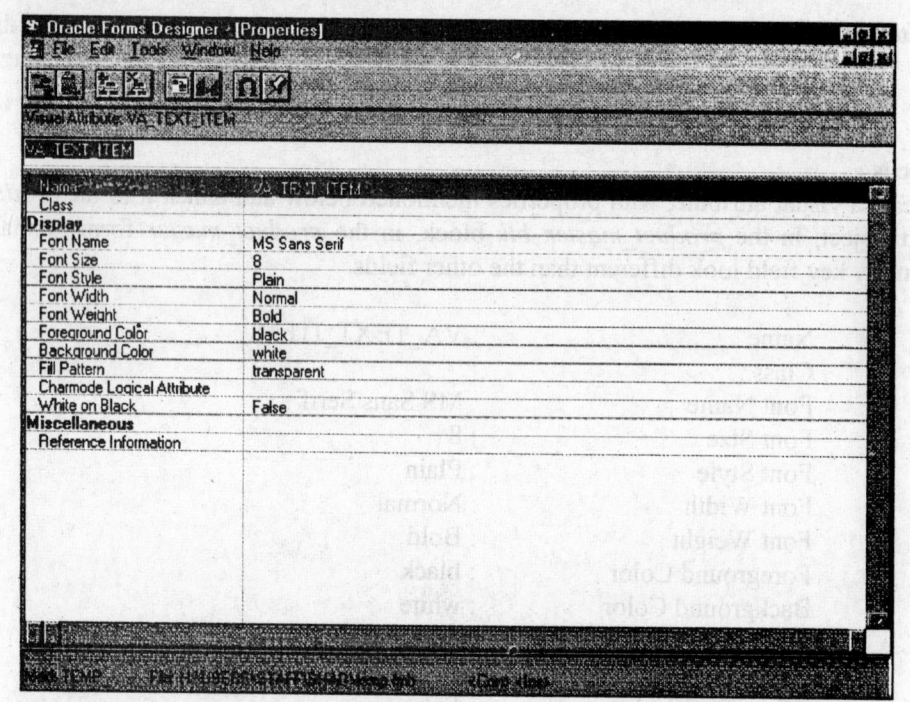

Diagram 9.5 : Adding properties in the visual attribute object

3. In the Object Navigator or the Layout editor, select the *product_no* text object and open its property sheet. Set the *Visual Attribute Name* property to the name of the visual attribute object created i.e. *VA_Text_Item*.

4. Similarly change the *Visual Attribute Name* property for all the text items in the product_master_blk to *VA_Text_Item*.

5. Save the form and open the Layout Editor to see the effect of the changes made. You will find the font and color attribute of the *product_no* text object changed to that of the visual attribute object as shown in the diagram 9.6.

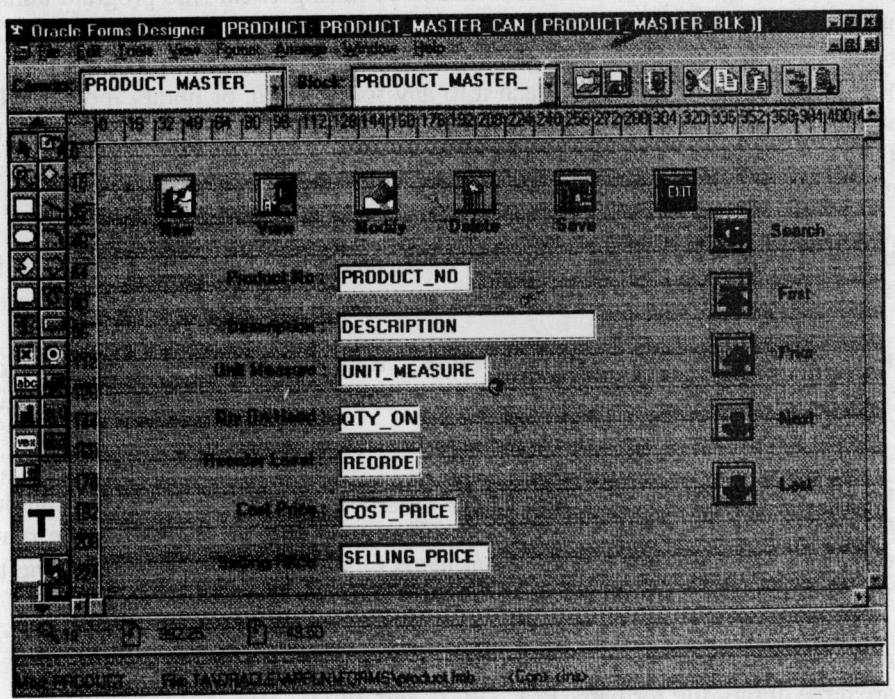

Diagram 9.6 : Final Layout

10. LIBRARIES AND ALERTS

A library is a collection of subprograms, including user-named procedures, functions and packages. Libraries provide a convenient means of storing client-side program units and sharing them among multiple applications.

Once you create a library, you can attach it to any form, menu, or library module. Then, you can call the library program units from triggers, menu item commands, and user-named routines you write in the form, menu, or library module to which you have attached the library.

The same library can be attached to multiple forms and menus. Conversely, a single form or menu can have more than one attached library.

Libraries can also be attached to other libraries. When a library is attached to another library, program units in the first library can be referenced by program units in the second library.

Libraries support dynamic loading i.e. library program units are loaded into a computers memory only when an application needs it. This can significantly reduce the runtime memory requirements of an application, but tends to slow an application. Thus the trade off is between speed vs memory.

LIBRARY FILE FORMATS
There are three library file formats, .PLL, .PLX, and .PLD.

1. **.PLL**
   A library .PLL file contains both library source code and the compiled, platform-specific p-code (executable code). The .PLL file is created or updated when you save your library module. In addition, when you save your library module, the changes are reflected in each module to which the library is attached.

2. **.PLX**
   A library .PLX file is a platform-specific executable that contains no source. When you are ready to deploy your application, you will probably want to generate a version of your library that contains only the compiled p-code, without any source. A .PLX file can only be generated from the command line.

   Note: When you attach a library to a module in the Designer, you attach the .PLL version of the library. At runtime, Oracle Forms looks for a .PLX file by that name in the default search paths. If no .PLX file is present, Oracle Forms looks for the .PLL file by that name.

3. **.PLD**
   The .PLD file is a text format file, and can be used for technical documentation of the library files.

CREATING AND ATTACHING A LIBRARY TO A MODULE

You create a library by opening, defining, compiling, and saving a library module.

One can define the following types of PL/SQL subprograms in a library :

- Procedures
- Functions
- Package Specifications
- Package Bodies

Creating a Library :
1. In the Navigator, create a library module. To create a library, choose **File, New, Library** or select the libraries node and then click on **Create**.

Note : You cannot change the name of a library module by editing it in the Navigator, as you can with forms and menus. Instead, the library name is updated automatically when you save the library.

2. To create a program unit, expand the desired library node, select the *Program Units* node, and then click **Navigator, Create**. The *New Program Unit* dialog appears.

3. Specify the *Program Unit Name* and its *Type* (either Procedure, Function, Package Spec, or Package Body). Click on OK. The *PL/SQL* Editor is displayed.

4. In the PL/SQL Editor, define your program unit and then click on **Compile** to compile and apply your modifications. click on **Close** to close the editor.

Note: Because Oracle Forms cannot execute uncompiled program units at runtime, you must compile your library program units at design time.

5. Choose **File, Compile** to compile any uncompiled library program units, or click on **File, Compile All** to compile all library program units.

6. Click on **File, Save** to save the library module to a file or to the database.

Attaching a Library to Another Module :
After you save a library module to the file system or database, you can attach it to a form, menu, or library module.

Note: Attached libraries are read-only. You cannot edit an attached library; you can only reference the program units within it. To edit a library module, open the library module in the Object Navigator and use the PL/SQL Editor to edit program units.

1. In the Object Navigator, open the desired form, menu, or library module by clicking on **File, Open** and then specify the module type to open.

Note: When you attach a library to a module in the Designer, you attach the .PLL version of the library. At runtime, Oracle Forms looks for a .PLX file by that name in the default search paths. If no .PLX file is present, Oracle Forms looks for the .PLL file by that name.

2. Expand the module and then select the **Attached Libraries** node. Click on **Navigator**, **C**r**eate** to attach a library. The Attach dialog appears as shown in diagram 10.1.

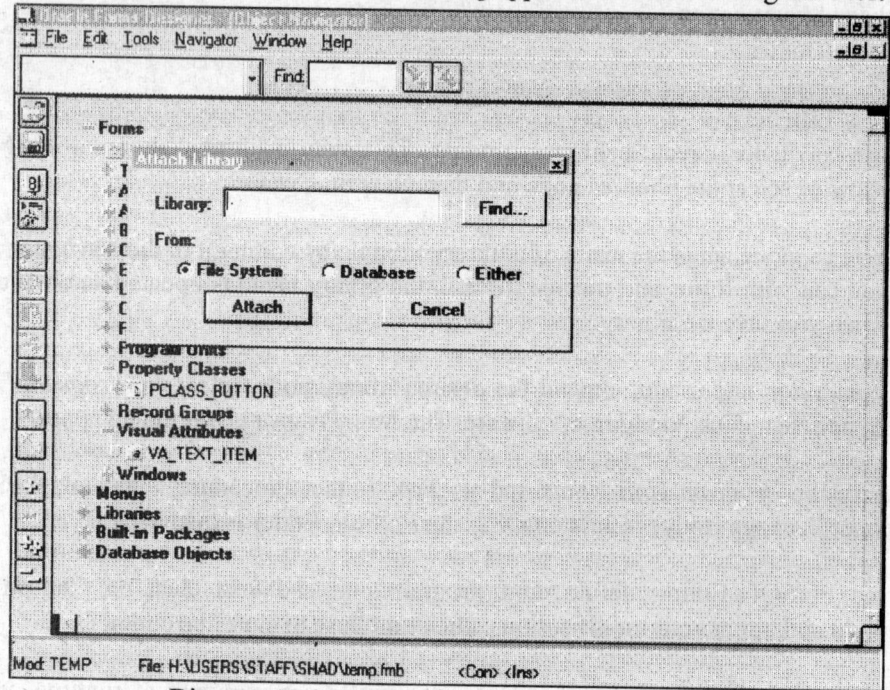

Diagram 10.1 : Attach Library Dialog Box

The Attach dialog includes the following :

Library: The name of the library you want to attach to the current module.

Find : Invokes the File or Database dialog allowing you to specify the library file you want to attach.

From : Specifies where Oracle Forms should look for the library file specified in the Library field. Choose File System or Database if you want Oracle Forms to look for the library in one or the other. Choose Either if you want Oracle Forms to look in both the file system and the database for the indicated library. This setting overrides the Module Access design option.

Order : Applies only when at least one library is already attached to the current module. Choose *Before* or *After* to specify whether you want the attached library to be inserted before or after the other libraries already attached to the module.

When a program unit i.e. procedure / function is called, Oracle Forms looks for the program unit under the *program unit* node of the current form. If the program unit is not found, it searches in the attached libraries.

If there are multiple libraries attached to a form, when resolving a procedure call at runtime, Oracle Forms searches the attached libraries in the order in which they are sequenced.

Attach :   Attaches the library named in the Library field to the current module and closes the dialog.

Cancel   Closes the dialog without attaching a library.

3. Specify the name of the library to attach as shown in diagram 10.2.

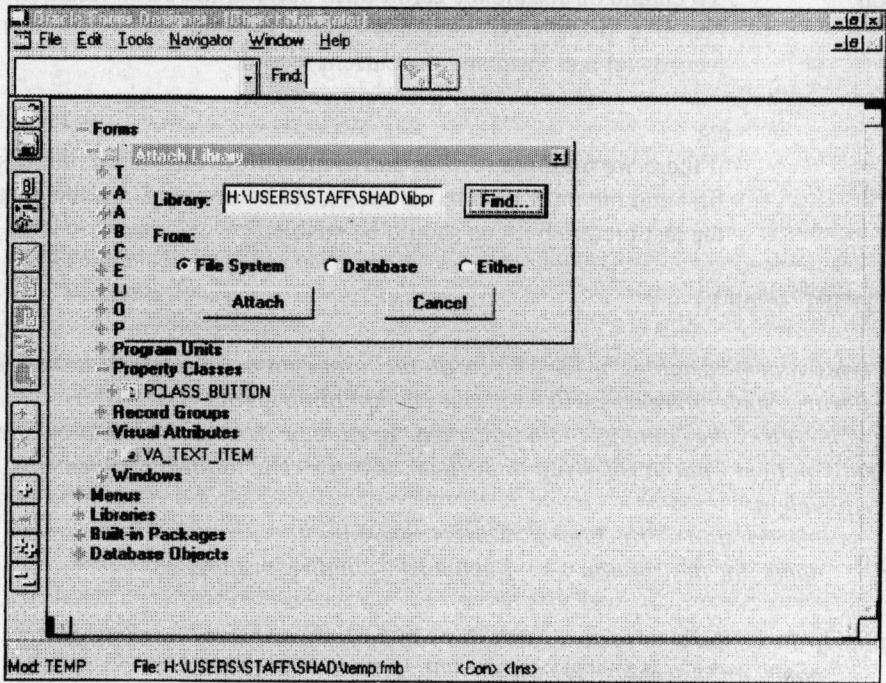

Diagram 10.2 : Specifying the library path

4. Save the active form or menu module to incorporate the library attachment in the module definition. Generate and run the form to check the library attachment.

HANDS ON

Create the *scroll_control* procedure in the new library called *libproc*. Attach this library to the form **product_master** and call the procedure in the **product_master** form.

Solution :
1. Create a new library as explained in step 1 of CREATE A NEW LIBRARY.

2. In the *Program Unit* dialog box of step2 and step3 select the procedure option and type the name of the procedure as *scroll_control*. In the PL/SQL editor of the scroll_control procedure type the following procedure.

The Procedures is defined below :

Procedure Name : **SCROLL**
Function : To enable or disable the scroll push buttons and scroll menu items i.e. first, prior, next and last based on the total number of records on the form and the current record.

e.g.
if there are multiple records and the record pointer is on the first the first and the prior picture button should be disabled and the next and the last picture buttons should be enabled.

```
PROCEDURE scroll IS
BEGIN
    /* Forms system variables or the objects on the form cannot be referenced directly in
    the library. Such references will result into compilation errors. The NAME_IN
    function returns the contents of an indicated variable or item. It is used to get the
    value of an item without referring to the item directly. The following statements
    are equivalent:
            :description = 'Keyboard' -- direct reference
            name_in('description') = ' Keyboard ' -- indirect reference

    Similarly the contents of system variables can be referenced indirectly as follows :
            name_in('system.last_record') = 'TRUE' */

    /* Setting the enabled property to false for all the buttons if there is only one
    record. */
    if name_in('system.last_record') = 'TRUE' and name_in('system.cursor_record') = '1' then
        set_item_property('button_palette.push_button_next', enabled, property_off);
        set_item_property('button_palette.push_button_last', enabled, property_off);
        set_item_property('button_palette.push_button_first', enabled, property_off);
        set_item_property('button_palette.push_button_prior', enabled, property_off);
```

```
   * Setting the enabled property for the buttons last and next to false and first and
     prior to True if focus is on the last record. */
   elsif name_in( 'system.last_record' ) = 'TRUE' then
       set_item_property('button_palette.push_button_next', enabled, property_off);
       set_item_property('button_palette.push_button_last', enabled, property_off);
       set_item_property('button_palette.push_button_first', enabled, property_on);
       set_item_property('button_palette.push_button_prior', enabled, property_on);

   /* Setting the enabled property for the buttons last and next to True and first and
      prior to False if focus is on the first record. */
   elsif name_in('system.cursor_record') = '1' then
       set_item_property('button_palette.push_button_first', enabled, property_off);
       set_item_property('button_palette.push_button_prior', enabled, property_off);
       set_item_property('button_palette.push_button_last', enabled, property_on);
       set_item_property('button_palette.push_button_next', enabled, property_on);
   else
       /* Setting the enabled property for all the buttons to True if focus is not on the
          first or the last record. */
       set_item_property('button_palette.push_button_next', enabled, property_on);
       set_item_property('button_palette.push_button_prior', enabled, property_on);
       set_item_property('button_palette.push_button_last', enabled, property_on);
       set_item_property('button_palette.push_button_first', enabled, property_on);
       end if ;
END;
```

3. Compile the *scroll_control* procedure and save the library with the file name *libproc.pll*

4. Attach the library *libproc* to the forms **product_master** as explained in the topic ATTACHING A LIBRARY MODULE.

5. Use the *scroll_control* procedure where required in the two forms. Generate and run the two forms to check the *scroll_control* procedure in two forms by scrolling through the records.

HANDS ON

Create the *item_enable_disable* procedure in the *libproc* library. Call the procedure in the **product_master** form.

Procedure Name : **ITEM_ENABLE_DISABLE**
Function : To enable the fields so that the contents of the field can be modified or new values can be entered. To disable fields so that the contents of the field cannot be modified.

e.g. programming convention requires :
The primary key field should be *enabled* in data insert mode and *disabled* in the data modify mode.

```
PROCEDURE ITEM_ENABLE_DISABLE( blk_name IN char, item_on_off
IN NUMBER) IS
        nxt_itemname varchar2(70);

BEGIN
    /* get_block_property is a function that gets the value of specified block property. The
       First_Item property holds the name of the first enterable item in the block. */
    nxt_itemname := blk_name||'.'|| get_block_property(blk_name, first_item);

    /* set a loop that gets the next navigation item and sets the updateable property to
       true or false. Next Navigation Item holds the name of the next navigational item in
       the block */
    loop
      set_item_property(nxt_itemname, updateable, item_on_off);
          nxt_itemname := blk_name||'.'||get_item_property(nxt_itemname,next_navigation_item);
       /* if the Next Navigation Item is the first item, exit the loop. */
          if (blk_name||'.'|| get_block_property(blk_name,first_item)) = nxt_itemname THEN
             exit;
          end if;
    end loop;
END;
```

Note :

Procedure *item_enable_disable* has been generalized so that it can be used in any form. It takes in two parameters i.e. the *Name of the Block* and the *Value for the property*. The call to the *item_enable_disable* procedure will change as follows :

item_enable_disable (block name , property_value)

The call to the item_enable_disable will have to be changed in all the triggers in the *product_master* form.

e.g.
item_enable_disable is called in the When-Button-Pressed Event of *push_button_add*. It make all the fields in the product_master_blk updateable.

The call to this function will be as follows :

item_enable_disable ('product_master_blk' , property_on)

ALERTS

When processing errors while programming, it is necessary to communicate with the user to inform the user that an error has occurred e.g. if the user has entered the cost price of a product as 0, then the system must display an error message as 'Cost Price cannot be 0'.

Often programmers offer choice to the user on how to actually process an event e.g. if the user clicks on the delete button the system must ask for confirmation to delete the current record. If the user clicks on the 'Yes' or 'OK' button the record must be deleted.

Showing an error message and offering different choices is done in Oracle Forms Designer using an object called **Alert**.

An alert is a modal window that displays a message notifying the operator of some application condition. Use alerts to advise operators of unusual situations or to warn operators who are about to perform an action that might have undesirable or unexpected consequences.

There are three styles of alerts: **Stop, Caution, and Note**. Each style denotes a different level of message severity. Message severity is represented visually by a unique icon that is displayed in a alert window.

Oracle Forms has many built-in alerts that display pre-defined messages. You can also create your own custom alerts that display in response to application-specific events.

When an event occurs that causes an alert to display, the operator must respond to the alert's message by selecting one of the predefined alert buttons. Selecting any button immediately dismisses the alert and passing control back to the program that called it.

When you create an alert, you need only specify basic information such as the message you want the alert to display and the text labels for the alert buttons.

Once you create an alert, you must write a trigger or user-named routine to display the alert in response to a particular event. In addition, the action that each button initiates is determined by the PL/SQL code you write.

An Alert can be displayed by the SHOW_ALERT function. The SHOW_ALERT function returns alert_button1, alert_button2 or alert_button3 based on the button clicked by the user. This return value can be used to determine the action that has to be taken.

Creating an Alert :
1. In the Object Navigator, create an alert object by selecting the Alerts node and then choose **Navigator, C_r_eate**.

2. In the Properties window, set the **Alert Style** property to the style that corresponds to the severity of your message: either Stop, Caution, or Note as shown in diagram 1. At

206 COMMERCIAL APPLICATION DEVELOPMENT USING ORACLE 7, DEVELOPER 2000

runtime, an icon representing the style you select displays next to the message in the alert window.

3. Set the **Message** property by entering the message you want the alert to display at runtime as shown in diagram 10.3. You can enter up to 200 characters.

4. Define one or more buttons for the alert by entering a text label in the Button 1, Button 2, and Button 3 fields. (The default text labels are "OK" for Button 1 and "Cancel" for Button 2.)

> **Note :**
> **At least one button must have a label. Buttons that do not have labels are not displayed. Buttons are displayed in the alert in the order that they appear in the Properties window. That is, Button 2 is displayed to the right of Button 1, and so on.**

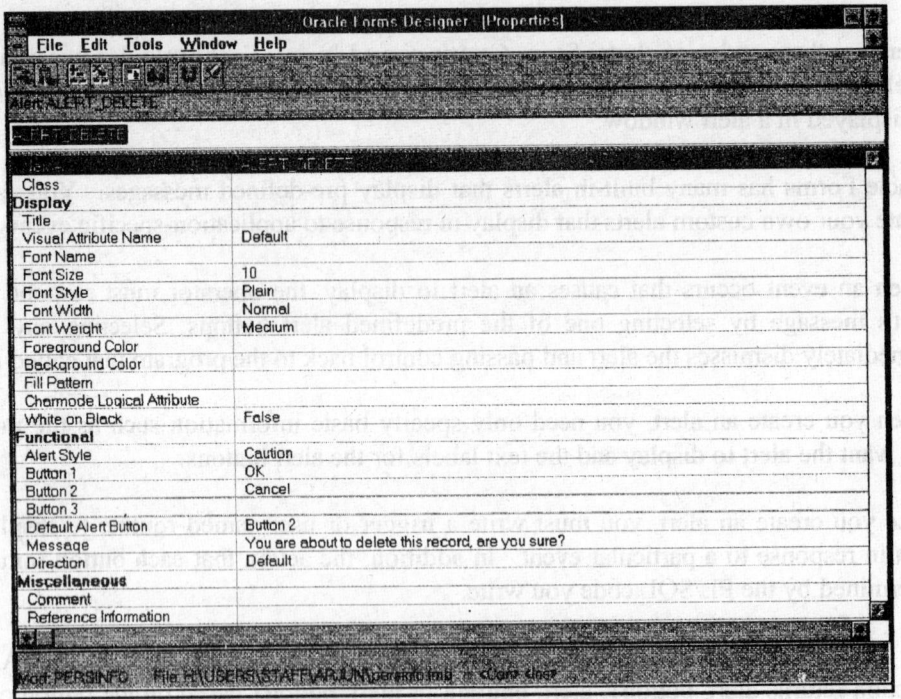

Diagram 10.3 Properties window for alert

5. Choose the Default Alert Button, either Button 1, Button 2, or Button 3. The default button is the button that is selected implicitly when the operator presses [Accept]. On most window managers, the default button has a distinctive appearance.

Displaying an Alert :
To display an alert, your application must execute the SHOW_ALERT built-in subprogram from a trigger or user-named subprogram. SHOW_ALERT is a function that returns a numeric constant. The general syntax is as shown below.

   Show_Alert(alert_name);

The constant returned by the SHOW_ALERT function indicates which alert button the operator selected and is one of the following :

- ALERT_BUTTON1
- ALERT_BUTTON2
- ALERT_BUTTON3

You can assign the return value of the SHOW_ALERT function to a variable, and then take different actions in your trigger depending on the value of that variable; that is, depending on which button the operator selected.
Example :
In Sales Order System you might create an alert that displays the following message :

   "You are about to delete this record, are you sure?"

Button 1 is labeled OK and button 2 is labeled Cancel. This **alert_delete** is invoked from a When-Button-Pressed trigger attached to a push_button_delete button.

If the user presses the delete button, a window displays the above message. The operator can select OK (button 1) to confirm the deletion or CANCEL (button2) to cancel the deletion operation.

Focus :
Create an alert that displays the a delete confirmation message with two buttons labeled as **Yes** and **No**. If the user clicks on Yes, the program must delete the current record.

Solution :
1. Open the product form in the forms designer. Locate the node labeled **Alerts** and click on **navigator, create**. It creates an alert object named *Alert1* as shown in diagram 10.4.

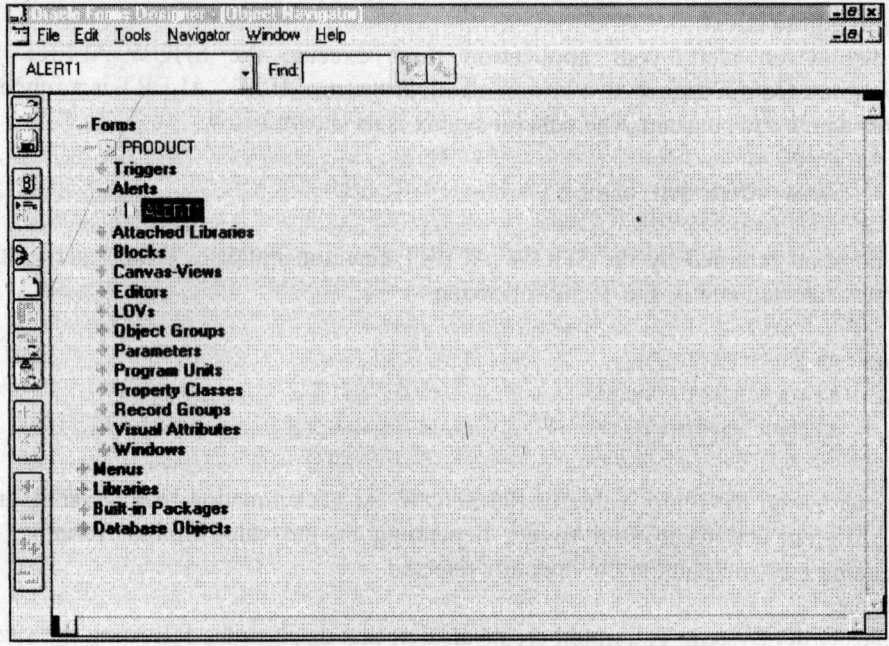

Diagram 10.4 : Creating a new Alert Object

2. In the Properties window, set the following properties :
   Name   : ALERT_DELETE
   Alert Style   : Caution
   Message   : You are about to delete this record, are you sure?
   Button 1   : Yes
   Button 2   : No
   Default Button : Button2

3. To display the alert the following trigger need to be added where it is required.

Trigger Name : **WHEN-BUTTON-PRESSED**   Form : product
Block   : product_blk   Item : pushbutton_delete
Function   : Displays the alert message box before deleting a record.
Text   : DECLARE
                   chk_button number;
               BEGIN
                   go_block('product_master_blk');
                   chk_button := show_alert('alert_delete');
                   if chk_button = alert_button1 then
                       delete_record ;
                   end if;
               END;

HANDS ON

CLIENT MASTER DATA ENTRY SCREEN
Create an application via which the user can manipulate the data being loaded into the table **client_master**. This is a single table taken from a Sales Order System.

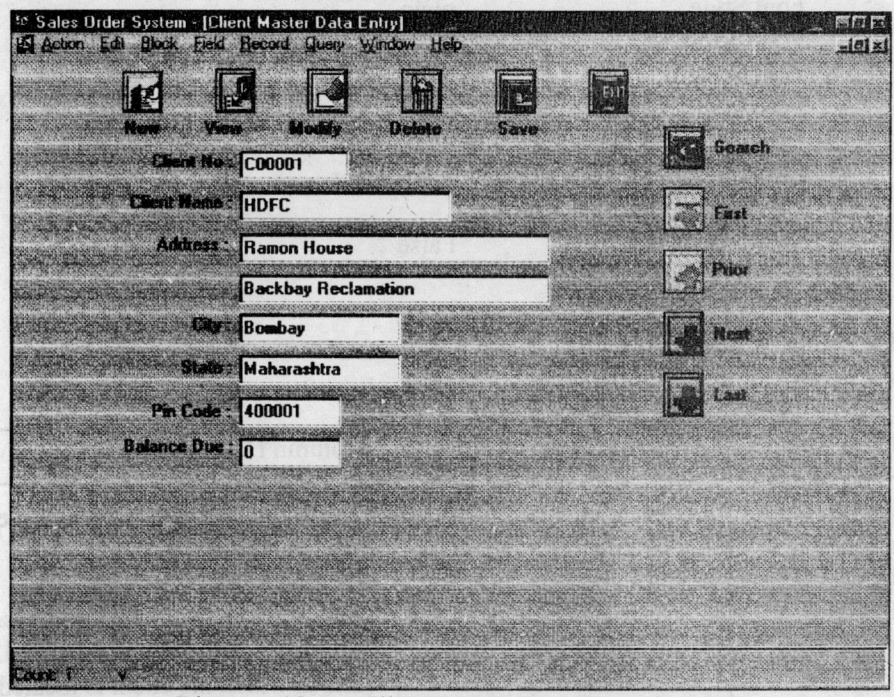

Diagram 10.5 : Client Master Data Entry Screen

Provide the user with complete data manipulation operations (Add, View, Modify, Delete). In the view mode, allow the user to browse through the data table, one record at a time i.e. First, Last, Previous, Next operations have to be provided for.

Make use of property class object to create buttons and standardize the visual properties of all the text objects with visual class object.

The properties of the property class are as follows :

Name	: PClass_Button
Class	:
Item Type	: Button
Canvas	: Client_Master_Can
Width	: 23
Height	: 23
Enabled	: True
Navigable	: True
Mouse Navigate	: True
Iconic	: True

The properties of visual attribute are :

Name	: VA_Text_Item
Class	:
Font Name	: Ms Sans Serif
Font Size	: 8
Font Style	: plain
Font Width	: Normal
Font Weight	: Bold
Foreground Color	: black
Background Color	: white
Fill Pattern	: transparent
Charmode Logical Attribute	:
White On Black	: False
Reference Information	:

Table Name : Client_master
Description : Stores information about clients.

Column Name	Data Type	Size	Column Description
client_no	varchar2	6	Access key via which we shall seek data.
name	varchar2	20	client's name.
address1	varchar2	30	First line in the client's address.
address2	varchar2	30	Second line in the client's address.
city	varchar2	15	City in which the client is located.
state	varchar2	15	State in which the client is located.
pincode	number	6	pin code
bal_due	number	10,2	Balance amount payable by the client.

Integrity Constraints :
- PK_Client_No Primary Key on Client_no.

Validations in the client master data entry screen are as follows :
- client_no is a Primary Key i.e. duplicate values are not allowed in client_no. It cannot be left blank.
- first letter of client_no must start with 'C'.
- client name cannot be left blank
- balance due should have a default value of 0. Field balance due is not enterable.

SOLUTION
1. Create the default form as specified in CREATING A FORM.

2. Create a new block to include the push buttons.

3. Position and Size the items as shown in diagram 10..5.

4. Create a new property class object *PClass_Button*.

5. Add following properties to the property class object.

Name	: PClass_Button
Class	:
Item Type	: Button
Canvas	: Client_Master_Can
Width	: 23
Height	: 23
Enabled	: True
Navigable	: True
Mouse Navigate	: True
Iconic	: True

6. Create an item in the block *button_palette* and assign following properties to the item.

Name	: push_button_Add
Class	: PClass_Button
Icon Name	: add

7. Similarly create 10 other items with properties as mentioned below.

Name	: push_button_View
Class	: PClass_Button
Icon Name	: retrieve

Name	: push_button_Modify
Class	: PClass_Button
Icon Name	: modify

Name	: push_button_Delete
Class	: PClass_Button
Icon Name	: trash

Name	: push_button_Save
Class	: PClass_Button
Icon Name	: Save

Name	: push_button_Exit
Class	: PClass_Button
Icon Name	: close
Name	: push_button_Search
Class	: PClass_Button
Icon Name	: view
Name	: push_button_first
Class	: PClass_Button
Icon Name	: first
Name	: push_button_prior
Class	: PClass_Button
Icon Name	: prior
Name	: push_button_next
Class	: PClass_Button
Icon Name	: next
Name	: push_button_last
Class	: PClass_Button
Icon Name	: last

8. Create a Visual Attribute object *Visual_Attribute_Text* in the Object Navigator.

9. Assign following properties to the visual attribute object.

Name	: VA_Text_Item
Class	:
Font Name	: Ms Sans serif
Font Size	: 8
Font Style	: plain
Font Width	: Normal
Font Weight	: Bold
Foreground Color	: black
Background Color	: white
Fill Pattern	: transparent
Charmode Logical Attribute	:
White On Black	: False
Reference Information	:

10. Assign the visual attribute object *Visual_Attribute_Text* to the *Visual Attribute Name* property of the text objects in *Client_Master_Blk* listed below.

CLIENT_NO
NAME
ADDRESS1
ADDRESS2
CITY
STATE
PINCODE
BAL_DUE

Place and align the items on the canvas as shown in diagram 10.5.

11. Set the next navigational item property of the last text item i.e. pin code to the name of the first text item i.e. client no. Similarly in the detail block set the next navigational item property of the last text item i.e. device to the name of the first text item i.e. contact no.

12. Attach the library *libproc* as explained in the chapter LIBRARIES. This library contains two procedures i.e. scroll control and item_enable_disable which will be called in the triggers.

TRIGGERS
The Triggers are defined below :

Trigger Name   : **WHEN-BUTTON-PRESSED**   Form : client_master
Block   : button_palette   Item : push_button_first
Trigger Level : Item Level
Function   : Go to the first record in the client_master table.
Text   : BEGIN
                 /* go to the next block i.e. client_master_blk */
                 next_block ;
                 /* position the cursor on the first record of the current block */
                 first_record ;
                 END ;

Trigger Name   : **WHEN-BUTTON-PRESSED**   Form : client_master
Block   : button_palette   Item : push_button_prior
Trigger Level : Item Level
Function   : Go to the previous record in the client_master table.
Text   : BEGIN
                 next_block;
                 /* position the cursor on the prior record of the current block */
                 previous_record ;
                 END ;

Trigger Name   : **WHEN-BUTTON-PRESSED**   Form : client_master
Block   : button_palette   Item : push_button_next
Trigger Level : Item Level
Function   : Go to the next record in the client_master table.
Text   : BEGIN
                     next_block;
                     /* position the cursor on the next record of the current block */
                     next_record ;
                 END ;

Trigger Name   : **WHEN-BUTTON-PRESSED**   Form : client_master
Block   : button_palette   Item : push_button_last
Trigger Level : Item Level
Function   : Go to the last record in the client_master table.
Text   : BEGIN
                     next_block ;
                     /* position the cursor on the last record of the current block */
                     last_record ;
                 END ;

Trigger Name   : **WHEN-BUTTON-PRESSED**   Form : client_master
Block   : button_palette   Item : push_button_add
Trigger Level : Item Level
Function   : Insert a record in the client_master table.
Text   : BEGIN
                     next_block;
                     /* Insert a new record in the current block and position the
                        cursor on that record */
                     create_record ;
                     item_enable_disable('client_master_blk', property_on);
                 END ;

Trigger Name   : **WHEN-BUTTON-PRESSED**   Form : client_master
Block   : button_palette   Item : push_button_view
Trigger Level : Item Level
Function   : Retrieve all records and go to the first record in the client_master table.
Text   : BEGIN
                     next_block;
                     /* execute query retrieves records for the current block. */
                     execute_query ;
                     item_enable_disable('client_master_blk', property_off);
                 END;

Trigger Name	: **WHEN-BUTTON-PRESSED**	Form	: client_master
Block	: button_palette	Item	: push_button_modify
Trigger Level	: Item Level		
Function	: Set the primary key i.e. client_no not enterable and set all other fields enterable so that the record in the client_master table can be modified.		
Text	: BEGIN		

```
    next_block;
    item_enable_disable('client_master_blk', property_on);
    /* set the updateable property of client_no to false.
       set_item_property sets the value of specified property. It takes
       in three parameters. The parameters are :
           Item Name optionally prefixed by block name
           Property Name
           Property Value
       If a properties takes a boolean value the user can pass
       property_on i.e. True or property_off i.e. False */
    set_item_property('client_master_blk.client_no', updateable,
           property_off) ;
END ;
```

Trigger Name	: **WHEN-BUTTON-PRESSED**	Form	: client_master
Block	: button_palette	Item	: push_button_delete
Trigger Level	: Item Level		
Function	: Delete the current record in the client_master table.		
Text	: BEGIN		

```
    next_block;
    /* delete the current record in the block */
    delete_record ;
END ;
```

Trigger Name	: **WHEN-BUTTON-PRESSED**	Form	: client_master
Block	: button_palette	Item	: push_button_save
Trigger Level	: Item Level		
Function	: Save the changes to client_master table.		
Text	: BEGIN		

```
    /* form status, a system variable holds the status of the form. It
       can take three values. These are :
       CHANGED (at least one record has changed in the form.
               changes may be in the form of insert, update or
               delete)
       NEW (contains only blank records i.e. the user has insert new
               rows but not values entered for the fields. Oracle
               doesn't post blank records into the database
       QUERY ( contains records that have been queried but no
               changes have been made. If the user changes the
```

*value in any field, status changes to CHANGED. If the commit is successful, status changes to QUERY */

   if :system.form_status = 'CHANGED' then
   /* If the form status is changed then commit changes */
    commit_form ;
    if :system.form_status = 'QUERY' then
     item_enable_disable('client_master_blk',
      property_off);
    end if ;
   end if;
  END ;

Note : Trigger *When-Button-Pressed* on field push_button_modify, push_button_delete, push_button_save calls a procedure named *Item_Enable_Disable*. This procedure is explained in the section PROCEDURE.

Trigger Name	: **WHEN-BUTTON-PRESSED**	Form	: client_master
Block	: button_palette	Item	: push_button_exit
Trigger Level	: Item Level		
Function	: Quit the client_master form.		
Text	: BEGIN		

   /* *Close the form. If there are any changes in the form the system asks for confirmation to save changes* */
   exit_form ;
  END ;

Trigger Name	: **WHEN-BUTTON-PRESSED**	Form	: client_master
Block	: button_palette	Item	: push_button_search
Trigger Level	: Item Level		
Function	: To search for a specific record.		
Text	: BEGIN		

   go_block('client_master_blk');
   go_item('client_no');
   /* *enter query function flushes the current block and puts the form in the query mode. The user can enter the value in any field and execute a query. The query will use the values entered by the user in the where clause* */
   enter_query;
  END;

PROCEDURES
The Procedures written in the library *libproc.pll* are defined below :

Procedure Name : **SCROLL_CONTROL**
Function   : To enable or disable the scroll push buttons i.e. first, prior, next and last based on the total number of records on the form and the current record.

      e.g.
      if there are multiple records and the record pointer is on the first record the first and the prior picture button should be *disabled* and the next and the last picture buttons should be *enabled*.

PROCEDURE scroll IS
BEGIN
    /* Forms system variables or the objects on the form cannot be referenced directly in the library. Such references will result into compilation errors. The NAME_IN function returns the contents of an indicated variable or item. It is used to get the value of an item without referring to the item directly. The following statements are equivalent:
        :description = 'Keyboard' -- direct reference
        name_in('description') = 'Keyboard' -- indirect reference

    Similarly the contents of system variables can be referenced indirectly as follows :
        name_in('system.last_record') = 'TRUE' */

    /* Setting the enabled property to false for all the buttons if there is only one record. */
    if name_in('system.last_record') = 'TRUE' and name_in('system.cursor_record') = '1' then
        set_item_property('button_palette.push_button_next', enabled, property_off);
        set_item_property('button_palette.push_button_last', enabled, property_off);
        set_item_property('button_palette.push_button_first', enabled, property_off);
        set_item_property('button_palette.push_button_prior', enabled, property_off);

    /* Setting the enabled property for the buttons last and next to false and first and prior to True if focus is on the last record. */
    elsif name_in('system.last_record') = 'TRUE' then
        set_item_property('button_palette.push_button_next', enabled, property_off);
        set_item_property('button_palette.push_button_last', enabled, property_off);
        set_item_property('button_palette.push_button_first', enabled, property_on);
        set_item_property('button_palette.push_button_prior', enabled, property_on);

```
        /* Setting the enabled property for the buttons last and next to True and first
           and prior to False  if focus is on the first record.  */
        elsif name_in('system.cursor_record') = '1' then
               set_item_property('button_palette.push_button_first', enabled, property_off);
               set_item_property('button_palette.push_button_prior', enabled, property_off);
               set_item_property('button_palette.push_button_last', enabled, property_on);
               set_item_property('button_palette.push_button_next', enabled, property_on);
        else
               /* Setting the enabled property for all the buttons to True  if focus is
                  not on the first or the last  record.  */
               set_item_property('button_palette.push_button_next', enabled, property_on);
               set_item_property('button_palette.push_button_prior', enabled, property_on);
               set_item_property('button_palette.push_button_last', enabled, property_on);
               set_item_property('button_palette.push_button_first', enabled, property_on);
        end if ;
END;
```

Note :

The scroll control procedure must fire when the user moves from one record to the other. The change in the record position may be due to insert, retrieve, delete or scrolling.
Trigger *When-New-Record-Instance* fires when the system performs insert retrieve, delete or scrolling operations.

Trigger Name	: **WHEN-NEW-RECORD-INSTANCE**	Form	: client_master
Block	: client_master_blk	Item	:
Trigger Level	: Block Level		
Function	: calls procedure scroll_control that enables or disables the scroll push buttons i.e. first, prior, next and last based on the total number of records on the form and the current record.		
Text	: BEGIN		
	scroll_control ;		
	END ;		

Procedure Name : **ITEM_ENABLE_DISABLE**
Function   : To enable the fields so that the contents of the field can be modified or new values can be entered. To disable fields so that the contents of the field cannot be modified.

                  e.g. programming convention requires :
                  The primary key field client_no should be *enabled* in data insert mode and *disabled* in the data modify mode.

```
PROCEDURE ITEM_ENABLE_DISABLE(blk_name IN char, item_on_off IN
NUMBER) IS

        nxt_itemname varchar2(70);

BEGIN
    /* get_block_property is a function that gets the value of specified block property.
       The First_Item property holds the name of the first enterable item in the block. */
    nxt_itemname := blk_name||'.'|| get_block_property(blk_name, first_item);

    /* set a loop that gets the next navigation item and sets the updateable property to
       true or false. Next Navigation Item holds the name of the next navigational item in
       the block */
    loop
        set_item_property(nxt_itemname, updateable, item_on_off);
        nxt_itemname := blk_name||'.'||get_item_property(nxt_itemname,next_navigation_item);
        /* if the Next Navigation Item is the first item, exit the loop. */
        if (blk_name||'.'|| get_block_property(blk_name,first_item)) = nxt_itemname THEN
            exit;
        end if;
    end loop;
END;
```

VALIDATIONS

To modify the form to include the following validations :
- client_no is a Primary Key i.e. duplicate values are not allowed in client_no. It cannot be left blank.
- first letter of client_no must start with 'C'.
- client name cannot be left blank
- balance due should have a default value of 0. Field balance due is not enterable.

Trigger Name	: WHEN-VALIDATE-ITEM	Form	: client_master
Block	: client_master_blk	Item	: client_no
Trigger Level	: Field Level		
Function	: Check for primary key i.e. client_no should not be left blank nor should it be duplicated.		
Text	: BEGIN		

```
            if :client_master_blk.client_no is null or
                :client_master_blk.client_no = '' then
                /* message is a packaged procedure at display a message */
                message('Client No cannot be left blank');
            else
                select client_no into :client_master_blk.client_no
                    from client_master
                    where rtrim(client_no) = :client_master_blk.client_no;
                message('Client No. cannot be duplicated ');
            end if;
```

```
                    /* raise form_trigger_failure aborts the trigger and positions e
                       the cursor on the same field */
                    raise form_trigger_failure;
           EXCEPTION
                    /* when a select statement returns no records it fires an
                       exception named no_data_found. In this validation, if the
                       select statement retrieves no records, the value entered by the
                       user is unique and thus no action has to be taken. */
                    when no_data_found then null;
           END;
```

Note :
If the column is defined as a primary key at the table level, Oracle Forms sets the *Required* attribute to *True*. If the *Required* attribute is set to *True*, Oracle will display an error message if the user tries to leave the field blank. The *When-Validate-Item* will not be fired.

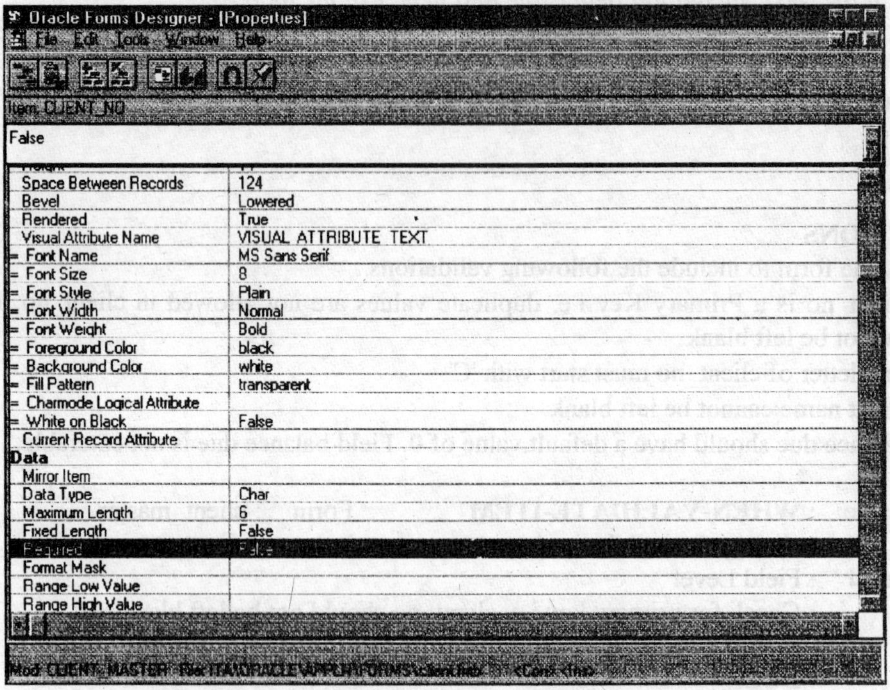

Diagram 10.6 : Setting the Required property to False.

We have incorporated the not null check in the trigger and so we need to set the *Required* attribute to *False*. Select item client_no in the Object Navigator and click on **Tools**, **Properties**. It will display all the properties of client_no. Set the *Required* attribute to *False* as shown in diagram 10.6.

The validation to check that the first letter of client_no is 'C', will be performed with the primary key validation. Thus we need to add PL/SQL code in the *When-Validate-Item* trigger:

Trigger Name	: **WHEN-VALIDATE-ITEM**
Block	: client_master_blk
Trigger Level	: Item Level
Function	: Check for primary key i.e. client_no should not be left blank nor should it be duplicated. The first letter of client_no should be 'C'.
Form	: client_master
Item	: client_no

Text   : BEGIN
```
    if :client_master_blk.client_no is null or
            :client_master_blk.client_no = '' then
                message('Client No cannot be left blank');
        else
            if :client_master_blk.client_no not like 'C%' then
                message('the first letter of Client No must be C.');
            else
                select client_no into :client_master_blk.client_no
                    from client_master
                    where rtrim(client_no) = :client_master_blk.client_no;
                message('Client No. cannot be duplicated ');
            end if;
        end if;
            raise form_trigger_failure;
    EXCEPTION
        when no_data_found then null;
    END;
```

- Client Name should not be left blank.

Trigger Name	: **WHEN-VALIDATE-ITEM**
Block	: client_master_blk
Trigger Level	: Item Level
Function	: Check to see that client name is not left blank.
Form	: client_master
Item	: name

Text   : BEGIN
```
    if :client_master_blk.name is null or
        :client_master_blk.name = '' then
            message('Client Name cannot be left blank');
            raise form_trigger_failure;
    end if;
    END;
```

Making the balance due field not enterable :

Bal_due column in the client_master table, shows the balance amount due from the client. This column will be updated when an invoice for the client is generated or when the client makes payment against an invoice.

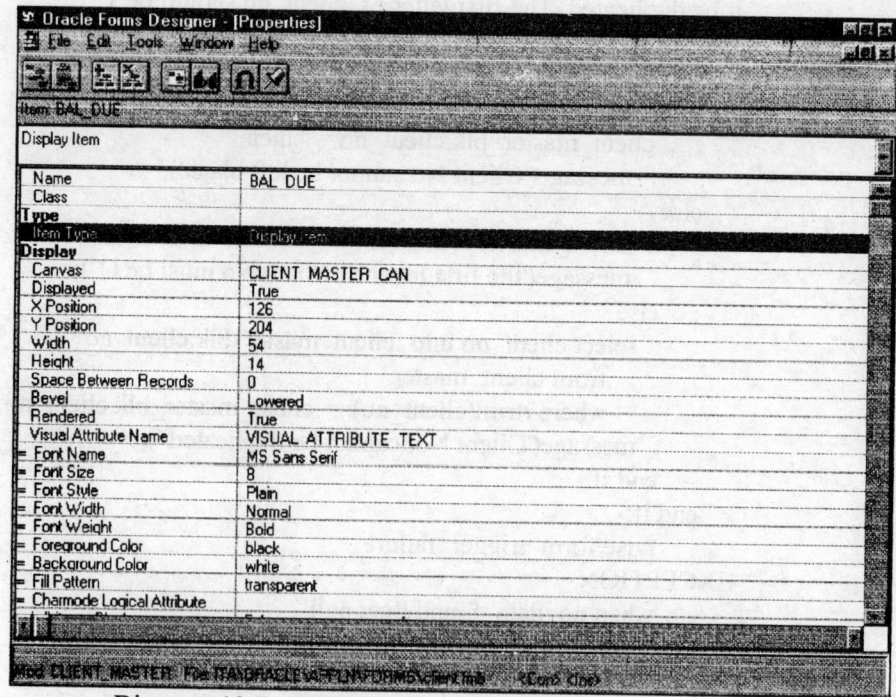

Diagram 10.7 : Changing the item type property of bal_due

Thus this field will not be enterable from the client master data entry form. Oracle gives you an object that can only be used to display data. Select the bal_due field in the Object Navigator. Select **Tools**, **Properties** from the main menu. It displays the properties of the bal_due field. Set the *Item Type* property to *Display Item* and the *Default* property to *0* as shown in diagram 10.7.

DISPLAYING CONTEXT SENSITIVE HELP

Oracle Forms can display context sensitive help text (HINT) by using the methods mentioned below :

- Display help on the message line at runtime.
- Display Balloon Help for the when the forms cursor touches iconic push button object on the data entry screen.

Display Context Sensitive Help on the message line at runtime :
Context sensitive help text can display in Oracle forms by setting the *Autohint* and the *Hint* property of the individual items. The values of the properties are as follows :

    Autohint   : True
    Hint   : Hint String

Hint text is usually advice to the operator on how to enter valid data in the item

Example :
The hint text for an item client no might be "Enter a Unique 6 digit Client Number." The values of the properties are as follows :

Autohint :   True
Hint   :   Enter a Unique 6 digit Client Number.

Oracle form displays the hint message automatically when its focus is on an item which has the Hint property defined and the Auto Hint property is True.

Displaying balloon Help :
The Hint String is displayed in the message line only when the focus is on that field. Whilst using iconic push buttons, we need to display the help message when the mouse cursor moves from one push button to the other.

The hint displayed when the mouse cursor moves from one push button to the other is called *Balloon Help*.

The balloon help is applicable to iconic push buttons only.

The steps in displaying *Balloon Help* are as follows :

1. Balloon Help displays the *Text String* as specified in the *Label* property. Set the *Label* property of all the iconic push buttons.

Example :
Display hint as 'Add a new record', when the mouse cursor is on add button.

To achieve the above objective, we need to set the *Label* property of *push_button_add* to *Add a new record*.

2. The functions and procedures for the balloon help are included in the library named *HINT.PLL*, package *HINT*. To use these functions we need to attach the hint.pll library to the form. This file is located in the c:\orawin\forms45\plsqllib directory. Refer to ATTACHING LIBRARY to the form in the LIBRARIES chapter.

3. Write the necessary code to activate the hint.

Trigger Name   : **WHEN-MOUSE-ENTER**   Form : client_master
Block   :   Item :
Trigger Level : Form Level
Function   : Set timer for the button help.
Text   : BEGIN
                    hint.showbuttonhelp ;
                 END;

Trigger Name   : **WHEN-TIMER-EXPIRED**   Form : client_master
Block   :   Item :
Trigger Level : Form Level
Function   : When the Timer Expires, show button help.
Text   : BEGIN
                    hint.showbuttonhelphandler ;
                 END;

11. MASTER DETAIL FORM

A Master Detail form has at least two blocks. These blocks are related to each other. The relationship is between the data being manipulated in each block. This relationship is called a **Master-Detail** relationship.

The relationship between the blocks is modeled upon a primary key, foreign key relationship between the tables on which the blocks are based.

Consider a sales order system. There is a client master table that stores the information about clients who purchase goods from an organization.

As and when a client places an order on the organization supplying material information such as the purchase order, date, client information, material id, material description, qty, unit price etc. has to be kept track of. This information is essentially divided into 2 unique blocks, client information(i.e. who is purchasing ?), material information (i.e. what is being purchased).

Hence the *sales_order* and the *sales_order_details* table are connected by a Master / Detail based on a primary key to foreign key columns present in each of the respective tables. The form includes blocks based on each of these tables. There is a master-detail relationship between the blocks in which the *sales_order* block is the master block and the *order_details_blk* block is the detail block. Both these blocks are related by *order number*.

A master-detail relationship is set by using an object called a *Relation Object*. A Relation object is an Oracle form object which stores master-detail relation information. When you create a relation, Oracle Forms generates the triggers and PL/SQL procedures required to enforce this relationship between the master and detail blocks.

The master-detail relationship automatically does the following :

- Ensures that the detail block displays only those records that are linked with the current (master) record in the master block

- Coordinates querying between the two blocks.

- Prevents you deleting data from the master block when associated data in the detail block exists.

- Prevents you inserting data into the detail block where there is no related data in the master block.

If we look at the relationship between the records contained in the sales_order and the sales_order_details tables clearly, there can be multiple items purchased by a single client. Hence, this information needs to be stored in two tables with a specific (one to many) relationship defined between the tables.

CREATING A MASTER-DETAIL FORM

1. Connect to the Oracle Database and create the master block as explained in CREATING A FORM.

2. Create a new block for the detail section. Click on **Tools** and select **New Block**.
   Specify the name of Base Table, the name of the block and the name of the canvas on which items of the blocks must be placed. The completed screen is displayed in diagram 11.1.

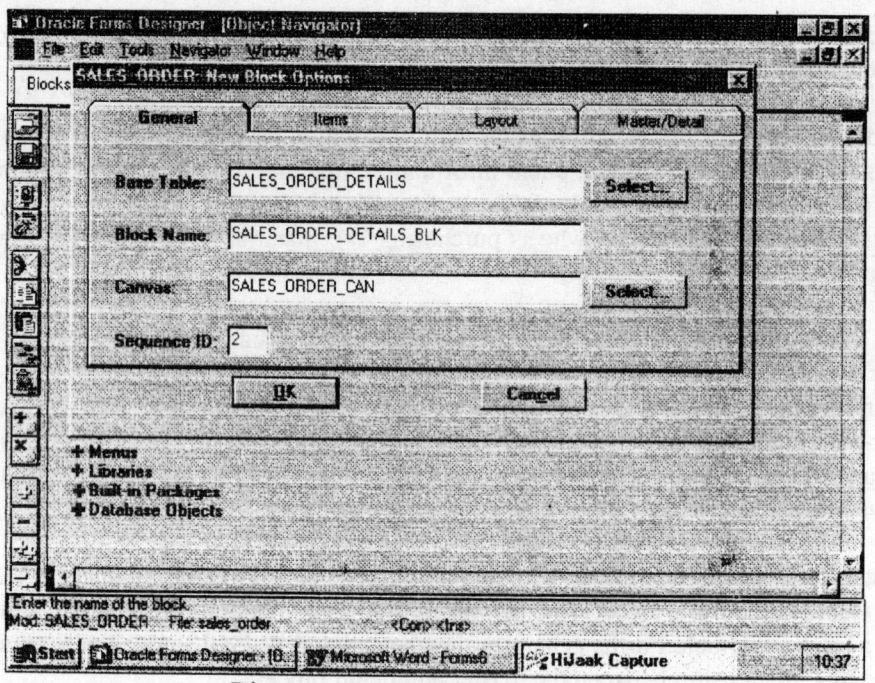

Diagram 11.1 : Creating a new block

3. Select the columns in the detail table by selecting the tab folder marked *Item* and Clicking on the pushbutton **Select Columns**. Set the *labels* for the columns in the detail section. If a column is not to be a part of the base table then, click on the column name then set the **Include** checkbox **off**.

> **Note :** To set the master-detail relationship, at least one field in the detail table should be selected. This is the common field between the two base tables..

4. Specify the presentation style or form. The default form may be created with the Items and its label in *Tabular* or *Form* style.

The Orientation of the Items within each style may again be either Horizontal or Vertical. Most of the time in details section we will use *Tabular* style and *Vertical*.

5. Specify the number of records to be displayed in the detail section. By default the number of records displayed is *1*. The completed screen is shown in diagram 11.2.

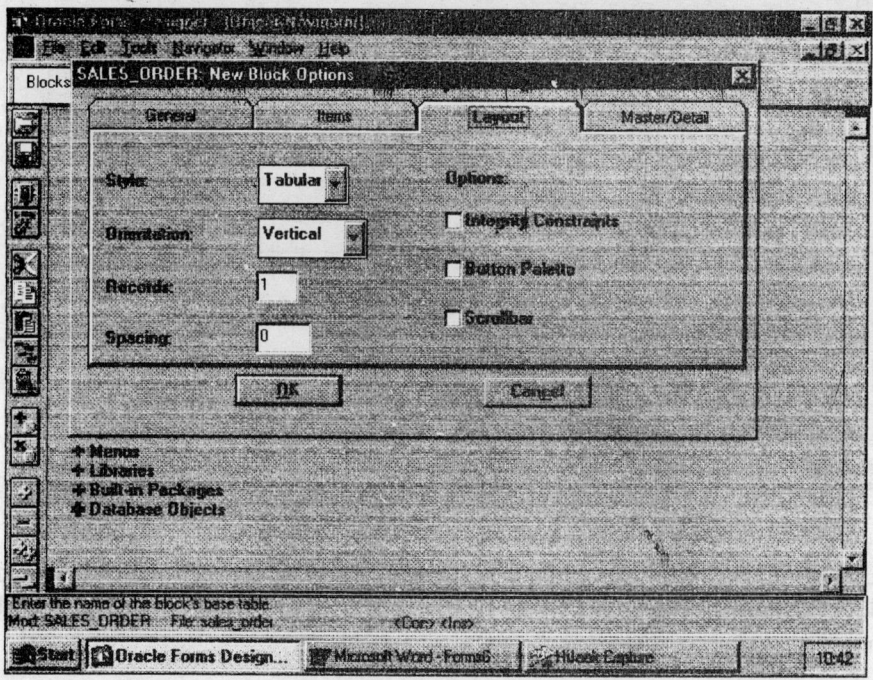

Diagram 11.2 : Form Presentation Style and No. of records

6. Select the tab folder marked *Master-Detail* to set the master detail relationship. Specify the name of the master block and the join condition as displayed in diagram 11.3.

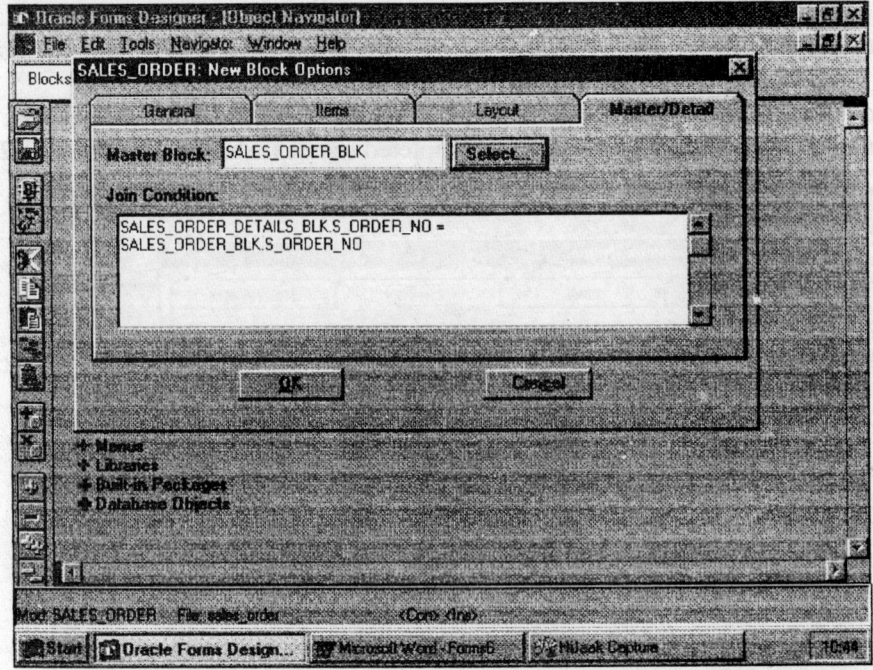

Diagram 11.3 : Specifying Master Detail Relationship

Oracle Creates a relation object when you create a relation between the master and the detail block as shown in diagram 11.3. This object is immediately visible in the object navigator.

The Relation Object :
A Relation object is an Oracle form object which stores master-detail relation information. A relation is a logical object that specifies the relationship between a master block and a corresponding detail block. In the Object Navigator, the relation object appears as a node under the block that is the master block in the relation.

When you create a relation, Oracle Forms generates the triggers and PL/SQL procedures required to enforce the relationship between the master and detail blocks. The actual code that Oracle Forms generates depends on how the properties of the relation are set. The behavior of the detail block is determined by the properties set in the relation object.

The master-detail relationship automatically does the following:

- Ensures that the detail block displays only those records that are linked with the current (master) record in the master block

- Coordinates querying between the two blocks.

- Prevents you deleting data from the master block when associated data in the detail block exists.

- Prevents you inserting data into the detail block where there is no related data in the master block.

For example, when the operator changes the current record in the master block by navigating to a different sales order record, Oracle Forms updates the detail block with a new set specifically associated with the new record in the master block. When the operator queries a particular sales order in the master block, Oracle Forms automatically retrieves the records specific to that sales order.

6. Click on **OK**. The master-detail form is ready. Save the form by selecting the **Save** menu item from the **File** menu item.

RUNNING A MASTER DETAIL FORM
Run the Form by selecting the **Run** option under the **File** option.

The default master data entry screen is displayed as shown in diagram 11.4.

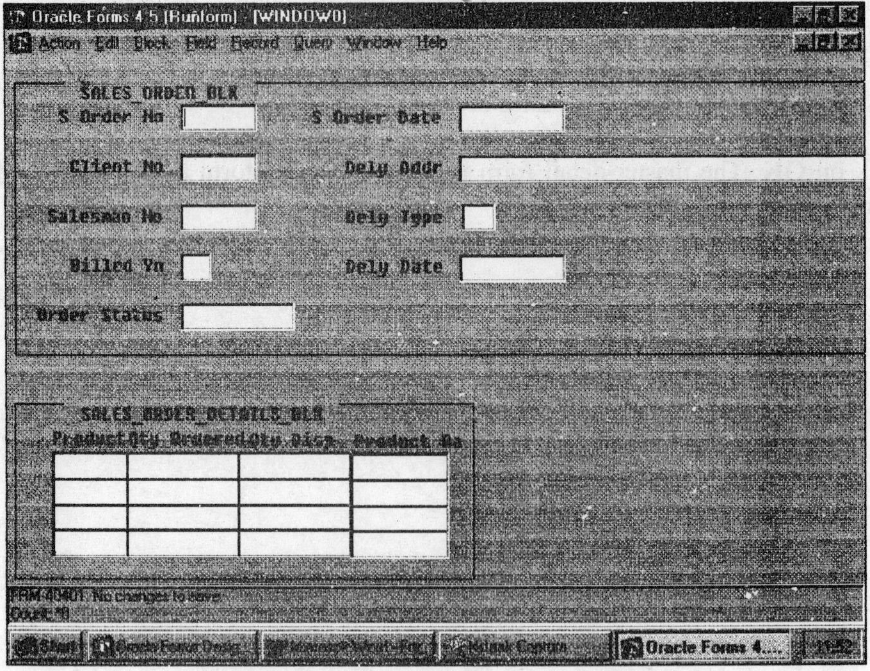

Diagram 11.4 : Default master detail form

Data Retrieval and Manipulation Operations :
At runtime the form comes with a default Menu system. The default menu system provides all options for Navigating within the form and performing data manipulation tasks such as First, Last, Previous, Next, Insert, Delete, Update, Save and Exit.

DATA RETRIEVAL :
Data can be retrieved by selecting the menu item **Query** and clicking on **Execute**. This would retrieve all the records from the master table. As soon as all the records of the master table are retrieved ,Oracle will display the first record in the master block. The Primary Key of this record is then used to retrieve the detail records for the detail block.

This controlled data retrieval for the detail block is taken care of by the **RELATIONAL OBJECT.**

If a conditional query must be performed then select **Query** and click on **Enter**. It clears the block and allows the user to enter an Item Value. Type in the Item value in the appropriate item. By doing so, a condition is automatically defined at the block level. Execute the query by Clicking on **Execute** from **Query** Menu item.

The status line at the bottom of the screen will indicate the number of records retrieved.

NAVIGATION :

If several records are queried, Click on **Records** and select **Previous** or **Next** to move to the previous or the next record.

when the operator changes the current record in the master block, Oracle Forms updates the detail block to display only those records associated with the records visible in the master block.

INSERTING DATA:

To insert a row click on **Insert** from the menu item **Records**. Enter the values in the different items required. In this manner several records can be inserted.

If the data entry operator is currently working with the master block and the insert instruction is given by the operator, both the master and detail blocks are cleared and blank records are inserted in both the blocks.

If the cursor is in the detail block, an insert record instruction given by the operator will cause a blank record to be inserted into the detail section only, leaving the master block as is.

DELETING DATA :

Records can be deleted by clicking on **Delete** from the **Records** menu item. Oracle will not delete a record in the master block unless all the corresponding detail records are deleted.

SAVING DATA :

Records are saved by clicking on **Save** from the **File** menu item.

SALES ORDER DATA ENTRY SCREEN

A salesman fills a sales order form for an order placed by a client. A client can ask for the delivery to be in *Part* or *Full* depending on his needs. The Order form includes information like order no, the date of order, client information along with the products ordered by the client.

Design a data-entry screen that allows data manipulation in the *sales_order* and *sales_order_details* tables. Both these tables are linked by *s_order_no* (order number). In the master section of the sales order form as soon as the client number is keyed in, the client name must be displayed from the client master table.

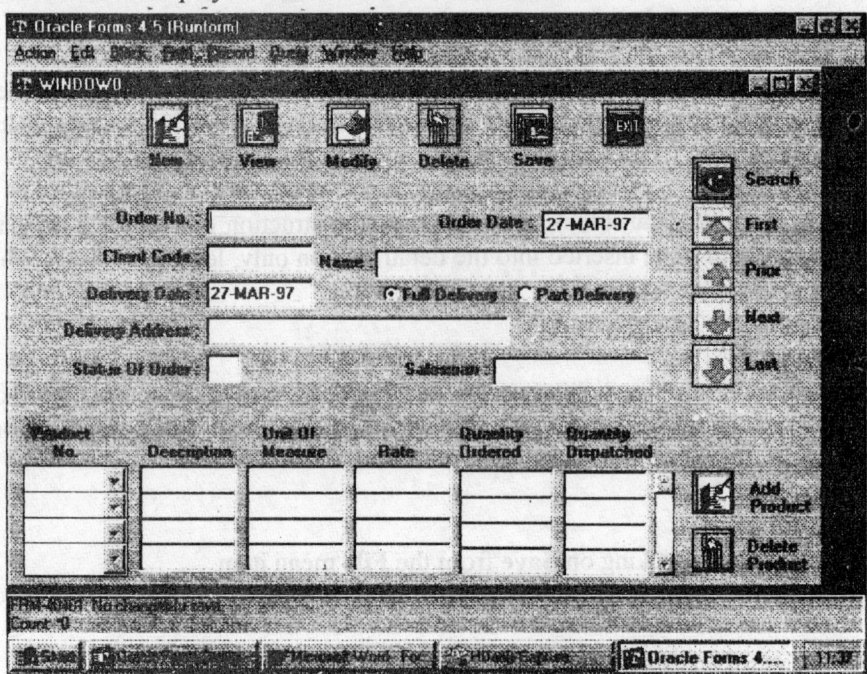

Diagram 11.5 : Sales Order Data-Entry Screen

Provide the user with complete data manipulation operations (Add, View, **Modify**, Delete). In the view mode, allow the user to browse through the data table, one record at a time i.e. First, Last, Previous, Next operations have to be provided for.

Add mode	: All the fields in the master and detail block must be updateable.
Modify mode	: The user is allowed to modify all the fields other than primary key. The user is allowed to modify an order only if the delivery challan for the same is not generated.
View mode	: No fields must be updatable.
Delete Mode	: Delete cascading must be on. The user is allowed to delete an order only if the delivery challan for the same is not generated.

Include a search operation that searches a table to match the order number entered by the user. In the detail section, the user must display the description and unit of measure from the product master table.

MASTER DETAIL FORM 233

Table Name : sales_order (Master)
Description : Use to store information about orders placed by the clients.

Column Name	Data Type	Size	Attributes
s_order_no	varchar2	6	Unique primary key allotted to each order.
s_order_date	date		Date on which the order is placed.
client_no	varchar2	6	Client No., who places the order.
dely_addr	varchar2	30	Address where the delivery of the goods has to be made.
salesman_no	varchar2	6	salesman No., who gets the order from the client.
status	varchar2	2	Order Status (In Process IP, FullFilled F)
dely_type	char	1	To note whether the delivery is to be made in parts (P) or full (F).
dely_date	date		Date when the delivery for the goods is to be made.

Integrity Constraints :
- PK_s_order_no Primary Key s_order_no
- FK_sales_order Foreign Key client_no References client_master(client_no)
- FK_salesman_no Foreign Key salesman_no References salesman_master (salesman_no)

Table Name : sales_order_details
Description : Use to store information about order details.

Column Name	Data Type	Size	Attributes
s_order_no	varchar2	6	Order No. for which details have to be stored.
product_no	varchar2	6	Product No. for which details have to be stored.
product_rate	number	8,2	The rate agreed upon.
qty_ordered	number	8	Quantity of goods ordered.
qty_disp	number	8	Quantity of goods dispatched.

Integrity Constraints :
- PK_so_details Primary Key (s_order_no, product_no)
- FK_so_details Foreign Key product_no References product_master(product_no)
- FK_sales_order Foreign Key s_order_no References sales_order(s_order_no)

The Lookup master tables used in this example are :

Table Name : client_master
Description : Stores information about clients.

Column Name	Data Type	Size	Column Description
client_no	varchar2	6	Access key via which we shall seek data.
name	varchar2	20	client's name.
address1	varchar2	30	First line in the client's address.
address2	varchar2	30	Second line in the client's address.
city	varchar2	15	City in which the client is located.
state	varchar2	15	State in which the client is located.
pincode	number	6	pin code
bal_due	number	10,2	Balance amount payable by the client.

Table Name : salesman_master
Description : stores information about salesmen working in the company.

Column Name	Data Type	Size	Column Description
salesman_no	varchar2	6	Unique primary key allotted to each salesman.
name	varchar2	20	Name of the salesman.
address1	varchar2	30	Address of the salesman.
Address2	varchar2	30	Address of the salesman.
city	varchar2	15	City the Client belongs to.
state	varchar2	15	State the client belongs to.
pincode	number	6	Pincode corresponding to the address.
sal_amt	number	8,2	Salesman earning in currency format.
commission	number	2,2	Commission the salesman earns per order. It is a percentage of Order value.
tgt_to_get	number	6,2	Target to be achieved by each salesman every year. This target is set by the sales manager every year.
ytd_sales	number	6,2	Target actually achieved by each salesman every year.
remarks	varchar2	60	Any specific comment for the salesman regarding his performance etc.

Table Name : product_master
Description : stores information about products supplied by the company.

Column Name	Data Type	Size	Column Description
product_no	varchar2	6	Access key via which we shall seek data.
description	varchar2	25	Description of the product.
unit_measure	varchar2	10	Unit by which the product is measured.
qty_on_hand	number	8	Quantity which is available in the stock.
reorder_lvl	number	8	Quantity level when the stock should be re-ordered.
cost_price	number	8,2	Cost price of the product.
selling_price	number	8,2	Selling price of the product.

The push buttons must be connected to a property class named *PClass_Button*. The properties in the property class must be as follows :

Name	PClass_Button
Item Type	Button
Canvas	sales_order_can
Width	23
Height	23
Iconic	True

All the data items must be connected to Visual Attribute object named VA_Data_Items. The properties in the Visual Attribute must be set as follows :

Name	VA_Data_Items
Font Name	MS Sans Serif
Font Size	8
Font Style	Plain
Font Width	Normal
Font Weight	Bold

Validations in the sales order form data entry screen are as follows :
- *s_order_no* is a Primary Key i.e. duplicate values are not allowed in *s_order_no*. It cannot be left blank.
- *s_order_date* cannot be greater than system date. Set the default value of *s_order_date* to system date.
- *client_no* must be present in the client master table. Implement this validation by using LOV FOR VALIDATION.
- The client name must be displayed using a display item when the user selects a valid value for *client_no* or when the user executes a query.
- *dely_address* cannot be left blank
- *salesman_no* must be present in the *salesman_master* table. Implement this validation by using LOV FOR VALIDATION.

- Status is a not enterable field. It will be updated from some other data entry screen. Use a display item for the non-enterable field.
- *dely_type* must be a radio group with buttons having label as **Part** and **Full** and value as **P** and **F**.
- *dely_date* must be greater than or equal to *s_order_date*. Set the default value of *dely_date* to system date.
- *product_no* must be present in the product master table. Implement this validation by using List Item.
- The Sales Order Form must display the description, *unit_measure* in the detail block using display items when the user exits the *product_no* field or when the records are retrieved by the user.
- The *Rate* must be populated in the *product_rate* text item from the product master table when the user exits the *product_no* field or when the records are retrieved by the user.
- Product Rate must not be left blank.
- Quantity Ordered must not be left blank. Quantity ordered cannot be 0.
- *qty_disp* is not enterable field. Use a display item for not enterable field. The default value should be set to **0**.

SOLUTION

1. Create the default form as specified in CREATING A MASTER DETAIL FORM. The *Master / Detail* section of the detail must be set as follows :

Master Block	Sales_Order_Blk
Join Condition	Sales_Order_Blk.S_Order_No = Order_Details_Blk.S_Order_No

2. Create a new property class object *PClass_Button* and add following properties to the property class object.

Name	: PClass_Button
Item Type	: Button
Canvas	: Sales_Order_Can
Width	: 23
Height	: 23
Iconic	: True

3. Create a new block to include the pushbuttons.

4. Create an item in the block *button_palette* and assign following properties to the item.

Name	: push_button_Add
Class	: PClass_Button
Icon Name	: addnew

5. Similarly place push buttons for the data manipulation operation as shown in diagram 11.5

6. Create a new visual attribute object *VA_Data_Items* and add following properties to the visual attribute object.

Name	: VA_Data_Items
Font Name	: MS Sans Serif
Font Size	: 8
Font Style	: Plain
Font Width	: Normal
Font Weight	: Bold

7. Position and Size the items as shown in diagram 11.5.

8. Set the Next-Navigation item of the last item in the master block to *s_order_no*. Similarly, in the detail block's last item Next-Navigation item property to the name of the first item.

   Attach the library *libproc* as explained in the topic ATTACHING A LIBRARY TO ANOTHER MODULE. Once the library is attached to the form, the program units defined in the library can be referenced in the triggers.

   The *Item_Enable_Disable* procedure is changed as explained below :

```
PROCEDURE ITEM_ENABLE_DISABLE(blk_name IN char, item_on_off
IN NUMBER) IS
        nxt_itemname varchar2(70);
        to_nxt_item varchar2(30);
        count number;
        itemtype varchar(70);
BEGIN
        /* get_block_property is a function that gets the value of specified block property.
        The First_Item property holds the name of the first enterable item in the
        block. */

    nxt_itemname := blk_name||'.'|| get_block_property(blk_name, first_item);

        /* set a loop that gets the next navigation item and sets the updateable property to
        true or false. Next Navigation Item holds the name of the next navigational
        item in the block */
```

```
        loop
            itemtype:=get_item_property(nxt_itemname,item_type);

            if itemtype <> 'DISPLAY ITEM' and
                    get_item_property(nxt_itemname,item_canvas) is not null then
                set_item_property(nxt_itemname,updateable,item_on_off);
            end if;

            nxt_itemname:=blk_name||'.'||get_item_property(nxt_itemname,
                        next_navigation_item);

            if (blk_name||'.'||get_block_property(blk_name,first_item))=nxt_itemname
            then
                exit;
            end if;
        end loop;
END;
```

The *scroll_control* procedure is as follows :

```
PROCEDURE scroll_control IS
BEGIN
    if name_in('system.last_record') = 'TRUE' and name_in('system.cursor_record') = '1' then
        set_item_property('button_palette.push_button_next', enabled, property_off);
        set_item_property('button_palette.push_button_last', enabled, property_off);
        set_item_property('button_palette.push_button_first', enabled, property_off);
        set_item_property('button_palette.push_button_prior', enabled, property_off);

    elsif name_in( 'system.last_record' ) = 'TRUE' then
        set_item_property('button_palette.push_button_next', enabled, property_off);
        set_item_property('button_palette.push_button_last', enabled, property_off);
        set_item_property('button_palette.push_button_first', enabled, property_on);
        set_item_property('button_palette.push_button_prior', enabled, property_on);

    elsif name_in('system.cursor_record') = '1' then
        set_item_property('button_palette.push_button_first', enabled, property_off);
        set_item_property('button_palette.push_button_prior', enabled, property_off);
        set_item_property('button_palette.push_button_last', enabled, property_on);
        set_item_property('button_palette.push_button_next', enabled, property_on);
    else
        set_item_property('button_palette.push_button_next', enabled, property_on);
        set_item_property('button_palette.push_button_prior', enabled, property_on);
        set_item_property('button_palette.push_button_last', enabled, property_on);
        set_item_property('button_palette.push_button_first', enabled, property_on);
    end if ;
END;
```

TRIGGERS
The Triggers are defined below :

Trigger Name	: **WHEN-BUTTON-PRESSED**	Form	: sales_order
Block	: button_palette	Item	: push_button_first
Trigger Level	: Field Level		
Function	: Go to the first record in the sales_order table.		
Text	: BEGIN		

        next_block ;
        first_record ;
END ;

Note : The Buttons first, prior, next and last allow the user to scroll in the master block. The detail records will change when the master record will change because of the Master Detail Relation.

In the above trigger, the next_block packaged function is used to make the Sales_Order_Blk the current block. For the next block to function properly, ensure that the sequence of blocks is as follow :

- sales_order_blk
- order_details_blk
- Button_palette

Thus when the user clicks on push_buttton_first, the current block is Button_palette. The Packaged procedure *Next_Block* will change the focus to sales_order_blk since it is the next block in the sequence. One can use the *Go_Block* packaged procedure to move to the specified block.

Trigger Name	: **WHEN-BUTTON-PRESSED**	Form	: sales_order
Block	: button_palette	Item	: push_button_prior
Trigger Level	: Field Level		
Function	: Go to the previous record in the sales_order table.		
Text	: BEGIN		

        next_block;
        previous_record ;
END ;

Trigger Name	: **WHEN-BUTTON-PRESSED**	Form	: sales_order
Block	: button_palette	Item	: push_button_next
Trigger Level	: Field Level		
Function	: Go to the next record in the sales_order table.		
Text	: BEGIN		

```
                next_block;
                next_record ;
          END ;
```

Trigger Name	: **WHEN-BUTTON-PRESSED**	Form	: sales_order
Block	: button_palette	Item	: push_button_last
Trigger Level	: Field Level		
Function	: Go to the last record in the sales_order table.		
Text	: BEGIN		

```
                next_block;
                last_record ;
          END ;
```

Trigger Name	: **WHEN-BUTTON-PRESSED**	Form	: sales_order
Block	: button_palette	Item	: push_button_add
Trigger Level	: Field Level		
Function	: Insert a record in the sales_order table.		
Text	: BEGIN		

```
          next_block;
          create_record ;
                /* Item_enable_diable is a user-defined procedure that enables
                    the fields so that the contents of the field can be modified
                    or new values can be entered in the add or modify mode and
                    disable fields so that the contents of the field cannot be
                    modified in view mode. It takes in two parameters i.e. name of
                    the block and the property value. This procedure is included in
                    the library libproc */
                item_enable_disable('sales_order_blk', property_on);
                item_enable_disable('order_details_blk', property_on);
          END ;
```

MASTER DETAIL FORM **241**

Trigger Name	: **WHEN-BUTTON-PRESSED** Form : sales_order
Block	: button_palette Item : push_button_view
Trigger Level	: Field Level
Function	: Retrieve all the records and go to the first record in the sales_order table. Make all the fields not updateable in the master and the detail block.
Text	: BEGIN

```
        next_block;
        execute_query;
        item_enable_disable('sales_order_blk', property_off);
        item_enable_disable('order_details_blk', property_off);
END ;
```

Trigger Name	: **WHEN-BUTTON-PRESSED** Form : sales_order
Block	: button_palette Item : push_button_modify
Trigger Level	: Field Level
Function	: The user is not allowed to modify the sales order if the delivery challan for the same is already generated. If the delivery challan is not generated, set the primary key i.e. s_order_no not enterable and set all other fields enterable so that the record in the sales_order table can be modified.
Text	: DECLARE

```
        orderno varchar2(6);
    BEGIN
        /* if the challan for the order is generated, display a message */
        select distinct s_order_no into orderno from challan_header
        where s_order_no = :sales_order_blk.s_order_no;
        message('Challan for the Order No. "' ||
                :sales_order_blk.s_order_no || '" already exists...
                You cannot Modify this record.');
    EXCEPTION
        when no_data_found then

                /* if the challan for the order is not generated, allow
                 the user to modify all fields other than s_order_no */
                next_block;
                item_enable_disable('sales_order_blk', property_on);
                item_enable_disable('order_details_blk', property_on);
                set_item_property('sales_order_blk.s_order_no',
                        updateable, property_off);
    END;
```

Relation Object and its Properties :

A master-detail relationship is set by using an object called the *Relation Object*. When you create a relation by using the fourth tab of the block creation tool, Oracle Forms generates the triggers and PL/SQL procedures required to enforce coordination between the master and detail blocks. The actual code that Oracle Forms generates depends on how the properties of the relation are set. One of the property of a relation object is **Master Deletes**.

Master Deletes Property :

Specifies how the deletion of a record in the master block effects records in the detail block:

Non-Isolated : The *Master Deletes* property is set to *Non-Isolated* by default. Prevents the deletion of a master record when associated detail records exist in the database.

Isolated : Allows the master record to be deleted and does not delete associated detail records in the database.

Cascading : Allows the master record to be deleted and automatically deletes any associated detail records in the detail block's base table at commit time. The *default* value for this property is *Non-Isolated*.

Setting the properties of the relation object :

1. Click on the relation object in the master block. It displays the relation object in the object navigator as shown in diagram 11.6.

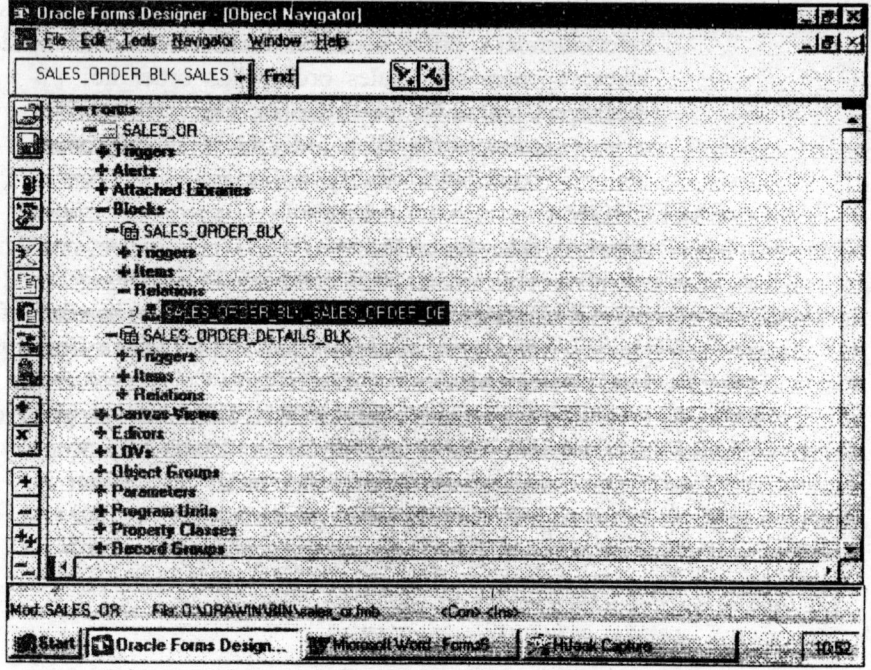

Diagram 11.6 : Relation Object in the Object Navigator

MASTER DETAIL FORM 243

2. Right click on the relation object and select **properties** from the popup menu. It displays the properties of the relation object. Set the **Master Deletes** property to **Cascading** as shown in diagram 11.7.

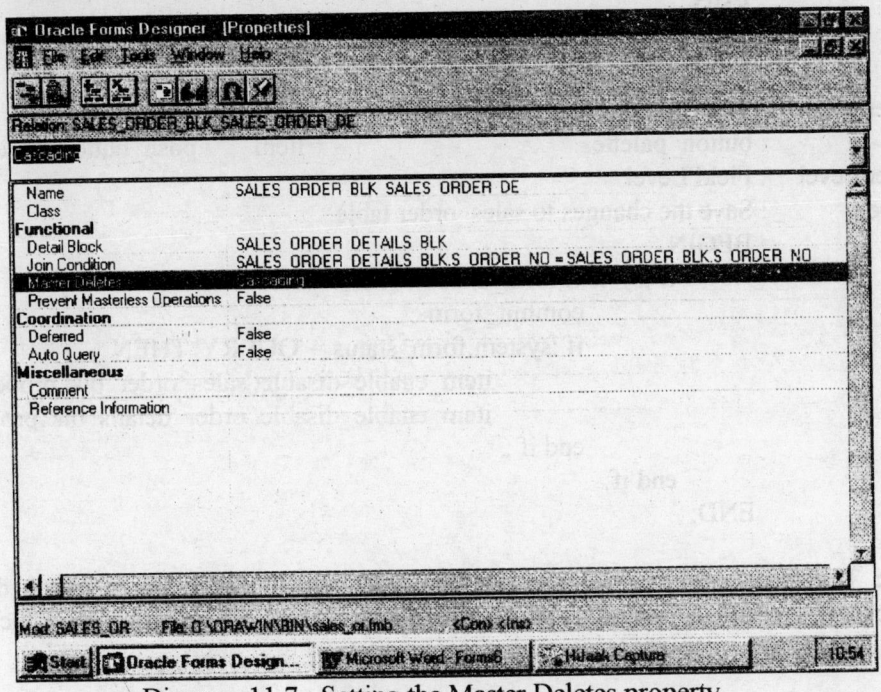

Diagram 11.7 : Setting the Master Deletes property

Thus if the **Master Deletes** property is set to **Cascading** then the trigger for delete master will be as follows :

Trigger Name : **WHEN-BUTTON-PRESSED**   Form : sales_order
Block   : button_palette   Item : push_button_delete
Trigger Level : Field Level
Function   : The user is not allowed to delete a sales order if the delivery challan for the same is already generated. If the delivery challan is not generated, delete the current record in the sales_order table.
Text   : DECLARE
                    orderno varchar2(6);
                BEGIN

                    /* if the challan for the order is generated, display a message */
                    select distinct s_order_no into orderno from challan_header
                        where s_order_no = :sales_order_blk.s_order_no;
                    message('Challan for the Order No. "' ||
                        :sales_order_blk.s_order_no || '" already exists...
                        you cannot delete this record.');
                EXCEPTION
                    when no_data_found then

```
                    /* if the challan for the order is not generated, delete the order */
                    next_block;
                    delete_record ;
            END;
```

Trigger Name	: **WHEN-BUTTON-PRESSED**	Form	: sales_order
Block	: button_palette	Item	: push_button_save
Trigger Level	: Field Level		
Function	: Save the changes to sales_order table.		
Text	: BEGIN		

```
                    if :system.form_status = 'CHANGED' THEN
                            commit_form ;
                            if :system.form_status = 'QUERY' THEN
                                    item_enable_disable('sales_order_blk',property_off);
                                    item_enable_disable('order_details_blk',property_off);
                            end if ;
                    end if;
            END;
```

Note : Trigger *When-Button-Pressed* on field push_button_modify, push_button_delete, push_button_save calls a procedure named *Item_Enable_Disable*. This procedure is included in the library *libproc*.

Trigger Name	: **WHEN-BUTTON-PRESSED**	Form	: sales_order
Block	: button_palette	Item	: push_button_exit
Trigger Level	: Field Level		
Function	: Exit sales_order form.		
Text	: BEGIN		

```
                    exit_form ;
            END ;
```

Trigger Name	: **WHEN-BUTTON-PRESSED**	Form	: sales_order
Block	: button_palette	Item	: push_button_deldet
Trigger Level	: Field Level		
Function	: Delete the current record in the sales_order table.		
Text	: BEGIN		

```
/* if the challan for the order is generated, display a message */

    select distinct s_order_no  into : sales_order_blk.s_order_no
    from challan_header
    where s_order_no = :sales_order_blk.s_order_no;
    message('Challan for the Order No. "' ||
            :sales_order_blk.s_order_no || '" already exists...
            You cannot delete the detail record.', acknowledge);
EXCEPTION
    when no_data_found then

    /* if the challan for the order is not generated, delete the
       current detail record */

    go_block('order_details_blk');
    delete_record ;
END;
```

Trigger Name	: **WHEN-BUTTON-PRESSED**	Form	: sales_order
Block	: button_palette	Item	: push_button_adddet
Trigger Level	: Field Level		
Function	: Insert a record in the sales_order table.		
Text	: DECLARE		

```
        s_order_no varchar(6);
BEGIN

    /* if the challan for the order is generated, display a message */
    select distinct s_order_no  into s_order_no from challan_header
    where  s_order_no = :sales_order_blk.s_order_no;
     message('Challan for the Order No. "' ||
            :sales_order_blk.s_order_no || '" already exists...
            You cannot add detail records.' );
EXCEPTION
    when no_data_found then

        /* if the challan for the order is not generated, add a
           blank record in the detail block */
        go_block('order_details_blk');
        create_record ;
        item_enable_disable('order_details_blk', property_on);
END ;
```

Enable or disable the scroll pushbuttons i.e. first, prior, next and last based on the total number of records on the form and the current record.

e.g.
if there are multiple records and the record pointer is on the first record the first and the prior picture button should be *disabled* and the next and the last picture buttons should be *enabled*.

This function is incorporated in the form by using a procedure. It is included in the *libproc* library.

The scroll control procedure must fire when the user moves from one record to the other. The change in the record position may be due to insert, retrieve, delete or scrolling. Trigger *When-New-Record-Instance* fires when the system performs insert retrieve, delete or scrolling operations.

Trigger Name   : **WHEN-NEW-RECORD-INSTANCE** Form   : sales_order
Block   : sales_order_blk   Item   :
Trigger Level : Block Level
Function   : calls procedure scroll_control that enables or disables the scroll pushbuttons i.e. first, prior, next and last based on the total number of records on the form and the current record.
Text   : BEGIN
                    scroll_control ;
                 END ;

VALIDATIONS
The triggers for the validation on the master block (sales_order) are defined below :
- s_order_no is a primary key. It must not be left blank nor should it be duplicated.

Trigger Name	: **WHEN-VALIDATE-ITEM**	Form	: sales_order
Block	: sales_order_blk	Item	: s_order_no
Trigger Level	: Field Level		
Function	: Check for primary key i.e. s_order_no should not be duplicated.		
Text	: BEGIN		

```
            select s_order_no into :sales_order_blk.s_order_no
                from sales_order
                where s_order_no = :sales_order_blk.s_order_no;
            message('Order No. "' || :sales_order_blk.s_order_no || '"
                    already exists...try again.');
            raise form_trigger_failure;
        EXCEPTION
            when no_data_found then null;
        END;
```

Being a primary key, s_order_no must not be left blank. To force the user to enter a value in the s_order_no field, we need to set the *Required* property to *True*. Oracle will display an error message if the user moves from that field without entering any value.

- s_order_date must be less than or equal to system date. The default value of Order date must be set to system date.

Trigger Name	: **WHEN-VALIDATE-ITEM**	Form	: sales_order
Block	: sales_order_blk	Item	: s_order_date
Trigger Level	: Field Level		
Function	: Check that order date is not left blank and it is less than or equal to the system date.		
Text	: BEGIN		

```
            if :sales_order_blk.s_order_date > sysdate then
                    message('Order Date cannot be greater than Current Date.');
                    raise form_trigger_failure;
            end if;
        END;
```

To set the default value of s_order_date to system date set the following property of s_order_date.

      Default Value   : $$date$$

$$date$$ is a system variable that records the current date in the 'DD-MON-YY' format. It can be used to designate a default value for an item only via the default value item characteristics. The item must be of *char* or *date* data type.

- dely_date must be greater than or equal to s_order_date. Set the default value of dely_date to system date.

To set the default value of dely_date to system date set the following property of dely_date.

      Default Value   : $$date$$

Trigger Name	: **WHEN-VALIDATE-ITEM**	Form	: sales_order
Block	: sales_order_blk	Item	: dely_date
Trigger Level	: Field Level		
Function	: Check that delivery date is not left blank.		
Text	: BEGIN		

```
            if :dely_date < :s_order_date then
                    message('Delivery Date cannot be less than Order Date.');
                    raise form_trigger_failure;
            end if;
       END;
```

Creating a Display Item :

In the master section, as soon as the user enters client number in the client_no field, the system must display the corresponding client name from the client_master table. Thus we need to create a display item to display the client_name i.e. an item in which the user cannot navigate.

1. Open the layout editor of the *sales_order* form. Create a new display field *name* by selecting the *display item* tool from the toolbar and dropping it on the form. Set the following properties of the display field *name*.

Name	: client_name
Item Type	: Display Item
Data Type	: Char
Maximum Length	: 20
Base Table	: False

2. Create a label object for the display field *Client_Name*.

WORKING WITH LOV OBJECTS

During data entry, often a user has to enter data which already exists in some other table. e.g. while creating a sales order, the client number needs to be entered. This client number must exist in the client master table. As soon as the client number is entered, a check for the existence of client number in the client master table must be performed.

If the entered value passes this check, the client name can be displayed else the entered value can be rejected.

Oracle provides a method via which list of values for a column can be provided. This method is called LIST OF VALUES or LOV

A List of window is an object that opens up a separate window displaying the values from one or more tables when the user clicks on the appropriate key sequence. Thus as programmers we need to define what has to be displayed in the LOV object and on which column the LOV must be displayed. Thus List of values consist of two distinct operations :

- Defining the data that will be displayed in the list.
- Connecting the List of Values to a specific column field.

Let us look at the current example. The Validation that we need to take care of is as follows :

- Client number must be present in the client master table. When the user selects a valid client number the client name must also be displayed.

The value entered into the field client number in the sales_order table must be present in the client master table. We will create an LOV that displays all the client numbers from the client master table. This list of values will be connected to column client number in the sales_order_blk. Since the data entry operator is now selecting from a pre-determined number of values i.e. selected dynamically from the table column, no validation code needs to be written.

Since the **client_no** field is not informative enough to give details of the client, a new display item can be created which will display the client name whenever client_no is entered. The LOV can display the client name along with the client numbers.

The steps are as follows :

- Create a display item to display the client name.
- Provide a list of values that gives a list of client numbers along with the client names.

Creating A List of Values :
1. In the Object Navigator, position the cursor on the *LOV* node and choose **Navigator, Create**. A *NEW LOV* properties screen is displayed.
2. List of values retrieves data based on the select statement specified for the LOV. Enter the following select statement in the *Query Text* property of the LOV.

   SELECT client_no, name INTO :client_no, :client_name FROM client_master ;

   As soon as the user selects a value from the LOV it must be displayed in the client number field. Thus the select statement includes an INTO clause that passes the selected values to the client number and client_name field. The completed *NEW LOV* screen is as shown in diagram 11.8.

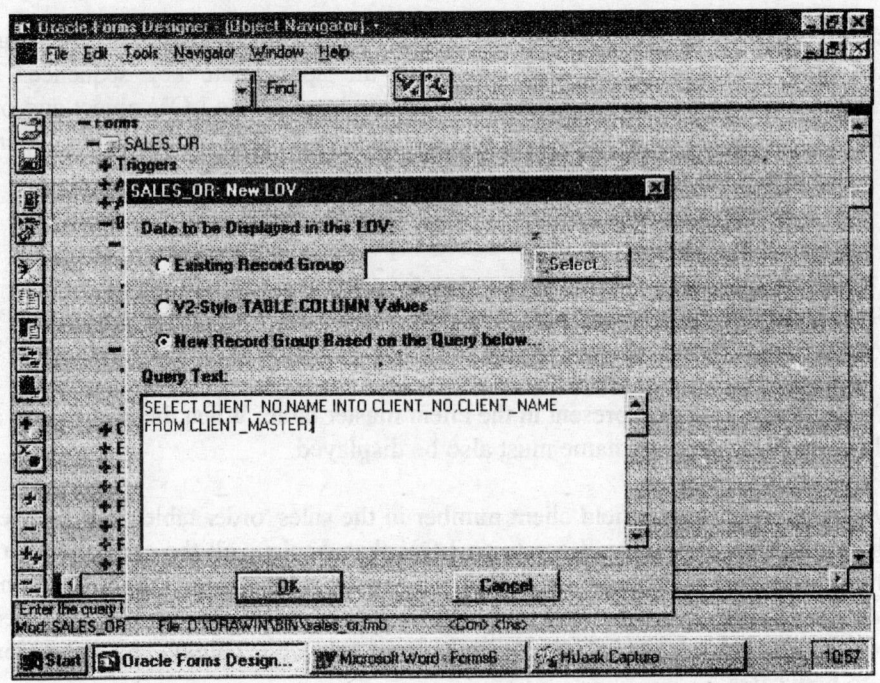

Diagram 11.8 : Creating a new LOV for *Client Number*

3. Click on OK. A List of values with a default name is displayed in the Object Navigator. Change the name of the list of values to *Client_List*.

4. The LOV **client_list** is connected to the field client no by selecting the LOV **client_list** in LOV property of the field **client_no** as shown in the diagram 11.9.

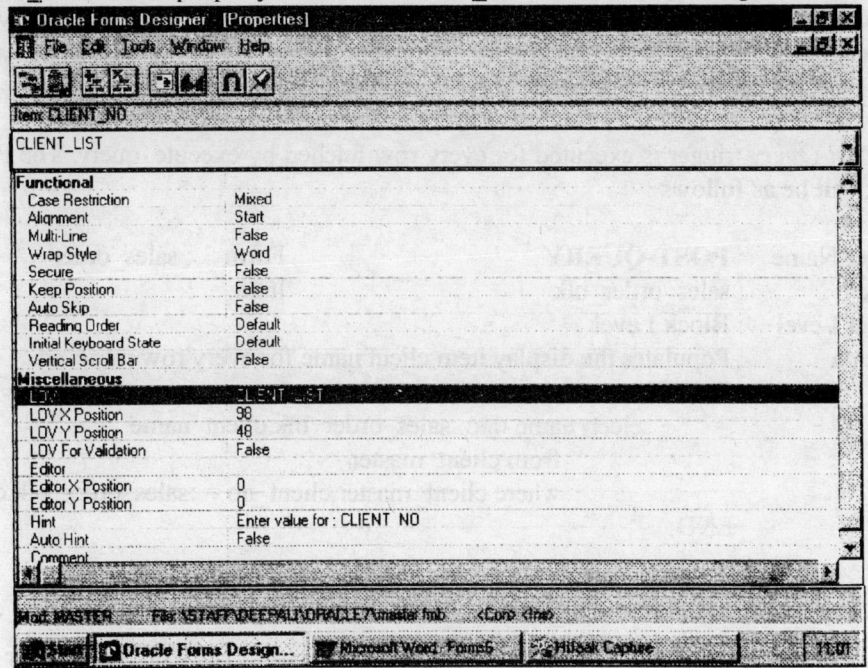

Diagram 11.9: Connecting the LOV to the field *Client No*

5. The following properties are set in the screen 11.9.

LOV	: Client_List
LOV X Position	: 98
LOV Y Position	: 48

   The LOV property connects the field to the List of Values. The LOV X Position and LOV Y Position properties specifies the X and Y co-ordinates where the List of values must be displayed.

6. When the user is on the client number field, the user can press the key sequence to show the list of values or enter the value without using the list of values. If the user enters the value directly, the system must check if the value is present in the list of values. If not, the list of values must be displayed.

   Set the *LOV For Validation* property of client number to *True* so that the system check the value entered with the list of values.

TRIGGERS FOR POPULATING NAME IN VIEW MODE :

The list of values will populate the client number and client name when the user selects a value from the list. In the view mode the client number will be populated when an execute_query is fired. Since the client name is not connected to the base table, we need to write PL/SQL block that populate client name for every record retrieved.

The *Post-Query* trigger is executed for every row fetched by execute_query. The PL/SQL block will be as follows :

Trigger Name	: **POST-QUERY**	Form	: sales_order
Block	: sales_order_blk	Item	:
Trigger Level	: Block Level		
Function	: Populates the display item client name for every row retrieved.		
Text	: BEGIN		

```
        select name into :sales_order_blk.client_name
               from client_master
               where client_master.client_no = :sales_order_blk.client_no;
        END;
```

- salesman number must be present in the salesman master table.

Create the list of values for the salesman number field. The properties of the list of values will be as follows :

Name	: salesman_list
Query	: SELECT salesman_no INTO :salesman_no FROM salesman_master ;

The properties of the salesman number field will be as follows :

LOV	: salesman_list
LOV X Position	: 304
LOV Y Position	: 119
LOV For Validation	: True

- Status is a not enterable field. It will be updated from some other data entry screen. Use a display item for not enterable field.

Order status column in the sales_order table, shows the status of the order i.e whether the order is completely delivered or it is in process. This column will be updated when a delivery challan is generated.

Thus this field will not be enterable from the sales order data entry form. Select the order status field in the Object Navigator. Select **Tools**, **Properties** from the main menu. It displays the properties of the status field. Set the *Item Type* property to *Display Item*.

- dely_type must be a radio group with buttons having label as **Part** and **Full** and value as **P** and **F**.

A client may request the delivery of goods in Part or Full. The order form must specify whether the delivery is in part or full. The dely_type field in the sales_order table records the delivery type information. It can take only two values i.e. **P** - Part and **F** - Full.

If a field can take only fixed values, the user must be provided with appropriate values to choose from. This will make the form more user friendly. It will also eliminate data entry errors.

USING A RADIO BUTTON GROUP

Oracle provides an object via which appropriate values for a column can be provided. This object is called a RADIO BUTTON GROUP. It consists of two distinct operations :
- Defining the *radio button group*
- Defining the radio buttons for the group.

Let us look at the current example. The value in the field dely_type in the sales_order table can take specific values like 'P' and 'F'. We will create a Radio button group and the radio buttons.

1. Open the property sheet of dely_type and set the following properties :

Item_type   : Radio Group
Default Value   : F

2. Open the Layout editor and place the radio buttons as shown in diagram 11.5. Each time you place a radio button, the system will ask for the name of *Radio Group* as shown in diagram 11.10.

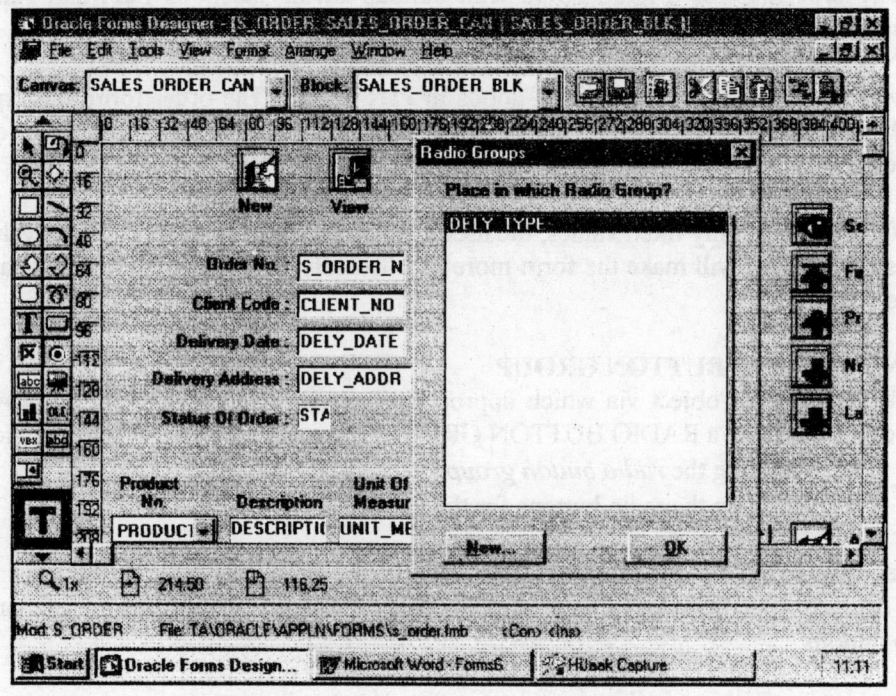

254 COMMERCIAL APPLICATION DEVELOPMENT USING ORACLE 7, DEVELOPER 2000

Diagram 11.10 : Creating a Radio Button

1. Click on OK. Set the properties of each of the radio buttons as follows :

Name   : RB_Part
Label : Part
Value : P

Name   : RB_Full
Label : Full
Value : F

- The following fields cannot be left blank : s_order_date, dely_address, dely_date, client_no, salesman_no.

- Set the *Required* property of the following fields to *True* : s_order_date, dely_address, dely_date, client_no, salesman_no.

MASTER DETAIL FORM

The validation on the detail block (order_details_blk) are defined below :
In the detail section, the combination of product_no and s_order_no is the primary key. Thus the product_no for a specific order should not be repeated.

This check should be performed as and when the user exits product_no item and goes to the next item field, next record or previous record either using key board or mouse.

If the user enters a valid value, it must display description, unit of measure and the product rate. Description and unit of measure are not in the sales_order_details table. This we need to create two display items to display description and unit of measure.

Select the order_details_blk in the layout editor and place the display items for description and unit of measure. Since the detail block displays multiple records and the description and unit of measure are included in the detail section, the form will display multiple records for both the display fields.

A function is written in the *libproc.pll* library to check for duplicate values in the detail section. This function is called from the different key and mouse triggers.

In the current example, the function checks to see that the product_no is not repeated for an order.

Open the *libproc* library and include function *f_dup_detail*.

Function Name	: **F_DUP_DETAIL**
Function	: In the detail section, the combination of s_order_no and product_no is the primary key. Thus the product_no for a specific order should not be repeated.
	This check should be performed as and when the user exit product_no item and goes to the next item, next record or previous record.
	A procedure is written to check that the product_no is not repeated for a specific order and the same is called from the different key and mouse triggers.

```
FUNCTION F_DUP_DETAIL (blk_col_name char) RETURN NUMBER IS
        Is_duplicate char(5);
        current_rec_no number(3);
        last_rec_no number(3);
        cur_val varchar2(20);
        row_count number(3);
        form_name varchar(40);
BEGIN
        is_duplicate := 'FALSE';
```

```
/* store the current record position */
current_rec_no := to_number( name_in('system.cursor_record'));

/* store the current record's product number */
cur_val := name_in(blk_col_name);
form_name := get_application_property(current_form_name);
set_form_property(form_name,validation,property_false);
last_record; /* position cursor on the last record */
/* check if current record is the only record in the detail block */
if name_in('system.cursor_record') <> '1' then

        /* find maximum number of records in the detail block */
        last_rec_no := to_number(name_in('system.cursor_record'));
        first_record;
        /* set up a loop from one to maximum number of records to compare
           each record's product_no with the variable cur_val */
        for row_count in 1..last_rec_no loop

                /* Ensure comparison is not made with the entered product_no,
                   stored in variable cur_val */
                if current_rec_no <> row_count then
                        if cur_val = name_in(blk_col_name) then
                                is_duplicate := 'TRUE';
                                exit;
                        end if;
                end if;

                /* Ensure that the cursor doesn't go to a record that does not exist */
                if last_rec_no <> row_count then
                        next_record;
                end if;
        end loop;
end if;

/* Reposition the cursor to the record number when function was called */
go_record(current_rec_no);
set_form_property(form_name,validation,property_true);
/* check if a duplicate is found; if yes, return 1 else return 0 */
if is_duplicate = 'TRUE' then
        return(1);
else
        return(0);
end if;
END;
```

MASTER DETAIL FORM 257

Trigger Name	: **KEY-NEXT-ITEM**	Form	: sales_order
Block	: order_details_blk	Item	: product_no
Trigger Level	: Field Level		
Function	: Check that product number is not duplicated for a specified order.		
Text	: BEGIN		

```
            if :order_details_blk.product_no is null then
                    message('Product No cannot be left blank');
                    raise form_trigger_failure;
            else

                    /* f_dup_detail is a function that checks that the combination
                       of s_order_no and product_no is unique. It returns 0 it the
                       combination is unique else it returns 1.This function is
                       included in the libproc library */

                    if f_dup_detail('order_details.product_no') = 0 then
                            select description, unit_measure, selling_price
                            into :description, :unit_measure, :product_rate
                            from product_master
                            where product_no = :order_details_blk.product_no;
                            next_item;
                    else
                            message('You cannot include product "' ||
                                    :product_no || '" twice in order "' ||
                                    :sales_order_blk.s_order_no || '".');
                            raise form_trigger_failure;
                    end if;
            end if;

    EXCEPTION
            when no_data_found then
            message('Product code "' || :product_no || '" is invalid...try again.');
            raise form_trigger_failure;
    END;
```

Trigger Name	: **KEY-UP**	Form	: sales_order
Block	: order_details_blk	Item	:
Trigger Level	: Block Level		
Function	: Check that product number is not duplicated for a specified order.		
Text	: BEGIN		

```
            if :system.cursor_block = 'order_details_blk' and
               :system.cursor_record <> 1 then
                    if :order_details_blk.product_no is null then
                            message('Product No cannot be left blank');
                            raise form_trigger_failure;
                    else
```

```
                    if f_dup_detail('order_details_blk_blk.product_no') = 0 then
                        select description, unit_measure, selling_price
                            into :description, :unit_measure, :product_rate
                            from product_master
                            where product_no = :product_no;
                        previous_record;
                    else
                        message('You cannot include product ''' || :product_no
                            || ''' twice in order ''' ||
                            :sales_order_blk.s_order_no || '''.');
                        raise form_trigger_failure;
                    end if;
                end if;
            end if;
        EXCEPTION
            when no_data_found then
            message('Product code ''' || :product_no || ''' is invalid...try again.');
            raise form_trigger_failure;
        END;
```

Trigger Name	: **KEY-DOWN**	Form	: sales_order
Block	: order_details_blk	Item	:
Trigger Level	: Block Level		
Function	: Check that product number is not duplicated for a specified order.		
Text	: BEGIN		

```
            if :system.cursor_block = 'order_details_blk' and
                :system.last_record < > 'TRUE' then
                if :order_details_blk.product_no is null then
                    message('Product No cannot be left blank');
                    raise form_trigger_failure;
                else
                    if f_dup_detail('order_details_blk_blk.product_no') = 0 then
                        select description, unit_measure, selling_price
                            into :description, :unit_measure, :product_rate
                            from product_master
                            where product_no = :product_no;
                        next_record;
                    else
                        message('You cannot include product ''' || :product_no
                            || ''' twice in order ''' ||
                            :sales_order_blk.s_order_no || '''.');
                        raise form_trigger_failure;
                    end if;
                end if;
            end if;
```

MASTER DETAIL FORM 259

```
            EXCEPTION
                when no_data_found then
                    message('Product code "' || :product_no || '" is invalid...try again.');
                    raise form_trigger_failure;
            END;
```

Trigger Name	: **WHEN-MOUSE-CLICK**	Form	: sales_order
Block	: order_details_blk	Item	:
Trigger Level	: Block Level		
Function	: Check that product number is not duplicated for a specified order.		
Text	: DECLARE		

```
                itemtype varchar(30);
            BEGIN
                if :order_details_blk.product_no is null then
                    message('Product No cannot be left blank');
                    raise form_trigger_failure;
                else
                    if f_dup_detail('order_details_blk_blk.product_no') = 0 then
                        select description, unit_measure, sell_price
                        into :description, :unit_measure, :product_rate
                        from product_master
                        where product_no = :order_details_blk.product_no;
                        if :system.mouse_item <> 'order_details_blk.product_no' then
                            itemtype:=get_item_property(:system.mouse_item,item_type);
                            if itemtype <> 'DISPLAY ITEM' then
                                Go_Item(:system.mouse_item);
                            end if;
                        end if;
                    else
                        message('You cannot include product "' || :product_no
                            || '" twice in order "' || :sales_order_blk.s_order_no || '".');
                        raise form_trigger_failure;
                    end if;
                end if
            EXCEPTION
                when no_data_found then
                    message('Product code "' || :product_no || '" is invalid...try again.');
                    raise form_trigger_failure;
            END;
```

TRIGGERS FOR POPULATING DESCRIPTION AND UNIT_MEASURE IN VIEW MODE :

Description and *Unit_measure* are not connected to the base table and thus these will not be populated automatically. These items must be populated by writing PL/SQL code. When the user enters a product_no and tabs out, Oracle Forms fires the *Key-Next-Item* trigger. The *Key-Next-Item* trigger validates the values in the product_no field and if the user has entered a valid value, it displays the description, unit_measure and rate.

In the view mode the product number product_rate, qty_ordered and qty_dispatched will be populated when an execute_query is fired. Since the description and unit of measure are not connected to the base table, we need to write PL/SQL block that populate description and unit of measure for every record retrieved.

The *Key-Next-Item* trigger fires only when the user presses the key sequence to tab out of the field i.e. when the user presses the TAB or the ENTER key.

Thus *Post-Query* trigger is executed for every row fetched by execute_query. The PL/SQL block will be as follows :

Trigger Name   : **POST-QUERY**   Form : sales_order
Block   : order_details_blk   Item   :
Trigger Level   : Block Level
Function   : Populates the description, unit of measure for every row retrieved.
Text   : BEGIN
          select description, unit_measure
              into :description, :unit_measure from product_master
              where product_no = :product_no;
    END;

- Product Rate must not be left blank.

Trigger Name   : **WHEN-VALIDATE-ITEM**   Form : sales_order
Block   : order_details_blk   Item   : product_rate
Trigger Level   : Field Level
Function   : Check that product rate is not left blank.
Text   : BEGIN
          if (:order_details_blk.product_rate) is null then
              message('Rate Ordered Cannot Be Left Blank');
              raise form_trigger_failure;
        end if;
    END;

- Quantity Ordered must not be left blank. Quantity ordered cannot be 0.

Trigger Name	: **WHEN-VALIDATE-ITEM**	Form	: sales_order
Block	: order_details_blk	Item	: qty_ordered
Trigger Level	: Field Level		
Function	: Check that qty_ordered is not left blank.		
Text	: BEGIN		

```
            if (:order_details_blk.qty_ordered) is null then
                    message('Quantity Ordered Cannot Be Left Blank');
                    raise form_trigger_failure;
            elsif (:order_details_blk.qty_ordered) = 0 then
                    message('Quantity Ordered Cannot Be 0');
                    raise form_trigger_failure;
            end if;
    END;
```

- qty_disp is not enterable field. Use a display item for not enterable field. The default value should be set to **0**.

Quantity dispatched column in the sales_order_details table, shows the total quantity dispatched to the client. This column will be updated when a delivery challan is generated or when a faulty goods note showing the goods returned by the client is generated.

Thus this field will not be enterable from the sales order data entry form. Select the qty_disp field in the Object Navigator. Select **Tools**, **Properties** from the main menu. It displays the properties of the qty_disp field. Set the *Item Type* property to *Display Item* and the *Default* property to *0*.

CREATING AND USING A LIST ITEM

So far we have seen how a LOV can be used to show a list of values. List Item also displays a list of values.

A list item is a list of text elements that can be displayed as either a poplist, text list, or combo box. A list item displays a fixed number of elements from which a operator can select a single text element. Each element in a list is a text string up to 30 characters long. At runtime, you can programmatically evaluate, add, or remove list elements. The runtime behavior of the list item is as explained below.

POPLIST :
The poplist style list item appears initially as a single field (similar to a text item field). When the operator selects the list icon, a list of available choices appears as shown below.

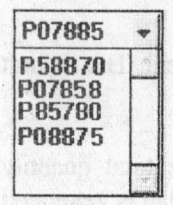

```
P07885  ▼
P58870
P07858
P85780
P08875
```

TEXT LIST
The text list style list item appears as a rectangular box which displays a fixed number of values. When the text list contains values that cannot be displayed (due to the displayable area of the item), a vertical scroll bar appears, allowing the operator to view and select undisplayed values.

```
P00001   ▲
P03453
P06734
P07865
P07868   ▼
```

COMBO LIST
The combo box style list item combines the features found in list and text items. Unlike the poplist or the text list style list items, the combo box style list item will both display fixed values and accept one operator-entered value. The combo box list item appears as an empty box with an icon to the right. The user can enter text directly into the combo field or click the list icon to display a list of available values.

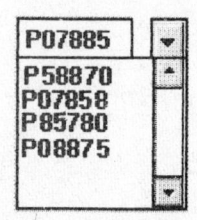

```
P07885  ▼
P58870   ▲
P07858
P85780
P08875
         ▼
```

MASTER DETAIL FORM 263

LIST ELEMENT VALUES :
When you create a list item you must associate a data value with each element in the list. When an operator selects an element, the value of the list item changes to the value associated with that element. Similarly, when a value is fetched from the database or assigned to the list programmatically, the element whose value matches the fetched or assigned value becomes the selected element in the list.

Creating A List Item :
A list item can be created in two ways as explained below.
METHOD 1
1. Click and drag the list item tool until the item's bounding box is the desired size. The default list item is displayed as a poplist.

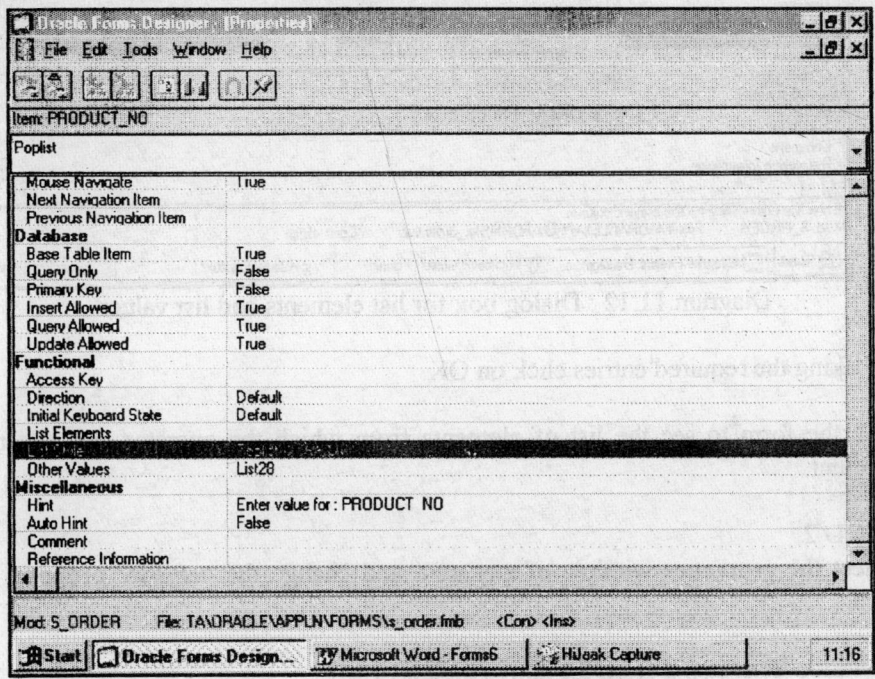

Diagram 11.11 : Properties window for list item

1. Open the properties window for the list item and change the **liststyle** to popup/combo/tlist as shown in diagram 11.11.

2. Double click on list elements property a dialog box appears as shown in diagram 11.12. Here enter the list element and its corresponding value box list item value.

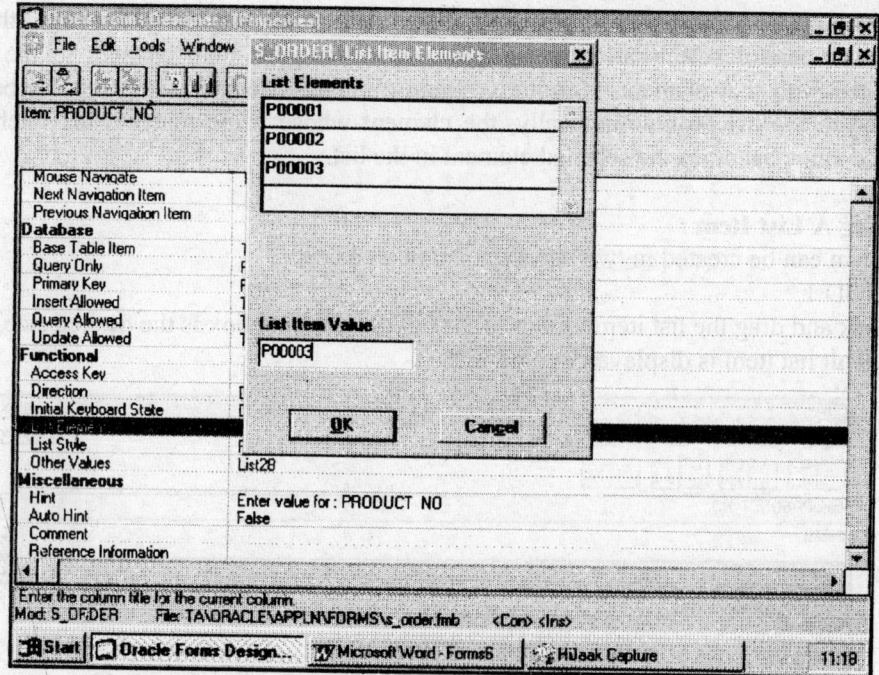

Diagram 11.12 : Dialog box for list elements and list values

After making the required entries click on OK.

1. Run the form to see the list of elements from which the operator can select a list element.

METHOD 2
1. Select the properties window of any item and change the *itemstyle* property to *list item*.

2. Continue from step 2 from the above method 1.

- Changing the Text Item for product_no to a List Item. For the sales order form make the item product_no a list item and allow the operator to select from product codes present in product master as shown in diagram 11.13.

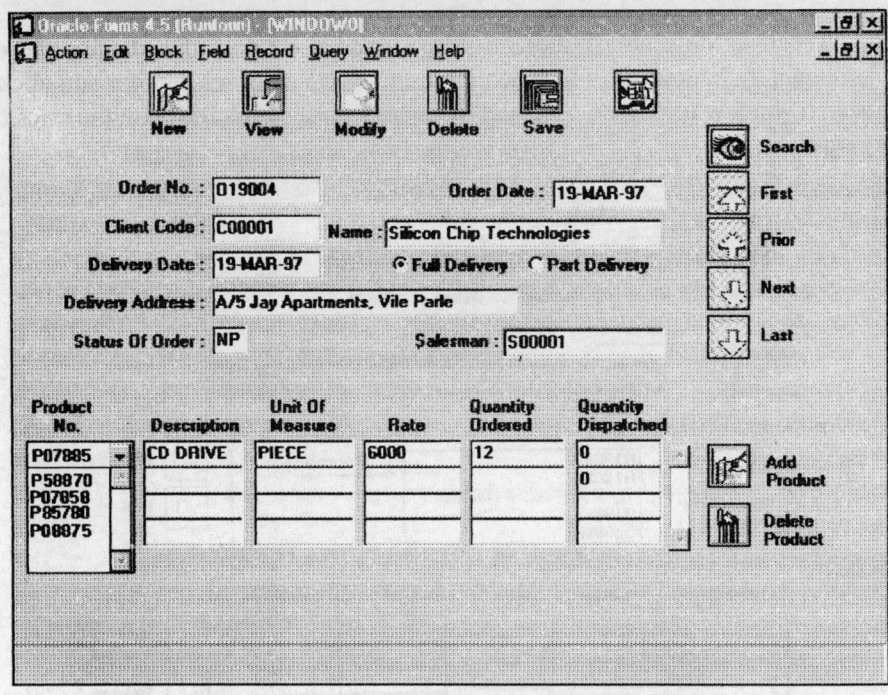

Diagram 11.13 : Sales Order data-entry form

1. Make the **item style** property **listitem** and **list style** property as **poplist**.

2. Write the following code in the WHEN-NEW-FORM-INSTANCE trigger as shown below.

```
Trigger Name  : WHEN-NEW-FORM-INSTANCE      Form  : sales_order
Block         :                              Item  :
Function      : Makes sure that the group doesn't already exist and then creates the
                group. After creating the group the group is populated with list elements
                and list values using a query. This group is then populated into the
                popuplist.
Text          : DECLARE
                    rg_name varchar2(40) := 'prod_rec';
                    status number;
                    groupid recordgroup ;
                BEGIN
                    groupid := create_group_from_query(rg_name,
                        'select product_no, product_no from product_master');
                    status := populate_group(groupid);
                    populate_list('product_no', groupid);
                END;
```

INCLUDING SEARCH FUNCTION IN THE MASTER DETAIL FORM

To modify the form to include search function that searches a record to match the s_order_no entered by the user.

When the user clicks on search button, it must popup a window that display the order number as shown in diagram 11.14. When the user selects an order number and clicks on OK, the search window must be closed and the record must be displayed in the sales order data entry screen.

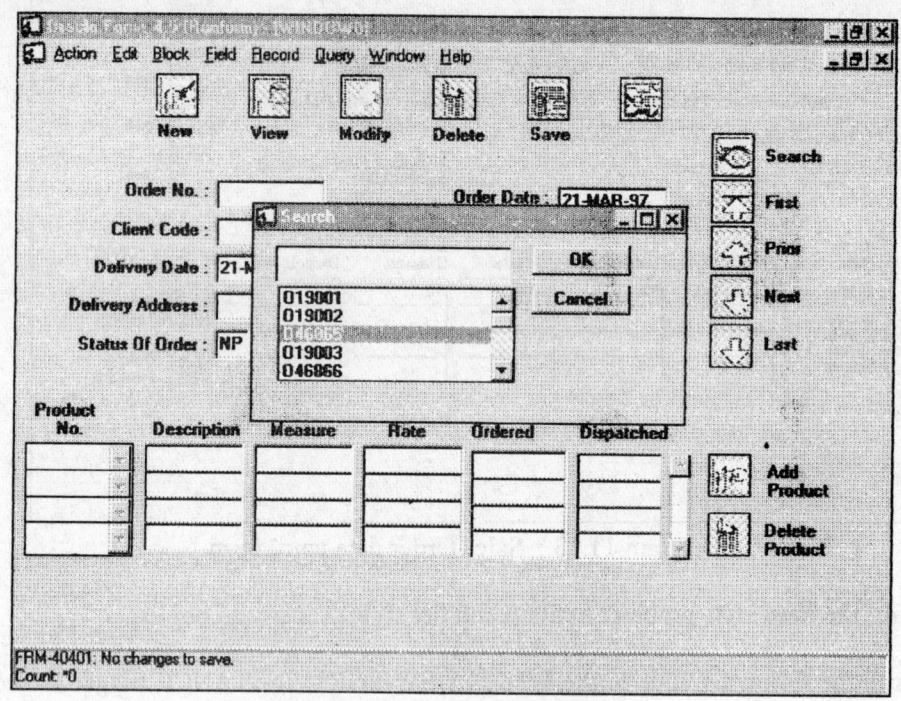

Diagram 11.14 : Search Window

Include a text item in the search window. The list must display the order numbers as per the pattern entered in the text item.

The steps to achieve the above objective are as follows :

1. Right click on button_palette block. It displays a popup menu. Click on *Layout Editor*. It displays the form layout. Click on the toolbox and select icon labeled *button* and place it on the form. Set the *Name* and *Label* property as

   Name   : push_button_search
   Label   : Search

2. Open a new form and save it as search.fmb.

3. Create a control block named search_blk.

4. Click on the toolbox in the layout editor and select icon labeled *text item* and place it on the form. Set the *following* properties of the text item.

Name   : search_pattern

5. Click on the toolbox in the layout editor and select icon labeled *list Item* and place it on the form. Set the *following* properties of the list item.

Name   : search_list
List Style   : Tlist

6. Place two push buttons as shown in diagram 11.14 and set the following properties.

Name   : push_button_ok
Label   : OK
Enabled   : False
Name   : push_button_cancel
Label   : Cancel

7. Size the canvas by setting the following properties.

Width   : 236
Height   : 101
View Width   : 236
View Height   : 101

8. Set the following properties of the window :

Name   : search_win
X Position   : 130
Y Position   : 100
Width   : 236
Height   : 101
Title   : Search
Window Style   : Dialog
Fixed Size   : True

As shown in diagram 11.14, the search window must be displayed as a popup window in the center of the screen. The *X Position* and *Y Position* attribute sets the position of the window on the VDU. The *Height* and *Width* attribute sets the size of the window.

The *Fixed Size* attribute is set to *True* to ensure that the user does not resize the search window.

9. Write the PL/SQL code in the search form as shown below :

Trigger Name	: **PRE-FORM**		Form	: search
Block	:		Item	:
Function	: To populate the list item with s_order_no as display value and data value.			
Text	: DECLARE			

```
        rg_name varchar(40) := 'Search_List';
        groupid recordgroup;
        status number;
BEGIN
        /* Create a record group that includes all the records from the
        sales_order table. The select statement select two values the
        first value will be used a display value and the second value will
        be used as data value in the list item */
        groupid := create_group_from_query(rg_name,
                'select s_order_no, s_order_no
                        from sales_order');

        /* populate the group with the records fetched by the
           select statement */
        status := populate_group(groupid);

        /* populate the list with the records in the group */
        populate_list('search_list', groupid);
END;
```

Trigger Name	: **WHEN-VALIDATE-ITEM**		Form	: search
Block	: search_blk		Item	: search_pattern
Function	: To change the list to display records as per the pattern entered by the user.			
Text	: DECLARE			

```
        rg_name varchar(40) := 'Search_List';
        groupid recordgroup;
        status number;
BEGIN
        /* find a record group by the name of 'search_list' */
        groupid := find_group(rg_name);

        /* if the record group exists then populate the group
           id_null is a packaged procedure that checks whether the
           record group id is null or not. It takes a recordgroup
           as the parameter */
        IF not id_null(groupid) THEN
                /* if the search pattern is null then populate the
        record group with all the records from the
```

```
                    sales_order table else populate the record
                    group with select statement having appropriate
                    where clause. */
                    if :search_pattern = '' or :search_pattern is null then
                        status := populate_group_with_query
                                (rg_name, 'select s_order_no, s_order_no
                                           from sales_order');
                    else
                        status := populate_group_with_query
                                (rg_name, 'select s_order_no,
                                           s_order_no from
                                sales_order where lower(s_order_no)
                                like lower(''' || :search_pattern || '%'')');
                    end if;

                /* populate the list with the records in the group */
                populate_list('seach_list', groupid);
            end if;
        END;
```

Note :

1. If the record group with a specific name exists, we simply need to populate that group with appropriate data. In this case, if the record group 'search_list' is existing, we need to populate the record group with / without a where clause.

2. In the Create_group_from_query function, we need to pass the following select statement as a string value :

    SELECT s_order_no, s_order_no FROM sales_order
        WHERE lower(s_order_no) like lower('search pattern%')

    where search pattern is the value in the search pattern text item.

Thus the select statement string is divided into a fixed part i.e. select statement upto *lower'* and a variable part i.e. the value of the search pattern.

The concatenation character i.e. || is used to concatenate strings. Thus the select statement will change to

    'SELECT s_order_no, s_order_no FROM sales_order
        WHERE lower(s_order_no) like
        lower(' || :search_pattern || '%)'

Single quotes are used to enclose string values. In the above select statement we need to have the single quotes as a part of the string itself. Two single quotes within a string will include a single quote in the string. Thus the select statement will change as follows :

```
                    'SELECT s_order_no, s_order_no FROM sales_order
                        WHERE lower(s_order_no) like
                        lower('''|| :search_pattern || '%'')'
```

Trigger Name   : **WHEN-BUTTON-PRESSED**   Form : search
Block   : search_blk   Item : push_button_ok
Function   : To assign the selected list value to global variable and quit the
                 search form. The value in this global variable will be used in the
                 default_where property of the sales_order_blk.
Text   : BEGIN

   /* *Assigning the selected order_no to a global
   variable. The value in the global variable can then be
   used in the sales order form.*

   *Any variable prefixed with **global.** is considered to a
   global variable. Global variables are not explicitly
   declared. They are of Datatype char size 255* */
                    :global.search_value := :search_list;
                    exit_form;
                 END;

Trigger Name   : **WHEN-BUTTON-PRESSED**   Form : search
Block   : search_blk   Item : push_button_cancel
Function   : To assign spaces to global variable and quit the search form.
Text   : BEGIN
                    :global.search_value := ' ';
                    exit_form ;
                 END;

Trigger Name   : **WHEN-LIST-CHANGED**   Form : search
Block   : search_blk   Item : search_list
Function   : To set the enable property of the OK button to true
Text   : BEGIN
                    set_item_property('push_button_ok',enabled,property_on);
                 END;

3. Write the PL/SQL code in the search button in sales order form as shown below :

Trigger Name	: **WHEN-BUTTON-PRESSED**	Form	: sales_order
Block	: button_palette	Item	: push_button_search
Function	: To open the search form. Pass the valid value accepted in the search form to the default_where property of the sales order block and execute the query.		
Text	: BEGIN		

```
            /* call_form is used to open another form. It takes the
            form name(along with the path ) as the parameter.
            By default, when a form ( called form ) is opened from
            another form (calling form), the calling form is made
            invisible. In this example we need to display the search
            form as popup form. The sales order form must not be
            invisible. This can be achieved by passing no_hide
            parameter to call_form. */
                call_form('c:\orawork\search.fmx', no_hide);

            /* If the search_value is not spaces then set the
            default_where property of the sales_order_blk
            to the sales_order_no entered go to sales_order_blk
            and execute the query set the default_where property
            of the sales_order_blk to null string. */
            if not (:global.search_value = ' ') then
                set_block_property('sales_order_blk',
                    default_where, 'where s_order_no = ''' ||
                    :global.search_value || '''');
            go_block('sales_order_blk');
            execute_query;
            set_block_property('sales_order_blk',
                    default_where, '');
            end if;
        END;
```

When *Execute_Query* is fired, Oracle creates the select statement from the properties of the block and the items included in the block. One such property is *Default_Where*. The *Default_Where* property includes the where clause of the select statement. If the *Default_Where* is set the record set retrieved on the form will be restricted to the records that satisfy the condition the *Default_Where* clause.

Default_Where property can be set at design time or it can be set programmatically by using *Set_Block_Property*. *Set_Block_Property* takes in three parameters. These are the *name of the block*, the *property name* and the *property value*.

In the current example, the execute query must populate the block with a global select statement when the user clicks on view. If the user clicks on search, appropriate where clause must be included in the select statement. Thus we need to specify the where clause programmatically as follows :

```
set_block_property('sales_order_blk', default_where,
    'where s_order_no = ''' || :global.search_value || '''');
```

HANDS ON

When goods are delivered to the client, a delivery challan against a sales order is generated for the goods delivered.

Challan Information like challan number, challan date and order number is recorded in the master table. The information about the products delivered like product number and quantity of goods delivered is recorded in the detail table.

Design a data-entry screen that allows data manipulation in the **challan_header** and **challan_detail** tables. Both these tables are linked by **challan_no** (challan number).

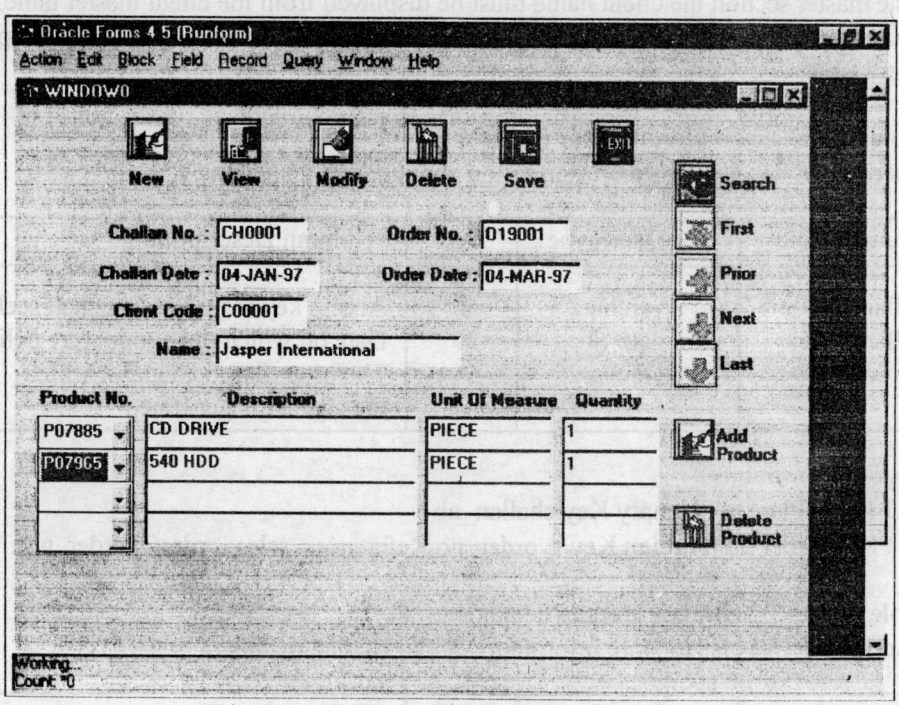

Diagram 11.15 : Delivery Challan data-entry screen

Provide the user with complete data manipulation operations (Add, View, Modify, The data entry screen must provide for add master, add detail, delete master, delete detail, modify, view, search and exit. The navigation buttons are first, previous, next and last.

Add mode   : All the fields in the master and detail block must be updatable.
Modify mode   : In the modify mode the user is allowed to modify the challan date and the quantity delivered to the client.
View mode   : All the fields in the master and detail block must not be updatable.
Delete Mode   : Delete cascading must be on.

Include search function that searches a record to match the challan number entered by the user.

In the master section the client name must be displayed from the client master table. In the detail section, the user must display the description and unit of measure from the product master table.

Table name   : **challan_header** (Master)
Description : Use to store information about delivery challans.

Column Name	Data Type	Size	Column Description
challan_no	varchar2	6	Access key via which we shall seek data.
challan_date	date	25	Date on which the goods were delivered.
s_order_no	varchar2	6	The order number against which the challan is generated

Integrity Constraints :
- PK_challlan_no Primary Key challan_no
- FK_s_order_no Foreign Key s_order_no References sales_order(s_order_no)

Table name   : **challan_details**(details)
Description : Use to store information about challan details.

Column Name	Data Type	Size	Column Description
challan_no	varchar2	6	Challan No. for which details have to be stored.
product_no	varchar2	6	Product No. for which details have to be stored.
quantity	number	8	Quantity of goods delivered.

Integrity Constraints :
- PK_challan_details Primary Key (challan_no, product_no)
- FK_product_details Foreign Key product_no References product_master(product_no)
- FK_challan_datails Foreign Key s_order_no References sales_order(s_order_no)

MASTER DETAIL FORM 275

Additional details :
Whenever a record is inserted ,updated,deleted ;two tables are affected -product_master and sales_order_details.

- The quantity dispatched would increase or decrease the Qty_On_Hand of Product_master and the Qty_Disp of Sales_Order_Details by a corresponding value.
- Whenever an insert is performed a decrease is recorded in Qty_on_Hand of Product_Master and an increase in Qty_Disp of Sales_Order_Details.
- Whenever a delete is performed an increase is recorded in Qty_on_Hand of Product_Master and a decrease in Qty_Disp of Sales_Order_Details.
- Whenever an update is recorded the old value of quantity is added to qty_on_hand of Product_master and the new value is subtracted . Also old value of quantity is subtracted from Qty_disp of Sales_order_details and new Quantity must be added.

The push buttons must be connected to a property class named *PClass_Button*. The properties in the property class must be as follows :

Name	PClass_Button
Item Type	Button
Canvas	challan_can
Width	40
Height	23
Iconic	True

All the data items must be connected to Visual Attribute object named VA_Data_Items. The properties in the Visual Attribute must be set as follows :

Name	VA_Data_Items
Font Name	MS Sans Serif
Font Size	8
Font Style	Plain
Font Width	Normal
Font Weight	Bold

Validations in the delivery challan form data entry screen are as follows :
- challan_no is a Primary Key i.e. duplicate values are not allowed in challan_no. It cannot be left blank.
- s_order_no must be present in the Sales_order table and the user can select only orders that are not completely fulfilled i.e. the order status is not 'FP'. Implement this validation by using **LOV**.
- Challan_Date cannot be greater than system date or less than the s_order_date. Set the default value of challan_date to system date.
- Product_no must be present in the sales_order_details for a particular order table. Implement this validation by using **LOV**. The list of products must include only the products in stock i.e. the qty_on_hand must be greater than 0 and the list must include only those products that are not delivered in full i.e. qty_ordered is greater than the qty_disp.

- The data entry form must display the description, unit_measure in the detail block from the product master table when the user exits the product_no field or when the records are retrieved by the user.
- A single product cannot be repeated for an order.
- Qty delivered cannot be greater than qty_on_hand in the product master and cannot be greater than the qty_ordered.

Cross Table Updations :
- The qty_disp must be set in the sales_order_details table for the order and the product delivered as follows :

    Add mode   : qty_disp = qty_disp + quantity
    Modify mode   : qty_disp = qty_disp - old quantity + new_quantity
    Delete mode   : qty_disp = qty_disp - quantity

- If the order is completely delivered the status flag in the sales_order table must be set to **FP**, else if the order is not completely delivered the status flag in the sales_order table must be set to **IP**.
- The qty_on_hand must be updated in the product master table for the product delivered as follows :

    Add mode   : qty_on_hand = qty_on_hand - quantity
    Modify mode   : qty_on_hand = qty_on_hand + old quantity - new_quantity
    Delete mode   : qty_on_hand = qty_on_hand + quantity

MASTER DETAIL FORM 277

SOLUTION :
1. Create the default form as specified in CREATING A MASTER DETAIL FORM. The *Master / Detail* section of the detail must be set as follows :

           Master Block   Challan_Header_Blk
           Join Condition   Challan_Header_Blk.Challan_No =
                                                 Challan_Details_Blk.Challan_No

2. Create a new property class object *PClass_Button* and add following properties to the property class object.

                   Name   : PClass_Button
                   Item Type   : Button
                   Canvas   : Challan_Can
                   Width   : 40
                   Height   : 23
                   Iconic   : True

3. Create a new block named *button_palette* to include the push buttons.

4. Create an item in the block *button_palette* and assign following properties to the item.

                   Name   : push_button_Add
                   Class   : PClass_Button
                   Icon Name   : add

5. Similarly place push buttons for the data manipulation operation as shown in diagram 11.15.

6. Create a new visual attribute object *VA_Data_Items* and add following properties to the visual attribute object.

                   Name   : VA_Data_Items
                   Font Name   : MS Sans Serif
                   Font Size   : 8
                   Font Style   : Plain
                   Font Width   : Normal
                   Font Weight   : Bold

7. Position and Size the items as shown in diagram 11.15.

8. Set the **Next Navigation Item** property of the last item i.e. **name** to the name of the first item i.e. **challan_no**. Similarly, in the detail block set the **Next Navigation Item** property of the last item i.e. **quantity** to the name of the first item i.e. **product_no**.

9. Attach the library *libproc.pll* as explained in the topic ATTACHING A LIBRARY TO ANOTHER MODULE. Once the library is attached to the form, the program units defined in the library can be referenced in the triggers.

TRIGGERS
The Triggers are defined below :

Trigger Name   : **WHEN-BUTTON-PRESSED**   Form : challan
Block   : button_palette   Item : push_button_first
Trigger Level : Field Level
Function   : Go to the first record in the challan_header buffer.
Text   : BEGIN
                     go_block('challan_header_blk');
                     first_record ;
                 END ;

Trigger Name   : **WHEN-BUTTON-PRESSED**   Form : challan
Block   : button_palette   Item : push_button_prior
Trigger Level : Field Level
Function   : Go to the previous record in the challan_header buffer.
Text   : BEGIN
                     go_block('challan_header_blk');
                     previous_record ;
                 END ;

Trigger Name   : **WHEN-BUTTON-PRESSED**   Form : challan
Block   : button_palette   Item : push_button_next
Trigger Level : Field Level
Function   : Go to the next record in the challan_header buffer.
Text   : BEGIN
                     go_block('challan_header_blk');
                     next_record ;
                 END ;

Trigger Name   : **WHEN-BUTTON-PRESSED**   Form : challan
Block   : button_palette   Item : push_button_last
Trigger Level : Field Level
Function   : Go to the last record in the challan_header buffer.
Text   : BEGIN
                     go_block('challan_header_blk');
                     last_record ;
                 END ;

MASTER DETAIL FORM 279

Trigger Name	: **WHEN-BUTTON-PRESSED**	Form	: challan
Block	: button_palette	Item	: Push_button_add
Trigger Level	: Field Level		
Function	: Insert a record in the challan_header table and set the updateable property of all the fields of the challan_header and the challan_detail block to ON.		
Text	: BEGIN		

```
        go_block('challan_header_blk');

        /* The user must be allowed to enter only a single master detail
        record. Thus after every record, ask the user to save changes
        if the user clicks on 'YES' then save current changes and clear
        the form. The clear_form package procedure checks if there are
        changes in the form. If so then it asks for confirmation to save
        the data. Based on the user options i.e. if the user clicks on 'YES'
        the form data is saved, the form buffer cleared and a blank
        record is inserted in the master and detail block. */
        clear_form;

        item_enable_disable('challan_header_blk', property_on);
        item_enable_disable('challan_details_blk', property_on);
    END ;
```

Trigger Name	: **WHEN-BUTTON-PRESSED**	Form	: challan
Block	: button_palette	Item	: push_button_view
Trigger Level	: Field Level		
Function	: Retrieve all the records and go to the first record in the challan_header table. Make all the fields not updateable in the challan_header and the challan_detail block.		
Text	: BEGIN		

```
        go_block('challan_header_blk');
        execute_query;
        item_enable_disable('challan_header_blk', property_off);
        item_enable_disable('challan_details_blk', property_off);
    END ;
```

Trigger Name	: **WHEN-BUTTON-PRESSED**	Form	: challan
Block	: button_palette	Item	: push_button_modify
Trigger Level	: Field Level		
Function	: In the modify mode the user is allowed to modify only the Challan date and the quantity delivered to the client.		
Text	: BEGIN		

```
        go_block('challan_header_blk');
        item_enable_disable('challan_header_blk',property_on);
        item_enable_disable('challan_details_blk',property_on);

        set_item_property('challan_header_blk.challan_no',
                   updateable, property_off);
        set_item_property('challan_header_blk.s_order_no',
                   updateable, property_off);
        set_item_property('challan_details_blk.product_no',
                   updateable, property_off);
    END;
```

The Relation Object :
A master-detail relationship is set by using an object called the *Relation Object*. In the previous example, we have seen how to create a relation object.

When you create a relation, Oracle Forms generates the triggers and PL/SQL procedures required to enforce coordination between the master and detail blocks. Sometimes we need to change the triggers and procedures that Oracle forms has created. Thus we need to have a closer look at the triggers and procedures that we wish to change.

In the current example, we need to perform cross table updation, when records are inserted, updated or deleted from the challan tables. To achieve this, we need to need to change the triggers created by the **Master Deletes** property. Let us have a look at the triggers written for the **Master Deletes** property in the relation object.

MASTER DELETES PROPERTY
Specifies how the deletion of a record in the master block affects records in the detail block:

Non-Isolated : The *Master Deletes* property is set to *Non-Isolated* by default. Setting this property prevents the deletion of a master record when associated detail records exist in the database. Oracle Forms creates **On-Check-Delete-Master** trigger automatically when you define a master-detail relation and set the **Master Deletes** property to **Non-Isolated**. The **On-Check-Delete-Master** trigger is written at the **block** level and it is written on the **master** block. It fires when there is an attempt to delete a record in the master block of a master-detail relation.

The **On-Check-Delete-Master** trigger uses cursors to find if the records are present in the detail table. If records are present then it displays a message informing the user that the master record cannot be deleted since detail records are present.

Isolated : Allows the master record to be deleted and does not affect associated detail records in the database.

Cascading : Allows the master record to be deleted and automatically deletes any associated detail records in the detail block's base table at commit time. The *default* value for this property is *Non-Isolated*.

Oracle Forms creates **Pre-Delete** trigger automatically when you define a master-detail relation and set the **Master Deletes** property to **Cascading**. The **Pre-Delete** trigger is written at the **block** level and it is written on the **master** block. It fires when there is an attempt to delete a record in the master block of a master-detail relation.

The **Pre-Delete** trigger fires a delete statement to delete the records present in the detail table. This trigger fires when the user fires a commit either by pressing the commit key or by pressing the save button or clicking the save menu option. It also fires if the user selects 'YES' when Oracle forms asks for confirmation to save information. The **Pre-Delete** trigger fires for every record deleted in the master block.

In the current example, the **Master Deletes** property is set to Non-Isolated thus it will create **On-Check-Delete-Master** trigger in the **challan_header_blk**.

In the current example, since the code to delete the current detail records is written in the **when-button-pressed** trigger of **push_button_delete**, we need to delete the **On-Check-Delete-Master** trigger.

To delete the trigger, position the cursor on the **On-Check-Delete-Master** trigger and press the delete key. Click on 'YES' when Oracle Forms asks for confirmation to delete the trigger.

Trigger Name : **WHEN-BUTTON-PRESSED**   Form : challan
Block : button_palette   Item : push_button_delete
Trigger Level : Field Level
Function : Delete all the challan_details records for the current challan_header record. Delete the current challan_header record.
Text : DECLARE
            total_records number(8);
            row_cntr number(8);
        BEGIN
            select count(challan_no) into total_records
                from challan_details
                where challan_no = :challan_header_blk.challan_no;
            go_block('challan_details_blk');
            first_record;
            for row_cntr in 1..total_records
            loop
                    delete_record;
            end loop;

```
                        go_block('challan_header_blk');
                        delete_record ;
                    END;
```

Trigger Name	: **WHEN-BUTTON-PRESSED**	Form	: challan
Block	: button_palette	Item	: push_button_save
Trigger Level	: Field Level		
Function	: Save changes to the database.		
Text	: BEGIN		

```
                        if :system.form_status = 'CHANGED' then
                            commit_form ;
                        if :system.form_status = 'QUERY' then
                            item_enable_disable('challan_header_blk',
                                                property_off);
                            item_enable_disable('challan_details_blk',
                                                property_off);
                        end if ;
                    end if;
                    END;
```

Trigger Name	: **WHEN-BUTTON-PRESSED**	Form	: challan
Block	: button_palette	Item	: push_button_exit
Trigger Level	: Field Level		
Function	: Quit challan data entry screen.		
Text	: BEGIN		

```
                        exit_form;
                    END;
```

Trigger Name	: **WHEN-BUTTON-PRESSED**	Form	: challan
Block	: button_palette	Item	: push_button_deldet
Trigger Level	: Field Level		
Function	: Delete the current record in the challan_details table.		
Text	: BEGIN		

```
                        go_block('challan_details_blk');
                        delete_record ;
                    END ;
```

Trigger Name	: **WHEN-BUTTON-PRESSED**	Form	: challan
Block	: button_palette	Item	: push_button_adddet
Trigger Level	: Field Level		
Function	: Add a record in the challan_details table.		
Text	: DECLARE		

```
              ord_stat char(2);
       BEGIN
           if :challan_header_blk.s_order_no is not null then
               select status into ord_stat
                   from sales_order
                   where s_order_no = :challan_header_blk.s_order_no;
               if ord_stat <> 'FP' then
                   go_block('challan_details_blk');
                   create_record;
               else
                   message('The Order Has Been FulFilled.
                           Select another Challan');
               end if;
           end if;
       END;
```

PROCEDURES

The Procedures are defined below :

Procedure Name	: **SCROLL_CONTROL**
Function	: To enable or disable the scroll pushbuttons i.e. first, prior, next and last based on the total number of records on the form and the current record.
	e.g.
	if there are multiple records and the record pointer is on the first record the first and the prior picture button should be *disabled* and the next and the last picture buttons should be *enabled*.

```
PROCEDURE scroll_control IS
BEGIN
       if :system.last_record = 'TRUE' and :system.cursor_record = '1' then
           set_item_property('button_palette.push_button_next', enabled, property_off);
           set_item_property('button_palette.push_button_last', enabled, property_off);
           set_item_property('button_palette.push_button_first', enabled, property_off);
           set_item_property('button_palette.push_button_prior', enabled, property_off);
       elsif :system.last_record = 'TRUE' then
           set_item_property('button_palette.push_button_next', enabled, property_off);
           set_item_property('button_palette.push_button_last', enabled, property_off);
           Set_Item_Property('button_palette.push_button_first', enabled, property_on);
           set_item_property('button_palette.push_button_prior', enabled, property_on);
```

284 COMMERCIAL APPLICATION DEVELOPMENT USING ORACLE 7, DEVELOPER 2000

```
    elsif :system.cursor_record = '1' then
            set_item_property('button_palette.push_button_first', enabled, property_off);
            set_item_property('button_palette.push_button_prior', enabled, property_off);
            set_item_property('button_palette.push_button_next', enabled, property_on);
            set_item_property('button_palette.push_button_last', enabled, property_on);
    else
            Set_Item_Property('button_palette.push_button_first', enabled, property_on);
            Set_Item_Property('button_palette.push_button_prior', enabled, property_on);
            Set_Item_Property('button_palette.push_button_next', enabled, property_on);
            Set_Item_Property('button_palette.push_button_last', enabled, property_on);
    end if ;
END;
```

Trigger Name	: **WHEN-NEW-RECORD-INSTANCE**	Form	: challan
Block	: challan_header_blk	Item	:
Trigger Level	: Block Level		
Function	: Set the enabled and disabled property of the scroll buttons based on the current record and the total records on the form.		
Text	: BEGIN		

```
            scroll_control;
        END;
```

Procedure Name : **ITEM_ENABLE_DISABLE**
Function   : To enable the fields so that the contents of the field can be
                  modified or new values can be entered. To disable fields so that the
                  contents of the field cannot be modified.

                e.g.

                programming convention requires :The primary key field challan_no
                should be *enabled* in data insert mode and *disabled* in the data
                modify mode.

ITEM_ENABLE_DISABLE (Procedure Body)
```
PROCEDURE ITEM_ENABLE_DISABLE(blk_name IN char,
                item_on_off IN NUMBER)  IS
        nxt_itemname varchar2(70);
        count number;
        itemtype varchar(70);
BEGIN
    /* get_block_property is a function that gets the value of specified block property. The
        First_Item property holds the name of the first enterable item in the block. */

    nxt_itemname := blk_name||'.'|| get_block_property(blk_name, first_item);

    /* set a loop that gets the next navigation item and sets the updateable property to
```

```
   true or false. Next Navigation Item holds the name of the next navigational item in
   the block */
loop
       itemtype := get_item_property(nxt_itemname,item_type);
       if itemtype <> 'DISPLAY ITEM' and
         get_item_property(nxt_itemname,item_canvas) is not null then
                set_item_property(nxt_itemname,updateable,item_on_off);
       end if;
       nxt_itemname:=blk_name||'.'||get_item_property(nxt_itemname,
                                 next_navigation_item);
       if (blk_name||'.'||get_block_property(blk_name,first_item))=nxt_itemname then
                exit;
       end if;
   end loop;
END;
```

Creating a Display Item :

1. Open the layout editor of the **challan** form. Create a new display field **name** by selecting the **display item** tool from the toolbar and droping it on the form. Following are the properties of the display field **name**

Name	: Name
Item Type	: Display Item
Data Type	: Char
Maximum Length	: 30
Base Table	: False

2. Create a label object for the display field **Name**. Repeat the steps for creating display items for **s_order_date** and **client_no** in the challan_header block.

3. Select the challan_detail block. Create a new display field **description** by selecting the **display item** tool from the toolbar and droping it on the form. Following are the properties of the display field **description**

Name	: Description
Item Type	: Display Item
Data Type	: Char
Maximum Length	: 30
Base Table	: False

4. Create a label object for the display field **Description**. Repeat the steps for creating display items for **unit_measure**.

TRIGGER FOR POPULATING THE DISPLAY ITEMS

Trigger Name : **POST-QUERY**   Form   : challan
Block   : challan_header_blk   Item   :
Function   : Populates the display item name for every row retrieved
Trigger Level : Block Level
Trigger Text   : BEGIN
                   Select client_master.client_no, name, s_order_date
                   into :client_no, :name, :s_order_date
                   from client_master, sales_order
                   where rtrim(sales_order.s_order_no) = :s_order_no and
                   rtrim(client_master.client_no)= rtrim(sales_order.client_no);
                EXCEPTION
                   when no_data_found then
                       message('Invalid order number was been entered');
                       raise form_trigger_failure;
                END;

Trigger Name	: **POST-QUERY**		Form	: challan
Block	: challan_details_blk		Item	:
Function	: Populates the display item description and unit_measure for every row retrieved.			
Trigger Level	: Block Level			
Trigger Text	: BEGIN			

```
        select description, unit_measure
            into :challan_details_blk.description,
                 :challan_details_blk.unit_measure
            from product_master
            where rtrim(product_no) =
                 :challan_details_blk.product_no;
        EXCEPTION
            when no_data_found then null;
        END;
```

VALIDATIONS :

The triggers for the validation on the master block (challan_header_blk) are defined below :

- challan_no is a Primary Key i.e. duplicate values are not allowed in challan_no. It cannot be left blank.

Trigger Name : **WHEN-VALIDATE-ITEM** Form : challan
Block   : challan_header_blk   Item : challan_no
Function   : challan_no is a Primary Key i.e. duplicate values are not allowed in challan_no. It cannot be left blank.
Trigger Level : Field Level
Text   : BEGIN
                   select challan_no
                       into :challan_header_blk.challan_no
                       from challan_header
                       where challan_no = :challan_header_blk.challan_no;
                   message('Challan No. "' || :challan_header_blk.challan_no
                               || '" already exists...try again.');
                   raise form_trigger_failure;
               EXCEPTION
                   when no_data_found then null;
               END;

- s_order_no must be present in the Sales_order table and the user can select only orders that are not completely fulfilled i.e. the order status is not 'FP'. Implement this validation by using **LOV**.

Create an LOV named order_list as follows :
1. In the Object Navigator, position the cursor on the *LOV* node and choose **Navigator, Create**. A *New LOV* properties screen is displayed.

2. List of values retrieves data based on the select statement specified for the LOV. Enter the following select statement in the *Query Text* property of the LOV.

        select s_order_no into :s_order_no from sales_order
            where order_status <> 'FP'

As soon as the user selects a value from the LOV it must be displayed in the s_order_no field. Thus the select statement includes an INTO clause that passes the selected values to s_order_no field. The completed *NEW LOV* screen is as shown in diagram 11.16.

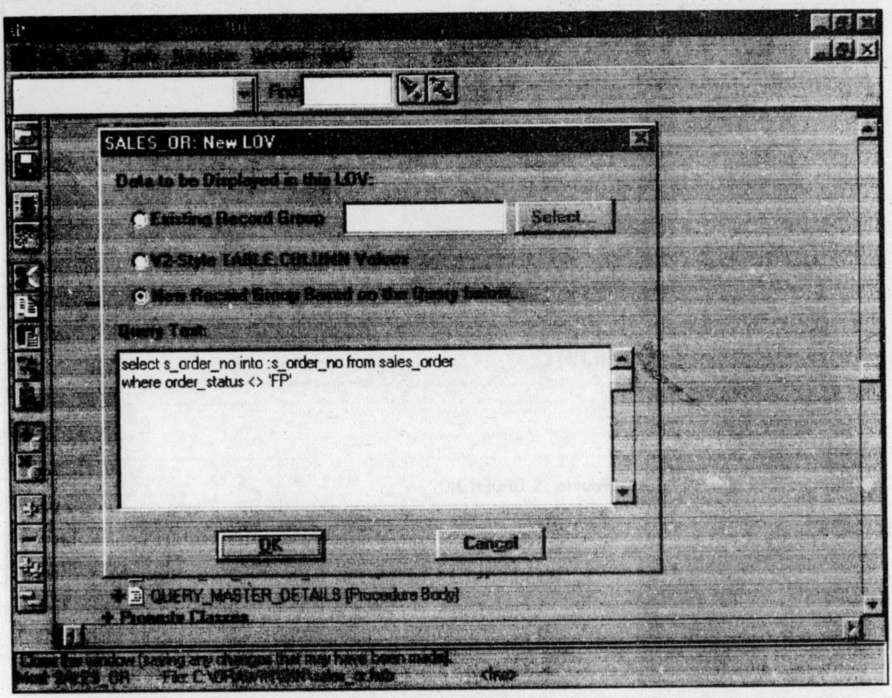
SALES_OR: New LOV
Select...
select s_order_no into :s_order_no from sales_order
where order_status <> 'FP'
OK
Cancel
QUERY_MASTER_DETAILS (Procedure Body)

Diagram 11.16 : Creating a new LOV for *Sales Order Number*

3. Click on OK. A List of values with a default name is displayed in the Object Navigator. Change the name of the list of values to *Order_List*.

4. The LOV **order_list** is connected to the field s_order_no by selecting the LOV **order_list** in LOV property of the field **s_order_no** as shown in the diagram 11.17.

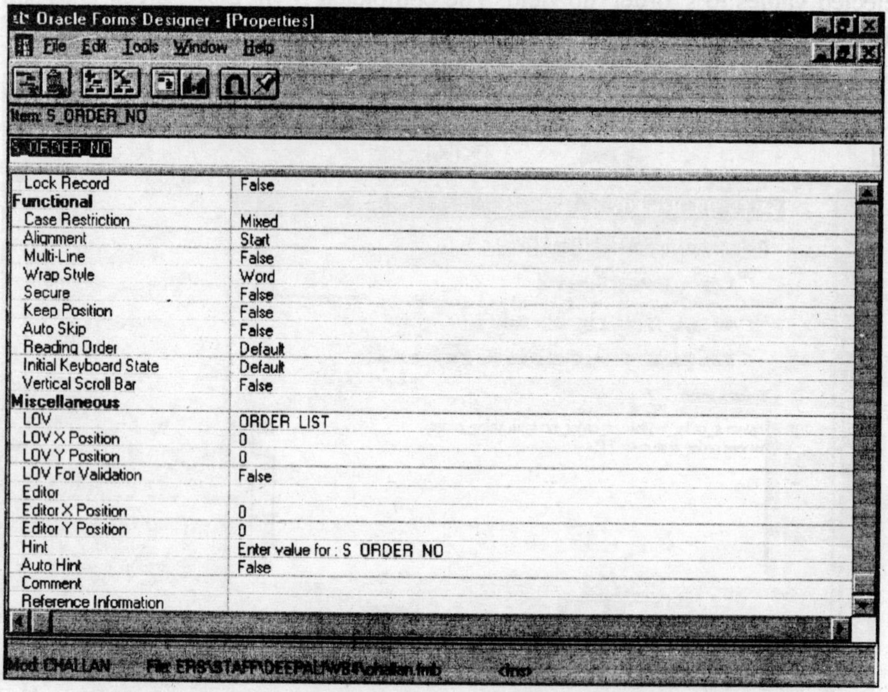

Diagram 11.17 : Connecting the LOV to the field *S_order_no*

5. The following properties are set in the screen 11.17.

   LOV   : Order_List
   LOV X Position   : 98
   LOV Y Position   : 48

   The LOV property connects the field to the List of Values. The LOV X Position and LOV Y Position properties specifies the X and Y co-ordinates where the List of values must be displayed.

6. When the user is on the order number field, the user can press the key sequence to show the list of values or enter the value without using the list of values. If the user enters the value directly, the system must check if the value is present in the list of values. If not, the list of values must be displayed.

   Set the *LOV For* **Validation** property of order number to **True** so that the system check the value entered with the values in the LOV.

MASTER DETAIL FORM 291

Trigger Name	: **WHEN-VALIDATE-ITEM**	Form	: challan
Block	: challan_header_blk.	Item	: s_order_no
Function	: Check the s_order_no is not left blank. Display client_no, name and the order date based on the order number selected.		
Trigger Level	: Field Level		
Text	: ――		

```
            ___ no is null then
              . Number cannot be left blank');
              _ger_failure;
        is
        /* Displaying Data in the Display Items */
        select client_master.client_no, name, s_order_date
            into :client_no, :name, :s_order_date
            from client_master, sales_order
            where rtrim(sales_order.s_order_no) = :s_order_no and
                rtrim(client_master.client_no) =
                    Rtrim(sales_order.client_no);
    end if;
    EXCEPTION
        when no_data_found then
            message('Invalid Order Number was been entered');
            raise form_trigger_failure;
END;
```

- Challan_Date cannot be greater than system date or less than the s_order_date. Set the default value of challan_date to system date.

Trigger Name	: **WHEN-VALIDATE-ITEM**	Form	: challan
Block	: challan_header_blk.	Item	: challan_date
Function	: Challan_Date cannot be greater than system date or less than the s_order_date. Set the default value of challan_date to system date.		
Trigger Level	: Field Level		
Text	: BEGIN		

```
        if :challan_header_blk.challan_date is null then
            message('Challan Date cannot be left Blank');
            raise form_trigger_failure;
        elsif :challan_header_blk.challan_date > sysdate then
            message('Challan Date cannot be greater than today"s date');
            raise form_trigger_failure;
        elsif :challan_header_blk.challan_date <
                :challan_header_blk.s_order_date then
            message('Challan date cannot be less than order date');
            raise form_trigger_failure;
        end if;
END;
```

The triggers for the validation on the detail block (challan_detail_blk) are defined below :

- Product_no must be present in the sales_order_details for a particular order table. Implement this validation by using **LOV**. The list of products must include only the products in stock i.e. the qty_on_hand must be greater than 0 and the list must include only those products that are not delivered in full i.e. qty_ordered is greater than the qty_disp.

Create an LOV named product_list as follows :
1. In the Object Navigator, position the cursor on the *LOV* node and choose **Navigator, Create**. A *New LOV* properties screen is displayed.

2. List of values retrieves data based on the select statement specified for the LOV. Enter the following select statement in the *Query Text* property of the LOV.

```
select sales_order_details.product_no, description, unit_measure
    into :product_no, :description, :unit_measure
    from product_master, sales_order_details
    where product_master.product_no = sales_order_details.product_no and
    s_order_no = :s_order_no and qty_ordered > qty_disp and
    qty_on_hand > 0
```

MASTER DETAIL FORM **293**

As soon as the user selects a value from the LOV it must be displayed in the product_no, description and unit_measure fields. Thus the select statement includes an INTO clause that passes the selected values to product_no, description and unit_measure fields. The completed *NEW LOV* screen is as shown in diagram 11.18.

```
select sales_order_details.product_no, description, unit_measure
into :product_no, :description, :unit_measure
from product_master, sales_order_details
where product_master.product_no = sales_order_details.product_no and
s_order_no = :s_order_no and qty_ordered > qty_disp and
qty_on_hand > 0
```

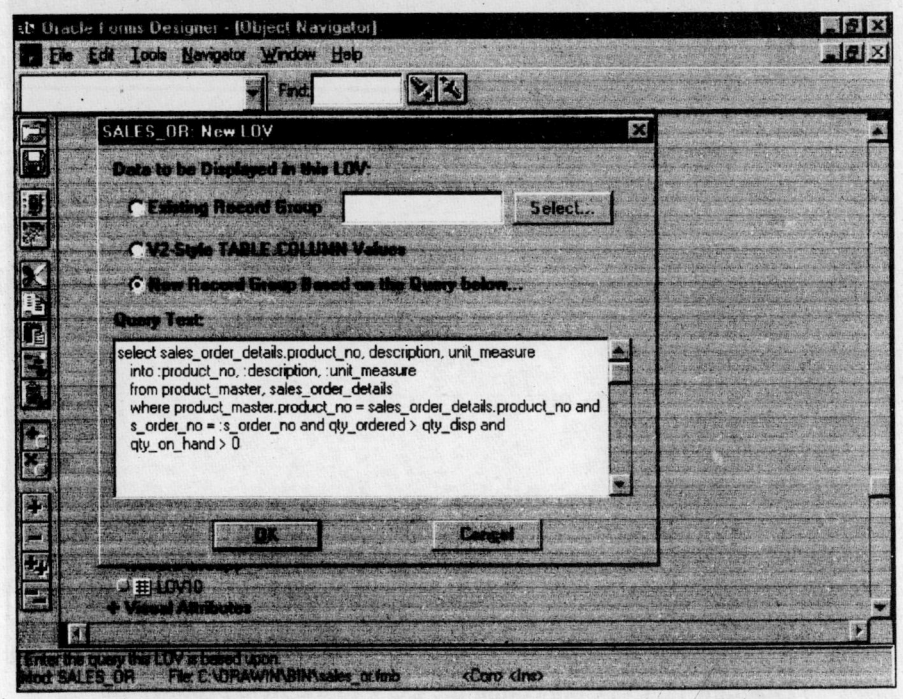

Diagram 11.18 : Creating a new LOV for *Product Number*

3. Click on OK. A List of values with a default name is displayed in the Object Navigator. Change the name of the list of values to *Product_List*.

294 COMMERCIAL APPLICATION DEVELOPMENT USING ORACLE 7, DEVELOPER 2000

4. The LOV **product_list** is connected to the field product_no by selecting the LOV **product_list** in LOV property of the field **product_no** as shown in the diagram 11.19.

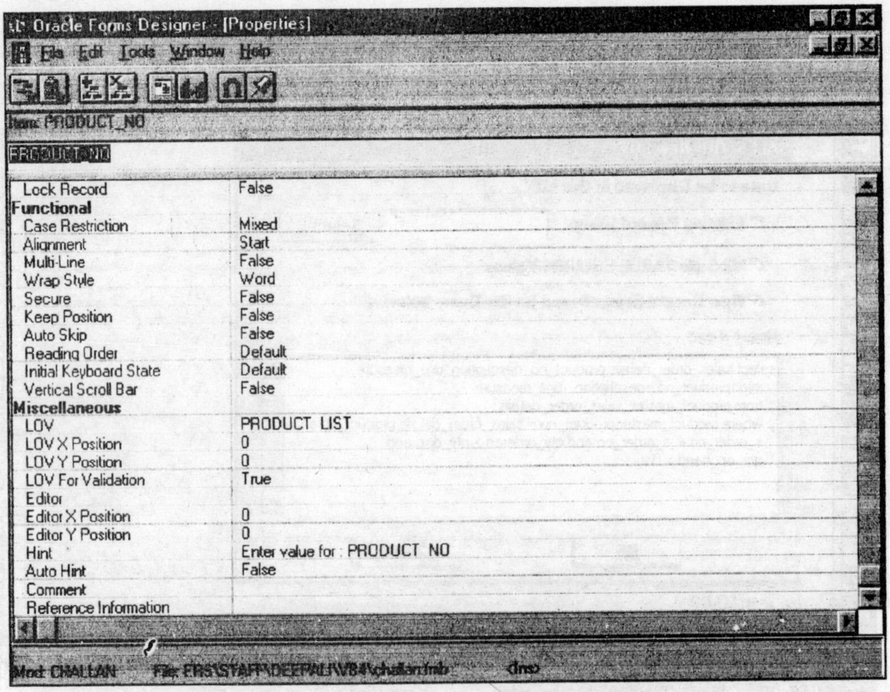

Diagram 11.19 : Connecting the LOV to the field *product_no*

5. The following properties are set in the screen 11.19.

   LOV   : product_List
   LOV X Position   : 200
   LOV Y Position   : 48

   The LOV property connects the field to the List of Values. The LOV X Position and LOV Y Position properties specifies the X and Y co-ordinates where the List of values must be displayed.

6. When the user is on the product number field, the user can press the key sequence to show the list of values or enter the value without using the list of values. If the user enters the value directly, the system must check if the value is present in the list of values. If not, the list of values must be displayed.

   Set the *LOV For* **Validation** property of product number to **True** so that the system checks the value entered with the values in the LOV.

- A single product cannot be repeated for an order.
  In the detail section, the combination of product_no and challan_no is the primary key. Thus the product_no for a specific challan should not be repeated.

  This check should be performed as and when the user exits product_no item and goes to the next item field, next record or previous record either using key board or mouse.

  If the user enters a valid value, it must display calculate the quantity that can be dispatched and set the value of the quantity field to the calculated value.

  A function is written in the *libproc* library to check for duplicate values in the detail section. This function is called from the different key and mouse triggers.

  In the current example, the function checks to see that the product_no is not repeated for a challan.

  Open the *libproc* library and include function *f_dup_detail*.

The function definition is as follows :

Function Name	: **F_DUP_DETAIL**
Function	: In the detail section, the combination of challan_no and product_no is the primary key. Thus the product_no for a specific order should not be repeated.
	This check should be performed as and when the user exit product_no item and goes to the next item, next record or previous record.
	A procedure is written to check that the product_no is not repeated for a specific challan and the same is called from the different key and mouse triggers.

```
FUNCTION F_DUP_DETAIL (blk_col_name char) RETURN NUMBER IS
        Is_duplicate char(5);
        current_rec_no number(3);
        last_rec_no number(3);
        cur_val varchar2(20);
        row_count number(3);
        form_name varchar(40);
BEGIN
        is_duplicate := 'FALSE';

        /* store the current record position */
        current_rec_no := to_number( name_in('system.cursor_record'));
```

```
                /* store the current record's product number */
                cur_val := name_in(blk_col_name);
                form_name := get_application_property(current_form_name);
                set_form_property(form_name,validation,property_false);
                last_record; /* position cursor on the last record */
                /* check if current record is the only record in the detail block */
                if name_in('system.cursor_record') <> '1' then
                            /* find maximum number of records in the detail block */
                            last_rec_no := to_number(name_in('system.cursor_record'));
                            first_record;
                            /* set up a loop from one to maximum number of records to compare
                                each record's product_no with the variable cur_val */
                            for row_count in 1..last_rec_no loop

                                        /* Ensure comparison is not made with the entered product_no,
                                            stored in variable cur_val */
                                        if current_rec_no <> row_count then
                                                    if cur_val = name_in(blk_col_name) then
                                                                is_duplicate := 'TRUE';
                                                                exit;
                                                    end if;
                                        end if;

                                        /* Ensure that the cursor doesn't go to a record that does not exist */
                                        if last_rec_no < > row_count then
                                                    next_record;
                                        end if;
                            end loop;
                end if;

                /* Reposition the cursor to the record number when function was called */
                go_record(current_rec_no);
                set_form_property(form_name,validation,property_true);
                /* check if a duplicate is found; if yes, return 1 else return 0 */
                if is_duplicate = 'TRUE' then
                            return(1);
                else
                            return(0);
                end if;
END;
```

Trigger Name	: **KEY-NEXT-ITEM**	Form	: Challan
Block	: challan_details_blk	Item	: product_no
Function	: A single product cannot be repeated for an order		
Trigger Level	: Field Level		
Trigger Text	: DECLARE		

```
                qty_on_hand number(8);
                quantity number(8);
        BEGIN
            if :challan_details_blk.product_no is null then
                    message('Product No cannot be null');
                    raise form_trigger_failure;
            else
                if :system.record_status <> 'QUERY' then
                    if f_dup_detail('challan_details_blk.product_no') = 1 then
                        message('You cannot include product ''' || :product_no ||
                        ''' twice in the challan ''' || :challan_header_blk.challan_no
                        || '''.');
                        raise form_trigger_failure;
                    else
                        select qty_on_hand into qty_on_hand
                           from product_master
                           where product_no = :challan_details_blk.product_no;

                        select (qty_ordered - qty_disp) into quantity
                           from sales_order_details
                           where rtrim(sales_order_details.s_order_no) =
                                           :s_order_no and
                                 rtrim(sales_order_details.product_no) = :product_no;
                        if qty_on_hand < quantity then
                                :challan_details_blk.quantity :=qty_on_hand ;
                        else
                                :challan_details_blk.quantity :=quantity;
                        end if;
                        next_item;
                    end if;
                end if;
            end if;
        EXCEPTION
            when no_data_found then
                    message('product code'''||:challan_details_blk.product_no||
                    '''is invalid... try again.');
                    raise form_trigger_failure;
        END;
```

Trigger Name : **KEY-UP**
Block : challan_details_blk
Function : A single product cannot be repeated for an order
Trigger Level : Block Level
Trigger Text : DECLARE
              qty_on_hand number(8);
              quantity number(8);
          BEGIN
              if :system.cursor_block = 'challan_details_blk' and
                 :system.cursor_record <> 1 then
                  if :challan_details_blk.product_no is null then
                      message('Product No cannot be null');
                      raise form_trigger_failure;
                  else
                      If :system.record_status <> 'QUERY' then
                          if f_dup_detail('challan_details_blk.challan_no') <> 1 then
                              select qty_on_hand into qty_on_hand
                              from product_master where product_no =
                                      :challan_details_blk.product_no;

                              select (qty_ordered - qty_disp) into quantity
                              from sales_order_details where rtrim(
                              sales_order_details.s_order_no) = :s_order_no
                              and rtrim(sales_order_details.product_no) = :product_no;

                              if qty_on_hand < quantity then
                                  :challan_details_blk.quantity:=qty_on_hand ;
                              else
                                  :challan_details_blk.quantity:=quantity;
                              end if;
                              previous_record;
                          else
                              message('You cannot include product "' ||
                                  :product_no || '" twice in the challan "' ||
                                  :challan_header_blk.challan_no || '".');
                              raise form_trigger_failure;
                          end if;
                      end if;
                  end if;
              end if;
          EXCEPTION
              when no_data_found then
                  message('Product code"' || :challan_details_blk.product_no
                      ||'"is invalid... try again.');
                  raise form_trigger_failure;
          END;

MASTER DETAIL FORM 299

Trigger Name	: **KEY-DOWN**	Form : Challan
Block	: challan_details_blk	Item :
Function	: A single product cannot be repeated for an order.	
Trigger Level	: Block Level	
Trigger Text	: DECLARE	

```
        qty_on_hand number(8);
        quantity number(8);
    BEGIN
        if :system.cursor_block = 'challan_details_blk' and
           :system.last_record <> 'TRUE' then
            if :challan_details_blk.product_no is null then
                message('Product No cannot be null');
                raise form_trigger_failure;
            else
                If :system.record_status <> 'QUERY' then
                    if f_dup_detail('challan_details_blk.challan_no') <> 1 then
                        select qty_on_hand into qty_on_hand
                        from product_master where product_no =
                            :challan_details_blk.product_no;

                        select (qty_ordered-qty_disp) into quantity
                        from sales_order_details where rtrim(
                        sales_order_details.s_order_no) = :s_order_no
                        and Rtrim(sales_order_details.product_no) = :product_no;

                        if qty_on_hand < quantity then
                            :challan_details_blk.quantity := qty_on_hand;
                        else
                            :challan_details_blk.quantity:= quantity;
                        end if;
                        next_record;
                    else
                        message('You cannot include product "' || :product_no
                            || '" twice in the challan "' ||
                            : challan_header_blk.challan_no || '".');
                        raise form_trigger_failure;
                    end if;
                end if;
            end if;
        end if;
    EXCEPTION
        when no_data_found then
        message('Product code"' || :product_no || '"is invalid... try again.');
        raise form_trigger_failure;
    END;
```

Trigger Name	: **WHEN-MOUSE-CLICK**	Form	: Challan
Block	: challan_details_blk	Item	:
Function	: A single product cannot be repeated for an order		
Trigger Level	: Block Level		
Trigger Text	: DECLARE		

```
            qty_on_hand number(8);
            quantity number(8);
            itemtype varchar(30);
        BEGIN
            if :system.record_status <> 'NEW' and
               :system.mouse_item <> 'challan_details_blk.product_no' then
               if :challan_details_blk.product_no is null then
                   message('Product No cannot be null');
                   raise form_trigger_failure;
               else
                   if :system.record_status <> 'QUERY' then
                      if f_dup_detail('challan_details_blk.challan_no') <> 1 then
                         select qty_on_hand into qty_on_hand
                         from product_master
                         where product_no = :challan_details_blk.product_no;

                         select (qty_ordered-qty_disp) into quantity
                         from sales_order_details
                         where rtrim(sales_order_details.s_order_no) =
                             :s_order_no and
                         rtrim(sales_order_details.product_no) =:product_no;

                         if qty_on_hand < quantity then
                            :challan_details_blk.quantity:=qty_on_hand ;
                         else
                            :challan_details_blk.quantity:=quantity;
                         end if;

                         if :system.mouse_item <>
                             'challan_details_blk.product_no' then
                            itemtype := get_item_property(
                                :system.mouse_item,item_type);
                            if itemtype <> 'DISPLAY ITEM' then
                                Go_Item(:system.mouse_item);
                            end if;
                         end if;
                      else
                         message('Product code"' || : :challan_details_blk.product_no ||
                                "'is invalid... try again.');
                         raise form_trigger_failure;
                      end if;
                   end if;
```

```
            end if;
        end if;
EXCEPTION
        when no_data_found then
        message('product code'' || :challan_details_blk.product_no ||
                '''is invalid... try again.');
        raise form_trigger_failure;
END;
```

- Qty delivered cannot be greater than qty_on_hand in the product master and cannot be greater than the qty_ordered in sales_order_details table.

To check for that the quantity is not greater than the qty_ordered, we need to keep a track of the old quantity for the modify mode. Thus we can create a display item named old_qty in the challan_details block. The properties of old_qty are as follows :

Name	: old_qty
Item Type	: Display Item
Data Type	: Number
Maximum Length	: 8
Base Table	: False
Canvas	: NULL

Write the following triggers :

Trigger Name	: **PRE-TEXT-ITEM**
Block	: challan_details_blk.
Function	: Set the contents of old_qty to the contents of quantity. If quantity is null then set the value to 0.
Trigger Level	: Field Level
Text	: BEGIN

Form	: challan
Item	: quantity

```
BEGIN
        if :quantity is null then
                :old_qty := 0;
        else
                :old_qty := :quantity;
        end if;
END;
```

302 COMMERCIAL APPLICATION DEVELOPMENT USING ORACLE 7, DEVELOPER 2000

Trigger Name	: **WHEN-VALIDATE-ITEM**	Form : challan
Block	: challan_details_blk.	Item : quantity
Function	: Check that quantity is not left blank or 0. Quantity is not greater than quantity ordered and qty_on_hand.	
Trigger Level	: Field Level	
Text	: DECLARE	

```
        max_qty number(8);
        qty_on_hand number(8);
    BEGIN
        if :challan_details_blk.quantity is null then
            message('Quantity cannot be Null');
            raise form_trigger_failure;
        elsif :challan_details_blk.quantity = 0 then
            message ('Quantity cannot be zero');
            raise form_trigger_failure;
        else
            select (qty_ordered - qty_disp), qty_on_hand
            into max_qty,qty_on_hand
            from sales_order_details,product_master
            where sales_order_details.s_order_no =
                    :challan_header_blk.s_order_no and

                sales_order_details.product_no =
                    :challan_details_blk.product_no and

                sales_order_details.product_no =
                    product_master.product_no;

            if :challan_details_blk.quantity - :old_qty > max_qty then
                message('Qty dispatched should be less than Qty ordered');
                raise form_trigger_failure;
            end if;
        end if;
    END;
```

Trigger Name	: **WHEN-NEW-FORM-INSTANCE**	Form : challan
Block	:	Item :
Function	: To maximize the window during runtime.	
Trigger Level	: Form Level	
Trigger Text	: BEGIN	

```
        Set_window_property(forms_mdi_window, window_state, maximize);
        Set_window_property ('challan_window ', window_state , maximize);
    END;
```

CROSS TABLE UPDATIONS

A very commonly used technique in commercial applications is that when data is being manipulated using a data entry form, data in several other tables will get affected immediately depending upon the processing taking place on the data entry form.

A very simple example of this is as described below. :

product_no	quantity

Product_no	qty_on_hand

Challan_details table
(When goods are dispatched records in inserted in the challan_details table)

Product_master table
(The qty_on_hand in the product_master table will reduce when goods are dispatched)

Cross table updation that is required in the challan data entry form is explained below :

Details:
Whenever a record in the challan_details table is inserted, updated or deleted three tables are affected : product_master , sales_order_details and sales_order.

- The quantity dispatched would increase or decrease the Qty_on_hand of Product_master and the Qty_Disp of Sales_order_details by a corresponding value.

- Whenever an insert is performed a decrease is recorded in the Qty_on_hand of Product_master and an increase the Qty_Disp of Sales_order_details Whenever a delete is performed an increase is recorded in the Qty_on_hand of Product_master and a decrease the Qty_Disp of Sales_order_details.

- Whenever an update is recorded, the old value of quantity is added to qty_on_hand of Product_master and the new value is subtracted. Also old value of quantity is subtracted from Qty_disp of Sales_Order_Details and new quantity must be added.

- Whenever an insert, update or delete is recorded, the order_status in the sales_order table must be updated as follows :
    * if the sum of quantity_ordered and quantity dispatched for all the products is equal then the order_status must be set to 'FP'.
    * If the sum of quantity dispatched is equal to 0 then the order_status must be set to 'NP'
    * else set order_status to must be set to 'IP'.

Trigger Name : **POST-INSERT**   Form : Challan
Block   : challan_details_blk   Item :
Function   : Cross table updation when a record is inserted in the challan detail table.
Trigger Level : Block Level
Trigger Text : DECLARE
                    current_quantity number(8);
                BEGIN
                    current_quantity := :Challan_details_blk.quantity;
                    update product_master
                        set qty_on_hand =
                            qty_on_hand - current_quantity
                        where rtrim(product_no) = :challan_details_blk.product_no;

                    update sales_order_details
                        set qty_disp = qty_disp + current_quantity
                        where rtrim(s_order_no) = :challan_header_blk.s_order_no
                        and rtrim(product_no) = :challan_details_blk.product_no;

                    /* Procedure called to set the status field of the sales_order table */
                    update_order_status;
                EXCEPTION
                    When No_data_found Then
                        message('Error while updating details of new records');
                        raise form_trigger_failure;
                END;

MASTER DETAIL FORM 305

Trigger Name	: **POST-UPDATE**	Form	: Challan
Block	: challan_details_blk	Item	:
Function	: Cross table updation when a record is updated in the challan detail table.		
Trigger Level	: Block Level		
Trigger Text	: DECLARE		

```
            old_qty Number(8);
            current_qty number(8);
        BEGIN
            current_qty := :challan_details_blk.quantity;

            select quantity into old_qty
                from challan_details
                where rtrim(challan_no) =:challan_details_blk.challan_no
                and rtrim(product_no) = :challan_details_blk.product_no;

            update product_master
                set qty_on_hand = qty_on_hand + old_qty - current_qty
                where rtrim(product_no) = :challan_details_blk.product_no;

            update sales_order_details
                set qty_disp = qty_disp - old_qty + current_qty
                where rtrim(s_order_no) = :challan_header_blk.s_order_no
                and rtrim(product_no) = :challan_details_blk.product_no;

            update_order_status;
            /* Procedure called to set the status field of the sales_order table */
        END;
```

For cross table updation for delete mode we need to change the **when-button-pressed** trigger on the push_button_delete and push_button_deldet. The triggers will be as follows :

Trigger Name	: **WHEN-BUTTON-PRESSED**	Form	: Challan
Block	: challan_details_blk	Item	: push_button_delete
Function	: Delete the corresponding detail records and the master record.		
	Cross table updation when a record is deleted in the challan detail table.		
Trigger Level	: Field Level		
Trigger Text	: DECLARE		

```
            old_qty Number(8);
            total_records number(8);
            row_cntr number(8);
    BEGIN
        select count(challan_no) into total_records
            from    challan_details
            where challan_no = :challan_header_blk.challan_no;
        go_block('challan_details_blk');
        first_record;
        for row_cntr in 1..total_records
        loop
            select quantity into old_qty
            from challan_details where rtrim(challan_no) =
                        :challan_details_blk.challan_no and
            rtrim(product_no) = :challan_details_blk.product_no;

            update product_master
            set qty_on_hand = qty_on_hand + old_qty
            where rtrim(product_no) = :challan_details_blk.product_no;

            update sales_order_details
            set qty_disp  = qty_disp - old_qty
            where rtrim(s_order_no) = :challan_header_blk.s_order_no
            and rtrim(product_no) = :challan_details_blk.product_no;

            /* Procedure called to set the status field of the sales_order
            table */
            update_order_status;

            delete_record;
        end loop;
        go_block('challan_header_blk');
        delete_record ;
    EXCEPTION
        when no_data_found then
            message('Error while updating details of delete records');
    END;
```

Trigger Name	: **WHEN-BUTTON-PRESSED**	Form	: Challan
Block	: challan_details_blk	Item	: push_button_deldet
Function	: Delete the current detail record.		
	Cross table updation when a record is deleted in the challan detail table.		
Trigger Level	: Field Level		
Trigger Text	: DECLARE		

```
              old_qty Number(8);
         BEGIN
              go_block('challan_details_blk');
              select quantity into old_qty
                   from challan_details
                   where rtrim(challan_no) =
                           :challan_details_blk.challan_no and
                   rtrim(product_no) = :challan_details_blk.product_no;

              update product_master
                   set qty_on_hand = qty_on_hand + old_qty
                   where rtrim(product_no) =
                           :challan_details_blk.product_no;

              update sales_order_details
                   set qty_disp = qty_disp - old_qty
                   where rtrim(s_order_no) =
                           :challan_header_blk.s_order_no
                   and rtrim(product_no) =
                           :challan_details_blk.product_no;

              /* Procedure called to set the status field of the sales_order
              table */
              update_order_status;

              delete_record;
         EXCEPTION
              when no_data_found then
                   message('Error while updating details of delete records');
         END;
```

The **post-insert**, **pre-update** on challan_details_blk and the **when-button-pressed** trigger on push_button_delete and push_button_deldet call a procedure named **update_order_status**.

The **update_order_status** is used to update the order status field in the sales_order table based on the quantity ordered and the quantity dispached in the sales_order_details.

UPDATE_ORDER_STATUS (Procedure Body)
```
    PROCEDURE update_order_status IS
        total_qty_ordered number(8);
        total_qty_disp number(8);
    BEGIN
        select sum(qty_ordered), sum(qty_disp)
                into total_qty_ordered, total_qty_disp
                from sales_order_details
                where s_order_no = :challan_header_blk.s_order_no;
        if total_qty_ordered = total_qty_disp Then
                update sales_order
                  set order_status = 'FP'
                  where rtrim(s_order_no) = :challan_header_blk.s_order_no;
        elsif total_qty_disp = 0 then
                update sales_order
                  set order_status = 'NP'
                  where s_order_no = :challan_header_blk.s_order_no;
        else
                update sales_order
                  set order_status = 'IP'
                  where s_order_no = :challan_header_blk.s_order_no;
        end if;
END;
```

12. PARAMETER PASSING IN FORMS

We can open a form from some other form by using the OPEN_FORM or the CALL_FORM built-in package procedure.

Example :
When the user clicks on the search button in the *Sales Order* form, it opens the search form that displays the Sales Order numbers.

We can pass parameter values from the calling form to the called form, when a form is invoked by using the OPEN_FORM or CALL_FORM procedures.

The two basic steps in parameter passing are :
- Specifying a list of parameters in the calling form and passing the parameters in the OPEN_FORM or CALL_FORM procedure.
- Defining the parameters in the called form and using the same.

SPECIFYING THE PARAMETER LIST IN THE CALLING FORM :
Parameter can be passed from the calling form to the called form by using a **parameter list**. A Parameter list is a three-column data structure that contain the name, the type (*Text_Parameter* or *Data_Parameter*) and the value of each parameter on the list.

The steps in passing the parameters in the calling form are :
- Create a Parameter list
- Add parameters to the parameter list
- Pass the parameter list to the called form.

Creating a Parameter List :
The Built-in package procedure CREATE_PARAMETER_LIST creates the parameter list and returns the pointer to the parameter list. It accepts a single parameter i.e. the name of the parameter list. This name will be assigned to the list.

Thus we need to declare a variable of type PARAMLIST in the declare section as follows :

    DECLARE
        client_param_list paramlist;

The list can be referenced either by the name of the parameter list or the variable name that holds the pointer to the parameter list.

Example : Create a parameter list with the name as 'client_list' and assign it to 'client_param_list'.
        client_param_list := create_parameter_list('client_list');

If the creation of parameter list is successful, it assigns a unique id to the parameter list.

Adding Parameter to the Parameter List :
The Built-in package procedure ADD_PARAMETER adds parameters to the parameter list It accepts the following parameters :
- Name of the parameter list (The Parameter List variable can also be specified)
- The Name of the parameter
- The Type of parameter
- The Value of the parameter

Types of Parameters :
The user can pass single values as the parameter or an entire record group as the parameter. The parameter type specifies whether the parameter holds a single value or is it a record group. The Parameters type can be any one of the following :
- TEXT_PARAMETER.
- DATA_PARAMETER

TEXT PARAMETER :
When the user wants to pass a single value as a parameter the parameter type must be defined as TEXT_PARAMETER. If you are passing a text parameter, the maximum length is 255 characters. Datatype of the value is CHAR.

Example : Passing the client_no from the client master form to the client contact information form.

DATA PARAMETER :
When the user wants to pass a record group as a parameter the parameter type must be defined as DATA_PARAMETER.

The value for a DATA_PARAMETER will be a string specifying the name of a record group defined in the current form.

To pass parameter values from one form to another, each parameter and its value must be in a parameter list.

Example : Create a parameter list with the name as 'client_list' and assign it to 'client_param_list'. Add the parameter named 'client_no' and specify the value as 'C00001'.

```
DECLARE
    client_param_list paramlist;
    client_param_list := create_parameter_list ('client_list');
BEGIN

    add_parameter(client_param_list, 'client_no',
            text_parameter, 'C00001');
END;
```

Specifying the parameters in the called form :
The parameters whose values are being passed must have been defined in the called form at design time. The called form must be expecting a value for each of the parameters included in the parameter list it receives from the calling form.

You can define parameters in a form in the Object Navigator at design time and also programmatically at runtime. The properties of a parameter include Name, Datatype, Length, and Default Value.

The steps in defining the parameters at design time are as follows :
1. Select the **Parameters** node in the Object Navigator and click on **Create** menu item under the **Navigator** menu item. It creates a parameter as shown in diagram 12.1.

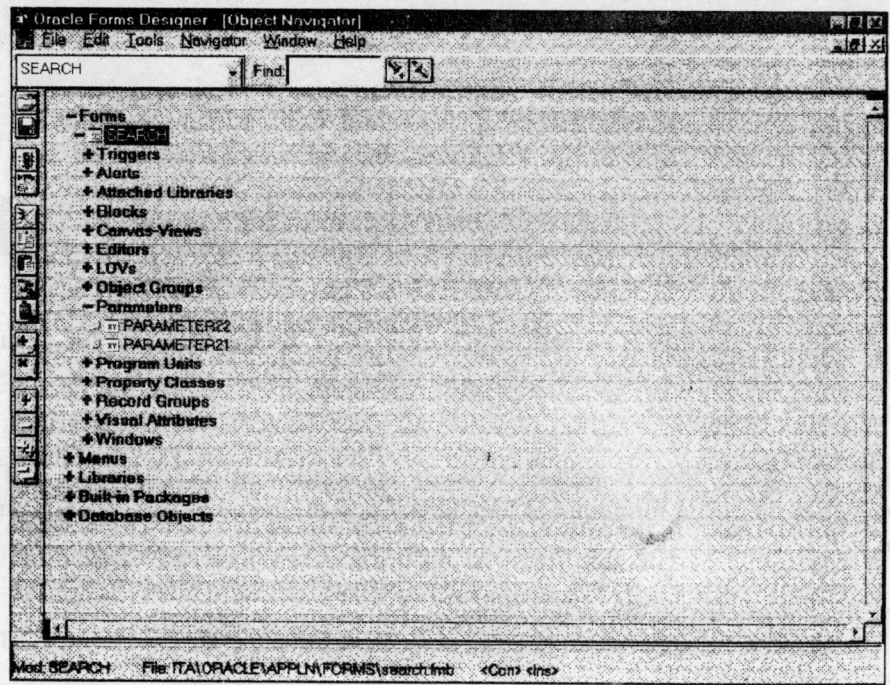

Diagram 12.1 : Creating a new parameter

2. Open the property sheet of the parameter and specify the name, data type and the maximum length of the parameter as shown in diagram 12.2.

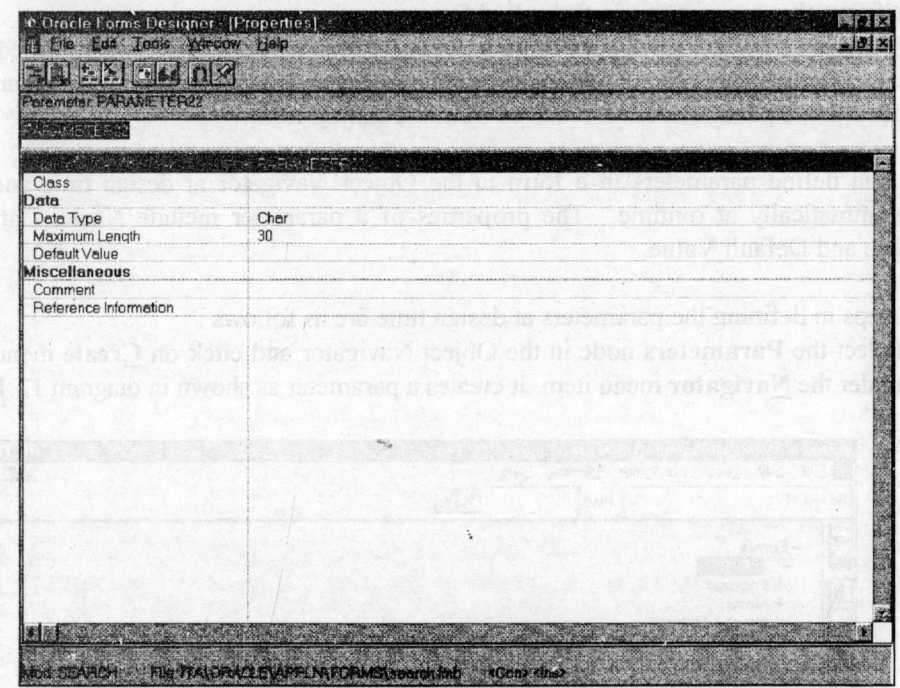

Diagram 12.2 : Setting the properties of the parameter

The number of parameters in the called form must be the same as the number of parameters added to the parameter list. The names of the parameters must also be the same.

Thus if the calling form is passing a single parameter named 'client_no', the no of parameters in the called form must at least be one and the name of that parameter must be client_no.

Using the parameters in the called form :
The Parameters in the called form can be referenced by using prefix 'PARAMETER.' before the parameter.

Example :
To get the value of the parameter client_no the syntax will be :

:PARAMETER.CLIENT_NO

DIFFERENCES BETWEEN GLOBAL VARIABLES / PARAMETER VARIABLES

Parameter values are not visible across multiple forms. Thus, even if a named parameter is defined in multiple forms, each form has a separate context, and setting the value of the named parameter in a form has no effect on the value of the parameter in another form.

For this reason, parameters are useful in multiple-form applications primarily as inputs to a form when it is first invoked.

If your application requires variables whose values are visible across all called forms, you should use *global* variables. Global variables are visible across called forms, and remain active until they are explicitly deleted with the ERASE built-in procedure, or until the session ends. *Global* variables can be referenced by using prefix 'GLOBAL.' before the variable name.

Example :
To get the value of the "global variable", client_no, the syntax will be :
:GLOBAL.CLIENT_NO

Focus :
When the user clicks on search button, the system must pop up a window that displays a product description list from the product_master table. When the user select a product description and clicks on OK, the search window must be closed all the details for the selected product description must be displayed in the product_master data entry screen.

Include a text item in the search window. The list must display the product description as *per the pattern* entered in the text item.

The search window must accept the SQL statement that populates the list of values and the name of the display field.

e.g.
If the search window is called from the product master form, it must pass the SQL statement that displays the product description and takes the product_no as the data value for the list item. The display field in this case is product description. The search window will be displayed as shown in diagram 12.3.

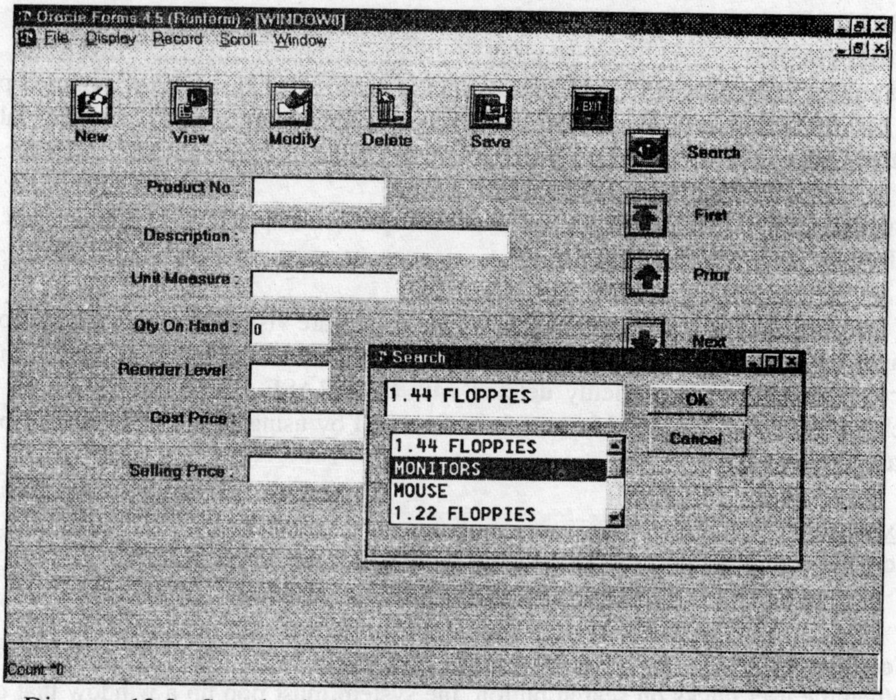

Diagram 12.3 : Search window called from Product Master Form

Similarly, if the search windows is called from the client master form, it must pass the SQL statement that displays the client name and takes the client_no as the data value for the list item. The display field in this case is client name.

Solution :

Modifications in the calling form :
1. Open the Product Master Form and check to see that the form has a Search button with the following properties.

2. Write the PL/SQL code in the search button in product_master form as shown below :

Trigger Name : **WHEN-BUTTON-PRESSED** Form : product_master
Block : button_palette Item : push_button_search
Function : To open the search form. Pass the valid value accepted in the search form to the default_where property of the product_master block and execute the query.
Text : DECLARE
    pl_id paramlist; /* parameter list declaration */
    pl_name varchar(40) := 'search_paramlist';

  BEGIN
    pl_id := get_parameter_list(pl_name);

```
            if id_null(pl_id) then
                    pl_id := create_parameter_list(pl_name);
                    if not id_null(pl_id) then
                            add_parameter(pl_id,'search_sql', text_parameter,
                                            'select description, product_no
                                            from product_master');
                            add_parameter(pl_id,'display_value',text_parameter,
                                            'description');
                    end if;
            end if;
/* call_form is used to open another form. It takes the
form name(along with the path ) as the parameter.
In this example we need to pass the parameter list to
the search form. The parameter list will the last
paramter in the call_form built-in procedure.

The product master form must not be
invisible. This can be achieved by passing no_hide parameter
to call_form. */
            call_form(' c:\orawork\search.fmx', no_hide, no_replace,
                                            no_query_only,pl_name);

        /* If the product number is not spaces then
        set the default_where property of the
        product_master_blk to the product_no entered
        go to product_master_blk and
        execute the query
set the default_where property of the
product_master_blk to null string. */
            IF not (:global.search_value = ' ') THEN
                    set_block_property('product_master_blk',
                            default_where, 'where product_no = '''
                                    || :global.search_value || '''');
            next_block ;
            execute_query;
            set_block_property('product_master_blk',
                    default_where, '');
            END IF;
    END;
```

When *Execute_Query* is fired, Oracle creates the select statement from the properties of the block and the items included in the block. One such property is *Default_Where*. The *Default_Where* property includes the where clause of the select statement. If the *Default_Where* is set the record set retrieved on the form will be restricted to the records that satisfy the condition the *Default_Where* clause.

Default_Where property can be set at design time or it can be set programatically by using *Set_Block_Property*. *Set_Block_Property* takes in three parameters. These are the *name of the block*, the *property name* and the *property value*.

In the current example, the execute query must populate the block with a global select statement when the user clicks on view. If the user clicks on search, appropriate where clause must be included in the select statement. Thus we need to specify the where clause programmatically as follows :

```
set_block_property('product_master_blk',default_where,
    'where product_no = ''' || :global.search_value || '''');
```

The :global.search_value is a global variable. The value of this global variable is assigned in the OK button to the value selected by the user and in the CANCEL button to null.

Creating a search form :
1. Open a new form and save it as search.fmb.

2. Create a control block named search_blk.

3. Click on the toolbox in the layout editor and select icon labeled *list item* and place it on the form. Set the *following* properties of the list item.

Name	: search_list
Item Type	: List Item
List Style	: Tlist

4. Click on the toolbox in the layout editor and select icon labeled *Text Item* and place it on the form. Set the *following* properties of the list item.

Name	: search_pattern
Item Type	: Text Item

5. Place two push buttons as shown in diagram 12.1 and set the following properties.

Name	: push_button_ok
Label	: OK
Enabled	: False

Name	: push_button_cancel
Label	: Cancel

PARAMETER PASSING IN FORMS **317**

6. Create two parameters as follows :

    Name   : search_sql
    Data Type   : Char
    Maximum Length : 255

Specify the name, data type and the maximum length of the parameter as shown in diagram 12.4.

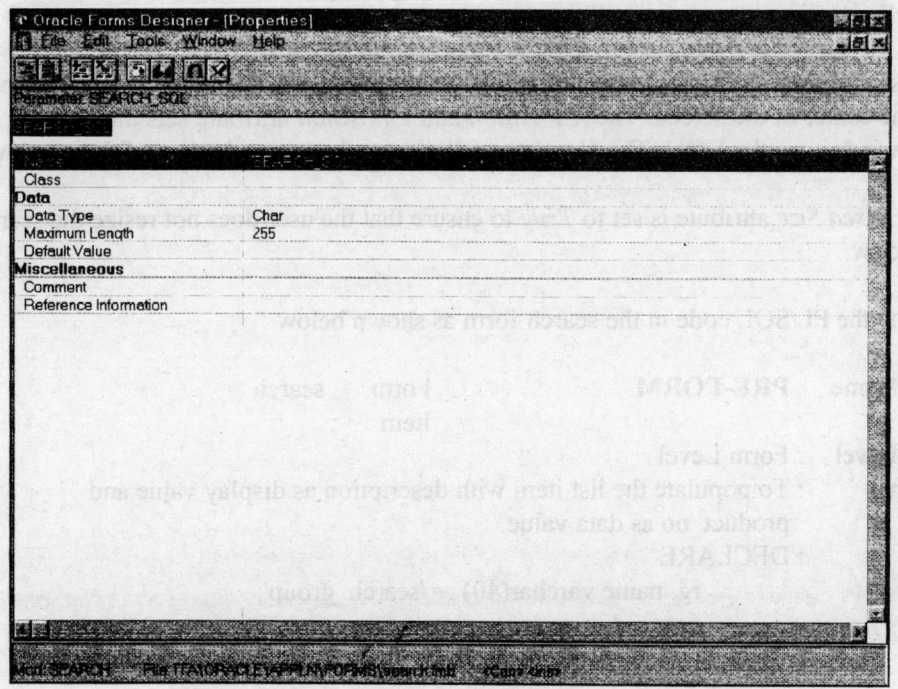

Diagram 12.4 : Setting the properties of the parameter

Similarly create another parameter and set the the following properties :

    Name   : display_value
    Data Type   : Char
    Maximum Length : 40

7. Size the canvas by setting the following properties.

    Width   : 236
    Height   : 101
    View Width : 236
    View Height : 101

8. Set the following properties of the window :

Name	: search_win
X Position	: 130
Y Position	: 100
Width	: 236
Height	: 101
Title	: Search
Window Style	: Dialog
Fixed Size	: True

As shown in diagram 12.3, the search window must be displayed as a popup window in the center of the screen. The *X Position* and *Y Position* attribute sets the position of the window on the VDU. The *Height* and *Width* attribute sets the size of the window.

The *Fixed Size* attribute is set to *True* to ensure that the user does not resize the search window.

9. Write the PL/SQL code in the search form as shown below :

Trigger Name	: **PRE-FORM**	Form	: search
Block	:	Item	:
Trigger Level	: Form Level		
Function	: To populate the list item with description as display value and product_no as data value.		
Text	: DECLARE		

```
       rg_name varchar(40) := 'search_group';
       groupid recordgroup;
       status number;
BEGIN
       /* Create a record group that includes all the records from the
       product_master table. The sql statement will be the search.sql
       parameter passed by the calling form */
       groupid := create_group_from_query(rg_name,
       :parameter.search_sql);

       /* populate the group with the records fetched by the
          select statement */
          status := populate_group(groupid);

       /* populate the list with the records in the group */
       populate_list('search_list', groupid);
END;
```

PARAMETER PASSING IN FORMS 319

```
Trigger Name  : WHEN-VALIDATE-ITEM   Form  : search
Block         : search_blk            Item  : search_pattern
Function      : To change the list to display records as per the pattern entered
                by the user.
Text          : DECLARE
                    rg_name varchar(40) := 'Search_group';
                    groupid recordgroup;
                    status number;
                BEGIN
                    /* find a record group by the name of 'search_list' */
                    groupid := find_group(rg_name);

                    /* if the record group exists then populate the record
                    group id_null is a packaged procedure that checks
                    whether the record group id is null or not. It takes a
                    recordgroup as the parameter */
                    if not id_null(groupid) then
                        if :search_pattern = '' or :search_pattern is null then
                            status := populate_group_with_query(rg_name,
                                      :parameter.search_sql);
                        else
                            status := populate_group_with_query(rg_name,
                                      :parameter.search_sql || ' where
                                      lower(' || :parameter.display_value ||
                                      ') like lower(''' || :search_pattern
                                      || '%')');
                        end if;
                    else
                        /* if the search pattern is null then populate the
                        record group with all the records from the product
                        master table else populate the record group with t
                        selecstatement having appropriate where clause. */
                        IF :search_pattern = '' or :search_pattern is null THEN
                            groupid := create_group_from_query(rg_name,
                                       :parameter.search_sql);
                        ELSE
                            groupid := create_group_from_query(rg_name,
                                       :parameter.search_sql || ' where
                                       lower(' || :parameter.display_value || ')
                                       like lower(''' || :search_pattern || '%')');
                        END IF;
                        status := populate_group(groupid);
                    END IF;
```

```
                    /* if the no of rows retrieved > 0 then
                       populate the list with the records in the group */
                    IF get_group_row_count(groupid) > 0 THEN
                        populate_list('search_list', groupid);
                    END IF;
                END;
```

Note : 1. If the record group with a specific name exists, we simply need to populate that group with appropriate data. In this case, if the record group 'search_list' is existing, we need to populate the record group with / without a where clause.

Trigger Name	: **WHEN-LIST-CHANGED**	Form	: search
Block	: search_blk	Item	: search_list
Function	: To set the enable property of the OK button to true		
Text	: BEGIN		

```
                        set_item_property('push_button_ok', enabled, property_on);
                    END;
```

Trigger Name	: **WHEN-BUTTON-PRESSED**	Form	: search
Block	: search_blk	Item	: push_button_ok
Function	: To assign the selected list value to global variable and quit the search form. The value in this global variable will be used in the default_where property of the main block.		
Text	: BEGIN		

```
                    /* Assigning the selected product_no to a global
                       variable. The value in the global variable can then be
                       used in any form.
                       Any variable prefixed with global. is considered to a
                       global variable. Global variables are not explicitly
                       declared. They are of Datatype char size 255 */
                        :global.search_value := :search_list;
                        exit_form;
                    END;
```

Trigger Name	: **WHEN-BUTTON-PRESSED**	Form	: search
Block	: search_blk	Item	: push_button_cancel
Function	: To assign spaces to global variable and quit the search form.		
Text	: BEGIN		

```
                    /* set the value of the global variable to single space and
                       quit form */
                        :global.search_value := ' ';
                        exit_form ;
                    END;
```

13. USING MULTIPLE CANVASES ON A FORM

In all the forms we have looked at earlier, either as an example to learn concepts or as hands on exercise, we have always worked with :

A single Form with
- One command window
- One canvas object
- Multiple blocks

Sometimes the number of columns in a table exceed the size of the standard canvas or the system requires that information on the form be displayed either on a click of a button or on some condition set by the user.

For Example,
- It is quite common to include a button labeled **More...** which when clicked displayed additional information. This helps in reducing space crunch on a form.

- In the sales order system the contact information of the client can be displayed when the user clicks on the button labeled **Contact Info...** (diagram 13.1)

The forms designer allows system developers to include multiple canvases on the same form. Additional fields can be included in the second canvas and code can be written to make the canvas visible / invisible as required.

HANDS ON

CLIENT MASTER DATA ENTRY SCREEN

To modify the client master data entry screen to manipulate the data being loaded into the **client_master** and the **client_contact** table.

Provide the user with complete data manipulation operations (Add, View, Modify, Delete): In the view mode, allow the user to browse through the data table, one record at a time i.e. First, Last, Previous, Next operations have to be provided for.

Make use of property class object to create buttons and standardize the visual properties of all the text objects with visual class object.

The client Contact information must be presented in a tabular format as shown in diagram 13.1. Contact information must be displayed only when the user clicks on the push button for contact information.

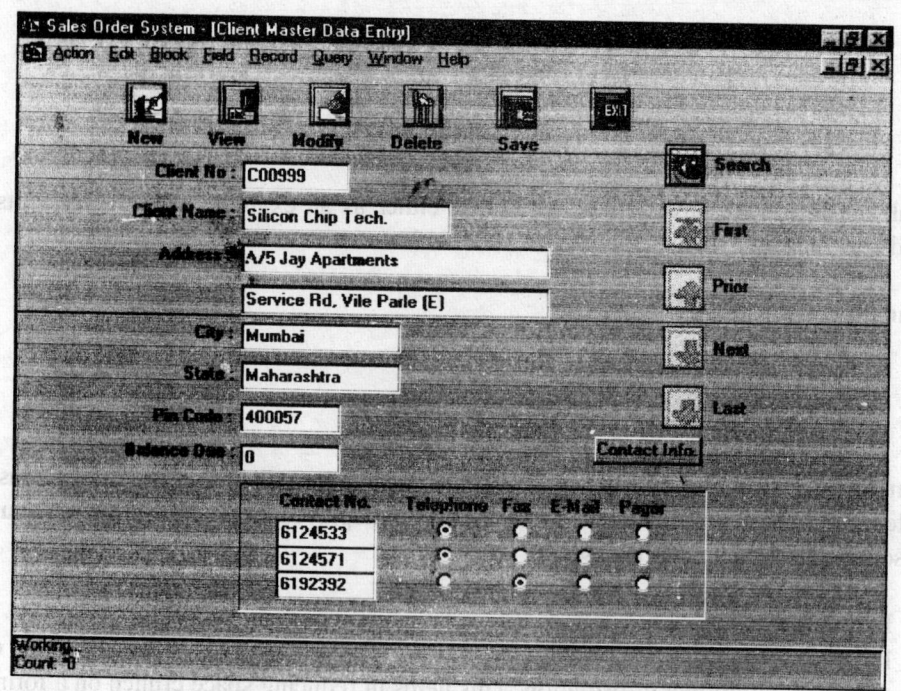

Diagram 13.1 : Client Master Data Entry Screen

Table Name : Client_master
Description : Use to store information about clients.

Column Name	Data Type	Size	Column Description
client_no	varchar2	6	Access key via which we shall seek data.
name	varchar2	20	client's name.
address1	varchar2	30	First line in the client's address.
address2	varchar2	30	Second line in the client's address.
city	varchar2	15	City in which the client is located.
state	varchar2	15	State in which the client is located.
pincode	number	6	pin code
bal_due	number	10,2	Balance amount payable by the client.

Table Name : Client_Contact
Description : Use to store information about clients contact information.

Column name	Data Type	Size	Column Description
client_no	varchar2	6	Access key via which we shall seek data.
contact_no	varchar2	15	Correspondence No. for the client.
device	varchar2	10	Type of contact no. (Tel, Fax, Email address, Pager No.)

Validations in the client contact information data entry screen are as follows :

- Client_no, contact_no or device cannot be left null.
- Client_no must be present in the client_master table.
- Device field can take only following values - 'Tel', 'Fax', 'Email', 'Pager no'

SOLUTION

1. Open the client_master form.

2. Position and Size the items as shown in diagram 13.1.

3. Create a new canvas and set the following properties.

Name : Client_Contact_Can
Canvas View Type : Stacked
View Width : 256
View Height : 70
Display X Position : 250
Display Y Position : 126

4. Change the *Background Color* of *Client_Master_Can* to *gray12*.

5. Create a new block for the client_contact information as follows :

General :
   Base Table : Client_Contact
   Block Name : Client_Contact_Blk
   Canvas Name : Client_Contact_Can

Layout :
   Presentation : Tabular
   No of Records : 3

Master/Detail :
   Master Block : Client_Master_Blk
   Join Condition : Client_Master_Blk.client_no = Client_Contact_Blk.client_no

6. Set the *Master Deletes* property in the relation object to *Cascading*.

7. Write the necessary triggers.

8. The when-button-pressed trigger on push_button_add, push_button_delete, push_button_view and push_button_modify calls the item_enable_disable procedure included in the library to enable or disable the items in the client_master_blk based on the mode of operation.

9. Since we have included the client_contact_blk, we need to enable or disable the items in the client_contact_blk. Thus we need to call the item_enable_disable twice i.e. for client_master_blk and for client_contact_blk as follows :

Trigger Name : **WHEN-BUTTON-PRESSED**   Form : client_master
Block : button_palette   Item : push_button_add
Trigger Level : Item Level
Function : Insert a record in the client_master table.
Text : BEGIN
    next_block;
    /* Insert a new record in the current block and position the cursor on that record */
    create_record ;
    item_enable_disable('client_master_blk', property_on);
    item_enable_disable('client_contact_blk', property_on);
END ;

Similarly change the when-button-pressed trigger for push_button_delete, push_button_view and push_button_modify

VALIDATIONS
To modify the form to include the following validations :

- Contact_No or Device cannot be left null.
- Device field can take only following values - 'Tel', 'Fax', 'Email', 'Pager No'.

Trigger Name	: **WHEN-VALIDATE-ITEM**	Form	: client_master
Block	: client_contact_blk	Item	: contact_no
Function	: Check to see that contact_no is not left blank.		
Text	: BEGIN		

```
        IF :client_contact_blk.contact_no is null OR
           :client_contact_blk.contact_no = '' THEN
           message('Client's Contact Number cannot be left blank');
           raise form_trigger_failure;
        END IF;
     END;
```

Trigger Name	: **WHEN-VALIDATE-ITEM**	Form	: client_master
Block	: client_contact_blk	Item	: device
Function	: Check to see that device is not left blank.		
Text	: BEGIN		

```
        IF :client_contact_blk.device is null OR
           :client_contact_blk.device = '' THEN
           message('Device cannot be left blank');
           raise form_trigger_failure;
        END IF;
     END;
```

Device field can take only following values - 'Tel', 'Fax', 'Email', 'Pager no' :
If a field can take only fixed values, the user should be provided with a list of values to choose from. This will make the form more user friendly. It will also eliminate the data entry errors.

Oracle provides an object via which list of values for a column can be provided. This object is called a RADIO BUTTON. List of values consist of two distinct operations :

- Defining the *radio button group*.
- Defining the radio buttons for the group.

Let us look at the current example. The value in the field device in the client_contact table can take specific values like 'Tel', 'Fax', 'Email', 'Pager no' We will create a Radio button group and the radio buttons.

1. Open the property sheet of device and set the following properties :

Item_type   : Radio Group
Default Value   : Tel
Other Values   :

2. Open the Layout editor and place the radio buttons. Each time you place a radio button, the system will ask for the name of *Radio Group* as shown in diagram 13.2.

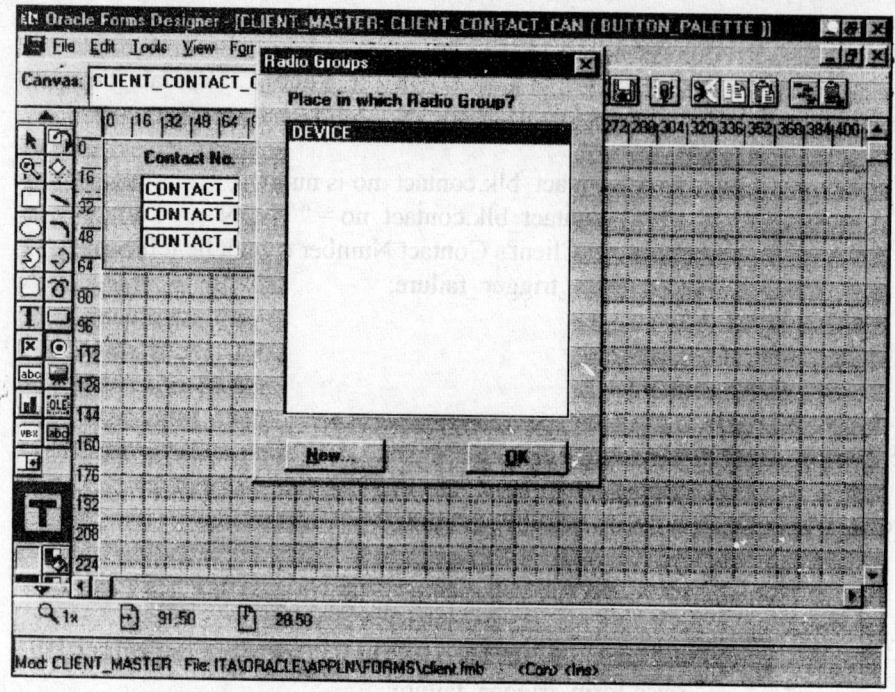

Diagram 13.2 : Including a radio button on the form

1. Click on OK. Set the properties of each of the radio buttons as follows :

Name   : RB_TEL
Label   : Tel.
Value   : Tel

Name   : RB_FAX
Label   : Fax.
Value   : Fax

Name   : RB_EMAIL
Label   : E-Mail
Value   : E-Mail

Name   : RB_PAGER
Label   : Pager No.
Value   : Pager No.

Making the Contact information visible when the user clicks on push_button_contact :

The steps are as follows :
1. Place a pushbutton and set the name and the label property as follows :

Name   : push_button_contact
Label   : Contact Info…

2. Write following code in the when-button-pressed event of push_button_contact.

Trigger Name : **WHEN-BUTTON-PRESSED**   Form : client_master
Block   : button_palette   Item : push_button_contact
Function   : Making the Client_Contact can visible.
Text   : BEGIN
                /* The show_view packaged procedure displays the specified
                canvas in the window. To hide the canvas the user can use
                the hide_view function. */
                show_view('client_contact_can');
              END;

14. WORKING WITH MENUS

Every form runs with one of the following:

- The Default menu that is built into the form
- A custom menu that the user defines as a separate module and then attaches to the form for runtime execution

At runtime, an application can have only one menu module active at a time, either the Default menu or a custom menu.

The Default menu is part of the form module. Custom menu modules, however, are separate from form modules. So, when you deliver a single-form application that uses a custom menu, you have to provide :

- An .FMX form module.
- An .MMX menu module.

In a multi-form application, you may need to deliver several form modules and several menu modules. Multiple forms can share the same menu, or each form can invoke a different menu.

USING THE DEFAULT MENU

A default menu is used for the data entry form automatically unless otherwise specified. The only time you need to explicitly specify that a form should use the Default menu is if the form's menu assignment has been modified via a program.

To explicitly specify the Default menu:

1. Open the form module to which the default menu is to be attached using the Object Navigator. The Properties window now displays the properties for this form module.

2. In the Menu Module property of the Properties window, type DEFAULT and Click on the Intersection/Union Icon (The 'U' shaped icon). If you want the form to run without a menu, leave the Menu Module field blank.

3. Select **F**ile, **S**ave or **F**ile, Save **A**s to save the form module.

4. Select **F**ile, **A**dministration, **G**enerate to generate the form module.

USING THE CUSTOM MENU

A Custom menu is build by creating a Menu Module and then defining the objects in the menu.

A Menu Module includes the following types of objects (diagram 14.1).

1. The Menu Module itself.
2. The Menus: the Main Menu, Individual Menus and Submenu
3. Menu items attached individual menu and menu items attached to submenus with their associated commands and procedures.

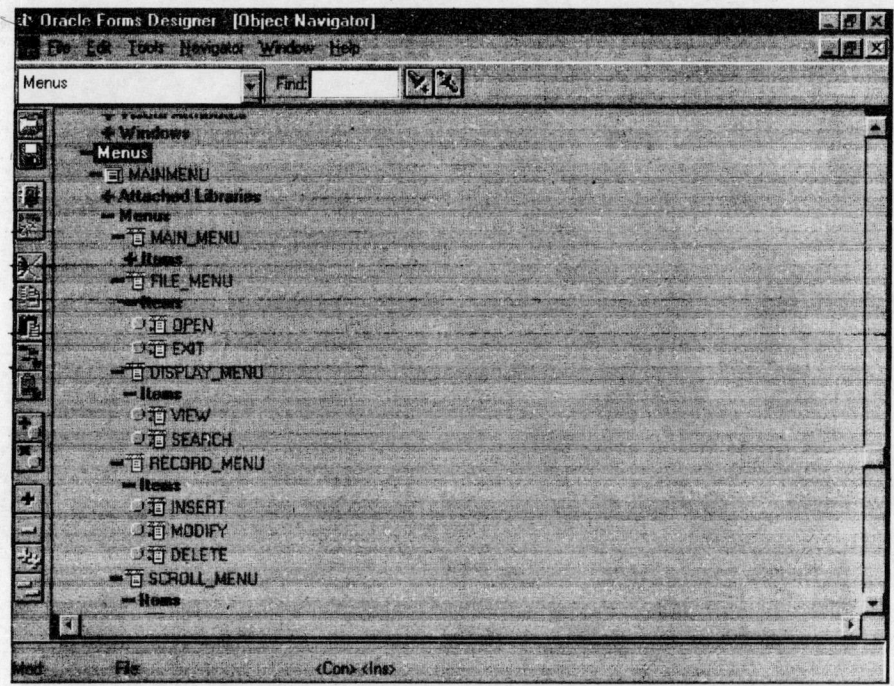

Diagram 14.1 : Menu Module Along with Objects in it.

Creating A Menu Module :

You can create a menu module in two ways, depending on whether you are starting from scratch or modifying an existing menu module.

To create a new menu module (diagram 14.2)

1. Choose **File, New, Menu**. Or, in the Navigator, select the Menus node and click on the Create icon in the toolbar. Oracle Forms creates a new menu module in the Navigator with a default name such as MODULE2 as shown in diagram 14.2.

2. Replace the default name with a more meaningful name. Click once to select the default name, click again to enter edit mode, drag to select the name, then type the new name.

Once you have opened a menu module, you can create:
   1) A Main Menu (displayed as a horizontal menu bar)
   2) Individual Menus consisting of menu items (displayed vertically)
   3) Submenus (displayed to the right of menu items)

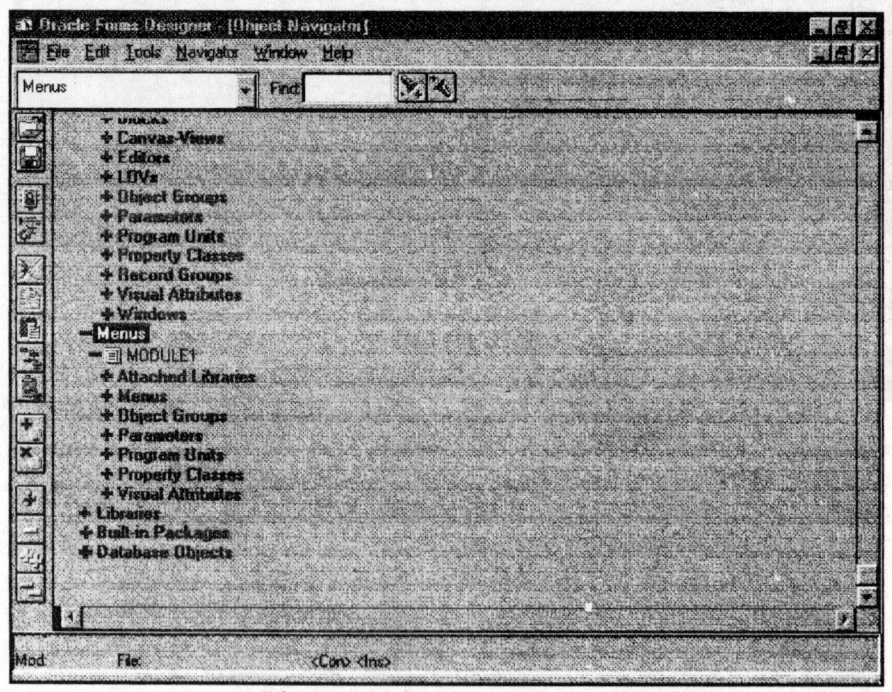

Diagram 14.2 : New menu module screen.

CREATING A MAIN MENU

To create a main menu

1. Choose **Tools, Menu Editor**. The Menu Editor opens, showing a new menu called MAIN_MENU, with one item, labeled **<New Item>** as shown in diagram 14.3. **<New Item>** is selected, so you can edit it.

2. Type a menu label (such as Action) to replace the default label.

3. Choose **Menu, Create Right** to add a new item to the main menu. Or, click the Create Right icon, or press Enter to leave edit mode and press Control-Right arrow. The Menu Editor creates a menu item **<New Item>** and selects it so you can edit the label.

4. Type to replace the default label. The label is the name of the menu item as it will appear at runtime. The label may differ from the name, which you can use programmatically and which must follow PL/SQL naming conventions. You can also edit these items in the Properties window.

5. To add additional items to the main menu, repeat steps 3 and 4.

Diagram 14.3 : Main Menu Screen.

Once the main menu is complete, you're ready to create the individual menus, which means adding menu items to the menu. For each parent item on the main menu (such as Action, Edit, Block, Field and so on), you'll create a list of related child menu items.

CREATING A MENU

To create a menu:

1. In the main menu, select the parent item, such as Action.

2. Choose **Menu, Create Down** to add a new item to the Action menu. Or, click the Create Down icon, or press Enter to leave edit mode and press Control-Down arrow. The Menu Editor creates a menu item **<New Item>** as shown in diagram 14.4 and selects it so you can edit the label.

3. Type to replace the default label.

4. Repeat steps 2 and 3 to add further menu items to the current menu. In the Properties window, the Command Type property of the parent item (Action) is changed from PL/SQL to Menu.

You'll notice that when you add the first menu item, Oracle Forms places a shaded rectangle, or handle, to the left of the first item, such as Action. The handle lets you move all the items on the menu as a unit or display the Menu-level properties in the Properties window. Menu items can call submenus, which are displayed to the right of the item.

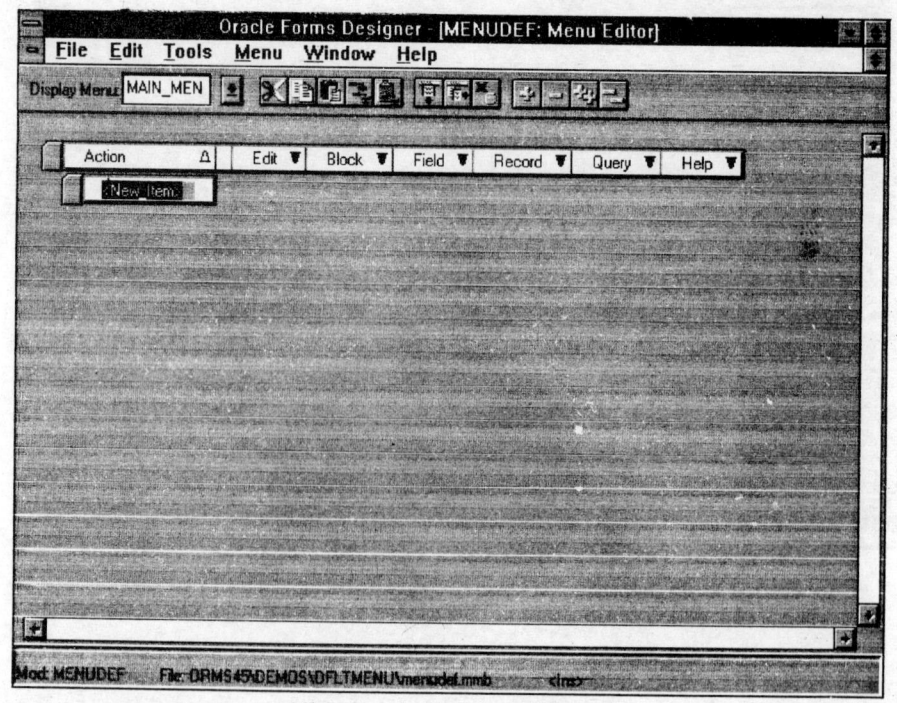

Diagram 14.4: Menu Screen

CREATING A SUBMENU

To create a submenu:

1. Select the parent item on the individual menu, such as Copy.

2. Choose **Menu, Create Right** to add the first item on a new submenu. Or, click the Create Right icon, or press Control-Right arrow. The Menu Editor creates a submenu item **<New Item>** and selects it so you can edit the label as shown in diagram 14.5.

3. Type to replace the default label. Choose **Menu, Create Down** to add another item to the submenu.

4. Type to replace the default label.

5. Repeat steps 4 and 5 to add further submenu items.

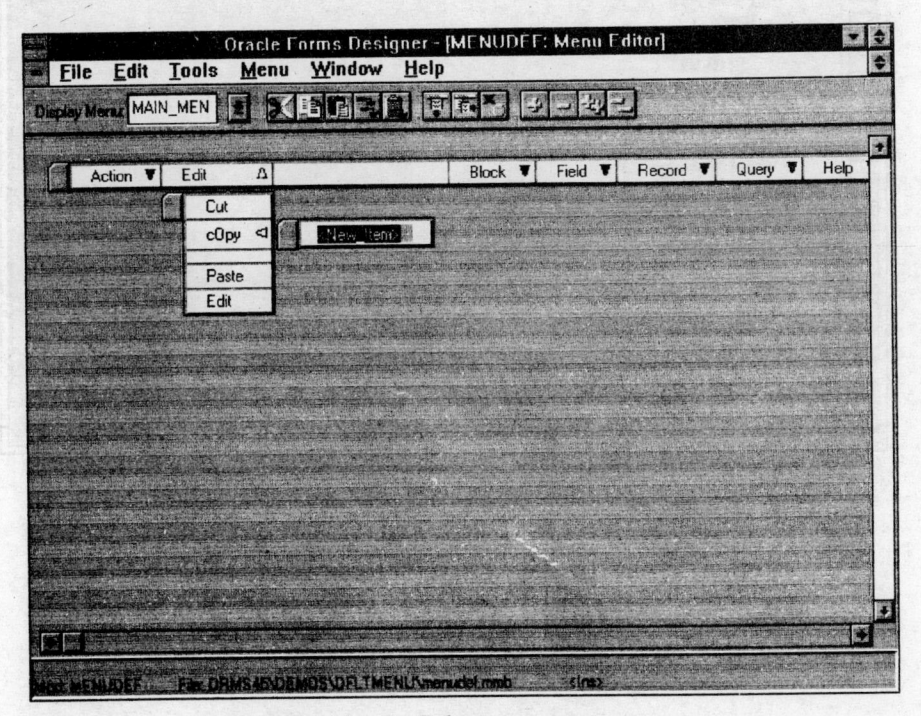

Diagram 14.5 : Submenu screen.

ASSIGNING NEW NAMES TO ALL THE MENUS UNDER THE MAIN MENU

1. Open the Object Navigator screen and click on Menus node. All the menus and submenus present under the MAIN MENU are displayed with default name such as ITEM1, ITEM2, ITEM3 etc. as shown in diagram 14.6.

2. Identify each of the menu by clicking on the menu node and then the item node. Check the items present under the menu. Name the menu accordingly(i.e. if items are PREVIOUS, NEXT AND CLEAR then name the menu as BLOCK)

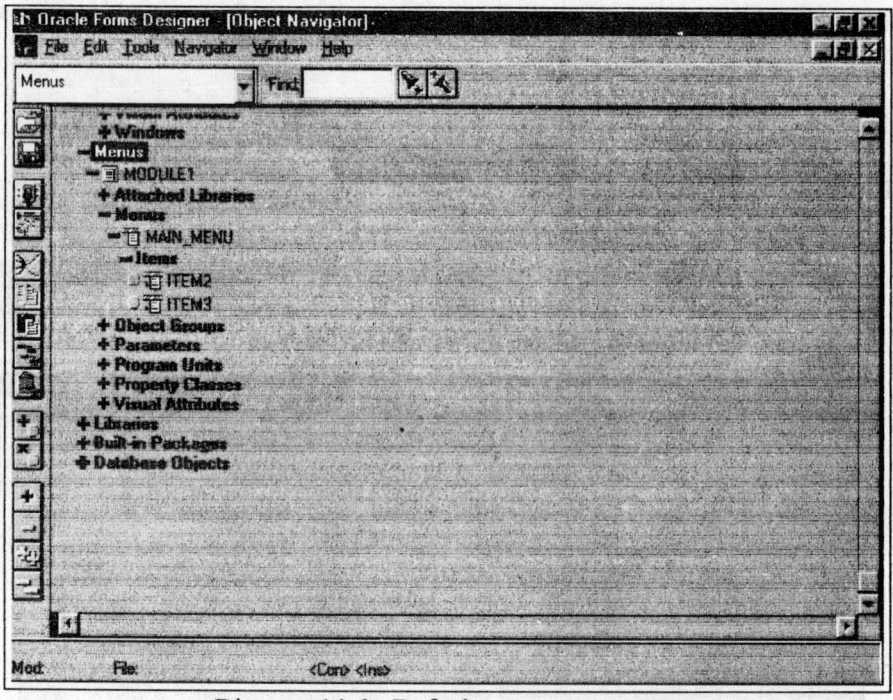

Diagram 14.6 : Default menu name screen.

DELETE ITEMS FROM A MENU OR SUBMENU

To delete items from a menu or submenu:

1. Select the item.

2. Choose **Menu, Delete** (or click on the Delete icon). Oracle Forms displays an alert asking if you are sure you want to delete.

3. Click Yes.

ASSIGNING COMMANDS TO MENU ITEMS

Every menu item must have a valid Command Type property:

- Null
- Menu
- PL/SQL,
- Plus
- Current Forms
- Macro.

Most menu items execute PL/SQL commands, so their Command Type is PL/SQL. If a menu item has submenus, however, its Command Type must be changed to Menu. (For example, all items on the main menu must have Command Type set to Menu.) Null is used for separator items.

To Assign a Command to a Menu Item

1. Select the desired menu item in the Menu Editor.

2. In the Properties window, check that the item's Command Type property is set to the appropriate command type:

   - If the menu item executes a command   Choose PL/SQL.
   - If the item invokes a submenu   Choose MENU.
   - If the item is a separator   Choose NULL.

   Note: The other three types--Plus, Form, and Macro--are included for backward compatibility only, and are not recommended for use in current applications.

3. In the Properties window, double-click in the Command Text property (or click on the More... button) to display the PL/SQL Editor as shown in diagram 14.7.

4. In the PL/SQL Editor, type the PL/SQL code.

5. Click Compile.

6. Click Close.

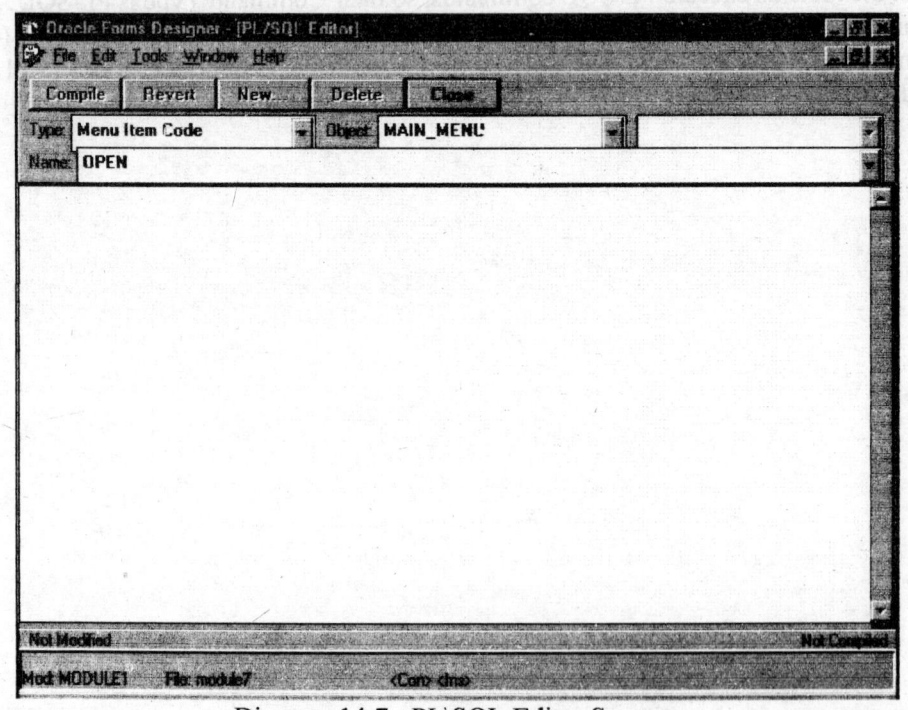

Diagram 14.7 : PL\SQL Editor Screen.

ATTACHING A MENU MODULE TO A FORM

Before you attach a menu to a form, you must: generate the menu module, set the form's Menu Module property, and generate the form.

To attach a menu to a form:

1. Make the menu module the current module in the Designer.

2. Select **F**ile, **S**ave or File, **S**ave **A**s to save the menu module (.MMB file).

3. Select **F**ile, **A**dministration, **G**enerate to generate the menu module.

   Oracle Forms creates a runtime .MMX menu file. Menu runfiles have an .MMX extension and are stored in the file system, not in the database. (The .MMB menu module in the Designer, however, can be saved to the file system or to the database. In the Designer by Default it is set to file system)

4. Select the form in the Navigator. The Properties window displays the form module properties.

5. In Properties window, set the Menu Module property to the filename of the runtime .MMX menu file that you generated in step 3.

   Once a menu is attached to a form, Oracle Forms automatically loads the .MMX menu file when the form is run.

6. Check that the Use File property is set to True (the default value).

7. Select **F**ile, **S**ave or File, **S**ave **A**s to save the form module.

8. Select **F**ile, **A**dministration, **G**enerate to generate the form module.

OPENING A FORM THROUGH THE MENU

You can open a form through a menu using **OPEN_FORM** built-in procedure. The syntax of OPEN_FORM is as shown below :

Open_Form(form_name)

form_name   : Name of the form in characters.

For example, to open a form 'product.fmx' through a menu, write the following code in the Clicked event of the corresponding menu item.

open_form('product.fmx');

Invoking Other Products From Oracle Forms Or Menus

You can invoke other products from Oracle Forms with the **RUN_PRODUCT** built-in procedure. The syntax for RUN_PRODUCT is shown here:

RUN_PRODUCT(product, document, commmode, execmode, location, list, display);

By default, when you invoke Oracle Reports or Oracle Graphics with RUN_PRODUCT, the called product logs on to ORACLE using the current form operator's USERID.

Oracle Forms uses the parameters you pass to RUN_PRODUCT to construct a valid command line invocation of the called product. RUN_PRODUCT takes the following parameters :

Product   : A numeric constant that specifies the Oracle tool to be invoked i.e. FORMS, REPORTS, GRAPHICS, or BOOK.

Document   : Specifies the document or module to be opened by the called product.

Commmode   : Specifies the communication mode to be used when running the called product. Valid numeric constants for this parameter are SYNCHRONOUS and ASYNCHRONOUS.

SYNCHRONOUS specifies that control returns to Oracle Forms only after the called product has been exited. The operator cannot work in the form while the called product is running. Synchronous is required when passing a record group to a called product as a DATA_PARAMETER; for example, when invoking Oracle Graphics to return an Oracle Graphics display that will appear in a form chart item.

ASYNCHRONOUS specifies that control returns to the calling application immediately, even if the called application has not completed its display. Do not use ASYNCHRONOUS when passing a record group to a called product as a DATA_PARAMETER; for example, when invoking Oracle Graphics to return an Oracle Graphics display that will appear in a form chart item.

Execmode : Specifies the execution mode to be used when running the called product, either BATCH or RUNTIME. When you run Oracle Reports and Oracle Graphics, execmode can be either BATCH or RUNTIME. When you run Oracle Forms, always set execmode to RUNTIME.

Location : Specifies the location of the document or module you want the called product to execute, either the file system or the database.

List : Specifies the name or ID of a parameter list to be passed to the called product.

Display : Specifies the name of the Oracle Forms chart item that will contain the display generated by Oracle Graphics.

For example, to invoke Oracle Report '*sales.rep*', you could make the following call in the clicked event of corresponding menu item :

**run_product(reports, 'sales.rep', asynchronous,
runtime, filesystem, null);**

HANDS ON

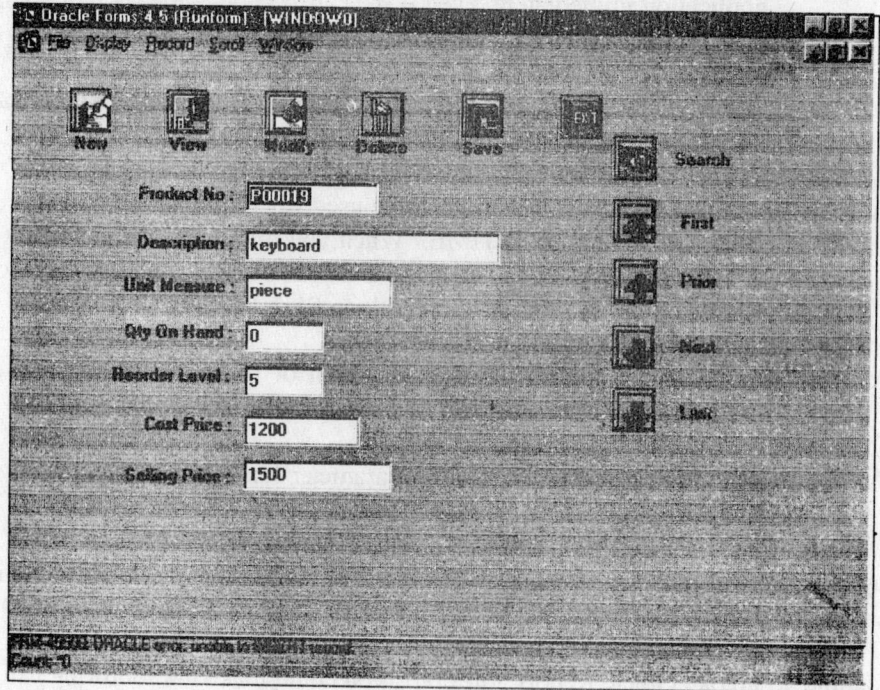

Diagram 14.8 : Product Data Entry Screen.

Focus :
Creating a menu for the application product allowing Data manipulation and Navigation.

Solution :

1. Create new menu module by choosing **File, New, Menu** and replace the default name to MAINMENU.

2. Choose **Tools, Menu Editor** to create a main menu.

3. Attach all the required items to main menu.

4. To each of the parent item attach the required items and submenu wherever required. The completed layout in the menu editor will be as shown in diagram 14.9.

5. Write the necessary commands to the items.

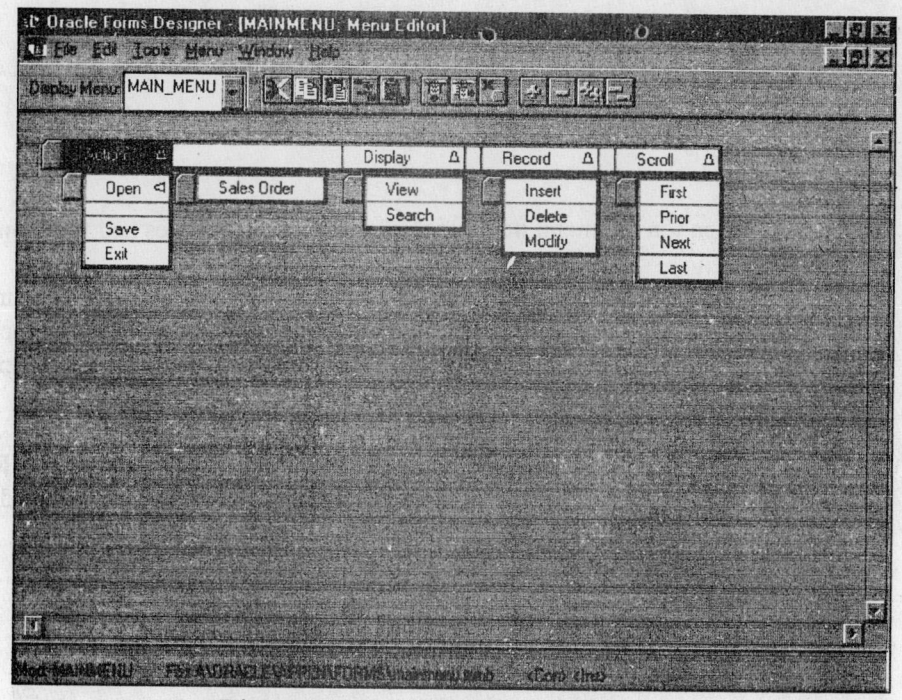

Diagram 14.9 : Completed Menu Layout

6. Attach the menu module to the Product_master form using the Properties Window of the Product_master form.

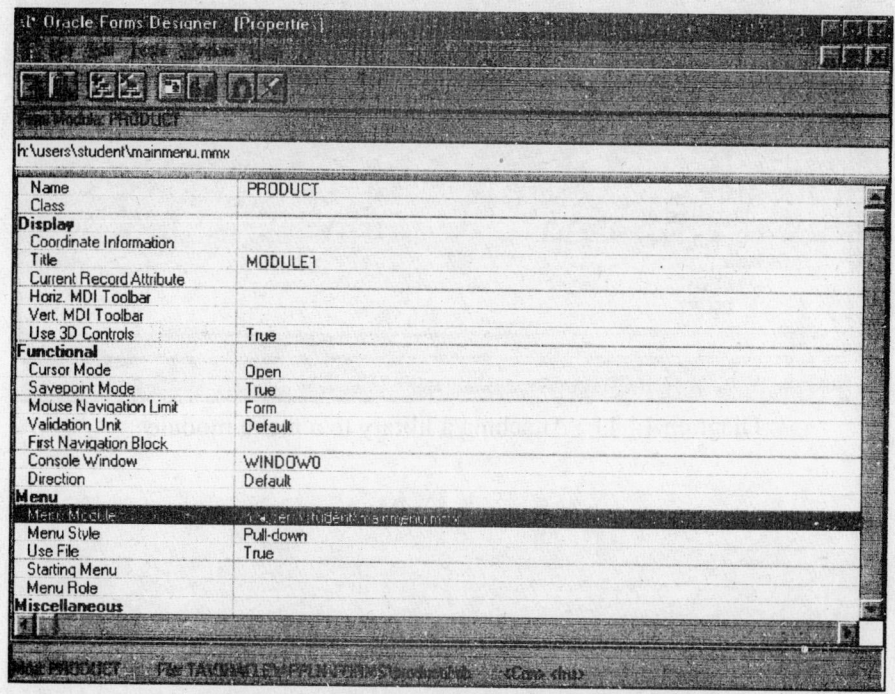

Diagram 14.10 : Form Property Window

7. Save and Generate the menu.

8. Save and Generate the form.

9. Run the form to check whether the menu works correctly.

PROCEDURES

The code blocks written ion the menu item uses user-defined procedures and functions.

Creation of user-defined procedures in a menu is similar to the creation of procedures in Forms. Since the form as well menu module uses the same procedure we can attach the library in which these procedures are defined. A library can be attached to the menu as follows :

1. Just like forms, the menu module has a node named ATTACHED LIBRARIES. Double click ion the Attached Libraries node. It displays the *Attached Library* dialog box. Specify the name of the library as *libproc.pll* as shown in diagram 14.11.

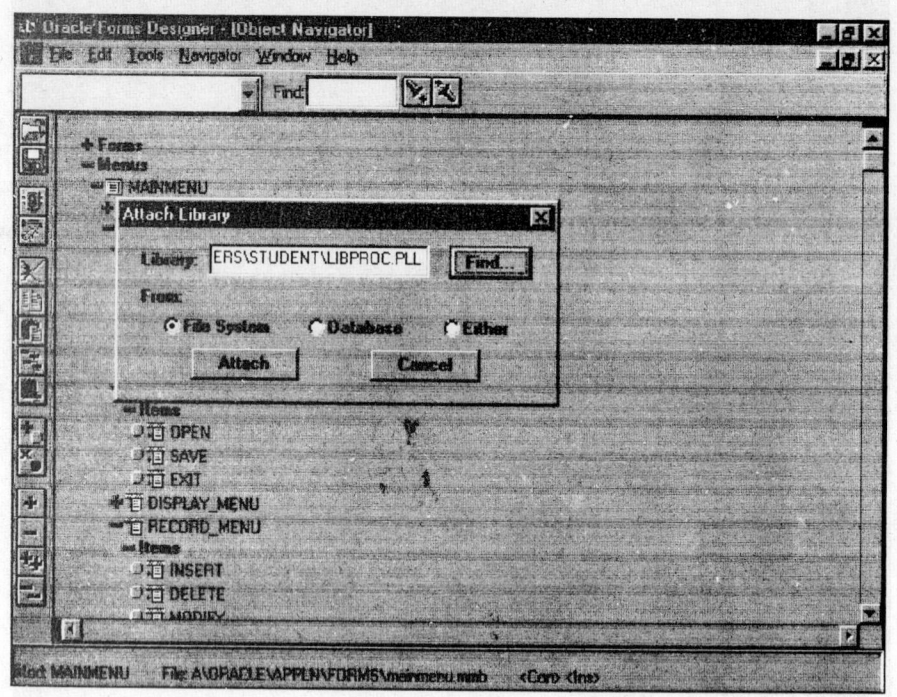

Diagram 14.11 : Attaching a library to a menu module

The Procedures used in the library are defined below :

Procedure Name : **ITEM_ENABLE_DISABLE**
Function : To enable the fields so that the contents of the field can be modified or new values can be entered. To disable fields so that the contents of the field cannot be modified.

e.g. The primary key field product_no should be enabled in insert mode and disabled in the modify mode.

```
PROCEDURE ITEM_ENABLE_DISABLE( blk_name IN char, item_on_off
IN NUMBER)  IS
        nxt_itemname varchar2(70);
        to_nxt_item varchar2(30);
        count number;
BEGIN
    /* get_block_property is a function that gets the value of specified block property. The
    First_Item property holds the name of the first enterable item in the block. */
    nxt_itemname := blk_name||'.'|| get_block_property(blk_name, first_item);

    /* set a loop that gets the next navigation item and sets the updateable property to
    true or false. Next Navigation Item holds the name of the next navigational item in
    the block */
    loop
      if get_item_property(blk_name|| '.' || nxtitemname, canvas) is not null then
          set_item_property(nxt_itemname, updateable, item_on_off);
          nxt_itemname := blk_name||'.'||get_item_property(nxt_itemname,next_navigation_item);
          /* if the Next Navigation Item is the first item, exit the loop. */
      end if;
      if (blk_name||'.'|| get_block_property(blk_name,first_item)) = nxt_itemname then
            exit;
      end if;
    end loop;
END;
```

> **Note :**
> This procedure is included in the library. Thus we need not create the procedure as specified above. We can attach the library as explained in the section ATTACHING LIBRARY TO A MODULE in the LIBRARIES chapter.

OBJECTS AND SCRIPTS :

1. Object   : File
   Menu Item   : Open
   Script   : open_form('h:\users\student\sales.fmx');

2. Object   : File
   Menu Item   : Exit
   Script   : exit_form;

3. Object   : Display
   Menu Item   : View
   Script   : DECLARE
   ```
   blk_name varchar(60);
   form_name varchar(60);
   item_name varchar(60);
   BEGIN
       execute_query ;
       form_name := get_application_property(current_form_name);
       blk_name := get_form_property(form_name, first_block);
       item_enable_disable(blk_name, property_off);
   END;
   ```

4. Object   : Display
   Menu Item   : Search
   Script   : DECLARE
   ```
   blk_name varchar(60);
   form_name varchar(60);
   item_name varchar(60);
   BEGIN
       enter_query;
       form_name := get_application_property(current_form_name);
       blk_name := get_form_property(form_name, first_block);
       item_enable_disable(blk_name, property_off);
   END;
   ```

5. Object   : Record
   Menu Item : Insert
   Script   : DECLARE
                    blk_name varchar(60);
                    form_name varchar(60);
                    item_name varchar(60);
                BEGIN
                    create_record ;
                    form_name := get_application_property(current_form_name);
                    blk_name := get_form_property(form_name, first_block);
                    item_enable_disable(blk_name, property_on);
                END;

6. Object   : Record
   Menu Item : Modify
   Script   : DECLARE
                    blk_name varchar(60);
                    form_name varchar(60);
                    item_name varchar(60);
                BEGIN
                    form_name := get_application_property(current_form_name);
                    blk_name := get_form_property(current_form_name, first_block);
                    item_enable_disable(blk_name, property_on);
                    item_name := get_block_property(blk_name, first_item);
                    set_item_property(item_name, updateable, property_off);
                END;

Note:
Menu Item Modify calls a procedure named ITEM_ENABLE_DISABLE. This procedure is explained in the section PROCEDURE.

It is assumed that the data block is the first block and the primary key is the first item in the block. Alternately the user can check for every block whether the base table is null or not to determine the blocks is a data block.

To check for the primary key the user will have to set the primary key property true and in the trigger the user will have to loop through all the items and check for the item where the primary key is true.

7. Object   : Record
   Menu Item : Delete
   Script   : delete_record ;

8. Object   : Record
   Menu Item : Save
   Script   : DECLARE
                     blk_name varchar(60);
                     form_name varchar(60);
                     item_name varchar(60);
                 BEGIN
                     if name_in('system.form_status') = 'CHANGED' then
                         commit_form ;
                         if name_in('system.form_status') = 'QUERY' then
                             form_name := get_application_property
                                     (current_form_name);
                             blk_name := get_form_property(form_name, first_block);
                             item_enable_disable(blk_name, property_off);
                         end if;
                     end if;
                 END;

9. Object   : Scroll
   Menu Item : First
   Script   : first_record ;

10. Object   : Scroll
    Menu Item : Prior
    Script   : previous_record ;

11. Object   : Scroll
    Menu Item : Next
    Script   : next_record ;

12. Object   : Scroll
    Menu Item : Last
    Script   : last_record ;

CHECKED, ENABLED AND DISPLAYED PROPERTY OF MENU ITEMS

The displayed, enabled and checked property specifies the state of the menu item. The three properties are explained below.

Checked Property :
Specifies the state of a check-box or radio-style menu item, either CHECKED or UNCHECKED. This property is set programmatically only for the menu items with the **Menu Item Type** property set to **Check** or **Radio**.

Enabled Property :
Specifies whether the menu item should be displayed as an enabled (normal) item or disabled (grayed) item. This property is set programmatically. One cannot programmatically enable or disable a menu item that is hidden as a result of the following conditions:

- The menu module **Use Security** property is TRUE.
- The menu item **Display w/o Privilege** property is set to FALSE.
- The current operator is not a member of a role that has access to the menu item.

Displayed Property :
Determines whether the menu item is visible or hidden at runtime. This property is set programmatically.

Getting the Value of the Menu Property :
The state of the menu item for the above three property can be obtained using the following functions:-

get_menu_item_property(menuitem_id, property)
get_menu_item_property(menu_name.menuitem_name, property)

The above function returns the state of the menu item given the specific property. The return value is either TRUE or FALSE depending on the state of property(i.e. if above function is used to check the enabled property of menu item, then it returns TRUE if the menu item is enabled and FALSE if it is disabled.)

The Parameters which are passed are explained below:

MENUITEM_ID
Specifies the unique ID Oracle Forms assigns when it creates the menu item. Use the FIND_MENU_ITEM built-in to return the ID to an appropriately typed variable. The datatype of the ID is MenuItem. menu_name. menuitem_name Specify the CHAR name you gave to the menu item when you defined it. If you specify the menu item by name, include the qualifying menu name, for example, menu_name.menuitem_name.

PROPERTY
Specify one of the following constants to retrieve the required property information about the menu item:

1. Checked   : To checked the state of check-box or radio-box menu item.

2. Enabled   : To check the enabled/disabled status of the menu item

3. Displayed : To check whether a menu item is visible/invisible

Setting the Properties of the menu item :
To set the above three property of a menu item use the following function

set_menu_item_property(menuitem_id, property, value);
set_menu_item_property(menu_name.menuitem_name, property, value);

The above function modifies the required property to TRUE or FALSE

The Parameters which are passed are explained below:

MENUITEM_ID:
Same as explained in for the function GET_MENU_ITEM_PROPERTY.

PROPERTY
Specify one of the following property which is to be set for the menu item.

1. Checked   : To set the menu item to checked/unchecked state.

2. Enabled   : To enable/disable the menu item.

3. Displayed : To make the menu item visible/invisible.

VALUE
Specify one of the following constants:

- PROPERTY_TRUE Specifies that the property is to be set to the TRUE state.
- PROPERTY_FALSE Specifies that the property is to be set to the FALSE state.

Focus :

Create a menu where the scroll menu items like first, next, last and prior will be enabled or disabled according to current record position(i.e. if the current record is the first record then first and prior menu items will be disabled. If the current record is the last record then the last and prior menu items will be disabled. If the current record is the only record then all the scroll menu items will be disabled. The menu item first will be checked if the current record is the first record and the menu item last will be checked if the current record is the last record.

The Scroll_control procedure is called in the WHEN-NEW-RECORD-INSTANCE of the product_master_blk form. WHEN-NEW-RECORD-INSTANCE will fire whenever there is a change in the row focus.

Similarly create a procedure named menu_scroll as follows and call the same in the WHEN-NEW-RECORD-INSTANCE trigger :

Solution :

1. Make the **Menu Item Type** property for first and last menu items equal to **check.**

2. Create a procedure named menu_scroll in the common library as shown below.

The Procedures is defined below :

Procedure Name : **MENU_SCROLL**

```
PROCEDURE menu_scroll IS
BEGIN
    if name_in('system.last_record')= 'TRUE' and  name_in('system.cursor_record') = '1' then
    /* Setting the enabled property for all the menu items if there is only one record. */
        set_menu_item_property('scroll_menu.next',enabled,property_false);
        set_menu_item_property('scroll_menu.last',enabled, property_false);
        set_menu_item_property('scroll_menu.first',enabled, property_false);
        set_menu_item_property('scroll_menu.prior',enabled, property_false);

    elsif name_in('system.last_record') = 'TRUE' then
        /* Setting the enabled property for the menu items  last and next to off  if focus is
           on the  last record. */
        set_menu_item_property('scroll_menu.next',enabled, property_false);
        set_menu_item_property('scroll_menu.first',enabled, property_true);
        set_menu_item_property('scroll_menu.prior',enabled, property_true);
        set_menu_item_property('scroll_menu.last',enabled, property_false);
```

```
                    /* Setting the checked property for the menu item  last  on and first to off  if
                    focus is on the last record. */
                    set_menu_item_property('scroll_menu.last',checked,property_true);
                    set_menu_item_property('scroll_menu.first',checked,property_false);

              elsif name_in('system.cursor_record') = '1' then
                    * Setting the enabled property for the menu items first and prior to off  if focus
                    is on the first record. *
                    set_menu_item_property('scroll_menu.prior',enabled, property_false);
                    set_menu_item_property('scroll_menu.next',enabled, property_true);
                    set_menu_item_property('scroll_menu.last',enabled, property_true);
                    set_menu_item_property('scroll_menu.first',enabled, property_false);

                    * Setting the checked property for the menu item  first on and last to off  if focus
                    is on the  last record. */
                    set_menu_item_property('scroll_menu.last',checked,property_false);
                    set_menu_item_property('scroll_menu.first',checked,property_true);

              ELSE
                    set_menu_item_property('scroll_menu.first',enabled, property_true);
                    set_menu_item_property('scroll_menu.prior',enabled, property_true);
                    set_menu_item_property('scroll_menu.next',enabled, property_true);
                    set_menu_item_property('scroll_menu.last',enabled, property_true);
              END IF ;
      END;
```

The menu_scroll procedure will be called in the form as shown below :

Trigger Name	: **WHEN-NEW-RECORD-INSTANCE** Form Name	: product
Block Name	: product_master_blk Item Name	:
Trigger level	: Block level	
Text	: menu_scroll ;	

Note :
The When-new-record-instance trigger will be written in all the forms where the menu is attached.

15. TOOLBARS

BASIC CONCEPTS

Toolbars are graphical objects that are added to the application and typically provide graphical shortcuts for commonly used menu commands.

Toolbars are displayed in an area directly beneath the menu bar. Each window in your application can display its own toolbar. When the window is active, the associated toolbar appears beneath the menu bar for that window.

When you create a canvas-view, you specify its type by setting the **Canvas-View Type** property. It defines how the canvas-view is displayed in the window to which it is assigned. The default type is **Content**.

Horizontal /Vertical Toolbar canvas is used to create toolbar for individual windows. Horizontal toolbars are displayed at the top of a window, just under its menu bar. Vertical toolbars are displayed along the left side of a window.

Once you create a toolbar canvas-view, you can add items and boilerplate graphics to it in the Layout Editor.

When you create a toolbar canvas, you assign it to a window by setting the **canvas-view Window** property, and then register it with that window by setting the **window's Vertical Toolbar** or **Horizontal Toolbar** property, as appropriate. You can also create more than one toolbar for the same window, and display them in response to navigation events and programmatic control, much like stacked canvas-views assigned to the same window.

Creating a Toolbar :
1. In the Object Navigator, position the cursor on the **Canvas-Views** node.

2. Choose Navigator and click on **Create** icon to insert a new canvas-view in the object hierarchy.

3. In the Properties window of the canvas-view, set the properties of the canvas-view as follows:

Canvas-view Type   :   Set to Horizontal Toolbar or Vertical Toolbar.

Window   :   Specify the window on which you want the toolbar to display.

Width/Height   :   Oracle Forms will display whatever size toolbar you create, one that completely obscures the window's content canvas-view.

For example:
A horizontal toolbar is usually as wide as the window to which it is assigned, but its height is usually just large enough to display a single row of items.

4. For the window to which you assigned the toolbar canvas-view, set the Horizontal Toolbar or Vertical Toolbar property by specifying the name of the toolbar canvas-view you created in step 2.

5. Add items and boilerplate graphics to the toolbar canvas as you would for any other canvas.

Let's create a toolbar and see each step involved in the process in detail.

Focus :
Creating a menu for the form which will allow the user to close the current form, perform all operations that the form allows (i.e. inserting, deleting, saving and abort as well as scrolling through the records). In this exercise, we will go step-by-step to create a toolbar, as shown in diagram 15.1.

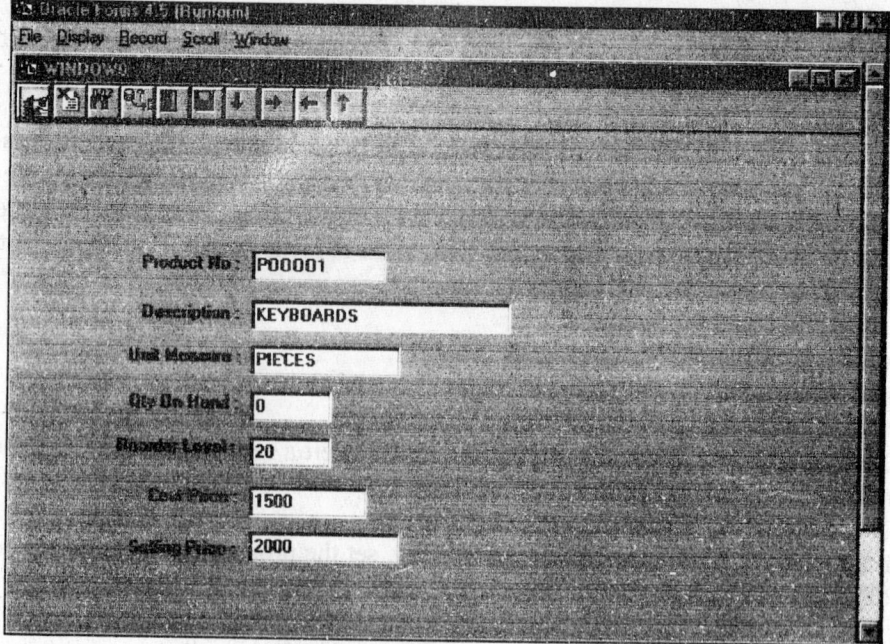

Diagram 15.1 : Product Form

1. Create a new Canvas and set the following properties as shown in the diagram 15.2.

Name	:	Toolbar_Can
Canvas-view Type	:	Horizontal \ Vertical
Window	:	Window0
Width/Height	:	400/21

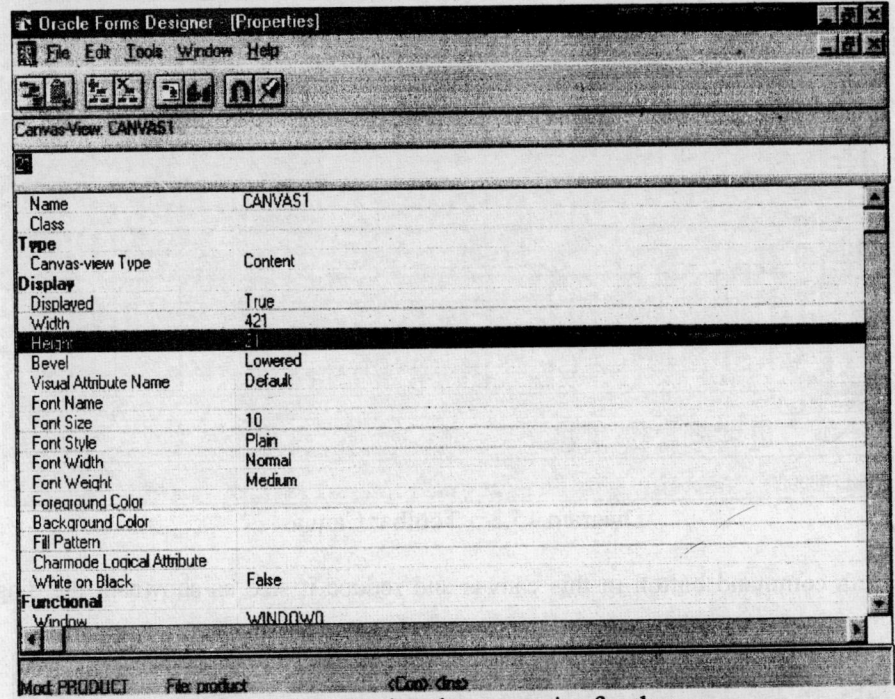

Diagram 15.2 : Setting the properties for the canvas

1. Select the toolbar canvas and click on layout editor a screen comes up as shown in diagram 15.3.

354 COMMERCIAL APPLICATION DEVELOPMENT USING ORACLE 7, DEVELOPER 2000

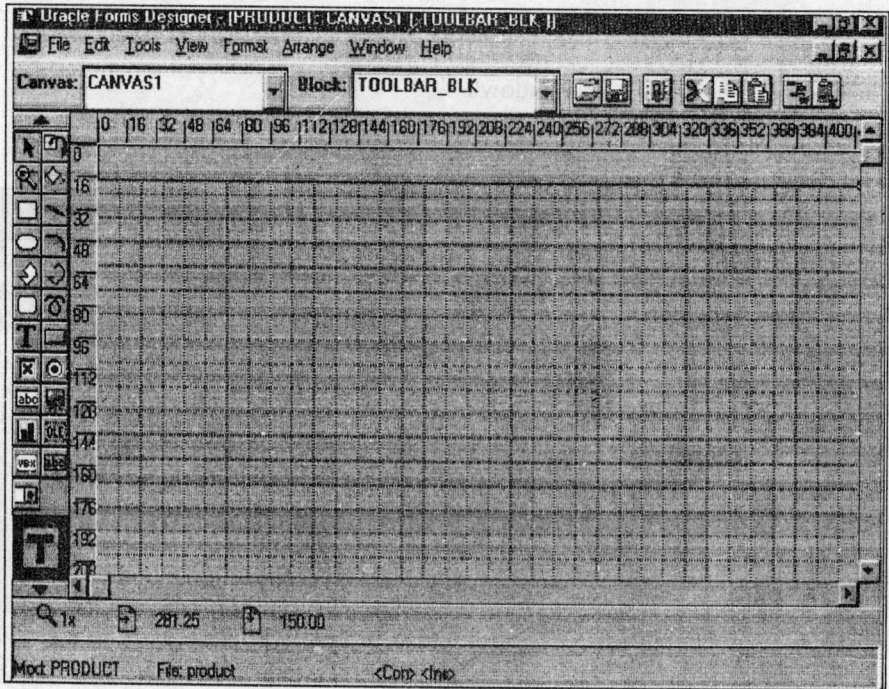

Diagram 15.3 : Toolbar Canvas

2. Place a command button in this canvas and reduce it size as shown in the diagram 15.4.

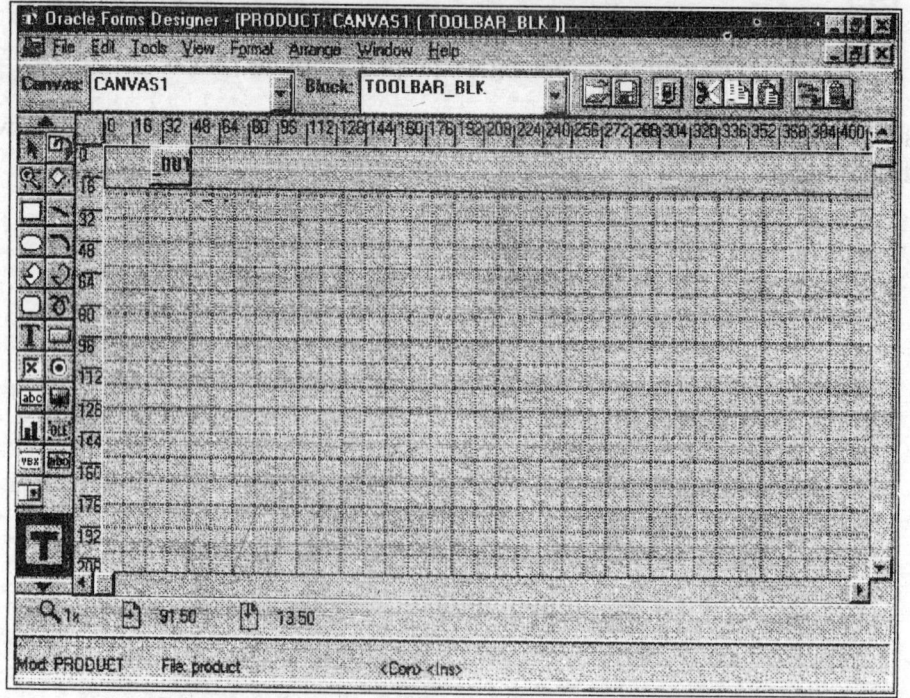

Diagram 15.4 Toolbar Canvas with a single button

TOOLBARS **355**

4. In properties window for the command button set the **Iconic** property to true and give the required icon name i.e. for *Insert* give the name as *AddRow* as shown in diagram 15.5, for *Delete* give the name as *DelRow*.

Command Button	Icon Name Property
INSERT	ADDROW
DELETE	DELROW
VIEW	QUERY
MODIFY	UPDATE
SAVE	TBSAVE
EXIT	EXIT
FIRST	UP
PRIOR	LEFT
NEXT	RIGHT
LAST	DOWN

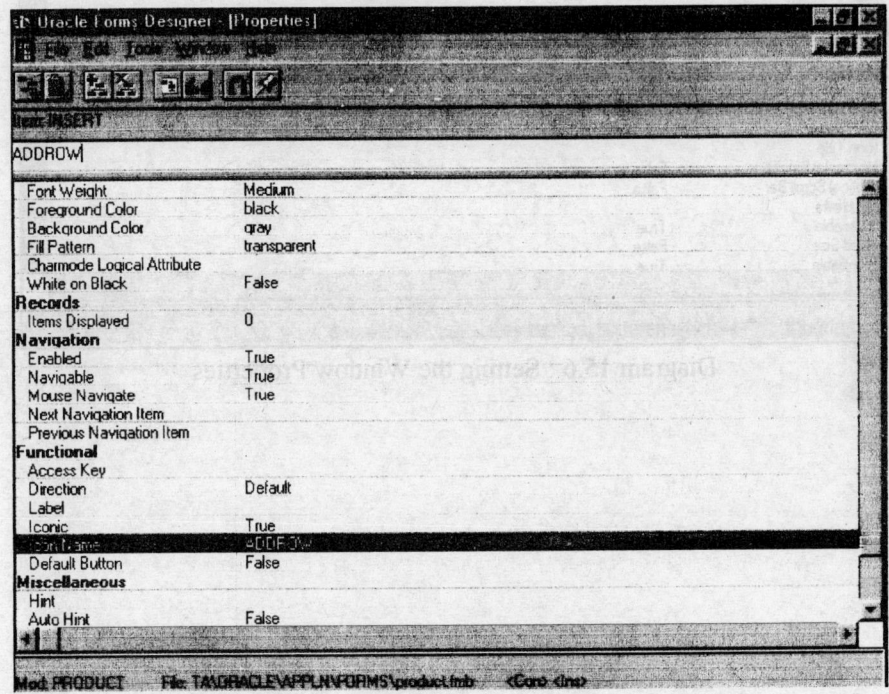

Diagram 15.5 Properties window for command button

5. Repeat the steps 3 & 4 for the remaining commands (View, Modify, Delete, First, Next, Previous, Last, Open and Exit).

356 COMMERCIAL APPLICATION DEVELOPMENT USING ORACLE 7, DEVELOPER 2000

6. Open the properties window for the window0 where the toolbar canvas will be placed and set the following properties as shown in diagram 15.6.

View   : Product_can
Horizontal Toolbar : Toolbar

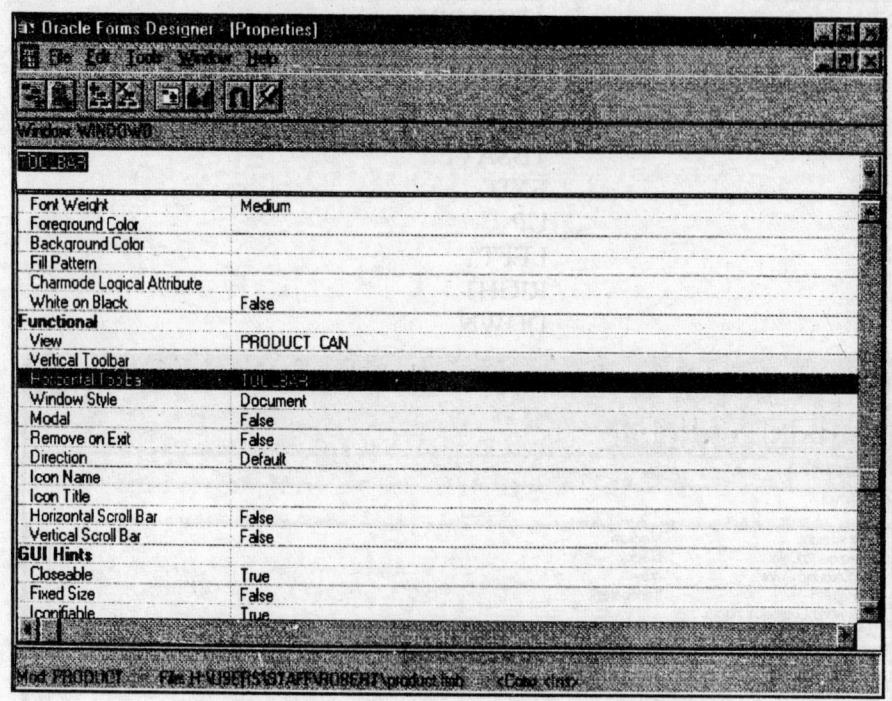

Diagram 15.6 : Setting the Window Properties

TRIGGERS AND PROCEDURES :

Trigger Name	: **WHEN-BUTTON-PRESSED**	Form	: product
Block	: toolbar_blk	Item	: tool_button_first
Trigger Level	: Field Level		
Function	: Go to the first record in the product table.		
Text	: BEGIN		
	next_block;		
	first_record ;		
	END ;		

Trigger Name	: **WHEN-BUTTON-PRESSED**	Form	: product
Block	: toolbar_blk	Item	: tool_button_prior
Trigger Level	: Field Level		
Function	: Go to the previous record in the product table.		
Text	: BEGIN		
	next_block;		
	previous_record ;		
	END ;		

Trigger Name	: **WHEN-BUTTON-PRESSED**	Form	: product
Block	: toolbar_blk	Item	: tool_button_next
Trigger Level	: Field Level		
Function	: Go to the next record in the product table.		
Text	: BEGIN		
	next_block;		
	next_record ;		
	END ;		

Trigger Name	: **WHEN-BUTTON-PRESSED**	Form	: product
Block	: toolbar_blk	Item	: tool_button_last
Trigger Level	: Field Level		
Function	: Go to the last record in the product table.		
Text	: BEGIN		
	next_block;		
	last_record ;		
	END ;		

Trigger Name	: **WHEN-BUTTON-PRESSED**	Form	: product
Block	: toolbar_blk	Item	: tool_button_add
Trigger Level	: Field Level		
Function	: Insert a record in the product table.		
Text	: DECLARE		

```
        form_name Varchar(60);
        block_name varchar(60);
    BEGIN
        next_block;
        create_record;
        form_name := get_application_property(current_form_name);
        block_name := get_form_property(form_name,first_block);
        item_enable_disable(block_name, property_off);
    END;
```

Trigger Name	: **WHEN-BUTTON-PRESSED**	Form	: product
Block	: toolbar_blk	Item	: tool_button_view
Trigger Level	: Field Level		
Function	: Retrieve all the records and Go to the first record in the product table.		
Text	: DECLARE		

```
        form_name Varchar(60);
        block_name varchar(60);
    BEGIN
        next_block;
        execute_query
        form_name := get_application_property(current_form_name);
        block_name := get_form_property(form_name,first_block);
        item_enable_disable(block_name,property_off);
    END;
```

Trigger Name	: **WHEN-BUTTON-PRESSED**	Form	: product
Block	: toolbar_blk	Item	: tool_button_modify
Function	: Set the primary key i.e. product_no not enterable and set all other fields enterable so that the record in the product table can be modified.		
Text	: DECLARE		

```
        form_name Varchar(60);
        block_name varchar(60);
        item_name varchar(60);
    BEGIN
        next_block;
        form_name := get_application_property(current_form_name);
        block_name := get_form_property(form_name,first_block);
        item_enable_disable(block_name,property_on);
        item_name := get_block_property(block_name,first_item);
        set_item_property(item_name,updateable,property_off);
    END;
```

Trigger Name	: **WHEN-BUTTON-PRESSED**	Form	: product
Block	: toolbar_blk	Item	: tool_button_delete
Function	: Delete the current record in the product table.		
Text	: DECLARE		

```
        form_name Varchar(60);
        block_name varchar(60);
    BEGIN
        next_block;
        form_name := get_application_property(current_form_name);
        block_name := get_form_property(form name,first_block);
        chk_button:=show_alert('alert1');
        if chk_button=alert_button1 then
        item_enable_disable(block_name,property_on);
        delete_record;
        item_enable_disable(block_name,property_off);
        end if;
    END;
```

Trigger Name : **WHEN-BUTTON-PRESSED**   Form : product
Block : toolbar_blk   Item : tool_button_save
Function : Save the changes to product table.
Text : DECLARE
    form_name Varchar(60);
    block_name varchar(60);
BEGIN
    form_name := get_application_property(current_form_name);
    block_name := get_form_property(form_name,first_block);
    if :system.form_status = 'CHANGED' then
        commit_form ;
        if :system.form_status = 'QUERY' then
            item_enable_disable(block_name,property_off);
        end if ;
    end if;
END ;

Trigger Name : **WHEN-BUTTON-PRESSED**   Form : product
Block : toolbar_blk   Item : tool_button_exit
Function : Exit product form.
Text : BEGIN
    exit_form;
END ;

16. WORKING WITH REPORTS

After validated data is stored in Oracle tables, it is necessary to extract this data and display it on VDU or printer. Business managers then can make business decisions based on how they interpret the displayed data.

The process of data extraction and its display is called Report creation. For this purpose Oracle provides you a GUI based report writer tool called Oracle Reports 2.5. Oracle Reports is a tool for developing, displaying, and printing production-quality reports.

FEATURES
Oracle Reports enables you to create a wide variety of reports, such as master/detail reports, nested matrix reports, form letters, and mailing labels. The major features include

- Data model and layout editors in which you can create the structure and format of your report
- Object navigator to help you navigate among the data and layout objects in your report
- Packaged functions for creating computations
- Support for fonts, colors, and graphics
- Conditional printing capabilities
- Fully-integrated Previewer for viewing your report output
- **Non-procedural Approach** The unique non-procedural approach of Oracle Reports lets you concentrate on design improvements instead of programming. It's easy-to-use, fill-in-the-form interface and powerful defaults make developing and maintaining even the most complex reports fast and simple.
- **Portability with GUI Conformance Oracle** Reports adheres to the native look-and-feel of your host environment. You can create reports on bit-mapped platforms and run them on character-mode, bit-mapped, and block-mode platforms with the guarantee of identical functionality and complete compatibility across all systems.
- **Full Integration with Other Oracle Products You** can integrate Oracle Reports with other Oracle products such as Oracle Forms, Oracle Graphics and Oracle Mail. For example, you can include graphics and charts in a report, and send output to other users via Oracle Mail.
- **Open Architecture Oracle** Report's open architecture enables you to incorporate user-defined routines written in COBOL, C and most other programming languages, as well as the powerful PL/SQL language. You can always present information exactly the way you want.

BASIC CONCEPTS

In the following few pages, the tool in general and its basic components are explained. There are three steps to building a report with Oracle reports

- Create a new report definition.
- Define the data model (choose the data, data relationships and calculation you will use to produce the report output).
- Specify a layout (i.e. design). You can use default, or customize it if desired.

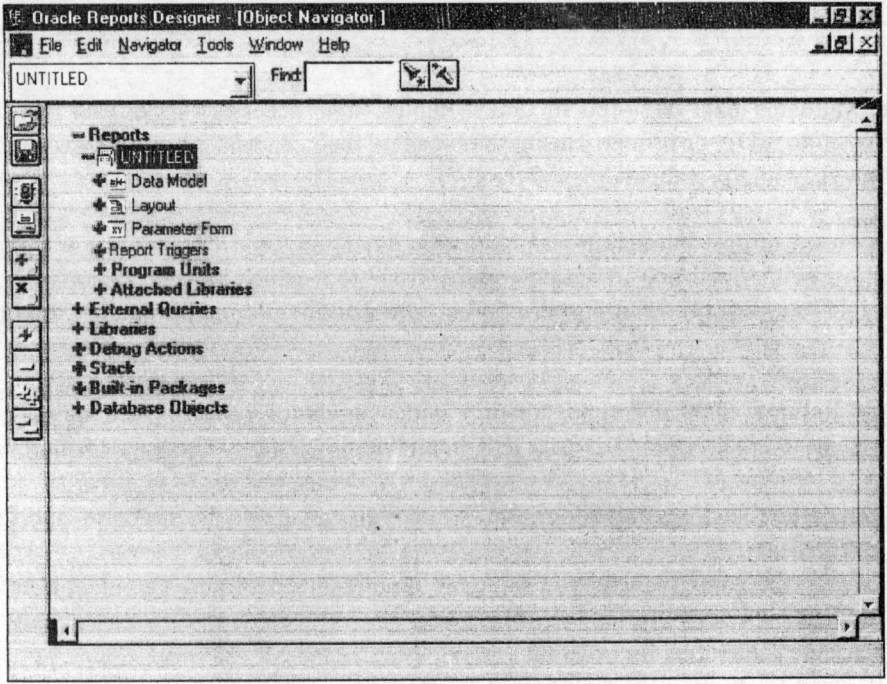

Diagram 16.1 : List of Report Objects.

Using the Object Navigator you can navigate through all objects contained within all currently open reports. It enables you to navigate to the following Oracle Report windows.

- The *Data Model editor*, in which you define the data for the report (i.e. defining Query, groups, computation fields etc. for the report).
- The *Layout editor*, in which you create the report layout (i.e. designing the looks of the reports).
- The *Parameter Form Editor*, is used to customize the appearance of the Runtime Parameter Form (a window that optionally appears at runtime and enables you to enter parameter values that affect report execution).

DEFINING A DATA MODEL FOR A REPORT

To specify the data for the report, a data model should be defined. A data model is composed of some or all of the following data definition objects

- Queries
- Groups
- Columns
- Parameters
- Links

A sample data model in the data model editor is as shown in diagram 16.2.

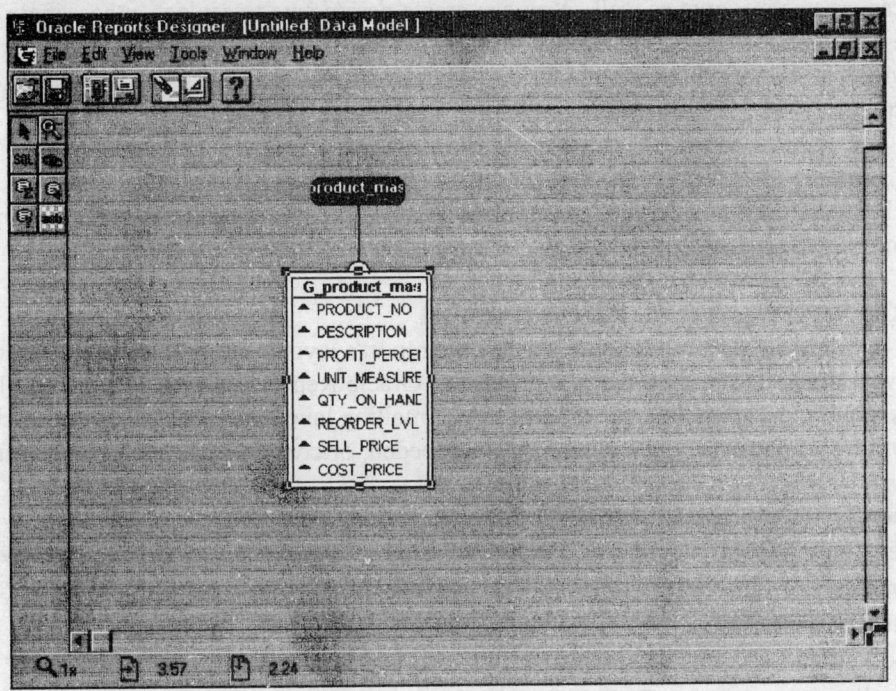

Diagram 16.2 : Sample Data Model

Queries :
Queries are ANSI-standard SQL SELECT statements that fetch data from a standard database such as Oracle, DB2 etc. These SELECT statements are fired each time the report is run. You can select any number of queries to select data from any number of tables.

Groups :
Groups determine the hierarchy of data appearing in the report, and are primarily used to create breaks in the report. Oracle report automatically creates a group for each query, but you are not limited to this default. You can create a new group in the data model and include a column that you want to use as the break column.

Columns :
Columns contain the data values for a report. Default report columns, corresponding to the table columns included in each query's SELECT list are automatically created by Oracle Reports, then each column is placed in the group associated with the query that selected the column. If you want to perform summaries and computations on database column values, you can create new columns. You can also reassign one or more columns to a group or groups you've created.

Parameters :
Parameters are variables for your report that enable you to change selection criteria at runtime. Oracle Reports automatically creates a set of system parameters at runtime, but you can create your own as well. You can create parameters to replace either single literal values or entire expressions in any part of a query. You can reference parameters elsewhere in the report, such as in PL/SQL constructs providing conditional logic for the report.

Data Links :
Data links are used to establish parent-child relationships between queries and groups via column matching.

SPECIFY THE LAYOUT FOR A REPORT
After defining the data model, you specify the report's layout; i.e., you position objects, as you want them to appear in the report output. Oracle Reports provides six default layout styles tabular, master/detail, form letter, form, mailing label, and matrix. You can choose one of these default layouts and modify it as needed, or create your own report layout.

A report layout can contain any of the following layout objects
- repeating frames
- frames
- fields
- boilerplate
- anchors

In the diagram 16.3, a sample layout, in the Layout Editor is shown.

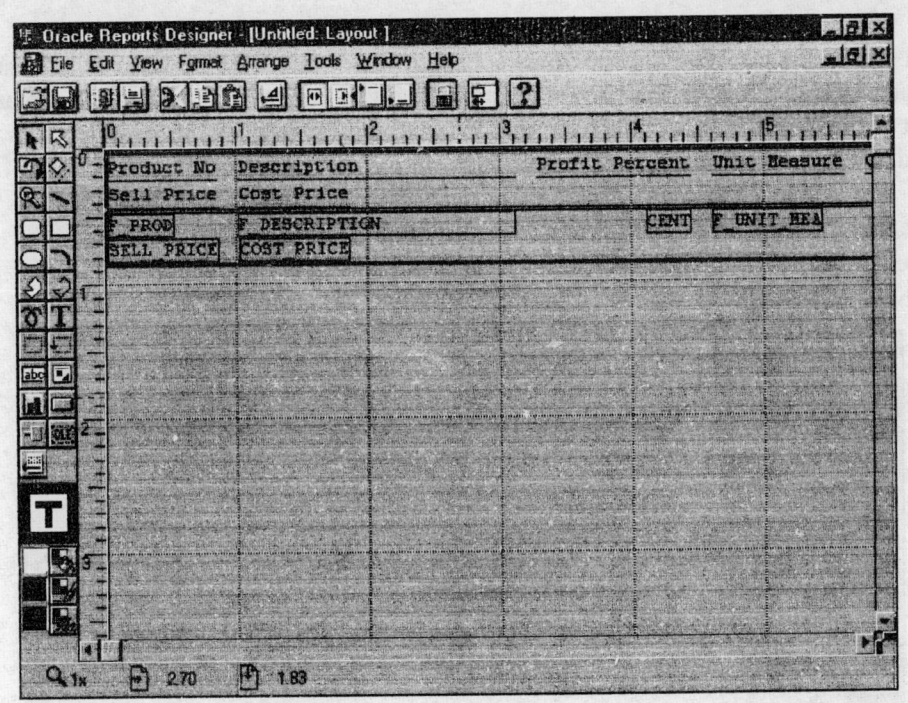

Diagram 16.3 : Sample Layout

Repeating Frames :
Repeating frames act as placeholders for groups (i.e. repeating values) and present rows of data retrieved from the database. Repeating frames repeat as often as the data is retrieved.

Frames :
Frames surround other layout objects, enabling you to control multiple objects simultaneously; e.g., ensuring that they maintain their positions relative to each other in the output.

Fields :
Fields act as placeholders for columns. They define the formatting attributes for all columns displayed in the report. A field is one of the objects that can be located inside a frame or repeating frame.

Boilerplate :
Boilerplate consists of text and graphics that appear in a report each time it is run; e.g., a label appearing above a column of data is boilerplate text. Graphics drawn in the layout as well as text added to the layout are boilerplate

Anchors :
Anchors fasten an edge of one object to an edge of another object, ensuring that they maintain their relative positions. For example, you can anchor boilerplate text to the edge of a variable-sized repeating frame, guaranteeing the boilerplate's distance and position in relation to the repeating frame, no matter how the frame's size might change.

SPECIFY A RUNTIME PARAMETER FORM FOR A REPORT

When you are almost ready to run your report, you can optionally customize the Runtime Parameter Form using the Parameter Form editor. The Parameter Form editor contains a subset of the Layout editor's functionality, and determines the positions of objects, as they should appear in the Runtime Parameter Form.

A Runtime Parameter Form can contain any of the following objects
- fields
- boilerplates

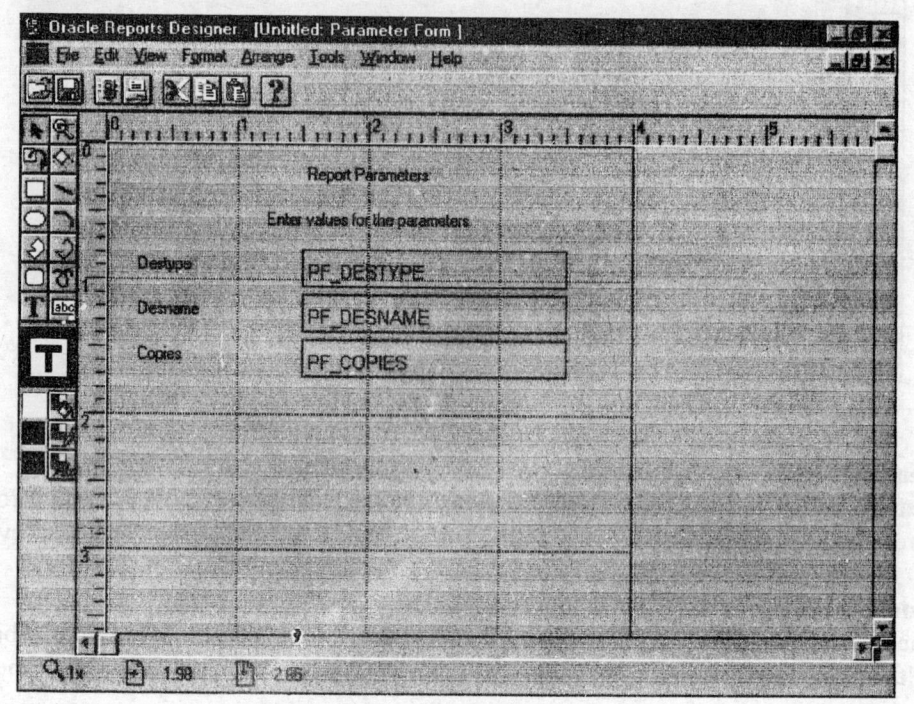

Diagram 16.4 : Parameters Form Editor

In diagram 16.4, a sample layout in the parameter form editor is shown.

Fields :
Fields in the parameter form editor act as placeholders for parameters. They define the formatting attributes for all parameters displayed in the Runtime Parameter Form.

Boilerplate :
Boilerplate in the Parameter Form editor refers to text and graphics that appear in the Runtime Parameter Form each time it is run; e.g., a label denoting a particular parameter is boilerplate text. Lines or boxes drawn in the layout are also considered boilerplate, as well as any added text.

USE THE ORACLE REPORTS INTERFACE

Use the following interface components to define report objects
- Property Sheets
- Object Navigator
- Editors
- Tool palettes and Toolbars

Property Sheets :
A property sheet is a window that displays the settings for defining an Oracle Reports object. Each object (query, group, frame, field, parameter, etc.) has a property sheet.

An example of the property sheet of a computed field is as shown in the diagram 16.5.

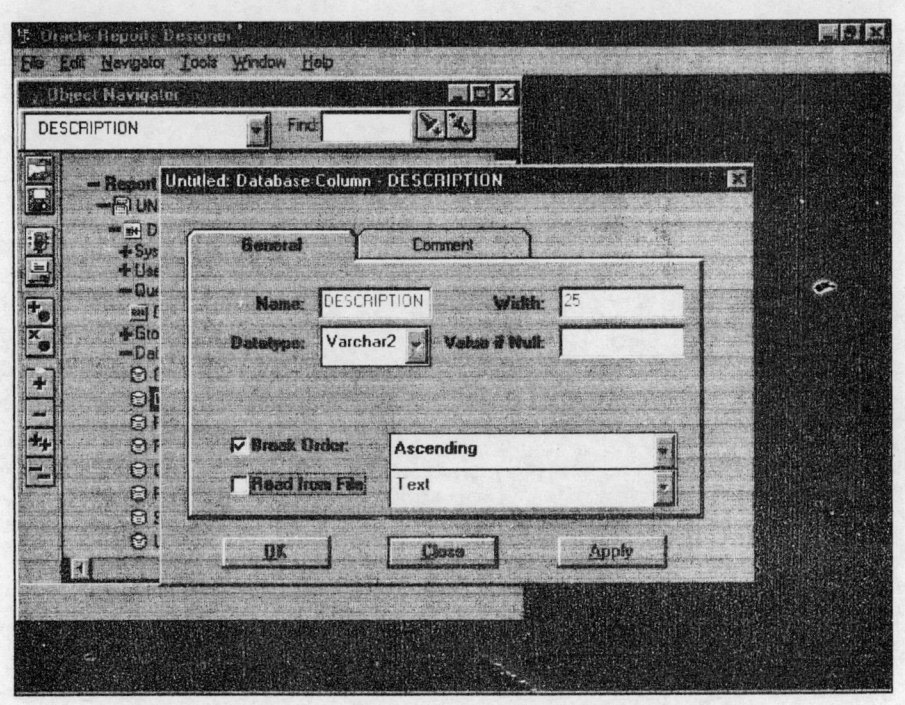

Diagram 16.5 : Property Sheet of a Database Column

Object Navigator :
The Object Navigator, as previously mentioned, shows a hierarchical view of objects in your report. Use it to gain an overview of a report's organization. Each item listed is called a node, and represents an object or type of object your report can contain or reference.

Editors :
An editor is a work area that contains graphical representations of related objects. You use the Data Model editor to manipulate (create, delete, move, resize, copy, paste, etc.), data model objects, the Layout editor to manipulate layout objects, and the Parameter Form editor to manipulate parameter form objects.

Palettes and Toolbars :
The Tool palettes and toolbars contain tools used to manually create or manipulate objects in the editors. Each editor has a tool palette and a toolbar; each tool appears as an icon on the palette or toolbar. Some tools, such as the Select tool, are common to all the palettes. Other tools are specific to the editors in which they appear. Toolbar items also have menu equivalents.

CREATING A DEFAULT TABULAR REPORT

Creating a tabular *'Productwise Sales Report'* from sales_order, sales_order_details and *Product_master* tables. In this exercise, we will go step-by-step to create a report, as shown in diagram 16.6. You will learn to create a new report, select data for it, save the report, run and view it. It also shows the default capabilities of Oracle Report Writer.

For ease of understanding, we are using the tables described below, populated with around 50 records so that we can see how the report writer tool handles "Pages" either on the VDU or the printer.

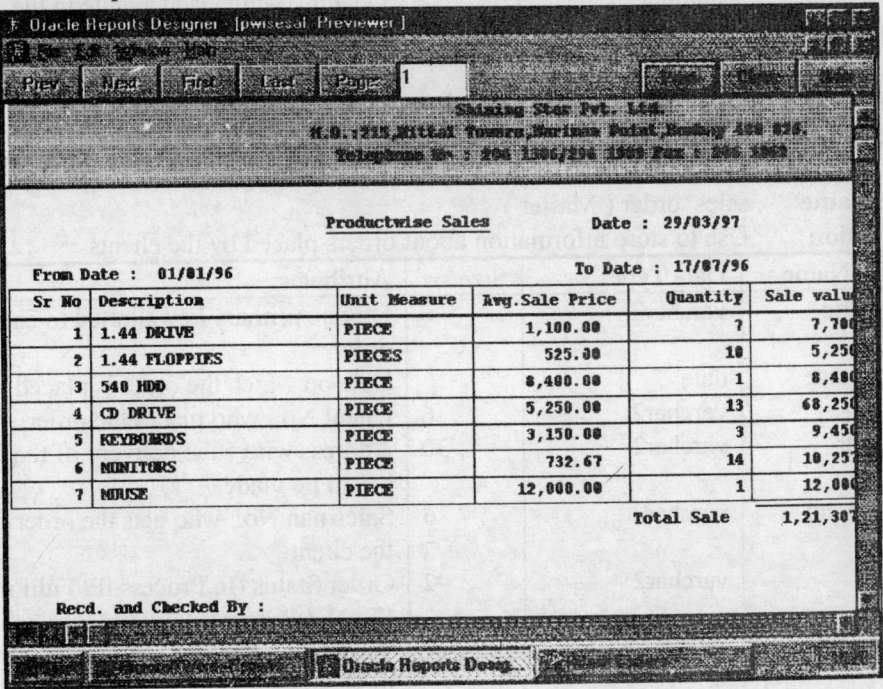

Diagram 16.6 : Productwise Sales Report

The definitions of the tables used are as mentioned below :

Table Name : product_master
Description : stores information about products supplied by the company.

Column Name	Data Type	Size	Column Description
product_no	varchar2	6	Access key via which we shall seek data.
description	varchar2	25	Description of the product
unit_measure	varchar2	10	Unit by which the product is measured.
qty_on_hand	number	8	Quantity which is available in the stock.
reorder_lvl	number	8	Quantity level when the stock should be re-ordered.
cost_price	number	8,2	Cost price of the product.
selling_price	number	8,2	Selling price of the product.

Table Name : sales_order (Master)
Description : Use to store information about orders placed by the clients.

Column Name	Data Type	Size	Attributes
s_order_no	varchar2	6	Unique primary key allotted to each order.
s_order_date	date		Date on which the order is placed.
client_no	varchar2	6	Client No., who places the order.
dely_addr	varchar2	30	Address where the delivery of the goods has to be made.
salesman_no	varchar2	6	Salesman No., who gets the order from the client.
status	varchar2	2	Order Status (In Process IP, FullFilled FP, Not Processed NP)
dely_type	char	1	To note whether the delivery is to be made in parts (P) or full (F).
dely_date	date		Date when the delivery for the goods is to be made.

Table Name : sales_order_details
Description : Use to store information about order details.

Column Name	Data Type	Size	Attributes
s_order_no	varchar2	6	Order No. for which details have to be stored.
product_no	varchar2	6	Product No. for which details have to be stored.
product_rate	number	8,2	The rate agreed upon.
qty_ordered	number	8	Quantity of goods ordered.
qty_disp	number	8	Quantity of goods dispatched.

To create the report shown in the diagram 16.6, we will follow following steps :
- Create a new report definition.
- Connect the database and define the data.
- Specify a default report layout.
- Save and run the report.
- View the report output.
- Create formulae columns, specify a default report layout.
- Create summary columns, specify a default report layout.
- Create user parameters.
- Arrange the layout and run the report.

Creating a new Report Definition :
The screen that will be displayed, as soon as the Oracle Report is invoked is as shown in diagram 16.7. The Object Navigator will display a new report definition.

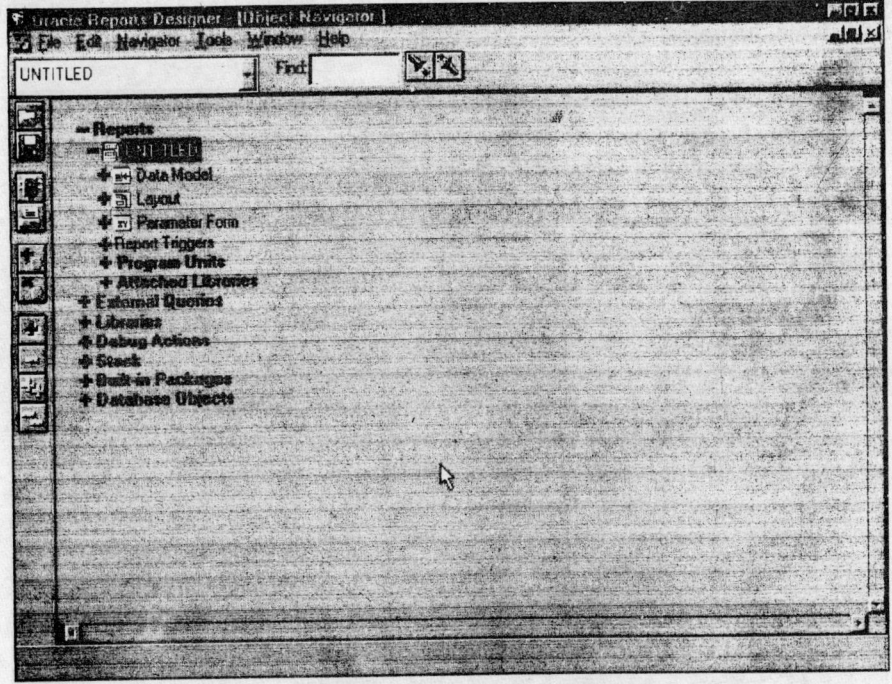

Diagram 16.7 : New Report Definition

Connecting to the Database :
1. Select **File**, **Connect** menu options. The *Connect* dialog box will appear, prompting you for your username and password.

2. Click in the *User Name* field and type your username.

3. Click in the *Password* field and type your password. Your password will not be visible when you type it.

4. Database Field is used to type in the connect string, if you are connecting to a remote database (located on another server).

5. Select the **Connect** button.

Specifying the Data for the Report :
After invoking the Report designer and connecting to the database, the next step is to specify the data for the report. The '*Data Model editor*' allow the user to specify the Query for the data retrieval. Data Model editor can be accessed by selecting the **Data Model Editor** menu item in the **Tools** menu.

In the '*Data Model editor*', you'll create one or more query objects. Query objects are data model objects that fetch data for the report from a base table. The steps are as follows :

1. Click on **Tools, Data Model Editor** menu. It will display the Data Model editor as shown in the diagram 16.8.

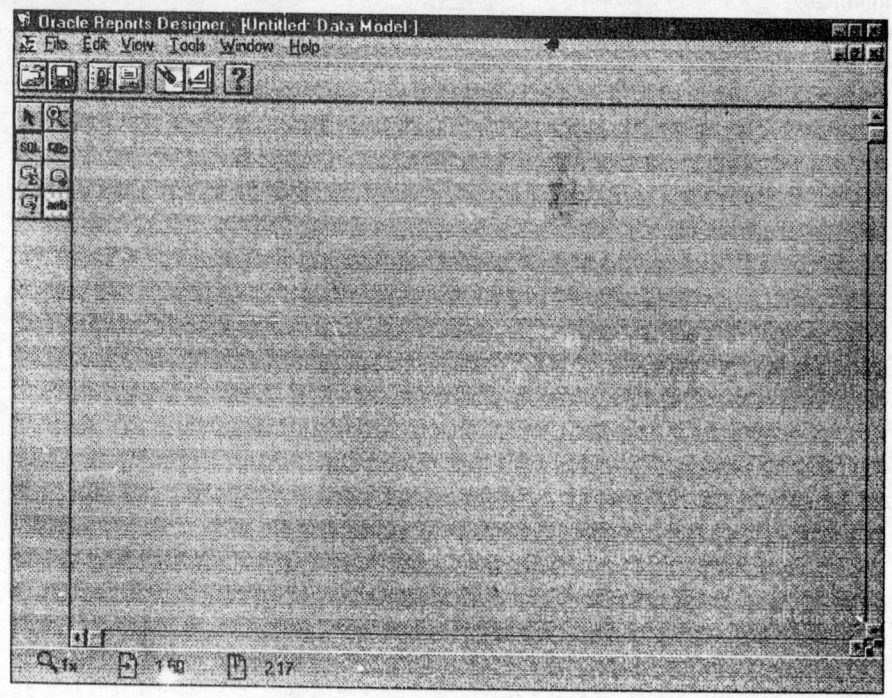

Diagram 16.8 : Data Model Editor.

2. Select the **Query** tool by clicking on it once in the Tool palette. Move the mouse pointer into the Data Model editor. Click once.

WORKING WITH REPORTS 373

A query object, represented by a rounded rectangle, will appear as shown in diagram 16.9.

> **Note :**
> If you are uncertain whether you've found the right tool, place the mouse pointer over the tool. After a moment, the name of the tool is displayed.

Diagram 16.9 : Query Object placed in the Data Model Editor

1. Double-click on the Query Object to display its property sheet (As explained before, a property sheet is a window displaying all properties of a single Oracle Reports object.), a window as shown in the diagram 16.10 will appear.

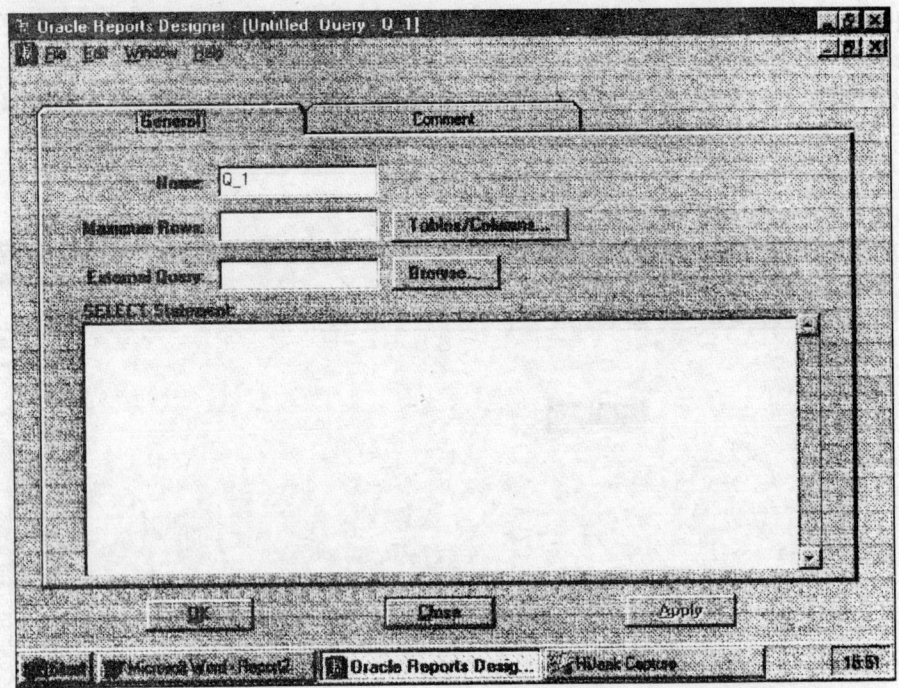

374 COMMERCIAL APPLICATION DEVELOPMENT USING ORACLE 7, DEVELOPER 2000

Diagram 16.10 : Property Sheet of the Query Object

4. Specify the **Name** of the query object as *Q_productwise_sales*. In SQL field specify the select statement :

    select   product_master.description,
          product_master.unit_measure,
          avg(sales_order_details.product_rate) "avg_product_rate",
          sum(sales_order_details.qty_ordered) "sum_quantity"
    from   sales_order, product_master,
          sales_order_details
    where (product_master.product_no = sales_order_details.product_no) and
          (sales_order_details.s_order_no = sales_order.s_order_no)
    group by product_master.description ,
          product_master. unit_measure
    order by product_master.description asc

    This select will actually get the data of the report from a base table.

    One can build a "Select" using the *Table and Column Name* dialog box, as explained in the steps 6, 7, and 8 below.

5. Click on **Tables/Columns** button. The *Table and Column Names* dialog box will appear, listing all of the database tables to which you have access (See diagram 16.11).

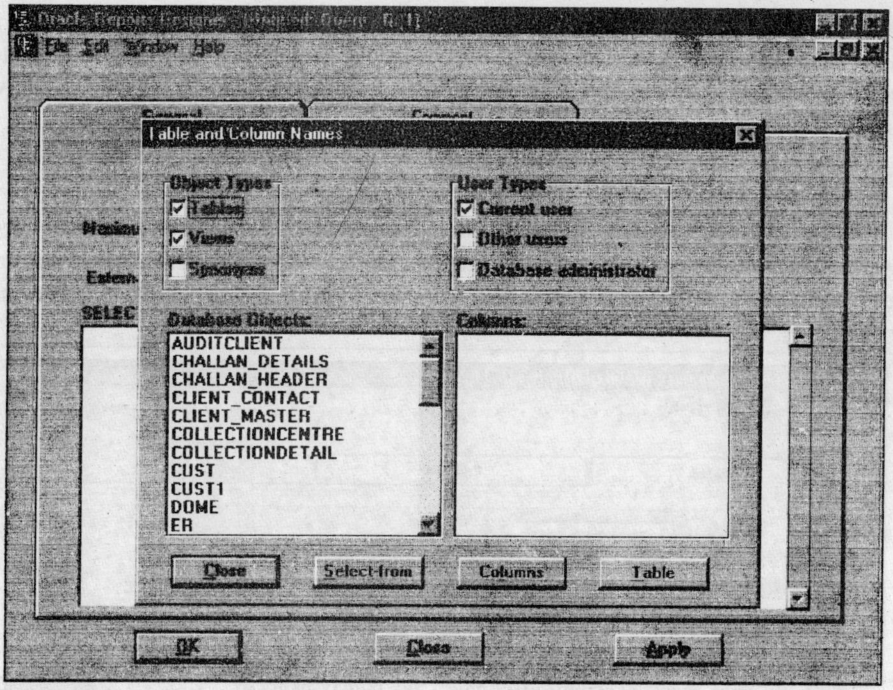
Table and Column Names
Object Types
Tables
Views
Synonyms
User Types
Current user
Other users
Database administrator
Database Objects:
AUDITCLIENT
CHALLAN_DETAILS
CHALLAN_HEADER
CLIENT_CONTACT
CLIENT_MASTER
COLLECTIONCENTRE
COLLECTIONDETAIL
CUST
CUST1
DOME
ER
Columns:
Close
Select-from
Columns
Table
OK
Close
Apply

Diagram 16.11 : Tables displayed in the Table and Column dialog box.

7. Select product_master and all its columns will appear in the columns list of values as shown in diagram 16.12.

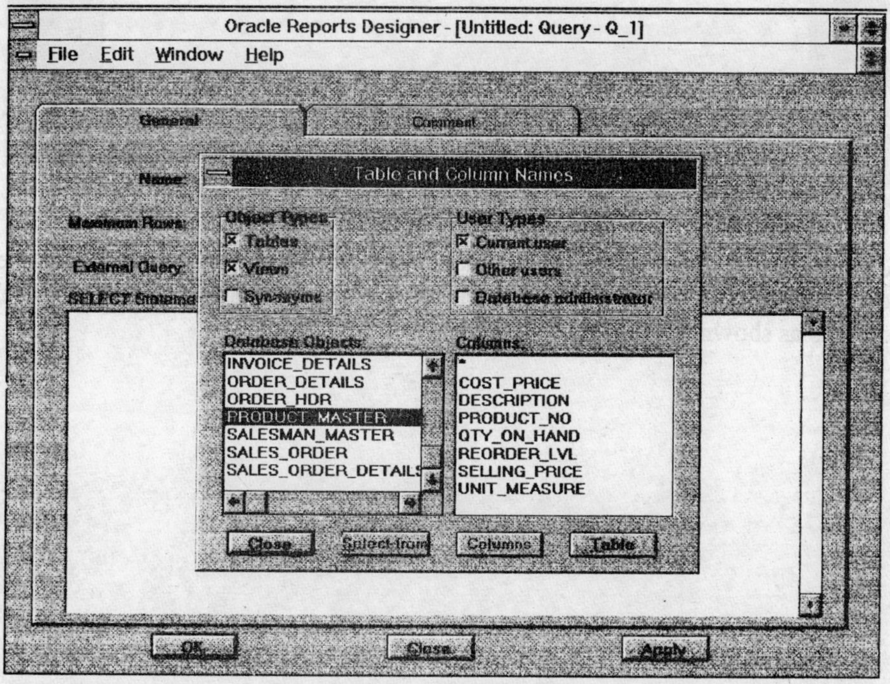
Oracle Reports Designer - [Untitled: Query - Q_1]
File
Edit
Window
Help
General
Comment
Name:
Maximum Rows:
External Query:
Table and Column Names
Object Types
Tables
Views
Synonyms
User Types
Current user
Other users
Database administrator
Database Objects:
INVOICE_DETAILS
ORDER_DETAILS
ORDER_HDR
PRODUCT_MASTER
SALESMAN_MASTER
SALES_ORDER
SALES_ORDER_DETAILS
Columns:
*
COST_PRICE
DESCRIPTION
PRODUCT_NO
QTY_ON_HAND
REORDER_LVL
SELLING_PRICE
UNIT_MEASURE
Close
Select from
Columns
Table
OK
Close
Apply

Diagram 16.12 : Creating Query using Tables and Columns Option

376 COMMERCIAL APPLICATION DEVELOPMENT USING ORACLE 7, DEVELOPER 2000

8. Select columns and tables by clicking on them and build the select statement given above. Close the Table and Column Names dialog box Click on the **Close** button to close the window and return to property window with a complete query as shown in diagram 16.13.

Note:
To select multiple, non-consecutive items from a list keep the <Shift> key pressed and click on the item. Select-from button is used to build a full select statement, table and column buttons will allow to select only the table or column names respectively.

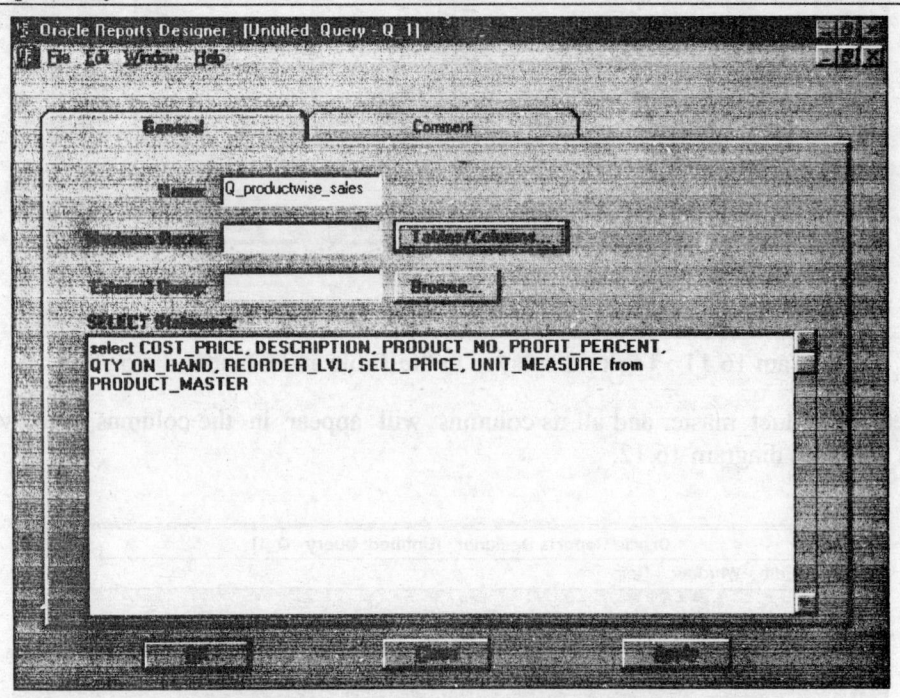

Diagram 16.13 : Completed Query Property Sheet

9. After specifying the complete query click on OK to close the Query property sheet. A default group, G_productwise_sale, will be created, containing a list of the selected columns as shown in the diagram 16.14.

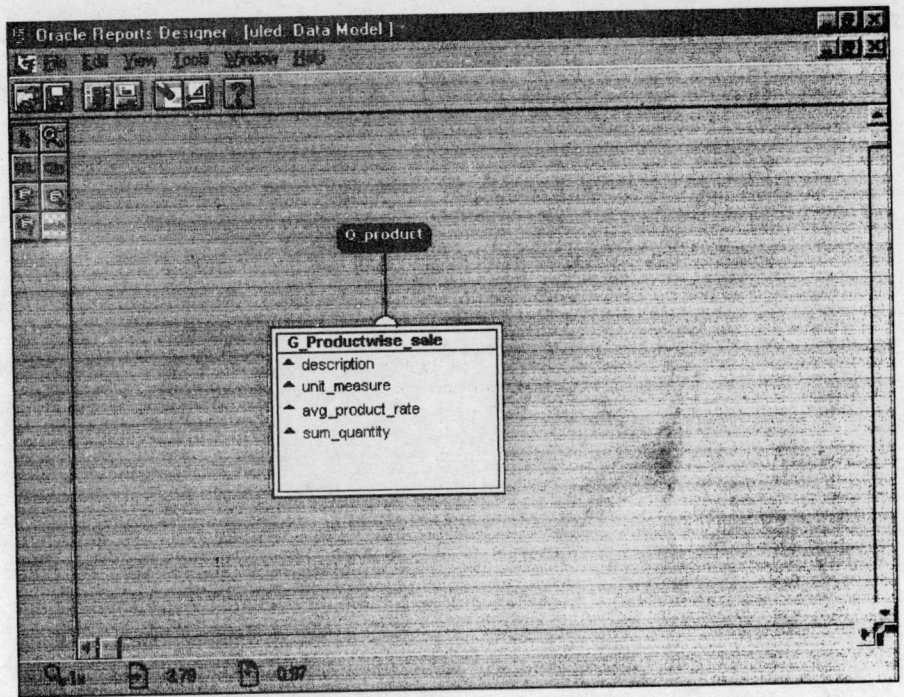

Diagram 16.14 : Data Model Editor After Creating a Query

Specify a Default Layout for the Report :
After specifying the data for the report, create its layout (i.e. the Design).

1. Select **Tools**, **Default Layout** from the menu (or the Default Layout tool). The *Default Layout* dialog box appears.

   Using this dialog box, you can specify several layout settings. Oracle Reports uses these specifications to create a complete, executable report. Specify the settings on the Style tab as shown in diagram 16.15.

   - Set the **Style** as **Tabular**. The Style of a report layout determines the initial layout style of your report.

   - Use **Current Layout Settings**, which determines if Oracle Reports should use its own defaults when creating boilerplate, or if it should use any changes you've made to the default attributes (e.g., new font, font size, type style, and so on).

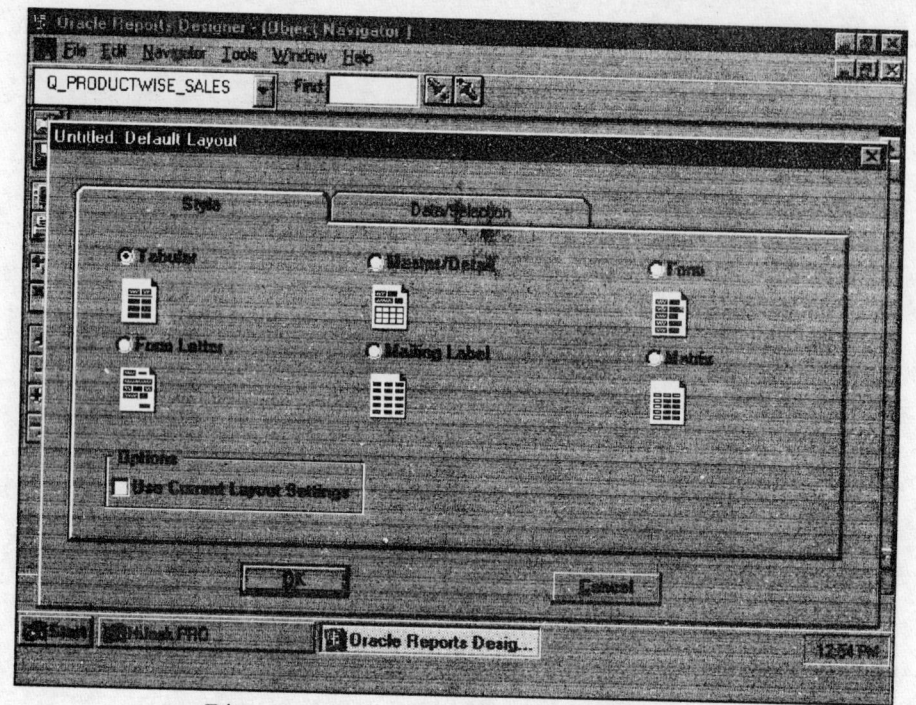

378 COMMERCIAL APPLICATION DEVELOPMENT USING ORACLE 7, DEVELOPER 2000

Diagram 16.15 : Specifying a default layout

2. Select the *Data/Selection* Tab. Change the **labels** of *avg_product_rate* and *sum_quantity* columns to *Avg. Sale Price* and *Quantity* respectively. Also change their **width** from *40* to *10* as shown in diagram 16.16.

- **Group and Repeat** determine the groups to be included in the report output and the direction in which to display their data. In the current example, repeat direction will be set as **Down**.
- Column Label, Width (W and Height (H), determine the columns to be included in the report output, their labels, and the widths and heights of the fields that will display them.

3. You can deselect a field by clicking it. Deselecting a column prevents it from appearing in the report. The column can be used to order the output, but you won't display it in the report for this lesson.

WORKING WITH REPORTS   379

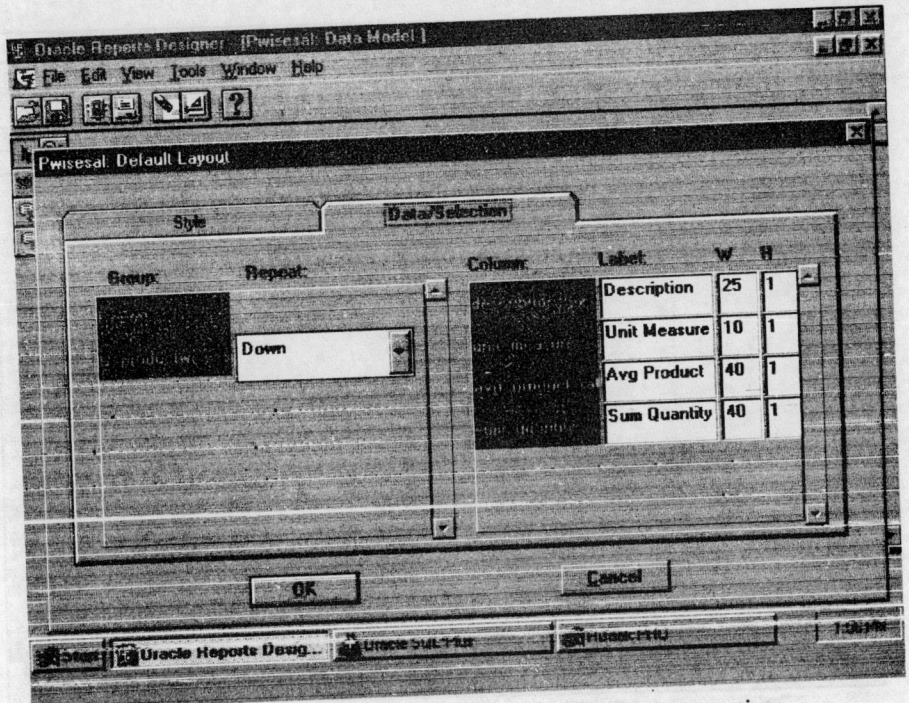

Diagram 16.16 : Specifying Data/Selection properties

4. Click on **OK** to accept the current properties. Layout editor is displayed as shown in diagram 16.17.

   Examine the objects in the Layout editor. Oracle Reports used the properties in the *Default Layout* dialog box to generate these objects, which, in turn, will determine how their associated data objects appear when you run the report.

   The layout objects are as shown in diagram 16.17 are :
   - Boilerplate (e.g., description) for labeling the data.
   - Frames (e.g., the rectangle enclosing the boilerplate labels) for grouping other layout objects.
   - Fields (e.g. *f_description*) for displaying the data.
   - Repeating frames (e.g., the horizontal rectangle enclosing all the fields), for controlling each record.

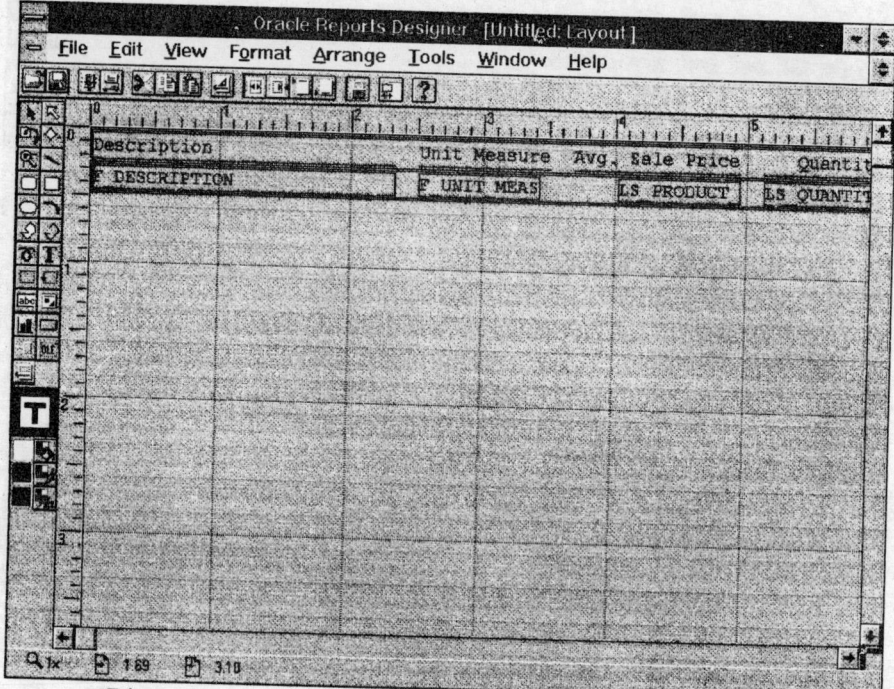

380 COMMERCIAL APPLICATION DEVELOPMENT USING ORACLE 7, DEVELOPER 2000

Diagram 16.17 : Objects displayed in the Layout editor

Each type of layout object governs a different aspect of the report's format and final appearance. For example, notice the small arrow in the upper-left corner of the repeating frame. This arrow points down, indicating that the rows will display sequentially down the page.

Now all that we need to do is to **Save**, **Run** and **View** the report.

Save and run the Report
While you work on your report, Oracle Reports preserves your changes in a memory buffer. You can save your changes to a file or to the database. During the tutorial, save to a *File* to conserve database space.

WORKING WITH REPORTS **381**

5. Select **File**, **Save** from the menu (or the Save tool). The *Save* dialog box as shown in the diagram 16.18 will appear.

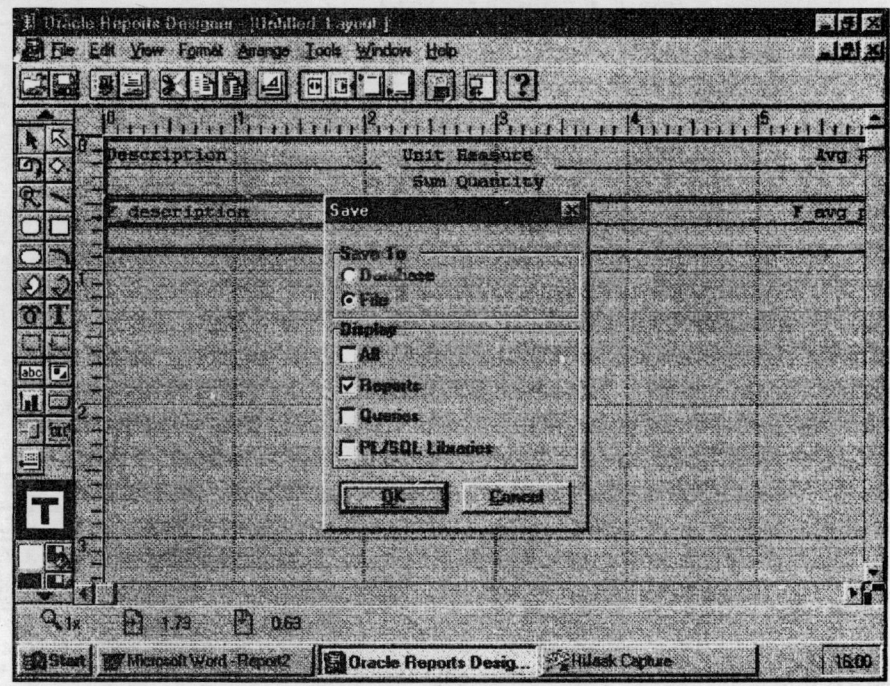

Diagram 16.18 : Saving a report

6. Select the **File** radio button and **ensure** that either **'All'** or **'Reports'** is checked.

Hint: *The Preferences dialog box (Tools, Tools Options : Preferences) provides a setting enabling you to specify that a module (e.g. your report) always be saved to either a database or a file. If you set this preference, the Save dialog box does not appear.*

7. Click on **OK**. The *Save To File* dialog box appears.

> **Note :**
> **Default filename of a report is *Untitled.rdf*. RDF stands for Report Definition File. You can both open and run .rdf files; they are binary and portable.**

4. Specify the report name as pwisesal.rdf. Specify the path for the report file and click on **OK**. The report file will be saved with the specified named.

5. Select **File, Run** (or the Run tool) to run the report. Oracle Reports displays the *Runtime Parameter Form*, as shown in diagram 16.19.

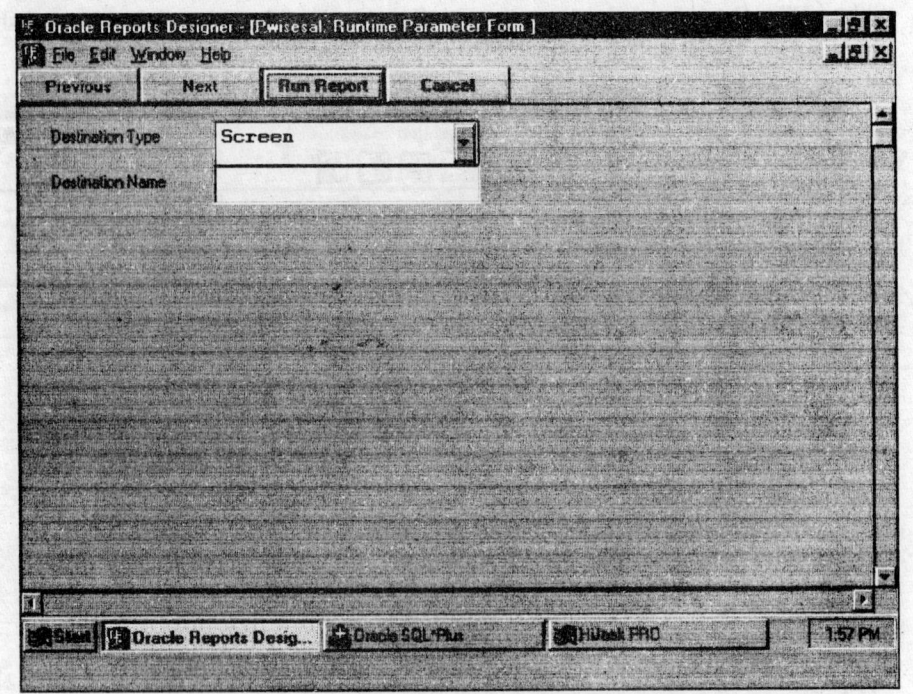

Diagram 16.19 : Runtime Parameter Screen

The *Runtime parameter form* prompts for runtime options that can be set just before the report is executed; e.g., User can specify the *report destination* as *File*, *Screen* or *Printer*, the *number of copies to print*, etc.

Oracle Reports provides several system parameters, two of which are included in the Runtime Parameter Form by default. These are :

- The **Destination Type** i.e. Screen, Printer, File or Preview.
- The **Destination Name**. Destination Name will be the name of the printer if the destination type is printer. If the destination Type is file then the destination Name will be the name of the file along with the file path.

You can include any or all of the other system parameters in the Runtime Parameter Form, or create your own.

8. Click on **Run Report** to accept the default values. The report output will be as shown in diagram 16.20.

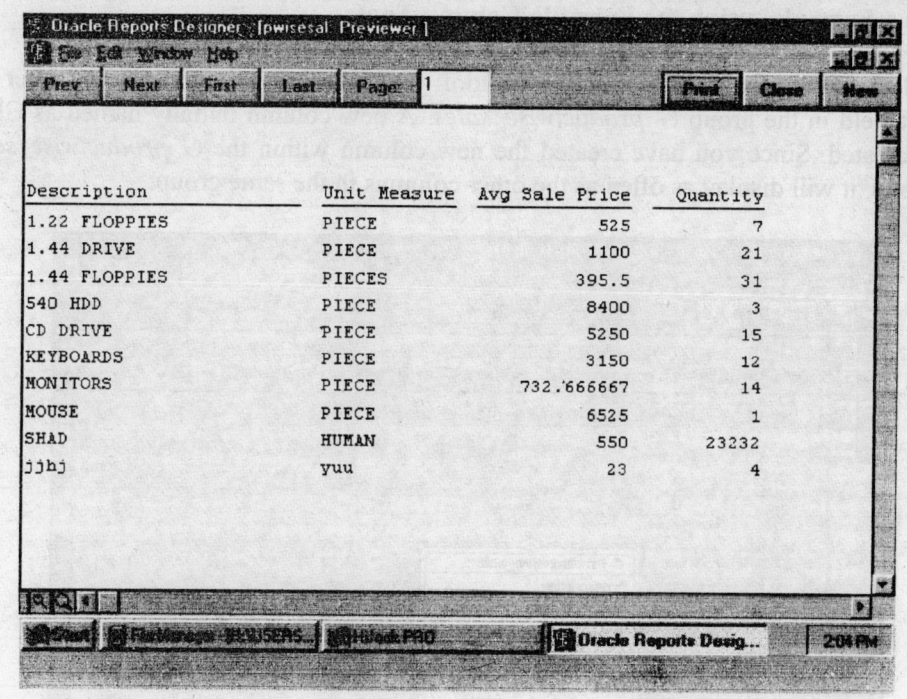

```
 Description           Unit Measure    Avg Sale Price    Quantity
 1.22 FLOPPIES         PIECE                      525           7
 1.44 DRIVE            PIECE                     1100          21
 1.44 FLOPPIES         PIECES                   395.5          31
 540 HDD               PIECE                     8400           3
 CD DRIVE              PIECE                     5250          15
 KEYBOARDS             PIECE                     3150          12
 MONITORS              PIECE                732.666667         14
 MOUSE                 PIECE                     6525           1
 SHAD                  HUMAN                      550       23232
 jjhj                  yuu                         23           4
```

Diagram 16.20 : Report Output

CREATING COMPUTED COLUMNS

Computed columns calculate values based either on PL/SQL expressions or on data provided by database columns. There are two types of computed columns that can add to a report:

Summaries columns :

Summary columns compute their values using built in functions of Oracle Reports. Summaries operate on one value over multiple records (e.g. *average* of product_rate).

Formula columns :

Formula columns compute their values using PL/SQL expressions. Formula can operate on multiple values per record (e.g. avg_price * quantity).

Create a Formula using the Formula Column Tool :

1. Select the *formula* column tool in the tool palette and place it after the last field in the group *G_productwise_sales*. A new column initially named as CF_1 is created. Since you have created the new column within the *G_productwise_sales* group, it will display as often as the other columns in the same group.

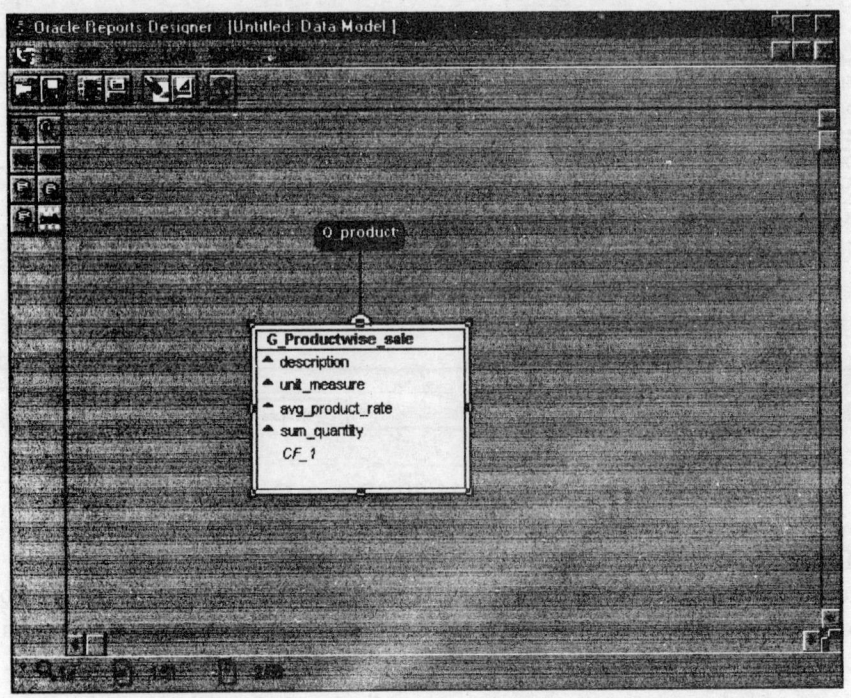

Diagram 16.21: Creating a Formula Column for Sales Value

2. Display the new column's property sheet as shown in diagram 16.22. Change the name of the column to *cf_sale_value*.

3. Ensure that the data type is number and enter the formula as explained below.

4. Click on **Formula**, **Edit**. Report Designer tool invokes the Program Unit editor.

WORKING WITH REPORTS 385

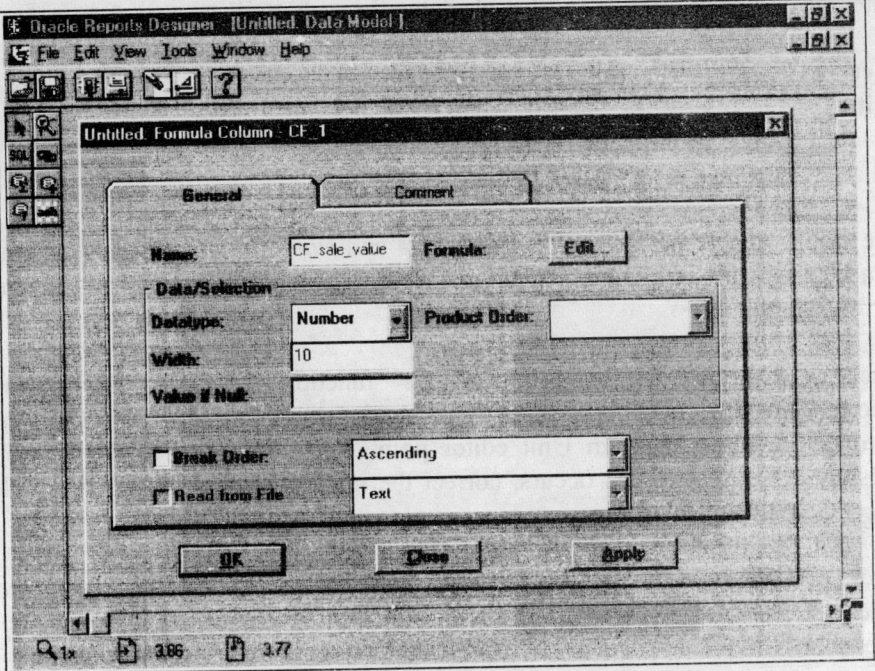

Diagram 16.22 : Property Sheet of Formula Column

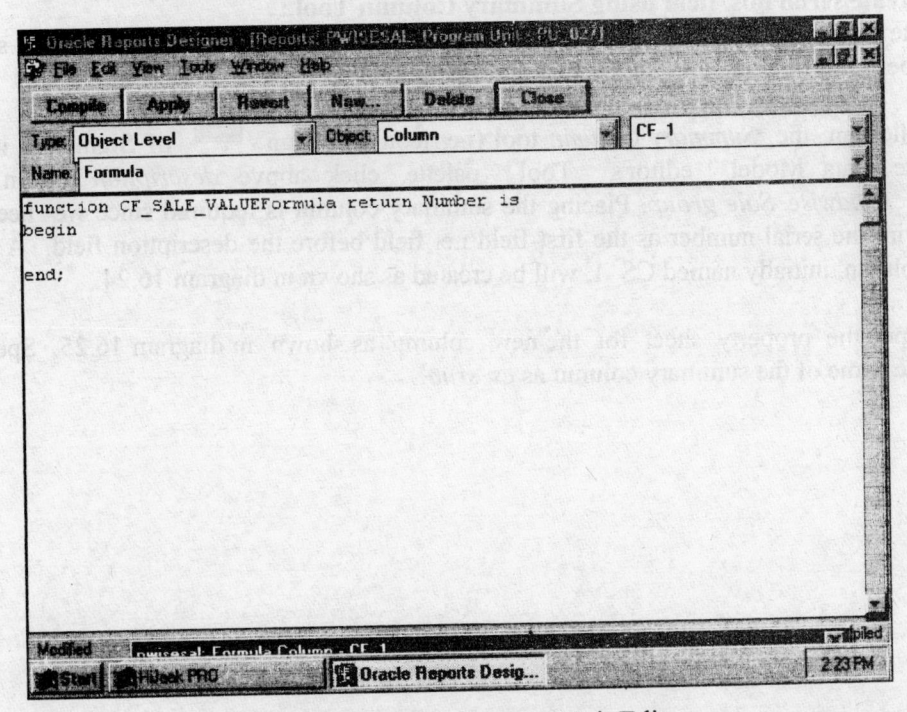

Diagram 16.23: Program Unit Editor

5. Enter the complete formula for the sale value for each product :

   function CF_sale_valueFormula **return** Number **is**
   begin
       return :avg_product_rate * :sum_ quantity ;
   end;

   The colons appear before *avg_product_rate* and *sum_ quantity* because it functions as a bind variable reference; i.e. the values of *sum_quantity* are substituted into the formula at runtime.

6. Click on **Compile**. If you typed the function correctly, the status line reports, "*Successfully Compiled.*" Otherwise, the status line reports "*Compiled with Errors,*" and the Program Unit editor points out your error in the Compilation Messages field. (If this occurs, correct the mistake in the Source Text field and select Compile again.)

7. Click on **Close** to close the Program Unit editor, then accept the property sheet. *cf_sale_value* is now listed as a column belonging to G_Prodwise_Sale. The column name appears in italic, indicating that it is a user-created column.

To create serial nos. field using Summary Column Tool :
Create a computed column that displays the serial number for every record. The serial number must be printed as the first column of the report.

1. Click on the *Summary Column* tool (i.e. icon with sign ![sigma] of Sigma on it) in the Data Model editor's Tool palette, click above *description* within the G_Prodwise_Sale group. Placing the summary column is required since we need to print the serial number as the first field i.e. field before the description field. A new column, initially named CS_1, will be created as shown in diagram 16.24.

2. Open the property sheet for the new column as shown in diagram 16.25. Specify the name of the summary column as *cs_srno*.

WORKING WITH REPORTS 387

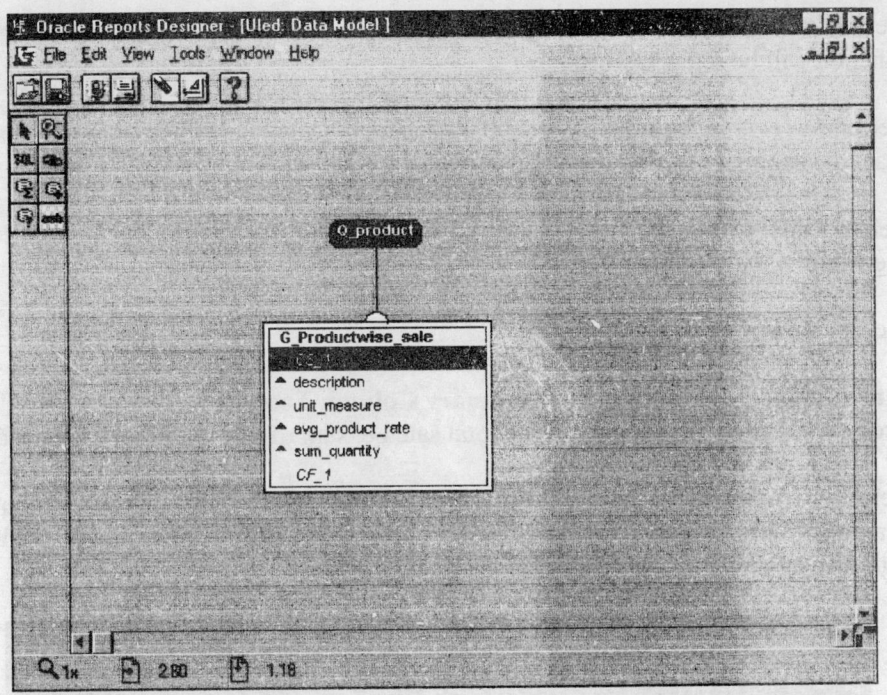

Diagram 16.24 : New Summary column for Serial Number

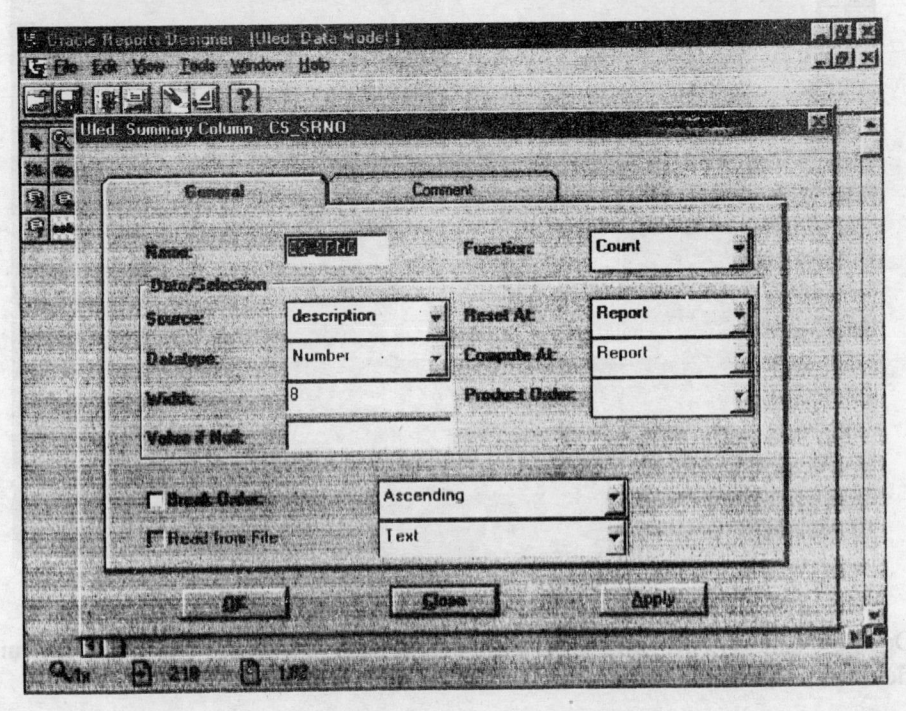

Diagram 16.25: Property Sheet for Serial Number column

The value in the Function field tells Oracle Reports what type of computation the summary will perform. The Sum function is the default function assigned to user-created summary columns. In this case we need the count for the records thus the function will be set as **Count**.

3. Select *description* from the Source list of values. This tells Oracle Reports that you want the summary to find the count of the *description* column.

4. Select **Report** from the **Reset At** list of values. This tells Oracle Reports not to reset the value of the summary to zero.

5. Accept the property sheet for *cs_srno*.

Create a Report Summary using Summary Column Tool :
To create a summary that computes the total sale i.e. sum of sale value for each product :

1. Select the *Summary Column* tool and click place the column as shown in diagram 16.26. A new column is created. As it belongs to the report as a whole, it will display only once, at the end of the report.

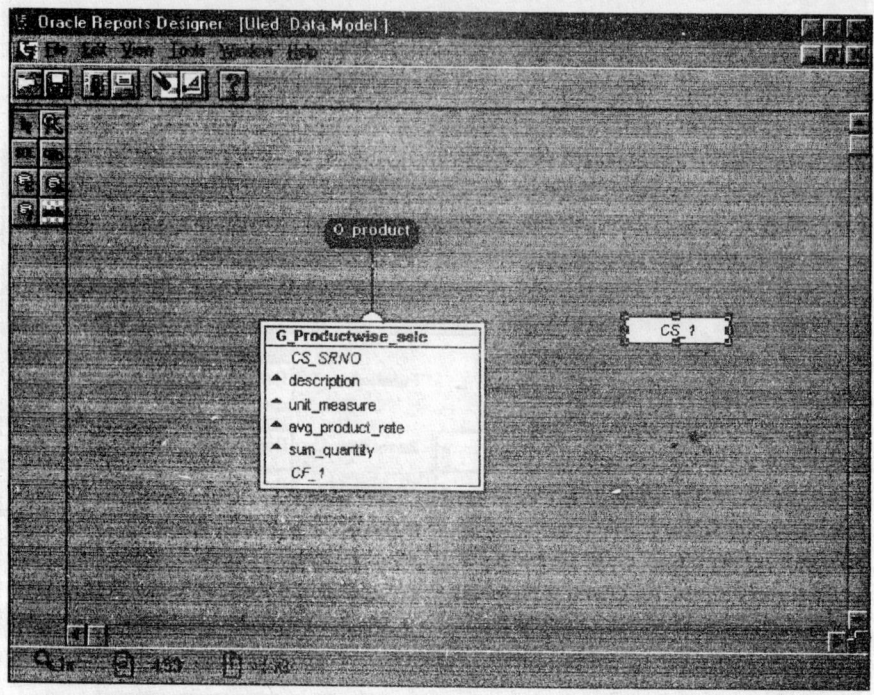

Diagram 16.26 : Report Level Summary column that displays Total Sales

2. Open the column's property sheet and name it as *cs_totsal* and check that the function field has value **Sum**.

3. Select *cf_sale_value* from the Source list of values. Thus indicating that it is the sum of *cf_sale_value*.

4. Ensure that the reset level is set to **Report**. A reset level of Report means that *cs_totsal* never resets to zero. Oracle Reports will continue to accumulate the values of *cf_sale_value* until the end of the report.

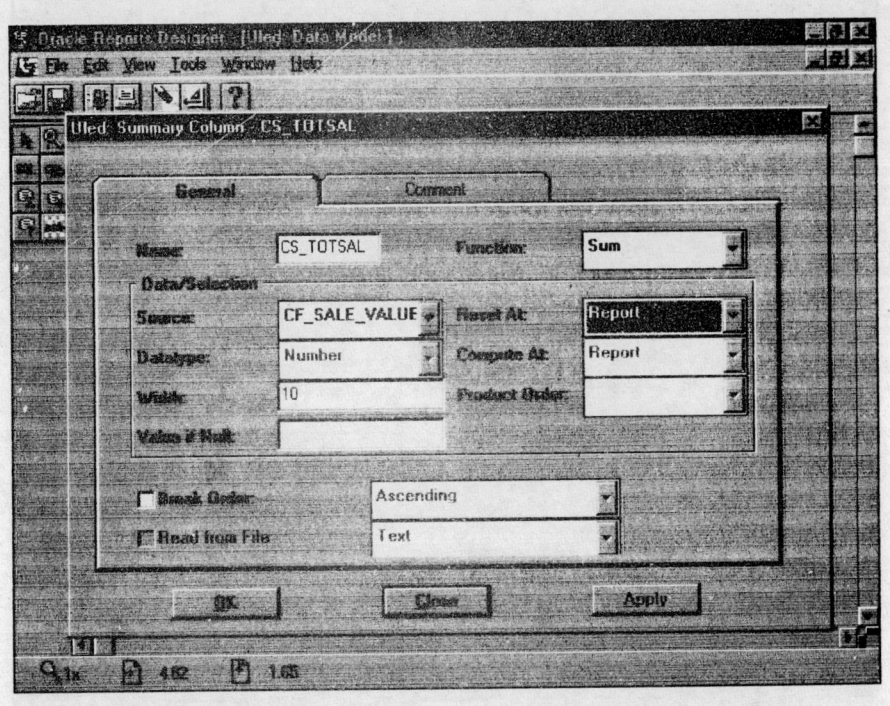

Diagram 16.27 : Property Sheet for new summary column

5. Create a default layout for the report. Change the labels for the fields as mentioned below :

Column	Label
cs_srno	Sr. No.
cf_sale_value	Sale Value
cs_totsal	Total Sale

6. It will ask you whether to replace the existing. Select Yes and the layout editor will open up with the layout as shown in diagram 16.28.

7. Save and run the report it will look as shown in the diagram 16.29.

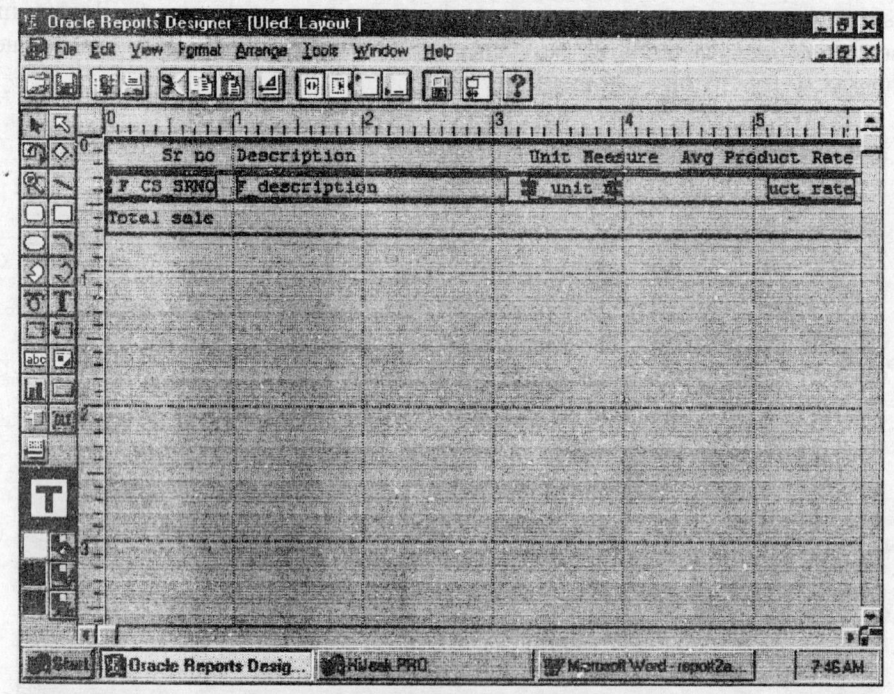

Diagram 16.28: Final Layout of the report

Sr no	Description	Unit Measure	Product Rate	Quantity	Sale Value
1	1.44 DRIVE	PIECE	1050	3	3150
2	1.44 FLOPPIES	PIECES	525	19	9975
3	540 HDD	PIECE	8400	1	8400
4	CD DRIVE	PIECE	5250	4	21000
5	KEYBOARDS	PIECE	3150	3	9450
6	MONITORS	PIECE	1050	6	6300
7	MOUSE	PIECE	12000	1	12000
				Total	70275

Diagram 16.29: Output of the report

CREATING USER PARAMETERS

The report created so far does not give the user, the flexibility to pass values of his/her choice. To make the report dynamic, it will be essential to define parameters such that they can accept input values from the operator giving him/her greater control over the kind of data retrieved.

Focus :
In the *Pwisesal* report, define parameter fields which will accept values for date range (i.e. start date and end date) from the user at runtime and the report must display the productwise sales for the date range specified by the user.

1. Expand the *Data Model* node in the object navigator. One of the nodes under the *Data Model* node will be *User Parameters* node.

2. Select the **User Parameters** node and click on the **Create** button on the vertical toolbar to create a user parameter for passing start date. A default parameter with name P_1 will be created as shown in the diagram 16.30.

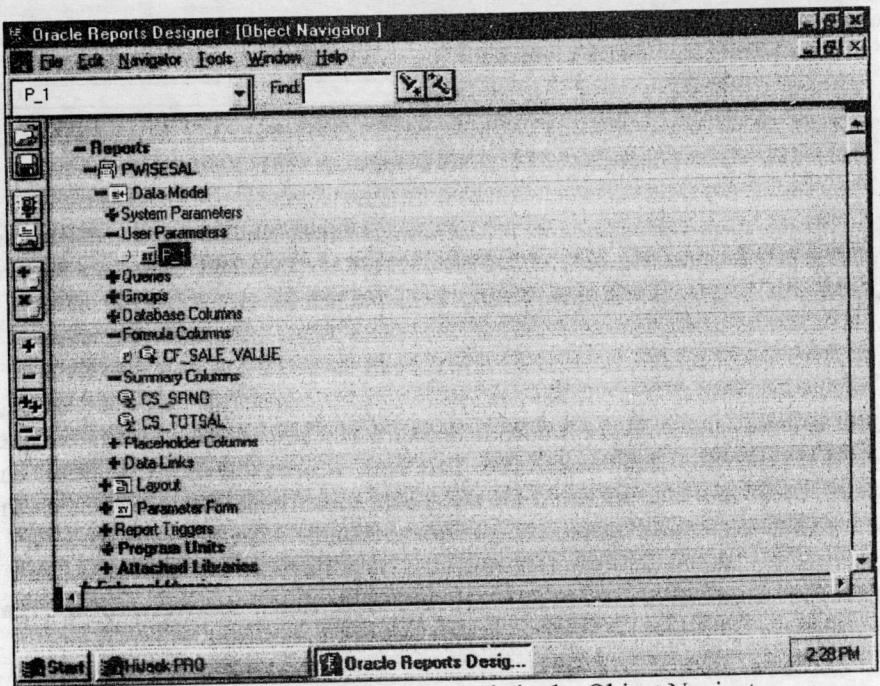

Diagram 16.30 : User Parameter node in the Object Navigator

3. Double-click on the icon next to the parameter P_1 to open up its property sheet. A small window shown in the diagram 16.31 will open up.

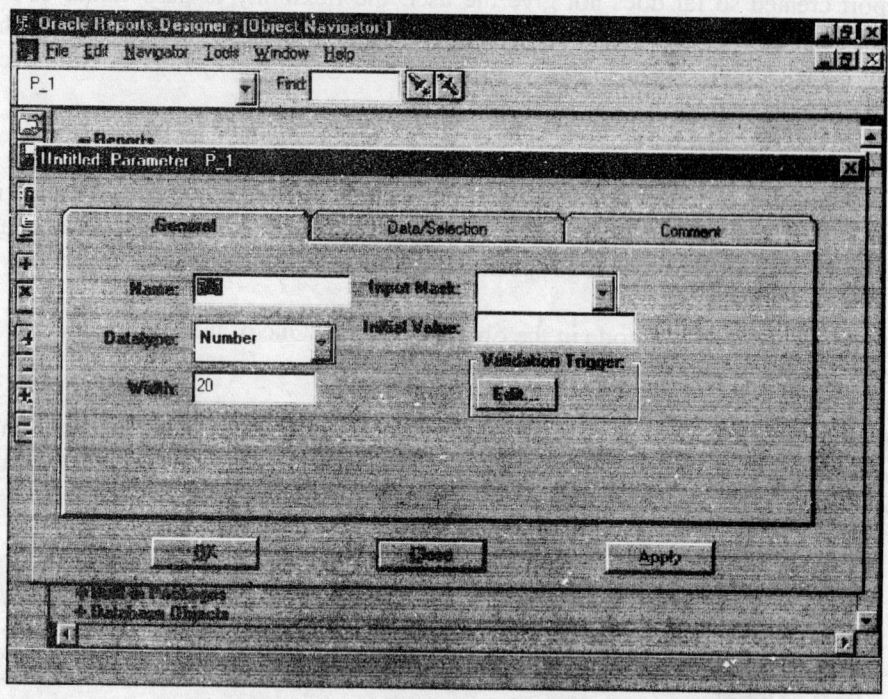

Diagram 16.31 : Property Sheet Of User Parameter

4. Specify the *Parameter Name* as *p_startdate*. Choose the *Data Type* of the parameter as *Date* and select an *Input Mask* of 'DD/MM/YY'. A default value can be specified if required by making an entry for *Initial Value*. Click on **OK**.

Similarly create another user parameter for end date.

6. Now that the parameter fields have been defined. They must be used in the query such that the query becomes conditional. This can be done by invoking the Data Model Editor. One way is to access from the **Tools** menu item. Double click on the query object so that the query definition screen is invoked.

Add the clause **and (("sales_order"."dely_date" between p_startdate and p_enddate))** to current select statement as shown in diagram 16.32.

WORKING WITH REPORTS 393

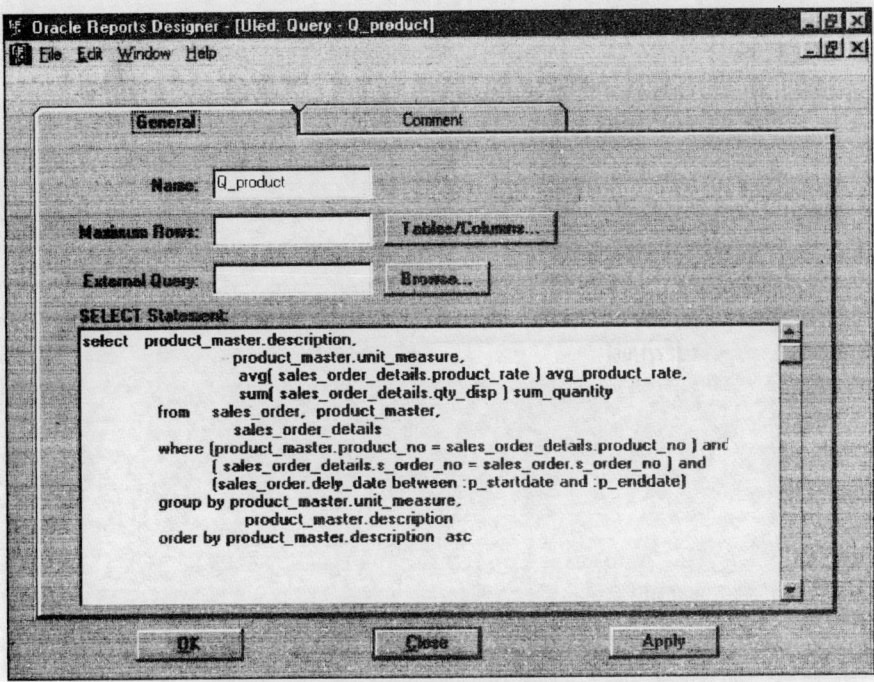

Diagram 16.32: Query with Parameters added in the WHERE clause

8. Save and run the report. The parameter form will display the parameters as shown in diagram 16.33.

Diagram 16.33: User Parameter Form At Run Time

7. Enter the values for the parameters as shown in diagram 16.34 and click on the **Run Report** push Button to view the output.

394 COMMERCIAL APPLICATION DEVELOPMENT USING DEVELOPER 2000

Diagram 16.34: User Parameter Form At Run Time With Filled Parameter Data

8. The report format for the dates specified will be as shown in diagram 16.35.

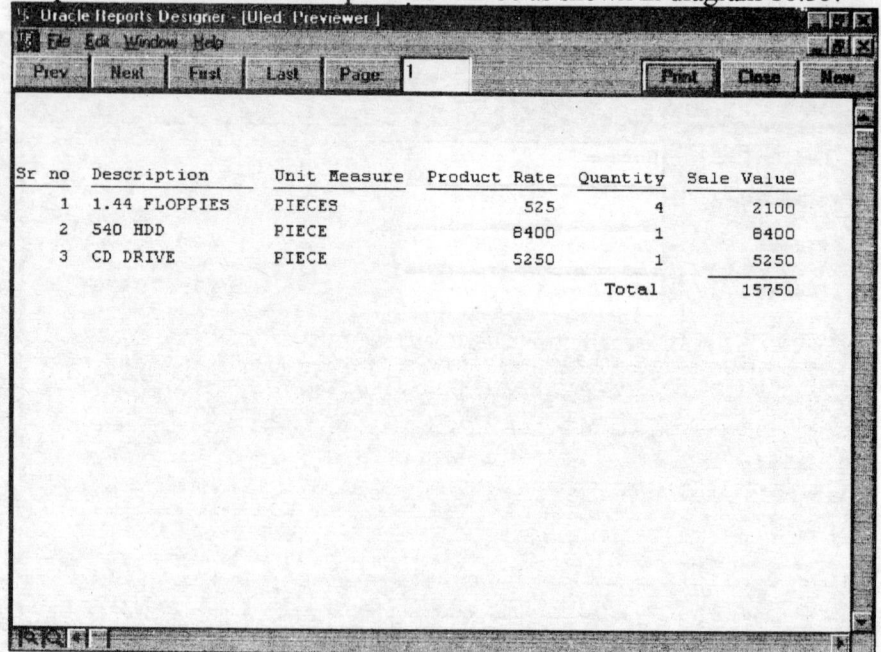

Diagram 16.35: Report Output

9. As shown in the diagram 16.33, the User Parameter form gives parameter names as default labels for the date range. So to make it more meaningful to the user, lets us see how to change the design of the form.

WORKING WITH REPORTS 395

10. Select **Tools, Default Parameter Form** from the menu bar and a small window shown in the diagram 16.36 will pop up.

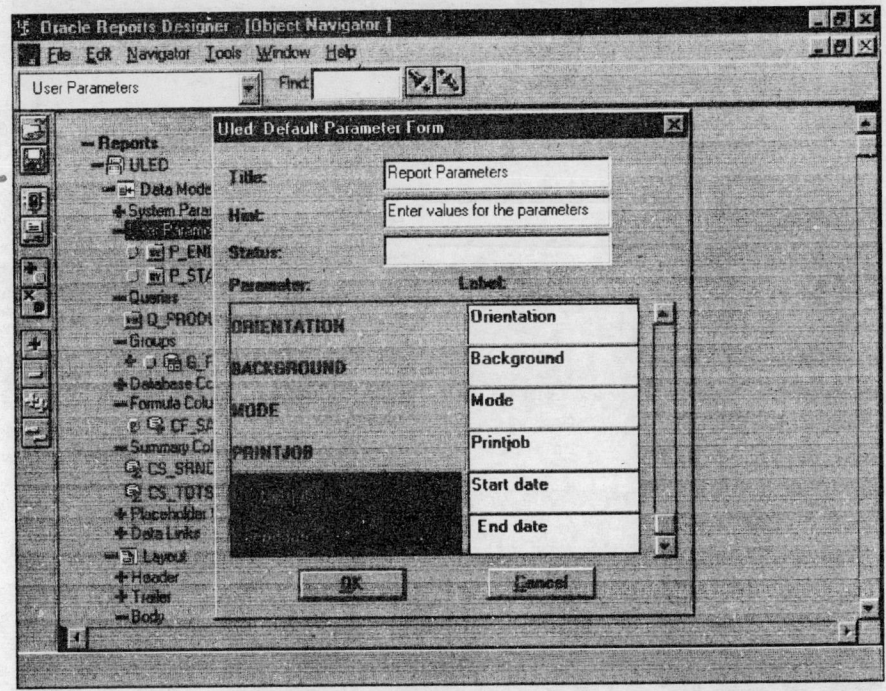

Diagram 16.36 : Changing the Label of Parameter

> **Note :**
> Highlighted parameters (selected) from the list of parameters are the ones you will see when you run the report. Click on the parameter name to select or deselect a parameter. Use scrollbar to scroll down or up the list.

11. Scroll down and change the labels of the parameters, P_startdate and P_enddate to '*Start Date :*' and '*End Date :*' respectively and click on OK to accept the changes.

12. Save and run the report again and see the change in the parameter form.

396 COMMERCIAL APPLICATION DEVELOPMENT USING DEVELOPER 2000

Diagram 16.37: Runtime Parameter Form

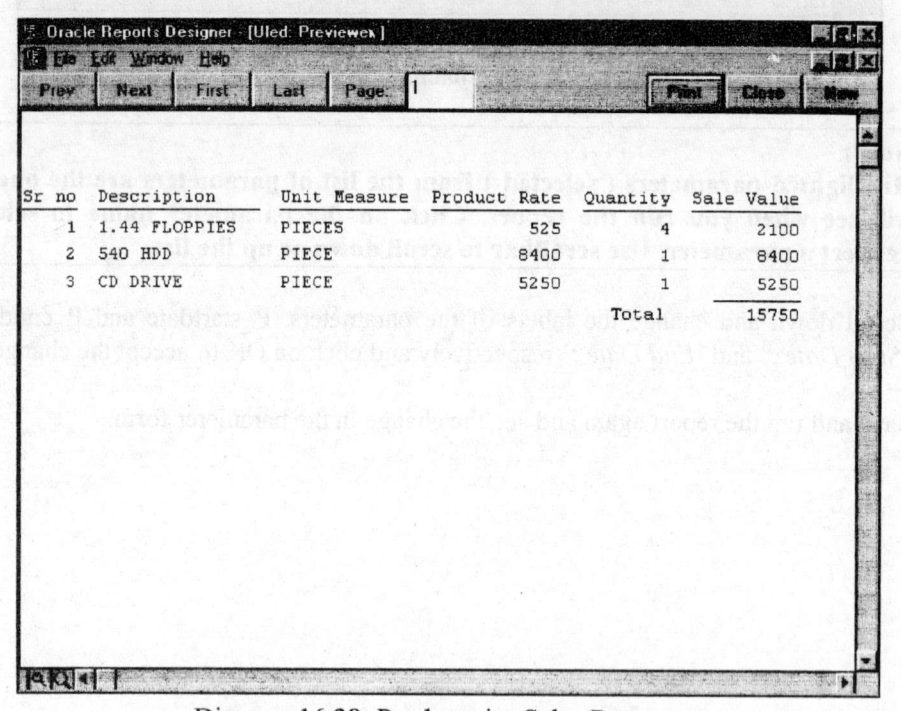

Diagram 16.38: Productwise Sales Report

CUSTOMIZING REPORT LAYOUT

You've added columns that you want to show in the output, so you need to update your layout. This time you can change the default layout to improve the overall appearance and readability of your report.

Let us look at some of the useful tools available for achieving our goal.

Change Layout Settings :
Oracle Reports offers a variety of options for displaying text and graphics. You can use any font (e.g. Courier), weight (e.g., bold), and style (e.g., italic) available on your system to create fields, boilerplate text etc.

- Go to the *Layout* editor.
- Select the item to be changed and click on **F_ormat, F_ont menu items**. Oracle Reports displays a standard *Font Setting* dialog box. Specify a font name as *Courier New*, size as *10*, *bold*, as you would normally specify a font in an application.
- Similarly you can change the text by creating a new boiler text by placing the *Text* icon and specifying the required text. Also you can move the fields and texts inside the corresponding group frame, change the format of the field, align the fields with respect to each other etc. through the **F_ormat** and **A_rrange** options on the menu.
- Notice the Fill Color, Line Color, and Text Color tools located near the bottom of the Tool palette. The **Line Color tool**, is used to customize borders around layout objects. The **Fill Color tool**, is used to fill layout objects with colors and patterns and, **Text Color tool**, enables you to change the default text color.

The *Fill/Line/Text Display*, shows the currently-selected fill, border, and text.

The default fill and border for objects created by Oracle Reports are *transparent*, while the default for objects you create is a black, one-point line around a white fill.

Note :
Since you are changing the text defaults, when you re-default the layout, all objects with be created with white backgrounds and black borders. To prevent this, change the fill and border to transparent.

Fill Color Tool :
Select the Fill Color tool. When the color palette appears, select No Fill to set the fill color to transparent or select the appropriate fill color.

Line Color Tool :
Select the Line Color tool. When the color palette appears, select No Line to set the fill color to transparent or select the appropriate fill color.

Text Color Tool :

Select the Item and then click on the Text Color tool. When the color palette appears, select the appropriate text color.

Now let us see how we can modify the layout of our report to make it look as shown in the diagram 16.39.

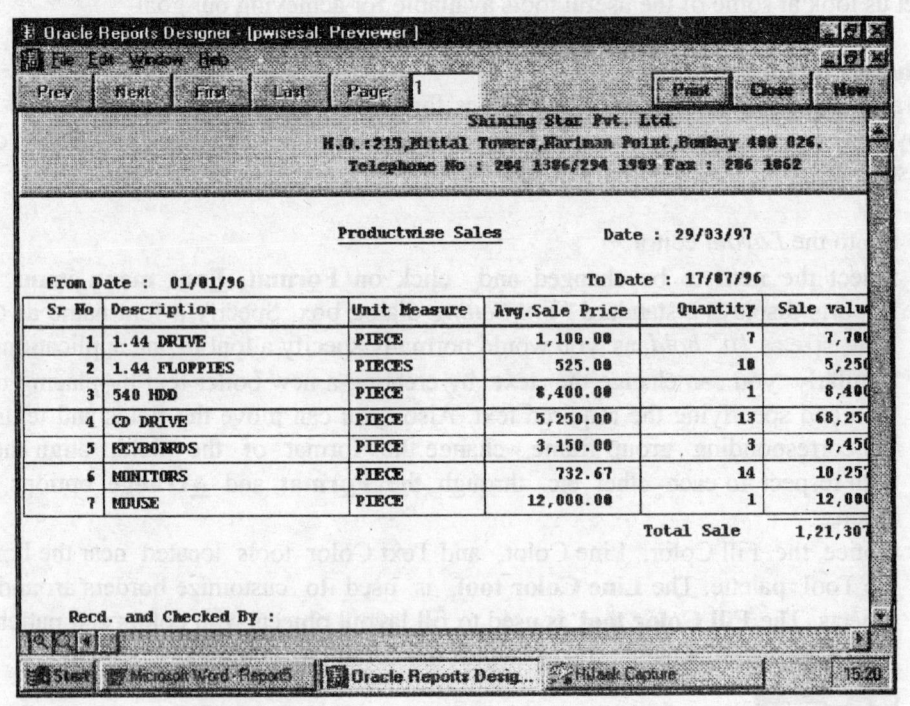

Diagram 16.39 : Productwise Sales Report

1. Look through the object navigator under Layout in report Pwisesal. Click on the '+' against the *Body* node. It will expand to display more nodes and items under this node like frames.

2. Select *m_prodwise_sale_grpfr* i.e. the main surrounding frame and then go to the Layout Editor and you will find a frame object will be selected there. Click-and-drag one of the frame's lower handles (the small boxes at the corners) down approximately 1.2 inch to make enough space for the heading i.e. the company name. Release the mouse button.

3. In the Object Navigator, click on the '+' sign next to main frame *m_prodwise_sale_grpfr* to expand that node if its not already expanded. Select *m_prodwise_sale_ftr*, *m_prodwise_sale_hdr* frames and the repeating frame *r_prodwise_sale*. Go to the Layout Editor as done before.

WORKING WITH REPORTS **399**

4. Now click-and-drag all these three selected objects down within the expanded main frame right till the bottom. You will find that as move these frames all the objects within these frames will also move along. Now the layout Editor will look as shown in the diagram 16.40.

> **Note: Use '*Shift*' key to for multiple selection of objects.**

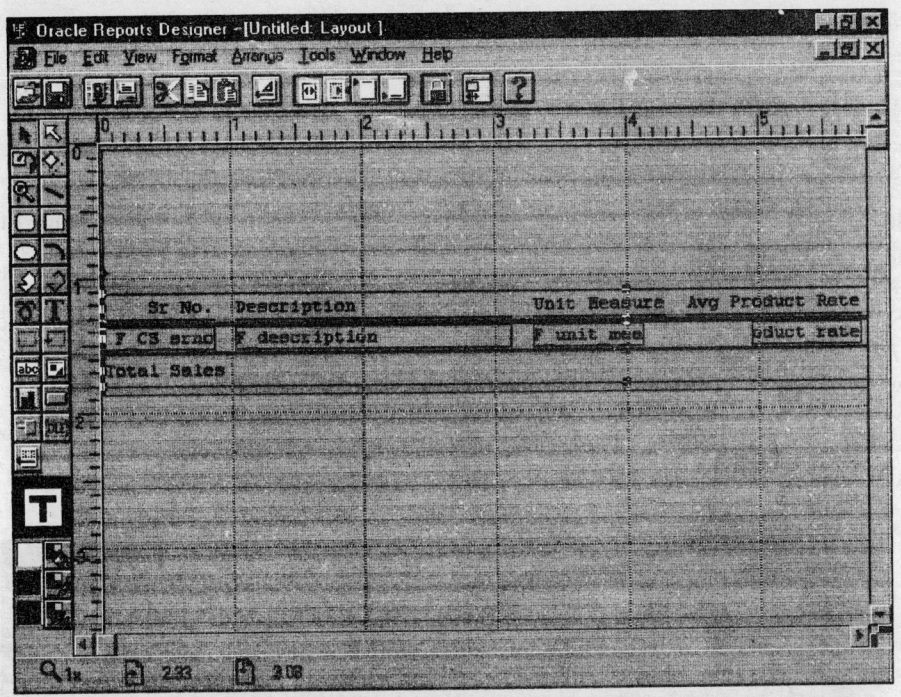

Diagram 16.40 : Expanded *m_prodwise_sale_grpfr* in Layout Editor

5. Click on Text button [T] on the vertical tool bar i.e. button on it and click on the empty space you have on top. Enter the name of the company and the address as follows :

Shining Star Pvt. Ltd.
H. O. : 215, Mittal Towers, Nariman Point, Bombay 400 026.
Telephone No : 204 1386 / 294 1909 Fax : 286 1862

6. Click on *Fill Color* button on the vertical tool bar and you will get a list of colors available. Select *light gray* color.

7. Click on **F**ormat, **B**evel menu items and select **R**aised to give a raise effect for the Company header.

400 COMMERCIAL APPLICATION DEVELOPMENT USING ORACLE 7, DEVELOPER 2000

8. Click on **Format**, **Alignment** menu items and select **Center** so that and the text you just typed in will move to the center of the object.

9. Now select **Format**, **Font** from the menu and you will get a list of all the fonts and styles available. Select the following and click on OK.

10. Now select **Format**, **Font** from the menu and you will get a list of all the fonts and styles available. Select the following and click on OK.

    Font   : Courier New
    Font Style   : Bold
    Size   : 9

11. Increase the size of the company header text such that it is slightly smaller than the main frame.

12. Similarly create another text object just below the text object created and type '*Productwise Sales*' and click outside the object.

    Underline   : On

Now the layout Editor will look as shown in the diagram 16.41.

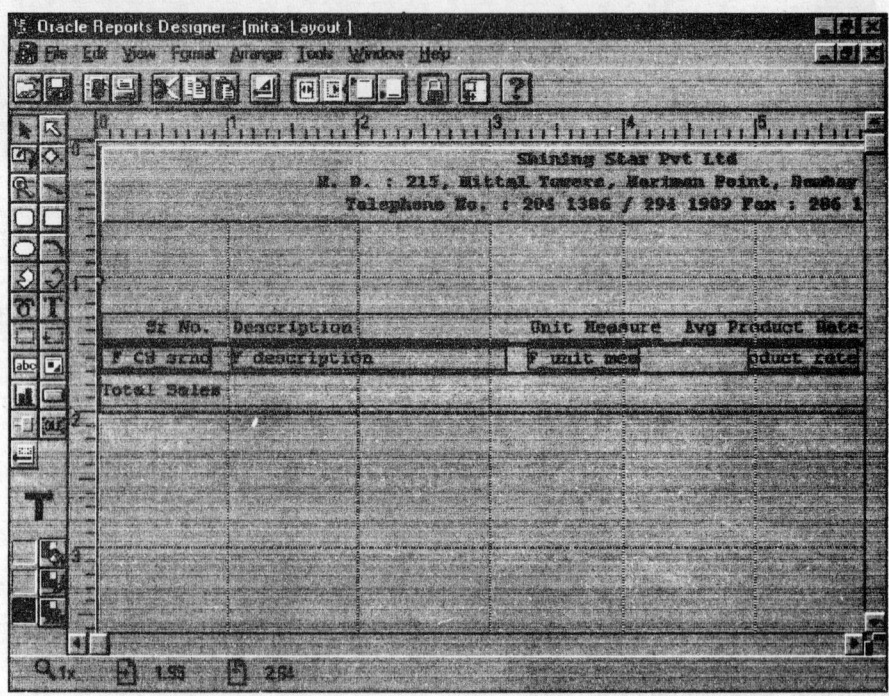

Diagram 16.41 : Adding a Text in the Layout Editor

13. Create another three text objects with text '**Date :**', '**From Date :**' and '**To Date :**'. and select all three text objects (using Shift key).

Font   : Courier New
Font Style   : Bold
Size   : 9

14. Align the objects so that the layout Editor looks as shown in the diagram 16.42

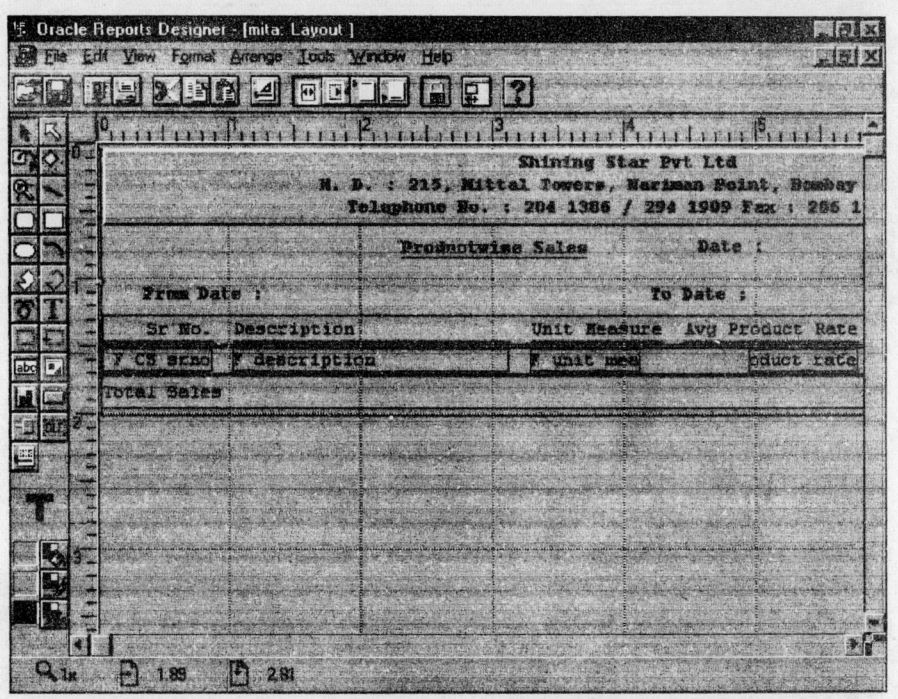

Diagram 16.42 : Including Boiler Text in the Report Header

15. We have put the labels for the current date and date range now let us create objects to display their actual values. Click on the [abc] field button on the vertical toolbar.

16. Click next to the '**Date :**' text to display current date and a small rectangle will be placed there. Click-and-drag and size the object.

17. Open the property sheet of the field created by clicking on **Tools**, **Properties** menu items. A window shown in the diagram 16.43 will come up.

18. Change the name of the field to F_curdt. Click on the list provided for and select **&Current Date** on the Object tab. Select Format Mask of 'DD/MM/YY' The completed screen will be as shown in diagram 16.44.

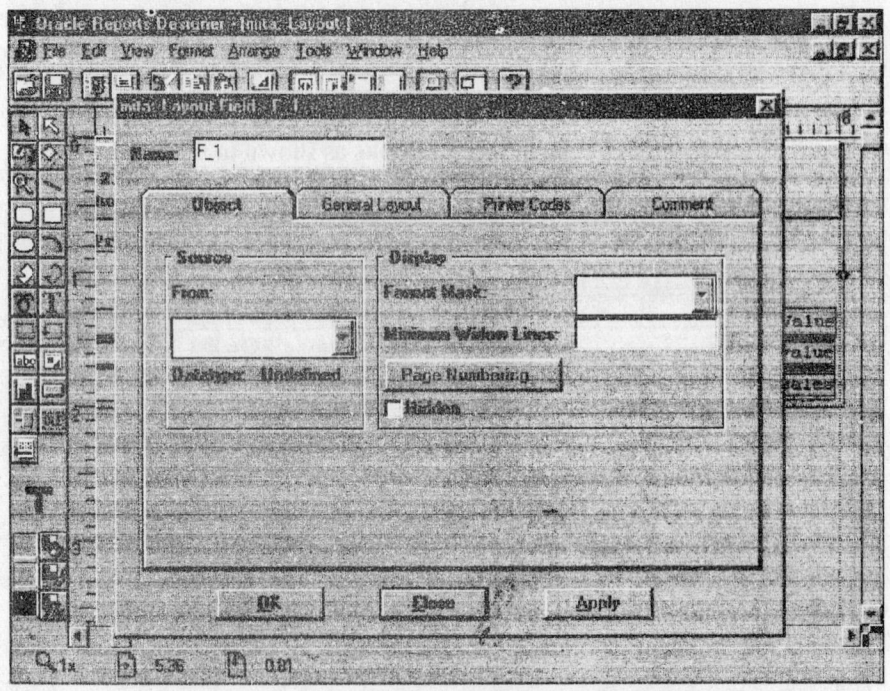

Diagram 16.43 : Property Sheet of a newly Added Field

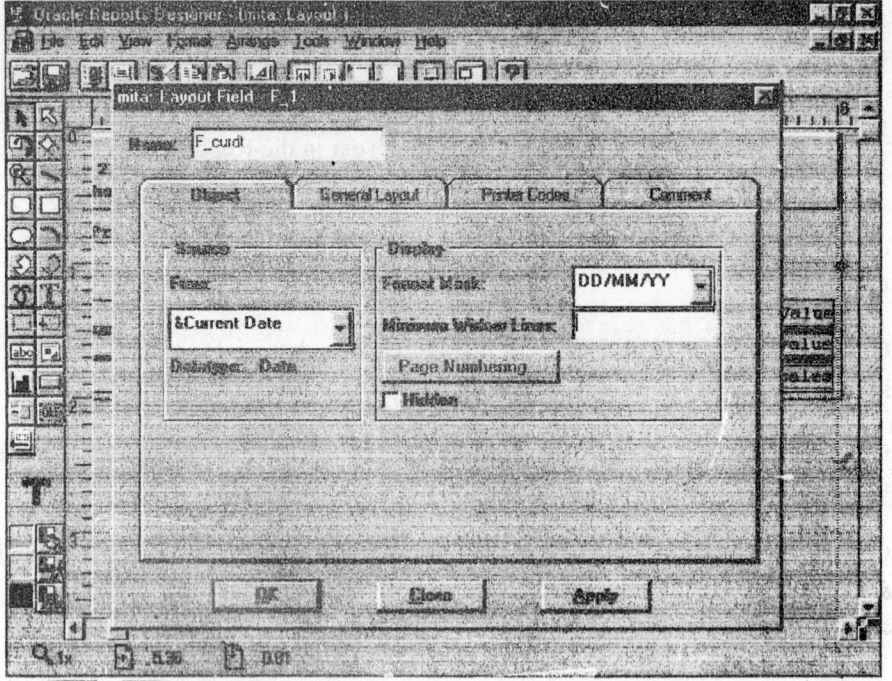

Diagram 16.44 : Property Sheet of the Current Date field

19. Similarly create two other fields and set their properties as follows :

   Object tab :
Name	: F_startdt
Source	: P_startdate (i.e. first user parameter)
Format Mask	: DD/MM/YY

   Object tab :
Name	: F_enddt
Source	: P_enddate (i.e. second user parameter)
Format Mask	: DD/MM/YY

20. By default, in Tabular presentation style, Oracle places line objects under the label objects. Select all the lines under the labels and delete them by pressing the *Delete* key. Similarly delete the line on top of the summary column *f_cs_totsal*.

21. Select all the labels (on top of the data columns) and change their format to as mentioned below :

Font	: Courier New
Style	: Bold
Size	: 9

22. Increase the size of the main frame and the footer frame. Place a text object with text **'Recd. and Checked by :'** and change font size to 9.

23. Click on the line button from the vertical tool bar, click-and-drag next to **'Recd. and Checked by :'** text. Run the report the output will be displayed as shown in diagram 16.45.

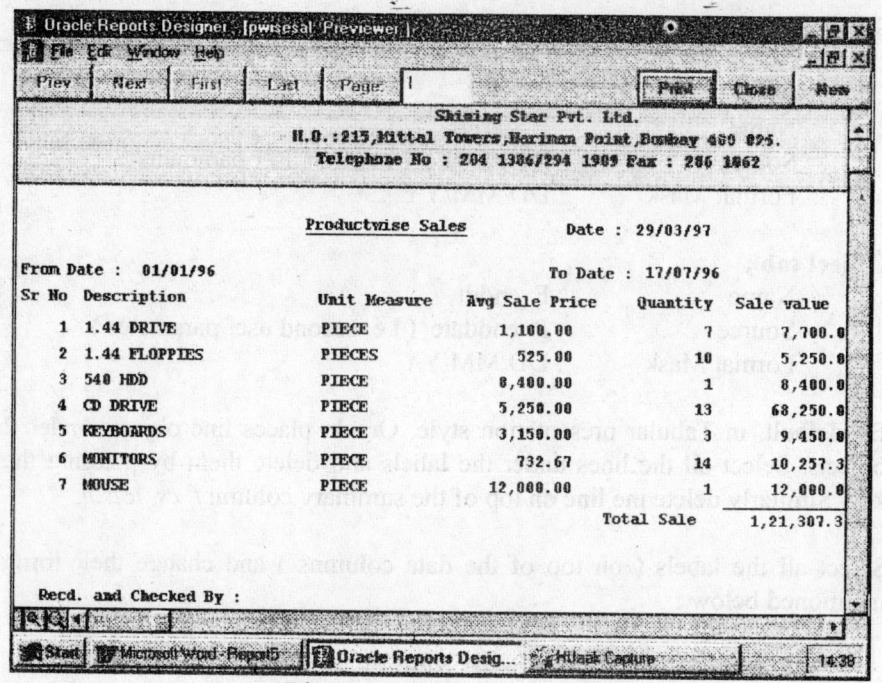

Diagram 16.45 : Report Output

Displaying Grid Lines for the report :

As seen in diagram 16.39 and diagram 16.45, the only difference between them is surrounding borders and lines between the data. Let us see how to get these borders around the data.

24. Go to Object Navigator, select *m_prodwise_sale_grpfr*, *m_prodwise_sale_ftr*, *m_prodwise_sale_hdr* and *r_prodwise_sale*. Go to the layout editor and you will find that all these frames will be selected there.

25. Click on the Line Color tool and select black color to give black border. Now run the report and see the difference. As shown in the report output, we have got the border around the data. We now need to draw lines between the columns.

26. Select the line tool from the vertical tool bar and draw a vertical line between columns *f_cs_srno* and *f_description*. You can size or change the inclination of the line by clicking-and-dragging one of the line's handles.

27. Similarly draw lines between other columns as well as their labels and run the report The report output will as shown in diagram 16.46.

Note :
None of the lines (or any other object) should cross their enclosing frames. If it does then you will get an error for that while running the report. In that case select the named object (in the error text) and move it inside the frame it is crossing.

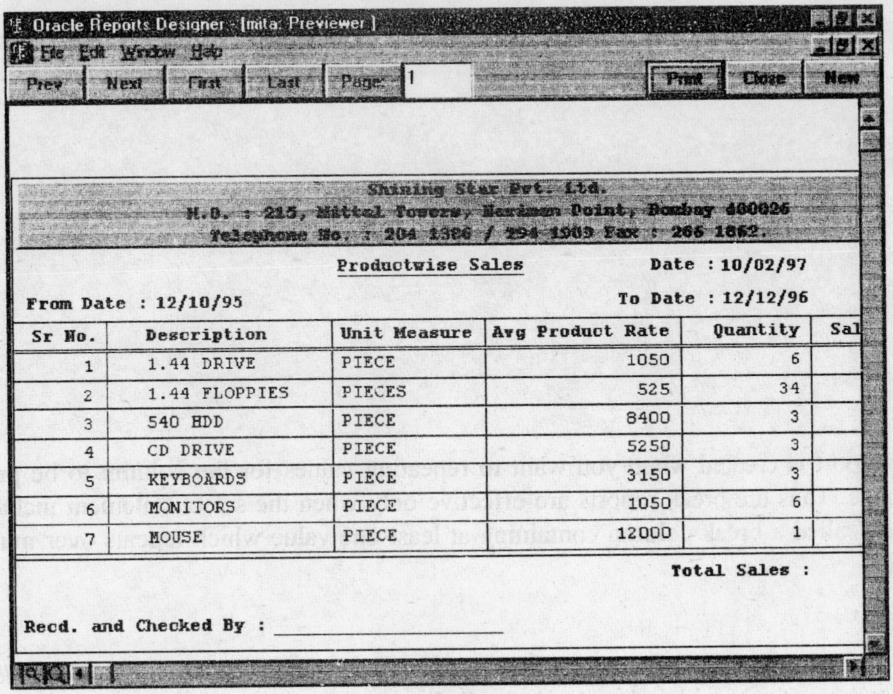

Shining Star Pvt. Ltd.
H.O. : 215, Mittal Towers, Nariman Point, Bombay 400026
Telephone No. : 204 1386 / 294 1303 Fax : 266 1862.

Productwise Sales   Date : 10/02/97

From Date : 12/10/95   To Date : 12/12/96

Sr No.	Description	Unit Measure	Avg Product Rate	Quantity	Sal
1	1.44 DRIVE	PIECE	1050	6	
2	1.44 FLOPPIES	PIECES	525	34	
3	540 HDD	PIECE	8400	3	
4	CD DRIVE	PIECE	5250	3	
5	KEYBOARDS	PIECE	3150	3	
6	MONITORS	PIECE	1050	6	
7	MOUSE	PIECE	12000	1	

Total Sales :

Recd. and Checked By : _____

Diagram 16.46 : Report Output with Borders and Lines included

17. CREATING A BREAK REPORT

Break report is created when you want to repeating values for the column to be printed only once. Thus the break reports are effective only when the select statement includes a column, called a break column containing at least one value which repeats over multiple records.

Focus :
Creating a control break *'Order Backlog Report'* from *Sales_order, Sales_order_details* and *Product_master* tables that displays all the pending orders along with the products that have not been delivered. In this exercise, we will go step-by-step to create a report, as shown in diagram 17.1.

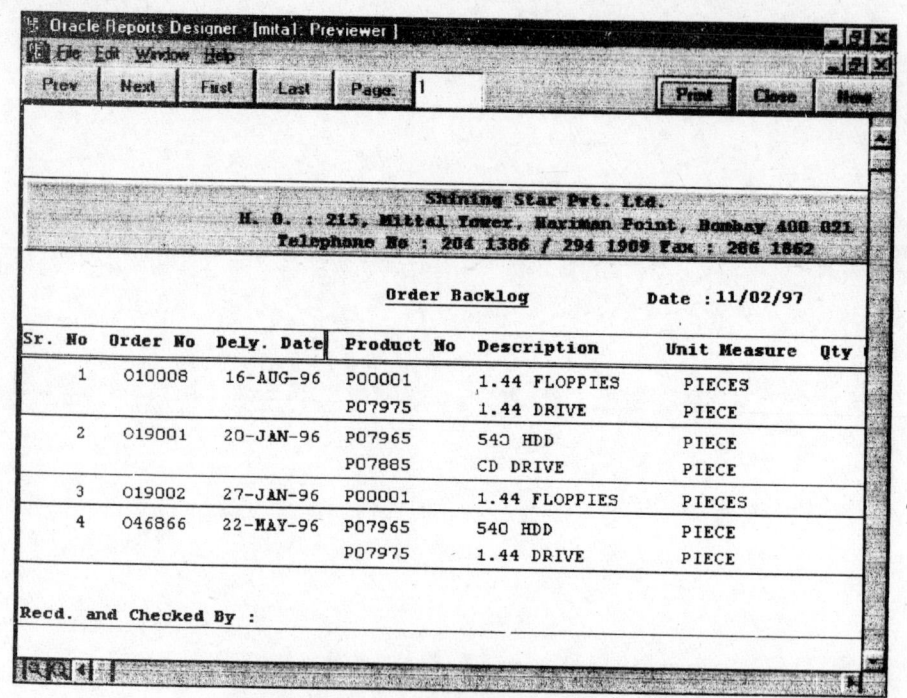

Diagram 17.1 : Control Break Report

The definitions of the tables used are as mentioned below :

Table Name : product_master
Description : stores information about products supplied by the company.

Column Name	Data Type	Size	Column Description
product_no	varchar2	6	Access key via which we shall seek data.
description	varchar2	25	Description of the product
unit_measure	varchar2	10	Unit by which the product is measured.
qty_on_hand	number	8	Quantity which is available in the stock.
reorder_lvl	number	8	Quantity level when the stock should be re-ordered.
cost_price	number	8,2	Cost price of the product.
selling_price	number	8,2	Selling price of the product.

Table Name : sales_order (Master)
Description : Use to store information about orders placed by the clients.

Column Name	Data Type	Size	Attributes
s_order_no	varchar2	6	Unique primary key allotted to each order.
s_order_date	date		Date on which the order is placed.
client_no	varchar2	6	Client No., who places the order.
dely_addr	varchar2	30	Address where the delivery of the goods has to be made.
salesman_no	varchar2	6	Salesman No., who gets the order from the client.
status	varchar2	2	Order Status (In Process IP, FullFilled FP, Not Processed NP)
dely_type	char	1	To note whether the delivery is to be made in parts (P) or full (F).
dely_date	date		Date when the delivery for the goods is to be made.

Table Name : sales_order_details
Description : Use to store information about order details.

Column Name	Data Type	Size	Attributes
s_order_no	varchar2	6	Order No. for which details have to be stored.
product_no	varchar2	6	Product No. for which details have to be stored.
product_rate	number	8,2	The rate agreed upon.
qty_ordered	number	8	Quantity of goods ordered.
qty_disp	number	8	Quantity of goods dispatched.

To create the report shown in the diagram 16.1, we will follow following steps :
- Create a new report definition.
- Define the data.
- Create a break group
- Create summary column
- Specify a default report layout.
- Save and run the report.
- Arrange the layout and run the report.

CREATING A NEW REPORT DEFINITION

1. Invoke the Oracle Reports designer and connect to Oracle as you did before. Open the *Data Model* editor. Select a **Query** object and drop it in the editor.

2. Open the property sheet of the query object, change its name to *Q_order_backlog* and enter the SQL statement as shown in the diagram 17.2. The SQL statement is as follows :

```
select   sales_order.s_order_no, dely_date ,
         sales_order_details.product_no , description,
         unit_measure, qty_ordered, qty_disp
from     sales_order, sales_order_details, product_master
where    sales_order.s_order_no = sales_order_details.s_order_no and
         sales_order_details.product_no = product_master.product_no and
         sales_order_details.qty_ordered > sales_order_details.qty_disp
```

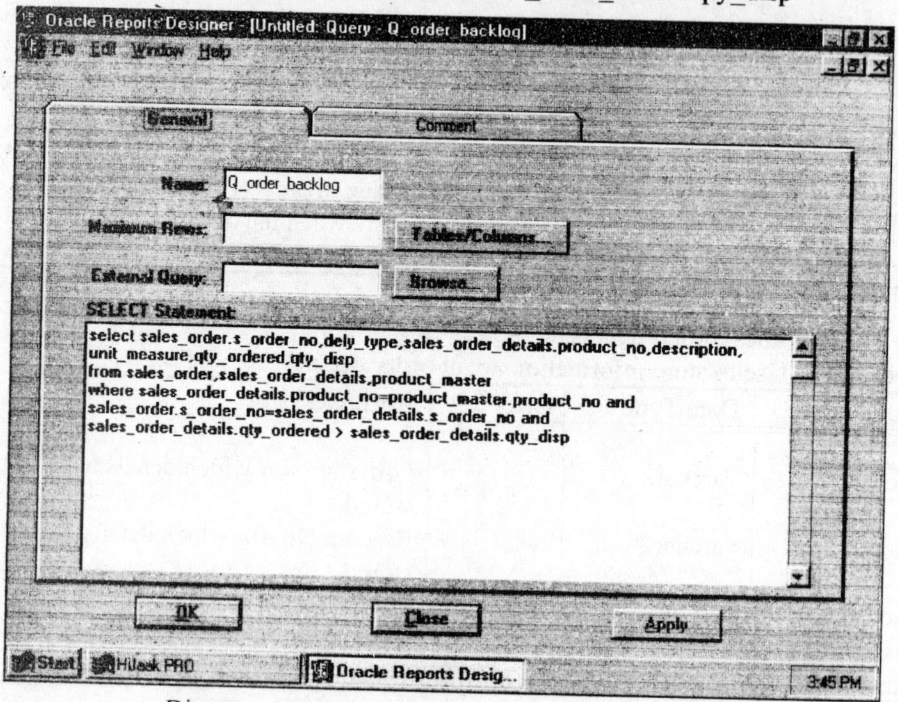

Diagram 17.2 : Property sheet of the Query Object

3. Click on OK to accept the SQL. A default group named *G_order_backlog*, will be created as shown in diagram 17.3

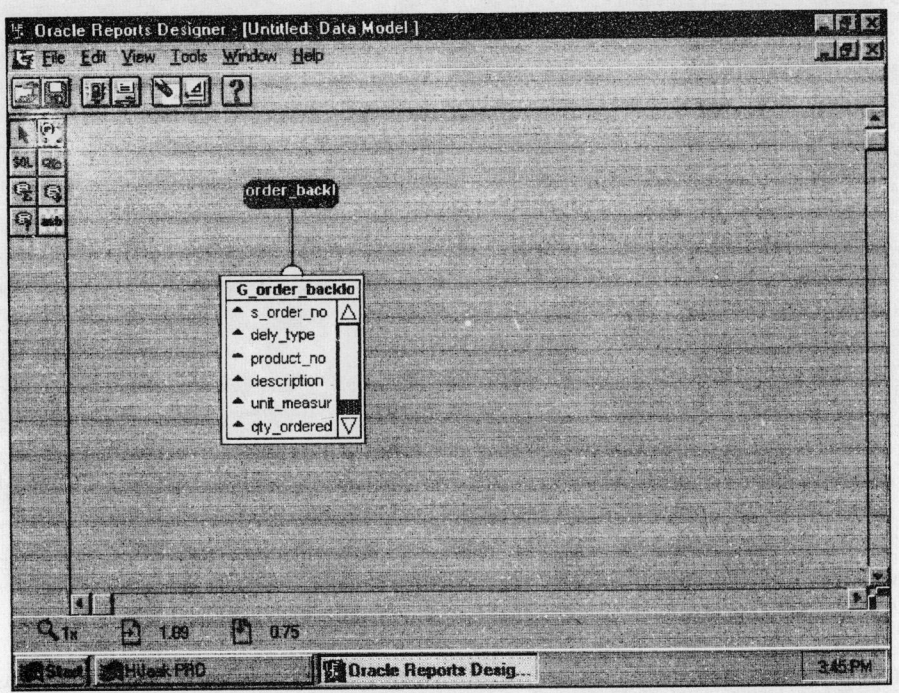

Diagram 17.3 : Data Model Editor after defining the Query

CREATING A BREAK GROUP

1. Select group named *G_order_backlog* by clicking on the title and drag it down by around 2 inches to make some space on top for create another group. This is required since the columns in the groups are printed in the order of their creation. At this point the *Data Model* editor will be as shown in the diagram 17.4.

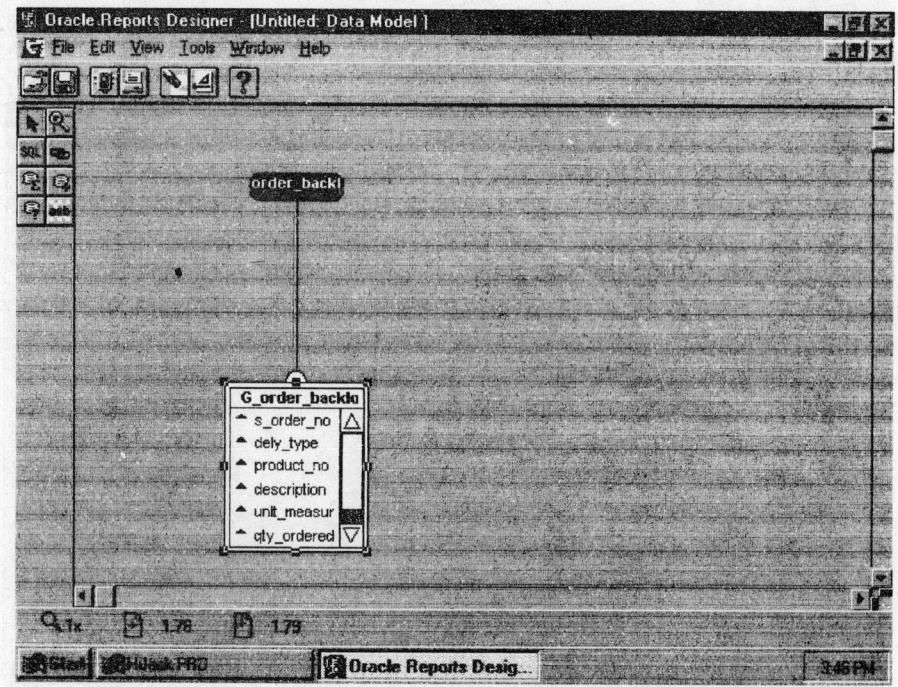

410 COMMERCIAL APPLICATION DEVELOPMENT IN DEVELOPER 2000

Diagram 17.4 : Data Model Editor After arranging the Query object

For our report, we will use *S_order_no* and *Dely_date* as control break columns as for each of their values (master table) i.e. for each order, there will be multiple products ordered (detail table).

2. Select the column *S_order_no* in the *G_order_backlog* group and drag the it above the *G_order_backlog* group. A new group, with default name G_1 and field *S_order_no* will be created above *G_order_backlog*, as shown in diagram 17.5.

By creating a break group above *G_order_backlog*, you are specifying that the break group ranks above *G_order_backlog* in the data hierarchy of the report. Thus, for each value of *S_order_no* fetched for the break group, all columns in the *G_order_backlog* group, will be displayed.

CREATING A CONTROL BREAK REPORT 411

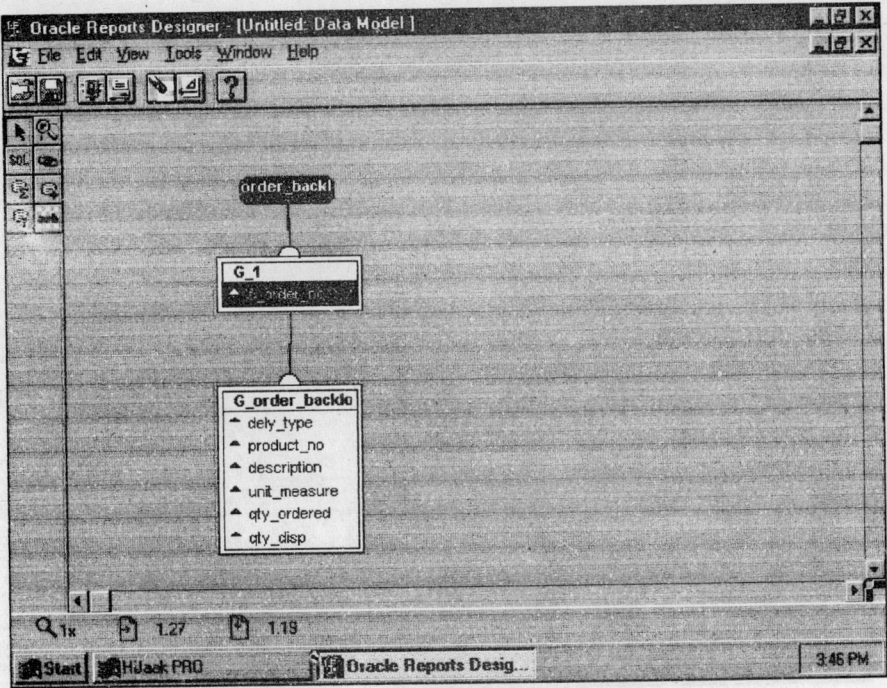

Diagram 17.5 : Creating A break group

3. We have included only *S_order_no*. We also have to include the column *Dely_date* in the new group. But for that first we need to create some space in the group box for group G_1 to add another column. Hence increase the height of the group box for group G_1 as done before.

4. Select the column *Dely_date* in the *G_order_backlog* group and drag the *Dely_date* column and place it below the *S_order_no* column in the G_1 group.

5. Double-click on the new group to display its property sheet. Specify the **Name** of the group as *G_order* as shown in diagram 17.6. Click on **OK** to accept the change.

We have got all the data that we want from the database now we only need to add serial numbers for orders as done in tabular report (refer to "Create a group summary" topic in "Creating tabular report").

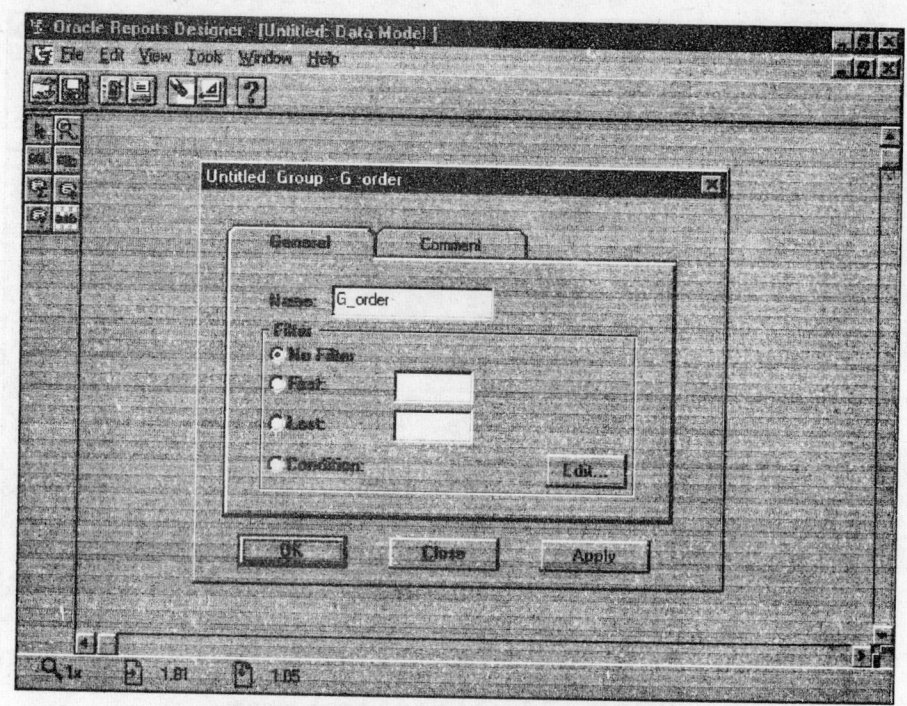

Diagram 17.6 : Changing the Group Name

CREATING SUMMARY COLUMN

1. As we need serial numbers for orders, a summary column must be added in the *G_order* group i.e. the group in which the *S_order_no* field is included. Thus add a summary column above the *s_order_no* column in the group *G_order* as shown in the diagram 17.7.

   The properties of the summary columns are :

Name	: CS_srno
Function	: Count
Source	: S_order_no
Reset At	: Report
Data Type	: Number
Width	: 3

   The summary column for serial number is placed above all the columns so that the first column in the layout editor will be serial number.

CREATING A CONTROL BREAK REPORT **413**

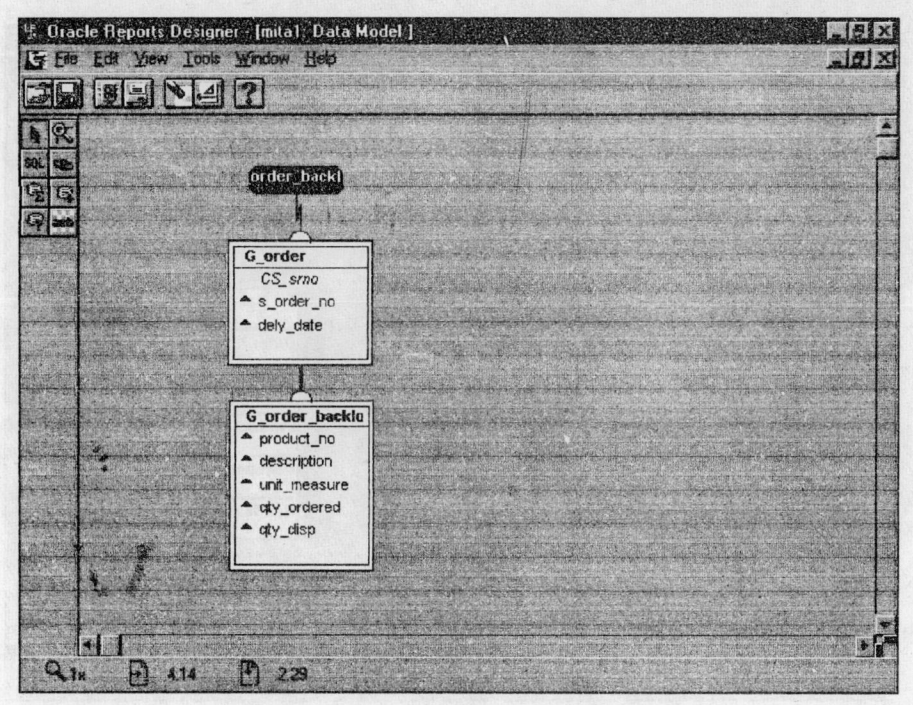

Diagram 17.7. : Adding a summary column

SPECIFYING DEFAULT LAYOUT

Now that we have all our data defined in place all that we need to do is specify default layout and arrange the layout.

1. Select **Tool**, **Default Layout**. Select the **Report Style** as **Tabular**.

2. In the **Data/Selection** tab make the following changes (refer to diagram 17.8) and click on OK to accept the changes.

    - Change the label of the S_order_no to "Order No".
    - Change the label of the CS_srno to "Sr. No".
    - Change the size of description to 15.
    - Change the width of the Qty_ordered to 7.
    - Change the width of the Qty_disp to 7.

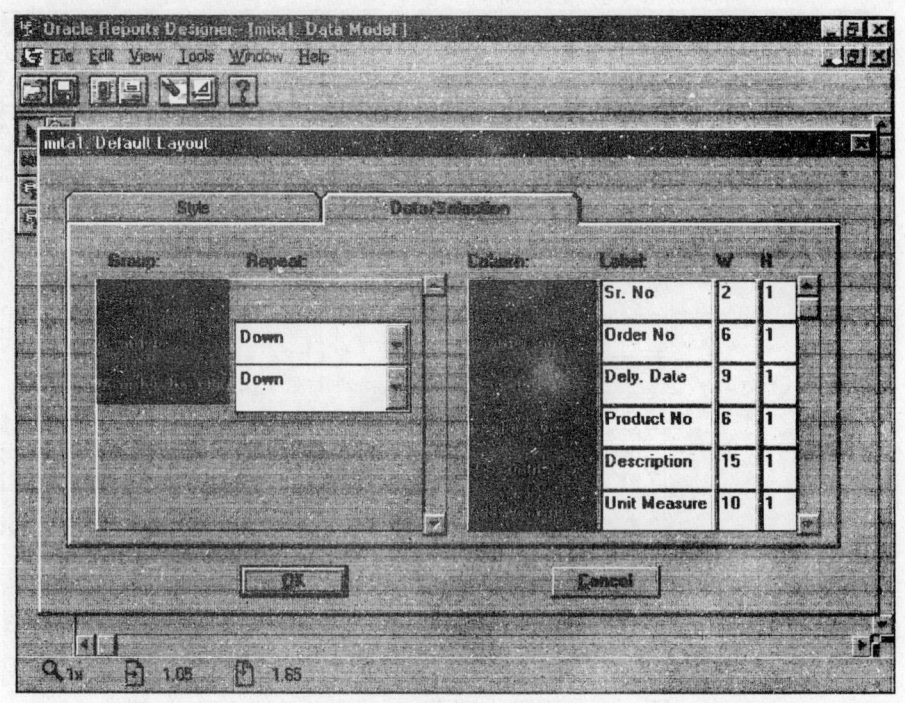

414 COMMERCIAL APPLICATION DEVELOPMENT IN DEVELOPER 2000

Diagram 17.8 : Data/Selection Tab of Default layout dialogue

3. The Report Layout will be as shown in diagram 17.9.

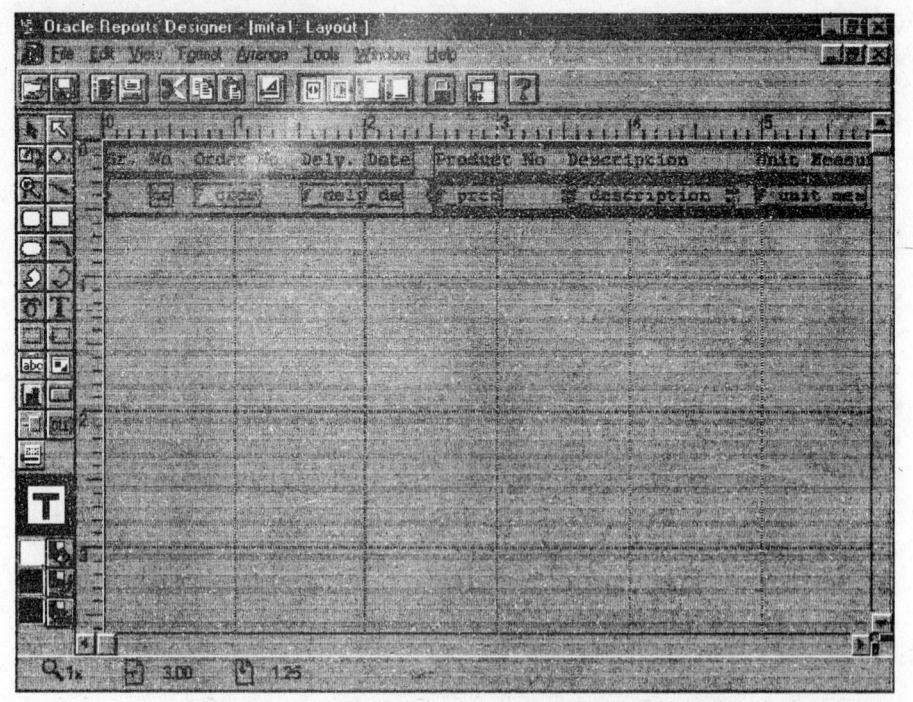

Diagram 17.9 : Report Layout in the Layout editor

The new layout, shown in diagram 17.9, resembles the default tabular layout. The major difference between the layouts is in the number of repeating frames generated for each.

About Repeating Frames :
Repeating frames contain the data owned by their corresponding groups. They are called repeating frames because they repeat as many times as necessary to display all the records.

The layout in diagram 17.9 contains two repeating frames i.e. *R_order*, which included the columns of the *G_order* group and *R_order_backlog*, which includes the columns of the *G_ Order_Backlog* group.

Placing the *G_order* group above the *G_ order_backlog* group in the Data Model editor ranks it higher in the data hierarchy and causes the *R_order* repeating frame to enclose the *R_order_backlog* repeating frame in the report's layout. Within one instance of *R_order*, *R_order_backlog* can repeat as many times as necessary to display all records related to current record in the repeating frame *R_order*. This is similar in action to a Do-loop in structured programming language.

In the *layout editor*, a repeating frame appears as a box surrounding one or more fields. The arrow on its border indicates the direction in which the repeating frame repeats. Both repeating frames in the layout show downward-pointing arrows on their borders, signifying that both will print down the page.

4. Save the report as "ordbcklg.rdf". Run the report and you will get the output as shown in the diagram 17.10.

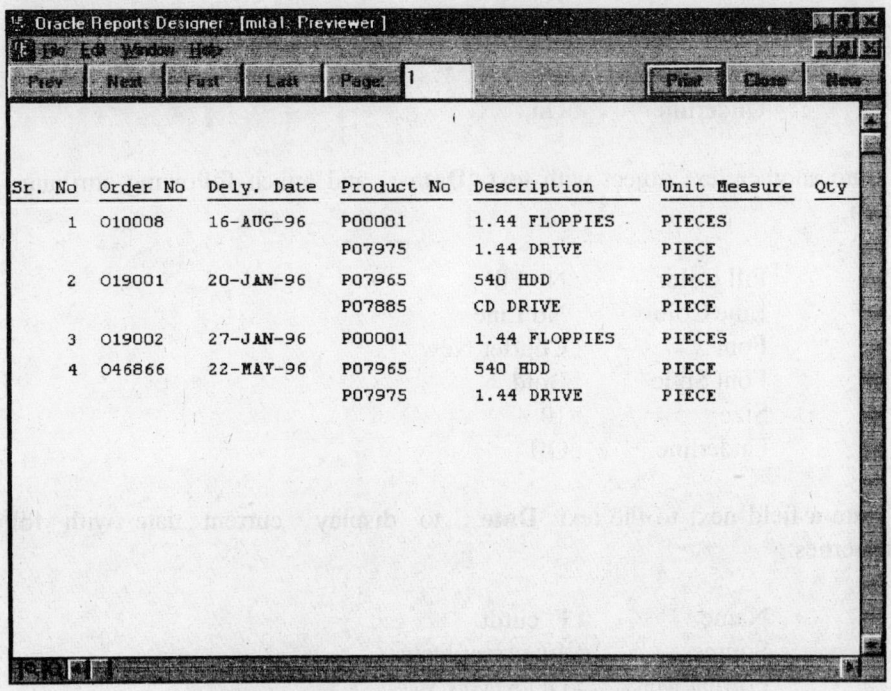

```
Sr. No   Order No   Dely. Date   Product No   Description     Unit Measure   Qty
     1   010008     16-AUG-96    P00001       1.44 FLOPPIES   PIECES
                                 P07975       1.44 DRIVE      PIECE
     2   019001     20-JAN-96    P07965       540 HDD         PIECE
                                 P07885       CD DRIVE        PIECE
     3   019002     27-JAN-96    P00001       1.44 FLOPPIES   PIECES
     4   046866     22-MAY-96    P07965       540 HDD         PIECE
                                 P07975       1.44 DRIVE      PIECE
```

Diagram 17.10 : Report output at Run Time

416 COMMERCIAL APPLICATION DEVELOPMENT IN DEVELOPER 2000

ARRANGING THE LAYOUT

We need to arrange the layout so that the output of the report looks as shown in the diagram 17.1.

1. Increase the size of the main surrounding frame *m_order_grpfr*.

2. Select *m_order_hdr*, *m_order_backlog_hdr* and *r_order* in the Object Navigator, go to the layout editor and move the selected frames down to make space for the heading.

3. Add a text and type the company name and address on top as done before. Change its font as mentioned below :

Fill Color	: Gray
Line Color	: black
Font	: Courier New
Font Style	: Bold
Size	: 9
Underline	: Off

4. Add another text below the text just added and type **"Order Backlog"**. Change its font as mentioned below :

Fill Color	: No Fill
Line Color	: No Line
Font	: Courier New
Font Style	: Bold
Size	: 11
Underline	: On

5. Create another text object with text '**Date :**' and attach following attributes to the them.

Fill Color	: No Fill
Line Color	: No Line
Font	: Courier New
Font Style	: Bold
Size	: 10
Underline	: Off

6. Create a field next to the text '**Date :**' to display current date with following properties.

Name	: F_curdt
Source	: &Current Date
Format Mask	: DD/MM/YY

CREATING A CONTROL BREAK REPORT 417

7. Add a text at the bottom and type "**Recd. and Checked by**" with following attributes and draw a line next to the text.

    Fill Color   : No Fill
    Line Color   : No Line
    Font   : Courier New
    Font Style   : Bold
    Size   : 9
    Underline   : Off

8. Select all the labels of the data columns. Change their fonts to as mentioned below :

    Font   : Courier New
    Font Style   : Bold
    Size   : 10
    Underline   : Off

The completed Layout will appear as shown in diagram 17.11.

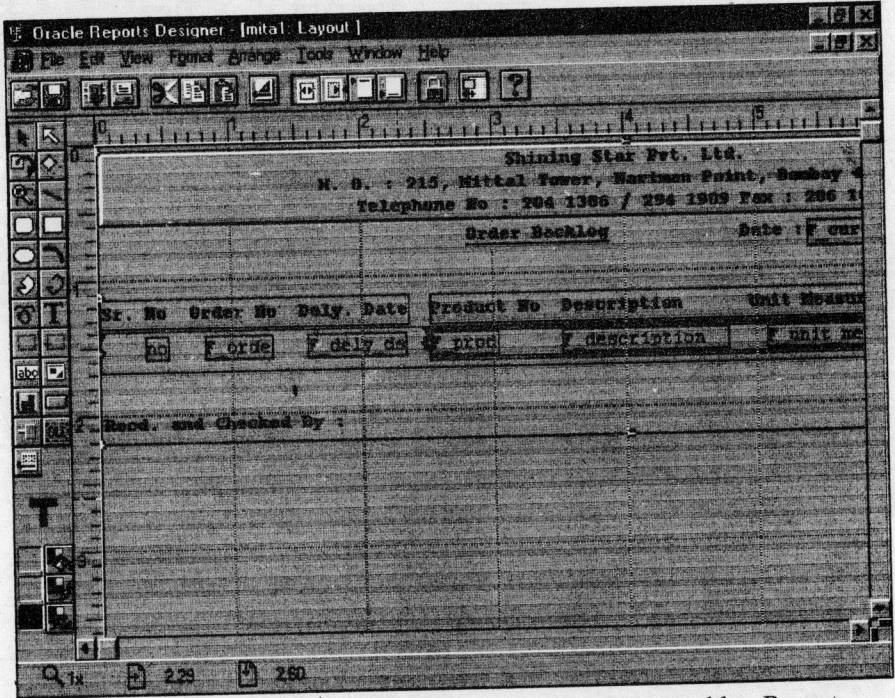

Diagram 17.11 : Complete Layout of the Order Backlog Report

418 COMMERCIAL APPLICATION DEVELOPMENT IN DEVELOPER 2000

9. Save and run the report and you will see the output as shown in the diagram 17.12.

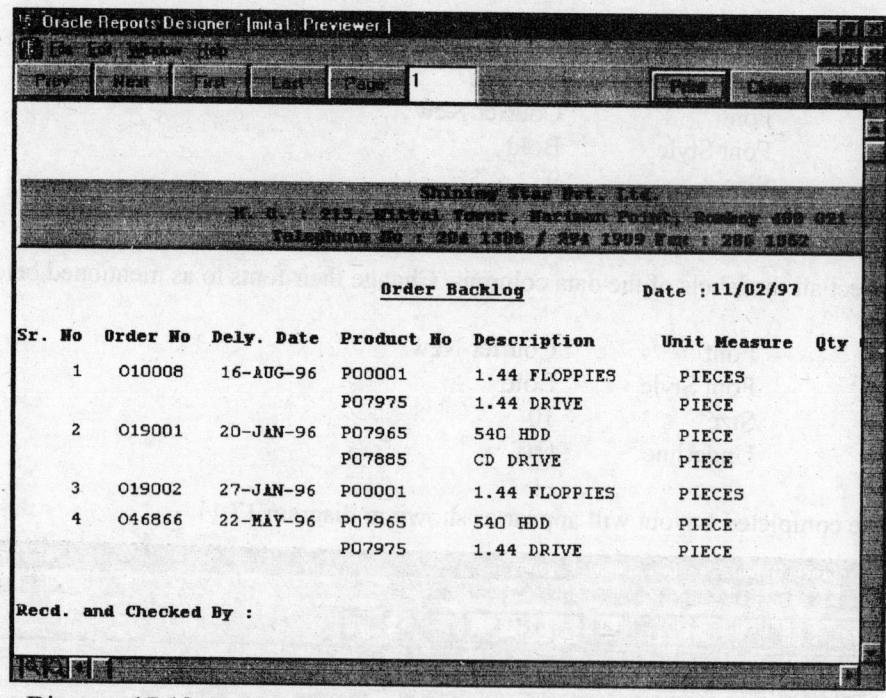

Diagram 17.12 : Report Output after completing the report Layout Settings

10. Select *m_order_grpfr*, *m_order_hdr*, *m_order_backlog_hdr*, *r_order* and *r_order_backlog* frames in Object Navigator, go to Layout Editor, select line color tool and select black color to display border around the data.

```
  Shining Star Pvt. Ltd.
  H. O. : 215, Mittal Tower, Nariman Point, Bombay 400 001
  Telephone No : 204 1388 / 204 1809 Fax : 202 2462
```

                    Order Backlog   Date : 11/02/97

Sr. No	Order No	Dely. Date	Product No	Description	Unit Measure	Qty
1	010008	16-AUG-96	P00001	1.44 FLOPPIES	PIECES	
			P07975	1.44 DRIVE	PIECE	
2	019001	20-JAN-96	P07965	540 HDD	PIECE	
			P07885	CD DRIVE	PIECE	
3	019002	27-JAN-96	P00001	1.44 FLOPPIES	PIECES	
4	046866	22-MAY-96	P07965	540 HDD	PIECE	
			P07975	1.44 DRIVE	PIECE	

Recd. and Checked By :

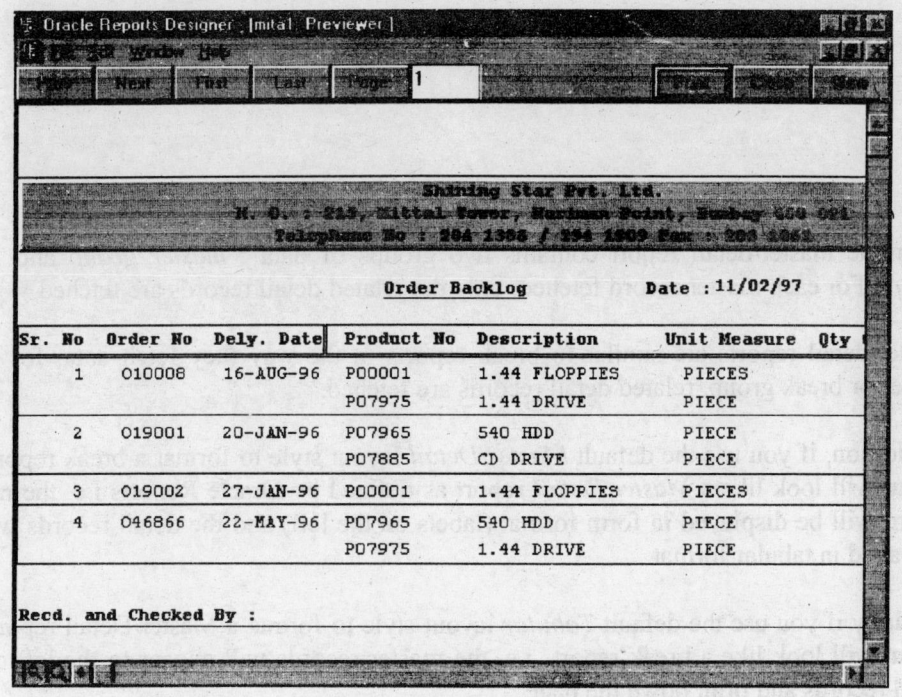

Diagram 17.13 : Report Output after Inserting Borders

18. MASTER/DETAIL REPORT

A simple master/detail report contains two groups of data : *master group* and *detail group*. For each master record fetched, only the related detail records are fetched.

Master/detail reports are similar to break reports in the way they fetch data; for every master or break group, related detail records are fetched.

In addition, if you use the default *Master/Detail* layout style to format a break report, the output will look like a *Master/Detail* report as defined by Oracle Reports i.e. the master record will be displayed in form format (labels on the left) and the detail records will be displayed in tabular format.

Similarly if you use the default *Tabular* layout style to format a Master/Detail report, the output will look like a break report i.e. the master records will appear to the left of the detail records and print down the page.

CONCEPTS

Break reports and master/detail reports can result in similar outputs but they require different data models objects. A break report uses <u>one</u> query and <u>two or more</u> groups, while a master/detail report uses <u>two</u> queries, each of which has one group.

A relationship between the two queries must be established. This relation is set by using a **Data Link**.

Data Link Object :
A *data link* object is a data model object which enables users to relate multiple queries. For a simple master/detail report, the users need to relate two queries using the primary and foreign keys of the tables from which you are selecting data. The Query with the primary key column i.e. the source for the master records is called the **Parent Query** and the Query with the foreign key column i.e. the source for the detail records is called the **Child Query**.

A primary key is a column for which each value uniquely identifies the record in which it is found. A foreign key is a column which contains the same values as the primary key for another table, and is used to reference records in that table.

Linking two tables via primary and foreign keys is similar to specifying a join condition. In fact, Oracle Reports defines a join by using the information in the data link object. The where clause for the join is added to the child query's SELECT statement at run time.

The join defined by a data link is an outer join i.e. in addition to returning all rows that satisfy the link's condition, an outer join returns all rows for the parent query that do not match a row from the child query.

Data Relationships :
Master/detail report is built using two queries related by a data link.

Layout :
Master/detail report uses a default master/detail layout style in which master records display across the page with the labels to the left of their fields and the detail records appear below the master records in standard tabular format.

You can also specify a maximum of 1 record per page to ensure that only one master record and its associated detail records are displayed per page of report output.

CREATING A MASTER/DETAIL REPORT

Focus :
Create a Master/Detail *'Sales Order Form Report'* from *'Sales_order'*, *'Sales_order_details'*, *'Client_master'*, *'Salesman_master'* and *'Product_master'* tables.

In this exercise, we will go step-by-step to create a report, as shown in diagram 18.1. You will learn to link 2 queries using Data Link to generate Master/Detail report.

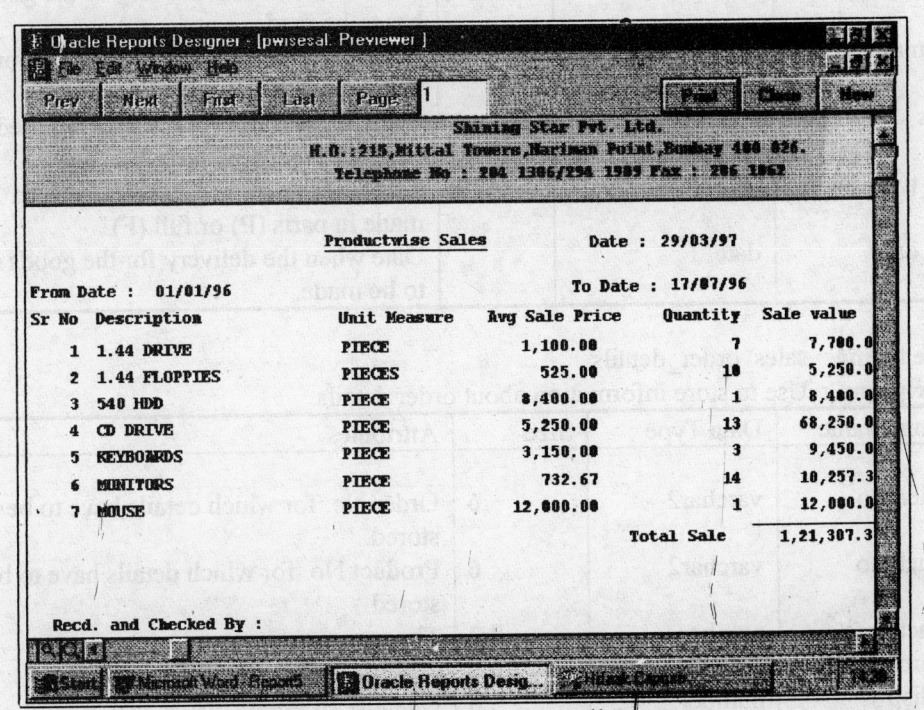

Diagram : 18.1 : Master / Detail Report

The definitions of the tables used are as mentioned below :

Table Name : product_master
Description : stores information about products supplied by the company.

Column Name	Data Type	Size	Column Description
product_no	varchar2	6	Access key via which we shall seek data.
description	varchar2	25	Description of the product
unit_measure	varchar2	10	Unit by which the product is measured.
qty_on_hand	number	8	Quantity which is available in the stock.
reorder_lvl	number	8	Quantity level when the stock should be re-ordered.
cost_price	number	8,2	Cost price of the product.
selling_price	number	8,2	Selling price of the product.

Table Name : sales_order (Master)
Description : Use to store information about orders placed by the clients.

Column Name	Data Type	Size	Attributes
s_order_no	varchar2	6	Unique primary key allotted to each order.
s_order_date	date		Date on which the order is placed.
client_no	varchar2	6	Client No., who places the order.
dely_addr	varchar2	30	Address where the delivery of the goods has to be made.
salesman_no	varchar2	6	Salesman No., who gets the order from the client.
status	varchar2	2	Order Status (In Process IP, FullFilled FP, Not Processed NP)
dely_type	char	1	To note whether the delivery is to be made in parts (P) or full (F).
dely_date	date		Date when the delivery for the goods is to be made.

Table Name : sales_order_details
Description : Use to store information about order details.

Column Name	Data Type	Size	Attributes
s_order_no	varchar2	6	Order No. for which details have to be stored.
product_no	varchar2	6	Product No. for which details have to be stored.
product_rate	number	8,2	The rate agreed upon.
qty_ordered	number	8	Quantity of goods ordered.
qty_disp	number	8	Quantity of goods dispatched.

MASTER DETAIL REPORT **423**

Table Name : client_master
Description : Use to store information about clients.

Column Name	Data Type	Size	Column Description
client_no	varchar2	6	Access key via which we shall seek data.
name	varchar2	20	client's name
address1	varchar2	30	First line in the client's address.
address2	varchar2	30	Second line in the client's address.
city	varchar2	15	City in which the client is located.
state	varchar2	15	State in which the client is located.
pincode	number	6	pin code
bal_due	number	10,2	Balance amount payable by the client.

Table Name : salesman_master
Description : Use to store information about salesman.

Column Name	Data Type	Size	Column Description
salesman_no	varchar2	6	Access key via which we shall seek data.
name	varchar2	20	salesman's name
address1	varchar2	30	First line in the client's address.
address2	varchar2	30	Second line in the client's address.
city	varchar2	15	City in which the client is located.
state	varchar2	15	State in which the client is located.
pincode	number	6	pin code
sal_amt	number	8,2	
tgt_to_get	number	6,2	
ytd_sales	number	6,2	
Remarks	varchar2	60	

To create the report shown in the Diagram 18.1, we will follow following steps :
- Create a new report definition by creating 2 queries for master and detail tables and link them.
- Create formula and summary columns.
- Specify a default report layout.
- Arrange the Layout.
- Save and run the report.

CREATING THE REPORT DEFINITION

Create two queries namely and *Q_detail*. Link both these queries add a data link defining *G_master*, the master group, as the parent of *G_detail* as shown in the Diagram 18.3, the detail query, represented by the line pointing from the column *s_order_no* of *sales_order* to the column *s_order_no* of table *sales_order_details*.

424 COMMERCIAL APPLICATION DEVELOPMENT USING ORACLE 7, DEVELOPER 2000

Queries Object :
1. Create a query named *Q_master* with the following SELECT statement:

    select   s_order_no, s_order_date, dely_date, dely_type,
                client_master.name "Client Name", Dely_Addr,
                salesman_master.name name "Salesman Name"
    from   sales_order, salesman_master, client_master
    where sales_order.client_no = client_master.client_no and
                sales_order.salesman_no = salesman_master.salesman_no

2. Create a second query approximately two inches to the right of the *Q_master*. Name the query as *Q_detail*, and enter the select statement as shown below :

    select   s_order_no, description,
                unit_measure, product_rate, qty_ordered
    from   sales_order_details, product_master
    where sales_order_details.product_no = product_master.product_no

The completed Data model editor will be as shown in the diagram 18.2.

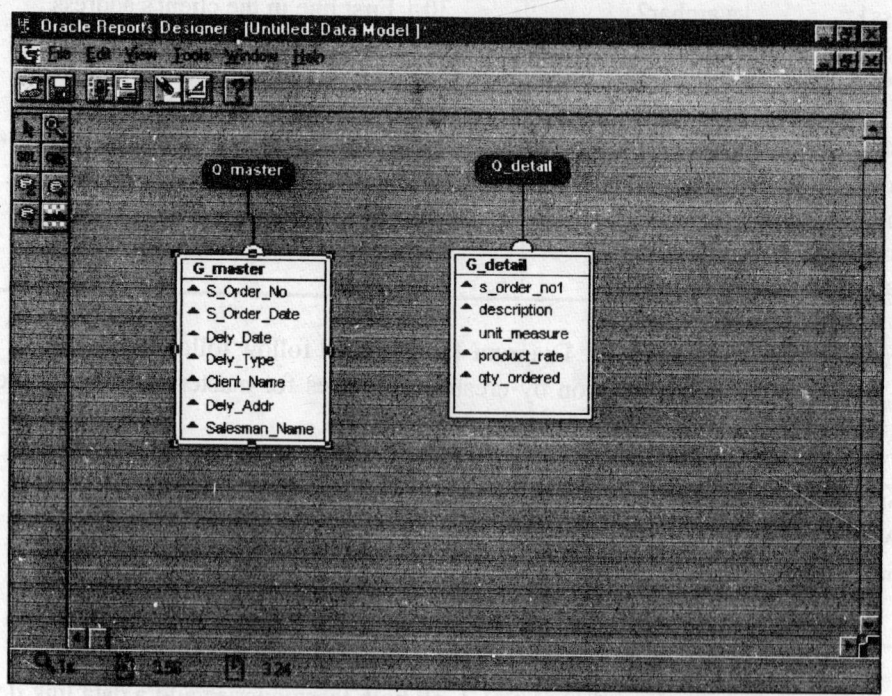

Diagram 18.2 : Data Model editor After creating two queries

Data Link Object :

3. Select the *Data Link* tool (icon with sign of two intersecting ellipses) and click-and-hold on the *s_order_no* column of the *G_master* group. Drag the mouse pointer to the *s_order_no* column of the *G_detail* group and release. A data link (arrow) will appear in the editor as shown in diagram 18.3. Notice the copy of the *s_order_no* column at the bottom of the master group, and the copy of the *s_order_no* column in the detail query.

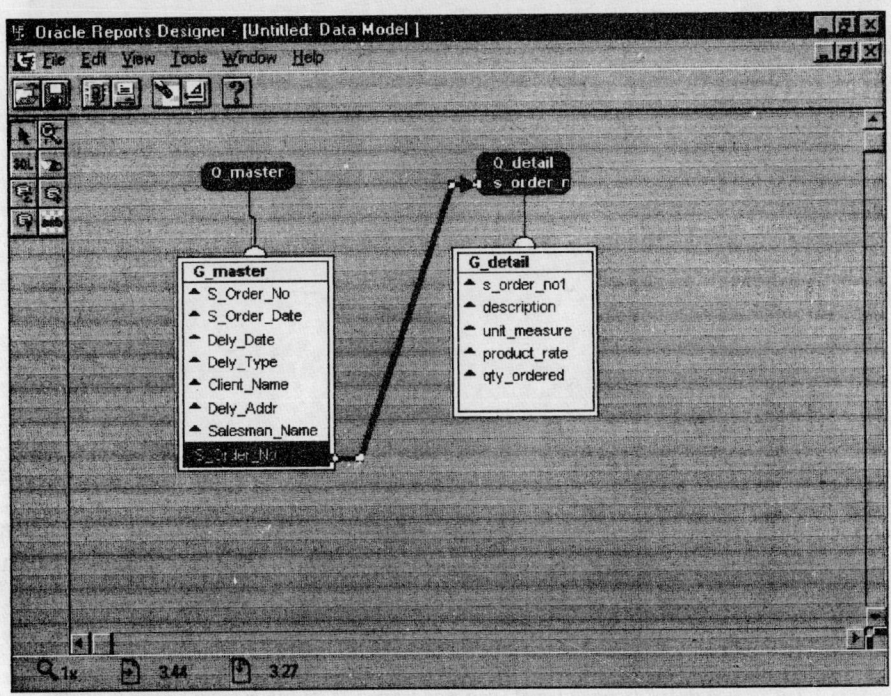

Diagram : 18.3 : Linking Queries using a Data Link Object

4. Open the Data Link property sheet by double-clicking on the data link. Examine the settings in the property sheet as shown in diagram 18.4). *G_master* is identified as the parent query, while *Q_detail* is listed as the child query.

The link / join is on the *s_order_no* column. The link is established by using a *where* clause and an *equality* sign. Notice that *where* already appears in the *SQL Clause* field. *where* is the default clause used in master/detail relationships. You can replace *where* with other SQL clauses such as *having* and *start with*.

Finally, notice that an *equal* sign (=) appears in the *Condition* field. An equality (i.e., table1.columnname = table2.columnname) is the default condition for master/detail relationships defined via a data link. You can replace the equal sign with any other supported conditional operator (to see what's supported, click on the field).

In terms of the data, the order header information make up the master record which is printed once for the products ordered in the sales order.

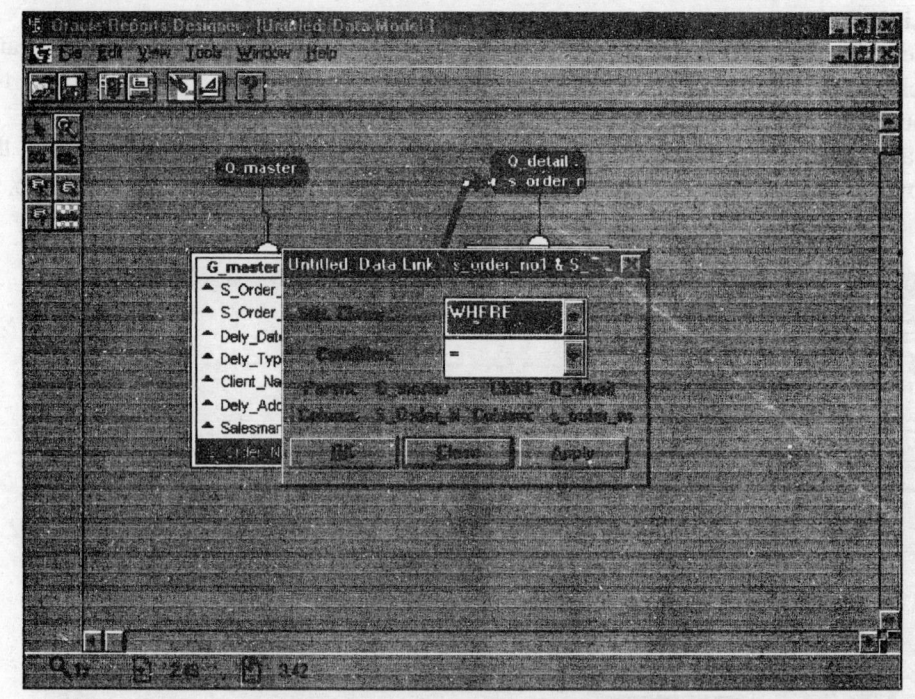

426 COMMERCIAL APPLICATION DEVELOPMENT USING ORACLE 7, DEVELOPER 2000

Diagram 18.4 : Data Link Properties

Linking the group *G_master* and the query *Q_detail* via the *s_order_no* columns in both the queries is analogous to writing both queries as the single query shown below :

    select   sales_order.s_order_no, s_order_date, dely_date,
                 dely_type, client_master.name "Client Name", dely_addr,
                 salesman_master.name "Salesman Name", description,
                 unit_measure, product_rate, qty_ordered
    from   sales_order, salesman_master, client_master ,
                 sales_order_details, product_master
    where   sales_order.s_order_no = sales_order_details.s_order_no and
                 sales_order.client_no = client_master.client_no and
                 sales_order.salesman_no = salesman_master.salesman_no and
                 sales_order_details.product_no = product_master.product_no (+)

CREATING FORMULA AND SUMMARY COLUMNS

After creating the required queries and linking them, we need to create the necessary formula and summary columns.

Formula Column :
1. Create a formula column in *G_detail* group, for *amount*, right at the bottom. Set the properties and attach the formula through program unit editor as follows :

    Name   : CF_amount
    Formula   : **function CF_amountFormula return Number is**
          begin
              return :product_rate * :qty_ordered ;
          end;

2. The dely_type field in the sales_order table holds 'F' for Full delivery and 'P' for part delivery. We need to change the values and display 'Full' if the value dely_type is 'F' and 'Part' if the value is 'P'. This can be done by creating a formula column that sets the value based on the value of the delt_type field.

Create a formula column in *G_master* group, immediately after the dely_type column. Set the properties and attach the formula through program unit editor as follows :

    Name   : CF_dely_type
    Formula   : **function CF_dely_typeFormula return Char is**
          begin
            if :dely_type = 'F' then
              return 'Full';
            else
              return 'Part';
            end if;
          end;

3. Create a summary column in the *G_detail* group for serial nos. The summary column must be the first column in that group. Change its properties as mentioned below :

    Name   : CS_srno
    Function   : Count
    Source   : Description
    Reset At   : G_master
    Data type   : Number
    Width   : 3

Note : As we want to number the products for every order. Reset At property is set to *G_master* as the value of *CS_srno* should be reset to zero for every new order i.e. for every new value of *G_master*.

4. Along with all the columns defined above, we also need total amount for the entire order. Create a summary column in *G_master* (as total amount will come only once for every order document). Attach following properties to the column.

Name	: CS_total
Function	: Sum
Source	: CF_amount
Reset At	: G_master
Data type	: Number
Width	: 10

At this point the *Data Model* editor will be as shown in the diagram 18.5.

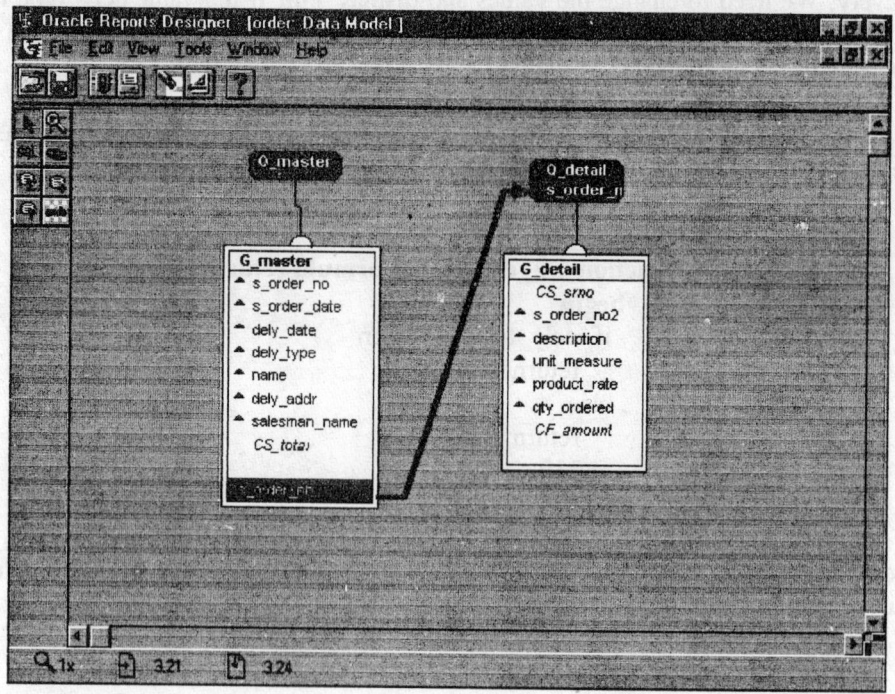

Diagram 18.5 : Data Model Editor with Formula and Summary Columns

DEFAULT LAYOUT

1. Select **Tools**, **Default Layout** (or the Default Layout tool) and specify the style as **Master/Detail**.

MASTER DETAIL REPORT **429**

2. Click on **Data/Selection** tab. Column *s_order_no* in the *G_detail* group must not be displayed in the report. Deselect this column by clicking on the *s_order_no*. Similarly deselect the *dely_date* field.

3. Make the following changes in the labels and widths of the columns and click on OK to accept the changes. You will get a layout shown in diagram 18.6.

Column	Label	Width
s_order_no	Order No :	
s_order_date	Date :	
dely_date	Delivery Date :	
cf_dely_type	Delivery In :	
dely_addr	Delivery Address :	
cs_total	Total (in Rs.) :	12
cs_srno	Sr. No.	3
unit_measure	Unit Of Measure	7
product_rate	Rate (in Rs.)	7
qty_ordered	Quantity	7
cf_amount	Amount (in Rs.)	12

Click on OK. The completed layout editor will be displayed as shown in diagram 18.6.

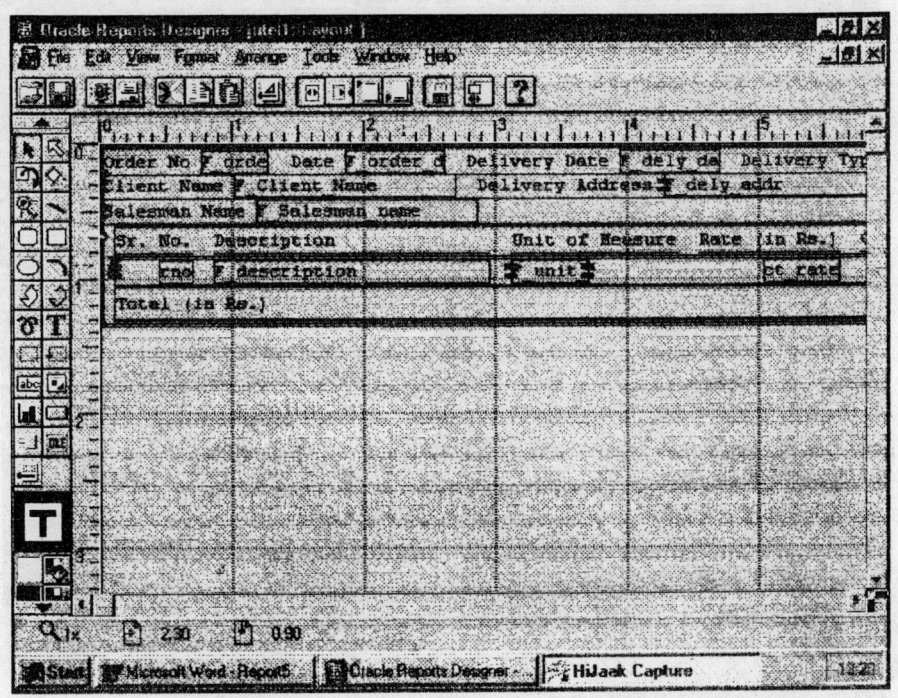

Diagram 18.6 : Layout Editor After creating default layout

Notice that the master/detail default layout creates master records across the page with the labels to the left of their fields, and the detail records below the master records in standard tabular format.

4. Save the report as *saleord.rdf* and run to see the output.

ARRANGING THE LAYOUT

1. Align the fields and labels, change the label text and their fonts. change the widths of the fields to ensure that they fit in the layout.

2. Select *r_master, m_detail_hdr, r_detail* from the Object Navigator. Then go to the Layout Editor, select the Line Color tool and select black color (for border) as done before in tabular and control break reports.

3. The length of the *dely_addr* field is 60. Since the display size is not enough to hold 60 characters, we need to inform Oracle Reports that if the text is larger than the display length, then the size of the field must be expanded vertically.

To do so, open the property sheet of *dely_addr* field, click on the **General Layout** tab and set the **Vertical Sizing** as **Expand** as shown in diagram 18.7.

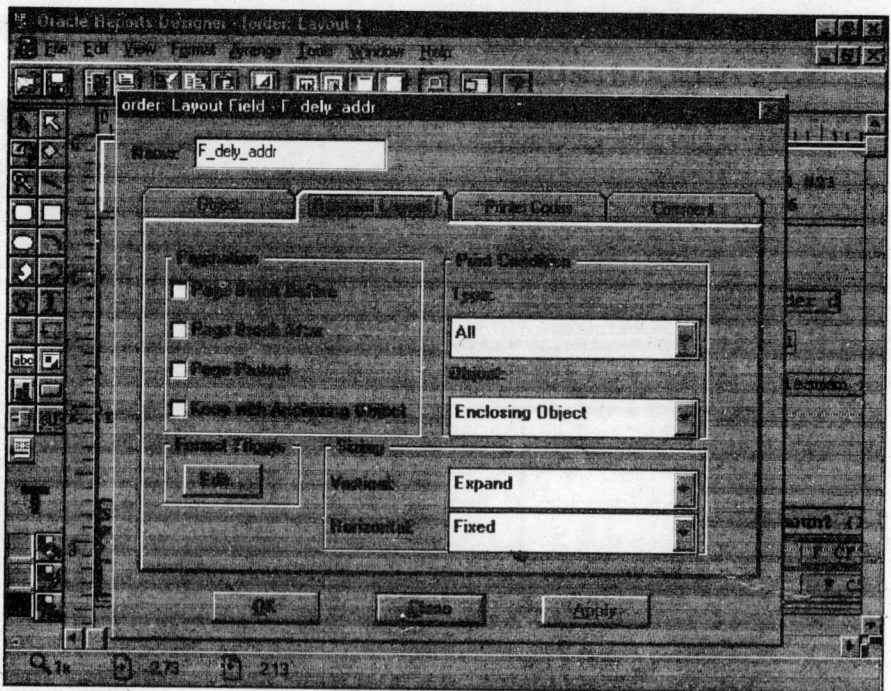

Diagram 18.7 : Setting the Vertical Sizing property for dely_addr

MASTER DETAIL REPORT **431**

The completed layout will be as shown in the diagram 18.8. Note that the dely_addr field displays = sign. It indicates that the field is expandable.

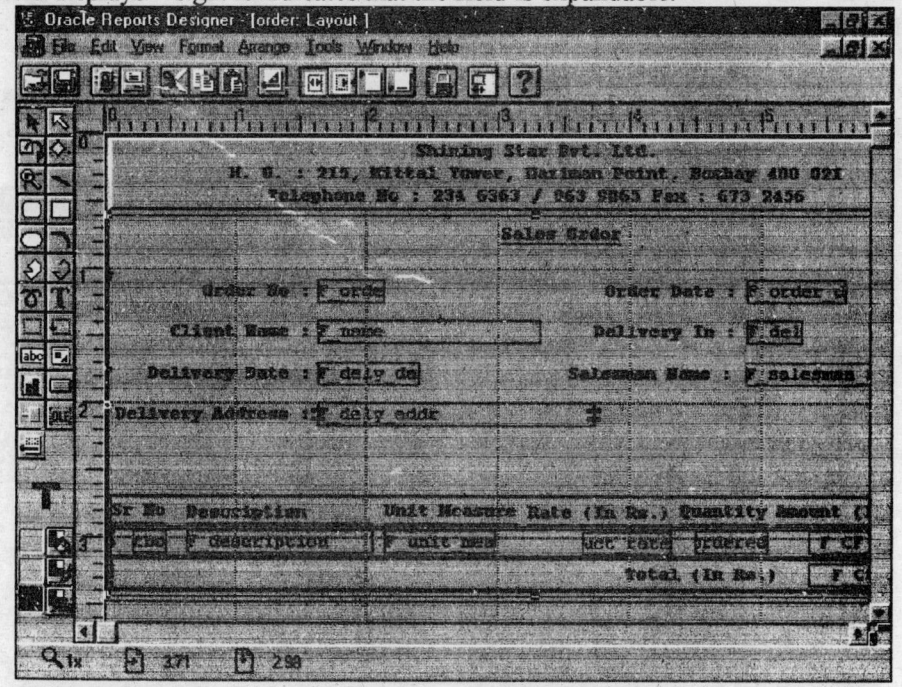

Diagram 18.8 : Arranging the layout

4. Run the report. The report output will be as shown in diagram 18.9.

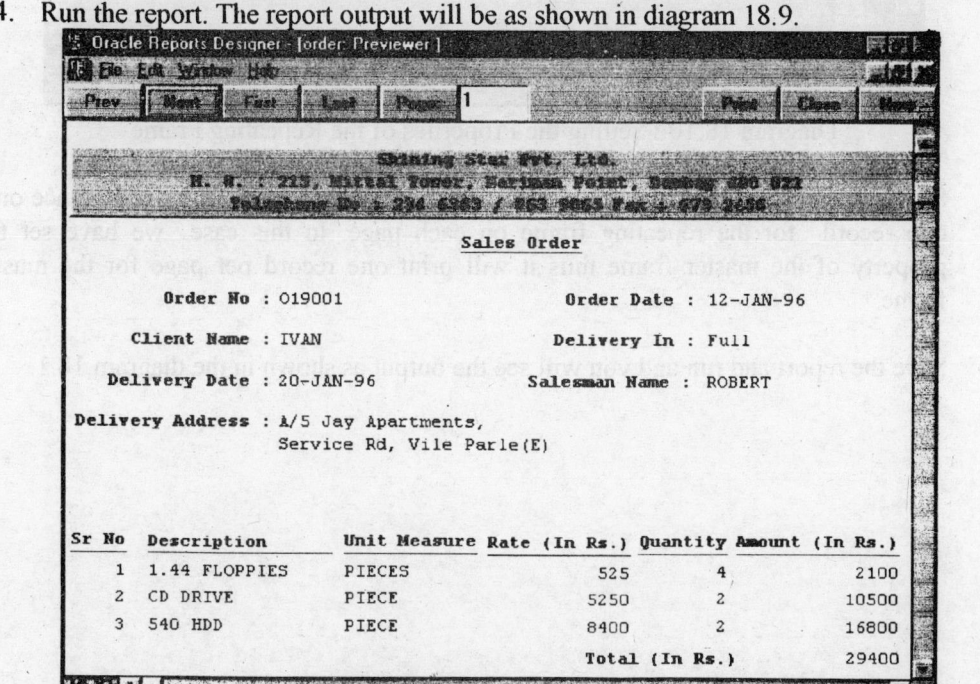

Diagram 18.9 : Report Output

5. The report output, displays multiple sales orders on the same page. The system must display only one sales order on a page. To achieve we need to set the properties as follows :

   Open the property sheet of repeating frame *r_master* and set the **Maximum Records per Page** as '1' as shown in diagram 18.10. Accept the changes in the property sheet by clicking on OK.

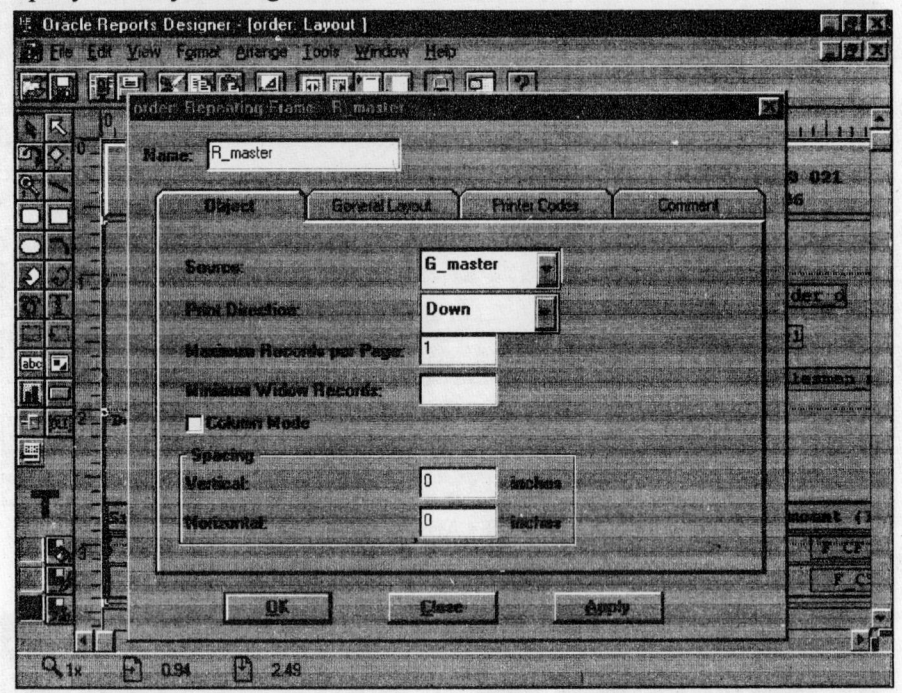

   Diagram 18.10 : Setting the Properties of the Repeating Frame

   Specifying a maximum of one record per page informs Oracle Reports to place only one record for the repeating frame on each page. In this case we have set the property of the master frame thus it will print one record per page for the master frame.

6. Save the report and run and you will see the output as shown in the diagram 18.1.

Accepting Parameter Values :

In the current example, the user will rarely view all the sales orders. Thus we need to accept s_order_no as the parameter and retrieve the data based on the s_order_no entered by the user. The steps are as follows :

1. Expand the *Data Model* node in the object navigator. One of the nodes under the *Data Model* node will be *User Parameters* node.

2. Select the User Parameters node and click on the **Create** button on the vertical toolbar to create a user parameter for passing *s_order_no*. A default parameter with name P_1 will be created.

3. Double-click on the icon next to the parameter P_1 to open up its property sheet. Specify the *Parameter Name* as *P_s_order_no*. Set the *Data Type* of the parameter as *Char* and *Size* as *6*. Click on **OK**.

4. Now that the parameter fields have been defined. They must be used in the query such that the query becomes conditional. This can be done by invoking the Data Model Editor. One way is to access from the **Tools** menu item. Double click on the *Q_master* object. The query definition screen is invoked.

5. Add the clause **and sales_order.s_order_no like :p_s_order_no** to current select statement.

6. Run the report. The Parameter form displays one more parameter i.e. *P_s_order_no*.

The values of the parameter *P_s_order_no* are dependent on the value of *s_order_no* in the *sales_order* table. Thus the parameter form can be made more user friendly by providing list of values for the parameter. The steps in creating a list of values for the parameters are as follows :

1. Go to the Object Navigator and open the property sheet of parameter *P_s_order_no*. Click on the **Data / Selection** Tab. It displays the screen as shown in diagram 18.11.

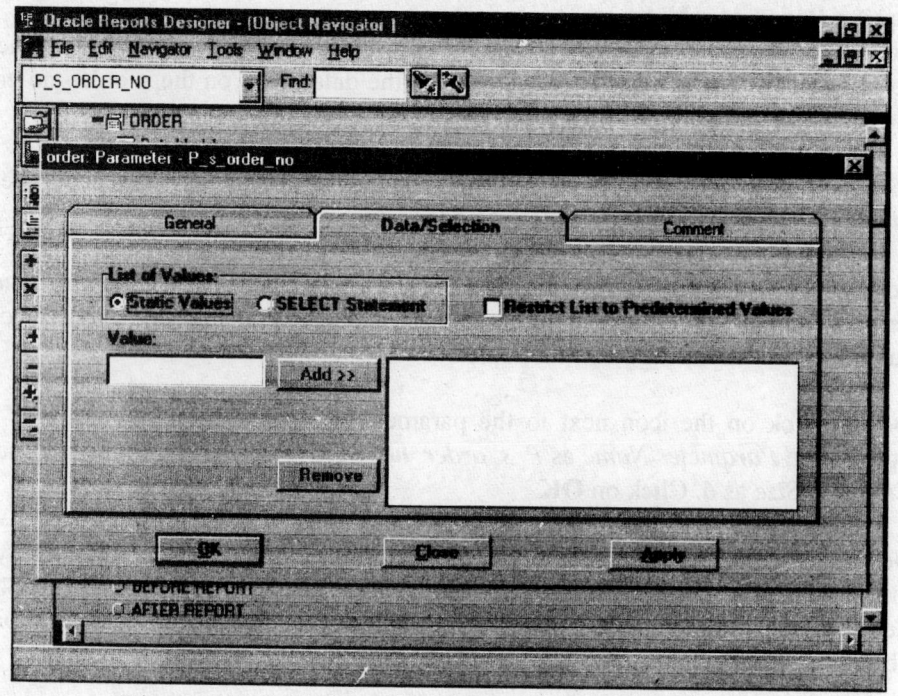

434 COMMERCIAL APPLICATION DEVELOPMENT USING ORACLE 7, DEVELOPER 2000

Diagram 18.11 : The Data / Selection tab of the Parameter

Providing List of values for the parameters :

2. The list of values can either be :

- **Static values** i.e. values that are hard coded in the report.
- Values from a **select statement**.

Since the list of values in the current example are based on column values we need to click on **Select Statement** radio button.

3. Enter the select statement as follows :

   select s_order_no from sales_order

4. Since the list of order number can be very large, the user must be allowed to either select from the list or enter the values i.e. the list must not be restricted to pre-determined values.

   Uncheck the check box for **Restrict List to Predetermined Values**. The completed screen will be as shown in diagram 18.12.

MASTER DETAIL REPORT 435

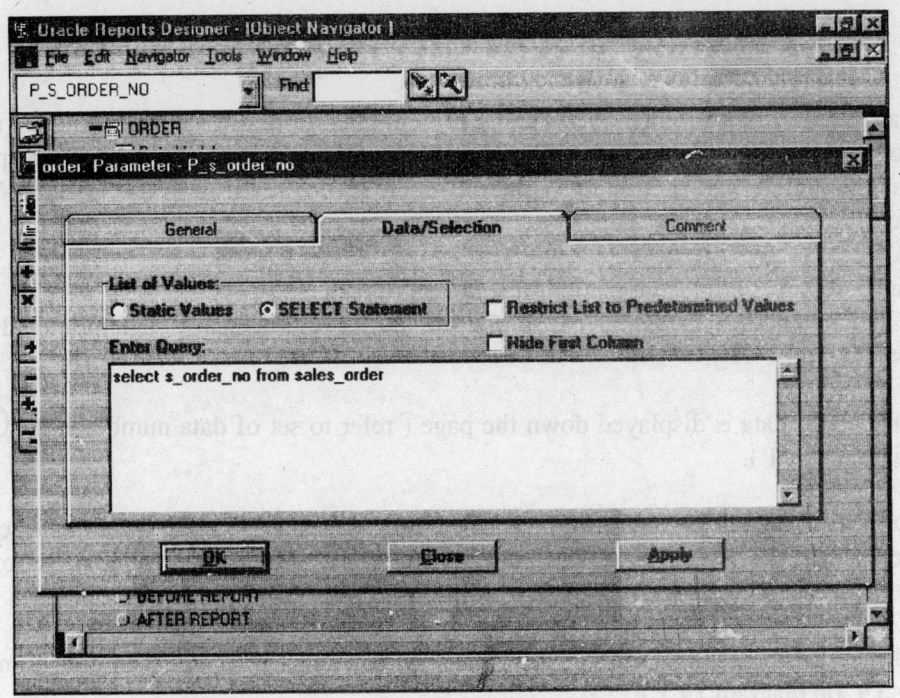

Diagram 18.12 : Completed Data / Selection Tab

5. Save and run the report. The parameter form will be displayed as shown in diagram 18.13.

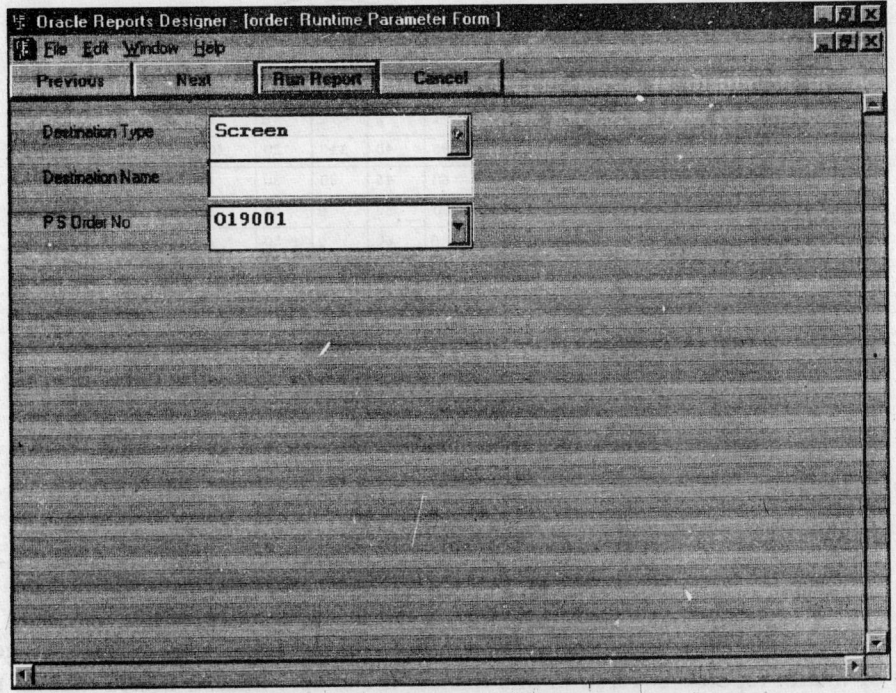

Diagram 18.13 : Parameter form displayed at Runtime

19. CREATING A MATRIX REPORT

A matrix report is a summary report that presents the desired data with headings across the top and the left side, the data in the middle like a spreadsheet. The totals are displayed across the bottom and right side. A matrix report is also referred to as **"CROSS-TAB"** report.

A matrix report is a cross-tabulation of four sets of data :
1. One set of data is displayed across the page (refer to set of data numbered as ① in diagram 19.1).

2. One set of data is displayed down the page (refer to set of data numbered as ② in diagram 19.1).

3. One set of data is the cross-product, which determines all possible locations where the across and down data relate and places a cell in those locations (refer to set of data numbered as ③ in diagram 19.1).

4. One set of data is displayed as the **"filler"** of the cells (refer to set of data numbered as ④ in diagram 19.1).

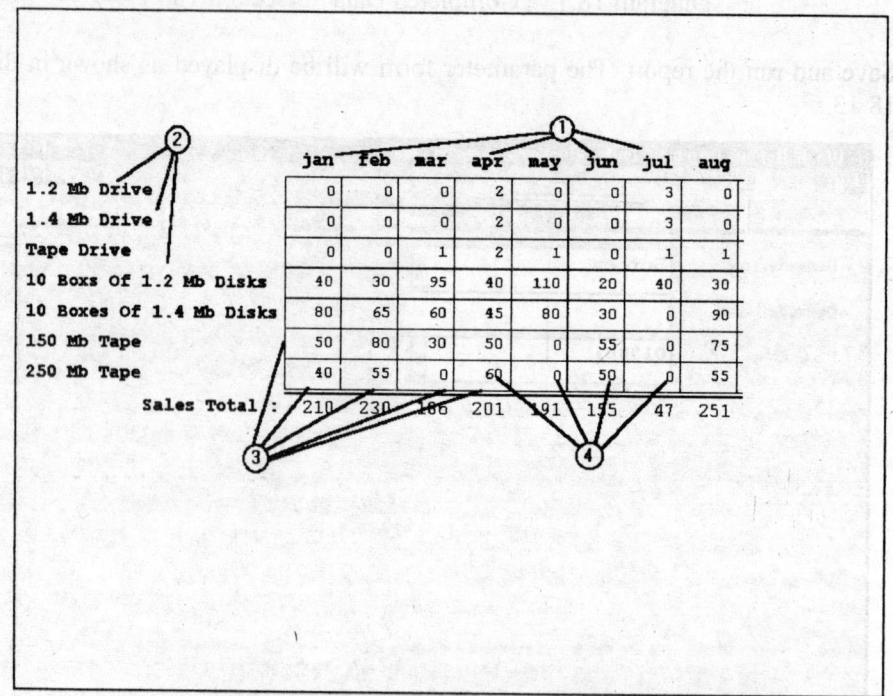

	jan	feb	mar	apr	may	jun	jul	aug
1.2 Mb Drive	0	0	0	2	0	0	3	0
1.4 Mb Drive	0	0	0	2	0	0	3	0
Tape Drive	0	0	1	2	1	0	1	1
10 Boxs Of 1.2 Mb Disks	40	30	95	40	110	20	40	30
10 Boxes Of 1.4 Mb Disks	80	65	60	45	80	30	0	90
150 Mb Tape	50	80	30	50	0	55	0	75
250 Mb Tape	40	55	0	60	0	50	0	55
Sales Total :	210	230	186	201	191	155	47	251

Diagram 19.1 : Sets Of data used in Matrix Report

With Oracle Reports, you can create many different matrix reports. The four general types of matrix reports covered in this manual are simple matrix, nested matrix, multi-query matrix with break, and matrix break.

Before discussing the particulars of matrix building, let's look at some of the issues involved in the matrix reports :

- Matrix Data Model
- Matrix Layout

MATRIX DATA MODEL
In building matrix data model, you should consider the following:

1. Number of queries
2. Group structure
3. Summary settings

Number Of Queries :
Although a matrix report always require at least four groups, they can be built with any number of queries. If you build a matrix report with only one query (usually the most efficient structure), you must create at least three groups manually in addition to the one created by default. If you build a matrix report with multiple (three or more) queries, you still need to create at least one group.

You can use two types of query structures for matrix data model.

One-Query Matrix :
One advantage to a one-query data model is that the resulting report is generally more efficient than a report based on a multi-query data model.

Multi-Query Matrix :
You may consider using a multi-query data model, as it often has simple queries and will be easier to maintain than the equivalent one-query data model. In addition, a multi-query data model is required for some types of matrices (e.g., some nested matrix reports).

Group Structure :
Matrix reports are built with four or more groups :
Two or more dimension groups :
   Dimension groups are contained within the cross product group. In the layout, the information in at least one group goes across the page, and the information in at least one group goes down the page, forming a grid. The information in these groups is sometimes referred to as "*Matrix Labels*", as they provide column and row labels for the matrix (refer to the group numbered as a in diagram 19.2).

One or more cross product groups :
   The cross product group represents all possible combinations of the values of the dimension groups. In the layout, the cross product group is represented by the intersection of the repeating frames for the across and down dimension groups. When the report is run, it expands, and each instance of data intersection becomes a separate cell. The rectangles are cells, and they show where each combination. (refer to the group numbered as b in diagram 19.2).

One cell, or filler group :

The cell group contains the actual information that is represented by the cells of the cross product. For each intersection of the values of the dimension groups (cell), the cell group contains zero, one, or multiple values. When the report is run, these values appear in the appropriate cells (refer to the group numbered as (c) in diagram 19.2).

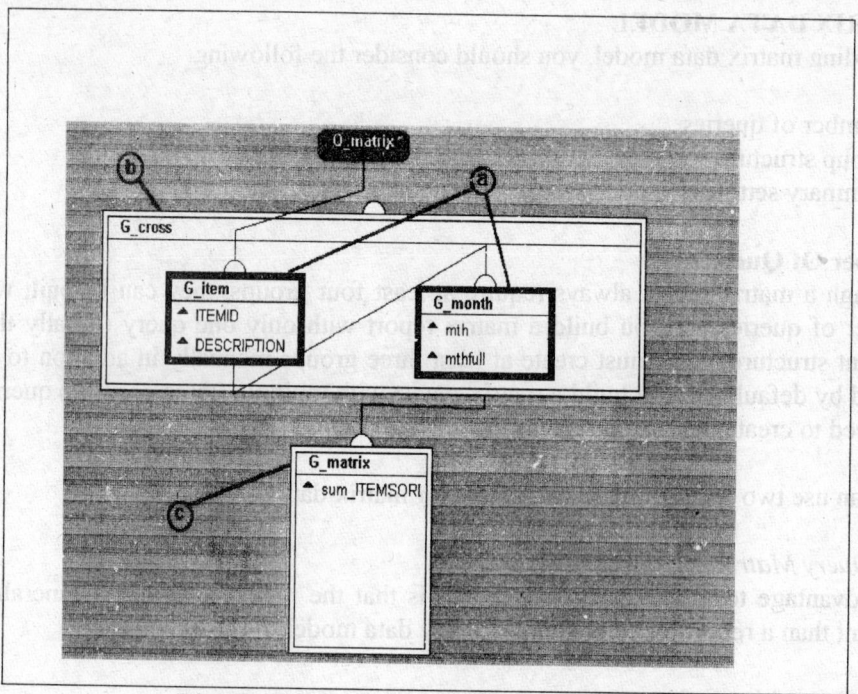

Diagram 19.2 : Groups used in Matrix Report

Summaries and Product Order :

Creating a summary for a matrix requires more information than creating a summary for other kinds of reports. While creating summary columns for the matrix, you need to indicate the following :

a) The frequency of the summary. The frequency specifies the dimension groups for which to compute the summary.

b) The order in which to compute the summary. The order specifies how to traverse the matrix in calculating the summary (top to bottom or left to right).

In Oracle Reports, you specify this information using the Product Order setting for your summary. All summary fields that are owned by the cross product group require that a Product Order be specified.

Matrix Layout :
A matrix layout model must consist of the following layout objects :
1. At least two repeating frames, one with a Print Direction of Down and one with a Print Direction of Across.

2. Several group, header, and footer (if summaries are included) frames.

3. A matrix object created for the cross product group, inside of which are the cells of the matrix.

4. Boilerplate for each column and row of values, as well as for summaries

Note : Displaying the boilerplate is optional, but Oracle Reports will generate it by default.

Matrix / Cross Product Object :
The matrix object defines the intersection of at least two repeating frames. The repeating frames are the dimensions of the matrix and the matrix object contains the field that will hold the **filler** or values of the cell group. You need one matrix object for each pair of intersecting repeating frames in the layout. One of the repeating frames must have a Print Direction of Down and the other must have a Print Direction of Across in order to form a matrix. Matrix object can be created by using the **cross product** button (shown above) on the toolbar.

Matrix reports are different from tabular reports because the number of columns is not known in advance; i.e., the number of columns in your report is not determined by the number of columns you specify in your SELECT statement plus the columns you create yourself. The number of columns in your report depends on the number of values contained in the columns providing the horizontal labels.

Focus : To create a simple one query matrix report of *Productwise Monthly Sales* shown in the diagram 19.3, using the tables listed below. The report should show the data based on the year entered by the user (i.e. create a user parameter for year). Enter test data for a full year in the tables listed below.

	Jan	Feb	Apr	May	Total
1.44 DRIVE	0	0	0	6	6
1.44 FLOPPIES	14	10	0	10	34
540 HDD	2	0	0	1	3
CD DRIVE	2	1	0	0	3
KEYBOARDS	0	3	0	0	3
MONITORS	0	4	2	0	6
MOUSE	0	0	1	0	1
Total :	18	18	3	17	56

Diagram 19.3 : Matrix Report

The definitions of the tables used are as mentioned below :

Table Name : product_master
Description : stores information about products supplied by the company.

Column Name	Data Type	Size	Column Description
product_no	varchar2	6	Access key via which we shall seek data.
description	varchar2	25	Description of the product
unit_measure	varchar2	10	Unit by which the product is measured.
qty_on_hand	number	8	Quantity which is available in the stock.
reorder_lvl	number	8	Quantity level when the stock should be re-ordered.
cost_price	number	8,2	Cost price of the product.
selling_price	number	8,2	Selling price of the product.

Table Name : sales_order (Master)
Description : Use to store information about orders placed by the clients.

Column Name	Data Type	Size	Attributes
s_order_no	varchar2	6	Unique primary key allotted to each order.
s_order_date	date		Date on which the order is placed.
client_no	varchar2	6	Client No., who places the order.
dely_addr	varchar2	30	Address where the delivery of the goods has to be made.
salesman_no	varchar2	6	Salesman No., who gets the order from the client.
status	varchar2	2	Order Status (In Process IP, FullFilled FP, Not Processed NP)
dely_type	char	1	To note whether the delivery is to be made in parts (P) or full (F).
dely_date	date		Date when the delivery for the goods is to be made.

Table Name : sales_order_details
Description : Use to store information about order details.

Column Name	Data Type	Size	Attributes
s_order_no	varchar2	6	Order No. for which details have to be stored.
product_no	varchar2	6	Product No. for which details have to be stored.
product_rate	number	8,2	The rate agreed upon.
qty_ordered	number	8	Quantity of goods ordered.
qty_disp	number	8	Quantity of goods dispatched.

Solution :
Steps to create the report shown in the Diagram 19.3 are as mentioned below :
- Create a new report.
- Create a query.
- Create Groups.
- Create Default Layout.
- Creating Summary columns.
- Adding zeroes in place of non-existent values.
- Adding a grid.
- Creating user parameter.

1. Create a new report and connect to the database.

   Creating Query :
2. Open the Data Model Editor and create a query named *Q_sales* with a select statement as follows :

   ```
   select     product_master.description,
              sum( sales_order_details.qty_ordered) "Quantity",
              to_char(sales_order.s_order_date,'mm') mth,
              to_char(sales_order.s_order_date,'Mon') mthfull
   from       sales_order_details, product_master, sales_order
   where      ( sales_order_details.s_order_no =   sales_order.s_order_no) and
              ( sales_order_details.product_no = product_master.product_no)
   group by   to_char(sales_order.s_order_date,'mm'),
              product_master.description,
              to_char( sales_order.s_order_date,'Mon')
   order by   to_char(sales_order.s_order_date,'mm') asc
   ```

   Here, *'to_char(sales_order.s_order_date ,'mm') mth'* is used to order by months i.e. month numbers and *'to_char(sales_order.s_order_date ,'Mon')'* is used to display months in character format. Both the formats are used here since you cannot order by month names (in characters) as it will give *'Apr'* before *'Jan'*. The completed Data Model editor will be displayed as shown in diagram 19.4.

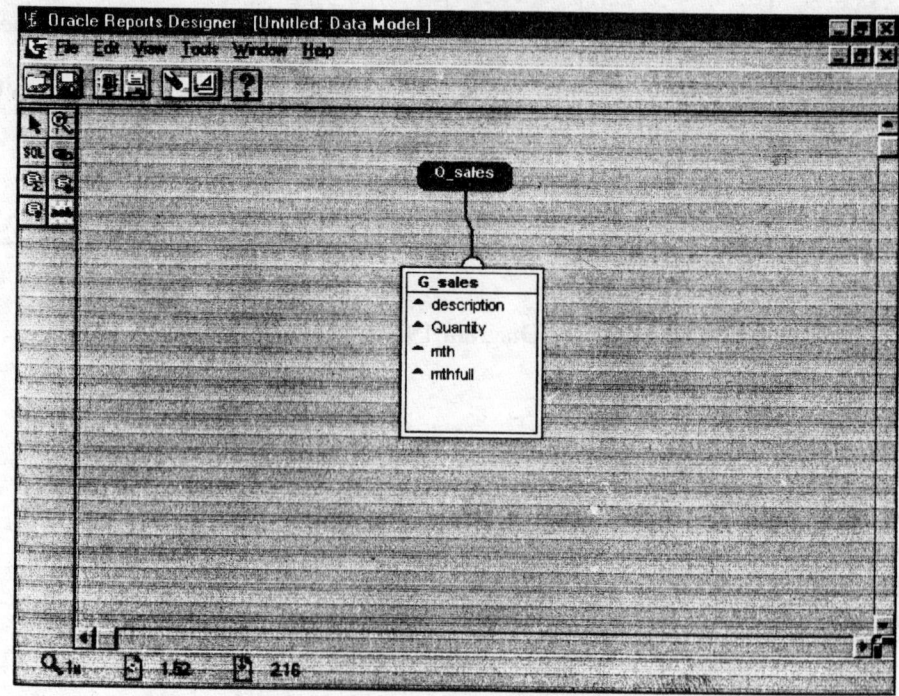

   Diagram 19.4 : Query and Group for the Matrix Report

CREATING A MATRIX REPORT **443**

Creating groups

3. Drag *G_sales* down an inch or two.

4. Drag the *description* column above and to the left of *G_sales* to create a new group. Rename the new group *G_product*.

5. Drag the *mth* column above and to the right of *G_sales* to create a new group. Rename the new group *G_month*.

6. Drag the *mthfull* column above and add it to the *G_month* group below the *mth* column.

Note : If column mthfull is the first column in the group, then the sorting within the group will be in the ascending order of *mthfull* i.e. month in character form. Thus we need to ensure that the mthfull column is the second column in the *G_month* group.

7. Select the **Cross Product tool** from the Tool palette. Draw a box around *G_product* and *G_month* to create the third group. Name this new group *G_Cross*. *G_Cross* is the cross product group in the matrix.

   G_product and *G_month* are now the child groups of the cross product. *G_sales*, which is not in the cross product group, remains a child group below the cross product in the group hierarchy. At this point the Data Model Editor will look as shown in the diagram 19.5.

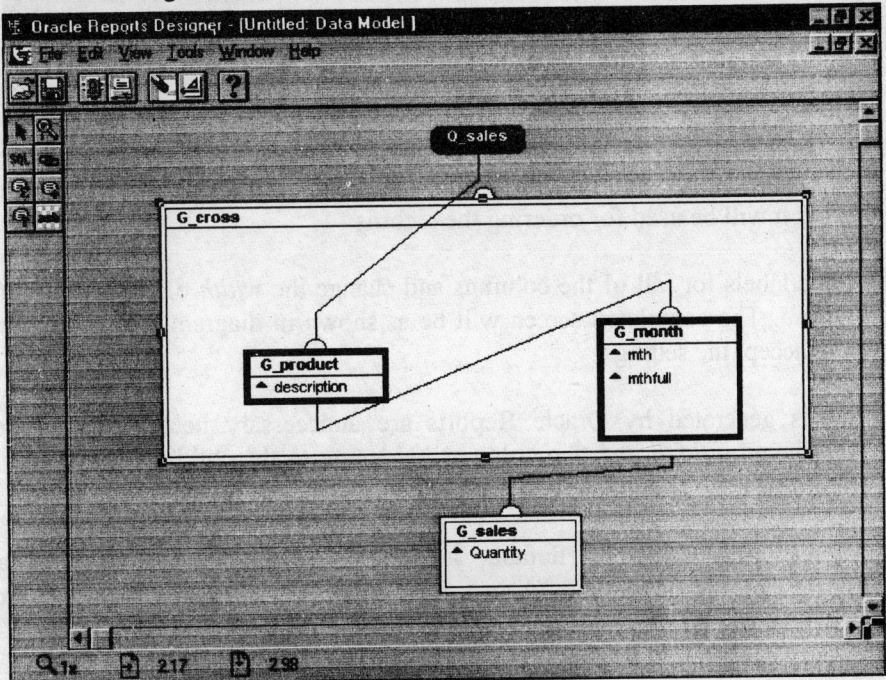

Diagram 19. 5 : Data Model Editor after creating Query and Groups

Creating Default Layout :

8. Select **Tools**, **Default Layout...** (or the Default Layout tool).

9. Select **Style as Matrix** as shown in diagram 19. 6.

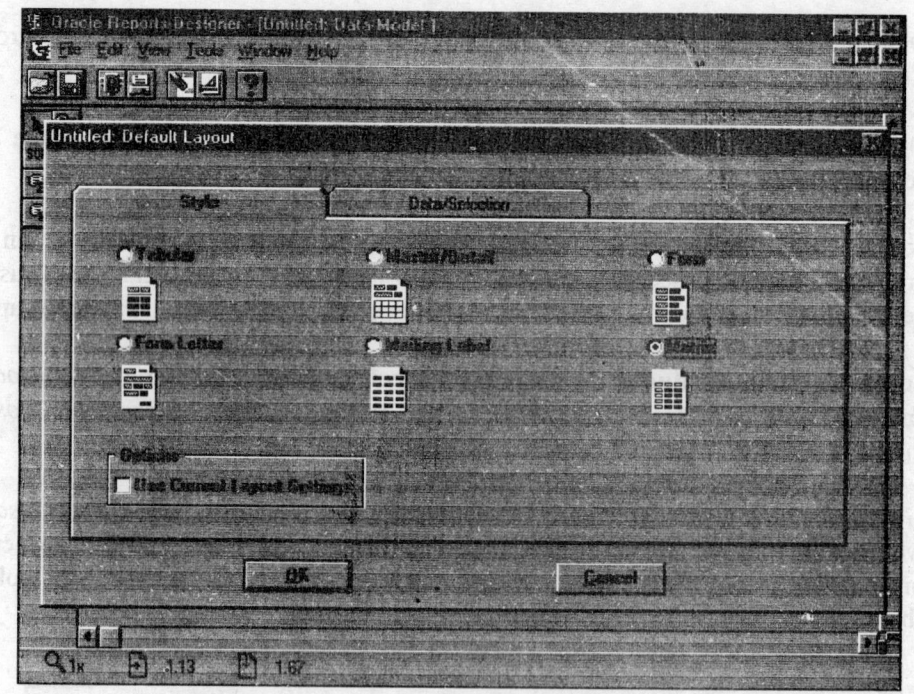

Diagram 19. 6 : Layout Style for Matrix Report

10. Go to **Data/Selection**. Change the setting for *G_month* to **Across**. Click on the column named *mth* (month number) to deselect it as mth must not to appear in the report but it will be used for ordering the records.

Delete the labels for all of the columns and change the *width* of *quantity* to *10* and *mthfull* to *5*. The completed screen will be as shown in diagram 19.7. Click on OK button to accept the settings.

The labels generated by Oracle Reports are unnecessary because the values of *description* and *mthfull*, the two columns belonging to the child groups of the cross product, furnish the labels for your report.

G_product prints down by default, and furnishes the vertical row of labels. Specifying the print direction as Across for *G_month* ensures that its values provide the horizontal row of labels.

CREATING A MATRIX REPORT **445**

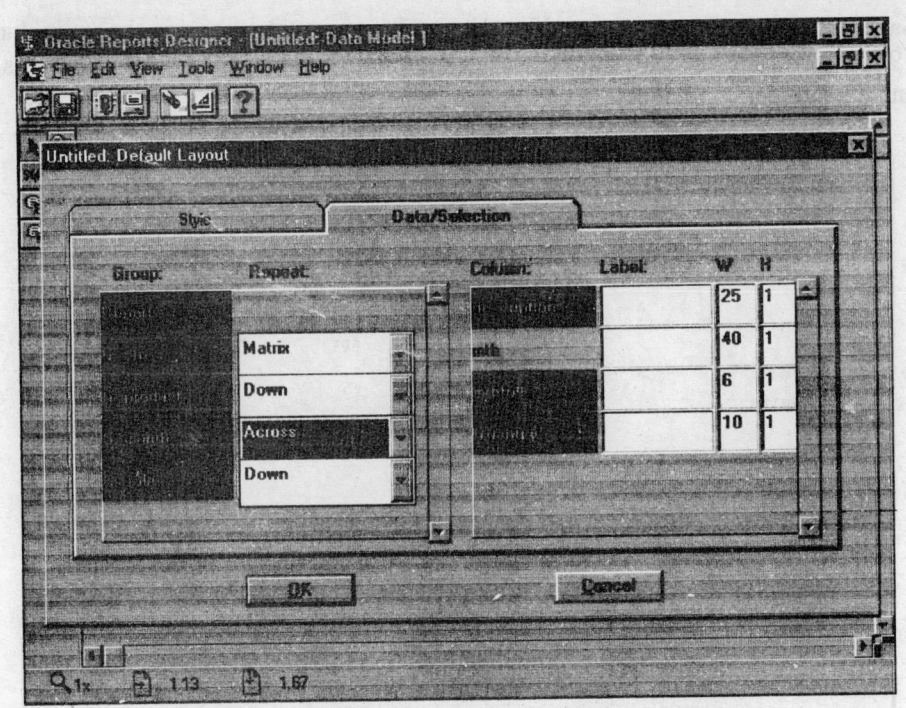

Diagram 19. 7 : Data Selection for Matrix Report

At this point the report layout will be as shown in diagram 19.8.

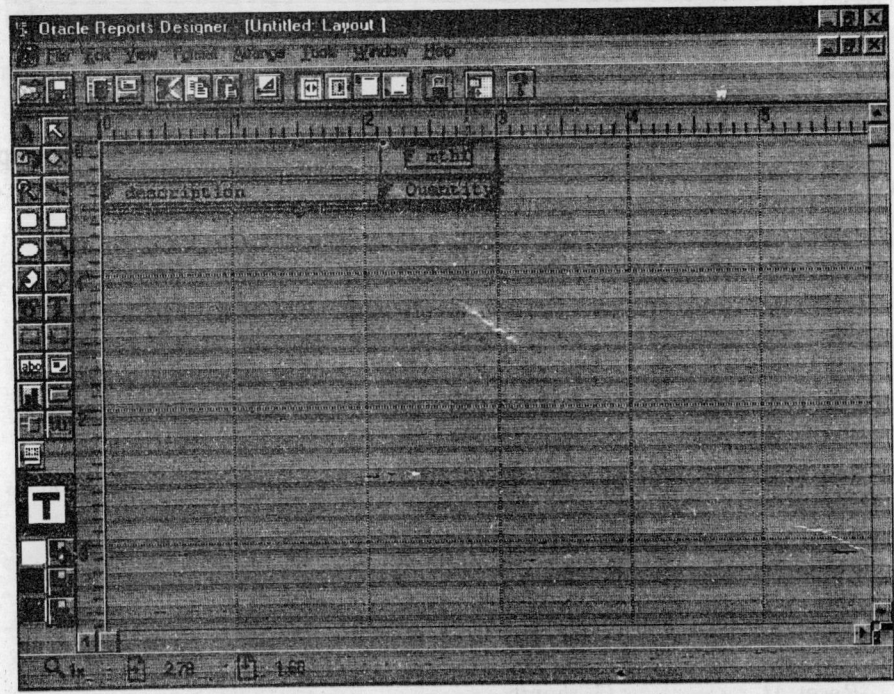

Diagram 19.8 : Layout of the Matrix Report

11. Save the report as *'ordbymon.rdf'* and run. The cross-tab report is shown in diagram 19.9. As you see, the grid shows sales of item with blank spaces where no values exist and no summaries included.

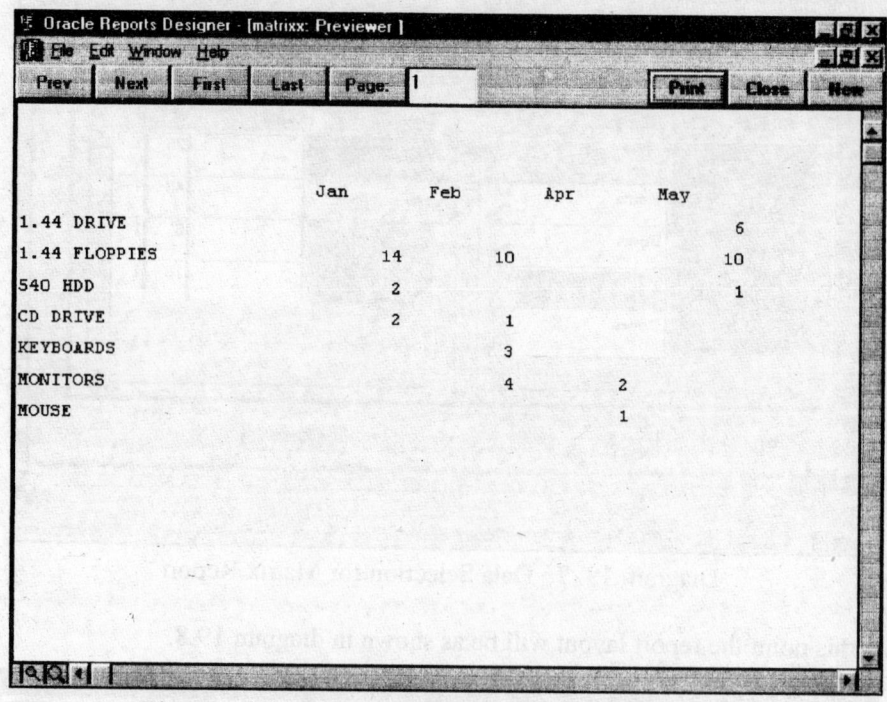

```
 Oracle Reports Designer - [matrixx: Previewer]
 File Edit Window Help
 Prev  Next  First  Last  Page: 1                    Print  Close  New

                        Jan         Feb         Apr         May
       1.44 DRIVE                                                       6
       1.44 FLOPPIES    14          10                      10
       540 HDD          2                                   1
       CD DRIVE         2           1
       KEYBOARDS                    3
       MONITORS                     4           2
       MOUSE                                    1
```

Diagram 19. 9 : Product Sale By Month Matrix Report

Creating Summary columns :

12. In the Data Model Editor, select the **Summary Column** tool from the Tool palette, and place it in the *G_Cross* group. Open the property sheet of the summary column and specify the following properties :

      Name   : CS_productwise
      Function   : Sum
      Source   : Quantity
      Reset At   : G_product
      Product Order   : G_product

13. Repeat the step 1 and create another summary column below *CS_productwise* in the *G_Cross* group and specify the following properties :

      Name   : CS_monthwise
      Function   : Sum
      Source   : Quantity
      Reset At   : G_month
      Product Order   : G_month

CREATING A MATRIX REPORT **447**

Note : Specify the same settings for the summary columns in both the one-query and three-query versions of the matrix report.

Notice the **Product Order** setting. This is required for summary columns belonging to the cross product. The Product Order informs Oracle Reports which groups to evaluate when computing a summary and in what order. In other words, you specify a Product Order of *G_product* for *CS_productwise* so the summary will include only the values for each product in the matrix, and a Product Order of *G_month* for *CS_monthwise* so the summary will include only the values per month.

14. Select the Summary Column tool, click in an empty area of the Layout editor, display the new column's property sheet and assign properties as mentioned below :

    Name   : sum _total
    Function   : Sum
    Source   : Quantity
    Reset At   : Report

Here the value for Product Order is not necessary, as you are not assigning the column to the cross product group. At this point the Data Model Editor will look as shown in the diagram 19. 10.

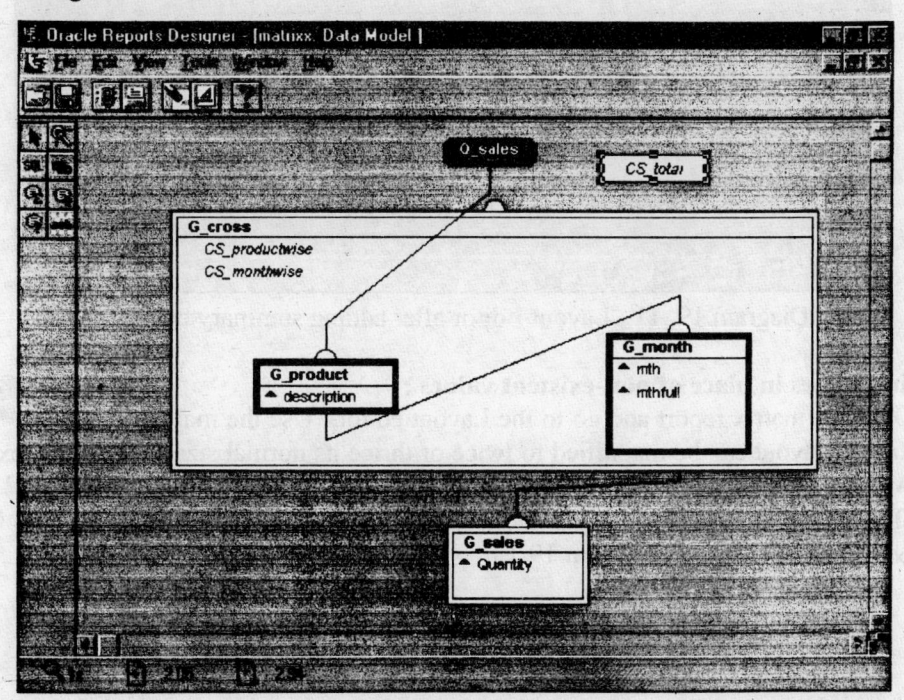

Diagram 19. 10 : Data Model Editor after adding summary columns

448 COMMERCIAL APPLICATION DEVELOPMENT USING ORACLE 7, DEVELOPER 2000

15. Create the default layout for the report as done before. There will be three summary fields included in the report.

16. After creating the default layout, select the field *F_mthfull*, then select **Format, Alignment**. Select **Center** as the alignment for *F_mthfull*.

17. Add two static texts i.e. **'Total :'** and **'Total'** and size, align and format (i.e. appropriate fonts and font sizes) all the objects as shown in the diagram 19. 11.

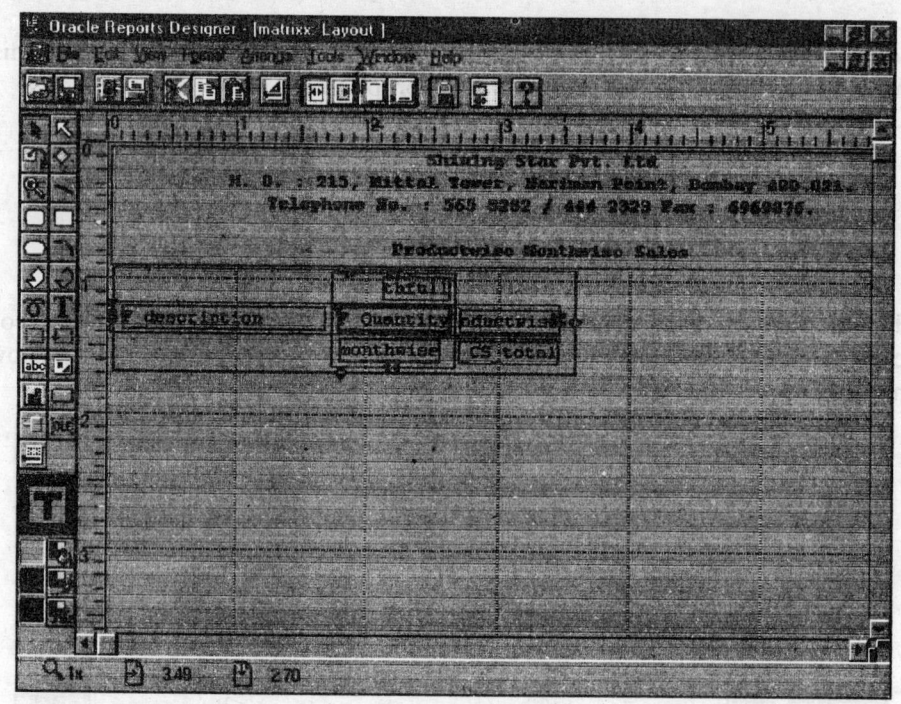

Diagram 19. 11 : Layout Editor after adding summary columns

Adding zeroes in place of non-existent values :

18. Open the matrix report and go to the Layout editor. Use the magnify tool so that the layout can be magnified to twice or thrice its normal size. Select the Text tool. And place it just outside the repeating frame *R_sales* as shown in diagram 19.12. Type **'0'** (zero). Note check to see that the text is just above the *R_sales* frame in the Object Navigator as shown in diagram 19.13.

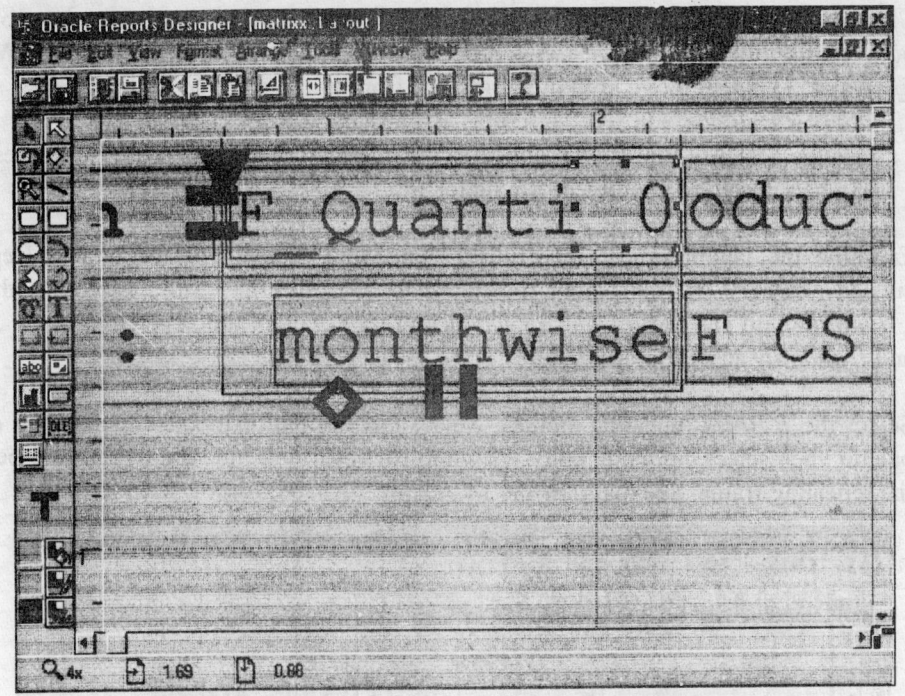

Diagram 19.12 : Text Object in the Layout Editor

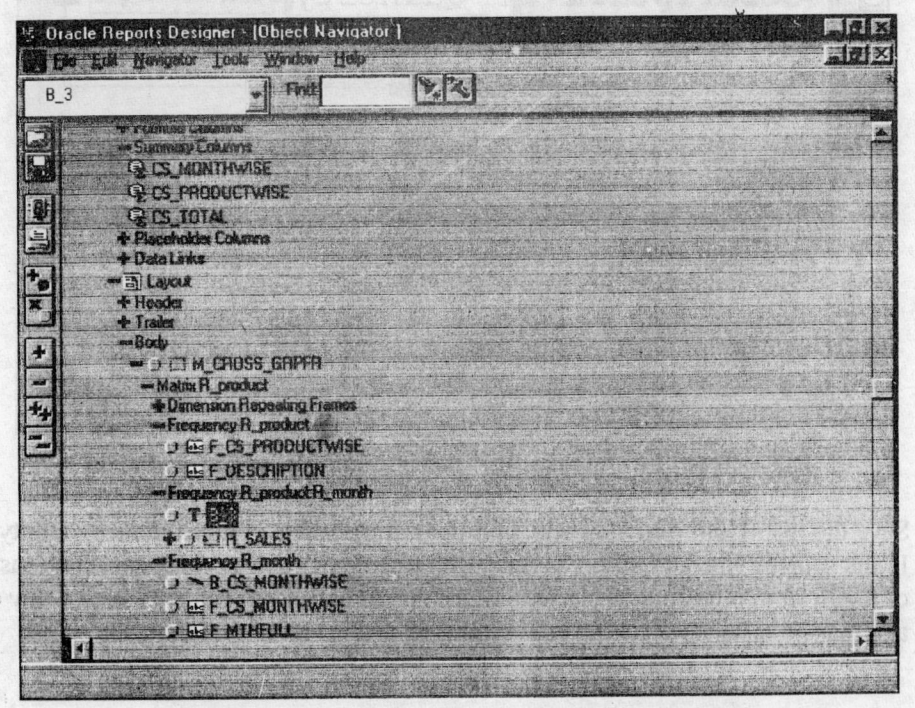

Diagram 19.13 : Text Object in the Object Navigator

450 COMMERCIAL APPLICATION DEVELOPMENT USING ORACLE 7, DEVELOPER 2000

19. Click once in an empty area of the Layout editor to deselect the boilerplate. Select both *f_quantity* and the *R_sales* repeating frame, then select **Arrange**, **Move Forward**. This will move both the objects in front of the piece of boilerplate.

Hint : Use the Magnify tool shown above to enlarge hard-to-see objects. The frames can also be selected in the Object Navigator.

20. Examine the layout objects carefully. Since the default fill for Oracle Reports created objects is transparent the zero is probably still visible behind both the *f_quantity* field and the *R_sales* repeating frame. To avoid this, one can give *R_sales* and *f_quantity* an opaque fill color.

    Select the *R_sales* repeating frame. Select the Fill Color tool to display the color palette, then select the white color. A white fill color will hide the boilerplate behind the repeating frame. See diagram 19. 14.

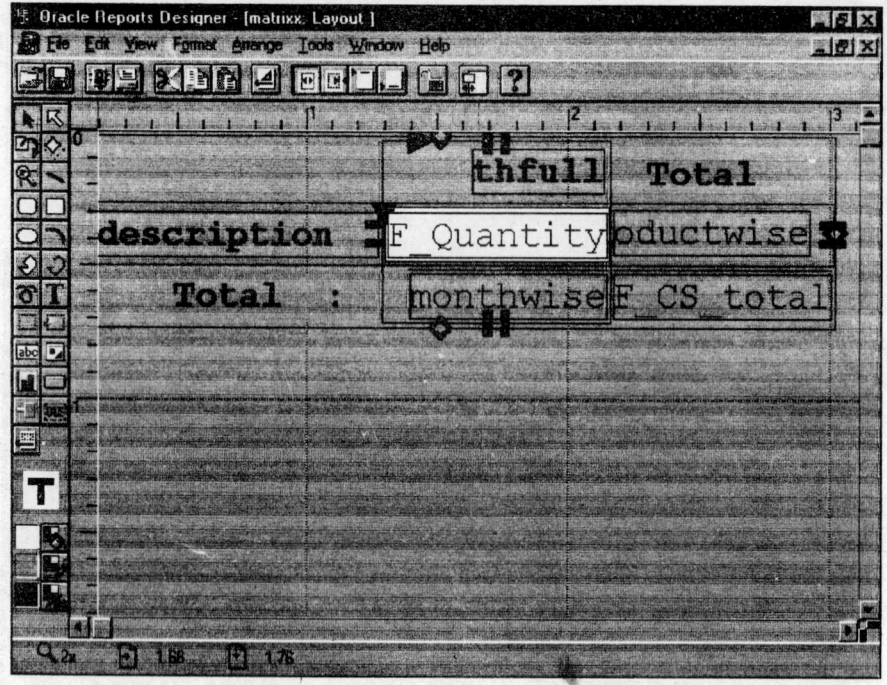

Diagram 19. 14 : Layout Editor after Adding Zeros for no values

21. Save the report and run. You will find that a zero will be placed in every empty cell. In the squares where *Quantity* is displayed, the zeroes are hidden beneath an instance of the *R_sales* repeating frame. Where the zeroes appear, no values for *Quantity* exist, and thus no instance of the *R_sales* repeating frame has been created.

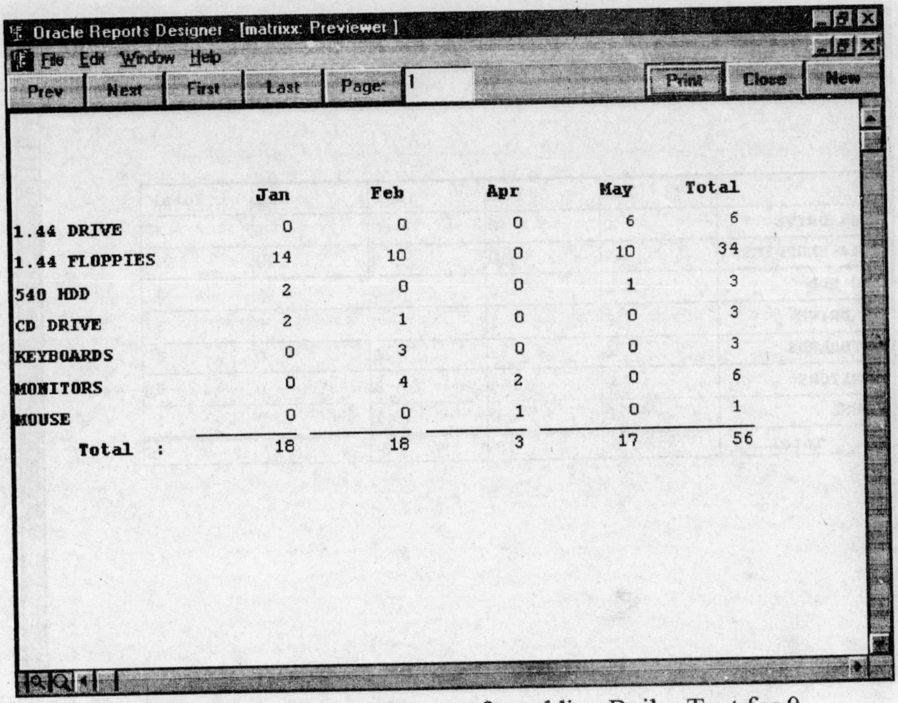

```
┌─ Oracle Reports Designer - [matrixx: Previewer]         _ □ X
│ File Edit Window Help                                    _ |₽| X
│ Prev   Next   First   Last   Page: 1          Print  Close  New

                Jan      Feb      Apr      May     Total
  1.44 DRIVE      0        0        0        6        6
  1.44 FLOPPIES  14       10        0       10       34
  540 HDD         2        0        0        1        3
  CD DRIVE        2        1        0        0        3
  KEYBOARDS       0        3        0        0        3
  MONITORS        0        4        2        0        6
  MOUSE           0        0        1        0        1
       Total :   18       18        3       17       56
```

Diagram 13.15 : Report Output after adding Boiler Text for 0.

Adding a grid.

22. Select the *M_cross_GRPFR,R_product*, *R_month* frame and select the Line Color tool to display the line color palette and make the border frames as black.

    A matrix object is a specialized type of frame that repeats for each instance of an intersection between the across and down dimensions. You can assign a border to it. In addition, if you have a color display, you can choose a color for the border.

23. Save and run the report. The report will look as shown as shown in the diagram 19.16.

452 COMMERCIAL APPLICATION DEVELOPMENT USING ORACLE 7, DEVELOPER 2000

	Jan	Feb	Apr	May	Total
1.44 DRIVE	0	0	0	6	6
1.44 FLOPPIES	14	10	0	10	34
540 HDD	2	0	0	1	3
CD DRIVE	2	1	0	0	3
KEYBOARDS	0	3	0	0	3
MONITORS	0	4	2	0	6
MOUSE	0	0	1	0	1
Total :	18	18	3	17	56

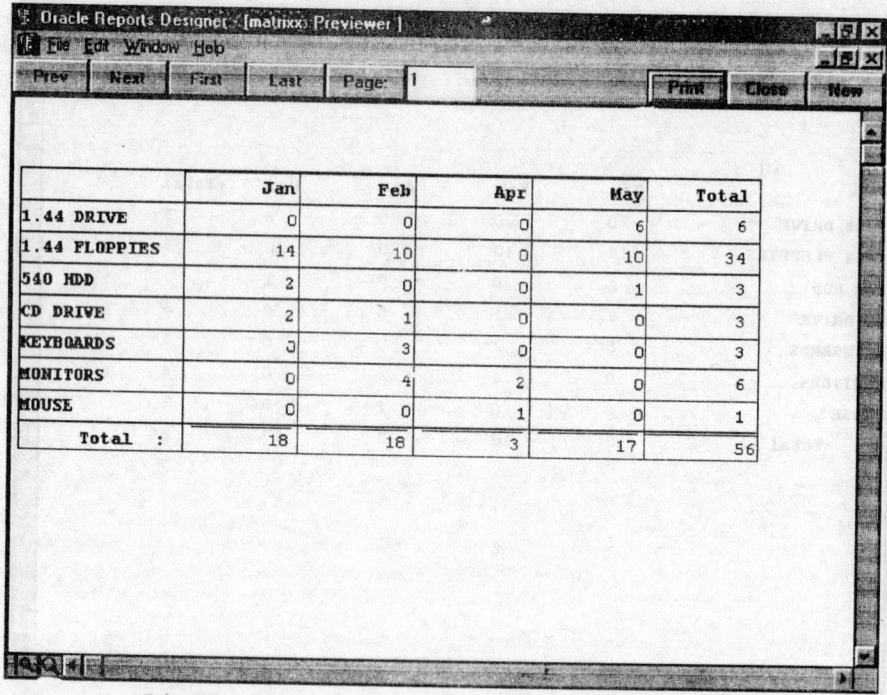

Diagram 19.16 : Report Layout after adding Borders

Creating user parameter :

24. Create a User Parameter and open its property sheet. In the **General** tab, rename the default parameter P_1 to *p_year*. Choose the data type of the parameter as *Character* and width as *4*.

25. Click on the **Data/Selection** tab and click on the radio button for *SELECT Statement*. SPecify the Select statement and click on OK to accept the information entered.

    Select distinct to_char(s_order_date,'yyyy') from sales_order

26. Invoke the Data Model Editor and double click on the query object and add the following WHERE clause to the query.

    and to_char(sales_order.s_order_date, 'yyyy') = :p_year

27. Invoke Default Parameter Form by selecting **Tools, Default Parameter Form**. Scroll through list of parameters and locate *p_year*. Change the label to *'Year :'* as shown in diagram 19.17. Click on OK after you have made necessary changes.

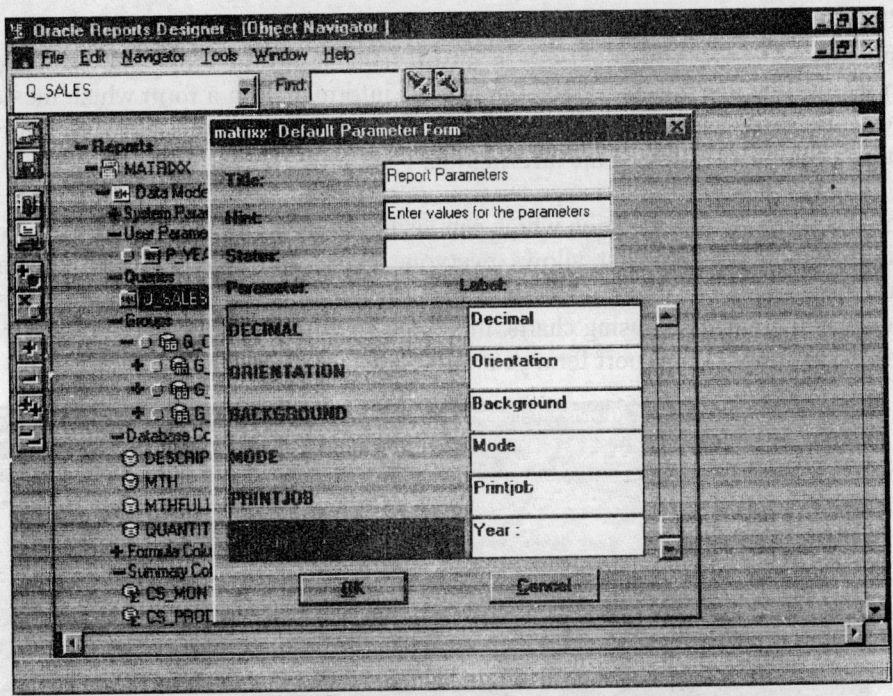

Diagram 19. 17 : Setting the Parameter Form

28. Save and run the report.

The Runtime Parameter window now will appear with one extra field i.e. **Year**, with an edit style that provides a list of values. Select the value from the list of values provided and click on **Run Report** to view the report for the corresponding value of the year selected.

20. WORKING WITH GRAPHS

INTRODUCTION
Corporations today are flooded with a lot of valuable information. The challenge is to interpret this massive information and relay this information in a form which the decision makers can easily understand. The form of representation of this massive information must be a compact version of the information.

Graph is a form of representation which can visibly show all the information in a compact version. Thus it's a tool that allows everyone in an organization to visually analyze information on-line. Using graphs one can retrieve data from a wide variety of sources and display it graphically, using charts, line drawing, bit-mapped images etc. An example of use of graph for sales report for a year is as shown in the diagram 20.1.

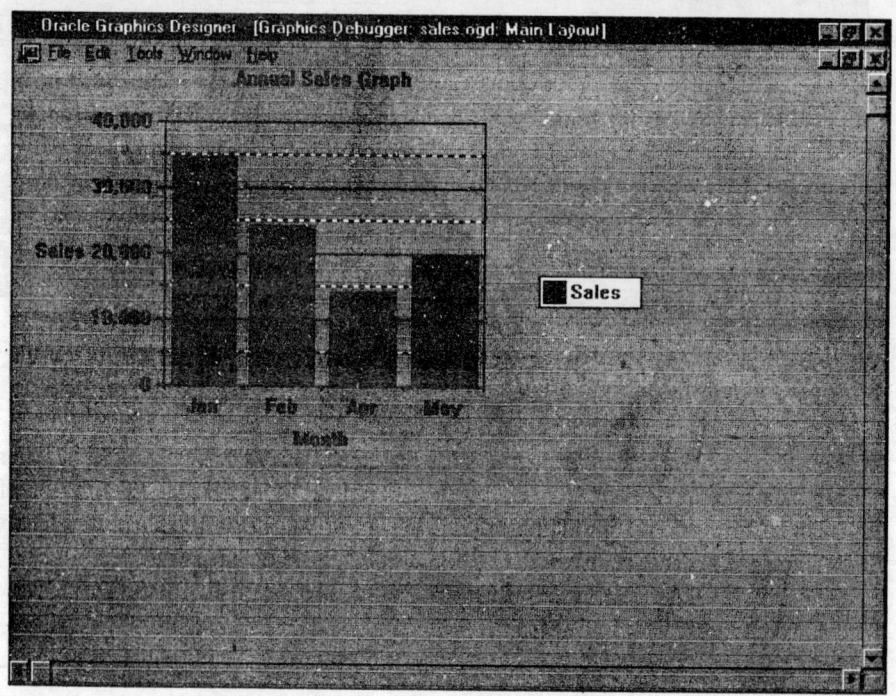

Diagram 20.1 : Annual Sales Graph

Functionality of Oracle Graphics :
Oracle Graphics provides many options for graphically portraying data. Here's what you can do:

- Retrieve data from a wide variety of sources and display it graphically, using charts, line drawings, bit-mapped images, text, and sound.
- Draw artwork such as lines, polygons, and freehand shapes using a full set of editing tools.

- Use PL/SQL to control flow, add interactive features, and animate artwork. Write, edit, and debug your programs within Oracle Graphics.
- Make charts and drawings dynamic, by linking them to data sources. Write procedures that update the display to reflect changes in the data.
- Include interactive features for end-users, such as mouse-activated buttons, or use timers to trigger certain operations automatically.
- Choose from 56 pre-defined chart templates that you can customize and reuse for multiple displays.
- Open multiple windows for working on more than one display at a time.

Working with Charts :
Graphs 2.5 comprises of the following components :
- Displays
- Layout
- Queries
- Chart Properties
- Templates

DISPLAY :
The primary object of *Graphics Designer* is the *Display*. The display module is nothing but a collection of objects such as *Layout, Template, Queries, Triggers*.

LAYOUT :
The Layout editor is the main work area in the Oracle Graphics Designer. It is where you design the layout of your display, by creating and modifying graphical objects (lines, polygons, rectangles, text, etc.). Every display contains exactly one layout, and every layout belongs to exactly one display. When you first run a *Display*, Oracle Graphics shows the contents of the layout. The user can view the information presented, or interact with the display with a mouse or keyboard.

QUERIES :
Is a SQL SELECT statement or file that Oracle Graphics needs in order to retrieve data for a chart. A chart can be associated with only one query at a time. When you draw the chart, Oracle Graphics uses the data from the current query, unless you specify a different one.

Chart Properties :

Chart properties define options for the chart as a whole, including its associated chart template and query. Chart properties are accessible through the **Chart property sheet** and are organized as follows :

Chart : Includes the chart's *Name*, *Title*, *Chart Type* and *Template*.

Data : Includes query related properties such as a *Query Filter Function* and the range of data to plot.

Categories : Includes the chart categories and any sub-categories to plot in the chart. Category (independent) data is plotted at fixed intervals. Category data is not considered to be mathematically related and is usually plotted along what is called the *Discrete* axis (i. e. X axis).

Values : Includes the chart values and associated field templates. Value (dependent) data generally starts at one value and continues until another value. Value data is considered to be mathematically related and is usually plotted along what is called the *Continuous* axis (i. e. Y axis).

PL/SQL : Includes any mouse events and associated procedures for the chart.

Chart Types :

The following list describes the available types of charts the user can create, and their usage :

Column

Column Charts type is used to compare sets of data ranges vertically. For example, a Column Chart can be used to show the quarterly sales revenue generated by each sales representative.

Pie

Pie Charts type is used to compare the ratios or percentages of parts of a whole. For example, a pie chart can be used to compare annual revenue by department or quarter.

Bar

Bar Chart type is used to compare sets of data ranges horizontally. For example, a bar chart can be used to compare monthly sales.

Table

Table Chart type is used to show data in a table format. For example, a table chart can be used to show an Employee Organization Chart.

Line

Line chart type is used to show vertical changes for a specific set of data. For example, a line chart can be used to gauge daily or weekly changes in a stock's value.

Scatter

Scatter chart type is used to show data along two value axes. Scatter charts are well suited for showing standard deviations. For example, a scatter chart can be used to plot the target and the actual sales for each salesmen. If there is a correlation between the two sets of data, the points will be grouped together fairly closely. One or more points well outside the group could indicate a disparity.

Mixed

Mixed chart combines multiple plot types such as column and line. For example, a mixed chart can be used to show daily sales revenue, with a line plot type to provide a summary view of the data.

High-low

HighLow chart type is used to show fields that correspond to high, low, and close (i.e. stock prices). For each row in your query, a high-low range is plotted on the chart.

Double-Y

Double Y chart type provides two independent Y-axes on which to plot data. Each Y-axis can show a different range of values. For example, you could use one axis to represent revenue, the second to represent income, and plot both over a course of time.

Gantt

Gantt chart type is used to to show sets of project data over a given amount of time. Gantt charts are generally used to show project milestone timelines.

Chart Templates :
Template is the format of a chart and its properties. A chart can be associated with only one chart template at a time. Each chart template can be associated with one or more field templates, which define the properties of the individual fields, such as bars, columns, pie slices, or lines.

Using a single chart template, you can create multiple charts with the same set basic of characteristics such as grid line settings or tick label rotation. For example, instead of specifying the properties for each chart individually, you can create a single chart template and associate it with multiple queries. To work with chart templates, you use the *Chart Template* Editor.

USING THE GRAPHICS DESIGNER

Tools Available with the Graphics Designer :
Before attempting create a chart, let us look what are the tools available with the Graphics Designer so that life is made a little simpler for the developer. These are

1. Object Navigator
2. Layout Editor
3. PL/SQL editor

OBJECT NAVIGATOR :
Queries and templates are the constituent parts of a Display. The Object Navigator allows you to navigate through the hierarchy of objects.

LAYOUT EDITOR
The Charts developed will be displayed in the layout editor. The sizing, positioning and alignment of the chart objects on the screen is done through this tool.

PL/SQL EDITOR :
More often than not, one needs to perform tasks which are specific to an application. One has to resort to writing code to customize application processing, to meet these specific requirements. The *PL/SQL* Editor gives you the interface to define code blocks which are called *Trigger Code* for appropriate trigger events.

CREATING A GRAPH

Focus :
To design a simple Line graph for sales order transactions. The Graph must display the gross earning for the year grouped by month.

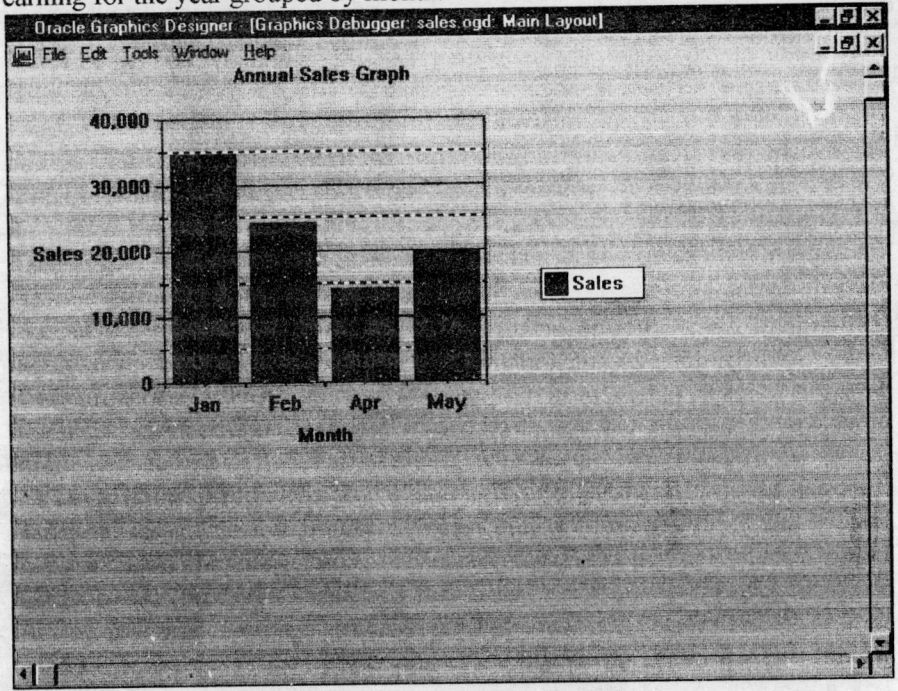

Diagram 20.2 : Annual Sales Graph

The table definitions are as follows :

Table Name : sales_order (Master)
Description : Use to store information about orders placed by the clients.

Column Name	Data Type	Size	Attributes
s_order_no	varchar2	6	Unique primary key allotted to each order.
s_order_date	date		Date on which the order is placed.
client_no	varchar2	6	Client No., who places the order.
dely_addr	varchar2	30	Address where the delivery of the goods has to be made.
salesman_no	varchar2	6	Salesman No., who gets the order from the client.
status	varchar2	2	Order Status (In Process IP, FullFilled FP, Not Processed NP)
dely_type	char	1	To note whether the delivery is to be made in parts (P) or full (F).
dely_date	date		Date when the delivery for the goods is to be made.

Table Name : sales_order_details
Description : Use to store information about order details.

Column Name	Data Type	Size	Attributes
s_order_no	varchar2	6	Order No. for which details have to be stored.
product_no	varchar2	6	Product No. for which details have to be stored.
product_rate	number	8,2	The rate agreed upon.
qty_ordered	number	8	Quantity of goods ordered.
qty_disp	number	8	Quantity of goods dispatched.

Solution :
1. Invoke *Oracle Graphics Designer* Tool. When you invoke the *Graphics Designer* Tool, it creates a new *display* with a default name *disp1* and opens up Object Navigator window with the focus on the display *disp1* as shown in the diagram 20.3.

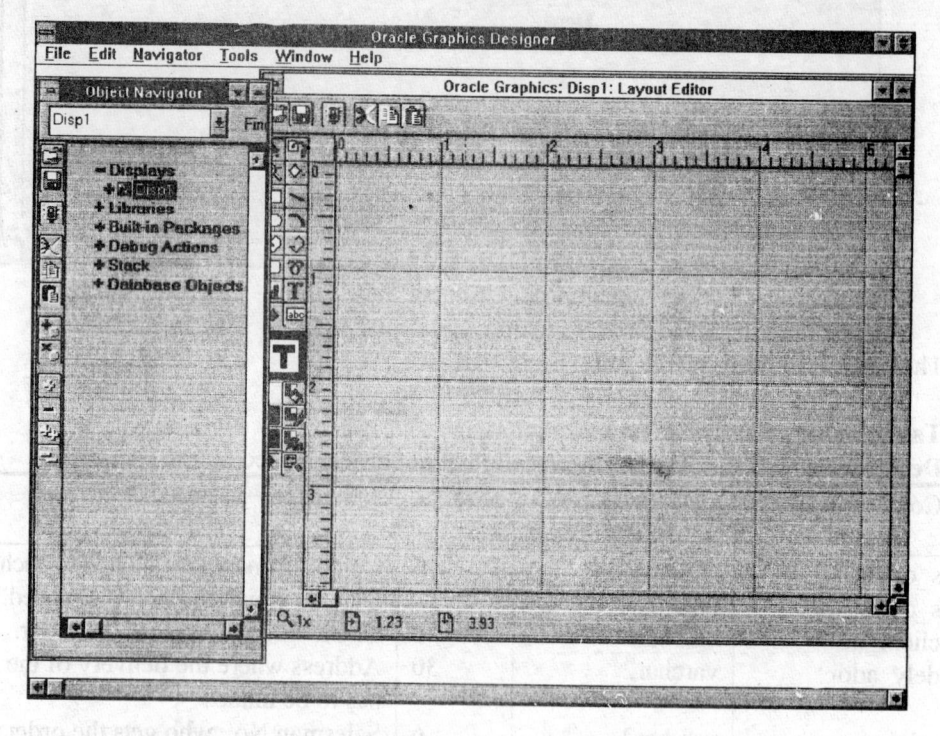

Diagram 20.3 : New Display opened in the Graphics Designer

2. Connect to the database by clicking on **File** and **Connect**.

Creating a Query for the graphs :
1. Double Click on the *Queries* option in object navigator window, the query property sheet is displayed.

The default name given to the query is *query0*, change the name of the query object. Select **SQL statement** in the **Type** option.

Enter the SQL Statement in the **SQL Statement** option.

```
select     to_char(s_order_date, 'Mon') "Month",
           to_char(s_order_date, 'mm'),
           sum(qty_ordered * product_rate) "Sales"
from       sales_order, sales_order_details
where      sales_order_details.s_order_no = sales_order.s_order_no
group by   to_char(s_order_date, 'Mon'), to_char(s_order_date, 'mm')
order by   to_char(s_order_date, 'mm')
```

The completed screen will be displayed as shown in diagram 20.4. Click on the **Execute** button.

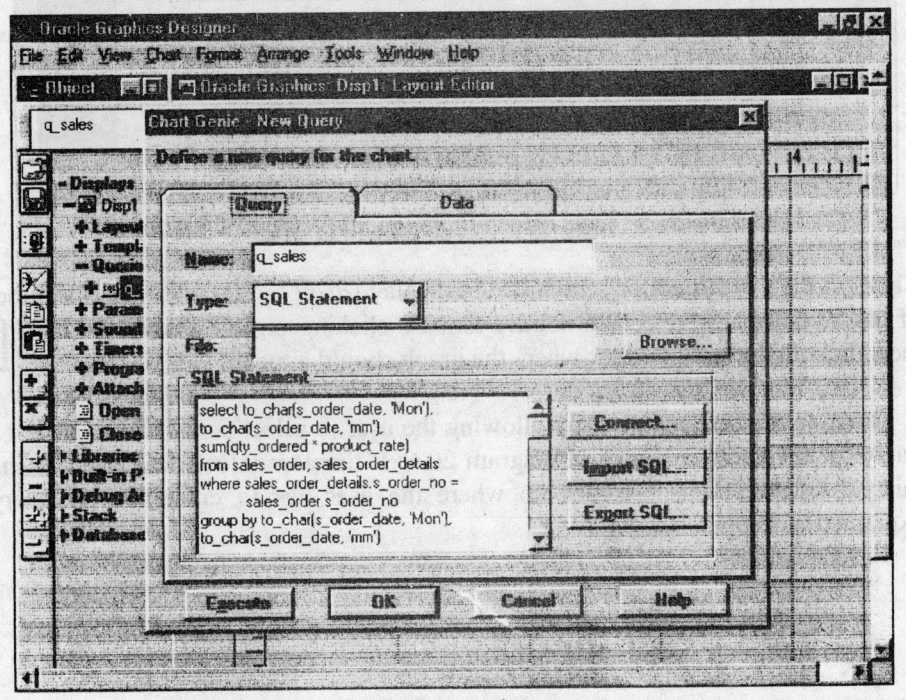

Diagram 20.4 : Query Properties screen

2. A screen comes up displaying the data that has resulted from the execution of the select statement as shown in diagram 20.5. Click on the OK button to accept the query.

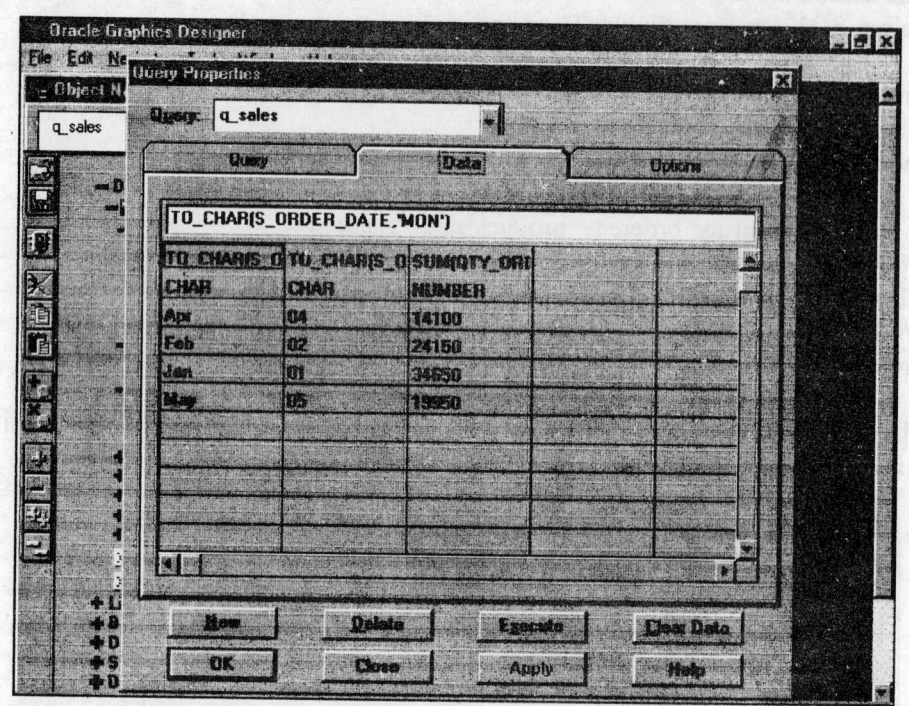

462 COMMERCIAL APPLICATION DEVELOPMENT USING ORACLE 7, DEVELOPER 2000

Diagram 20.5 : Data screen in the query properties window

3. Click on the *Layout* editor screen of the display (*displ* by default). From the toolbar of the layout editor select the **Chart** tool by clicking on the **chart** icon and then click on the layout editor where the graph should appear.

A *Chart Genie* screen comes up allowing the user to select an existing query or new query for the chart as shown in diagram 20.6. If the user selects new query then, the query properties screen comes up where the user has to create a new query as explained in step 3.

WORKING WITH GRAPHS 463

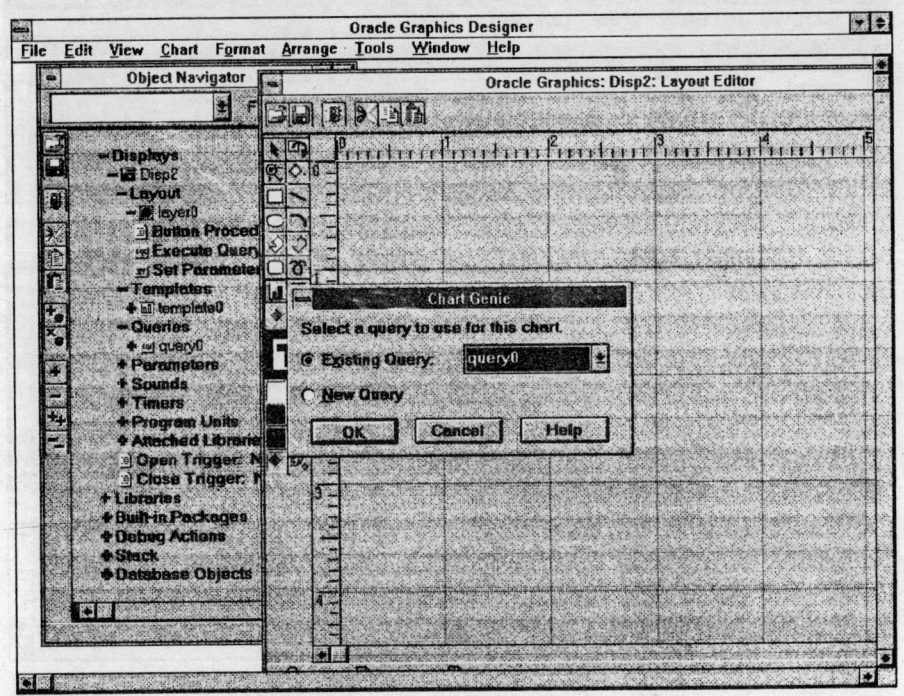

Diagram 20.6 : Query Genie screen

4. Select the required query and click on OK. It displays the Chart properties as shown in diagram 20.6. Enter the *Name, Title* for the chart and select the required *Type Of Graph* and its *Subtype* as shown in diagram 20.7.

    Name   : ch_sales
    Title   : Annual Sales Graph
    Type   :

    Sub Type   :

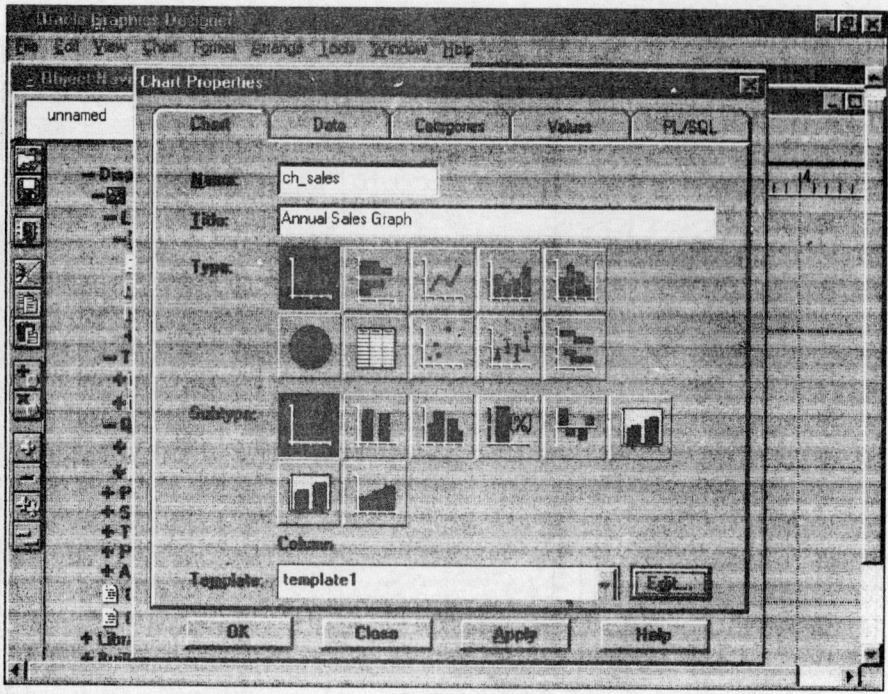

464 COMMERCIAL APPLICATION DEVELOPMENT USING ORACLE 7, DEVELOPER 2000

Diagram 20.7 : Chart Properties Screen

5. Click on the **Categories** and select "Month" column and click on *insert* to include it in the chart categories.

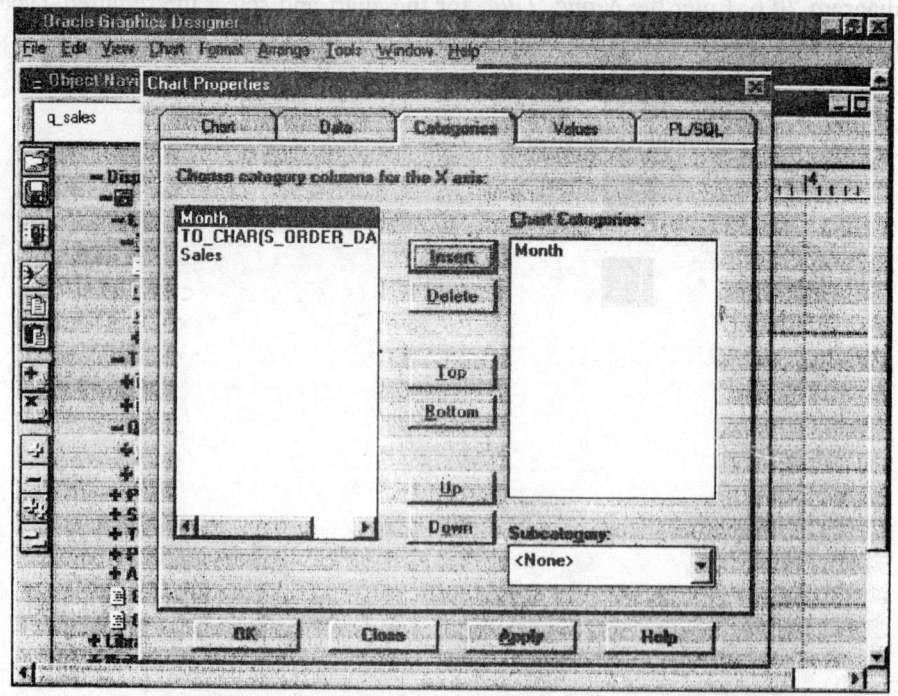

Diagram 20.8 : Specifying the column for the Categories Axis

6. Click on **Values** item from the menu and select "Sales" column and click on *insert* to include it in the chart Values.

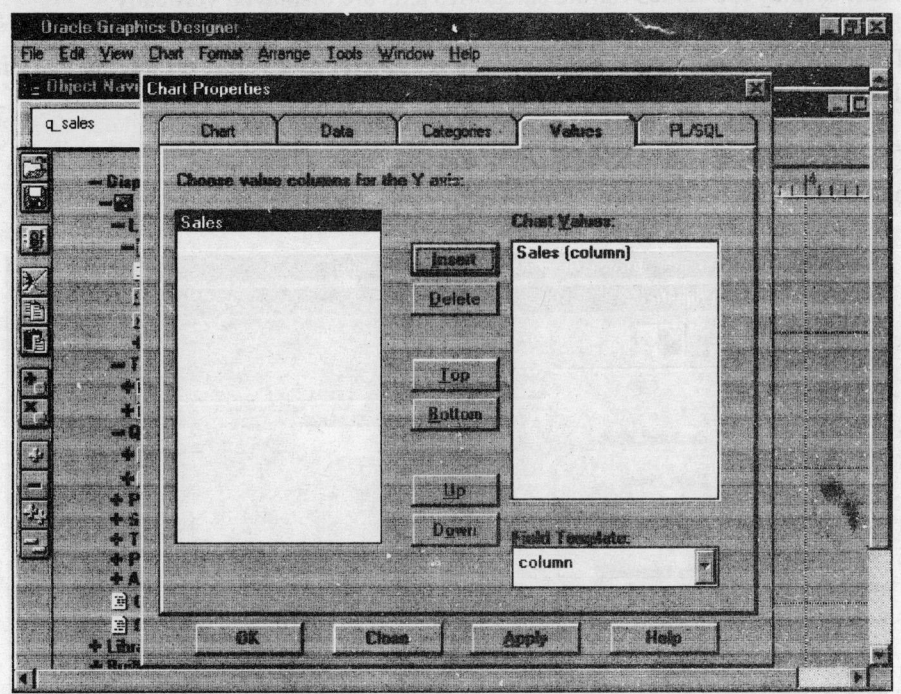

Diagram 20.9 : Specifying the column for Values Axis

7. Click on **Apply** and then OK button to accept the values. The completed graph will be displayed as shown in diagram 20.10.

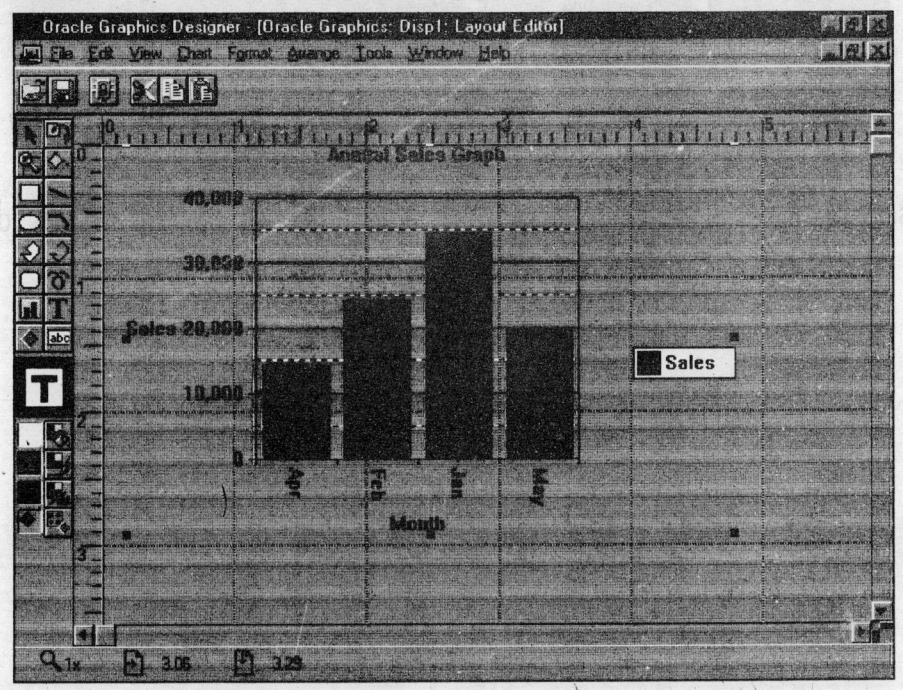

Diagram 20.10 : Graph displayed in the Layout Editor

8. Save the display as **sales.odg**. Compile and run the display to see the graph. As seen in the display the values for the categories axis are displayed vertically.

To change it to horizontal display, double click on the values in the layout editor. It displays the X or categories properties.

Change the **Tick Label Rotation** to horizontal by clicking on the appropriate radio button as shown in diagram 20.11.

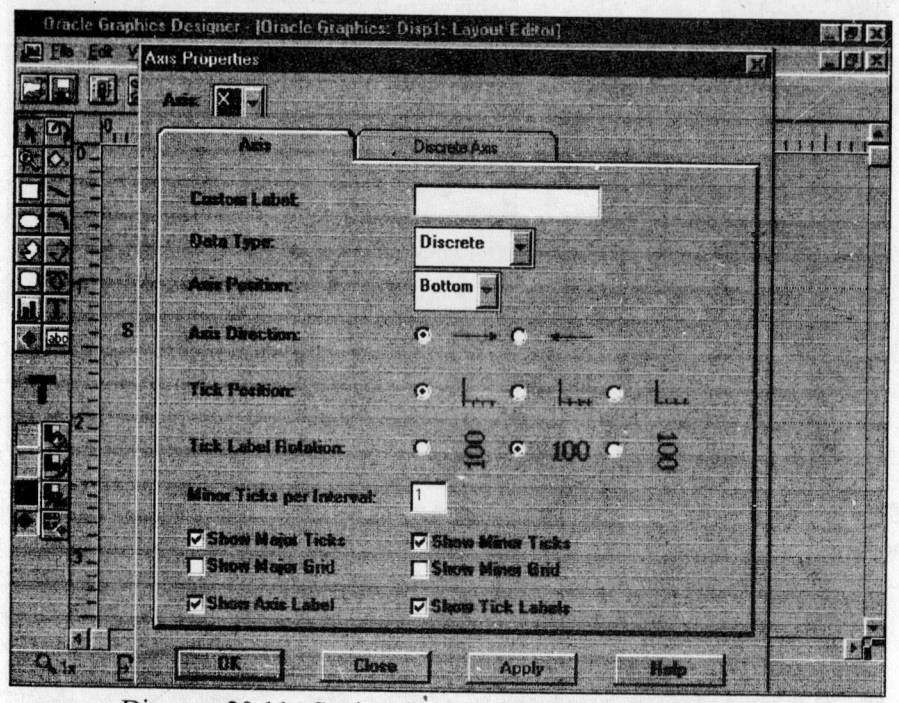

Diagram 20.11 : Setting the Tick Label Rotation Property

9. Save and run the graph. The graph runtime output will be as shown in diagram 20.12.

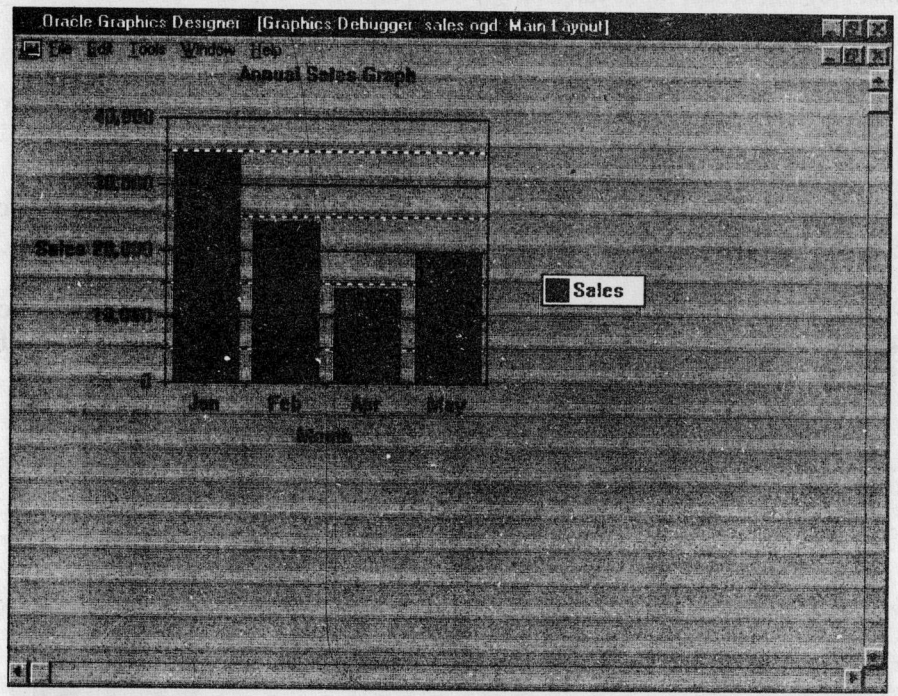

Diagram 20.12 : Sales Graph Displayed at Run time

PASSING PARAMETERS IN ORACLE GRAPHICS

The graphs created so far are static. It does not give the user the flexibility to pass values of his/her choice. To make the graphs dynamic, it would be essential to define parameters such that they can accept input values from the operator.

Focus :
Create an Annual Sales Report which will allow the user to pull reports based on the Year of his/her choice.

Using the *Annual Sales* report created in the first exercise, we will demonstrate how to define a parameter field which will accept a value for *year* from the user at runtime.

1. Open the *Annual Sales* graph and click on the **Parameters** node in the object navigator. A default parameter by the name *Param0* will be displayed along with the property sheet as shown in diagram 20.13.

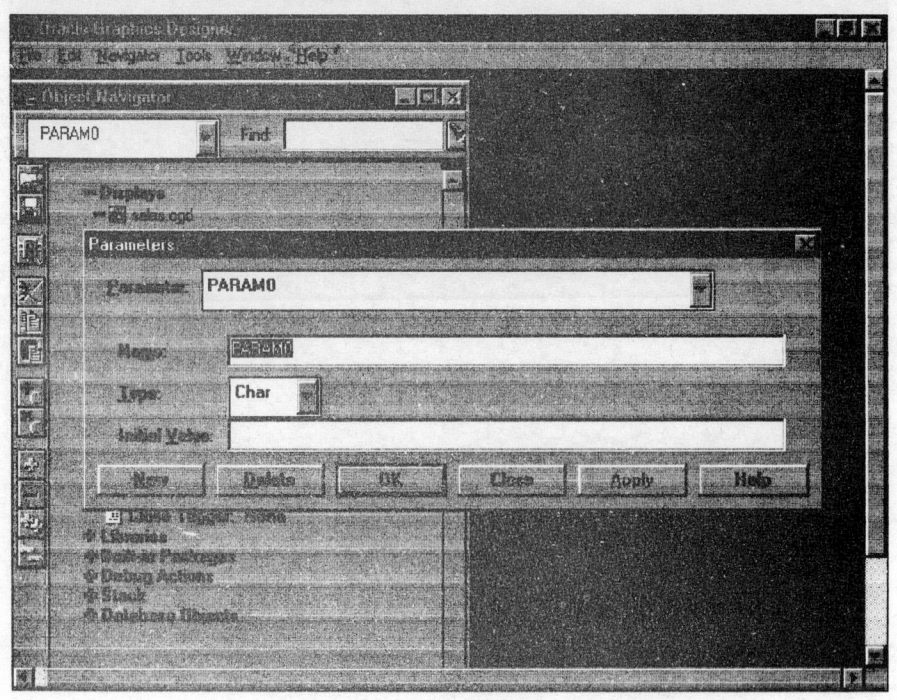

Diagram 20.13 : Creating a New Parameter

2. Enter the *Parameter Name* as *P_year* and *Data Type* as *Char* and Click on **OK**.

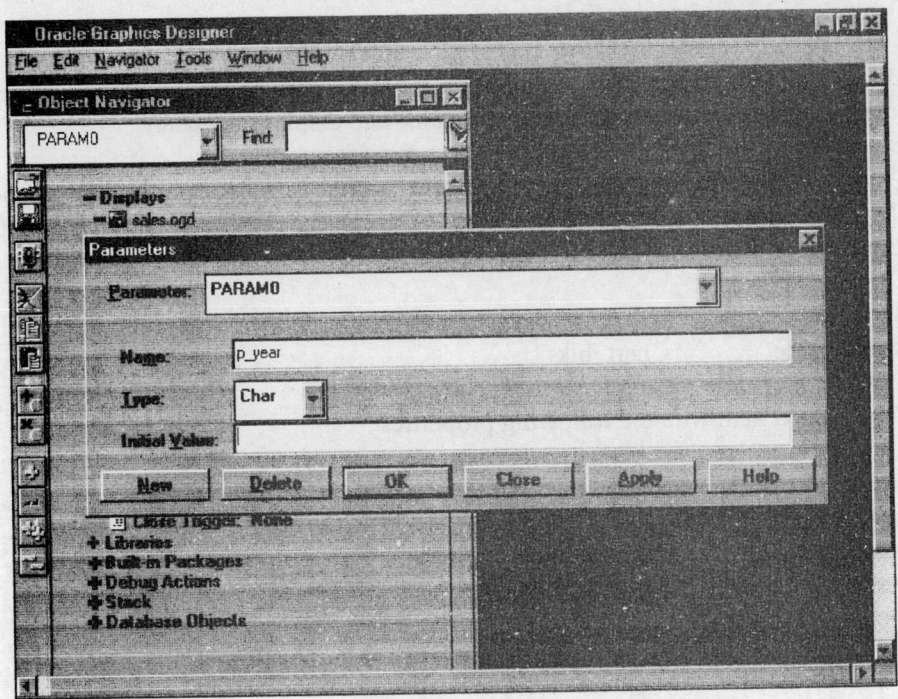

Diagram 20.14 : Parameters Properties set for p_year

3. Select *Q_Sales* and add the following WHERE condition, **and to_char(s_order_date , 'yyyy') = :p_year** as shown in the diagram 20.15.

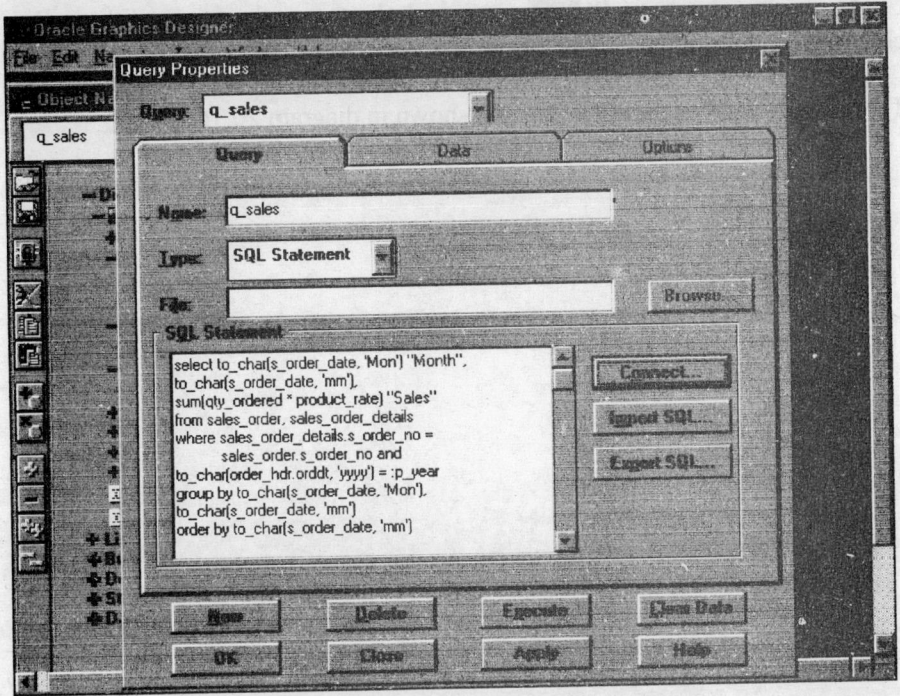

Diagram 20.15 : Query Properties screen

4. Compile and Generate the display.

5. The Oracle Graphics tool does not have its own parameter form. Thus we need to create a form that accepts the parameter value and displays the chart.

    Create a new form **gr_call**. Since the form is used to accept parameters we need a block that is not connected to the table. Create a control block **chart_blk** with the following properties.

Base Table	: None
Block Name	: Chart_blk

6. Create a text item with the following properties :

Name	: **Year**
Base Table	: False
Data Type	: Char
Maximum Length	: 4

7. Place a button item **Graph Open** with the following properties.

Name	: Graph_open
Label	: Graph Open

8. Click on the **chart tool** icon and place it on the *Layout* Editor. Resize the chart item and change the name of the chart item to *ch_sales*.

    The completed layout editor will be as shown in diagram 20.16.

WORKING WITH GRAPHS 471

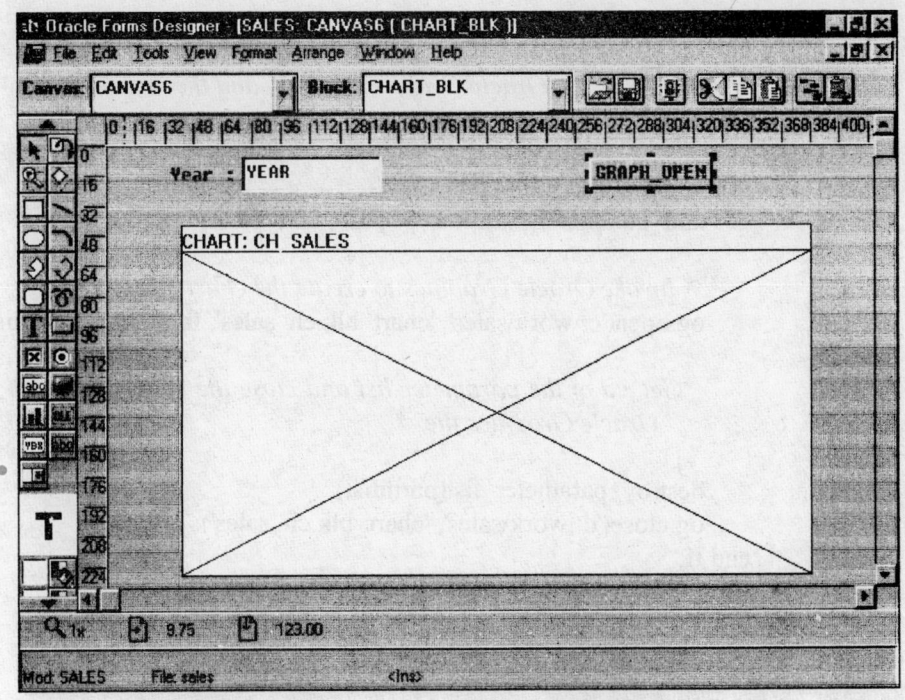

Diagram 20.16 : Layout Editor with a chart tool

9. Create a LOV **year_list** and attach it to the text item **year**. The select statement for the LOV is as given below.

    select distinct to_char(s_order_date, 'yyyy') into :year from sales_order ;

10. The function required to call a graph are included in a library named OG.PLL under \orawin\forms45\plsqllib directory. Thus we need to include this library before writing the PL/SQL code. Click on *Attached libraries* node in the Object Navigator. It displays the *Attach Library* dialog box. Specify the name of the library as **og.pll** and click on **Attach**. In the command button **Graph_Open** , enter the following PL/SQL code.

Trigger Name	: **WHEN-BUTTON-PRESSED**	Form	: gr_call
Block	: chart_blk	Item	: graph_open
Function	: Open the sales Graph and pass the year parameter to the same.		
Text	: DECLARE		

```
         parmlist   ParamList;
      BEGIN
         /* Create a parameter list for data passing */
         parmlist := Create_Parameter_List('plist');
```

```
            /* Add a parameter to the parameter list to
            ** specify the relationship between the named query
            ** 'query0' in the Oracle Graphics display and the named
            ** record group in the form, 'chart_data'. */

            if not id_null(parmlist) then
                add_parameter(parmlist, 'p_year', text_parameter, :year);

                /* Invoke Oracle Graphics to create the chart */
                og.open('c:\work\sales', 'chart_blk.ch_sales', false, true, parmlist);

                /*Get rid of the parameter list and close the connection with the
                    Oracle Graphics file. */

                destroy_parameter_list(parmlist);
                og.close('d:\work\sales', 'chart_blk.ch_sales');
            end if;
        END;
```

The runtime screen will be as shown in diagram 20.17.

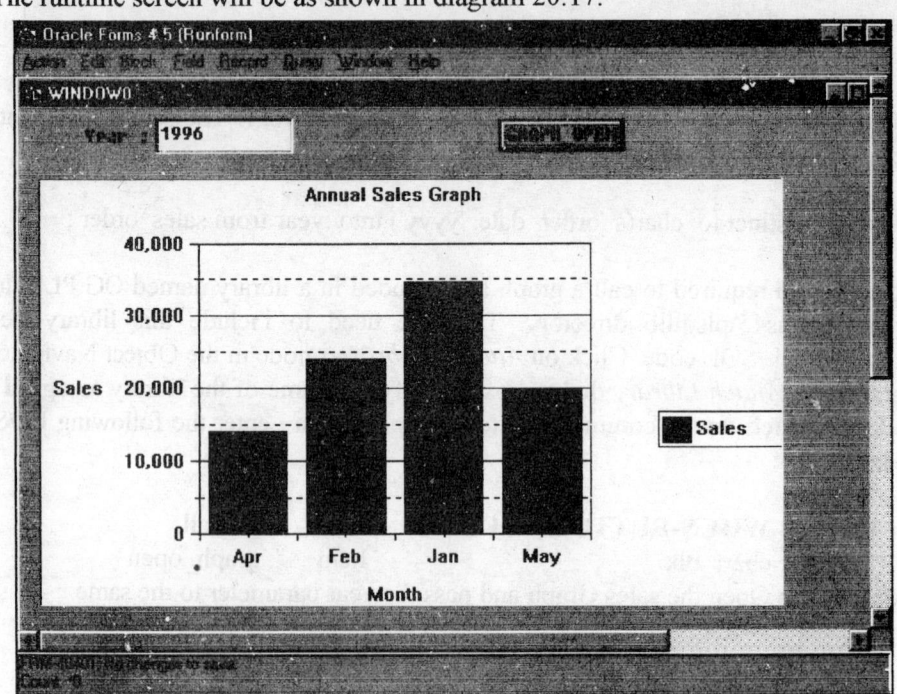

Diagram 20.17 : Oracle Graph displayed at Run Time

21. DRILL DOWN CHARTS

Oracle Graphics provides the capability to create individual displays that are based on multiple charts that are linked through parameters. One example of a multiple chart application is a drill-down chart, which displays a secondary chart based on the data passed from one chart to the next.

Problem Definition :
Create an *Annual Sales Pie Chart Report* which will allow the user to pull reports based on the relative percentage of sales for each customer. Based on the selection of a particular customer (when the user clicks on a particular slice in the Pie Chart) open a *Line Graph* showing the yearly sales of the customer as shown in the diagram 21.1.

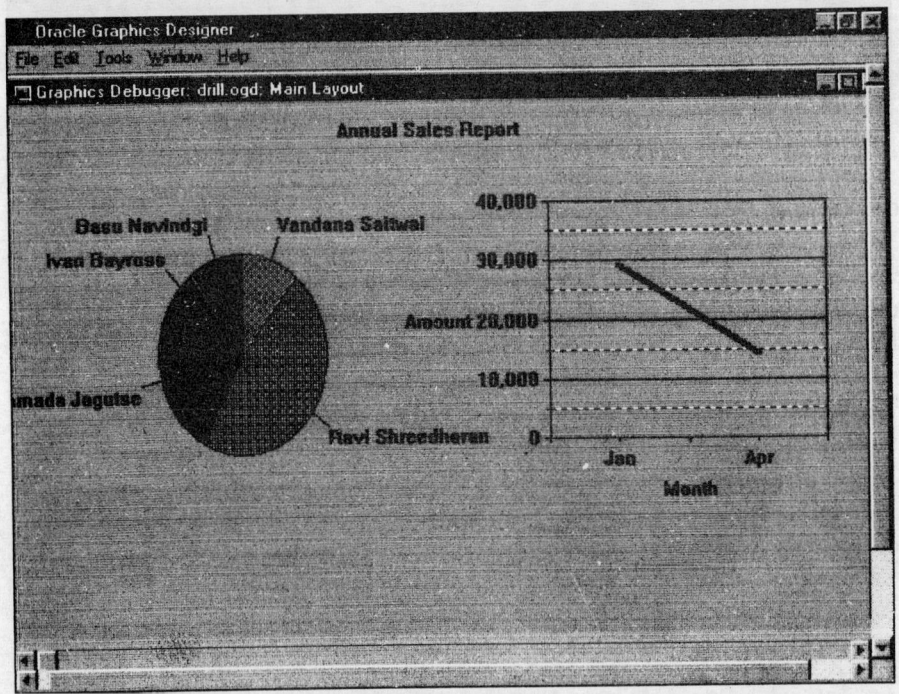

Diagram 21.1 : Drill-Down Chart

474 COMMERCIAL APPLICATION DEVELOPMENT USING ORACLE 7, DEVELOPER 2000

Solution :

1. Open the graphics designer tool and save the default display as **drilgrap.ogd.**

2. Click on the display and select **query** from the Object Navigator. Enter the name of the query as **q_customer** and click on **execute** and OK to accept the query. Enter the following query as shown below and in the diagram 21.2.

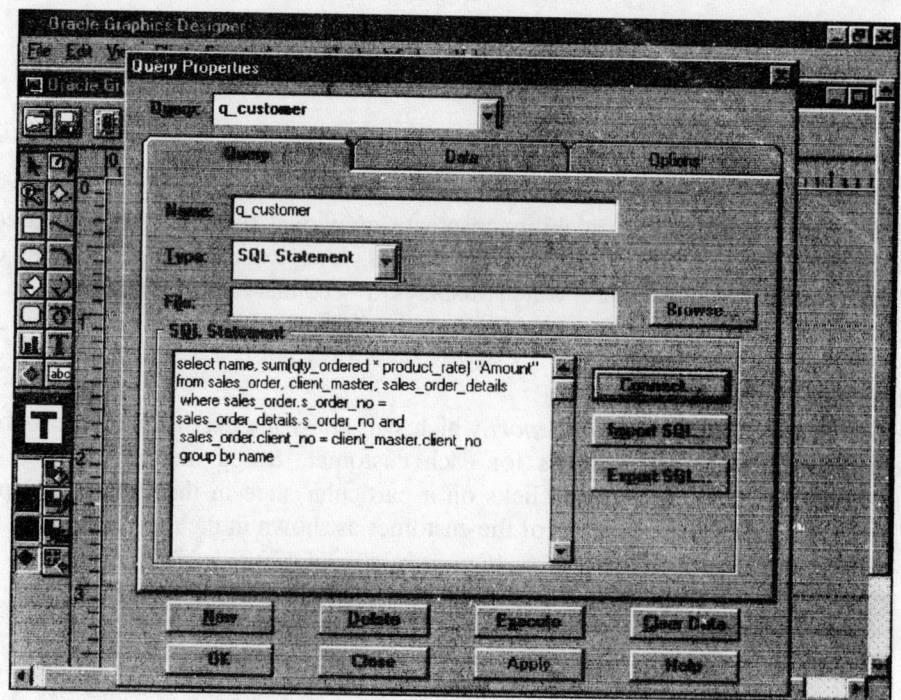

Diagram 21.2 : Query for the Pie Chart

The completed query in diagram 21.2 is as follows :

```
select      name, sum(qty_ordered * product_rate) "Amount"
from        sales_order, client_master, sales_order_details
where       sales_order.s_order_no = sales_order_details.s_order_no and
            sales_order.client_no = client_master.client_no
group by    name
```

3. Create the chart object as explained in step 6 of CREATING A GRAPH. Name the chart as **ch_customer** and the title as **Annual Sales Report**. From type option select the **Pie** type graph and select the same from the subtype as shown in diagram 21.3.

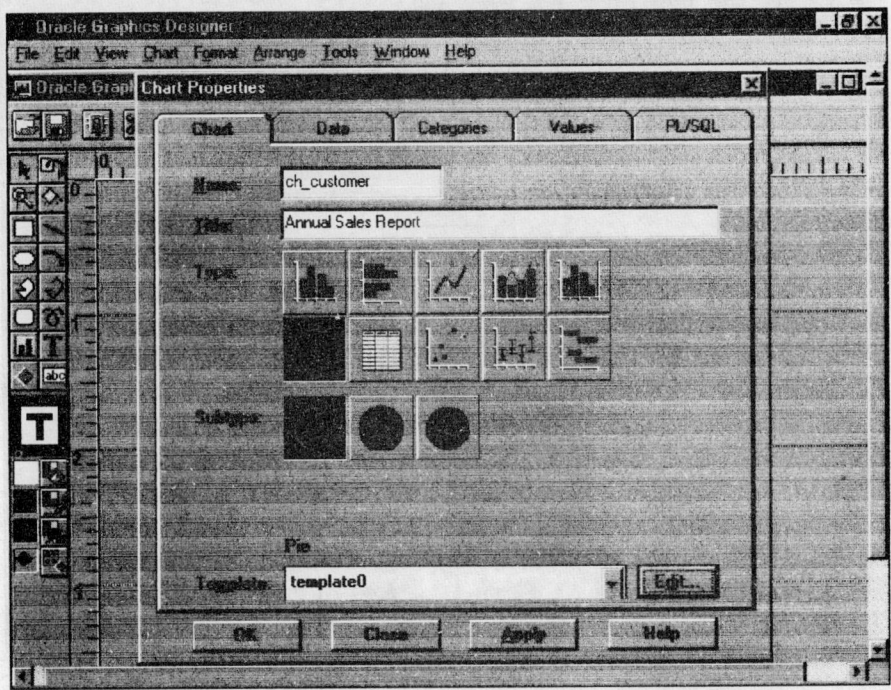

Diagram 21.3 : Creating the Pie chart from q_customer

4. In **Categories** option select the **Name** column as shown in diagram 21.4.

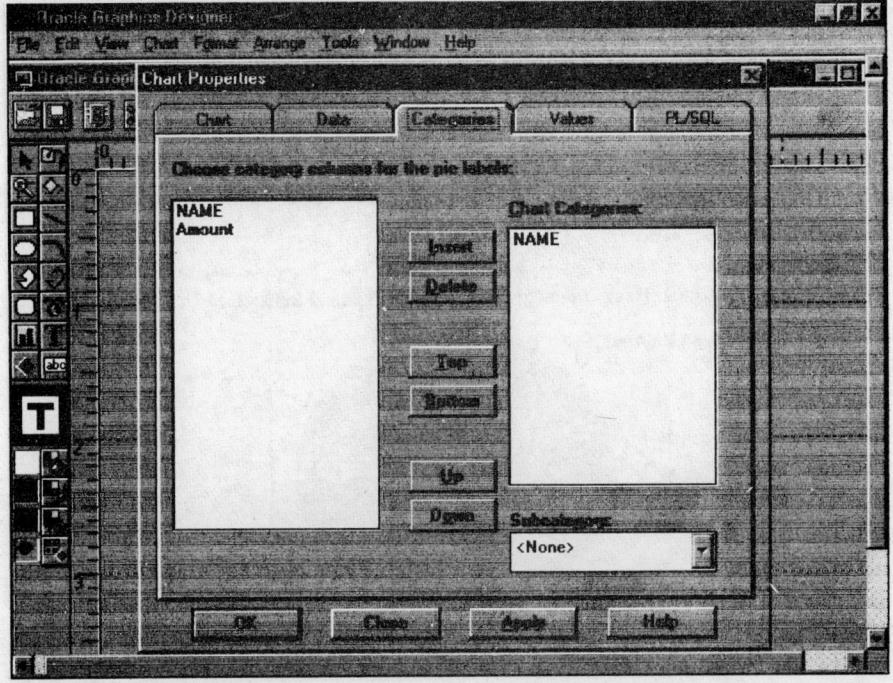

Diagram 21.4 : Specifying Categories as Name

476 COMMERCIAL APPLICATION DEVELOPMENT USING ORACLE 7, DEVELOPER 2000

5. In the **Values** option select the **Amount** column as shown in diagram 21.5. Click on **apply** and OK to accept the graph.

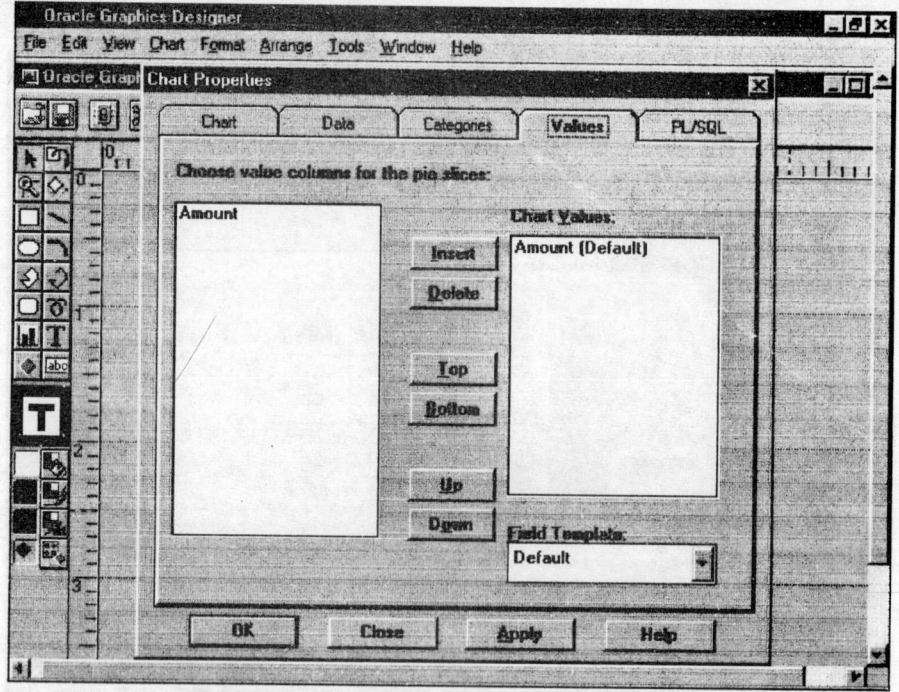

Diagram 21.5 : Specifying Values as Amount

The Completed Layout will be displayed as shown in diagram 21.6.

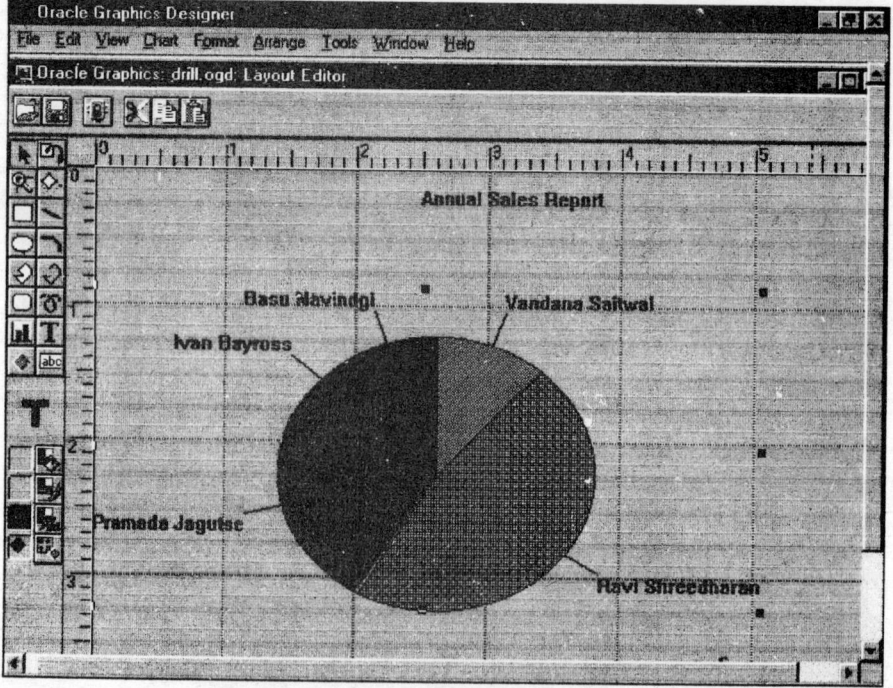

Diagram 21.6 : Completed Graph Layout

6. Create a Parameter **p_customer** of data-type **CHAR** as shown in diagram 21.7.

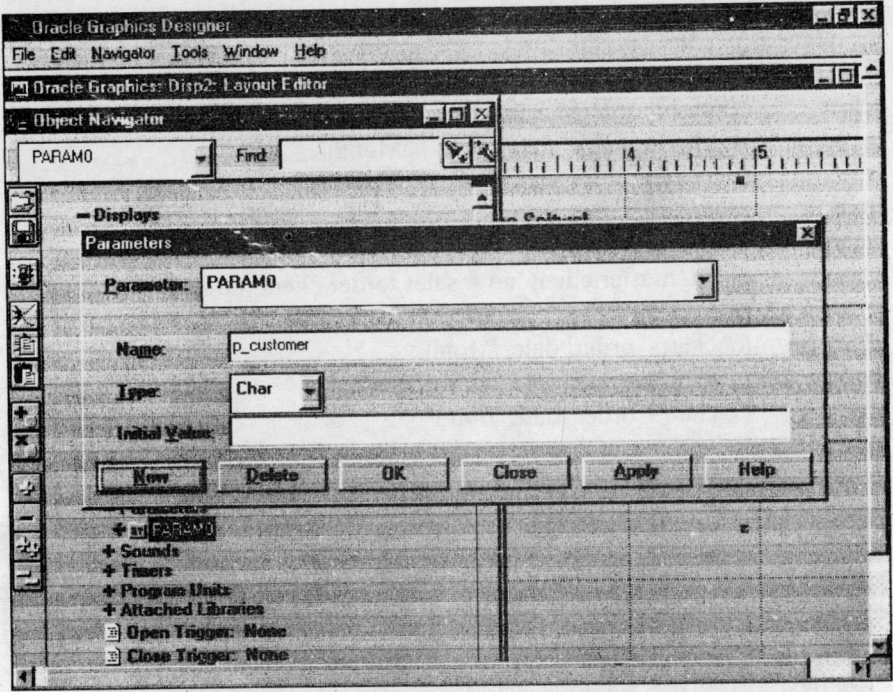

Diagram 21.7 : Creating a Parameter named p_customer

The Object Navigator will be displayed as shown in diagram 21.8.

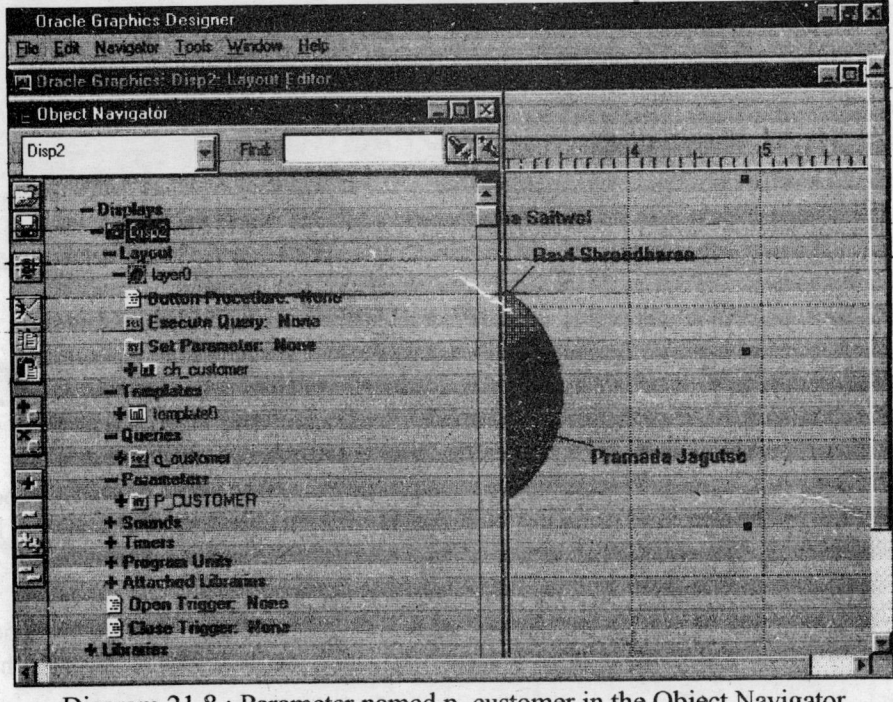

Diagram 21.8 : Parameter named p_customer in the Object Navigator

478 COMMERCIAL APPLICATION DEVELOPMENT USING ORACLE 7, DEVELOPER 2000

7. Arrange and size ch_customer to make space for the second chart. Create a line graph as explained in the hands on for Annual Sales Report with the following query. Name the query as **q_sales** and the chart as **ch_sales**.

```
select      sum(qty_ordered * product_rate ) "Amount",
            to_char(s_order_date, 'Mon') "Month",
            to_char(s_order_date, 'mm') "Num"
from        sales_order_details, sales_order, client_master
where       sales_order.s_order_no = sales_order_details.s_order_no and
            client_master.client_no = sales_order.client_no and
            rtrim(name) = :p_customer
group by    to_char(s_order_date, 'Mon'),
            to_char(s_order_date, 'mm')
order by    to_char(s_order_date, 'mm')
```

The completed layout will be as shown in 21.9.

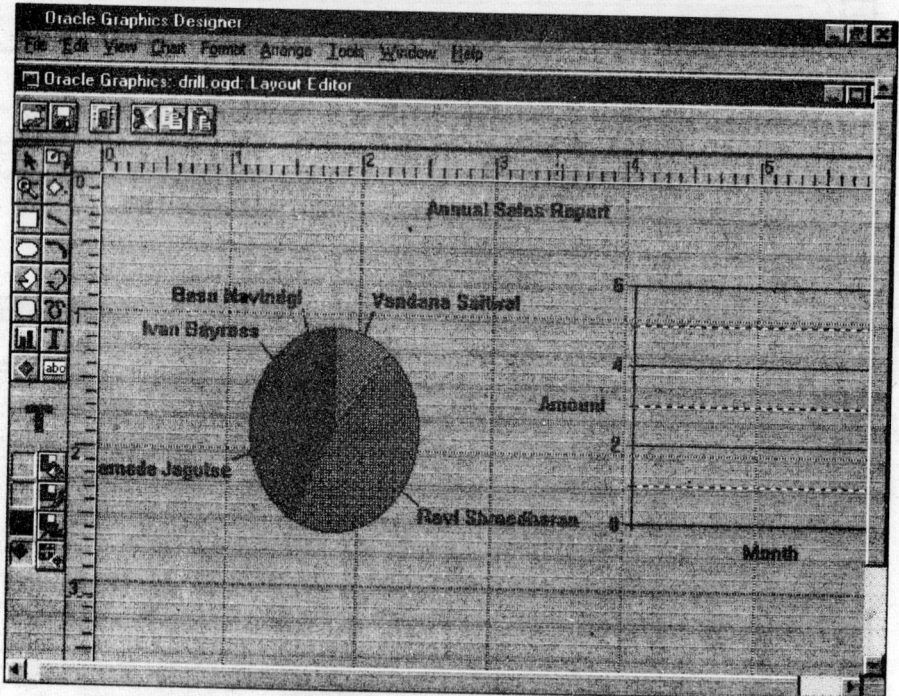

Diagram 21.9 : Completed layout after creating the second chart

Observe that the new chart does not display any data at design time. This is because chart ch_sales accepts a parameter named p_customer. This parameter does not have a value at design time. Thus the default value is NULL.

The query for this chart i.e. q_sales includes a field named **Name** which does not have any record that has a Null value. Thus no data is displayed in the second chart.

WORKING WITH GRAPHS **479**

So far we have seen how to pass parameters from the form to the Oracle Graphics tool. In this case ch_sales chart accepts a parameter named p_customer. Thus value must be the name of the customer. The name of the customer is determined by the pie section that the user clicks on.

Thus we need to link the first chart i.e. ch_customer to the second chart i.e.ch_sales.

8. To link the two charts in a drill-down relationship, click within the pie chart to select the pie chart and then click one of the pie segments. The selected graph will be as shown in diagram 21.10.

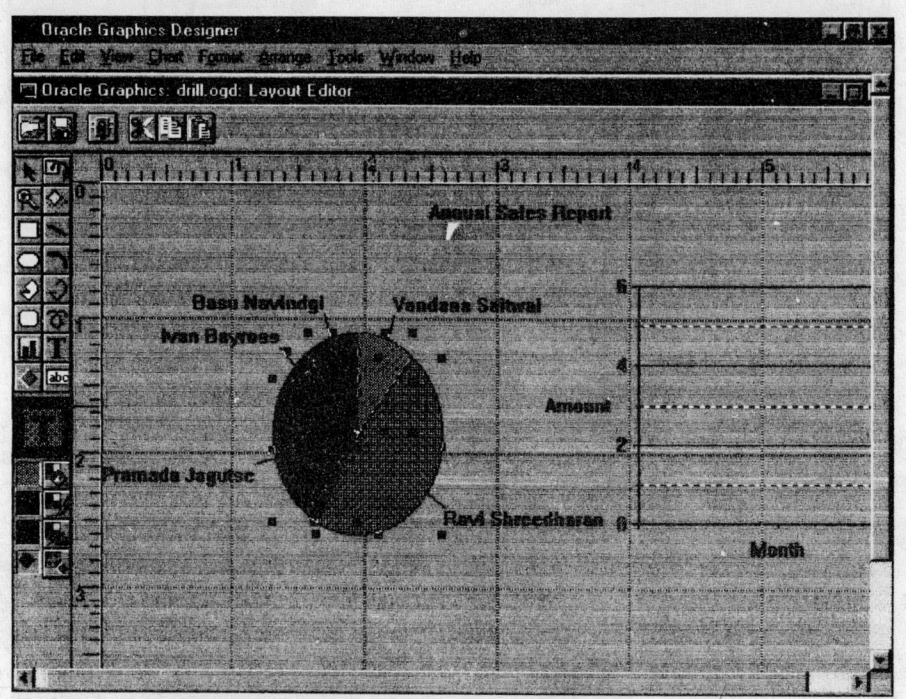

Diagram 21.10 : Pie chart selected in the layout editor

480 COMMERCIAL APPLICATION DEVELOPMENT USING ORACLE 7, DEVELOPER 2000

9. This will present the object definition property sheet as shown in the diagram 21.11.

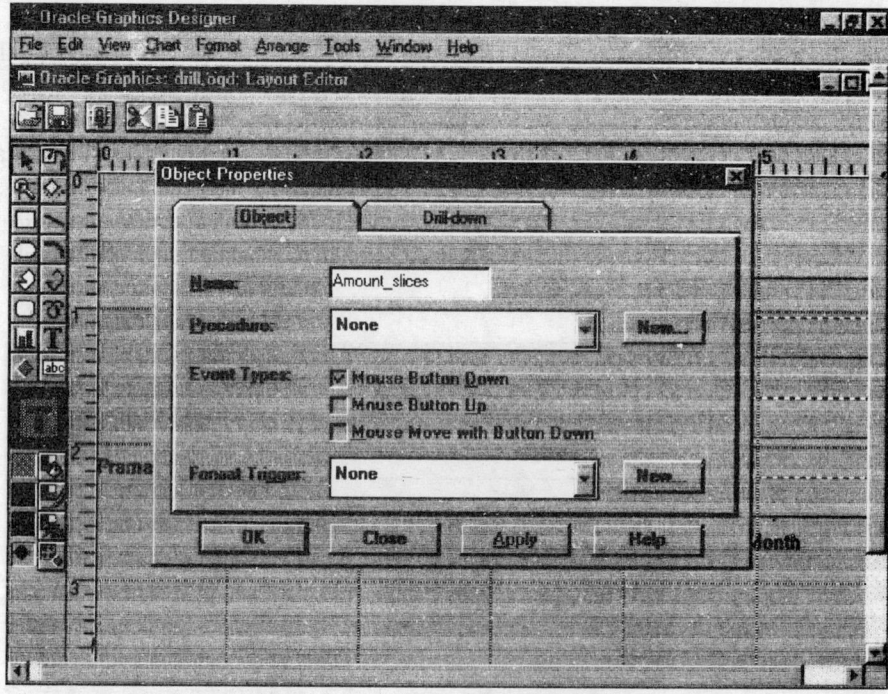

Diagram 21.11 : Object Properties Screen

10. Click on the **Drill-down** tab. It displays the drill-down tab as shown in diagram 21.12.

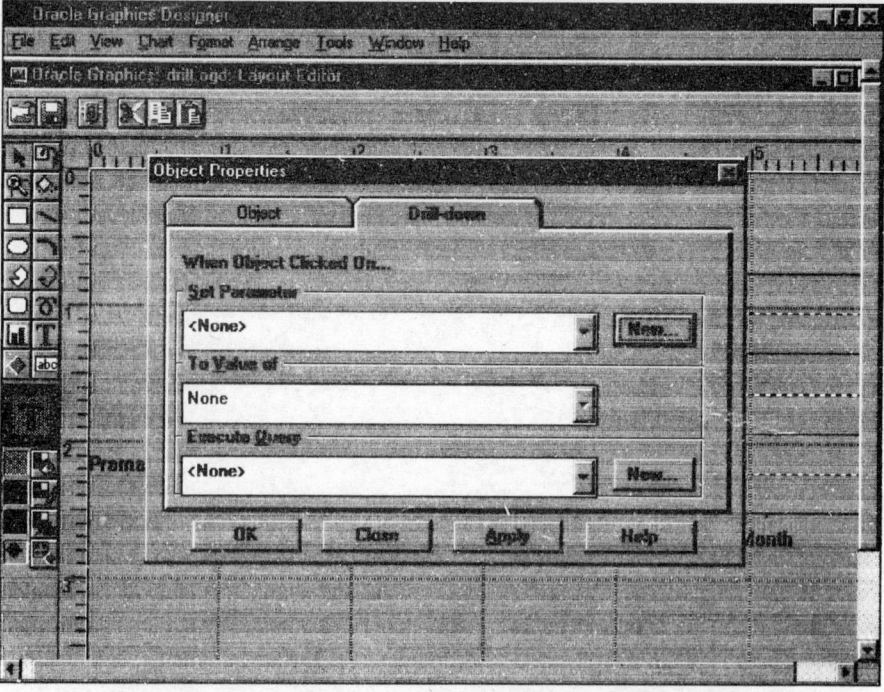

Diagram 21.12 : Drill-down tab in the Object Properties Screen

11. Set the **Set Parameter** value to **p_customer**. The Set Parameter field is used to specify the name of the parameter that has to be set to the value from the chart. In this case the value from the ch_customer chart.

12. Set the **To Value Of** to **Name**. This parameter specifies the name of the column on the chart from which the value must be taken.

13. Set the **Execute Query** to **q_sales**. This parameter specifies the name of the query for which the parameter value will be used.

The completed screen will be as shown in diagram 12.13. Click on **Apply** to accept it.

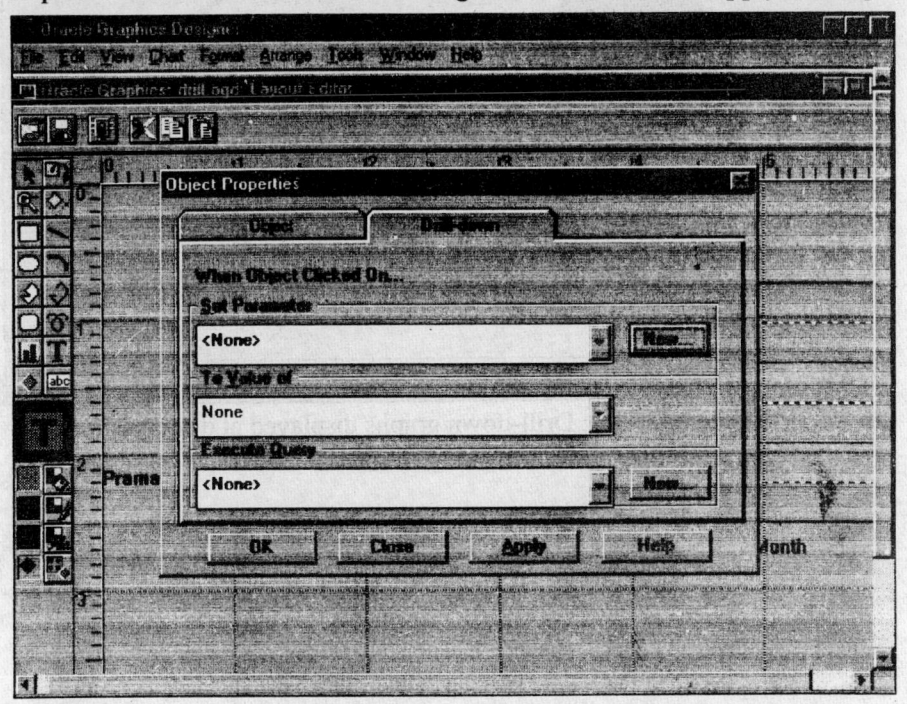

Diagram 12.13 : Completed Drill-down tab in the Object properties screen

482 COMMERCIAL APPLICATION DEVELOPMENT USING ORACLE 7, DEVELOPER 2000

14. Save, Compile and run the display to view the graph. The completed graph will be as shown in diagram 12.14.

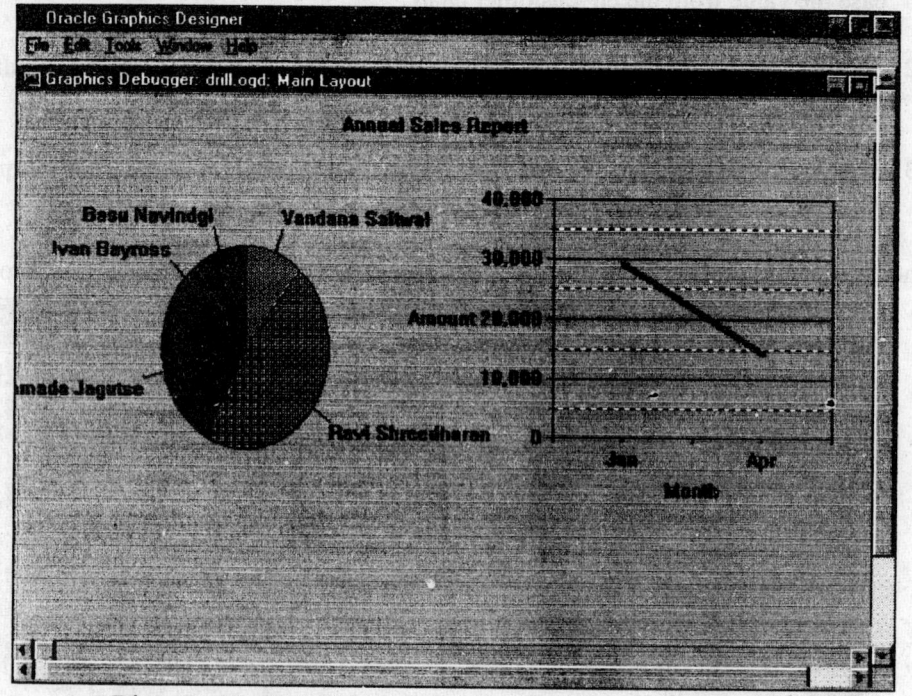

Diagram 21.14 : Drill-down graphs displayed at design time

INDEX

A

ABS 38
access authorization 4
Active Data Set 96, 98
Adding new columns in the table 24
Alerts 198, 205
   modal window 205
   Creating an Alert 205
   Displaying an Alert 207
Alert Properties
   Alert Style 205
      STOP, CAUTION, NOTE 205
   Default Alert Button 206
   Message 206
Altering A Sequence, ALTER SEQUENCE 60
Altering the table, ALTER TABLE 24
ALTER TABLE - Defining Integrity constraints 32
ANSI SQL 5
Arithmetic operators 33
Attributes 5
AVG 37

B

Balloon Help 223
Behavior of an Oracle Form 168
BETWEEN clause 35
Blocks 146
   Base Table 146
   Control Block 146
Block Properties
   Default_Where 315
   No of Records 323

C

CACHE 59
Canvas, Canvas-view 149, 189
Canvas Properties
   Canvas View Type 323, 351
      Stacked 323
      Content 351
      Horizontal 351
      Vertical 351
   Height 267
   View Height 267
   View Width 267
   Width 267
   Window canvas-view 149
Catalog facilities 8

Class	189
Creating a Form	153
Cell Data Type	2
Cell Length	2
Cell Name	2
CHAR	17
Characteristics of a Relational DBMS model	5
CHECK Integrity constraints	29
Closing a Cursor	101
Closing Transactions	89
Column Level Constraints	25
COMMIT	89
Computations in Expression	33
Concurrency Control	92
Conditional control	85
Constants	82
Constructing an English Sentence	51
Context Sensitive Help	223
COUNT, COUNT(*)	37
Creating a Sequence, CREATE SEQUENCE	58
Creating a table, CREATE TABLE	18
Creating a table from a table	19
Cross Table Updations	303
CURRVAL	60
Cursor *For* Loops	104
CURSORS	96
CYCLE	59

D

Data Constraints	25
Data Language	8
Data Retrieval and Manipulation	159
Data Security	6
Datatypes	17
data validationin	11
database	4
DataBase Administrator	7
Database Concepts	4
Database Distribution	9
$$DATE$$	247
Date Datatype	17
DBA	7
DBMSystems	2
DCL, DDL, DML	11
Declaring a Cursor	99
Declaring Exceptions	114
Default Forms Environment	158
Designer Options	158
Runtime Options	158
Default Value	27
Delete, DELETE FROM	6, 8, 21

Deleting a Stored Function, DROP FUNCTION 131
Deleting a Stored Procedure, DROP PROCEDURE 125
Displayed 189
Display Item 222
Displaying user Messages 84
   dbms_output 84
   PUT_LINE 84
   DBMS_OUTPUT.PUT_LINE 85
   SERVEROUTPUT 85
DISTINCT 22, 37
Dropping Integrity constraints 32
Dropping Indexes, DROP INDEX 55
Dropping A Sequence, DROP SEQUENCE 60
Dropping Tables, DROP TABLE 24
Dropping Views, DROP VIEW 57

E

E.F. TED CODD'S Laws 8
Elimination of duplicates rows 22
Enabled 189
Equi Joins 43
Error Handling In PL/SQL 114
EXCEPTIONS 114
   Pre-determined internal PL/SQL exceptions 115
   EXCEPTION_INIT 117
Explicit Cursors Management 97, 98
Explicit Cursor Attributes 97
   %FOUND 102
   %ISOPEN 103
   %NOTFOUND 102
   %ROWCOUNT 104

F

Fetching a record from the Cursor 100
Field 2, 16
Foreign Key 28
FOR LOOP 86
Foreign Key/References constraint 28
Forms Designer 11
Forms Designer 145, 146
   Parts of Forms Designer Window 151
      Layout Editor 152
      Menu Editor 152
      Object Navigator 151, 152
      PL/SQL Editor 152
      Properties Window 152
      Textual Menu 151
      Toolbox 151
Forms Built-in
   Add_Parameter 310
   Call_Form 271

Clear_Form 279
Create_Group_From_Query 265
Create_Parameter_List 309, 315, 471
Create_Record 172
Delete_Record 173
Destroy_Parameter_List 472
Execute_Query 170
Enter_Query 184
Exit_Form 174
Find_Group 268, 319
First_Record 171
Get_Application_Property 255, 344
Get_Block_Property 204, 345
Get_Form_Property 345
Get_Group_Row_Count 320
Get_Item_Property 204
Get_Parameter_List 314
Go_Block 184
Go_Item 184
Id_Null 268, 472
Last_Record 171
Message 179
Name_In 202
Next_Block 171
Open_Form 309
Populate_Group 265
Populate_Group_With_Query 269
Populate_List 265
Previous_Record 171
Run_Product 338
Set_Block_Property 271
Set_Form_Property 255
Set_Item_Property 172
Set_Window_Property 302
Show_View 327
Forms Generator 145
FORMS_MDI_WINDOW 302

G

Generating a Form 158
Global Variables 270
GOTO STATEMENT 87
Granting Permissions, GRANT 61
Graphics Designer, Oracle Graphics 10, 12
Graphs - Working with 454
   Chart Genie 463
   Chart Types 456, 463
      Bar, Column, Pie, Table 456
      Double-Y, Gantt, High-low, Line 457
      Mixed, Scatter 457
   Creating a Graph 459

    Chart Properties 456, 463
        Categories 464
        Name 463
        Subtype 463
        Tick Label Rotation 466
        Title 463
        Values 465
    Chart Templates 455, 457
    Creating a Query 455, 460
Display 455
Functionality of Oracle Graphics 454
Graph Built-in
    og.close 472
    og.open 472
    og.pll 471
Multiple Chart Applications 473
Object Definition Property 480
    Drill-down Tab 480
        Link The Two Charts 479
        Execute Query 481
        To Value Of 481
Set Parameter 481
Passing Parameters in Graphs 468
    LOV 471
Using the Graphics Designer 458
Grouping Data, GROUP BY 42

H

HAVING 42
Hint Built-in
    showbuttonhelp 224
    showbuttonhelphandler 224
HINT.PLL 224
Human data 1

I

Iconic 189
identifier 84
Implicit Cursor 107
Implicit Cursor Attributes 107
    %FOUND 108
    %ISOPEN 109
    %NOTFOUND 108
    %ROWCOUNT 109
IN and *NOT IN* 36
INCREMENT BY 58
Indexes, CREATE INDEX 54
Information Representation: 8
INITCAP 39
Insert, INSERT INTO 6, 8, 19
Integrity Constraints 9

Integrity Constraints at the form level 163
Interactive SQL ....
INTERSECT Clause 11, 13
Invoking Other Products From Oracle Forms Or Menus 53
Iterative Control 338
Items 85
    Control Items 147
    Item Types 147
        Display Item, Text Item 147
        Button, Chart Item, Check Box, Image Item 148
        List Item, *OLE container*, Radio Group 148
        VBX Control ....
    Setting the Properties of the Items 149
    Item Properties 161
        Autohint 223
        Base Table 301
        Canvas 191, 301
        Default Value 183, 222
        Font Type, Font Size and Font Weight 185
        Foreground and Background Color 185
        Height, Weight 189
        Hint 223
        Icon Name 191
        Item Type 189
        Label 184
        Mouse Navigate 189
        Maximum Length 301
        Name 184
        Query Allowed 184
        Primary Key 345
        Required 179

J

Joins 43

K

Key-Delrec 163

L

LENGTH 39
LIKE Operator 35
Library File Formats ....
    PLL 198
    PLD 198
    PLX 198
Libraries 198
    Attaching a Library 198
    Attached Libraries 199
    Creating a Library 200
    dynamic loading 199
    Library source code 198

Literals
- Character ... 80
- Logical (boolean) ... 80
- Numeric ... 80
- String ... 80

Library ... 146

List Item ... 262
- Creating A List Item ... 263
- Liststyle ... 263
  - Combo List ... 262
  - Poplist ... 262
  - Text List ... 262

LOCKS ... 92
- Explicit locking ... 93
- Implicit locking ... 92
- Types of locks ... 92
- LOCK TABLE statement ... 94

Logical Accessibility ... 8
logical comparisons ... 83
Logical Operators ... 34
Logical data independence ... 9
Long ... 17
LOV object ... 249, 288
- Creating A List of Values ... 250
- Attaching an LOV Object to an Item ... 250
- Item Properties for Attaching an LOV Object
  - LOV ... 251
  - LOV For Validation ... 251
  - LOV X Position ... 252
  - LOV Y Position ... 252
- LOV Properties
  - Query Text ... 288

LOWER ... 38
LPAD ... 40
LTRIM ... 39

M

Managing data ... 1
Manipulating Dates ... 43
Master-Detail relationship ... 225
- Join Condition ... 227, 236
- Master Block ... 227, 236
- Master Deletes ... 242, 243, 280
  - Cascading ... 242
  - Isolated ... 242
  - Non-Isolated ... 242

MAX ... 37
MAXVALUE ... 58
Menu ... 146
- Attaching A Menu Module To A Form ... 337
- Command Type ... 335

Creating A Menu Module ... 330
    Create a Submenu ... 333
    Using The Custom Menu ... 328
    Using The Default Menu ... 328
Menu Built-in
    Get_Menu_Item_Property ... 347
    Set_Menu_Item_Property ... 348, 349
Menu Editor ... 331
Menu Module Property ... 328
Menu Properties
    Checked Property ... 347
    Displayed Property ... 347
    Enabled Property ... 347
Menu Types
    Custom menu ... 328
    Default menu ... 328
MIN ... 37
Minus Clause ... 54
MINVALUE ... 58
Modifying existing columns in the table ... 24
Multiple Canvases on a Form ... 321

N

Name ... 189
Named Visual Attributes ... 191
Navigable ... 189
NEXTVAL ... 60
NOCACHE ... 59
NOCYCLE ... 59
NOMAXVALUE ... 59
NOMINVALUE ... 58
Non Subversion ... 9
NOORDER ... 59
NULL (is Null and is not null) ... 80
NULL values ... 8, 25
Number Datatype ... 17

O

Object Privileges ... 61
Opening a Cursor ... 100
Opening A Form Through The Menu ... 338
Oracle 6.0, Oracle 7.1 ... 5
Oracle Forms ... 10,11
Oracle Functions ... 37
Oracle Kernel ... 10
Oracle Report Writer ... 10
Oracle Server ... 6
Oracle Tools ... 10
Oracle Transactions ... 89
ORDER ... 59
ORDER BY ... 22

P

Parameterized Cursors ... 109
Parameter Passing In Forms ... 309
   Parameter List ... 309
   Parameter Types, Types of Parameters ... 309
      Data_Parameter ... 309, 310
      Text_Parameter ... 309, 310
   Adding Parameter ... 310
   Creating a Parameter List ... 309
   Creating the parameters in the called form ... 311
Using the parameters ... 312
Parent-Child relationships ... 5
Pattern Matching ... 35
Physical data independence ... 9
POWER ... 38
PRAGMA ... 117
Pre-defined Exceptions
   no_data_found ... 179
Primary Key ... 26, 163
Procedural Language, PL/SQL ... 11, 15, 76
   block structure ... 83
   character set ... 79
   Comments ... 80
   Data Types ... 77, 80
   Portability ... 77
Program Unit ... 174
Property Class ... 185, 186
   Add Property ... 190
   Creating Property Class object ... 187
Property class inheritance ... 186

Q

QBE (Query By Example) ... 5

R

RAISE_APPLICATION_ERROR ... 143
Raise FORM_TRIGGER_FAILURE ... 179
Radio button group ... 253, 325
   Radio Buttons ... 253
   Radio Button Properties
      Label ... 254
      Value ... 254
Range Searching ... 35
Record ... 3
redundant data ... 6
Referencing a Sequence ... 59
Referencing a table belonging to another user ... 62
Relational Database Management ... 8
Reports in SQL*PLUS, Report Formatting commands ... 65
Report Writer, *reporting section, Reports Designer* ... 11

Reports - Working with 361
   Creating A Break Report 406
      Creating a break group 409
   Creating A Default Tabular Report 369
   Creating Computed Columns 383
      Formula Columns 383, 427
      Summary Columns 383, 411, 427
   Creating Master/Detail Report 420
      Child Query 420
      Data Link Object 420
      Data Link property sheet 420, 426
      Data Relationships 426
      Detail Group 421
      Master Detail Layout 420
      Master Group 421
      Parent Query 420
   Data Model 362, 363
   Layout Editor 362
   Parameter Form Editor 362
Creating a Matrix or Cross-Tab Report 436
   Adding a grid 451
   Creating groups for the Matrix report 444
      Cross Product Groups 437
         Filler, Filler Group 436, 438
   Matrix / Cross Product Object 439
   Matrix Layout 439
   Matrix Data Model 437
      Number Of Queries in the matrix Report 437
         Multi-Query Matrix 437
         One-Query Matrix 437
      Group Structure 437
   Summaries and Product Order, Creating Summary columns 439, 447
   Adding zeroes in place of non-existent values 448
   Cross-tabulation of data 436
   Product Order 448
Report Layout - Customizing 398
   Alignment 400
   Displaying Grid Lines for the report 404
   Field Sizing 430
      Vertical Sizing, Expand, Fixed Size 430
   Fill Color Tool 398
   Font 400
   Format 400
   Line Color Tool 398
   Text Color Tool 398
   Displaying Fields that are not a part of the table 401
      Current Date 401
      Displaying Parameters in the Report Layout 403
      Displaying one record per page - Maximum Records Per Page Property 432
Report Features 361
Report Interface 367

    Editors 368
    Object Navigator 367
    Palettes and Toolbars 368
    Property Sheets 367
Use The Oracle Reports Interface 367
Report Layout 364
    Anchors 364, 366
    Boilerplate 364, 366
    Current Layout Settings 381
    Data Selection 382
    Fields 362, 364, 366
    Frames 364, 366
    Repeating Frames 364, 415
    Report Styles 381
        Tabular 381
    Specify The Layout For A Report 364, 381
Reports Data Model Editor
    Columns 363, 364
    Data Links 364
    Groups 363, 375
    Links 363
    Parameters 363, 364
    Queries 363, 372
    Query Tool 372
    Specifying the Data for the Report 372
Report Parameters
    Boilerplate 367
    Creating User Parameters 394
    Fields 367
    Report System Parameters 381
        Destination Name 382
        Destination Type 382
    Report - Print Direction
        Across 445
        Down 364
    Specify A Runtime Parameter Form 367, 381
    User Parameter Properties 392
        Data Type 392
        Initial Value 392
        Input Mask 392
        Parameter Name 392
        List of values for the User Parameters 434
            Restrict List to Predetermined Values 434
            Select Statement 434
            Static values 434
REVOKE 62, 63
Rollback 89
ROUND 38
RPAD 40
RTRIM 39
Runform, Running a Form 145, 158

S

Savepoint, SAVEPOINT	90,90
SELECT command	22
Select...For Update command	93
Selecting a data set from a view	56
Self Joins	46
Sequences	58
SET SERVEROUTPUT ON	85
Set theory	5
SHOW_ALERT	205, 207
Alert_button1, Alert_button2, Alert_button3	205
Sorting, ORDER BY	22
SQL*Plus	10, 11, 13
SQRT	38
START WITH	59
Stored Functions	126
Declarative part	126
Executable part	126
Exception Handling part	126
Syntax	128
Stored Procedures	119
Declarative part	119
Executable part	119
Exception Handling part	119
Syntax	121
Subqueries	52
SUBSTR	39
SUM	38
System Variables	
cursor_block	258
cursor_record	176
form_status	173
last_record	176
mouse_item	259

T

%TYPE	77, 80
Table	3, 16
Table Data Input / Output Validations	178
Table Level Constraints	25
TK21_ICON	191
TO_CHAR	40, 41
TO_DATE	40
TO_NUMBER	40
Toolbars	351
Trigger	166
Interface Events	166
Internal Processing Events	166
The sequence of trigger execution	166
Writing Triggers	166

Triggers Names 165
   Key-Next-Item 166
   On-Check-Delete-Master 280
   Post-Insert 304
   Post-Query 252
   Post-Text-Item 166
   Post-Update 305
   Pre-Delete 281
   Pre-Form 268
   Pre-Text-Item 166
   When-Button-Pressed 166, 168
   When-Validate-Item 178
   When-List-Changed 270
   When-Mouse-Enter 224
   When-New-Form-Instance 302
   When-New-Record-Instance 177
   When-Timer-Expired 224
Tuples 5

U

Update, UPDATE 6, 8, 20
UNION Clause 53
Unique Key 27
UPPER 39

V

VARCHAR / VARCHAR2 17
Variables 81
   Assigning Values to 81
   Picking up a Variable's Parameters from a table cell 82
View, Views 6, 55
View Updatability 8, 56
Visual Attribute
   Named Visual Attributes 185, 191, 194
      Applying a Named Visual Attribute To An Object 194
      Creating Named Visual Attributes 194
   Custom Visual Attributes 194
   Default Visual Attributes 194
   Setting the Visual Attributes of an object 191

W

WHERE clause 23
WHILE LOOP 86
Windows in the Forms Designer 149
Window Properties
   Fixed Size 267
   Height 267
   Title 267
   Width 267
   Window Style 267

X Position 267
Y Position 267
Horizontal Toolbar 351
Vertical Toolbar 351
WITH GRANT OPTION 61, 62
Working with Forms 145
Writing Procedures in Forms Designer 174